Warfare in Hi

THE

BATTLE OF AGINCOURT

SOURCES AND INTERPRETATIONS

WARFARE IN HISTORY
ISSN 1358–779X

Series editor
Matthew Bennett, Royal Military Academy, Sandhurst

This series aims to provide a wide-ranging and scholarly approach to military history, offering both individual studies of topics or wars, and volumes giving a selection of contemporary and later accounts of particular battles; its scope ranges from the early medieval to the early modern period.

New proposals for the series are welcomed; they should be sent to the publisher at the address below.

Boydell and Brewer Limited, PO Box 9, Woodbridge, Suffolk, IP12 3DF

THE
BATTLE OF AGINCOURT

SOURCES AND INTERPRETATIONS

Anne Curry

THE BOYDELL PRESS

First published 2000
The Boydell Press, Woodbridge
Reprinted in paperback 2009

Transferred to digital printing

ISBN   978 1 84383 511 0

The Boydell Press is an imprint of Boydell & Brewer Ltd
PO Box 9, Woodbridge, Suffolk IP12 3DF, UK
and of Boydell & Brewer Inc.
668 Mt Hope Avenue, Rochester, NY 14620, USA
website: www.boydellandbrewer.com

A CIP catalogue record for this book is available
from the British Library

Library of Congress Catalog Card Number 00–042919

This publication is printed on acid-free paper

Printed in Great Britain

Contents

List of Illustrations

Preface

It was during my undergraduate days at Manchester that I first became interested in the Hundred Years War, thanks to the stimulating teaching and encouragement of John Roskell and Richard Davies. Since then I have benefited from discussion with many others in the field. In the particular context of the battle of Agincourt, Matthew Bennett has been a constant source of ideas and good humour, Christopher Allmand and Robert Hardy of inspiration and encouragement. It was a privilege to be invited to join the Battlefields Trust 'expedition' to Crécy and Agincourt in October 1998 and to be amongst so many experts and enthusiasts. Thanks here particularly to Chris Scott. I would like to express my gratitude to Richard Barber and Caroline Palmer at Boydell & Brewer for their advice and patience.

There is nothing like having to teach the subject to make one realise both how much and how little one knows: my students have never failed to ask those difficult questions and to provide their own insights which have kept the subject live and exciting for me (and, I hope, for them). A special thanks to them, and in particular to Rachel Gibbons who has helped with materials in France. Elizabeth Berry deserves both praise and gratitude for much typing beyond the call of duty. Thanks are also due to Adrian Ailes, Nick Barrett, Françoise Beriac, Colin Fox, Rebecca Griffiths, David Grummitt, Ralph Houlbrooke, David Knott, Gareth Prosser, Jenny Stratford and Roy Wolfe for assisting in the search for materials, to Andrew Gurr and Ron Knowles for advice on the sixteenth-century literary materials, and to Marianne Ailes, Peter Davies, Sarah Hamilton, and Iveta Mednikova for help with translations. Brian Kemp, Peter Noble and Tim Ryder have offered much useful advice and, along with Christie Davies, Leonard Dressel, Peter Must and other members of the 'Blue Room Luncheon Club', have helped to keep me sane by reminding me that there is more to life than medieval warfare. This task has been assisted too by my long-suffering family, John and Tom, who have indulged my interests and absences, and who deserve my constant gratitude and love.

Source Acknowledgments

The author and publishers are grateful to the following writers and publishers for their permission to reprint from materials for which they hold copyright. Every effort has been made to trace the copyright holders; we apologise for any remission in this regard, and will be pleased to add any necessary acknowledgements in subsequent editions.

C. Given-Wilson, *The Chronicle of Adam Usk* (Oxford, 1997). By kind permission of Professor Given-Wilson.

C. Hibbert, *Agincourt* (London, 1964). By kind permission of Mr Hibbert.

J. Keegan, *The Face of Battle* (London: Jonathan Cape, 1976). Copyright John Keegan 1976.

Oxford University Press, for *Gesta Henrici Quinti: The Deeds of Henry the Fifth*, translated from the Latin with an introduction and notes by Frank Taylor and John S. Roskell (1975). Copyright Oxford University Press, 1975.

The Public Record Office for documents in its custody.

Note on translations

It is to be remembered that translation is not an exact art, and that this book is not intended as a full critical edition of any of the sources. Thus it is possible that similarities and differences have not been detected and that they are not reflected fully in the translations. As many of the chronicles are interlinked, a comprehensive and critical study of the texts in their original languages would be necessary to be completely certain of how the wording of one work relates to that of another. In sixteenth-century materials, there has been some modernising for the sake of clarity but names of people and places have been left in their original spellings where identification is not certain and 'earl' has been retained as in the works themselves, rather than substituting 'count'. There are occasional problems of identification in some of the medieval texts also.

General Editor's Preface

Ask an English-speaking audience for the name of a medieval battle, and, after Hastings, Agincourt is most frequently on their lips. Further, unlike 1066, conceived of as a defeat for anglophones, Henry V's victory of 1415 is often seen as a great victory for 'us', in which 'we' (the English) beat 'them', the old enemy: the French. In some ways Agincourt appears a re-match, a re-vindication of a natural superiority upset by the unlucky arrow catching King Harold in the eye; and – poetic justice – it is the archers who play the decisive role! I say 'appears', because the whole Anglo-Saxon approach to the battle has been conditioned by Shakespeare's play, and, in the last half-century by the cinematographic reconstructions of Laurence Olivier and Kenneth Branagh. So does a work intended for a select group at the Jacobean court find its way before the mass audiences of the modern era. Not that the Bard intended an anglocentric emphasis in his study of military leadership: his focus is assuredly British, a unifying theme played upon in the wartime film.

Such matters are still surprisingly sensitive today. Following a BBC television programme on the longbow (as a decisive weapon), contributors, including the author of this book, were harangued by a Welshman angry that they had referred only to 'English' archers at Agincourt and not Welsh! It was only possible to get off the hook by explaining that, in fifteenth-century terms, the soldiers of the king of England were generically 'English', whatever their geographical location in his realm. Of course, it was actually more complicated than that, as national and regional variation was often as keenly felt as today and expressed the variety of legal relationships with the royal government, and in terms of the military obligation which provided the forces for the invasion of France.

All these themes are tackled in Dr Anne Curry's interpretation of the historical event known as the Battle of Agincourt. As she points out, its significance is far more than a single day's conflict, as it was part of the ongoing relationship between England and France, revolving around English claims to sovereignty over French soil. Henry V represented his 1415 campaign as an attempt to recover Normandy as rightfully his (although it had been in French hands since King John had lost the duchy in the early thirteenth century). Henry fought determinedly to gain and retain the territories in northern France. By a combination of this endeavour – and a slice of luck provided by the assassination of John the Fearless in 1419 which gave him the Burgundian alliance – he managed the remarkable achievement of having himself accepted as heir to the French Crown. It can be argued that the exertions killed him, as he died at the siege of Meaux (1422) trying to assure his inheritance. Some historians have accused him of presenting a poisoned chalice to the Lancastrian dynasty by virtue of trying to conquer a large, rich country with the resources of a smaller, poorer one.

How far the victory at Agincourt contributed to Henry's successes is one of Dr Curry's themes; but essentially she wishes to play down the importance of the battle alone. Her study of the sources brings out how contemporaries interpreted the event, as well as the extensive after-life which preceded Shakespeare's play and was then fed by it. Succeeding generations of historians sought to use the battle to justify their view of the proper relationship between ruler and ruled, England and France, the political and material economy, and divine intention. Only in the last century did the battle become a purely 'military' event, to be dissected and reconstructed by old soldiers, and they, by keeping their noses too close to the ground, often saw it with the anachronistic perspective of practitioners who knew what was 'inherently probable' (to use Alfred Burne's phrase), as opposed to what the often hugely conflicting sources actually said.

It is the range of material explored by Dr Curry which makes this book so valuable. Previous accounts have depended too heavily upon narrative sources alone to describe the course of the Agincourt campaign and its repercussions. The author's thorough knowledge of documentary and record information makes it possible – for the first time – to understand the wealth of the evidence available. As a result it is possible to gain a greatly enriched understanding of medieval warfare in its social setting; the essential purpose of this series. By taking into account the various impetuses of researchers and historians over the centuries: most frequently genealogical; often concerned with the study of government; and also as part of a literary tradition, she has produced the most important book on the subject to date.

Matthew Bennett
Royal Military Academy Sandhurst
July 2000

Abbreviations

CPR	Calendar of Patent Rolls
DNB	*Dictionary of National Biography*
EHL	C.L. Kingsford, *English Historical Literature in the Fifteenth Century* (Oxford, 1913)
EHR	*English Historical Review*
Foedera	Thoms Rymer, *Foedera, conventiones, litterae et cuiuscunque generis acta publica* (3rd edition, The Hague, 1739–45, unless otherwise stated)
Gransden	Antonia Gransden, *Historical Writing in England, ii. c. 1307 to the Early Sixteenth Century* (London and Henley, 1982)
Nicolas	*History of the Battle of Agincourt* (1st edition, London, 1827; 2nd edition, 1832; 3rd edition, 1833). Unless otherwise stated, references are to the 3rd edition, which was reissued in facsimile by H. Pordes in 1971
POPC, 2	*Proceedings and Ordinances of the Privy Council of England*, vol. 2 ed. H. Nicolas (London, 1834)
Wylie	J.H. Wylie and W.T. Waugh, The *Reign of Henry the Fifth*, 3 vols (Cambridge, 1914–29)

Unpublished materials are to be found in the Public Record Office, Kew, unless otherwise stated.

Introduction

I shall begin by betting that everyone, or nearly everyone, who reads this book has seen the battle of Agincourt. By that I do not mean those who have visited the field where the battle was fought, and which is considered to have changed little since the fifteenth century save perhaps for the reduction of woodland cover on the flanks, the metalling of roadways, and new buildings.[1] I mean the battle as seen in the two most famous films of Shakespeare's *Henry V.* Olivier (Rank Films, 1944) takes 10 minutes to fight the battle, if we take our timings from the point where Mountjoye herald withdraws ('thou never shalt see herald more') to when he reappears to tell Henry that the victory is his. Branagh (Renaissance Films, 1989) takes slightly longer – 11 minutes – between these same points. The portrayals are rather different, and could themselves occupy a whole book for we would all bring our own perceptions to bear. To my mind, the specific wartime context of Olivier's film is revealed by the emphasis on group action, whether it be by the English archers or the charging French cavalry. Branagh's battle is fought between individuals, with many close ups of the leading characters (and actors) involved in hand-to-hand combat.

Which one is nearer the truth about the events of 25 October 1415? Or is it neither? Taking our cue from the Irishman who asked for directions, to answer that question one would not start with Shakespeare. Nor should one do so, even if the first duke of Marlborough claimed that was the only history he ever read, and even if his equally illustrious descendant, Winston Churchill, cites Shakespeare much as any other historical source in his *History of the English Speaking Peoples.*[2] Nor would one start with Shakespeare's own direct sources, sixteenth-century historians such as Hall, Grafton and Holinshed. The writers of

---

[1] There is no dispute about the location of the battle. As will be seen from the extracts in chapter 1, English writers of the fifteenth century always call it Agincourt as do most French writers, although the latter also have a tendency to locate it in relation to other settlements. Basin, for instance, has it 'fought near to the town of Hesdin in two villages, the one Agincourt, the other Ruisseauville'. The Berry Herald does not mention Agincourt at all but has the armies meet at Blangy. Philippe de Vigneulles writing in the early sixteenth century, names it as 'the battle of Blangy or Agincourt'. A Venetian, Antonio Morosini, places it simply 'in Artois', and Thérouanne is also found in one of the *Chronicles of London*. It is in the chronicles of Monstrelet, Le Fèvre and Waurin that we find reference to Henry V considering that battles should take their name from the nearest fortress, village or town where they occurred, and hence having it named as Agincourt after the castle which was close by. For references to these works, see chapter 1. There is a fuller discussion of the naming in J.H. Wylie and W.T. Waugh, The *Reign of Henry the Fifth* (3 vols, Cambridge, 1914–29) (henceforth Wylie), 2, pp. 178–9.

[2] For the duke's comment see A.R. Myers, 'The character of Richard III', in *English Society and Government in the Fifteenth Century*, ed. C.M.D. Crowder (London, 1967), p. 112.

the sixteenth century *did* consult earlier sources (and even began to use the systems beloved of modern historical empiricism – the bibliography and the footnote reference). But they could not consult them all, nor did they consult what we now consider the earliest and most reliable of the fifteenth-century texts, the *Gesta Henrici Quinti*.[3] Sixteenth-century writers produced their own versions which were eminently readable and encouragingly detailed, so much so that they were often taken up by later historians in preference to using chronicles produced nearer to the date of the battle. In this respect, therefore, we have a slightly strange situation in that the 'interpretations' of Agincourt of the sixteenth century have also assumed the status of 'sources' in their own right.

Shakespeare's *Henry the Fifth* and other literary interpretations of the battle have enjoyed a similar fate. Agincourt is not the only battle to be featured in works of literature, but the fame of its Shakespearean image has undoubtedly given it a prominence in the popular domain which few other engagements of any period have enjoyed. In addition to the ringing words of the playwright, some readers of this book may already be hearing in their heads the 'Agincourt Carol', considered to be an almost immediate celebratory response to the victory. Less well known, at least in Britain, are the French poetic responses which, not surprisingly, sing a rather different song. These literary images will thus provide the topic for discussion in chapter 3, where evidence for the contemporary reception of the battle will also be considered.

It is fair to say, and will be a point returned to in the conclusion, that Agincourt was not a decisive battle. It does not feature prominently in any of the well-known works on decisive battles in history. Shakespeare rushes us on to the treaty of Troyes (May 1420), whereby Henry V won the promise of the crown of France as well as the hand of Princess Catherine. In reality, there was much hard fighting and talking still to come over the intervening years, with the conquest of Normandy and of the approaches to Paris being undertaken by Henry between 1417 and 1420. To some degree, the victory of Agincourt was overtaken by other events, the visit of Emperor Sigismund to England in 1416, and the murder of the duke of Burgundy in 1419, to name but two major events.[4] The notion that Agincourt was the sole key to Henry's success found, and still finds, its way into the popular literature. In fact, he was much assisted by divisions within France between the Burgundians and Armagnacs (otherwise known as the Orleanists). These divisions were largely occasioned by a struggle for control of government in the face of the mad King Charles VI's incapacity to rule, and had reached the dimensions of civil war well before 1415. Even without being truly decisive, however, there is ample evidence to suggest that Agincourt had an impact on the English and French and was seen as a momen-

---

[3] *Gesta Henrici Quinti. The Deeds of Henry the Fifth*, ed. F. Taylor and J.S. Roskell (Oxford, 1975).
[4] For a general narrative account of the war, see E. Perroy, *The Hundred Years War* (New York, 1965, first pub. in French in 1945), and for this period in particular, C.T. Allmand, *Henry V* (London, 1992).

tous event. Its legends and myths have continued to maintain a hold on the English psyche (the French soon learned to seize on Joan of Arc in preference), spilling over into the desire to establish whether one's brave ancestors might have fought there. Whilst perhaps not quite in the league of 'Queen Elizabeth slept here', this has affected the study of the subject, not necessarily for the better.

As we shall see in chapter 4, much historical interpretation of Agincourt has been influenced by sentiments of national identity and pride. Much of this focuses on Henry himself, 'the perfect medieval hero', as Kingsford called him.[5] Added to this we have the effect of the 'gallant archer' syndrome, that the day was won by the common yet brave English (or Welsh) soldier, bending his bow against and bringing low the proud and haughty French nobleman. It is perhaps not jumping too far ahead to say that historical writing before the turn of this century did not make as much of the role of the archers as modern commentators have done with their debate over the positioning of the archers. Were they on the flanks, or in between the groups of men-at-arms, or, in Burne's view, both.[6] The role of the archer has perhaps been given extra force by virtue of the misconception that we are dealing here with a faceless multitude. It was once thought that we could not know the names of the archers at Agincourt. This is not true. There is a vast quantity of archival material concerning the administration of the English army in the Agincourt campaign and I am not the first to draw upon it. As we shall see in chapter 4, hesitant advances were begun by Sir Harris Nicolas in the early nineteenth century based upon copies and extracts made a century earlier for Rymer's edition of diplomatic documents. This contributed to his publication of the first focused study, the *History of the Battle of Agincourt*, in 1827.[7] Sir Joseph Hunter made great strides in identifying the relevant original documents in the middle of the nineteenth century, and contributed much to cataloguing and making accessible these materials in the newly founded Public Record Office.[8] The potential which the original administrative records offered was demonstrated in James Hamilton Wylie's amazingly detailed *Reign of Henry the Fifth*.[9] But, strangely, they have remained a lesser known element compared with the vast quantity of chronicle and early historical

---

[5] C.L. Kingsford, *Henry V* (New York and London, 1901), p. 401.

[6] A. Burne, *The Agincourt War* (London, 1956), pp. 79–80.

[7] This was issued in an expanded edition in 1832, with a third edition of 1833 almost identical to that issued the year before. A facsimile of the third edition was published by H. Pordes in 1971.

[8] *Agincourt. A Contribution towards an Authentic List of the Commanders of the English Host in King Henry the Fifth's Expedition to France in the Third Year of his Reign* (London, 1850).

[9] At Wylie's death in 1914, only the first volume, which ends with the departure from England in 1415, was complete and could be published immediately. The second, which contains the account of Agincourt, existed in partially corrected proofs and was published with the assistance of Wylie's family in 1919. The final volume dealing with the years from 1416 to 1422 was published in 1929, being written by W.T. Waugh, Professor of History at McGill University but based upon Wylie's notes wherever possible. For simplicity's sake, I shall use 'Wylie' for the work as a whole.

writing on the battle. Chapter 5 seeks to redress this by aiming to provide a straightforward analysis of what survives, and what it can tell us about the battle. It also gives a brief survey of administrative records which can be used for the study of the French army at Agincourt. It would be fair to say that the French have been less interested in the battle than the English. The only dedicated study, René de Belleval's *Azincourt* (1865), concentrates on establishing the presence of individuals at the engagement, but is forced to rely on the lists of dead and prisoners found in the chronicles.

My study of the battle is, in many ways, conceived along the same lines as that of Nicolas. Nowhere is this clearer than in the space given up in both works to accounts of the battle found in fifteenth-century chronicles. There are many of these, coming from both sides of the English Channel: indeed one of the main fascinations is seeing how the two sides differed in their treatment of the battle. Some chronicles were written close to the event, others were writing with considerable retrospection. Some chronicles are no doubt already well known to those interested in the topic. On the English side, for instance, the anonymous *Gesta Henrici Quinti*, written within a couple of years of the battle, has formed the basis of many modern works.[10] Of accounts written in French, perhaps the best known are those in the chronicles of Enguerran de Monstrelet and of Jean Waurin, both of which works are available in English translation. As noted earlier, sixteenth-century writers based their own accounts on certain fifteenth-century chronicles, and the latter have remained pre-eminent in any serious discussion of the battle. It is not surprising, therefore, that extracts from them, and a discussion of their value, will form the largest part of this current volume. These chronicles are extremely valuable sources, but they are not without their pitfalls, as we shall consider more fully at the beginning of the first chapter.

One of the principal difficulties has been deciding what starting point to take in the extracts. We might argue that the accession of Henry V in 1413 should be the point of departure for it seems clear that he was determined almost from the outset to invade France, no doubt to take advantage of the divisions within that kingdom. But that might create a need to look even further back, as the last few years of his father's reign had already seen armies sent in the context of French civil strife.[11] After much thought, it was decided not to include full details of the siege of Harfleur but to commence the study from the point Henry left Harfleur to begin his march towards Calais. The decision was made partly on the grounds of length. To have included full narratives of the siege would have led to a book which was even longer. When it comes to administrative records concerning the English army, however, it is necessary to ignore the distinction between siege and battle for the materials relate to the campaign as a whole. The failure to treat

---

10 See for instance, C. Hibbert, *Agincourt* (London, 1964); J. Keegan. *The Face of Battle. A Study of Agincourt, Waterloo and the Somme* (London, 1976); M. Bennett, *Agincourt 1415. Triumph Against the Odds* (Osprey Campaign series, 9, London, 1991); C.T. Allmand, *Henry V* (London, 1992).

11 A. Curry, *The Hundred Years War* (Basingstoke and London, 1993), pp. 91–4.

of the siege is regrettable, but could perhaps be justified on two further grounds. First the siege as a military exercise is relatively straightforward and uncontentious.[12] The second justification for starting with the departure from Harfleur is that it is only at that point that battle with the French became likely, if not − dare one say it − inevitable.

This does of course raise an important and perplexing point right from the start, for we cannot be completely sure what Henry's original intentions had been in undertaking a campaign to France. All of the sources are vague in this respect. The chroniclers tend to speak only in terms of the recovery of his just rights. The indentures by which retinue leaders committed themselves to royal service are also problematic. Some imply that even in late April 1415 the king was keeping his options open, for they speak of an expedition to France *or* to Gascony, a distinction having to be made as the rates of pay for the duchy were traditionally higher than for expeditions to elsewhere in France. When money was actually paid out in early June, it was for a campaign in Gascony, although the indenture clauses still permitted adjustment to be made later if the venue was changed. By the time Henry left England on 11 August 1415, he had decided on a landing in Northern France. He had with him, at perhaps around 12,000 men, the largest army which had left England since 1359, so we can be certain about one thing − he clearly intended to make an impact. But even so, we cannot know, nor perhaps did he, whether he was already committed to a battle-seeking strategy. The first target was Harfleur, but had the siege proved shorter and easier and had disease not set in, might not other towns have been besieged? It has also been suggested that Henry may have planned to move southwards towards Bordeaux. A letter to the *jurats* of Bordeaux written on 3 September at the siege of Harfleur by Jean Bordiu, archdeacon of the Médoc and chancellor of Gascony, boasted that Henry would take Harfleur within eight days and would then go on to attack Montivilliers, Dieppe, Rouen, and Paris before moving south to Bordeaux.[13] At a meeting of the *jurats* of 7 September, they spoke of the possibility of the king coming to their city, although there is nothing in the surviving letters of the king himself which mentions this intention.[14] This would certainly help to explain the double terms of the indentures. Whilst Bordiu may have been unduly optimistic, Henry had certainly envisaged a long campaign. The campaign indentures were theoretically for a year's service, although as we shall see in chapter 5, the issue of proposed duration is not so clear cut: Henry knew that he did not have enough money to pay his troops for the whole year,

---

[12] I concur with the verdict of Taylor and Roskell (*Gesta*, p. xxxiii) that 'for the course of the siege the *Gesta* is unsurpassed'.

[13] *Archives Municipales de Bordeaux, vol. 4. Registres de la Jurade. Délibérations de 1414 à 1416 et de 1420 à 1422* (Bordeaux, 1883), p. 257. M.G.A. Vale, *English Gascony 1399–1453* (Oxford, 1970), p. 75, claims that the *king* had said he would march to Bordeaux before he returned to England, but this expression comes from Bordiu's letter, not from the king's. See below, Text F 6.

[14] *Registres de la Jurade*, p. 250.

and thus had to include let-out clauses which would have truncated the length of campaigning. In this respect, the length of the campaign was, from the outset, dependent upon what happened during it. We might come to the same conclusion on the issue of whether Henry was intent from the start upon giving battle: he was, like most military leaders over the ages, an opportunist.

The French made no attempt to meet him in battle in order to rescue Harfleur, which surrendered on 22 September. Four days later, Henry summoned the Dauphin Louis to single combat, proposing that such a duel should determine the claim to the throne: if Henry were to prove the victor, he would inherit the throne of France when Charles VI died, an interesting anticipation of the outcome of the treaty of Troyes in 1420.[15] But no reply was received within the eight-day period allowed by the terms of Henry's summons, nor did any French army appear, although they were beginning to gather troops in earnest from at least 20 September. Whilst it is not surprising that the dauphin turned down Henry's offer, the French also needed time to gather their army, for, with the memory of Crécy and Poitiers still fresh, they were determined not to suffer an easy defeat. We must assume that the French were well aware of the damaging effect the siege had had on Henry's manpower. They no doubt decided to await his next movements before themselves deciding whether to seek battle, and certainly they would reap an advantage in letting him move away from Harfleur, for then he would be prevented from using in any field engagement the large garrison he had left in the town.

This brings us to the point of Henry's departure from Harfleur, which can be dated to between Sunday 6 and Tuesday 8 October. Although in retrospect Henry's decision to march north was portrayed as an act of courage, aimed at showing the French that he took his rights to their crown seriously, there are signs that it was also intended as a fairly swift retreat to Calais where easy shipping could be found for the return to England. Getting enough transport to Harfleur would have been difficult, and an early return home for the main force would have been demoralising, not least for those left in Harfleur and for the English people as a whole. Henry moved quite quickly to the Somme estuary, reaching it by 13 October. Indeed, as the accounts of the march in the *Gesta* and in leading French chronicles show, he did not dally in any place, and certainly chose not to launch any further sieges or assaults, keeping well away from the main fortified centres. Thus although he still had a good number of men with him, as many as some English *chevauchées* of the fourteenth century, he does not seem to have conducted this march as a means to offer his men opportunities for plunder. He chose not to cross at Blanchetaque because the French had a small army waiting for him there. He would have been in a very vulnerable position had his army, still weakened by dysentery, been attacked whilst crossing the causeways. He had no choice but to move eastwards, again keeping up a

---

15 T. Rymer, *Foedera* (3rd edition, The Hague, 1739–45), IV, ii, p. 147, translated in Nicolas, appendix VII, and in Hibbert, *Agincourt*, appendix V. This summons is often dated to 16 September but is much more likely to have been issued after the surrender of Harfleur.

good pace. He must have realised that this would make him vulnerable to a battle-seeking French. We cannot be too certain why the French did not attack him before he managed to cross the Somme. A French advance guard was already trailing him. It may be that the French 'high command' in Rouen were, as some of the chronicles tell us, not so sure of what the best policy should be, although one might be tempted to believe that accounts of the debate parallel explanations of Henry's march from Harfleur in the sense of being wise after the event, in this case to show that there were some who had advised against the battle in the first place. It is likely that the French were keen to raise as large an army as possible to be certain of success. Their main force had mustered at Rouen around 15–17 October. There was no harm in keeping Henry under pressure for a while longer, though there might be dangers in allowing him to get too near to Calais where he could be assisted by a large garrison, and by reinforcements from England, for it does seem as though attempts were made to raise more men at home in mid-October.[16] One aspect of the Agincourt campaign which is perhaps less well known is the fact that Calais itself was under pressure. According to at least one French chronicle, a sortie from Calais, possibly hoping to join up with Henry, was intercepted.[17]

Once Henry was across the Somme on 19 October, the French made their intentions clearer, being buoyed up by the arrival of large numbers of troops, no doubt, and were clearly sending out several reconnaissance parties, as was Henry himself. This must explain why the administrative records show us some men killed on days before the battle. Heralds were sent by the French on 20 October to fix a date and place, to which Henry seems to have given a rather equivocal reply that he was bent on marching to Calais. The *Gesta* has the French deciding not to fight on 21 October: Bennett suggests that 'the French challenge was intended to pin him in place while the advance guard made its withdrawal'.[18] The French were thus able to amass their various troops and to block Henry's route at Agincourt, choosing a site of battle which they presumably considered to their advantage. Henry had little choice but to fight. From his scouts' reports of the gathering of French troops, he must have known for at least a week or so that battle was likely. According to the *Gesta*, it was around 17 October that he had ordered the preparation of sharpened stakes for protection against an anticipated cavalry charge. It is most likely that Henry knew of French intentions from prisoners. A written French battle plan is now known to have existed, but it is unclear whether it came into Henry's hands before or after the battle. Nor is it certain whether Henry tried to negotiate his way out of the battle or not. As you will read, some accounts, significantly not those on the English side, have it so. The extracts will take as their end point Henry's arrival

---

16 See below, p. 425.
17 See below, p. 103 (Le Religieux de Saint-Denis).
18 Bennett, *Agincourt*, p. 54. See also C. Phillpotts, 'The French plan of battle during the Agincourt campaign', *English Historical Review*, 99 (1984), pp. 59–66.

at Calais on 29 October, although chapter 3 will give some material on his return
to England.

We shall return at the end of this work to see what conclusions can be drawn
in the light of all the evidence henceforward presented. No doubt those reading
on will focus on the issues of interest to them, whether it be the positioning of
the archers, whether Henry or the French made the first move, the killing of the
prisoners, or the reasons for French defeat. This book is not intended, however,
as a full study of the battle and its impact. Nor is it able to provide critical
editions of the narrative and documentary sources. Such studies still need to be
written. But it is hoped that this current work will bring a greater range of source
materials and issues to a wider audience, and, in particular, that it will heighten
awareness of the problems of the subject. Agincourt has suffered because of its
fame. There has been an over-reliance on certain works and, in particular, those
sixteenth-century works which were considered to have influenced Shakespeare.
In historical discussion of the battle, a critical eye has often been lacking and
there has been frequent reiteration of certain set interpretations. We all have a
view of how Agincourt was fought, but how much of this can be substantiated
from sound evidence? Just how reliable are the sources and the interpretations
before us?

That is not to say, of course, that we should seek to avoid the myth entirely.
The myths and legends of Agincourt begin in the period itself, as the extracts in
chapters 1 and 3 show, and have developed ever since. This in itself is undoubtedly part of the lasting fascination of the subject. It also stands as an integral
element in our national consciousness, offering a linking of arms across the
centuries. Several English chronicles, including Thomas Elmham's *Liber
Metricus* written close to the event, speak of St George being seen fighting in
the battle on the side of the English. In the First World War, there were stories of
angelic Agincourt bowmen giving support and inspiration for the British army at
Mons.[19] Such was the potency of the memory of this medieval victory for the
English. A ballad written around 1600 asks, rhetorically, 'Know ye not Agincourt?' But do we?

---

[19] A. Machen, *The Bowmen and Other Legends of the War* (London, 1915), cited in J. Winter,
Sites of Memory, Sites of Mourning. The Great War in European Cultural History (Cambridge, 1995), p. 67. See also J. Terraine, *The Smoke of the Fire. Myths and Anti-Myths of War
1861–1945* (London, 1980), pp. 17–19. I am grateful to Colin Fox for these references.

1

Fifteenth-Century Chronicle Sources

Many chronicles of the period include an account of the battle of Agincourt. Only one chronicle, however, the anonymous *Gesta Henrici Quinti*, can be seen to have been written, at least partly, as a *direct* result of the battle. In other cases, the account of the battle occurs within a broader chronological narrative covering many years of the century. As is clear from the size of the extracts provided in this chapter, there is much variation in the length and extent of coverage, and in level of detail. Given the constraints of space, only the major accounts are provided here. Although some chronicles, such as the works of Adam of Usk and John Streeche, are generally important for a study of the reign of Henry V, their descriptions of Agincourt are perfunctory and have thus been omitted. In France, it is clear that many accounts of the battle were derived from the chronicle of Enguerran de Monstrelet with only minor variations, sometimes of a local significance. This has also justified the omission of some accounts; but where relevant, materials which have been excluded are mentioned in the context of other works.

Anyone drawing on chronicle materials needs to be aware of certain key issues; their purpose and nature, authorship, date of composition, sources, reliability, dissemination, connections with, and influences on, other writings.[1] As these are specific to each work, there will be a discussion of such matters preceding each extract so that its particular strengths, emphases and weaknesses can inform the subsequent reading of the text itself. It is sensible, however, to begin with a broader discussion of the chronicle sources as a whole. This is doubly necessary because, as we have already noted, many historians of later

---

[1] Anyone working on chronicles is in constant debt to those who have produced critical editions. My comments on each text are largely drawn from the introductions to such editions. Two works of synthesis are also indispensable. C.L. Kingsford, *English Historical Literature in the Fifteenth Century* (Oxford, 1913) (henceforward *EHL*) was a seminal work of its time, providing discussion of individual works as well as much evaluation of the writings of the period. Antonia Gransden's *Historical Writing in England, ii. c. 1307 to the Early Sixteenth Century* (London and Henley, 1982) (henceforward Gransden) provides a supplement and up-date to the work of Kingsford in the light of later study, and also includes some discussion of French chroniclers whose works impinged on English history. For the French side we have a fairly comprehensive list, although little by way of commentary, in A.M.L.E. Molinier, *Les sources de l'histoire de France des origines aux guerres d'Italie*, 6 vols (Paris, 1901–6), vol. 4 (1904). Gérard Bacquet, *Azincourt* (Bellegrade, 1977) offers extracts from several chronicles in French with short commentaries on each author.

centuries, including those of our own, have drawn extensively on the chronicle accounts, accepting them as the definitive versions of the events of 25 October 1415.

We hit a problem right from the start. There are many accounts of the battle. As we shall see, some are intrinsically more reliable than others, but none is exempt from problems of interpretation. There is at base a fundamental difference between English and French accounts. In English chronicles, the emphasis is on triumph against the odds, on the bravery and brilliance of command of Henry himself, and on God's support for the English cause. As all were written with hindsight, their narratives are crafted to bring out the inevitability, as well as the surprising nature, of the English victory. They are works of triumphalism, and this remains the case even well after the event. French chronicles, on the other hand, are often works of defeat, of reflection and criticism. If the English writers endeavoured to find someone to praise (largely their king and God), then the French writers were looking for someone to blame. It is in their accounts that we have the stress on the foolish pride of the French nobility which led them to attack without caution and, in their desire to keep the glory to themselves, to reject or fail to use other troops which could have assisted them. The French were certain of victory because of their weight of numbers, and because the English army had been weakened by illness and an extended march. But their over-confidence proved their downfall. French chronicles stress the hand of unpredictable fortune, but also often seek to explain why their side lost. There are thus many more excuses for French failure put forward in French compared with English writings. The earliest French account by the Religieux of Saint-Denis is particularly keen to give as many reasons as possible why the French lost. These include the decision to move from an original sound position; the desire of all the nobility to get to the front; political divisions within France; the impetuousness in actual combat, especially of the young, who did not heed the advice of their elders; heavy rain, leading to heavy going, which was a disaster when in heavy armour; the lack of sleep on the night before the battle; disdain for the English, the rejection of the latter's overtures for withdrawal on 24 October. The *Chronique de Ruisseauville* also adds the observation that the French were positioned on newly sown land, the English on uncultivated, firm land. These are all negative factors, and only one positive one – the effectiveness of the English archers both with the bow and with the heavy war hammer – is given. Some French writings also display a desire to explain why God had forsaken them. This is not absent from English writings but it tends to be used in the latter as a component of triumphalism.

There are some further 'national' differences which are to be expected. The French show a greater interest in the burial of the French dead, the English in Henry's entry to London. There is also generally more interest (and knowledge of?) French actions and movements in French sources, although the fact that the English were marching through their country means they are not devoid of details on Henry's movements. Moreover, Le Fèvre was in the company of the English for this period, and Waurin also developed links and interests in English history. They, in company with Monstrelet, composed 'chivalric chronicles' where deeds of arms on both sides of a conflict were worthy of mention. These features, combined with the continuing French desire to explain the English victory by virtue of the deployment of the archers, means that French writers do give attention to English actions. Early English accounts, such as the *Gesta*, stress French folly and pride, but both there and in later texts, there is a definite feeling that the English *won* the battle rather than the French losing it, as well as an almost complete ignorance of French deployments.

The most obvious expression of national differences is in the variation seen in the numbers of troops involved on both sides (see Table 1). English accounts tend to exaggerate the size of the French army whilst perhaps minimising their own numbers. Setting aside the late account in the Greyfriars' Chronicle, with its rogue, but possibly more accurate, 26,000, all English accounts place the French army at the battle as numbering between 60,000 and 140,000. French writers are on the whole much more reluctant to hazard an opinion on numbers, especially on their own forces, which could of course be taken as testimony in its own right to the fact that they knew the odds had been heavily stacked against the English. Only Monstrelet, Le Fèvre and Waurin give a total figure for the French (50,000), although other writers give the sizes of some of the components of the army. As for the English, the *Chronique de Ruisseauville* mentions 8,000–9,000 men although it is not clear whether the archers are in addition; Monstrelet has 14,000 (of which 13,000 are archers), Le Fèvre and Waurin 11,000 (including 10,000 archers), and the Berry Herald 17,500, including 15,000–16,000 archers. The Religieux has Henry V mention 12,000 archers in his battle speech, but these figures are minuscule compared with those advanced by Juvenal des Ursins at 22,000 and 38,000, with again the vast majority (18,000 and 30,000) as archers, and the 80,000–100,000 leaving England according to Perceval de Cagny and Antonio Morosini. Intriguingly, in the *Chronique d'Arthur de Richemont*, written with information from Richemont who was captured at the battle, the English, at 11,000–12,000, *outnumber* the French, who are given as 10,000! Whilst both French and English give high numbers for French casualties, it is interesting to note that French writers give much higher numbers for English dead than do their English counterparts, who have an obsession with keeping the number around or below 30.

French writers also seek to set the reasons for the defeat within a broader discussion of contemporary political difficulties engendered by the civil war between the Burgundian and Armagnac factions. Almost all of the extant chronicles are pro-Burgundian, some more rabidly than others. Duke John the Fearless (d. 1419) was not present at the battle but his absence is either not mentioned at all in the chronicles, or is explained as the result of the hostility of the other princes of the blood. This is stated even by the anti-Burgundian, Jean Juvenal des Ursins, who is surprisingly oblique in his criticism of the duke.[2]

2 There is similarly veiled criticism of the Burgundians in the writings of Alain Chartier. See below, Texts E 4 and E 5.

Table 1. Chroniclers' estimates of numbers

Chronicle	English army	French army	English dead	French dead
Gesta	6,000[a]	60,000	4 named: 9–10	5,598–6,598
Liber Metricus	7,000[b]	60,000	2 named: 30	9,310
Walsingham	8,000	140,000	7 named: 28	3,080
Otterbourne	1,500 ships	60,000	2 named: 30	1,598
Usk	10,000	60,000	27	8,523
Streeche	8,000	100,000	–	–
Tito Livio	[c]	–	2 named: 98	10,004
Pseudo Elmham	–	–	2 named: 100	9,000–10,000
Capgrave, *De Illustribus Henricis*	7,000[d]	60,000	2 named: 30	8,614
Capgrave, *Abbreviacion*	8,000[e]	140,000	9 named: 28	4,078
Hardyng	9,000	100,000	4 named	1,508
Basset, College of Arms MS 9	16,500[f]	150,000	4 named: 10	2,400?
Benet	11,000	100,000	–	–
Brut	7,000	120,000	2 named: 26–28	11,000–12,000
London Chronicles	10,000	60,000–80,000	5 named: 23	5,000
Latin *Brut*	8,000	100,000	2 named: 100	11,000+
Religieux	12,000 archers	[g]	–	4,000
De Cagny	80,000–100,000	–	–	5,000–6,000
Ruisseauville	8,000–9,000	–	–	7,600–7,800
Des Ursins 1	20,000–22,000[h]	–	–	4,000
Des Ursins 2	38,000[i]	8,000[j]	–	–
Monstrelet, Waurin, Le Fèvre	11,000[k]	50,000	600(M): 1600 (Waurin Le Fèvre)	10,000+
Bourgeois de Paris	–	One and a half times English	–	–
Berry herald	16,500–17,500[l]	10,000 men-at-arms	2 named: 300–400	4,500–4,600
Tramecourt	–	–	–	10,000
Richemont	11,000–12,000	10,000	–	–
Morosini	100,000[m]	–	–	–

[a] Garrison at Harfleur 1,200; invalided home 5,000; march 900 men-at-arms plus 5,000 archers.
[b] On march 900 + 5,000.
[c] 2,000 in garrison of Harlfeur.
[d] 9,000 leave England; 5,000 on march.
[e] 1,500 ships; 8,000 on march
[f] 1,500 knights, 35 esquires and others in garrison of Harfleur.
[g] Gives size of vanguard as 5,000.
[h] Ie. 4,000 men-at-arms, 16–18,000 archers.
[i] Ie. 4,000 men-at-arms, 4,000 gros valets, 30,000 archers.
[j] In first two battles 5,000 and 3,000 respectively.
[k] Monstrelet says 13,000 archers, Waurin and Le Fèvre 11,000; but all state 900–1,000 men-at-arms.
[l] Comprising 1,500 knights and esquires and 15,000–16,000 archers.

Whilst the Norman, Pierre Cochon, suggests that John the Fearless had an agreement with Henry V, he is keen to tell us that the duke dropped it as soon as he heard news of the defeat. Emphasis is often placed by writers on those members of the duke's family who were present and died, such as his brother, Duke Anthony of Brabant, whose impetuous bravery is applauded in accounts on both sides of the Channel. In addition, John the Fearless is credited for punishing those who attacked the English baggage. In the case of Monstrelet, Le Fèvre and Waurin, all writing in the time of his heir, Philip the Good, there is an effort to explain the latter's absence from the battle as being due to his father's deliberate efforts to keep him away.

Many accounts make clear, however, the devastating effects of political divisions in France as the context, cause and effect of French defeat at Agincourt. There is explicit criticism of the Armagnac rulers by the Religieux and the Bourgeois of Paris, noting particularly their inability to keep the troops in order, so that they commited worse excesses than the English enemy. As the Bourgeois puts it, 'never since God was born did anyone, Saracen or others, do such destruction in France', adding that 'it was widely said that those who were taken prisoner had not been loyal or true to those who died in the battle', perhaps an implicit criticism of the role of the dukes of Orléans and Bourbon. Accounts of the supposed debate in the French court over whether the French should give battle, as presented in several writers, tend to vary in whom they see as responsible for the decision to fight, but Orléans, Bourbon, and the constable d'Albret are named as the leaders who sent the heralds to give summons to Henry. The *Geste des nobles françois* accuses the duke of Bourbon of acting prematurely without awaiting the arrival of the Bretons, but criticism of the duke of Brittany's failure to send troops is found in the works of the Norman, Thomas Basin, and of Perceval de Cagny, servant of the duke of Alençon, whose master's estates were also in the duchy of Normandy. These are occasioned in part by longer-standing animosities between the people of Normandy and those of Brittany, as well as the particular circumstances of the time where the duke of

Brittany was pursuing his own interests over Saint-Mâlo and was also absent from the battle.

Political influences are less apparent and indeed less present in English works, but they are not totally absent. This can be seen in relation to the portrayal of two members of the royal family. Humphrey, duke of Gloucester, was Henry V's youngest sibling and the only brother to be present at the battle, for Thomas, duke of Clarence had been invalided home from Harfleur and John, duke of Bedford had been left behind in England as keeper of the realm during the campaign. Early accounts mention Gloucester's bravery and also the fact that he had been wounded, heightening the story with the king, his brother, protecting him and saving his life. Stories always improve in the telling (another good example was the notion that St George was seen fighting for the English), but there seems little doubt that Gloucester's role is given greater prominence in the writings from the mid 1430s onwards. At the death of Henry V in 1422, Gloucester had become protector of the realm for the nine-month-old Henry VI, but his rule had not been without problems. Most notable was his feud with Henry Beaufort, bishop of Winchester. But there had also been clashes with his own brother, Bedford, over foreign policy, particularly the attitude to be taken to the Burgundian alliance. Bedford died in 1435 and the king was due to come of age in 1437. There is a strong suspicion that Gloucester commissioned the *Vita Henrici Quinti* from Tito Livio around 1437–8 to stress his close relationship with the young king's father, and also to encourage the young prince to emulate the deeds of his father, and also of his uncle who both in the Agincourt campaign and the later conquest of Normandy is given a distinctive and prominent role. This is sustained by the Pseudo-Elmham's *Vita et Gesta Henrici Quinti* which is partly derived from Tito Livio and may also have had links with Gloucester's circle, and by writings emanating from London, the *Brut* and the London Chronicles (where his role in the defence of Calais in 1436 is stressed), for Gloucester was always popular with the Londoners.

The second example is Edward, duke of York, who was Henry V's cousin and the most significant fatality of the battle. As with Gloucester, he is given some prominence in early writings and is consistently noted as commander of the vanguard, but there is a marked development of his role as time goes on, including accrediting him with the idea of the stakes. Unfortunately, without further detailed manuscript research, it is not easy to date the writings which give him such prominence, and where it is also stated that the king mistrusted him (no doubt because of the treason of his brother, Richard, earl of Cambridge in the Southampton plot on the eve of the army's departure from England). It is tempting to link them to pro-Yorkist feelings in the early 1450s.[3] As Gransden notes, almost all the chronicles from mid-century supported the Yorkist cause, adding that 'the London chronicles and the authors of the *Brut* continuations favoured the Yorkists because theirs was the party which promoted the war with

---

3   See below, p. 93.

France, a source of prosperity to the citizens of London'.[4] With the coming of a Yorkist to the throne of England in 1461, sentiments could be made even more explicit. Thus in John Benet's chronicle, which ends in 1462 and was probably compiled sometime before 1471, 'Edward duke of York held the battle (*aciem belli*) that day and fighting with great vigour against the enemy; he was killed there honourably, whom in our days we might with justification call the second Solomon'.[5]

What we are seeing here is the way in which history was rewritten to suit a contemporary purpose. The chronicles from which extracts are given were written at various times over the course of the sixty years or so following the battle. Approximate datings are given at the beginning of each extract, and the texts are presented as far as possible in the order in which they were completed. It might seem unequivocal that the earliest sources would be the most useful and reliable, for not only does memory fade with the passing of the years, but also stories and traditions develop to warp and overwhelm the initial version of events. This is not a wholly sound conclusion, however, for it is possible that some 'later' works existed in note form or at least in the minds of their authors earlier. This is a particular problem with the accounts in Monstrelet, Le Fèvre and Waurin which are relatively late in final composition, and yet offer much detail, some of it unique. We know so little on the actual mechanics of chronicle writing, and no sets of notes seem to have survived. Yet the welter of detail is surely so great that it is tempting to believe that it did not simply exist in the memory of writers until it was written down as a continuous narrative, but that, like a modern historical study, it involved some element of research and took up many sets of notes and drafts before completion. Very few medieval chronicles of this or any other period are considered to be in the hand of their author, so it is likely that they were dictated or copied, perhaps from a rough autograph draft. It is tempting to believe that in this set of material, College of Arms MS 9, the chronicle of Basset and Hanson, is one such draft.

This is linked to a further important issue. It might be assumed that eyewitness accounts are the most valuable to us, and are likely to be the most reliable. But, as with the issue of date of composition, we have the interesting situation whereby the majority of eyewitness accounts are late, at least in final composition. Four writers were present at the battle. The *Gesta* was written by a priest accompanying the English army and is the only account written in the first person. He tells us that during the battle he was sitting on a horse among the baggage at the rear of the battle. The *Chronique de Ruisseauville* may include mention of this: the writer, also unknown, tells us that 'when the English realised that fighting had started, they had in their rear two men like monks who wore big hats with large shells on them and who read their books and kept

---

4 Gransden, p. 467.
5 *John Benet's Chronicle for the years 1400 to 1462*, ed. G.L. Harriss and M.A. Harriss, Camden Miscellany, vol. 24 (Camden Society, fourth series, 9, London, 1972), p. 177. The account of the battle here is too perfunctory to merit inclusion.

making the sign of the cross over the English as long as the battle lasted.' The Latin prose account of the *Gesta* was produced quite quickly after the battle, perhaps in 1417, but may have the disadvantage of being an example of English royal propaganda. Our second eyewitness, John Hardyng, probably from Northumberland, tells us in the second version of his Middle English verse chronicle that he was at the battle of Agincourt with his master, Sir Robert Umfraville. It has been assumed that Hardyng was a soldier who participated in the battle although it has not been possible so far to substantiate this from the muster rolls for the campaign. A further problem arises in that the first version of his chronicle does not mention his presence at the battle. Both versions were written up at least thirty years after the event and provide extremely thin details on the battle, and the Latin prose account of the battle which Hardyng wrote in connection with the second version is almost entirely derived from the *Gesta*.

The two remaining eyewitnesses were both from Picardy. Jean Waurin tells us that he was aged 15 at the time of the battle, and was 'in the assembly on the French side'. His age, and indeed the way he writes about the battle, make it likely that he served as a page or squire rather than as an active soldier, although he did have an active military career later. Waurin tells us that the author of the other eyewitness account, Jean Le Fèvre, was aged 19 at the time of the battle, and was with the English army. It seems most likely that he was serving with the medieval equivalent of the diplomatic corps, the heralds and pursuivants. He tells us that he heard tell of the dead from the *officiers d'armes* who were at the battle on both sides, and as he later became King of Arms of the Burgundian order of the Golden Fleece, a link with the heralds at this stage seems feasible. Why exactly a Frenchman was with the English for so long (possibly since the leaving of Harfleur), remains puzzling. There is no indication in his account that he was a prisoner or hostage. Waurin also tells us that Le Fèvre was 'even one great cause of dissuading King Henry' from crossing the Somme at Blanchetaque, but it may be significant that Le Fèvre does not say the same, but names a Gascon servant of d'Albret as telling the English, falsely, that the ford was well guarded, and so blaming him for the disaster which followed on the grounds that otherwise Henry would have marched on peacefully to Calais and there would have been no battle. Was Le Fèvre trying to cover up his own 'act of treason'?[6] Be that as it may, neither Waurin nor Le Fèvre seems to have completed the relevant part of their chronicles, both in French, until the early 1460s, and as we shall see later, they were extremely dependent upon the existing work of Monstrelet, completed in the 1440s. As far as we can tell, Monstrelet was not an eyewitness of the battle.

There are therefore specific problems with all of the eyewitness accounts. In addition there is the general issue of how much one eyewitness could have seen. Is the author of the *Gesta* trying to reassure his readers by telling us that he was sitting *on a horse* in the rear, giving him perhaps the advantage of height? If one visits the site, and considers where the baggage might have been in the vicinity

---

6   The Religieux also speaks of French traitors who advised Henry to march into France.

of Maisoncelles, however, one wonders whether even on a horse he could have had much of a range of vision. It is difficult for us to picture a medieval battle, but an analogy with a modern-day rugby match might not go amiss. A lot happens simultaneously over a wide area. There would be much movement whose cause or purpose would not be apparent to an individual spectator. As Bradbury has already noted much would have happened simultaneously. A comparison with the French plan of battle 'shows that chronicle accounts of battles tend to prolong and separate moves that must often have been designed to coincide. There is a clear intention to make one major effort, that would strike at vital points, at the same time engaging all the English forces so that there could be no reinforcement against a successful breakthrough.'[7] Eyewitnesses could not see everything at once, nor was it easy for anyone to write up a narrative dealing with simultaneous actions.

A rugby pitch is a lot smaller than the field of Agincourt (even though as battles go, the latter was possibly fought over a relatively small expanse), and it is difficult to see it all with one's own eyes. Quite often one needs some of the action related by someone else, although everyone has their own view of what happened, and those actually playing (or fighting) might give a different account of events. Our eyewitnesses, as at a rugby match, were able to soak up the atmosphere, to ask questions at all stages (presupposing, of course, that they had in mind they were going to write it up afterwards, which does not necessarily follow, except perhaps in the case of the author of the *Gesta*), and to see the aftermath. In fact that is what Le Fèvre and Waurin say that they did 'see with their own eyes' – the dead. We would be suspicious nowadays, however, if two people said *exactly* the same thing, which is what Waurin and Le Fèvre did for the most part. They also say that they got information from the heralds. The latter were clearly an important source of information as they were responsible for compiling the lists of the dead and probably of the prisoners too. They would have been eyewitnesses to the same degree as our non-combatant writers, and research has shown just how important they were in the compilation of history in the period.[8] They might also be the recorders of chivalrous deeds as the medieval equivalent of being mentioned in despatches, or indeed of non-chivalrous actions, as well as of knightings on campaign and before battles.[9]

The deployment of troops would be a particularly difficult thing to see if one was not involved, and perhaps even if one was. It is likely, perhaps, that even eyewitnesses of battles would derive much of their information on such topics from those aware of plans of action, although whether they would have had

---

[7] J. Bradbury, *The Medieval Archer* (Woodbridge, 1985), p. 125.

[8] M. Keen, 'Chivalry, heralds and history', in *The Writing of History in the Middle Ages: Essays Presented to R.W.Southern*, ed. R.H.C. Davis and J.M. Wallace-Hadrill (Oxford, 1981), pp. 393–414.

[9] Basset (Text A 8) mentions that Henry dubbed several knights at Pont-Saint-Maxence when he anticipated battle, but no account tells us of English knightings before the battle of Agincourt. Monstrelet, although interestingly not Le Fèvre and Waurin, says that the duke of Orléans and others were dubbed knights on the evening of 24 October.

direct access to commanders is more dubious. There can be little doubt that those who were present at battles and who wrote about them had also to rely to a greater or lesser degree on what they were told, and what they heard. The *Gesta*, Le Fèvre and Waurin all contain references to this indirect form of information, which is of course the kind of material that other writers would also have had access to, albeit after the battle. Tito Livio, one assumes, gleaned information from the duke of Gloucester. The author of the Pseudo Elmham might have gained some from another soldier, Walter, Lord Hungerford. But both were writing several years later, and their informants were also reminiscing after many years. This would also be true for Jean Juvenal des Ursins who was in Paris at the time of the battle, and later in the company of veterans as well as in a position and with an inclination to carry out research into what had happened. He speaks of matters reported by someone called Tromagon, the king's yeoman of the chamber, who had been taken prisoner and had come to seek his ransom. But des Ursins is aware that there is more than one version of events, and at the end of his first narrative moves into a second with 'on this matter some others have written in the manner which follows'. Basin too is aware of different opinions: 'some of them reported – we are not sure whether it really was like this – that the king of England realising that so large and strong and army was coming to meet him, had offered to surrender Calais and to pay a great sum in gold so that he might be allowed to return home without his men suffering any harm'. Perceval de Cagny exaggerates the size of the English army but tries to give his figure authenticity by saying that this is what veterans have told him. Philippe de Vigneulles (d. 1527–8) tells us that some of his information came from old men he had talked to.[10]

Closer to the event, we do not know whom the Religieux, or, in England, Thomas Walsingham, spoke to. Both monkish authors lived through the general reportage of the battle in their countries, and would have been well aware of the atmosphere of, respectively, tragedy or triumph. Both were 'professional' monastic chroniclers who had regular sources of information, formal networks feeding material to them. The Religieux speaks of 'credible witnesses of whom I have enquired carefully', 'I know by accurate information', 'I have learned from a reliable source', showing an awareness of the need to give some validity to his account. Such chroniclers also had access to 'official channels' as they were able to include documents produced by the authorities. They do not do so with relation to Agincourt, although Monstrelet includes the text of an order of Charles VI to raise troops about which the Religieux clearly knew. It is highly likely that there was an official list of the French dead and prisoners agreed by the heralds of both parties. This would explain, for instance, some similarities between the various lists given in the chronicles, and also between them and the list provided in an entry in the ledger book of the city of Salisbury, which may itself derive from an official list circulating in England as part of a royal

10 *La Chronique de Philippe de Vigneulles*, ed. C. Bruneau, 2 vols (Metz, 1927–9), 1, pp. xvi–xvii.

news-letter.[11] There is not total consistency, however, and it is known that there were some missing believed dead, yet not definitely known to be so. Moreover, the lists only noted those 'of name' (sometimes described as noble or with 'cote armours', that is, in this context, heraldic identifications) so that it is not surprising that the chronicles provide us with different accounts of the total numbers of dead. It has also been speculated that some chronicle accounts of the entry of Henry V to London were derived from an official programme of some sort. That again might explain the basic similarity between the accounts, although there are always minor variations between one account and another.

For some writers there were also other chronicles to draw upon. The *Brut* and London Chronicles were often derived from existing versions which were then copied and continued. The complex inter-relationship of the writings of Monstrelet, Waurin and Le Fèvre has already been mentioned, and will receive further attention before their extracts are given. We can be certain too that the author of the Pseudo Elmham drew on the *Vita* of Tito Livio, and it seems likely that Tito Livio drew on the *Brut*. Hardyng used the *Gesta* for his prose account. It has also been thought that the *Gesta* was perhaps drawn on by Thomas Elmham in his *Liber Metricus*, but this remains shrouded in mystery partly because we are still unsure over the authorship of the *Gesta*, and also because it is not impossible that there was a lost common source for both. In these respects, therefore, the chronicle accounts are not wholly independent, even those of 'eyewitnesses'.

Accounts were not only affected by nationality and sources of information but also by their genre, which was in turn linked to audience and purpose. The religious element tends to be more stressed in works from a monastic environment. Clerical writers tend to be less interested, I suggest, in weaponry and in the positioning of the troops. The works of Thomas Walsingham, and to a lesser extent the Religieux of Saint-Denis, are products of a well-established, although by now declining, tradition of chronicle writing in Latin which stresses the workings of the divine will. That is not to say that all churchmen were willing to ascribe events merely to God's decree. Human agency was important even if man brought divine wrath upon himself through sin. Thomas Basin, bishop of Lisieux shows a remarkably objective stance.

This unlucky battle was fought near to the town of Hesdin in the fields of two villages, the one Agincourt, the other Ruisseauville, in the year of our lord 1415, on the day of Saints Crispin and Crispinian. A year had passed since the French had wretchedly sacked the city of Soissons, as we recounted above, and amongst other sacrilegious acts, had despoiled the venerable monastery which was dedicated to those blessed martyrs. So it was commonly believed that this disaster was divinely inflicted on the French because of their acts of impiety and their cruelty which they had committed in great numbers and to such a great degree by their sacking of that city and their plundering of the saints shrines. Everyone can think what they will. We, however, will be

[11] See below, pp. 263–5.

content to tell the facts in true narrative fashion leaving the discussion of the arcane workings of the divine will to those who presume to do so.

Writers were also influenced by access to monastic libraries containing Biblical and classical sources, and their narratives are littered with allusions to both. Walsingham chose to use a number of classical quotations in his account of the battle. Such a habit is found elsewhere in his writing but nowhere as intensively exploited as in his treatment of Agincourt. Classical influences are strong too in the *Vita* of Tito Livio, as the work of an Italian fully conversant with the new burgeoning humanist trend, and in the Pseudo Elmham which is more a hybrid continental and insular form of Latin composition. There would be much sense in a thorough assessment of classical influences on chroniclers' treatment of battles. I suspect we would find that many points derived more from classical *topoi* than from actual incidents. Dice throwing, for instance, occurs in Suetonius' account of Caesar, and there are other elements in Elmham's *Liber Metricus* which are redolent of Caesar's own *Gallic Wars*.[12] Moreover, Walsingham, Elmham and the early humanist authors, as well as the sixteenth-century writers, were keen to have Henry V appear to emulate the classical heroes.[13]

In the sixteenth century, works in English also took up some of these classical influences, particularly in terms of the battle oration. In the fifteenth century, however, these Latin works would have had a readership restricted to the educated, although this was by no means an exclusively ecclesiastical audience, and some of the stories they included, such as those of the tennis balls and of saintly intervention were in wider circulation. The *Brut* and London Chronicles were aimed at a bourgeois audience in London, and give a less rhetorical, more direct approach – in the case of the London Chronicles rendered rather terse by the format of key events of the mayoral year. They were no less, indeed often more, interested in the doings of the great and good. Thus they tend, as do all English writings, to mention very few of the English army by name, only those close to the king by birth or household service. They had a clear concept of who 'made history'. There is no 'popular' version which glories in the achievements of the archers. It is only in the 1400s, however, that a full tradition of chronicle writing in English emerged, testimony not only to the growth of a middle-class, largely urban audience but also to the rise of the vernacular in formal prose. In France, almost all chronicles, save those of the clergy, were in French and had been for almost a century. Only in France was there a tradition of chivalric chronicling, as evidenced by Monstrelet (who intended his work as a continuation of Froissart's *Chroniques*), Waurin and Le Fèvre. But in all traditions there was a tendency to relieve the monotony of bland reporting of events and to

---

12 I am grateful to my colleague, Dr Gill Knight, for these observations.

13 This is even more overt in an anonymous text of the mid-fifteenth century, 'Contentio Alexandri Hanibalis Scipionis et Regis Henrici Quinti', where Henry V claims superiority over the other three, Alexander, Hannibal and Scipio. W. O'Sullivan, 'John Manyngham: an early Oxford humanist', *Bodleian Library Record*, 7 (1962–7), pp. 28–39.

heighten the dramatic tension by the use of invented direct speech, something which was much boosted by humanist influences into the next century.

No account could contain everything, and each was determined by its particular circumstances of composition, and perhaps by constraints of sources and length. Chronicles were written for effect, for a message, and not just to convey information. If we wish to draw a modern comparison then it must be with newspapers which often tell the same story but in very different ways and with different emphases based on their perceived audience and their own conception of the message they wish to communicate.[14] Some chronicles, like some newspapers, have a limited circulation, as is witnessed by the fact they now only exist in one copy. Others, like the *Brut*, were much more widely circulated, and copied. Only the *Gesta* can be seen as anything approaching an official account. Indeed, 'official history, in the sense of government commissioned history, was extremely rare in medieval England'.[15] The shifting sands of political control in France, along with the madness of King Charles VI and Henry V's continuing success made an official French history unlikely. It is often difficult to know whether omissions or inclusions are totally deliberate, but some raise problems. One might have expected the duke of Alençon's impetuous bravery to feature prominently in the chronicle of Perceval de Cagny devoted to the history of the Alençon line, but it is not there, and the duke is even omitted from the list of dead in Fenin. Yet he features in sixteenth-century English histories as the man who threatened Henry himself. As des Ursins tells us, 'Of all those who conducted themselves well and valiantly and fought strongly, both the English and French gave the palm to the duke of Alençon, and it was clear on both sides that he had conducted himself so valiantly that one could not have performed better.' But we have here a chivalric archetype. Even the English came to allow the French one hero, for in doing so they could make their own royal hero all the greater.

Fenin has the killing of the prisoners as due to an attack on the English baggage, but most writers, if they mention it at all, link it to the possible attack of the third French battle or to a French regrouping in general. Sir Thomas Erpingham is assigned a special role of command (although not always specifically of the archers as has been sometimes claimed by historians) in Monstrelet, Le Fèvre and Waurin, but not in English sources. What are we to make of this? Likewise, only the *Gesta* has Lord Camoys as commander of the rearguard.

This leads us to the final problem, which is how historians use the chronicles. There has been a tendency, difficult to avoid we must admit, of heaping up the

14 Adam of Usk's account of the battle, written before 1430, is not substantial enough to merit inclusion here, but it is interesting to see how his Welshness influences him on two occasions. He is the first to tell us that Davy Gam was 'of Brecon', and he later notes that Welsh benefices were exempted from convocation's grant of taxation to Henry after the battle because they had been impoverished by the Anglo-Welsh wars (*The Chronicle of Adam Usk, 1377–1421*, ed. C. Given-Wilson (Oxford, 1997), pp. 255–9). Usk also provides an interesting narrative of the entry to London.
15 Gransden, p. 456.

information they all provide, taking it all as potentially true in order to create a full narrative. So Camoys *is* commander of the rearguard not simply because the *Gesta* says so, but because no other account offers a straight alternative, with many names, some wrong (like the duke of Exeter, who was not at the battle), being given elsewhere in fairly random fashion. The *Gesta* does not mention weather conditions, so those are plucked from other writers, as is the idea of the soldiers taking earth in their mouths, or kissing the ground before battle. But the chroniclers are not consistent. Most accounts have the French camp noisy but the opposite is given in Monstrelet yet not in Waurin and Le Fèvre. The battle lasts for different lengths of time. The English troops are drawn up differently, and usually confusingly. There is a lack of consistency over whether the English moved position or not. On such shifting sands, one might be relieved to find situations where the chronicles agree, but if they are works which merely copy others, that can hardly be used as confirmation that what they say is true. This is a major problem with Monstrelet, Waurin and Le Fèvre, and one which historians have tended to duck. There is a need for more work on the inter-relationship of all the texts before us. Moreover, this would require a full study of the texts in the original language, for similarities and differences may be disguised by the foibles and inaccuracies of translation. All in all – and these points will be returned to in the conclusion to the book – the bare bones of a narrative for the battle can be agreed, but the smaller points of detail remain less firm, even though they are precisely the ones which often seize the imagination. One might argue, therefore, that the chronicle sources are deceptively 'user friendly', but that they need to be approached with a certain degree of caution. But let us leave the last word to one of our chroniclers to show that they too knew how daunting a task it was to describe the battle. All students of the period can feel sympathy for John Capgrave when he wrote, 'I shall remain silent about the archers, and the stakes, and how they were ordered, and also on many other related matters, for they deserve a lengthy exposition.'

A. Chronicles written in England

A 1. The *Gesta Henrici Quinti* (*c.* 1417, Latin)

Reprinted from *Gesta Henrici Quinti. The Deeds of Henry the Fifth*, translated from the Latin with an introduction and notes by Frank Taylor and John S. Roskell (1975), by permission of Oxford University Press. Copyright Oxford University Press 1975.

It is generally agreed that the *Gesta* offers the most reliable account of the campaign. The *Gesta* was written close to the event. The last date in its text is 20 November 1416, and as it refers to Henry's intention to renew the war 'in the following summer' but gives no detail of the second Norman campaign, it has been assumed that the original text was completed in the spring of 1417. If this is so, then the *Gesta* must stand as the earliest full narrative of the campaign. It commences with the coronation of Henry as king on 9 April 1413, but it is not a complete narrative of the reign from that point onwards. It confines itself to three issues, Sir John Oldcastle and Lollard activity (the 'heresies and errors' mentioned towards the end of the extract), diplomatic and military activity regarding France and Burgundy, and the visit of the emperor in 1416. In all three, the overriding purpose is 'to present Henry V as a devoutly Christian prince who, with his people, enjoyed God's constant approval and the support of Him and His Saints, notably the Blessed Virgin and St George'.[16] This has led commentators to suggest that the work had a very specific aim, namely to justify Henry's policies, not only at home, but also at the Council of Constance, being held at the time to solve the papal schism. The English and French were already implacable enemies as supporters of rival popes and had been since the opening of the schism in 1378. Emperor Sigismund had ambitions to solve the problems in the papacy and also to assist in the bringing about of Anglo-French peace, but had, by his alliance with Henry in August 1416, somewhat sullied, especially in the eyes of the French, his reputation as an independent arbitrator. The *Gesta* thus may also have been aimed at justifying Sigismund's support for Henry by emphasising that God has shown his approval for the king of England both at home and abroad in affording him victories against the Lollards and the French respectively.

Not only is the *Gesta* useful because it is written so soon after the event, but also because it was written by a priest accompanying the English army throughout the campaign of 1415. In addition it seems to be a wholly independent account which did not draw on other works, unlike many of the sources we shall encounter. Because it is an early text, written by an eyewitness and with a focused and detailed treatment of the campaign, it is all too easy to assume that it tells us all we need to know. Its original manuscript does not survive, but there are signs that it was drawn on by other writers in the fifteenth century: 'Giles Chronicle' uses it verbatim,[17] and there are obvious but problematic links with Elmham's *Liber Metricus* and Hardyng's Latin account, both of which are discussed later in this volume. The *Gesta* was not known in the sixteenth century, however, and was drawn on only sporadically by historians of the eighteenth and early nineteenth centuries.[18] Harris Nicolas first realised its importance, and printed the relevant sections in translation as his 'base text' in his *History of the Battle of Agincourt* (1827). The full text was subsequently printed by Benjamin Williams in 1850.[19] The *Gesta* was already starting to dominate modern accounts of the battle before a full critical edition appeared in 1975, but since then there can be no doubt of its central position in every work on the subject, even to the extent that the numbers of troops it gives as on the march

---

[16] *Gesta*, p. xxiii.

[17] *Incerti Scriptoris Chronicon Angliae de Regni Regum Lancastriensum Henrici IV, Henrici V et Henrici VI*, ed. J.A. Giles (London, 1848).

[18] Goodwin used it, but only marginally, in his *The History of the Reign of Henry the Fifth, King of England* (London, 1704). It is noted there as Anon. Scrip. Hist in Bibliotheca D. Bernard.

[19] *Henrici Quinti Angliae Regis Gesta* (London, 1850).

from Harfleur (900 men-at-arms and 5,000 archers) have become the common orthodoxy on the size of the English army at the battle.

There are some issues, however, which impinge on the question of reliability. The first is that the work is anonymous. There is enough internal evidence to indicate that the author was in priest's orders and attached to the royal household; he is therefore often referred to as 'the chaplain'. It used to be thought that the author was Thomas Elmham, a monk of St Augustine's Abbey, Canterbury, whom we shall meet again when looking at his own *Liber Metricus*. Elmham is certainly referred to elsewhere as 'our chaplain', but there is no evidence that he was present on campaign in 1415; indeed at that stage he was prior of Lenton. His authorship has also been questioned on linguistic grounds. The established view is now, therefore, that Elmham did not write the *Gesta*, but there is as yet no firm agreement on who did. Perhaps the most likely candidate is John Stevens, an Oxford graduate and canon of Exeter cathedral who served as royal chaplain and in the Court of Arches. On the eve of the expedition he had been ordered by Archbishop Chichele to transcribe copies of the treaty of Bourges of May 1412 whereby the Armagnac princes of France had made generous offers to Henry IV in return for hope of his military assistance, offers which had since been reneged upon.[20] His familiarity with official documents may explain, for instance, why the summons to the dauphin with which the extract below begins is very similar to the wording of the actual text itself.

The lack of firm knowledge on authorship is not in itself a major stumbling block in terms of the reliability issue. It would seem that the author was close enough to the king and his entourage to know what policies were being pursued. Yet he makes little of the sending of the French heralds to Henry, with no indication of what the king said to them. As we noted in the introduction to this chapter, he cannot have observed everything at first hand. His account was therefore based on what he was told by others. There is some indication that he took notes on the campaign: the story of Sir Walter Hungerford's wish for more men is introduced by 'amongst other things which I noted as said at the time'. That is not to say however, that this was in any way a war diary. Moreover, the account had to be recast into a Latin narrative. This causes us some difficulties with the military detail, not least over the positioning of the archers. The use of words is problematic. The army leaves Harfleur in three 'acies', which the editors translate as 'battles', although companies might serve as well. On the eve of the battle, the king draws up his army 'in aciebus et alis', battles and wings. But on the day itself, he drew up only one 'bellum' (battle), placing his vanguard for a wing at the right and his rearguard as a wing to the left ('aciem suam anteriorem . . . pro ala a dextris, et aciem posteriorem . . . pro ala a sinistris'). He positioned 'wedges' of his archers in between each battle ('intermisisset cuneos sagittariorum suorum cuilibet aciei'). It is the last expression which has caused the most controversy because it makes it seem as though the archers were not on the flanks of the whole army but were positioned between the centre battle and

---

20 *Gesta*, p. 13. Taylor and Roskell provide a full discussion of authorship, pp. xviii–xxiii.

the other two battles. Even if the translation of 'cuneos' as wedges can be dismissed, and thus with it the notion of a 'herse' formation, we are still left with the awkwardness of men-at-arms on the flanks, unless, of course, some archers were included in the expression 'acies' which surely must be the case for the two pre-battle usages of this term. Here then the wording of the *Gesta* has confused rather than assisted an analysis of the battle, and it may well be that our clerical author was just not very good at describing military formations! His position in the baggage train thus enables him to tell us that Henry ordered the train to be placed in the rear but prevents him from saying anything conclusive about Henry's advance towards the enemy (he simply says that Henry advanced towards his enemy and the enemy to him; the change of English position is not clear at all) or the battle. His comments read as though they have been picked up from others and from his own viewing, perhaps, of the heaps of slain. He tells us that the armies array at dawn, that most of the day passed without anything happening until the battle began, and that it lasted two to three hours; but can we necessarily trust these timings, for in the heat of the moment and moved to the rear, he could all to easily have lost track of time. Others certainly seem to place the battle earlier in the day, but inactivity, which the author of the *Gesta* no doubt experienced, is always something which drags.

The issue of why the work was written is also an influence on the way the battle is treated. Given the possible circumstances of the *Gesta*'s purpose, as outlined above, it is difficult to remove the charge that it was a deliberate work of propaganda. Even if there is no direct proof that the king commissioned it, or that it was for external consumption, much of what it says, for instance on Henry's war aims, fits with statements in diplomatic and other documents produced for the king. Thus it is possible that the truth was manipulated or elaborated to make it fit the general purpose. A particular characteristic is the tendency of the author to break off the narrative in order to make a pious exhortation. A study of the placing of these interpolations shows that they come at moments of possible disaster, such as when battle looked likely on 21 October, and just before the actual battle itself, or at the taking of fateful decisions, as at the commencement of the march from Harfleur. The French lose because they are sinful, the English win because they are inspired and assisted by God. There is little place for acts of individual bravery, even by the king. There is no battle speech for Henry, and indeed there is much less use of direct speech in this account that in many others. It is notable, too, how the wounding of Gloucester is played down and is not used as an opportunity to applaud the king for the defence of his brother, as features in several other later accounts. This fits neatly with the king's deliberate and conscious portrayal of the battle as God's victory rather than his own, a theme which is continued through the lengthy account of the entry to London after the battle. Under such circumstances too, it is not surprising to find that although French prisoners are killed when it is feared that the French are regrouping, the act is portrayed as happening spontaneously, without the king being mentioned as giving the order. The king, and God, needed to appear without blemish.

Taylor and Roskell provide an assessment on the fullness of the *Gesta* with respect to the campaign of 1415.[21] They suggest that it provides a fairly full account of the siege of Harfleur and of the march to the Somme, save that it can be supplemented by other sources on some points. For instance, a fuller account of the terms and events of the surrender of Harfleur is to be found in the London-based vernacular chronicles. They see its account of the battle as by far the clearest. 'It is free from both verbosity, which mars the *Vita* of the Pseudo-Elmham, and the distraction of individual incidents, such as are found in some French chronicles.' It certainly does permit a chronological reconstruction of the march from Harfleur, the only English chronicle to allow this. In many ways, I would argue, its strength lies not so much in its recounting of the battle as in its account of the march, especially the crossing of the Somme and the preparation of stakes, and of the preparations on the eve of battle, which imply that the English anticipated a French attack that night. Note that Hungerford's wish for more men is placed on that day, not on the day of the battle itself. The *Gesta*'s account of the battle itself is not particularly substantial, reflecting no doubt the inherent difficulties of describing the event as well as the intention to use it as an example of the revelation of God's will. This may explain why it says nothing about the state of the ground or the weather (odd omissions, perhaps, for an English eyewitness), or about the French being weighed down by their armour. Nor is there any mention of the late arrival of the duke of Brabant, or of what happened after the battle or at Calais. There is a very short list provided of French dead and prisoners. But as noted earlier, this is an account with the personalities left out save for the Divine Creator himself.

*

And our king, in order to seek after and inquire into every means which appeared to offer a prospect of deliverance for both peoples, that is, his own and the adversary's, sent a single herald, called Guienne Herald, with [Raoul], Sire de Gaucourt, to his adversary's first-born son the dauphin, deferring to send to the adversary himself because the latter was afflicted with his usual mental disorder. The king's purpose was to notify the dauphin that he had been waiting for him at his town of Harfleur and would continue to wait for him there for a further eight days, and to invite an answer from him within that period in the hope that he might yet feel compunction at the shedding of human blood, cause his right to be con-ceded to him without further rigours of war, and reach peace with him; or that, at least sparing the many, they might bring to an end that controversy respecting the right and dominion over the kingdom, begun long ago, then interrupted, and now revived afresh but still unresolved, and (following an exchange of certain legal securities and conditions to be established by the councils of the two kingdoms) might do so without any other shedding of fraternal blood whatsoever, by a duel between them, man to man.

21 Ibid., pp. xxxiv–xxxvii.

However, after the eight days had elapsed and neither the herald nor any other intermediary whatsoever had returned, arrangements having been made in the meantime to stock up and guard the town, and certain barons and knights diligent in warfare placed at the captain's disposal along with the three hundred lances and nine hundred archers of the garrison, the king resolved to start out on the march for which he had already made arrangements, a march through his duchy of Normandy towards his town of Calais, which was said to be more than a hundred English miles distant.

But because the dysentery, which had carried off far more of our men, both nobles and others, than had the sword, so direly afflicted and disabled many of the remainder that they could not journey on with him any further, he caused them to be separated from those who were fit and well and gave them leave to return to England, and these (quite apart from those whom death had carried off, those who had been appointed to guard the town, and those who, out of sheer cowardice leaving or rather deserting their king in the field, had stealthily slipped away to England beforehand), numbered about five thousand, so that of what was left of the army there remained no more than 900 lances and 5,000 archers able to draw sword or fit to fight.

And although a large majority of the royal council advised against such a proposal, as it would be highly dangerous for him in this way to send his small force, daily growing smaller, against the multitude of the French which, constantly growing larger, would surely enclose them on every side like sheep in folds, our king – relying on divine grace and the justice of his cause, piously reflecting that victory consists not in a multitude but with Him for Whom it is not impossible to enclose the many in the hand of the few and Who bestows victory upon whom He wills, whether they be many or few – with God, as is believed, affording him His leadership, did nevertheless decide to make that march, which was an eight days' journey. And, commanding the army to lay in stores of provisions for a journey of eight days, on Tuesday [8 October], the day before the feast of St Denis, on the nones of October, with this army of his, so very small yet arrayed bravely enough in three 'battles', he resolutely and fearlessly began the march, leaving the town of Montivilliers, which was some two miles distant from Harfleur, half a mile away on his right. Among other most pious and worthy ordinances, he commanded that, under pain of death, no man should burn and lay waste, or take anything save only food and what was necessary for the march, or capture any rebels save only those he might happen to find offering resistance.

And, pressing forward on the march, we arrived on the following Friday [11 October] before the town of Arques, which had a fresh-water river running down to the port of Dieppe (about three miles to our left on the sea coast) and also narrow bridges and a castle, within the area and under threat of which our passage lay. The king himself appeared in the 'battles' and wings and had them take up their positions in full view of the castle. And its garrison shot stones at us from their guns to make us keep our distance and prevent us from coming close. The stones, however, by God's will, did not harm anyone. And after a short time the king sent to the garrison to ask for free passage, and they, after negotiating for terms and having given hostages, granted the king free passage and a fixed amount of bread and wine with which to refresh the army, in order to ransom their town and neighbourhood from being burnt. We therefore passed through that area by way of the middle of the town, the entrance to which we found strongly barricaded with large trees placed across our route and with other obstacles.

And on the next day, leaving it half a mile away to the left, we went past the town of Eu, a walled and strong town, in which a part of the French army assembled against us had taken up quarters. And this force made a sally against our men; however, they were soon put to flight, making back to the town as a refuge in their retreat, not without incurring losses in killed and wounded. But some of our men, too, did not return free from injury. And on the night after, the inhabitants of the town, following a parley and the giving of hostages, ransomed from burning those neighbouring towns in which we had spent the night, in return for a fixed amount of bread and wine with which to refresh the army.

And, meanwhile, a report was spread in the army by certain prisoners that a great host of the French had made ready to engage us, and some stated that in their opinion the engagement was bound to take place, on the Sunday or Monday following, at our crossing of the River Somme. But there were different opinions amongst us as to when battle would be joined. For some persisted in maintaining that, in view of the civil discord and deadly hatred existing between the French princes and the duke of Burgundy, the French would be unwilling to move away from the interior of the country and the source of their strength, for fear that, while they were doing so, a hostile force of the duke of Burgundy might either come upon them from behind or, in their despite, usurp dominion over their territories by force. Some, however, said the opposite: that the military strength and armed forces of the French, once so noble, could not possibly (if they still retained any heart or manliness) bear the stain of the great dishonour which, to their everlasting reproach, would be attributed to them throughout the world, namely, that they had become so irresolute and cowardly and had so much fallen away from their ancient nobility of character that against the king of England (who had entered their land, remained there for so long, besieged and taken a town, and, at length, with so small a following and so reduced an army, laid waste their country at so great a distance from it) they did not dare, nay rather feared, to exert their military strength.

Chapter 10.

Now on the morrow of these events, which was Sunday [13 October], we came near to the town of Abbeville where, on the following day, we were hoping to cross the River Somme. But then, all at once, we were told by our scouts and mounted patrols that the bridges and causeways had been broken, and that a great part of the French army was on the opposite bank to obstruct our passage. We therefore reined round along the shore of the river, expecting to have no alternative but to go into parts of France higher up and to the head of the river (which was said to be over sixty miles away), where rumour had it that a great host of the French was making ready to do battle with us with every sort of practice and stratagem of war and with engines and other subtle contrivances, and expecting, too, that they would not allow us to cross the river before then anywhere in between. Dejected therefore at these rumours of battle and bemoaning the obstruction of our passage, we moved off on the next day [14 October] to another crossing of the river. But there, too, the bridges and causeways had been broken down, and the French confronted us on the other side in great arrogance; and they disposed themselves in line of battle as if prepared to engage us there and then. However, the fact that the river at that point had a broad marsh on both sides prevented either of us from coming any closer, so that not one of us, even had he sworn to do so, could have inflicted injury on the other.

And then at that time we thought of nothing else but this: that, after the eight days assigned for the march had expired and our provisions had run out, the enemy, craftily hastening on ahead and laying waste the country-side in advance, would impose on us, hungry as we should be, a really dire need of food, and at the head of the river, if God did not provide otherwise, would, with their great and countless host and the engines of war and devices available to them, overwhelm us, so very few as we were and made faint by great weariness and weak from lack of food. I who am writing, and many of the rest of the army, looked up in bitterness to Heaven, seeking the clemency of Providence, and called upon the Glorious Virgin and the Blessed George, under whose protection the most invincible crown of England has flourished from of old, to intercede between God and His people, that the Judge Supreme, Who foresees all things, might take pity on the grief all England would feel at the price we would pay with our blood and, in His infinite mercy, deliver from the swords of the French our king and us his people, who have sought not war but peace, and bring us, to the honour and glory of His name, in triumph to Calais.

Without any other hope but this, we hastened on from there in the direction of the head of the river, leaving on the next day [15 October] the city of Amiens about a league to our left. And on the following day [16 October] we came to a part of the country where there was a town belonging to the duke of Burgundy called Boves, with a river, and bridge and a castle, and our passage lay under threat of hostile attack from these latter. However, after we had had a parley with those in command of the castle and they had given hostages, we occupied the town for our night's rest, and it was well stocked with wine by which the army was greatly refreshed; and from the castle we had a free passage and bread in return for ransoming the town and its vineyards from burning.

And when on the Thursday [17 October] we arrived at a field next to the walled town of Corbie which itself was to our left, there sallied out from it against our men a part of the French army which had assembled there also. But they were soon put to flight by our men, some of them being killed and two of their men-at-arms captured. And there was brought to the king in that field a certain robber, an Englishman who, in God's despite and contrary to the royal decree, had stolen and carried off from a church (perhaps thinking it was made of gold) a pyx of copper-gilt in which the Host was reserved, that pyx having been found in his sleeve. And in the next hamlet where we spent the night, by command of the king, who was punishing in the creature the wrong done to the Creator (as Phinehas did with Zimri), and after sentence had been passed, he met his death by hanging.

Chapter 11.

Meanwhile, as a result of information divulged by some prisoners, a rumour went the rounds of the army that the enemy command had assigned certain squadrons of cavalry, many hundreds strong and mounted on barded horses, to break the formation and resistance of our archers when they engaged us in battle. The king, therefore, had it proclaimed throughout the army that every archer was to prepare and fashion for himself a stake or staff, either square or round, but six feet long, of suffi-cient thickness, and sharpened at both ends; and he commanded that whenever the French army drew near to do battle and to break their ranks by such columns of horse, all the archers were to drive in their stakes in front of them in line abreast and that some of them should do this further back and in between, one end being driven into the ground pointing down towards themselves, the other end pointing up towards the enemy above waist-height, so that the cavalry, when their charge had brought them close and in sight of the stakes, would either withdraw in great fear or, reckless of their own safety, run the risk of having both horses and riders impaled.

Moving from that place, we were lodged on the following day [18 October] in quite small hamlets near the walled town of Nesle. And the king sent word to the townspeople to arrange for the ransoming of the neighbouring hamlets from burning. But when the inhabitants refused, he ordered these places on the morrow to be set on fire and utterly destroyed. And suddenly, by God's will, news was there brought to the king that nearly a league away was a suitable passage across the River Somme. The king, therefore, sent mounted patrols ahead to test the passage, the depth of the channel, and the current of the river, and soon followed with the army. However, before he reached the river at that point, about a mile short of it, he crossed a marsh through which ran a stream (R. Ingon) making its way down from nearby into the main river, and so he was hemmed in, as it were, in the angle between the two; but, by God's will, the enemy were not aware of this.

And when the River Somme itself was reached, there were found two places where it could be crossed over (the water at the fords reaching only a little higher than a horse's belly), the approach to which places was by two long but narrow causeways which, previously, the French had astutely broken up the middle in such a way that it was scarcely possible, and then only with difficulty, to ride across the broken parts in single file. And when, immediately, Sir John Cornwall and Sir Gilbert Umfraville, with their pennons and a number of lances and archers on foot, had been sent across the water and a bridgehead firmly established to protect the remainder of the army when climbing up the bank (in case of a sally by the French), the king ordered the broken parts to be filled in with wood, bundles of faggots, and straw until it was possible for three men to ride through abreast without difficulty. And he ordered that the baggage of the army should cross by one of the causeways and his fighting men by the other. At the entrance to the latter he positioned himself to one side and certain persons of his own choosing to the other side, lest the throng of men, tightly packed and not under control, should, in their eagerness to cross, become jammed and choke the narrow passage with obstructions of their own making. And straightway, using these two places, the army increased greatly in strength on the far side of the water.

Even so, before a hundred of our men had waded across the river, enemy cavalry, which had been ordered in accordance with a plan of the French to prevent our crossing, made their appearance and emerged in columns and platoons from near-by hamlets within one, two, and three miles on that side; and, while in the process of joining up (although, as was God's will, too late), they drew nearer to our men, sending their swifter riders on ahead, perhaps to find out whether it still seemed possible for them to drive us back. Our mounted patrols, however, immediately went out to meet them and, meanwhile (before they, being dilatory or lacking foresight, could in fact join up and continually add to their numbers), our strength in that fine bridgehead across the water had greatly increased. For this reason, the French, taking up a position at a distance and having estimated our capacity to stand firm and their own incapacity to resist, abandoned the place and vanished from our sight.

Now we started our crossing about one o'clock in the afternoon, and it was only an hour short of nightfall before we were all across. It was, then, a cheerful night that we spent in those hamlets very near by, from which, when first we began our movement across the river, the French had emerged; and we thought it a matter for great rejoicing on our part that we had shortened our march by, as many reckoned, about an eight days' journey. And we were of the firm hope that the enemy army, the army which was said to be waiting for us at the head of the river, would be disinclined to follow after us to do battle.

Nevertheless, on the morrow, namely the Sunday [20 October], the duke of Orléans and the duke of Bourbon, who are very closely related to the French king and were in command of the French army, sent a message to our king by three heralds that they would do battle with him before he reached Calais, although they did not assign a day or place. Whereupon our king, readily accepting this as an act of grace on God's part and relying entirely on divine help and the justice of his own cause, with great resolution and manly spirit gave encouragement to his army and made ready to do battle on the morrow [21 October]. Proceeding on his march when the morrow came, he found no one opposing him.

And, while we were passing the walled town of Péronne, which we left behind a short distance away to our left, we caught sight of cavalry of the French army coming from the town towards us as a decoy, in order perhaps to entice us within range of enemy shots and the damage these would do. However, as soon as our cavalry went out against them, they promptly turned tail and made back to the town. And after we had gone past the town, we found, about a mile away, the roads quite churned up by the French army as it had crossed ahead of us many thousands strong. And the rest of us in the army (for I will say nothing of those in command), fearing battle to be imminent, raised our hearts and eyes to heaven, crying out, with voices expressing our inmost thoughts, that God would have pity on us and, of His ineffable goodness, turn away from us the violence of the French.

Chapter 12.

From there we marched away in the direction of the River of Swords [R. Ternoise], leaving on the following Wednesday [23 October] the walled town of [?Doullens] a league away on our left flank. And when on the next day, namely the Thursday [24 October], we were moving down a valley towards the River of Swords, word was brought to the king by our scouts and mounted patrols that an enemy force of many thousands was on the other side of the river, about a league away to our right. We therefore crossed over the river as quickly as possible, but, just as we reached the top of the hill on the other side, we saw emerging from higher up the valley, about half a mile away from us, the grim-looking ranks of the

French. These, in compact masses, 'battles' and columns, their numbers being so great as not to be even comparable with ours, at length took up a position facing us and rather more than half a mile away, filling a very broad field like a countless swarm of locusts, and there was only a valley, and not so wide at that, between us and them.

And in the meantime, our king, very calmly and quite heedless of danger, gave encouragement to his army, and he drew them up in 'battles' and wings as if they were to go immediately into action. And then every man who had not previously cleansed his conscience by confession, put on the armour of penitence; and there was no shortage then save only one of priests. And amongst other things which I noted as said at that time, a certain knight, Sir Walter Hungerford, expressed a desire to the king's face that he might have had, added to the little company he already had with him, ten thousand of the best archers in England who would have been only too glad to be there. 'That is a foolish way to talk', the king said to him, 'because, by the God in Heaven upon Whose grace I have relied and in Whom is my firm hope of victory, I would not, even if I could, have a single man more than I do. For these I have here with me are God's people, whom He deigns to let me have at this time. Do you not believe', he asked, 'that the Almighty, with these His humble few, is able to overcome the opposing arrogance of the French who boast of their great number and their own strength?' as if to say, He can if He wishes. And, as I myself believe, it was not possible, because of the true righteousness of God, for misfortune to befall a son of His with so sublime a faith, any more than it befell Judas Maccabeus until he lapsed into lack of faith and so, deservedly, met with disaster.

And when for a short while the enemy from their positions had watched us, taken our measure, and noted how few we were, they withdrew to a field, at the far side of a certain wood which was close at hand to our left between us and them, where lay our road towards Calais. And our king, on the assumption that by so doing they would either circle round the wood, in order that way to make a surprise attack upon him, or else would circle round the somewhat more distant woodlands in the neighbourhood and so surround us on every side, immediately moved his lines again, always positioning them so that they faced the enemy.

And when at length, after some time had passed, it was almost sunset, the French, perhaps realizing that battle was not to be joined (which in any case was not feasible with night coming on), occupied the hamlets and scrub close by, intending to rest until morning. And when at last the light failed and darkness had fallen between us and them, and we, still standing our ground in the field, could hear the enemy after they had taken up quarters, each one of them calling out, as usual, for his fellow, servant, and comrade (perhaps separated from him in so great a host), and our men had begun to do the same, the king ordered silence throughout the whole army under pain of forfeiture of horse and harness on the part of a gentleman should he offend, and of loss of his right ear by a yeoman and anyone else of lower rank who presumed to infringe the royal order, without hope of obtaining pardon. And he at once moved off in silence to a hamlet near by, where we had houses, although very few of them, and gardens and orchards in which to rest, and heavy rain almost the whole night through. And when our adversaries noted how still and silent we were, thinking that, being so few, we were smitten with fear and perhaps intended to make off during the night, they had fires lit and set heavily manned watches across the fields and roadways. And, it was said, they thought themselves so sure of us that that night they cast dice for our king and his nobles.

And on the morrow, that is Friday, on the feast of Sts Crispin and Crispinian, the 25th of October, the French, in the early dawn, arrayed themselves in battle-lines, columns, and platoons and took up position in front of us in that field, called the field of Agincourt, across which lay our road towards Calais, and the number of them was really terrifying. And they placed squadrons of cavalry, many hundreds strong, on each flank of their vanguard, to break the formation and resistance of our archers. And that vanguard was composed of dismounted men drawn from all their nobles and the pick of their forces and, with its forest of spears and the great number of helmets gleaming in between them and of cavalry on the flanks, it was at a rough guess thirty times more than all our men put together. Their rearguard and its wings, columns and platoons, however, were all mounted as if more ready to flee than to tarry, and compared with our men they were a multitude hardly to be counted.

And meanwhile our king, after offering praises to God and hearing Masses, made ready for the field, which was at no great distance from his quarters, and, in view of his want of numbers, he drew up only a single line of battle, placing his vanguard, commanded by the duke of York, as a wing on the right and the rearguard, commanded by Lord Camoys, as a wing on the left; and he positioned 'wedges' of his archers in between each 'battle' and had them drive in their stakes in front of them, as previously arranged in case of a cavalry charge. The enemy, made aware of this by scouts riding out in between either on that account or for some other reason for caution known to God but not to me, astutely kept at a distance to our front and came no nearer to us.

When, by so delaying, they had used up much of the day, both armies standing still and neither moving a foot towards the other, the king realized that the enemy host were putting off the assault he had been expecting them to make, and would so stand astride our route as either to break up our array or infect our hearts with fear of their numbers, or else as if they would obstruct our advance and were awaiting reinforcements, perhaps on the point of arrival, or, at any rate, as if, aware of our serious lack of provisions, they would overcome us by hunger, not daring to do so with the sword. And so he decided to move against them sending for the army baggage in order to have it at the rear of the engagement lest it should fall as booty into the hands of the enemy. (He had previously arranged that this baggage, together with the priests who were to celebrate the divine office and make fervent prayer for him and his men, should await him in the aforesaid hamlet and closes, where he had been the night before, until the fighting was over.) And at that time French pillagers were watching it from almost every side, intending to make an attack upon it immediately they saw both armies engage; in fact, directly battle was joined they fell upon the tail end of it where, owing to the negligence of the royal servants, the king's own baggage was, seizing on royal treasure of great value, a sword and a crown among other precious objects, as well as all the bedding.

But once, however, the king thought that almost all this baggage had reached his rear, in the name of Jesus (to Whom is bowed every knee, of those in Heaven, on earth, and under the earth) and of the Glorious Virgin and of St George, he advanced towards the enemy, and the enemy, too, advanced towards him.

But then, indeed, and for as long as the conflict lasted, I, who am now writing this and was then sitting on a horse among the baggage at the rear of the battle, and the other priests present did humble our souls before God and, bringing to mind . . . which at that time the Church was reciting aloud, said in our hearts: 'Remember us, O Lord, our enemies are gathered together and boast themselves in their excellence. Destroy their strength and scatter them, that they may understand, because there is none other that fighteth for us but only Thou, our God.' And also, in fear and trembling, with our eyes raised to heaven we cried out that God would have compassion upon us and upon the crown of England, and not suffer the supplications and tears which the English Church had poured forth and, at this very hour and in her accustomed processions, did undoubtedly pour forth on our behalf, to come to nothing, but would admit them to the bosom of His mercy and not allow that devotion which our king had taken unto himself – to the worship of God, the extension of the Church, and the peace of kingdoms – to be brought to naught by his enemies, nay rather, in the manifest bountifulness of His mercy, would now and hereafter cause him to be more exalted and mercifully deliver him from these perilous events as from others.

Chapter 13.

And then, when the enemy were nearly ready to attack, the French cavalry posted on the flanks made charges against those of our archers who were on both sides of our army. But soon, by God's will, they were forced to fall back under showers of arrows and to flee to their rearguard, save for a very few who, although not without losses in dead and wounded, rode through between the archers and the woodlands, and save, too, of course, for the many who were stopped by the stakes driven into the ground and prevented from fleeing very far by the stinging hail of missiles shot at both horses and riders in their flight. And the enemy crossbows which were at the back of the men-at-arms and on the flanks, after a first but over-hasty volley by which they did injury to very few, withdrew for fear of our bows.

And when the men-at-arms had from each side advanced towards one another over roughly the same distance, the flanks of both battle-lines, ours, that is, and the enemy's, extended into the woodlands which were on both sides of the armies. But the French nobility, who had previously advanced in line abreast and had all but come to grips with us, either from fear of the missiles which by their very force pierced the sides and visors of their helmets, or in order the sooner to break through our strongest points and reach the standards, divided into three columns, attacking our line of battle at the three places where the standards were. And in the mêlée of spears which then followed, they hurled themselves against our men in such a fierce charge as to force them to fall back almost a spear's length.

And then we who have been assigned to the clerical militia and were watching fell upon our faces in prayer before the great mercy-seat of God, crying out aloud in bitterness of spirit that God might even yet remember us and the crown of England and, by the grace of His supreme bounty, deliver us from this iron furnace and the terrible death which menaced us. Nor was God unmindful of the multitude of prayers and supplications being made in England, by which, as it is devoutly believed, our men soon regained their strength and, valiantly resisting, pushed back the enemy until they had recovered the ground that had been lost.

And then the battle raged at its fiercest, and our archers notched their sharp-pointed arrows and loosed them into the enemy's flanks, keeping up the fight without pause. And when their arrows were all used up, seizing axes, stakes and swords and spear-heads that were lying about, they struck down, hacked, and stabbed the enemy. For the Almighty and Merciful God, Who is ever marvellous in His works and Whose will it was to deal mercifully with us, and Whom also it pleased that, under our gracious king, His own soldier, and with that little band, the crown of England should remain invincible as of old, did, as soon as the lines of battle had so come to grips and the fighting had begun, increase the strength of our men which dire want of food had previously weakened and wasted, took away from them their fear, and gave them dauntless hearts. Nor, it seemed to our older men, had Englishmen ever fallen upon their enemies more boldly and fearlessly or with a better will.

And that same just Judge, Whose intention it was to strike with the thunderbolt of His vengeance the proud host of the enemy, turned His face away from them and broke their strength – the bow, the shield, the sword, and the battle. Nor, in any former times which chronicle or history records, does it ever appear that so many of the very pick and most sturdy of warriors had offered opposition so lacking in vigour, and so confused and faint-hearted, or so unmanly. Indeed, fear and trembling seized them, for, so it was said among the army, there were some of them, even of their more nobly born, who that day surrendered themselves more than ten times. No one, however, had time to take them prisoner, but almost all, without distinction of person, were, as soon as they were struck down, put to death without respite, either by those who had laid them low or by others following after, by what secret judgment of God is not known.

God, indeed, had also smitten them with another great blow from which there could be no recovery. For when some of them, killed when battle was first joined, fall at the front, so great was the undisciplined violence and pressure of the mass of men behind that the living fell on top of the dead, and others falling on top of the living were killed as well, with the result that, in each of the three places where the strong contingents guarding our standards were, such a great heap grew of the slain and of those lying crushed in between that our men climbed up those heaps, which had risen above a man's height, and butchered their enemies down below with swords, axes, and other weapons.

And when at long last, after two or three hours, their vanguard had been riddled through and through and broken up and the rest were being put to flight, our men began to pull those heaps apart and to separate the living from the dead, intending to hold them as prisoners for ransom. But then, all at once, because of what wrathfulness on God's part no one knows, a shout went up that the enemy's mounted rearguard (in incomparable number and still fresh) were re-establishing their position and line of battle in order to launch an attack on us, few and weary as we were. And immediately, regardless of distinction of person, the prisoners, save for the dukes of Orléans and Bourbon, certain other illustrious men who were in the king's 'battle', and a very few others, were killed by the swords either of their captors or of others following after, lest they should involve us in utter disaster in the fighting that would ensue.

After but a short time, however, the enemy ranks, having experienced the bitter taste of our missiles and with our king advancing towards them, by God's will abandoned to us that field of blood together with their wagons and other baggage-carts, many of these loaded with provisions and missiles, spears, and bows. And when, at God's behest, the strength of that people had been thus utterly wasted and the rigours of battle had ended, we who had gained the victory came back through the masses, the mounds, and the heaps of the slain and, seeing them, reflected (though not without grief and tears on the part of many) upon the fact that so great a number of warriors, famous and most valiant had only God been with them, should have sought their own deaths in such a manner at our hands, quite contrary to any wish of ours, and should thus have effaced and destroyed, all to no avail, the glory and honour of their own country. And if that sight gave rise to compunction and pity in us, strangers passing by, how much more was it a cause of grief and mourning to their own people, awaiting expectantly the warriors of their country and then seeing them so crushed and made defenceless. And, as I truly believe, there is not a man with heart of flesh or even of stone who, had he seen and pondered on the horrible deaths and bitter wounds of so many Christian men, would not have dissolved into tears, time and again, for grief. Indeed, having previously been despoiled by English pillagers, none of them, however illustrious or distinguished, possessed at our departure any more covering, save only to conceal his nature, than that with which Nature had endowed him when first he saw the light.

Chapter 14.

Would that the French nation might soon attain to peace and unity with the English, repudiate their acts of injustice, and abandon those most wicked ways by which, lured and confused, they are being led astray, lest they be reproached by that saying of the prophet: 'God is a just judge, strong and patient, is He angry every day? Except you will be converted, He will brandish His sword; He hath bent His bow and made it ready, and in it He hath prepared the instruments of death.' And if they do not very soon come to their senses, then let them bear in mind what follows: 'Behold, he hath been in labour with injustice, he hath conceived sorrow and brought forth iniquity, he hath opened a pit and dug it, and he hath fallen into the hole he made. His sorrow shall be turned on his own head, and his iniquity shall come down upon his crown.' For God is merciful and One who waits in long-suffering; but, when He has exhausted the balm of His mercy and long-suffering, He is a stern avenger and oft takes away the powers of strong men when not accompanied by justice. This was made manifest in the multitude of our enemies, all of whom, by means of that little band of ours that was striving for justice, He delivered up, indiscriminately, to flight, to capture, or to the sword.

For there were of them, by their own reckoning, more than sixty thousand who drew the sword, whereas our little band did not exceed six thousand fighting men. Of that great host there fell the dukes of Bar, Brabant, and Alençon, five counts, more than ninety barons and bannerets, whose names are set down in a volume of records, and upwards of one thousand and five hundred knights according to their own estimate, and between four and five thousand other gentlemen, almost the whole nobility among the soldiery of France. And of the number remaining there were taken prisoner the dukes of Orléans and Bourbon, the counts of Richemont, Vendôme, and Eu, and also that most worthy knight the Sire de Bouccicaut, the Marshal of France, but few others of gentle birth.

And indeed there was great rejoicing among our folk and also considerable amazement because, out of all our little band, there were found slain upon the field no more than nine or ten persons, apart from the illustrious and most prudent prince, the Lord Edward, duke of York, the Lord Michael, earl of Suffolk (a brave young man), and two newly dubbed knights who had fallen in the line of battle. And our duke of Gloucester, Humphrey, the king's youngest brother, a brave prince, like as he gave, in part received. Fighting in the king's 'battle', he was seriously wounded. And no wonder among so many furiously wielded swords, spears, and axes! After his arrival at Calais, however he soon recovered, God be praised.

Our England, therefore, has reason to rejoice and reason to grieve. Reason to rejoice at the victory gained and the deliverance of her men, and reason to grieve for the suffering and destruction wrought in the deaths of Christians. But far be it from our people to ascribe the triumph to their own glory or strength; rather let it be ascribed to God alone, from Whom is every victory, lest the Lord be wrathful at our ingratitude and at another time turn from us, which Heaven forbid, His victorious hand. And let our England be zealous in pleasing God unceasingly, in purging herself of heresies and errors along with other acts of sedition and unrighteousness, in making acknowledgement, more fully and perfectly than before, in hymns, by confession, and with chants, and in singing psalms to the Lord Who hath done marvellous things in Israel and given the victory to His anointed. And let her pour forth prayers, supplications, and tears, in the sight of God's great clemency, that for our sake, with the shield of His omnipotence, He may long watch over, protect, visit, and defend our most victorious king and likewise his desire and devout concern for the extension of the Church and the peace of kingdoms. And let us together sing that . . . which the Church sings year in, year out: 'Thine is the power, Thine the kingdom, O Lord; Thou art above all nations. Give peace in our time, O Lord.'

And when, the battle over, our king, out of consideration for his men, had spent that night in the same place where he had lodged the previous night, on the morrow he resumed his march towards Calais, past that mound of pity and blood where had fallen the might of the French. And on the Tuesday [29 October], the morrow of Sts Simon and Jude, he came to Calais. And on the Saturday [16 November] after the festival of St Martin, when (Raoul), Sire de Gaucourt, and the other prisoners from Harfleur had arrived, as bound by their agreement, he returned to England, by the port of Dover, with his prisoners.

Nor do our older men remember any prince ever having commanded his people on the march with more effort, bravery, or consideration, or having, with his own hand, performed greater feats of strength in the field. Nor, indeed, is evidence to be found in the chronicles or annals of kings of which our long history makes mention, that any king of England

ever achieved so much in so short a time and returned home with so great
and so glorious a triumph. To God alone be the honour and the glory, for
ever and ever. Amen.

A 2. Thomas Elmham, *Liber Metricus de Henrico Quinto* (Metrical Life of Henry V) (*c.* 1418, Latin)

Translated from 'Liber Metricus de Henrico Quinto', in *Memorials of Henry the Fifth, King of England*, ed. C.A. Cole (Rolls Series, London, 1858), pp. 113–24.

Thomas Elmham was a monk of St Augustine's Canterbury.[22] He became prior
of Lenton (Notts.) in 1414, and in the following year was appointed vicar-
general of the Cluniac order in England and Scotland. His preface to the *Liber
Metricus* says that it is an abbreviation in verse of another book which he wrote
in prose. It was thought that this other book was the *Gesta* but it is now generally
agreed that the *Gesta* was more likely the source of it, and that Elmham's prose
work is itself now lost or unidentified. This would explain the similarities in fact
between the *Gesta* and the *Liber*, but also the variations, most notably that the
Liber includes the story of the dauphin's gift of tennis balls to Henry, probably
being the earliest known version of this. The compilation of the *Liber* is
commonly dated to 1418: it ends by celebrating the first 'quinquennium' of the
reign, with its last datable event being the celebration of Easter by the king in
Normandy in 1418. Henry V is spoken of as still alive so the work must at least
predate 1422. It is in elegiac verse form, as found in classical love poetry, rather
than in the hexameter form more commonly used for Latin epic. There is thus a
classical feel, and influences in vocabulary from Livy and Suetonius (though it
follows no single model); but the grouping and ordering of words is not as we
might expect of 'real' Latin. It is difficult to translate and to analyse because it is
written in contrived and often abstruse style with deliberate use of cryptograms.[23] This was deliberate. The king would not have the glory ascribed to
himself alone, thus the meaning of the work was put 'beyond the comprehension
of most men: only the learned, who would appreciate Henry's desire for reti-

---

[22] For his career and other writings, see Gransden, pp. 206–10; *EHL*, pp. 46–7, 49–50. The
work is discussed in the introduction to the *Gesta*, pp. xx–xxi. There is an introduction
provided in Cole's edition of the *Liber Metricus*, pp. xli–lvii, but it must be used with caution
as it assumes that Elmham was also the author of the *Vita et Gesta Henrici Quinti*, now
commonly called the Pseudo-Elmham.

[23] These include the use of chronograms where letters in words should be read as numbers.
This is also seen in verses on the siege of Harfleur and battle in other monastic chronicles,
including the *Chronicle of Mont-Saint-Michel* (see Text D 5 b.). See also A. Gransden, 'Silent
meanings in Ranulph Higden's *Polychronicon* and in Thomas Elmham's *Liber Metricus de
Henrico Quinto*', *Medium Aevum*, 46 (1977), pp. 231–40. I am grateful to my colleague, Dr
Gill Knight, for discussion of the text.

cence, would fully understand it'.[24] Although it includes much material in the form of aide-memoire, such as the lists of events of each year from 1413 to 1418 – Elmham claims at the outset that he has extracted the most important material from his prose work in a form that will be more easily remembered – the verses themselves are written in a style intended to impress Elmham's fellow intellectuals within the ecclesiastical fraternity. The strong anti-Lollard tone would also appeal to this group, as would the biblical and classical references.[25] With nine fifteenth-century manuscripts extant, the *Liber* seems to have been more widely circulated and copied than the *Gesta*, and to have even 'enjoyed a considerable vogue', likely being used by Capgrave, Otterbourne, Streeche and probably Tito Livio.[26] It does not seem, however, to have been much used by writers of the next, or indeed later, centuries.

Elmham's exact link with Henry V remains unclear: a letter of the king to the abbot of Cluny in November 1414 refers to him as 'capellanus noster' ('our chaplain'), but it is thought unlikely that a monk would in reality have been a member of the king's household chapel. However, towards the end of the *Liber*, Elmham notes that the king sent for his chapel to celebrate Easter in Normandy in 1418. This may imply that Elmham was connected with this institution in some way, although the text does not say, as Kingsford claimed, that Elmham himself joined the king in Normandy in 1418. There is no proof that Elmham was present on the 1415 campaign. His work is not in the first person, nor does it have the ring of an eyewitness account. Elmham himself claimed, for the contents of the *Liber* as a whole, that it included what he had either seen himself or else had heard by trustworthy account, either in writing or orally, from those who had been present.[27] Thus, given the similarities with the *Gesta*, we must assume that his account is basically derived from the latter. It goes on to give a similar account of the entry to London. For the campaign, it gives a very similar

[24] Gransden, 'Silent meanings', p. 236, with reference to the preface of the work (*Liber Metricus*, p. 80).
[25] One early fifteenth-century copy of the *Liber* is in Cotton Julius E IV (where is found also the J text of *Gesta*). As the editors of the *Gesta* note (p. xvi, n. 3) this manuscript was previously part of British Library, Cotton Tiberius B XII, a collection of materials made by Thomas Beckington, bishop of Bath and Wells (1443–65) with respect to the English claim to France.
[26] *Gesta*, p. xlix. Thomas Otterbourne, *Chronica Regum Angliae* (c. 1422–3) is printed in *Duo Rerum Anglicarum Scriptores Veteres*, ed. T. Hearne, 2 vols (Oxford, 1732). It provides a very perfunctory account of the campaign with only two points of note: that Harfleur was deliberately depopulated by Henry at its conquest and that the march to Calais was undertaken on foot (1, p. 276). Like Streeche and Elmham, however, it does include the story of the dauphin's gift of tennis balls. John Streeche was a canon of the Augustinian priory of St Mary's, Kenilworth, close to Kenilworth castle which was visited by Henry in 1414 and where Otterbourne places the receipt of the dauphin's gift. His account of the battle, also composed in the early years of the reign of Henry VI, is likewise short and inconsequential, save perhaps for the idea that Henry took his captives to Calais 'chained and bound' (J. Taylor, 'The Chronicle of John Streeche for the reign of Henry V (1414–1422), *Bulletin of the John Rylands Library*, 16 (1932), pp. 151–4).
[27] *Liber Metricus*, p. 81.

version of the siege and route of the march, but without the level of detail. It has
the same numbers of troops, but different numbers of dead at the battle. It adds
more details on Henry's summons to the dauphin, telling us that the king
proposed that whoever won the duel should become king after the death of
Charles VI. That is not in the *Gesta* but is closer to the text of the actual
summons. More detail is given over the coming of the French heralds to fix a
battle, including mention of the sire de Heilly having a beautiful lady, perhaps an
allusion to a story well known at the time but now lost. More direct speech is
given and the king is given a battle speech. There is also more invocation of St
George as well as the notion that he was seen in the air fighting for the English,
also a story in early circulation. More detail is given on the wound to Gloucester
and to the king's bravery in defending him. This could be another early story
picked up by Elmham, who also provides us with the jingle (chapter 40) summa-
rising Henry's successes in the third year of his reign which was also circulating
widely. As for the battle proper, we have the same problem over the deployment
of the archers as in the *Gesta*, but then a much thinner account of the action.
Already, then, a version of Agincourt was developing which was a mixture of
experience and legend.

*

Chapter 22. *The lord king sent a herald to the dauphin saying that he
would await him in his town of Harfleur in eight days and that, without
the spilling of blood, he would give up his due rights to him if they
determined between themselves alone the right and lordship of the
kingdom of France by a duel, and that even if the victory fell to the king,
that he would allow the crown to remain with the present king of France
until the latter's death.*

The king sent to the dauphin in Paris by means of a herald that he should
give him a delay of eight days. So that there might be peace, he sought
either to gain his rights without war or to give duel alone in the field, and
if the dauphin should concede victory, Henry would return the proper
right of the crown to him, which he would give to his father (i.e. the king
of France) during his own lifetime but for no longer, and on the latter's
death it should returned to Henry. But neither the king of the French nor
the dauphin sent a response through the messengers Henry had provided.
Soon, marching on foot, he moved off, journeying through Normandy
towards Calais, by which means his rights were made clear.

Chapter 23. *That many were made ill by the bloody flux, and the bishop
of Norwich and the earl of Suffolk died, and many returned to England.*

The suffering of this dysentery weakened many unto death. Five thousand
men prepared to leave him. The bishop of Norwich and the earl of Suffolk

died there from the disease and some fled. For many deserted the king, secretly returning home. Scarcely more than 900 lances were with him; scarcely 5,000 archers remained, and everyday the number with him grew smaller.

Chapter 24. *The lord king, unperturbed, took up his journey on the feast of St Denis, crossing before the town of Arques and to the town of Eu.*

However, the king, unperturbed, by the time of the feast of St Denis [9 Oct.], having made all the necessary arrangements, began his journey, prohibiting arson and plunder under the threat of punishment by death. Having taken up supplies, he set out for the main routeway. The town of Arques, a place in a narrow site, overlooked the river. A crossing was provided by defended bridges. The route he hoped to take was blocked by many obstacles. Eu was said to be occupied by the enemy and to be well defended. They spent the night by these towns so that the health of all the men might be redeemed for the price of bread.

Chapter 25. *There was a rumour among the people through certain captives that they would shortly be engaging with the enemy in battle.*

Rumour spread through the army that battle with the French was soon to be give. Abbeville was on the Somme at a place where shallows allowed crossing, but as the bridges had been broken, there was no possibility of getting across. On the other side of the river the enemy army showed itself. He had to head upstream.

Chapter 26. *The bridges and causeways were broken asunder by the enemy, and the French emptied the area of supplies.*

Everywhere the bridges and causeways were broken by the enemy. Their company continued to grow. There were scarcely supplies for eight days for the king. The French devastated the farms, the vineyards and food supplies. They were keen to harry the people by hunger so that they might ruin them completely by making them weak and without even fighting. Oh Father Christ! Oh George, saint and knight, under whose nourishment England flourishes, you bring treasure! He chose Boves, with its bridges, for encampment. In the quiet of night, bread was carried back from there.

Chapter 27. *Of the sortie into the field made from Corbie.*

From Corbie a serious sortie was launched. The French were put to flight by the enemy sword.

Chapter 28. *Of the robber hanged because he carried off a pyx containing the body of the Lord.*

Having been caught with a pyx containing the body of the Lord after the fighting, a man was hanged because of his crime by the order of the king.

Chapter 29. *There came a rumour from the French about the intended destruction of the archers. Concerning the order of the king against them.*

Indeed certain groups of prisoners declared that the enemy wished to draw near so that they might break the battle lines (*acies*) of the archers by use of force. The king ordered the latter to prepare shaped stakes to fix in the ground. Their sloping gave protection against the enemy as the sight of them might frighten the horses.

Chapter 30. *The king sent to ransom villages around the town of Nesle but, with the locals resisting, he burned them.*

Soon the king sent to ransom villages near Nesle. They did not respond. Out of anger, he set fire to them.

Chapter 31. *Of the crossing of the River Somme.*

It was said that there was a crossing near to the River Somme. His scouts told him about it. However before he came to cross that river he had to cross the marsh. A stream enclosed his men by a flow of water. There were two shallows close together over which were two long, narrow causeways. Scarcely one horseman could walk in front of another. A troop of nobles crossed over the first. By the foresight of the king, it was decided that it would be a good idea to have a guard of infantry with bows and missiles in the front of his army. He made a wider path over the broken causeways by means of wood and straw. By such means, a crossing was effected.

Chapter 32. *French troops tried to impede the crossing but they were put to flight by the cavalry.*

The French troops tried to repel them through the troops. A few cavalry put them to flight, by attacking them. Indeed, throughout the quiet of the night, the next day, Sunday [19 Oct.], was awaited. Then there was great glory.

Chapter 33. *The duke of Orléans and the duke of Bourbon sent to the Lord king to say that that they were preparing to give battle shortly.*

The dukes of Orléans and Bourbon sent their messengers to the king that they would give battle against him. No day nor place was assigned by them. The final point and the place was said to be Calais. The sire de Heilly, having broken from prison, fled secretly and came there, carrying a beautiful woman. Sir Jean de Graville was also with him. The king, keeping silent, excused them. With the help of Christ, preparing for battle the next day by giving courage to his men, he crossed from there to Péronne. The French taunted the English that they would retreat. The English sought camp, and their hearts were quaking with fear.

Chapter 34. *Of the crossing of the water of the Ternoise.*

On the fourth day of the week, the king crossed the Ternoise, and, on the fifth, news was carried to him that the other bank of the river held many thousands of the French. They appeared on his right.

Chapter 35. *The king carefully observed the army of the French from a distance over the River Ternoise and of the constancy of the king against the enemy.*

The king crossed the river far from the watching eyes of the French, noting the three battles (*agmina*) of troops. In comparison, the king's army seemed very small. The king ordered his battle lines (*acies*) with wings (*alis*). They all made true confession to God. There was a shortage of priests, so many confessed to each other. A certain knight expressed his wish that a thousand more archers could be there. The king answered him, 'Thus, foolish one, do you tempt God with evil? My hope does not wish for even one man more. Victory is not seen to be given on the basis of numbers. God is all-powerful. My cause is put into His hands. Here he pressed us down with disease. Being merciful, He will not let us be killed by these enemies. Let pious prayers be offered to Him.'

Chapter 36. *Of the boldness of the French on account of the small numbers of the king's men and of the foresight of the king against them.*

The French, seeing the very small numbers of troops (*acies*) with the king, soon established themselves at the rear of the woods (*nemoris posteriora loca*). The king, believing that the enemy wished to surround him, ranged his army against them. Black night was almost descending, and

did not allow for fighting. The king bivouacked in silence, and ordered his
men to keep silent. He silently approached the village where he might
pitch camp. That rainy night, the people there, without bread, overflowed
with the offering of prayers and vigils to the Lord. The enemies, ponder-
ing that the English were spending the night in silence, thought therefore
that the king was intending to flee. They rode quickly over the fields by
several routes. They threw the dice to determine which [of the English]
they should each have.

Chapter 37. *Of the battle of Agincourt on the day of the Sts Crispin and
Crispinian.*

It was the twenty-fifth day of the month of October ever afterwards giving
the English passionate memories of that day. On the sixth day, Crispin
with Crispinian willingly bore weapons in the name of Christ. The enemy
troops stood in the field in many companies, so that the wing could be
driven back by any of the archers (*trusa quod his quaevis arcubus ala
foret*). The companies of French infantry were in the front, outnumbering
the English by three to one in that field. The battle lines (*acies*) of the
companies (*turmis*) of cavalry were in the rear, with sixty thousand in that
field of men. On the side of the king there were scarcely 7,000. With regal
command, the king prepared his men for battle, placing the vanguard as
wing on the right, with the rearguard as a wing to the left. Amongst them
he intermingled troops of archers (*hic intermisit turmas simul architenen-
tium*). He ordered them to drive the stakes into the field. The enemy
position was drawn up facing the king. The king stood in his army without
fear. He ordered the baggage to withdraw to the rear so that it might be
placed at the back of the battle. This was done by assigning the duke of
York as supervisor. But he refused, with this pious purpose: 'Oh king!',
the duke said, 'I will carry arms against these enemies not with the last
but with the first.' The king said to those remaining, 'My fellow men,
prepare arms! English rights are referred to God. Memories noted many
battles given for the right of King Edward and Prince Edward. Many a
victory occurred with only a few English troops. This could never have
been by their strength alone. England must never lament me as a prisoner
or as to be ransomed. I am ready to die for my right in the conflict. St
George, George, saint and knight be with us! Holy Mary, bestow your
favour on the English in their right. At this very hour many righteous
English people pray for us with their hearts. France, hasten to give up
your fraud!' The king, bearing his own arms, put his own crown on his
head. He signed himself with the cross, thus giving courage to his men.
For the priests cried out from behind, sighing, 'Now have mercy on us,
God. Now have mercy, God. Spare the crown of the English. Support the
royal right! In your mercy, Virgin Mary, bestow your favour. As your right

dowry, George, knight, and Edward, pious king, give your aid. May all the saints give constancy to our king. My God accept our holy prayers.'

Both armies came together to battle. The field through the woods was too narrow for them. The brother of the king, the noble Duke Humphrey, was wounded in the groin. Gore flowed down from the sword. Having fallen to the ground, the king stood over him to assist him. He was in this battle the defender of his brother. The troops of the French rushed forward against the archers. In the face of a storm of arrows they began to turn back. Their nobility in the front, divided into three groups, advanced towards the banners in the three positions. Our arrows were carried and penetrated, and the enemy was worn out under the weight of their armour. Some of our king's trustworthy men, pressed down the enemy who penetrated the line with axes, and the latter fell over. The living were pushed towards death. The living went under the dead. The battle lines piled in. The English rose up against the companies of the French as they came to grips. The French fell before the power of the English. Flight from there was not open to them. They killed them, they captured them and keep them for ransoming but quickly there was a shout that a new battle would begin. Many new battle lines threatened to enter the fray to fight against the weary. There was indeed a great throng of people. The English killed the French they had taken prisoner for the sake of protecting their rear. Praise was given to God. The crown of the king was broken off his helmet by an axe. Here it is noted that Grace had bestowed its hand.

Chapter 38. *Of the death of the duke of York and others on the side of the king.*

Here the duke of York was overcome by the whirlwind of war. The king washed his body for burial with royal care. The young earl of Suffolk died there also. Scarcely thirty other English fell by the sword.

Chapter 39. *The smaller army overcame the greater. Concerning the number of dead and prisoners on the enemy side.*

Thus, from the heavens, the anger of God rose against the enemy so that the smaller army overcame the many thousand. A bishop, three dukes, six counts and no less than 800 barons, 1,000 knights and also 7,500 of the men of noble rank fell. There were captured three counts, two dukes and the marshal of the French, that noble Bouccicaut. They surrendered. Many from the ranks of the nobles were captured. The victor was Christ, bearing the joyful trophies.

Chapter 40. *St George was seen by certain people fighting for the English.*

In the field, St George was seen fighting in the battle on the side of the English. [Eleven French dead are named, 'with 1,200 barons and those with banners, 1,500 knights and 7,000 other nobles and esquires'. Eight prisoners are named 'and many other gentlemen.] The Virgin, the hand-maiden of the almighty, protected the English. All the glory be given to her not to us. St Maurice took Harfleur, St Crispin carried the battle of Agincourt. May the third year of our king be celebrated by these events.

Chapter 41. *After the battle the king returned to the village where he had spent the previous night, and in the morning he took up his march towards Calais.*

After the battle the king spent the night in that place where he had slept during the preceding night. In the morning he resumed the journey to Calais and passed the battlefield with a great show of pious compassion. On the third day he came to Calais. He stayed there of his own will for twenty days.

A 3. Thomas Walsingham, *St Albans Chronicle* (*c.* 1420–22, Latin)

Translated from *The St Albans Chronicle 1406–1420*, ed. V.H. Galbraith (Oxford, 1937, pp. 92–8.

Thomas Walsingham was a monk at the Benedictine abbey of St Albans who carried on that monastery's tradition of historical writing. He served as precentor from 1380 to 1394 and then had a two-year period as prior of Wymondham before returning to St Albans where he seems to have remained until his death in about 1422. His output was considerable, with his principal work being intended as a continuation of the *Chronica Majora* of Matthew Paris. This was initially written down to 1392 but later continued to 1420. Its textual history is somewhat complicated, so much so that it was once supposed that not all of the writings were by the same man. One account of the period under discussion here is to be found in the *Historia Anglicana*,[28] although it must be remembered that this edition is in fact a compilation of a series of works by Walsingham. The latter also wrote another chronicle covering the period from 1376 to 1420. Its account of the years 1406–20, which is found in Bodleian Library 462 and was edited by V.H. Galbraith as *The St Albans Chronicle*, is

---

28 Ed. H.T. Riley, 2 vols (Rolls Series, London, 1863–4), pp. 309–14.

longer than the version edited as part of the *Historia Anglicana*, and is therefore used as the text for translation here. In addition, around 1419–20, Walsingham compiled the *Ypodigma Neustriae* (the symbol of Normandy), as both justification and celebration of Henry V's conquest of Normandy, and intended the work to be presented to the king.[29] In reality, it is a history of England rather than of Normandy, and is heavily dependent on Walsingham's other writings.

All three provide similar accounts of the siege of Harfleur and battle of Agincourt; there are only very small variations in wording which do not need to be noted for current purposes. The *St Albans Chronicle* gives fuller accounts of the Southampton plot and the siege of Harfleur, although the latter is concerned mainly with negotiations for surrender than with military details. It also offers a slightly fuller narrative of Henry's entry into London after the battle. By the reign of Henry V, the quality and level of information in Walsinghan's writing had declined somewhat from his earlier days, perhaps the result of his advancing age (he is thought to have died around 1422.) This may explain the rather thin account of the battle, although it was written within a few years of the event. It is thought that he gleaned information for his chronicles not only from official texts (he includes much from the trial of Oldcastle, for instance) but also from those passing through St Albans. If that is so, then there is no evidence here of the use of newsletters and it would not seem that he picked up much information. He uses extracts from Virgil, Lucan, Persius and Statius for rhetorical effect and to embellish an otherwise fairly bald narrative.[30] He also adds much surmising about the state of the English troops before the battle, which may reflect the kinds of stories being spread around England after the victory as well as Walsingham's penchant for heightening the tension. His patriotism is apparent throughout, as is his praise for Henry himself. It is possible, of course, that the account was deliberately vague, that he was writing for effect here rather than merely to provide information. In this interpretation too we might speculate that he consciously interlaced extracts from Roman authors in order to place Henry's victory on a par with classical incidents.

The account does contain some interest. It is the earliest known English account to mention that the ground at Agincourt was newly sown and soft, and to mention the threat of the French to mutilate the English if they won, although no details of this are given. It also makes clear that the English had to advance

---

[29] Ed. H.T. Riley (Rolls Series, London, 1876), pp. 461–8. Galbraith notes differences between the *Historia Anglicana*, the *Ypodigma Neustriae* and the *St Albans Chronicle* in his edition of the latter, and provides the references for all the classical quotations.

[30] Galbraith, *St Albans Chronicle*, p. vi, comments that the pasages on Agincourt 'show a verbal memory of a variety of classical authors which is surely astonishing'. Lucan (AD 39–65) wrote an epic poem, the *Pharsalia*, on the civil war between Caesar and Pompey. Persius (AD 34–62) wrote satirical poems largely against Nero. The *Thebais* of Statius (*c.* AD 45–96), tells the story of the quarrel between the sons of Oedipus. The *Aeneid* of Virgil (70–19 BC) concerned the wanderings of the Trojan, Aeneas, and the ultimate founding of Rome. The *Ilias Latinas* was a Latin version of Homer's *Iliad* by an unknown poet, probably of the first century AD, and was a popular school text in the classical period.

towards the French with some difficulty, and that the initial French plan was to overwhelm the archers by a cavalry attack. But the English retaliate – without the aid of stakes, it must be noted! To some degree, the archers are given a greater role here than in the *Gesta*, and the king is given a greater personal role. Walsingham is the first English writer to note that in the attack on the baggage, a crown was taken and used to make the local people think that the French had won the battle; but there is no killing of the prisoners. The numbers of dead are oddly precise, perhaps being derived from some kind of official list, such an item being the kind of document we might expect Walsingham to acquire. Thus he is able to tell us that the number of the rank and file who died was not calculated by the heralds, a forerunner of the 'and none other of name' well known from Shakespeare.

*

Having arranged things at Harfleur as befitted him and was appropriate to his success, the king ordered that they should at once take route towards Calais on foot with only a few men, no more than, as was said, eight thousand archers and armed men, many of whom had contracted sickness at Harfleur, as we described before. However, although it is amazing that he dared to approach the thickest forest of the French with such a weak hand, yet it is much more amazing that he pierced through it even though it was fortified with so many obstacles. Indeed, throughout the whole time of the siege of the town of Harfleur, the French had called together the most powerful and brave men, chosen from those already in their company and from those in far distant regions, summoning help from all directions so that the number of them, as was said, grew to 140,000 warriors. These prepared themselves for the day, time and hour when they would attack the king and his very small band who were thin from hunger, from the bloody flux, and from fever. When the English made camp to share out their victuals, there was such a shortage of bread in the army that many had to eat hazelnuts and roast meat in the place of bread. They were all forced by adverse fortune to drink water for the space of nearly eighteen days. With these delicacies and provision, the athletes of the king of the England were nourished and fed – they who were about to fight a massive army of thousands. In addition, they were exhausted from the journey, weakened by the need to keep watch, and debilitated from the cold nights. It is amazing that they were able to survive, but God gave them strength and fortified those whom He considered to be suffering from great infirmity. The king passed over the river which blocked his way, but not without great difficulty since the French had broken the bridges by which he might have been able to effect a short-cut. Soon the French hastened to gather together with all their knights in order to block the way which the English army needed to take to reach Calais. On 24 October they stayed in a certain small town. However the undaunted king set forth resolutely on the journey he had begun and proceeded from there to within a thousand paces of where the other army had encamped on that night. However, the appearances of the two armies were not alike at all. While the French were revived, having gorged themselves on supplies, the English were fatigued and weakened by fasting. Yet it was certain that on the next day the English would fight and engage in combat with all the nobility of France. As a result they did not spend that night so much in sleeplessness as in strengthening their bodies and spirits with prayers and confessions. The French published abroad that they wished no one to be spared except certain named lords and the king himself. They announced that the rest would be killed or have their limbs horribly muti-lated. Because of this our men were much excited to rage and took heart, encouraging one another against the event. Therefore, 'Scarce was the morrow's dawn sprinkling the mountain tops with light when the trumpet with brazen song rang out afar its fearful call' [Virgil, *Aeneid*, xii.113–14, and ix.503].

Our men hastened from all sides to come to the presence of their leader, being doubly well prepared for the battle to come both by their bravery and their purity. The king saw that his men had advanced with alacrity, and immediately led forth his host into a field which was newly sown with wheat. Here it was extremely difficult to stand or to advance because of the roughness as well as the softness of the ground. Equally unsluggishly on the great morning did the French send out the vanguard into the field, comprising strong men arrayed in shining arms, with horse-men preceding them on noble and handsome horses; as I may put it, 'Golden are the chains that hang drooping from their breasts' [Virgil, *Aeneid*, vii.278], over which 'their trappings of gold and yellow gold they champ with their teeth' [Virgil, *Aeneid*, vii.279].

Because of the muddiness of the place, however, the French did not wish to proceed far into the field. They waited about to see what our men, whom they held cheap, intended to do. Between each of the two armies (*cuneum*) the field lay, scarcely 1,000 paces in extent. But not 'inspired with the same motive did each of the armies rush forward' [Lucan, *Civil War*, vii.385]. Because the French were holding their position without moving, it was necessary for the English, if they wished to come to grips with the enemy, to traverse the middle ground on foot, burdened with their arms. The king realised the astuteness of the French in standing firm in one place so that they might not be exhausted by advancing on foot through the muddy field.

'Borne high on horseback, he goes round the columns, encouraging his leaders and strengthening their resolve for battle' [*Ilias Latinas*, 496–7]. 'Oh most faithful companions!' he said. 'For the high feat of valour and for utmost hardships we march towards the field' [Lucan, *Civil War*, ix.381–2]. 'This day has demanded your virtue again. Therefore, all of you, set forth your whole strength. Put to the test whatever lance, what-ever shield, whatever sword, whatever arrows may be powerful in your hand. Whoever desires wealth, honour or profit, here he will soon deserve it. Here surely God has set everything in the middle of the field' [Lucan, *Civil War*, vii.348].

Having thus spoken, he ordered the banners to be raised, saying 'Because the enemy tried most unjustly to block our path, let us advance against them in the name of the Trinity and at the best hour of the whole year.' With the banners raised, he ordered his men to proceed in order. He made the archers go first from the right and also from the left. Seeing those who on the previous day had sworn to bring about their deaths or mutilations, they were made hot with indignation, and forgot all their exhaustion, misfortune and weakness: thus I may say that 'he expanded' in them 'their glassy bile' [Persius, *Satires*, iii.8] and, with rage, 'he lends strength and courage' [Virgil, *Aeneid*, ix.764].

It is also amazing that he who of late was not able to stretch the weakest bow could now draw at will the strongest without. The French saw that our men had crossed the field with considerable effort; considering, there-fore, that the moment was favourable to attack those tired men whom they thought would be captured with no quarter, they advanced in terrifying fashion into the field, sending the mounted men ahead who were to over-whelm our archers by the barded breasts of their horses, and to trample them under their hooves. But, by God's will, things turned out other than they had hoped. The archers simultaneously shot arrows against the advancing knights so that the leading horses were scattered in that great storm of hail. For 'no blow but fells, no missile flies without wound' [Statius, *Thebais*, ix.770–71], and there was no rest from the hand of the marksman for 'every dart finds its mark', since 'no stroke [was] without wounds' [Statius, *Thebais*, x.656]. The horses were pierced by iron; the riders, turning round by means of their bridles, rushing away, fell to the ground amongst their army, and all horses who escaped drew away from the field. Next, as the lines met, a huge cry was lifted to the heavens by our men, and the air was filled with a terrifying sound. Then the cloud of arrows flew again from all directions, and iron sounded on iron, while volleys of arrows struck helmets, plates and cuirasses. Many of the French fell, pierced with arrows, here fifty, there sixty. The king himself, not so much as a king but as a knight, yet performing the duties of both, flung himself against the enemy. He both inflicted and received cruel wounds, offering an example in his own person to his men by his bravery in scat-tering the opposing battle lines with a battle axe. To no less a degree the knights, emulating the royal acts, all laboured together to fell the opposing wood of the shuddering French with iron, until at last a way was achieved by their force. The French did not so much yield but instead fell to their death. Indeed when the French realised that they, who had been saying that they were unconquerable, were now brought low in the battle lines of war, soon 'Their hearts were dazed, and a cold shudder ran through their inmost marrow' [Virgil, *Aeneid*, ii.120–21], so much so that they stood immobile and senseless while our men wrenched axes from their hands and felled them in the same way as if they were cattle. 'Unlimited slaughter followed and as if there was no battle but only steel on one side and throats to be attacked nor were our men able to throw down all of the other side that could be slain' [Lucan, *Civil War*, 532–5, adapted]. Thus therefore all the honour of the French perished through the hand of a small number which they had but a short time before looked down on. Among those slain were the duke of Alençon, the duke of Brabant, the duke of Bar, along with five counts and the constable of France, the seneschal of Hainault and the master of the crossbowmen of the king of France, and other lords numbering almost a hundred. Of the knights and squires, 3,069 were brought to their deaths. The number of the rank and file was not calculated by the heralds. There were captured the dukes of Orléans and Bourbon, the counts of Artois and of Vendôme, and Arthur, the brother of the duke of Brittany, who titles himself the count of Richemont, and a certain Bouccicaut, a knight who was also the most honourable marshal of the whole kingdom of France, and others, as is said, up to 700. On our side there died Lord Edward, duke of York and Lord Michael, earl of Suffolk, four knights and one squire called Davy Gam, and twenty-eight of the rank and file.

While the king and his men were engaged in close combat against the multitude of the French, French thieves attacked from the rear, plundering and taking away abandoned baggage. Finding the royal crown therein, they made the French citizens rejoice but with vain delight, even going so far as to have bells rung and canticles of praise, 'Te deum laudamus', to be sung with great jubilation. They pretended that the king had been captured and would be coming there soon. But after the fight, when the French understood from the downcast herald the whole truth of the events, their song was turned into one of lamentation, and rejoicing was turned into mourning.

The king, ascribing all these good outcomes to God, as he ought, gave ceaseless thanks to Him who had bestowed an unexpected victory and had subjected savage enemies. The king passed the night in the same place, and on the next day, that is to say the Saturday, he continued the journey he had begun towards Calais.

A 4. Tito Livio Frulovisi, *Vita Henrici Quinti* (c. 1438, Latin)

Translated from *Titi Livii Foro-Juliensis Vita Henrici Quinti*, ed. T. Hearne (Oxford, 1716), pp. 12–22.

Tito Livio dei Frulovisi (Titus Livius Forojuliensis) was born in Ferrara, probably around 1400. As well as writing Latin comedies he also ran a school in Venice and is also described as 'physician'. After travels in Italy, he came to

England around 1436, and entered the service of Humphrey, duke of Gloucester, where he assisted with formal correspondence and composed Latin plays. In letters of denization granted at the request of the duke in March 1437 he is described as 'poet and orator', and was one of several humanist scholars in the duke's circle.[31] But he made enemies and within two years was seeking a new patron in the bishop of Bath and Wells.[32] Nothing seems to have come of this, so he returned to Italy, facing further vicissitudes which seem to have been caused by his own temper, a problem which had dogged him throughout his life.

Several compositions in Latin date to his stay in England. The poem *Humfroidos* celebrates duke Humphrey's successes against Philip, Duke of Burgundy, in 1436 and may have been commissioned by the duke or else written to please him. His most famous work, the *Vita Henrici Quinti* (c. 1438) was likely commissioned by Humphrey and was intended to glorify the duke as well as his royal brother, and to encourage the young Henry VI, to whom it was dedicated, to emulate his father's deeds as well as to have regard to his uncle. The work begins with a panegyric on Gloucester, who is likened to Lycurgus, the famous Spartan law-giver who guarded his nephew's son's right to the throne.[33] and gives much space to his military prowess on both the campaign of 1415 and on the later conquest of Normandy, so we must assume that information on the battle came from the veteran Gloucester himself. In this respect, therefore, the account must be of considerable significance to us as it stems from the experience of one of the leading commanders present, and someone exceptionally close to the English king. No other account has this connection. (It may explain the unique mention of the fact that d'Albret's ancestors had been vassals of the English king in Aquitaine, for instance, as Henry had taken an interest in his rights in that area.) It is not surprising, however, that the story of Gloucester's wounding and his royal brother's defence of him, found in earlier works, is given much greater elaboration here. There is always a danger that even Henry V's

---

31 As cited in Gransden, p. 210. On his links with the duke, see R. Weiss, 'Humphrey, Duke of Gloucester and Tito Livio Frulovisi', in *Fritz Saxl 1890–1948: A Volume of Memorial Essays from his Friends in England*, ed. D.J. Gordon (London, 1957), pp. 218–27. For general background see R. Weiss, *Humanism in England during the Fifteenth Century*, 3rd edition (Oxford, 1967), and D. Rundle, 'On the difference between Virtue and Weiss: humanist texts in England during the fifteenth century', in *Courts, Counties and the Capital in the Later Middle Ages*, ed. D.E.S. Dunn (Stroud, 1996), pp. 181–203.

32 Tito Livio seems to have sent a copy of the *Vita* to John Stafford, archbishop of Canterbury when the latter was also sought as a patron. (Rundle, 'On the difference between Virtue and Weiss', p. 191, n. 38.) A copy given to a fellow humanist, Decembri, was translated by him into Italian, see J.H. Wylie, 'Decembri's version of the Vita Henrici Quinti by Tito Livio', *EHR*, 24 (1909), pp. 84–9.

33 C.W.T. Blackwell, 'Humanism and politics in English Royal Biography: the use of Cicero, Plutarch and Sallust in the *Vita Henrici Quinti* (1438) by Titus Livius de Frulovisi and the *Vita Henrici Septimi* (1500–1503)', in I.D. McFarlane, ed., *Acta Conventus Neo-Latini Sanctandriani: Proceedings of the Fifth International Congress of Neo-Latin Studies* (Binghampton, 1986), pp. 431–40, at p. 433. Blackwell doubts, however, that the work was influenced by a reading of Plutarch's *Lives*.

decisiveness of command might have been embellished to assist in the purpose of the work, and we certainly cannot be sure that the words ascribed to Henry were definitely spoken by him. Kingsford suggested that Tito Livio also drew on a *Brut* in Latin composed in 1436–7, and perhaps also on the *Brut* in the vernacular, as well as on some official documents.[34]

This is the first *Vita* of an English king and shows a distinctly humanist style, with several classical models being followed not least in terms of oratory. Speeches are put into the mouth of Henry on several occasions. These help to give him a much more noble demeanour, and to build up his role in determining events whilst not denying the assistance he received from the Almighty. Incidents are also much more fully worked out compared with any previous account. We are given a much more extensive explanation of Henry's decision to march to Calais. There is also more on the billeting arrangements before the battle, and Tito Livio is the first to mention negotiations before the battle itself. Heilly turns up in the *Liber Metricus* but before the crossing of the Ternoise. Note, however, that the negotiations spoken of are not of the type given in some French narratives, where Henry supposedly offers to withdraw if the French will let him pass in peace. This is also the first English account to mention that the soldiers took earth in their mouths before the battle, and that Henry ordered the commemoration of the saints on whose day he had won his victory. The discussion at Calais as to whether more conquests should be undertaken is also first mentioned here.

There are also some distinctive features in terms of deployment of troops and the battle itself. Henry has three battles and two wings as soon as he leaves Harfleur, and these groupings persist to the battlefield. On 24 October, he draws up his army 'distributing to each leader the order and place for the battle'. It is tempting to believe that this is information from Gloucester who surely would have been one such leader. Livio tells us that the three lines were almost contiguous on the day of the battle, and that the men stood four deep, but interestingly he does not tell us who commanded the van and the rearguard. There are almost two stages to the engagement in his version, which indicates some degree of confusion on his part perhaps, and the difficulty of narrating something where many things are happening at once. Initially the French, with two wings of horsemen, come down on the English but are then driven back. Some discussions then follow both within the English camp and with de Heilly. Henry then decides to move forward, and all the army advances with their arms and each, not simply the archers, with a stake. Tito Livio introduces a slight difficulty in his remarks that 'the usual order of the English was maintained': the first battle line proceeded, then the second and the third followed straight after, making it seem as though they are arrayed one behind the other rather than alongside. But could this be simply the order in which they moved their position, for later he tells us that the English battleline was as wide as the field? Again he notes that all the English had stakes which they fixed in the ground against the

[34] *EHL*, pp. 53–4.

advancing cavalry. Unfortunately he says nothing about where the archers were, though arrows do force the French to retreat. The account of the heat of battle says very little, save to contradict itself by emphasising at one point that the English captured no one and at another that there were as many prisoners as the English army itself. The killing of the prisoners is obfuscated. Although this is the first English account to mention the duke of Brabant's late arrival it places it in a most odd location.

The work was certainly drawn on by the author of the Pseudo Elmham and also formed the basis of the *First English Life* of Henry V of 1513. Either through the latter, or by knowledge of the original Latin text, the account of Tito Livio found its way into many of the sixteenth-century histories and hence into later narrative accounts. Thus, until the rediscovery of the *Gesta* in the mid-nineteenth century, it was the most influential of the Latin works of the fifteenth century. The Latin text was edited by Thomas Hearne in 1716, but it is fair to conclude, I think, that the influence of Tito Livio's version of events was mainly felt second or third hand by transmission through the sixteenth-century histories.[35]

*

. . . the most vigorous duke of Clarence, the king's brother, advised it would be to the greater glory of the king that most of the army should be despatched by sea to England as soon as possible because the French were intent upon giving battle and the enemy had already collected together a great multitude of men whilst that the army of the English was reduced almost to nothing by terrible disease. Then the king said. 'No less does my wish hold to come to see my lands and places which are mine by inheritance. It is clear they may prepare a great army but our hope is in God that no injury will come to either the army or to myself. I shall not suffer that the haughty rejoice with pride for evil doings and unjustly possess what is mine against the will of God. They would say that I had taken flight on account of my fear and had thus abandoned my right. I have the spirit of a very strong man, more willing to enter all dangers rather than anyone should impugn the reputation of your king. We shall go with the judgment of God, unharmed and safe even if they try to hinder us, we shall triumph as victors with great praise.' As soon as the opinion of the king was heard, he moved the hearts of all, nor was there anyone who wished to contradict him in case his own fear might then be criticised by the most powerful king.

This royal decision was announced to all, and a march over land was prepared, with provisions for armed combat. First the king drew up three battles (*acies*) and two wings (*alas*), according to the custom of the English, from the army that remained to him, which was not very exten-

---

35 The references to Tito Livio in the first single volume study of the reign, T. Goodwin, *The History of the Reign of Henry the Fifth, King of England* (London, 1704), are to folio numbers which may imply, however, that an original manuscript was consulted at least in this case.

sive for many had died, others had been sent home on account of illness
and two thousand had been left behind in Harfleur. After this the army set
out in order on the march, but this was immediately discovered by the
enemy who moved on, despatching many horsemen and footmen to try to
lay waste the whole country of victuals for men and horses so that the
English would not be able to find any food. The English army moved on
slowly without any haste and were able to be refreshed with food and
drink, and forage for horses from towns and fortresses because the latter
had been made much afraid by the defeat of Harfleur.

However, when the English came to the town of Eu with their standards, many of the townsmen came out and attacked the English lines
with much noise and aggression. There was loud battle on both sides but
the French did not restrain the men of the English for very long, and being
forced back to the gates, the French defended themselves with arrows and
missiles. Then the English reached the passage of the River Somme which
the French call Blanchetaque. Because it had been defended in advance
by the enemy by means of sharp stakes fixed close together, it allowed the
English no chance of crossing. Thus they had to move upstream in search
of another crossing. The city of Amiens came up on the left and the castle
of Corbie, already aware that the English were coming by earlier indications. Another battle arose. Many cavalry and infantry ran together into
the English with a terrific sound and a great impetuosity, as is the custom
of the French. But they did not restrain the men of the English who forced
them back inside the walls.

Meanwhile it was announced to the most Christian king that a certain
silver vessel in which the body of Christ had been accustomed to be kept
had been stolen from a certain church. Then the king ordered his host to
halt until the religious sacrilege be expiated. The vessel was returned to
the church. Those who had committed the sacrilege were led out throughout the whole army and hanged on a high tree until dead. The host was
then ordered to proceed. In a few days, through the help of certain men of
the region who had been taken captive by the army, they came to a
passage of the river suitable for crossing, which had not previously been
known about, so that they were able to cross over to the other bank.

The disease which had infected the English and the number of knights
who remained with the king in the army were known to the French. They
had in mind the long distance the English had travelled and the many days
they had journeyed without any physical recuperation, and they also
thought of how they were congregated together in a great multitude. It did
not seem possible that so small a number could resist them, particularly as
there had come together to block the English march many princes from all
over France, that is to say the duke of Orléans, the duke of Brabant, the
duke of Bourbon, the duke of Alençon, the duke of Bar, the sire d'Albret
(then constable of France, whose ancestors, however, were men who had
been liege subjects of the king of England from his duchy of Aquitaine),

the count of Nevers, the dukes of Burgundy [sic] and Brabant [sic], the archbishop of Sens and many others. These men, placing their trust entirely in the multitude of the men they had, sent to the king three heralds, which are called 'araldos' in their language, with orders to announce the intention to give battle. When they had come to the army, they were led to the duke of York who presented them to the king. They bent their knee, and having been granted leave by him, they expounded their embassy in these words. 'Great is the strength of the military force, most illustrious prince, which is brought by your highness to the land of our lords. They hear that you intend to try to capture the lands, towns and castles of the kingdom of France by your strength. They hear also about your devastations of towns and of French people. On account of this matter, they have sworn to protect the rights of this kingdom and fatherland, and they inform you that before you reach Calais, they will have come to meet with you, and will make battle with you and avenge the injuries you have caused.'

Then the English king with brave heart, with a fixed expression, and with no anger, with no change in the colour of his face, answered with modest speech in these words, 'Whatever is pleasing to God shall be pleasing to all.' Having been asked by the herald what way he would go, he answered, 'Straight to Calais. If our enemy should try to impede our journey they will not do so without calamity and great danger. Indeed we do not seek them nor do we move either more slowly or quickly because of fear of them. However, we urge them not to impede our way, nor should they seek a great shedding of Christian blood.' Being content with this response, and having been given a hundred gold crowns of French money, they were sent from the king and returned happily to their own side.

After the king had been advised that he and his army had to cross another river by a bridge, and that they would not be able to cross the river without great loss and difficulty if the bridge was broken by the enemy, he despatched certain nobles and knights and other men assigned to them from his military force to hold the bridge. They attacked the French enemies who were trying to break the bridge with a bold and powerful assault but they defended the bridge unharmed after a great fight, and captured and injured many of the French. This was 22 October which is, according to the custom of the church, the commemoration of the blessed confessor Romanus [*recte*, 23 October]. And when the English army came over by the bridge on that stream of the river, the duke of York, having set out from the king with the vanguard (*aciei primae*) climbed up to the top of a hill and sent out scouts into the locality. They came back with certain rumours about the enemy. One scout, with worried face and with anxious gasping breath, announced to the duke that a great, countless multitude was approaching. As others of them came back and told the duke the same, he communicated the whole matter to the king. The latter stood with the main battle (*aciem mediam*) which he commanded.

Without trembling or showing any anger, he set spurs to his horse and rushed to see the approaching enemy. Once he had seen and obtained certain knowledge of the army which was too large to be counted, he returned to his men with steady heart, and unflinching for he placed all hope in the singular justice of God alone. After this he drew up and instructed his army, distributing to each leader the order and place for the battle to be conducted, and he kept his men drawn up and prepared in the field until evening. Since there was no light to be had through the night, he therefore ordered his men to seek a night's lodgings, and to rest and care that night for their bodies which were about to fight so harsh a battle. There was no place near to them in this area which was not familiar to them, but, by divine intervention, a suitable way was revealed to them by which they came into a village where they were nourished with food and drink much better than they had had on other days. By chance a certain little house was available to the king that night for lodgings. Yet from the time of the drawing up of the army right to when they were in this village, by virtue of royal command no sound was heard from the English as would have been customary, but instead the army advanced quietly into the village. Afterwards they lit watch fires and set up the watchmen. So also did the French, who were scarcely 250 paces away from the English.

On 25 October prayers, supplications, matins and masses were completed and sung by the royal priests according to religious observance with all proper devotion, at dawn. Then the most Christian king led out the battle lines (*acies*) of the army. But he ordered horses and all the baggage train to remain in the village where they had been lodging, leaving a few guards with them, and he took with him only the men and arms of the army. The arrangement of the army was this. No one battle (*acies*) was very distant from the others. The middle battle (*acies media*), over which the king presided himself and in which he would fight, was located in the field directly against the middle battle (*aciei*) of the enemy. To the right of it was the vanguard (*acies prima*) and also the right wing (*ala dextra*). To the left was the rearguard (*acies postrema*) with the left wing (*ala sinistra*). The three battles lines (*acies*) were nearly joined. With divine protection and with the king relying upon justice from God, fortune had prepared a suitable position and well-defended field protected to the rear by the place where they had lodged the night before, and on the two flanks hedges and thorn bushes which protected the royal army from ambush and assault by the enemy. The king put on a helmet and placed over it an elegant gold crown encrusted with various precious gems and with the insignia of the English and French kingdoms. He then seated himself on a white horse. Following him, the most noble horses were led forth with gold saddles, with fine harnesses and most valuable trappings as was the royal custom, with similar insignia of the English and French kingdoms all over. Thus with everything made ready and set in order, the undefeated king urged his men to battle and to the approaching contest. It is said that a certain man was heard to say, disclosing his prayer to the others, 'If only good God would grant us by his mercy that so all those knights who are in England might be with us in this battle.' To whom the most valiant king replied, 'Indeed, I do not wish a single man to be added to my army. We are small in number compared with the enemy. If God in his mercy favours my army with justice – which we hope – there is not one man amongst us who may attribute such a victory over so many of our enemies to our own strength, but only to help of God, for which thanks would be by you due to be given to the Almighty. If – God forfend – because of our sins we are rendered up to the sword and to our enemy, it will be, if we are few in number, less of a loss to the kingdom and our country. But, if we fight with a great multitude and win a victory, with our hearts overwhelmed by self pride we might offend the Almighty by ascribing the victory to ourselves rather than to Him. Also if we are many, and the enemy win the victory, it would be reckoned that the loss and detriment to our country and to our kingdom would be much greater. But be strong of heart and fight with all your might. May God and the justice of our cause defend us. May he render up to our hands and to our power that all the multitude of that exceedingly proud enemy which you can see, or at least most of it.'

In very truth, the French placed so much confidence in the fact that they had very powerful and splendid horses as well as superior arms that, on coming to the battle, several of the great princes had left behind their lesser knights and servants, as well as several banners and military symbols, because they were certain of a most speedy victory. Among such men was the duke of Brabant. Since his standards had been left behind, he seized a banner of his arms from a trumpet and set them up on a long lance, ordering them to be held above his battle lines for his banner. When they came upon the English army with as much military diligence as they could, they exceeded the English in number so much, coming thirty-one deep in their battle line. And when they came to fight, this great multitude was so wide in extent that the field was not able to hold the whole force. The English were scarcely four deep. The French army had two wings of one thousand horsed spearmen who beat down upon the English with a sudden assault. They had many military engines throwing big, small and medium-sized stones one after another at the English army. The enemy armies were distant from each other for scarcely two or three bow shots. For some time they remained stationary on both sides, except that several knights of the French passed between the two armies but were forced to return at a gallop in the face of the arrow shot which had been ordered by the king. A council was held so that it might be seen what might prudently be done for already some part of the day had gone by. Many said there was nothing to be gained by staying in that enemy territory where they had no comfort and where there was a lack of supplies to eat. The French were in their own territory where they had no enemies and where they would gain in strength and numbers as time passed. The great king saw that the enemy were not coming to him, and that three French nobles had advanced towards his presence, amongst whom was the sire de Heilly who had been captured previously by the English soldiers, and had given faith that he would return, but who had afterwards fled from England. He spoke to the king in this way; 'It has often been reported within your kingdom and mine that I fled away in a common manner, shamefully and in a way not fitting to a soldier of the order of a knight. I deny all this to you and to your men, and if any man now dares to prove it he should prepare himself for a duel, and through arms I shall prove in presence of your majesty and of certain others that such an accusation of dishonourable conduct should not be brought against me.'

Then the king said, 'No duel is to be fought at this point on account of this matter. That must await another time. So, go back and, at our summons, call your men before night intervenes. For we hope in God that just as you fled from us, heedless of military discipline and the honour of knighthood, so today you will come to us again as a prisoner, or else or you will depart from this life by the sword.'

But de Heilly said, 'O most vigorous king, I will not order them for your benefit nor will I act according to your command. We all remain, both ourselves and your army, in the territory of the supreme Charles, sovereign ruler of the French. It is his order we obey, not yours. We will come to you to fight with you when the time seems right to us.' The king replied, 'Go from here to your camp. We do not believe that you will return with such great speed as that with which we shall burst into your ranks.' Then he said to his men, 'Advance banners'. Then he stood with his battleline in the order in which they stood, having exhorted all his men to go into battle with the enemy. The usual order of the English, established by the king, was maintained; the first battle line proceeded, then the second and the third followed straight after. The priests and chaplains of the king were ordered to remain in divine prayers and supplications, and with the heralds in their tabards took up their offices. Then the whole English army knelt, each soldier took a little piece of earth in his mouth. Then they all set aside their burdens, and with only their arms and each one with a great sharp stake they moved towards the enemy with great clamour and vigour. When within twenty paces of the town of Agincourt they came to the French enemy, with a most sounding of trumpets, they all roused their souls to the fight, they fell upon the enemy and battle commenced. The English battle line was as wide as the field. The French had made two sharp wings like two horns and were even greater in width as they pressed upon the centre of the enemy. The order of the English would have been thrown into disorder by the French knights if the great part of the latter had not been killed or wounded with arrows and had been forced to retreat in terror. All the English fixed in the ground the stakes as a shield for themselves so that the advancing cavalry of the enemy was forced to pull back from fear or else was fixed, wounded and killed, both horses and men. The battle heightened, and every one who came into combat during the three hours did so without slaying or being slain himself. No-one looked for booty, but all sought victory. No-one was captured; many were killed. At the mid-point, the English were increasingly eager to kill for it seemed that there was no hope of safety except in victory. They killed those near them and then those who followed upon the latter. Soon no one from the French side came to the battle in their great pride but that they fell. Indeed it is said that once the French had yielded to death and the certain victory of the English was apparent, the English spared the French and captured them, including many princes, lords and nobles. The renowned king never spared himself from the laborious battle, nor did he shun danger by avoiding it, but like the unconquered lion fighting among the enemy with most ardent spirit he received many blows on his helmet and elsewhere. During this great assault the most serene brother of the king, Humphrey, duke of Gloucester fought bravely and without caution. Having been pierced by the point of a sword, he was thrown to the ground half dead. His brother the king himself put his feet astride the legs of Humphrey. For the renowned duke fell with his head against the king's feet but with his feet to the enemy. In this position the king fought most courageously for a long time so that his brother might be carried safely away from the enemy to his own men.

At length with victory achieved, and with the army of the French vanquished, killed and overthrown, Henry immediately prepared to fight another army of the enemy, no less than the first. Considering that the English were exhausted by so long and hard a fight, and because they saw that they held so many prisoners – so many that they came to the same number as themselves – they feared that they might have to fight another battle against both the prisoners and the enemy. So they put many to death, including many rich and noble men. Meanwhile, the most prudent king sent heralds to the French of the new army asking whether they would come to fight or would leave the field, informing them that if they did not withdraw, or if they came to battle, all of the prisoners and any of them who might be captured, would all be killed by the sword with no mercy. He informed them of this. They, fearing the English and fearing for themselves, departed with great sadness at their shame. Then the king gave thanks to God for the great victory accorded to him. Because that day was the commemoration by the church of the blessed Crispin and Crispinian, and it seemed to him that it was through their intercession to God that he had obtained so great a victory over the enemy, he ordered that for as long as he lived, commemoration of them was to be made in the masses which he heard every single day.

Here in the battle were killed on the French side the most serene dukes of Alençon, Bar and Brabant, and the sire de Heilly whom, as I said, had come to the king to purge himself of his flight, and many others numbering up to 10,000. Those captured were the duke of Orléans, the duke of Bourbon, Arthur, brother of the duke of Brittany and many others. Of the English, the duke of York, the earl of Suffolk and others numbering up to a hundred were killed in the first fight.

And when evening approached, by the advice of his entire council, the most victorious king with his army went into the same village in which they had received hospitality the night before, and learnt that the many horses and other baggage of the army had been carried off by French thieves. That night the most noble royal captive princes served the king at his feast. The following day he made his way across the middle of the field where he had fought which was covered with the amazing sight of all the bodies of the fallen, stripped of their belongings. He then came to his castle at Guines. From there he went to the town of Calais with all his army and prisoners. At Calais the most vigorous king was received by his people there with great and appropriate joy. There his knights and the others were restored with food, drink, sleep and rest, for a short time. The king consulted his men whether, as ought to follow a great victory, he should go on to besiege neighbouring towns and castles or whether, because much of his army was troubled by the bloody flux and were hampered by a lack of supplies, as well as having many wounded, he should lead the army back home where they could recover for a few months. The unanimous opinion was that two great victories showed that God had the king's rights close to his heart, and that divine aid would not be lacking in the future to give further honour to the king and his rights. As a result, all of them considered that they should go back home.

A 5. Pseudo Elmham, *Vita et Gesta Henrici Quinti* (*c.* 1446–49, Latin)

Translated from *Thomae de Elmham Vita et Gesta Henrici Quinti*, ed. T. Hearne (Oxford, 1727), pp. 49–73.

This is an anonymous work which exists in at least three fifteenth-century manuscript copies. When Thomas Hearne edited the text, he ascribed it to Thomas Elmham, author of the *Liber Metricus*, but it is generally agreed that there is no basis for believing it to be Elmham's work; hence it has come to be known as the Pseudo Elmham. Its last chapter is addressed to John Somerset, physician to Henry VI, and must have been composed after 1446. An early sixteenth-century copy of the work omits the reference to Somerset but includes a preface addressed to Walter, Lord Hungerford (d. 1449), and it is possible that this represents an earlier recension of the text. Remember that, according to the *Gesta*, it was Hungerford who expressed a wish for more men. Here, however, the desire is ascribed simply to some peers of the realm, which might indicate that Hungerford was not a source of information for the work, or that the author of the *Gesta* was himself mistaken.

There are textual links (especially in the section to 1419) with the *Vita* of Tito

Livio, which the author admits to using, but a full comparison between the works is yet to be undertaken, and the Pseudo Elmham is certainly more verbose, needing almost twice as many words as Tito Livio for the battle. There is a similar use of classical models and it is possible that the author was also a foreign visitor to England who was influenced by the development of humanist forms in style and Latinity. Both authors, for instance, give Henry V long speeches in the classical tradition. In addition to the *Vita*, the *Brut* may have been a source for the work as well as possibly also other narratives of the war which are now no longer extant. Kingsford also suggests that Monstrelet may have been a source.[36] This is difficult to substantiate, particularly as Monstrelet's own work was only first evidenced around the same time, but it would be an important early cross-channel link if true. It is possible that some information (especially on later campaigns and death of Henry) came from Hungerford, who was steward of the king's household and highly active in the fifteenth-century phase of the Hundred Years War, being present at Agincourt. Both Hungerford and John Somerset had links with Humphrey, duke of Gloucester, the latter being one of the duke's executors. There are also several abbreviated versions of the work extant, one of *c.* 1455 being bound in with a copy of the *Gesta*.[37] The work was used by sixteenth-century historians. Stow refers to it but ascribes it to Roger Wall, archdeacon of Coventry from 1442 to 1488, and copyist of one of the extant manuscripts of the work. Holinshed also used the text, believing it to be by an anonymous author who recast Livio into a different, more poetical style.

There is little to highlight from its account of the battle for it is close to that provided by Tito Livio with some poetic interjections. It does make clearer the French intention to break the English ranks by a cavalry charge, and makes more sense of Brabant's late arrival. The duke of York is called the constable and marshal of the army, although the functions he exercises are the same as in Tito Livio. It gives more place to Henry's decision to move forward, but omits any mention of negotiations with de Heilly. But whereas in Tito Livio the English seem to have taken their stakes with them when they moved forward, in the Pseudo Elmham the archers leave behind their stakes before they advance. Henry himself is perhaps more endangered than in any previous account, with specific mention of a piece being hacked off his helmet: Tito Livio tells us this indirectly in his account of the entry into London where he mentions the king's reluctance to show this helmet to his people. The aftermath of the battle, and in particular the discussion over whether to continue the war, receives more attention in the Pseudo Elmham, but in terms of added words rather than of detail, save for the idea that the plan was to attack Ardres.

*

---

36 *The First English Life of King Henry the Fifth*, ed. C.L. Kingsford (Oxford, 1922), p. xv.
37 *Gesta*, p. xvii.

[In the preceding section, there is an argument going on as to whether the king should withdraw the forces, avoiding the dangers of an inland route to Calais, or take the risks and not damage his glorious image.]

A march overland should also be avoided because, with many of his men taken away from this life by the serious plague during the siege, and with many also brought by the same illness to the gates of death (including the noble duke of Clarence, the dearest brother of the king, and other earls and nobles) and thus transferred to England with the permission of the king, and with such a large number of warriors assigned as a garrison for the town of Harfleur, the king's army (which, although having remained intact, was just a handful of warriors compared to the number of the French enemy), with so many people, as pointed out before, having been lost recently, was severely depleted. The majority of the councillors were of the opinion that a decision should be made not to march on. The noble king, with the firmness of his spirited heart in the Lord strengthened by faith in his troops, objected to that opinion, maintaining that his heart was moved to see those places which he claimed as his own on the grounds of hereditary right. He also maintained that he would rather throw himself and his men on the mercy of God in determining the outcome of the events, not shirking the dangers, than offer himself to the enemy as grounds for elevating their pride, diminishing the reputation of his honour by flight. And since, after his opinion had been expressed, nobody dared to contradict the king's decision, they concluded finally that the king and the army should pass from Harfleur to Calais, following the overland route.

Chapter 23. *On the disposition of the royal army, and the troubles caused by the French as far as they were able; on the various armed engagements during this journey, and on the crossing of the king and the army over the River Somme.*

The necessities of the journey were prepared in accordance with what circumstances had demanded. Then the king, immovably resolute in his intention noted earlier, constantly maintaining that the victory depended not on the weight of numbers but on divine will, decided that, in order to secure an easier journey, the wagons should be left behind and the loads of victuals and other things which were to be brought with them should be carried on the backs of the horses. Forming, according to the custom, three main battle lines and two wings from the men of his army who, as pointed out before, with the exception of those assigned as a guard of Harfleur, had survived the impact of disease, he committed himself with royal courage to the intended route through the middle of his territory of Caux. But having discovered by which route the king had arranged to pass with the army, the enemy, going ahead, was stripping its own country of victuals as much as they possibly could. The English, however, were providing the necessary food for themselves as well as they could, although not without a great effort. Meanwhile the king's army, proceeding by the will of fate marching each day without being disturbed, in due and appropriate order and without the inconvenience of excessive haste, received provisions from some fortified places, which were somewhat struck by fear. These were given in accordance to the size of the place but, were offered spontaneously by the guards of those places. But when the king's troops appeared with standards unfurled at the town of Eu, the nobles, armed, came forth bravely and with a rapid advance of their strong horses engaged courageously with the English, in a powerful conflict. With a frequent striking of the spears, there was much fighting and deeds of arms worthy of praise. But in the end the French were driven in headlong flight into the town by a thunderous charge of the English, who disregarded their insults. Some Englishmen were cruelly wounded by missiles hurled across the walls of the town.

The neighbouring fortresses, wanting to avoid the indignation of the king, refreshed his army with provisions. The accursed dishonesty of the enemy, desirous of doing mischief by refined tricks, blocked the ford at Blanchetaque by means of which the king's army would have crossed the River Somme by a short cut, with such a dense mass of stakes, that the king's army, debarred from that crossing, were compelled, moving upstream into enemy territory towards the source of the river to look for new fords about which they had no information. Leaving the town of Amiens slightly to the left, the fort of Corbie came into sight. When the English, with banners on display, had presented themselves at these places, mounted troops of armed men, assembling with fixed resolve for that purpose, went out of the town and engaged in a fight against the English with a martial impetus. Shield met with shield, spear with spear, horse with horse, mounted warrior with soldier, and mighty with noble. The horses and their riders were cast down on all sides during the long contest, and finally under the relentless, nay, unbearable impetus of the English, the French enemy drew back to their town. Around that time, in violation of the statutes of the king, some Englishman secretly stole from a church the box in which the body of Christ was accustomed to be kept; informed about that matter the king ordered all his battle lines to stop, and refused to proceed further before a just sentence of death was passed on the person who had committed the sacrilege. The robber, dragged before the whole army after the proclamation of his sentence, finished his miserable life by being hanged on a tree near the very church which he had robbed. After a few days of further marching, some Englishmen, looking for an unknown crossing over the river, noticed a place in the river which was, fortuitously, suitable for passing and which, as prisoners from that country asserted, had never been known of before. By such means the royal troops successfully crossed to the other side of the river.

Chapter 24. *The duke of Orléans and other princes of France make
known through a herald that they intend to fight against the king, and
they receive a reply from the king.*

The French considered the fact that, as mentioned before, the royal army
was severely depleted, and believed that the king himself, exhausted by
the long-lasting toils, was driven to a complete confusion. They thought
that they were strong because of the extraordinarily large number of soldiers gathered by martial fervour from all over the French kingdom and
the neighbouring areas. They did not believe that the English troops could
resist their multitude because they were small in number and exhausted by
the effects of famine, hardship, illness and other burdens. So the princes
and nobles in command of the French troops, namely the duke of Orléans,
the duke of Brabant, the duke of Bourbon, the duke of Alençon, the duke
of Bar, and the sire d'Albret, at that time constable of France (whose
ancestors, by the way, were lieges of the kings of England as they came
from the duchy of Aquitaine), and other nobles, perhaps placing their
hope for victory on their great number of troops, unanimously agreed to
inform the English king, through the mediation of the embassy of three
heralds, that they were going to give battle to the English.

The heralds arrived at the vanguard of the English arm. The reason for
their coming was first made known to the duke of York, who was constable and marshal of the army, and he informed the king. The heralds were
then introduced at royal command into the presence of the king, who was
waiting on horseback in the open country, surrounded by a few noblemen.
Falling on their knees, they stated the purpose of their mission. They
informed him that, as the princes and nobles of France had heard of and
knew his martial fame and fervent passion for warlike deeds, and especially because he was attempting with a mighty hand to lay waste or
subdue those parts which belonged to the crown of France, which they
were bound to defend, themselves and their numerous followers, and for
the preservation of the title of their King, they had resolved to fight the
English army before they reached Calais. Henry mildly, and with a courageous heart, and a steady countenance replied, 'As the Lord hath decreed,
let all things be fulfilled'. Being asked by the heralds by which road he
would proceed, he said, 'We intend to direct our steps straight towards our
town of Calais, from which road, if our enemies have determined to drive
us, let them attempt to do so at their peril, for we will neither seek them,
nor move faster or more slowly on their account.' The heralds, satisfied
with these replies, returned to those who sent them, after a hundred
crowns had been presented to each of them from the king's treasury.

Chapter 25. *How the king had his people watch a bridge, which the French intended to destroy; concerning the first sighting of the army of the French; and concerning the conduct of the king and of the army during the day and night immediately preceding the day of the battle of Agincourt.*

The king had learned by the report of certain persons that he and his people were to cross another river by means of a certain bridge. He had also learned that if that bridge were to be destroyed, the safe crossing over the deep bed of the river would become difficult for him and his men, so he sent some noble knights to watch that bridge, assigning to them men faithful to him. They found the men of the enemy in arms, endeavouring in vain to destroy the bridge. Putting the enemy to flight with a valorous attack, by the will of fate the English courageously preserved the bridge intact preventing it being broken into pieces by the enemy. They also took some prisoners and wounded others. It was Thursday (24 October), the morrow of the feast of St Romanus the Confessor. Having passed over the bridge, the duke of York, commander of the vanguard of the royal army, climbed to the top of a hill, and sent scouts over the country to bring back information if they discovered the enemy's forces. One of them spotted them, and being astonished at the size of the French army, returned to the duke with a trembling heart and with the utmost speed his horse would carry him. Almost out of breath, he said, 'Be prepared quickly for battle, for you are about to fight against such a huge host that it cannot be numbered.'

As soon as the duke had informed himself of the truth of the report, he acquainted the king, who received the news with a cheerful countenance. He neither changed into a cold tremor, nor into a heat of passion but, having directed the middle battalion (which he commanded in person) to halt, hastened to view the enemy as fast as his fine horse could carry him. The superior numbers of the French troops were like so many forests covering the whole of the country far and wide. The king saw them and reflected with unflinching hope and with a firm heart and without the doubt of hesitation. He was certain that all strength comes from God, in whose hands are the hearts of kings, and he believed with spirited firmness that the huge number of the enemy could not prevail against him and his small army contrary to the will of God. And because the divine mercy castigated with His own hand the royal army with such lashes of death, plague, famine, hardship and other troubles but had done so with some mercy, he kept a strong faith that God in his goodness did not want to seize them up to be thrown into the mouth of the wolves to be devoured.

Therefore devoutly committing himself and his army into God's protection, with the advice of experienced soldiers he chose a suitable position for his forces. Knowing from the shortness of the winter's day that evening would speedily approach, he drew up his army in regular order and array, and assigned them their stations. He exhorted them to prepare for battle, animating their hearts by his intrepid demeanour, and his consoling expressions. Thus, ready for fighting, the English troops awaited in the camp the arrival of the enemy until, with the brightness of Phoebus driven away, the night spread a gloomy darkness over the face of the earth. The enemy noted the keen expectation of such a small army [i.e. of the English] and its worthy preparations and, gathering themselves for a night's rest, refused to enter the contest of a harsh battle on that day.

When night closed in and it became so dark that they could scarcely see their own hands and knew not where to find a night's lodging, the king determined to seek such quarters for his army as God might provide. He ordered them to refrain from making their customary noise and clamour in case the enemy might thereby devise some means of annoying them. Then the army, without sending harbingers, proceeded in search of quarters for the night. Wonderful to relate, by the direction of a certain white road which they discovered in the dark, they came safely to a village suitable for their quarters where they were provided with what they needed in a more convenient manner than on previous nights. There they passed the night without confusion. Companions met with companions, and masters with servants: they caused watch-fires to be lighted all round the army in the same way as the enemy had done, who were not more than a quarter of an English mile from them. Around the middle of the night, the king, deeming that an acquaintance with the place where the battle would be fought on the next day would be very useful to him, sent some valiant knights by moonlight to examine the field. From their report he derived information, the better to enable him to array his forces.

Chapter 26. *The preparations for the battle and the ordering of the king's battle lines in the field, with other matters.*

The night being passed, but the sun (*Titan*) not yet risen above the horizon, at the dawn of the Friday on which the martyrdom of the blessed Crispin and Crispinian is celebrated, masses were heard and other observances completed, despite the fact that the furore of battle was imminent, and the king entered the field with due devotion. Aware that the winter day would be short, wishing to avoid showing either to the enemy or to his friends any signs of inactivity or fear, so that with cautious preparation and sensible precautions, without any enforced haste, he might provide for his army a suitable order in which to give battle he did not neglect to lead his battle lines (*acies*) into the field at the first show of dawn. Thinking that his adversaries would be more engaged in fighting than plundering, he ordered the horses of his men, and whatever other things his army had brought with them, save for their arms, to be left in the village in which they were quartered in the night, entrusting them to the custody of

a few soldiers. So that his army, as they were very small in comparison
with the French, might be able to fight without a wide separation between
them, he arrayed it for battle in this manner. To the middle battle, which
he himself commanded, and in which, under the mercy of God, he proposed to fight, he assigned a convenient station in about the middle of the
field, so that it might come in contact with the middle battle of the enemy.
On his right, at a very little distance, he placed the vanguard, and joined to
it the wing stationed on his right. On the king's left was the rearguard of
the army, to which the left wing was joined in like manner. Being so
arrayed, the providence of the divine favour was manifestly shown, which
provided for so small an army so suitable a field, enclosed within hedges
and trees, and with closes or hedges on the sides, to protect them from
being surrounded by the enemy's attacks. The King was clad in safe and
very bright armour: he wore on his head a splendid helmet, with a large
crest, and encompassed with a crown of gold and jewels, and on his body
a surcoat, with the arms of England and France; from which a celestial
splendour gleamed on the one side from three golden flowers, planted in
an azure field; on the other, from three golden leopards, sporting in a ruby
field. Sitting on a noble horse as white as snow having also horses in
waiting royally decorated with the richest trappings, his army were much
inspired to martial deeds. The nobles also, on the king's side, were
arrayed with coats of their arms, as it befitted such persons about to be
engaged in conflict.

When the king heard some wishing that other peers of the realm of
England might be present to assist in this business, by God's will, he
firmly replied: 'Truly I would not wish that the number should be
increased by one single person. For if in numbers we were equal to, or
perhaps stronger than our enemies, and they were delivered over in to our
own hands by the chances of war, our undiscerning judgment would
attribute the victory to the greatness of our strength, and so due praise
would by no means be rendered. But if, from God's manifold chastise-
ment of our crimes, the divine will should determine to deliver us into the
enemy's hands (the contrary to which I earnestly hope) certainly then our
army would be too large to be subjected, which God forbid, to so great a
misfortune. But if the divine compassion should deign to deliver up so
many adversaries to such a trifling number of fighting men, we should
think so great a victory certainly bestowed by God upon ourselves, and we
should render praise to him, and not to our number. Behold! he who is
splendidly and safely defended, and armed in body with bodily arms, is
protected in mind much more gloriously by stable hope and unbroken fortitude.'

Chapter 27. *The disposition and ordering of the French army and other matters, together with an account of the great and famous battle of Agincourt.*

The enemy, disdaining the sluggishness and inactivity of the King's army, endeavoured to prepare for the battle their numerous companies (*cuneos*), in great worth and with the greatest foresight, in proper order and with all the circumspection that they could. They thought that they would fight so that their arms would blaze out with such splendour, like the rays of the sun, shining with the deeds of their glory.[38] They arrayed their troops after their own manner, as the King had disposed his: yet the width of the plain was not sufficient to fit so numerous a people into suitable formation for battle. For the English army, in all its lines, was fortified sideways by only four ranks of men, one behind the other. All the French lines were strengthened with ranks of twenty or more fighting men, one behind another, throughout. Also in the outside flank of their army were placed a thousand cavalry, to break through the ranks of the English with the charge of their horses; also certain 'saxivora', intended to disperse the English as they came to fight, or at least put them out of order, were in like manner placed along the flanks of the army. But the number of standards and other ensigns, which, fastened on the points of lances, and rustling in the air with the wind, were displayed in the French army, seemed to exceed the lances in the English army. Never in times past (at least that can easily be recalled to memory), was there ever such an immense multitude within France of so many noble and mighty men, so strongly and splendidly equipped. Also the noble men of the enemy thought themselves so assured of victory that some, through great hurry, left their servants and others, who are generally required in such circumstances, behind them; thinking they were hastening to victory and honour, rushed suddenly to defeat and death. Amongst these was the duke of Brabant, who, not having brought his standards, formed one of a banner that was hanging to a trumpet, and was slain in the conflict.

The troops being thus drawn up over the fields on both sides, and being distant from each other the space of about three bow shots, each army waited for the other, but neither moved towards the other for a long space of time. Yet the French cavalry, entering a little way into the field, were forced to retreat precipitately into the army by some of the King's archers, at the king's orders. Certain French barons, according to a desire they expressed, came into the king's presence, and without being able to ascertain anything the king purposed to do, were ordered quickly to depart into their own army. Now the king considering that a great part of the short day

---

[38] This is probably drawn from Horace. Other works are also drawn upon, including the Psalms, and a full study of the allusions in this work, and in Tito Livio and Walsingham, would no doubt be frutiful in showing how these battle narratives were created.

was already past, and firmly believing that the French were not inclined to move from their position, consulted the most experienced officers of his army whether he should advance with his troops, in the order in which they stood, towards the enemy who refused to come towards him. Having fully considered the circumstances of so important an affair, they prudently determined that the king should march with his army towards the enemy, and charge them in the name of God. For they considered that the English army, very much wearied with hunger, disease and marching, was not likely to obtain any refreshment in the enemy's country, and that the longer they remained there, so much the more would they be subjected to the effects of debility and exhaustion: on the contrary, the army of the enemy situated amongst friends, readily obtained whatever was convenient for them, and through delay, gathered fresh and increased strength by virtue of new troops arriving. Therefore the King's advisers finally concluded that delay was injurious to the English, but advantageous to the French. The King thought it difficult and hazardous to depart from his position, yet to avoid greater dangers, with the greatest intrepidity he set his army an example how they should direct their march towards the enemy, preserving, however, the order of their former array. He commanded that his own chaplains, and all the priests of his army should be employed in prayer, and that the heralds should diligently attend only to their own duties, without using arms. Without more delay both the men-at-arms, without caring for their burdensome arms, and the archers leaving behind them in the field their sharp stakes, which they had before prepared in case of meeting the French horsemen, all having knelt, and taken mouthfuls of earth, with a war cry which penetrated the heavens, and with an amazing attack boldly flew across the field, and demonstrated by their actions how much they were animated by courage. When they had approached towards the enemy's ranks, to the distance of twenty paces, not far from Agincourt, and the sounds of the trumpets rending the very air, had roused the minds of the warriors to battle, the enemy now first stirring himself, proceeded to meet the English. Immediately the battle commenced with such fury in that way that at the first attack of such brave soldiers, by the dire shock of lances, and impetuous strokes of swords and other weapons, the joints of their strong armour were violently broken, and the men in the first ranks on both sides inflicted deadly wounds. But there, the warlike bands of archers, with their strong and numerous volleys, darkened the air, shedding as a cloud laden with a shower, an intolerable multitude of piercing arrows, and inflicting wounds on the horses, either caused the French horsemen (who were intent upon overriding them and fighting the English from the rear) to fall to the ground, or forced them to retreat, and so defeated their dreadful purpose.

O, deadly war, dreadful slaughter, mortal disaster, hunger for death, insatiable thirst for blood, insane attack, impetuous frenzy, violent insanity, cruel conflict, merciless vengeance, immense clash of lances, prating of arrows, clashing of axes, brandishing of swords, breaking of arms, infliction of wounds, letting of blood, bringing on of death, hacking up of bodies, killing of nobles! The air thunders with dreadful crashes, clouds rain missiles, the earth absorbs blood, breath flies from bodies, half-dead bodies roll in their own blood, the surface of the earth is covered with the corpses of the dead, this man charges, that one falls, this one attacks, that one dies, this one recovers, that one vomits forth his soul in blood, the killer is enraged, the dead crashed in grief; the living desires to surrender, the charge of the victors does not allow the time for withdrawal, cruelty reigns, piety exults, the brave and the strong are crashed, and mountains of corpses are piled up, a vast multitude is yielded up to death, princes and magnates are led off as captives.

In this deadly conflict, amongst other things it is to be remembered, that that brightly shining Titan of Kings so much exposed his precious person to every chance of war, that he thundered upon his adversaries violent terrors and unbearable assaults. Nor did the fury of Mars grant to the royal dignity an exemption from hostile assaults and heavy blows, for from the crown encircling the king's helmet a certain piece was hacked off. Indeed if the prince himself had been of inferior rank amongst the combatants, he would on account of his extraordinary gallantry, have deserved to be crowned with a laurel of honour above others. Also the noble duke of Gloucester, the king's brother, pushing forward perhaps too vigorously on his horse into the conflict, was grievously wounded and cast down to the earth by the blows of the French; for whose protection the king being determined, bravely leapt against the enemy, defended him with his own body, and snatched and guarded him from the enemy, sustaining dangers scarcely possible to be borne. It happened also that this most victorious prince, with that part of the army which he himself commanded, first conquered his adversaries, who being dispersed, when the king had turned aside with his soldiers to the aid of his vanguard, he saw before him another numerous company (*cuneos*) of French preparing themselves in the field for battle, against whom it was necessary for the king to march with his followers. Yet after a while all the king's battles, both the front and the rear, and each wing having overthrown their enemies, were victorious. The English already wearied, and for the most part bereft of arms fit to charge with, fearing because the French were arraying themselves for battle, that a new fight would be commenced, in case the men they had taken should rush upon them in the fight, murdered many of them, although noble, with the sword. But the king commanded, by a message of heralds to those French, who as we have said above, still occupied the fields, that they should either come to battle, or speedily withdraw from his sight, knowing that if they should again array themselves for a new fight, that both they and the prisoners yet remaining would perish without mercy, with the direst revenge that the English could inflict. Then, dreading the effect of so severe a resolution, all the adversaries confused with fear, shame, and grief, retreated with one accord from the field.

And the magnanimous king by the divine mercy gained a glorious triumph, having overcome his enemies. He remained in the field in which the battle was fought, and was gratefully mindful to return thanks most devoutly to the bestower of so great a victory. And because on the festival of St Crispin and Crispinian so great a victory was given him, he heard mention of them in one of his masses every day during his life. In this very great battle on the French side, there fell and were killed the duke of Alençon, the duke of Bar, the archbishop of Sens, as it is said, the duke of Brabant, the count of Nevers, the count of Dammartin, the count of Marlay, the count of Grandpré, the count of Salebruce, the count of Vaudemont, the sire d'Albret, and of others between 9,000 and 10,000 fighting men. There were captured the duke of Orléans, the duke of Bourbon, Arthur of Brittany, the count of Vendôme, the count of Eu, John de Meingre, called Bouccicaut. But on the side of the English, the duke of York, the earl of Suffolk, and about a hundred others were killed.

Chapter 28. *How the king had conducted himself after the triumph.*

When the king had stayed in the fields for a long time, and day had already declined towards evening, on the advice of his nobles and wise men, he returned to lodge with his army in the same village in which he had happened to lodge the previous night; but during the battle, French plunderers had seized as their spoils the goods of the English, both horses and other things. In the evening the captured princes of France served the nobles of the king, the princes who in the morning believed infallibly that they would take him prisoner. For such is the change of fortune wrought by the right hand of Him on high, to whom honour and glory be forever.

Chapter 29. *For the passage of the king with his captives to Guînes, Calais and England.*

When the night had passed, the king went back with his army and the captives through the field, in which the battle had been fought, because this was the convenient route for his journey. Incredible to hear, he found all the bodies of those who had been killed naked and completely despoiled. He made his way to his castle at Guînes, and thence on to his town of Calais, in which he was received by his people with utmost reverence and with immense joy. There he ordered the names of all the prisoners to be presented to him so that at least he might know about them. The king asked the advice of his people there as to whether he should try to seize by assault the town of Ardres or other forts in the marches near Calais before his army was finally demobilised. Finally, a reply was given and a decision was made that victories so miraculous, given to the king by divine providence and without serious trouble for himself and the army, should suffice for his honour for the present, and that they envisaged, by the will of fate, there were likely to be future times suitable to the fulfilment of his desire. Agreeing with the gist of this advice, the king passed over the sea to England, his kingdom, with the auspicious blowing of a favourable wind . . .

Exult, O fortunate England, rejoice and delight in the return of your king, on account of whose departure you were so anxious. Wipe away your tears, stop grieving! For he who departed, comes back with great gain. You had sent him forth as dawn, and you take him back on his return as noon in full splendour. Your single grape grew into a fertile bunch of grapes. Your star was transformed into a likeness of the sun. From a mere cupful is generated a sea, from a single bloom a flowery Tempe, from a single grain a bundle of wheat, from a laurel a fruitful grove, from a little spark a flame, and from the king a conqueror, by divine will. He it is who renews and increases with his industry the ancient fame of your nobility, which had been shrouded in a mist of oblivion, who made you a queen of kingdoms, who raised you to the Olympus of praise, who brought terror to the enemy and crowned you with the glory of supreme victory. Delight in the Lord, O Britannia, who provided this most noble prince and monarch of your kingdom.

A 6. John Capgrave, *De Illustribus Henricis* (*c.* 1446–53, Latin)

Translated from John Capgrave, *De Illustribus Henricis*, ed. F.C. Hingeston (Rolls Series, London 1858), pp. 114–18.

Capgrave was born in 1393 probably in King's Lynn. Around 1410 he entered the Augustinian friary in Lynn. The order had a reputation for learning and it is therefore not surprising to find that he spent five years studying theology in London before moving to Cambridge in 1422 to continue his studies. He wrote various biblical commentaries, some of which were dedicated to Humphrey, duke of Gloucester, as well as lives of various saints. He was probably prior at Lynn when Henry VI visited the Augustinian friary there in 1446. In 1453 Capgrave was elected prior provincial of the Augustinian order, a post he held until 1457. He died at Lynn in 1464.

The *De Illustribus Henricis* was dedicated to Henry VI and was intended to eulogise the king as well as to encourage his desire to emulate great deeds of the past by telling him of the 'great Henries' who had come before him. In part I Capgrave deals with the rulers of the Empire from Henry I to Henry VI, in part II with the kings of England from Henry I to Henry VI and in part III with 'the lives of illustrious men who have borne the name of Henry scattered throughout the whole world and of different degrees and dignities', the period covered being from 1031 to 1406. These include men of the name who had a religious signifi-cance, such as Henry of Urimaria of the Augustinian order. The work as a whole seems to have been completed between 1446 and 1453, although the fourth and fifth chapters of part II on Henry IV and Henry V were perhaps written soon after the death of the latter, with that on Henry VI being added between 1446 and 1447.

He is at pains in the work to convince the reader that he was an honest and reliable commentator especially in those sections, such as that dealing with Henry V, where he was selecting from his own experience and from what others had told him. The account of the reign is a fairly straightforward narrative which gives much place to the years from 1413 to 1418, covering military activities and the problem of Lollardy, a not surprising inclusion given Capgrave's relig-ious profession. It has been suggested that the treatment of Henry V is largely an adaptation in prose of Elmham's *Liber Metricus*, but it also mentions rain before the battle. It is also notable for ducking out of the issue of the positioning of the archers! The remark he makes is indeed intriguing, and implies that the role of the archers was already established in the public mind.

Capgrave also included a brief and unimportant mention account of the battle in his last work, his *Abbreviacion of Chronicles* (Middle English), completed around 1462–3 and dedicated to Edward IV.[39] This is more closely derived from Walsingham, and hence gives different numbers and names. There is an element, however, of the 'Chinese whispers' of history, perhaps arising out of the dangers of copyists, for Capgrave boosts by a thousand Walsingham's figure of the French knights and esquires who died.

*

The king sent a herald to the dauphin of France that he would wait for him in the town of Harfleur for eight days, ordering him to surrender to him land which rightly belonged to him, without any shedding of blood, or

---

[39] *John Capgrave's Abbreviacion of Chronicles*, ed. P. Lucas (Early English Text Society, original series, 285, 1983), pp. 245–6. 'On 24 October [sic] the hosts met less than a mile apart. The king gave comfort to his men that they should trust in God, for their cause was rightful. The French stood on the hill, and we in the vale. Between them was land newly ploughed, making for difficult footing. Suffice to say that the field fell to the king, and the French lost it, despite their great numbers and their pride. There were killed the duke of Alençon, the duke of Brabant, the duke of Bar, five counts, the constable of France and a hundred lords, 4,069 knights and squires, with the common people not being counted. The following were taken prisoner: the duke of Orléans, the duke of Bourbon, the counts of Eu and Vendôme, the duke of Brittany's brother who claimed to be earl of Richmond, and a knight called Bouccicaut, marshal of France, and others wearing coats of arms to the number of 700. On our side were killed Edward duke of York, the earl of Suffolk, 4 knights, a squire Davy Gam, and of the common people 28. During the battle, brigands on the French side took the king's carriage and led it away. Inside it they found the king's crown. They had bells rung and then sang 'Te Deum laudamus', saying that the king was dead. But only a few hours later, their joy was changed.'

else if this did not please him, that they would settle the right and lordship of the kingdom by personal combat between the two of them. But no reply came on this . . .

For many had become ill by bloody flux . . . Many went back to England so that scarcely 5,000 remained with the king. But the king, being fearless, passed near the town of Arques which was positioned on the route which he had to take and was well fortified with bridges and walls. Here there was rumour that battle was imminent. Then he moved on his host to Eu where he found all the bridges of the area destroyed and all the causeways broken so that no one could effect a crossing. He also found that all victuals had been either removed or hidden. Then he moved on to the town of Boves, and thence to a field called Corbie where the French, suddenly coming on, were put to flight by the actions of the archers.

Crossing a marsh and the River Somme, by a causeway where he again sustained an attack by the French, the duke of Orléans and the duke of Bourbon sent to him that he should prepare himself for battle to be fought very soon. No place and no date was given but with great pomp the envoys bearing the news returned. It was said that the envoys on this matter were the sire de Heilly who had broken prison from the castle at Wysbech, and fled, and the other Jean de Graville, knight. Then the intrepid king, committing his cause to God crossed the River Ternoise and, raising his eyes, spotted companies of French a long way off and a valley between the two armies. Then he ordered everyone to confess their sins in faith to the almighty, and to receive the salvation of penitence, considering that they might be the conquerors of men if first they had become the conquerors of their own vices. There were few priests. As a result he could not do what he wished quickly. Therefore all that day they remained in that place and the others did not attack. Night came and the king went to a village nearby. That night was very rainy. The people spent the night in the rain and without food. In the morning the French thought the king had fled and seduced by false hopes they played at dice over who should take possession of whom. What an amazing turn of events! It is said that there were 7,000 on the king's side, and 60,000 on the French. Yet the victory was given to the English. I shall remain silent about the archers and the stakes, how they were ordered, and also on many other related matters, for they deserve a lengthy exposition. Suffice to know that this victory, by the aid of God, was won on the feast of St Crispin and Crispinian and that there fell on our side the duke of York, the earl of Suffolk and of the common people, or so it is said, no more than 30. On the French side were killed the archbishop of Sens, three dukes, seven counts, the Lord d'Albret, constable of France, 100 barons, 1,500 knights, and 7,000 men of gentle birth. Two dukes, three counts and many other gentlemen were killed. It is claimed that St George was seen by some fighting on behalf of the king.

That night the king stayed put. On the third day he proceeded to Calais where he rested from his labours for 20 days. This victory was a matter of joy and exultation to one people and of grief and opprobrium to the other.

A 7. John Hardyng, *Chronicle* (1457, 1464, Middle English and Latin)

First version; English text modernised from British Library, Lansdowne MS 204, fols 210v–211.

Second version: English text modernised, and Latin text translated, from John Hardyng, *Chronicle (to 1461)*, ed. H. Ellis (London 1812), pp. 374–6, 389–91.

Hardyng was born in the north of England in 1378 and served from 1390 in the household of Henry Percy ('Hotspur'). After the latter's death at the battle of Shrewsbury, Hardyng entered the service of Sir Robert Umfraville in whose company he claims to have served at the siege of Harfleur and battle of Agincourt, and in the Scottish campaign of 1417, and possibly also in the naval engagement off Harfleur in 1416.[40] He later served on the Marches of Scotland and was constable of the castles of Warkworth and Kyme. In addition, he was much used as a spy against the Scots, and was also responsible for collecting documentary evidences relating to English claims of overlordship in Scotland. Some of these we know he delivered to Henry V at Vincennes in May 1422, but later research has shown them to have been, in the main, forgeries.

His Chronicle is in verse, composed in the seven-line royal or Chaucerian stanza form. Like the *Brut* it begins with the foundation of Albion and continues to Hardyng's own lifetime. He did not start writing his chronicle until around 1440, finishing the first version, which exists only in one manuscript, for presentation to Henry VI in 1457.[41] Dissatisfied at the level of reward accorded by the king for his services concerning Scotland, he changed his allegiance to the Yorkists, writing a revised version of the chronicle for Richard, duke of York and subsequently his son, Edward IV, to whom it was presented in 1464. Interestingly, Hardyng claims in the *proem* to the second version that he wrote in English for the benefit of Richard of York's wife, who had little knowledge of Latin, unlike her husband. In the invocation to Edward IV he also included his new queen Elizabeth Woodville, noting that 'women like to know all things

---

[40] Sir Robert was uncle to Gilbert Umfraville, one of the king's most trusted captains. At the end of the first version of his chronicle, Hardyng extols the virtues of Sir Robert: 'truly he was a jewel for a King, in wise counsel and knightly deeds of war' (C.L. Kingsford, 'The first version of Hardyng's Chronicle', *EHR*, 27 (1912), pp. 746–8). A John Hardyng served in the garrison of Argentan in the 1430s (Bibliothèque Nationale de France, manuscrit français 25771/770, 812, 888, 900; 25773/1185; 25774/1285).

[41] Kingsford, 'First version', pp. 462–82, 740–53.

belonging to their husbands' so that they can understand them properly, and so that the queen especially might rejoice in Edward's noble ancestors and their success.[42]

The second version was published in 1812 by Sir Henry Ellis, based upon the printed text of 1543 collated against the manuscript copy in British Library, Harley MS 661.[43] This second version is considerably shorter than the first (12,600 lines as opposed to 19,000). Not surprisingly the first 'Lancastrian' version gives a lengthier panegyric at the end of its account of the reign of Henry V,[44] but its account of the battle of Agincourt is shorter than in the second version although a further list of French casualties is given in the margin. Hardyng only mentions his own presence on the campaign in the second version, which might raise suspicions of his actually being there at all.

Hardyng added to his second version a prose account in Latin which gave a further account of the campaign. This mainly derived from the *Gesta*, or perhaps from some other source which was derived from the latter. The second version of Hardyng's chronicle was much read by others in the later fifteenth and sixteenth centuries and was printed twice by Richard Grafton in 1543, who added his own continuation to it. Thus Hall, Stow and Holinshed all came to use Hardyng.

Hardyng's accounts of the battle ought to be of great value to us as he was apparently present there, although his exact function in Umfraville's service is not clear and neither of his accounts of the battle contains any expression of real personal experience. His description of the naval engagement off Harfleur in 1416 is notably fuller than the account he gives of Agincourt. In his English versions there is mention only of the fact that many more French died from 'the press' than at the hands of their enemy. There is no fighting at all in the Latin prose account where he follows the *Gesta* but omits all of the latter's comments on the battle proper and is confused in his dating of events. His English versions both show possible influences of the *Brut*, and the numbers of troops he cites are no more reliable than those of any other commentator. That said, we might argue that, in his assessment that 9,000 English met with 100,000 Frenchmen, we have an intriguing insight into what the odds might have looked like to someone apparently present at the battle. Even odder is his notion in the latin version that 100,000 French died at the battle! Remember too that he did not write his works until thirty years or more after the event. He mistakenly calls the duke of Orléans Louis in his second version, and in the chapter which follows the extract from that version, claims that Emperor Sigismund accompanied Henry back to

---

[42] As noted in Gransden, p. 282.

[43] Several further manuscripts of the second version are known. See A.S.G. Edwards, 'The manuscripts and texts of the second version of John Hardyng's Chronicle', in *England in the Fifteenth Century: Proceedings of the 1986 Harlaxton Symposium*, ed. D. Williams (Woodbridge, 1987), pp. 75–84.

[44] Printed in Kingsford, 'First version', pp. 744–6. There is no specific mention of Agincourt here but the king is praised for his conquests and said to have crusading ambitions ('to conquer the land of all Syria').

England after the battle. Even if Hardyng *was* present at Agincourt it was not an event of which he chose to make much. He was much more interested in Anglo-Scottish affairs than Anglo-French, and in proving English claims to overlordship of Scotland. This is particularly apparent in the first version which alerts Henry VI to the deeds of Edward I and ends with a rather splendid map of Scotland.

*

First version

How the king Henry he did [behead] the earl of Cambridge, the Lord Scrope, Sir Thomas Gray of Wark and went to Normandy and won Harfleur and coming homeward he struck then the battle of Agincourt.

At Lammas after, the king to Normandy
At Southampton was with all his host to sail
Where then the earl of Cambridge certainly
The lord Scrope also and Sir Thomas Gray,
The king's death had cast for their avail
Of which the king was aware, and took all three
And beheaded them at Southampton by decree.

And held his way to Harfleur then anon
And won it so and made there captain
His own the duke of Exeter alone
And homeward went by Calais so again
At Agincourt the French met him certain
And with him fought with host innumerable
Where they were taken and won, without fable.

The duke was taken that day of Orléans
The duke also of Bourbon certainly
The earl of Vendôme that was of great credence
And Sir Arthur of Brittany verily
With many more of other prisoners
That taken were, as say chroniclers.

The dukes there of Bar and Alençon
And of Lorraine were in that battle slain
And for their lifes they paid no more ransom
Who for their wives no more came ever again
But on that ground there died they certain.
Forty thousand there laid their lives to wed
For their ransom me thought they had well sped.

On our side was of York duke Edward slain
A mighty lord and full of sapience
And fell else none of Englishmen certain
As I conceive that were of reverence
That was but grace of God's omnipotence
For Englishmen nine thousand did not exceed
That fought against a hundred thousand indeed.

On Saint Crispin and Crispinian's day*
This battle sore certainly was smitten
At Agincourt as they withstood his way
For which the king fought as well was written
With them anon where were slain unsmitten
Thousands more through their multitude
That would have fled from his highness (*excelsitude*).

The year of Christ a thousand and four hundred
And seventeen [sic] when this same battle
Was smitten so and of his reign no wonder
The third year was, that time without fail
And home they came them to their most avail
Through Picardy by Guines and Calais then
And there they shipped and unto England went.

* Beside this line is inserted in the margin 'Note the date of the battle of Agincourt, when it was'. In another hand is added in Latin a brief list of those French nobles captured and killed which includes those mentioned in the text along with a few others.

Second version

The 213th chapter. *How the king went into Normandy and besieged Harfleur and gained it with great pain and loss of men. But who may cast off running hounds and many hunting dogs without losing some of them?*

The king held forth by sea to Normandy,
With all his host at Chef de Caux landed they
And laid a siege to Harfleur mightily
On every side by land and water.
With bulwarks stout and bastions he began
In which he put the earl of Huntingdon,
The earl of Kent also of great renown

Which earls two, with others to them assigned
Cornwall and Grey, Steward also, and Porter,
Full great assaults made each day and repulsed,

Whilst at last they battered the town's towers there
And what the king with faggots that there were,
And his cunning digging under the wall,
With his guns casting they made the tower to fall

And their bulwark burnt with shot of wild fire
At which place then the two earls set up
Their banners both without any hire;
The king there with his guns the walls beat
The king did so of Clarence without stopping
On the far side, where he then lay
The earl of Mortagne did well there always

The lord Gaucourt that then was their captain
of Harfleur, though, with others of the town
offered then the town to the king full fain,
And he with others to stand at the king's direction
Then made he there his uncle of great renown,
Captain of it, duke of Exeter then,
And homeward went through France like a man

The 214th chapter. *How the king came homeward through Normandy and
Picardy and smote the battle of Agincourt, where I was with my master.*

A hundred miles to Calais had he then
At Agincourt, so homeward in his way
The nobles there of France before him were,
Proudly battled with a hundred thousand in array,
He saw he must needs with them make affray
He set on them and with them fought full sore
With nine thousand, no more with him there.

The field he had and held it all that night
But then came word of new host of enemies,
For which they slew all prisoners down right
Save dukes and earls in fell and cruel wise
And then the press of enemies did surprise
Their own people, that more were dead through press
Than our men might have slain in time no less.

On our side was the duke of York there slain,
The earl also of Suffolk worshipfully,
And knights two with others then truth to say,
And at the siege the earl of Suffolk indeed,

The father died of the flux continually,
But many folk at that siege yet died,
Of fruit and flux and cold were mortified.

On the French part the dukes of Bar and Lorraine
And of Alençon in battle there were dead,
And taken were of Christians for certain
The Duke Louis [*recte*, Charles] of Orléans their leader,
The duke of Bourbon in that same place.
The earl of Vendôme and also Arthur of Brittany
And Sir Bouccicaut marshal of France for certain.

And the earl of Eu was taken there also
Five barons also that were with their banners,
And fifteen hundred knights and esquires more
were slain that day in full knightly manner
With wounds so as then did appear
As wars would upon Crispin's day,
And Crispinian the saints in bliss be always.

Latin prose account

On the Monday [30 September] the king sent a herald, called Guienne, with the Sire de Gaucourt to the dauphin to indicate that he should wait at the town of Harfleur for another eight days following, seeking a reply from him within this time on whether he wished to come to a settlement with the English king and to submit to having his right determined, without the rigours of war or the shedding of much blood, by a duel between the two of them, and by the advice of both kings. But the eight days passed without reply, so Henry began his march towards his town of Calais which was more than 100 English miles distant from Harfleur, ordering his army to stock up with victuals for eight days.

On Tuesday 1 October he left Harfleur with his army, which did not number more than 900 lances and 5,000 archers. He passed the town of Montivilliers half a mile to his right. Establishing three battles and wings, he boldly began his march, and on the following Friday came before the castle and town of Arques which was situated on the river which flowed through Dieppe, keeping the town of Dieppe three miles to his left. On the Saturday he passed by Eu, leaving it half a mile to his left. On Sunday he approached close to the town of Abbeville where he was not able to effect a crossing of the River Somme because the bridges, fords and causeways had been broken. On Monday he made his way upstream of the Somme, keeping the city of Amiens to his left at a distance of one league. On Tuesday he travelled along the river upstream but could not find any crossing or ford. It was the same on Wednesday. On Thursday he came to Boves and then to the walled town of Corbie, passing it on his left in a valley, wherein the king ordered that each archer should make for himself a stake or staff squared or rounded (*palum vel baculum quadratum seu rotundum*), six feet in length and sharpened at both ends, to be fixed in front of them into the ground at one end and with the other end set at an angle towards the enemy at the time of battle.

On Friday the king lodged in small villages near to the walled town of Nesles where he was informed that he could cross the River Somme in two places. On this account he sent Lord Gilbert Umfraville, earl of Kyme, William Porter, John Cornwall and William Bourchier with their standards to guard the crossing of the army over the river, which they did from midday to one hour before night. On Saturday the king and his entire army crossed at the two places where there was a great marsh on either side of the river and at two causeways the whole army crossed between the marshland. The crossings were protected by their guards from midday to one hour of night.

On Sunday next the duke of Orléans and the duke of Bourbon sent three heralds to the king saying that they would give battle. On Monday the king came close to the walled town of Péronne, keeping it on his left by a mile. Then the king came to the River Ternoise and crossed it. On Tuesday and Wednesday the king and his army stayed in small villages where they had sight of the great army of the French. On Thursday the king suddenly moved his army by riding in full array towards them. At sunset the French camped in villages and gardens near the king. When the king saw this and that each was shouting for his servant, friend or companion, as was their custom, he ordered his army to [gap in manuscript] under certain penalty to [be] in the village of Agincourt near the enemy until morning.

On Friday, the feast of the Sts Crispin and Crispinian, at sunrise the French drew themselves up in their army in wings, companies and troops (*aciebus, turmis et cuneis*) before the king in the field of Agincourt, blocking his way to Calais. Meanwhile the king drew up his army near to the enemy, putting Edward, duke of York in the vanguard and Lord Camoys in the van, four wings on right and left (*pro alis dextra et sinistra)*. The king approached closer to his enemy and the enemy towards him and by a hard won fight, the king gained a victory. In this were killed the duke of Bar, the duke of Brabant, the duke of Alençon, 5 counts, 90 barons and bannerets, 1500 knights and a great multitude of the rank and file, according to the reckoning of the heralds totalling 100,000 men. There were captured on the French side the duke of Orléans, Louis, brother of the king of France [*recte*, Charles, nephew of Charles VI], duke of Bourbon, the count of Vendôme, Arthur of Brittany, count of Richemont, and the count of Eu, and the Lord Bouccicaut, marshal of France. On the English side were killed Edward, duke of York, Michael de la Pole, earl of Suffolk, a young man, two knights newly dubbed and 10 other people.

After the battle had ended, our king, out of his humanity and his great boldness, spent the night in the village of Agincourt and in the same place where he had rested on the previous night. On Saturday he took up his journey again, crossing the place where the battle had been fought, with great lamenting in his heart because so many Christians had been killed, to the number of 100,000, when the king had had no more than 9,000 men both sick and healthy. On Tuesday, on the eve of the feast of Saints Simon and Jude the king came with his whole army to Calais with great rejoicing and happiness amongst the people, where he had, with great devotion, praises sung to the one God for the victory,

A 8. The Chronicle of Peter Basset (1459, French)

Translated from London, College of Arms, MS 9, fols xxxi–xxxiii.

In the College of Arms MS 9 there is an unpublished chronicle in French covering the period from the capture of Harfleur in 1415 to the raising of the siege of Orléans in May 1429.[45] The preface to the work calls it a *Liber de Actibus Armorum* (*Book of Military Deeds*) concerning the conquest of the kingdom of France, the duchy of Normandy, duchy of Alençon, and the duchies of Anjou and Maine, compiled for Sir John Fastolf in 1459, in which year Fastolf died. Its authors are named as Peter Basset, an Englishman who, it was noted, had served in the wars for many years, Christopher Hanson, a German who had been in the service of Thomas Beaufort, duke of Exeter, and Luke Nantron, native of Picardy, one of the clerks of Sir John Fastolf. The whole work had been put into effect 'by the diligence of William Worcester, secretary of Fastolf'. This chronicle was probably part of a bigger project by William Worcester to record the military deeds of his master.[46] Fastolf had embarked on the campaign of 1415 in the retinue of Michael de la Pole senior, earl of Suffolk.

[45] For further discussion, see Gransden, pp. 329–30, B.J.H. Rowe, 'A contemporary account of the Hundred Years War from 1415 to 1429', *EHR*, 41 (1926), pp. 504–13, and J.G. Nichols, 'Peter Basset: a lost historian of the reign of Henry V', *Notes and Queries*, second series, 9 (1860), p. 424.

[46] Annals were attributed to William Worcester himself by Thomas Hearne and are published as such in J. Stevenson, *Letters and Papers Illustrative of the Wars of the English in France*, 2 vols in 3 parts (Rolls Series, London 1861–4), II, ii, pp. 743–93. It is unlikely, however, that these are the work of Worcester although their true nature is not clear. The entry for 1415 (p. 759) is given here to show that, in the annalistic tradition, Agincourt was seen as 'the event' of the year but that this did not always generate expansive treatment. The reference to Cecily Neville may be another example of the impact on historical writing of the Yorkist ascendancy later in the century. '1415 In this year on the morrow of St Laurence, King Henry V entered the sea with 1726 ships at Southampton and on the vigil of the Assumption landed at Chef de Caux, and on 22 September the town of Harfleur surrendered to him, and on 25 October next was the battle of Agincourt, on which day the French were defeated and many lords captured

The earl died at the siege of Harfleur and Fastolf was invalided home.[47] He was thus not present at the battle of Agincourt although he soon returned to serve under the earl of Dorset in the garrison of Harfleur. He went on to give many years of service in Normandy and especially in the conquest, and as governor, of Maine, before being disgraced by alleged cowardice at the battle of Patay in 1429. Significantly, the text ends shortly before this battle.

It is possible that Basset served on the campaign of 1415. He was certainly present on the 1417 expedition, mustering in the retinue of the earl of Norfolk. His military service can be traced, some of it spent in Fastolf's garrison of Alençon, until at least 1437. There is no truth, however, in John Bale's assertion that he was the chamberlain and intimate friend of Henry V, nor is there any known copy of a life of the king which Bale claimed Basset had composed in English. Hanson was also a serving soldier in the garrison of Saint-Suzanne in Maine, and later served in Fastolf's estate administration in England.

The chronicle was not put into its final form until the late 1450s. It may have been based on earlier sources and on the reminiscences of Sir John and his companions in arms. It abounds in lists of men serving on various campaigns, those commanding garrisons on both the French and English sides, and the dead and prisoners in battles and skirmishes. This tendency is revealed clearly in the sections on the siege of Harfleur and battle of Agincourt, although some of the forenames of English peers are incorrect. It is likely that these lists were partly derived from records kept by the heralds; in the case of the French dead and prisoners there is a specific reference to a list provided by Mountjoye, the French king of arms. The account is valuable for the list of knights which Henry made at the crossing of the Somme and for the comment that the reason that so many French nobles died at Agincourt was because of the killing of the prisoners. Was this Fastolf trying to redeem his own alleged unchivalric behaviour by implying that Henry V was himself culpable of a major offence against the chivalric code, or was this the version of events which was circulating later in the century? Whatever the case, one of the main claims to importance of this chronicle is that it was used extensively by Edward Hall in the sixteenth century: in the list of sources which Hall gives, he notes under English writers a Basset, although he gives him the first name of John. It is possible, of course, that Hall drew on the English life which Bale claimed was written by Basset, but there are major similarities between the listings in College of Arms, MS 9 and Hall. It is also possible that the chronicle now before us was a translation into French of an English work by Basset. It is noteworthy that this is the only chronicle in French concerning the war which is associated with an English author. It may be speculated that French was chosen as the language of chivalry despite the fact that historical writing in England by the early fifteenth century had already moved away from the use of French towards the vernacular. The chronicle was, it

and killed. In this year was born Cecily, wife of Richard, duke of York, daughter of the earl of Westmoreland, on 3 May.'
47 PRO, E101/46/24.

seems, consulted in the early seventeenth century by Ralph Broke, York Herald, who compiled a list of those at the battle, and was also known to Thomas Hearne in his editing of the Pseudo Elmham in 1727.[48]

*

In the year of grace 1415 between the feasts of St Michael and of All Saints, the very noble and victorious prince, Henry, king of England and of France, the fifth of that name, took and conquered the town of Harfleur. Surrender was made to him by the principal captain of the place, the sire de Gaucourt, and by the sire d'Estouteville, Sir Jean de Typtot, Sir Henry Chambroy, particular captains in the said town under the sire de Gaucourt, and several others, all of whom were taken as prisoners to England. The victorious prince and king ordered and appointed governor of the town his uncle, Thomas Beaufort, duke of Exeter and earl of Dorset, the which duke of Exeter was commissioned and established his lieutenant and keeper therein.

Sir John Fastolf had a noble retinue of 1500 knights and 35 esquires and other men of war for the guard, safekeeping and defence of the said town, part of whose names follow. That is to say, the baron of Carew of the county of Devon, Sir Hugh Luttrell of the county of Somerset, John Standish esquire, Thomas Lord esquire and several others. [gap] And because during the time that the victorious prince and king had laid siege before the town of Harfleur, several lords had fallen into great sickness, the king gave them licence to return to England. That is to say, to Thomas, duke of Clarence, brother of the king, John, earl marshal and earl of Nottingham, John, earl of Arundel and of Warenne, treasurer of England.

These things done and other notable statutes and ordinances being established and made, the said victorious prince the king accompanied by princes and lords whose names follow, that is to say Humphrey, duke of Gloucester, brother of the king, John [erased, Edward entered by a later hand] duke of York, John, earl of Huntingdon, John, earl of March, Thomas, earl of Oxford, Richard, earl of Devon, William, earl of Suffolk, Gilbert of Umfraville, count of Kyme, John, Lord Roos, Thomas, Lord Willoughby, John Lord Clifford, the Lord Fitzhugh, the Lord of Ferrers Groby, the Lord of Ferrers Chartley, the Lord Camoys, the Lord Bourchier, John de Beauchamp, Lord Despenser and of Bergavenney and later earl of Worcester, the Lord Harington, the Baron Carew of the land of Cornwall (the baron of Duddeley) [gap] and several others to the number of 800 lances and 8,500 archers or thereabouts. He left Harfleur and rode by land to Blanchetaque near to Saint Valéry in order to cross over the River Somme, but he found that the enemy to the number of

---

[48] Pseudo Elmham, p. xxxi. For Broke's list, now British Library, Harley MS 782, see below p. 407.

50,000 men of war were on the other side of the river to prevent his passage. For this reason, and also because of the danger of the tides the victorious prince left Blanchetaque and rode with all his host downstream of the River Somme to the Pont Saint Maxence in order to cross the river there. And there he found again the enemy in large number guarding the crossing. As the victorious prince thought that he might have battle there he made several knights some of whose names follow here: that is to say, John, lord of Ferrers Groby, Ralph de Greystoke, Peter Tempest, Christopher Moresby, Thomas Pickering, William Hodelston, John Hosbalton, John Mortimer, Philip Halle and William Halle, brothers, James de Ormond [gap] and several others, but the enemy did not give him battle at the said place. Thus the victorious prince left that place with all his host and rode on without having any battle until he reached a place which was a league from the city of Amiens in a town near a castle called Boves, where he lodged for two days and afterwards he passed the River Somme two leagues from the town of Péronne and rode on from that town towards the River Soudon up to a castle called Agincourt at which place he heard certain news that the enemy to the number of 150,000 men of war had come to give battle against him.

Thus the victorious prince made his deployments (*ordonnances*) and dressed himself to give battle. On the vigil of the feast of Saints Crispin and Crispinian, in the year 1415, the enemy gave battle in which the victorious prince and king had honour and victory. And of the enemy were killed or taken prisoners in the battle the princes and lords whose names follow. [Five prisoners are named, 38 dead] and several other knights to the number of 2,400, according to a declaration delivered by Mountjoye, King of Arms of France. And as Sire Guillaume de Tybouville, knight, lord of La Rivière Thibouville rallied the enemy to the number of 20,000 men of war and more under a white banner to give a new battle, the victorious prince the king had cried throughout his host that every man kill his prisoner. And that was the reason that so many nobles were killed.

In the said battle on the side of the victorious prince there died the lords whose names follow. That is to say, the duke of York, the earl of Suffolk, Sir Richard Kyghley, Davy Gam esquire, Welshman, and about 10 archers.

After the glorious victory thus obtained, the victorious prince ordered the burial of the lords and others killed in the battle both of his own side and of the side of his enemy. And then he rode peacefully with all his host to Calais where he stayed for several days to refresh himself and then he crossed the sea to his kingdom of England with great honour and victory.

A 9. The *Brut* (1430, 1436–37, 1460–70, Middle English)

The English *Brut* was essentially the vernacular descendant of the Anglo-Norman prose *Brut* produced in the late thirteenth and fourteenth centuries.[49] As the name suggests, the latter had as their initial inspiration the legends relating to the origins of Britain, where Brutus, son of Aeneas who had fled Troy, found his way to these islands. The earliest English versions of these works, dealing with the period from the origins of Britain to 1333, appeared around 1400. The *Brut* chronicles of the fifteenth century were continuations which took up the story where earlier works ended. The first continuation in English was probably compiled about 1430 and covered the years from 1377 to 1419. It is likely, however, that there were once earlier recensions. Kingsford speculates that in addition to one ending in 1419 (which formed the basis of the main compilation of 1430), another might have ended in 1415.[50] There were further versions of the *Brut* chronicles compiled in 1436–7, the mid-1460s and late 1470s. It was common for continuators to rewrite sections which preceded their own continuation; as a result, there are a number of different versions, and it is unlikely that any *Brut* is the work of one author alone.

The textual study of such works is thus extremely complex. F. Brie edited a two-volume compilation for the Early English Text Society in 1906–8. The first volume presents the English *Brut* to 1333, the second volume the continuations, drawing on 21 manuscripts and on the first printed edition of 1480.[51] His classification has since been criticised, with Matheson suggesting four new categories, and a further 52 manuscripts have been identified.[52] There can be no doubt, therefore, that the *Brut* was the most widely circulating chronicle in the fifteenth century and that there remain many *Brut* texts unedited. There was also a Latin version of the *Brut*,[53] and the English *Brut* was often abbreviated, perhaps for pedagogic reasons.[54]

The textual history is further complicated by links with the London Chroni-

---

[49] See the discussion in *Manual of Writings in Middle English 1050–1500*, 8 (Newhaven, Connecticut, 1989), pp. 2629–37.

[50] *EHL*, p. 133.

[51] The intended third volume which would have included a full textual discussion never appeared but Brie had earlier written *Geschichte und Quellen der mittelenglischen Prosachronik, 'the Brute of England', oder The Chronicles of England* (Marburg, 1905), where he listed and attempted to classify 120 manuscripts of the *Brut* (see review by J. Tait in *EHR*, 21 (1906), p. 616).

[52] *Manual of Writings in Middle English*, 8, pp. 2634–5, 2818–21. The new categories are 1. The common version to 1333 with continuations, some of which go to 1461, 2. extended versions, 3. the abbreviated versions drawing on the common and extended versions, 4. peculiar texts and versions. See also L.M. Matheson, *The Prose Brut: The Development of a Middle English Chronicle* (Medieval and Renaissance Texts and Studies, Arizona, 1998).

[53] *EHL*, pp. 129–33. Tito Livio is thought to have used the longer version of the Latin *Brut*. Kingsford suggests that it was the source for the version of the English *Brut* printed in *An English Chronicle from 1377 to 1461*, ed. J.S. Davies (Camden Society, 64, London, 1856).

[54] Examples are given in *Manual of Writings in Middle English*, 8, pp. 2632–3. The 'Chronicle of King Henryie ye fifte' in British Library, Cotton Claudius A VIII is essentially the

cles. As Gransden puts it 'The fifteenth-century *Brut* and London Chronicles have features in common with each other, and are in fact directly related, because the *Brut* chronicles were partly derived from the London ones.'[55] The *Brut* certainly seems to have been compiled in London. But some distinctions can be drawn. The London Chronicles developed from the lists of mayors and sheriffs of the city. As these officeholders were appointed on an annual basis, the London Chronicles had a strict chronological framework, as will be seen from the examples given later below. The *Brut* also provided a fuller narrative than the London Chronicles and maintained a link with its Anglo-Norman predecessors in the continuing interest in chivalry and deeds of war.

It might be thought that together they provide a more popular version of the campaign of 1415 than the works in Latin. A major difficulty is the relatively late date of composition. As we have seen, the first English *Brut* dealing with events after 1377 was compiled around 1430. Others, the version of the *Brut* continued to 1461 and many London Chronicles, belong to the Yorkist period and hence have a tendency to eulogise the Yorkists. Indeed the accession of Edward IV in 1461 may have been a stimulus to their compilation. We can see a small element of this in the increased place given to Edward, duke of York in the battle. Although Gransden suggests that 'ultimately all the *Brut* and London Chronicles are based on excellent contemporary sources of evidence', it is not always easy to separate out what might be of the period and what the legends and embellishments which developed with the power of hindsight. The *Brut* was drawn upon by many other writers including Tito Livio and the author of Pseudo Elmham. Waurin may also have had access to it, especially for the pre-Conquest sections of his *Receuil des Croniques*.[56] With up to 172 manuscripts and transcripts extant, the prose *Brut* is by far the most popular work written in English before 1500, save for the Wycliffite Bible. It was also the first English history to be printed, for Caxton printed the continuation to 1461 in 1480. He also drew on the *Brut* for the section covering 1377 to 1461 which he added to his printed edition of Higden's *Polychronicon* in 1482. The author of the *First English Life* says he drew on English chronicles: it is thought that this was most likely the *Polychronicon* printed by Caxton. A further 11 printed editions appeared over the next 50 years and were much used by the Tudor historians from Polydore Vergil onwards and thus through them by Shakespeare.

The *Brut* accounts are always eulogistic of Henry V. Although not written up till 1430 or later, it is highly likely that the account of the siege of Harfleur and battle of Agincourt drew on contemporary ballads. The link is clearest for the siege of Rouen with use of John Page's poem. Newsletters (London was always kept well informed by the government) and reports of eyewitnesses were also drawn on, as was that nebulous thing called popular tradition. Three versions are

---

section on the reign from the common version of the *Brut* but has a claim to being the only fifteenth-century English life of the king.
55 Gransden, p. 221
56 *EHL*, p. 136.

given below to give some impression of the most widely circulating accounts of the battle from the 1430s onwards.

Although not within the *Brut* tradition, here is a convenient place to mention two further chronicles in Latin which Kingsford discovered. The first, 'A Southern Chronicle', covers the period from 1399 to 1422, and is written in a hand of the second quarter of the fifteenth century.[57] Its account of Agincourt is short and insignificant except for the fact that it claims that the dauphin died at the battle. The 'Northern Chronicle' is in a mid-fifteenth-century hand and may derive from a northern monastery, perhaps Whalley Abbey. Elsewhere it makes frequent reference to the Percy earls of Northumberland.[58] It is a continuation of Higden's *Polychronicon* from 1399 to 1430. Its account of the battle is slightly longer but predictable. The size of the English army is given as 'scarcely 10,000', and the French 100,000 of whom 20,000 die. Four hundred men are said to have died on the English side. It provides two interesting observations – the distance of Agincourt from Calais (30 miles), and the length of the battle, claiming that it lasted from the third hour to the hour of vespers. The Latin *Brut*, printed by Kingsford, states that 'the battle lasted from the first hour until midday'.[59]

*

a. A continuation of the *Brut* from 1377 to 1419, Cambridge University Library, MS Kk I 12, mid-fifteenth century, modernised from *The Brut, or the Chronicle of England*, ed. F.W.D. Brie, 2 vols (Early English Text Society, original series, 131, 136, 1906, 1908), 2, pp. 377–80.

When the king saw that the town of Harfleur was well provided with both men and victuals, this worthy prince and king took his leave and set off in the direction of Calais by land. The French heard of his coming and were determined to stop his way so that he might not pass in that direction. To this end they broke all the bridges where ever there was a crossing for horse or man, with the result that no one could cross over the rivers, whether on horse or foot, without being drowned. As a result, our king, with all his people, made his way up river towards Paris. There was all the royal power of France ready to give him battle and to destroy all his people. But almighty God was his guide, and saved him and all his people, and withstood all his enemy's intent. Thanks be to God who preserved His own knight and king in his rightful title! Our king saw the multitude and number of his enemies who were preventing his way and intending to give him battle. Then our king, with a meek heart and a good spirit, lifted up his hands to almighty God, beseeching him to give His aid and succour, and, on that day, to save His true servant. Then our king

---

[57] *EHL*, pp. 275–6, 31–2.
[58] Ibid., pp. 285, 35–6.
[59] *EHL*, p. 132.

gathered all his lords together and other people about him, and bid them all to be of good cheer, for they should have a fair day and a gracious victory, and the better of their enemies. He prayed them all to make themselves ready for the battle, for he would rather be dead that day, in the battle or in the field, than be taken by his enemies; for he would never put the realm of England to ransom for his person. The duke of York fell on his knee and beseeched the king to grant his wish, that he would give him that day command of the vanguard in his battle order. The king granted his request and said 'Many thanks, cousin of York', praying him to make ready. Then he bade every man to provide himself with a wooden stake sharpened at both ends so that the stake could be put in the ground at an angle so that the enemy could not override them (for that was their wicked purpose), as they had arrayed them all there in order to override our company at their first charge suddenly in the opening stages of the battle.

All the night before the battle the French made many great fires and much revelry with shouting, and played for our king and his lords at dice, and bidding for an archer a *blanc* of their money, for they intended to have them as their own.

When the morning came and the day began, the king, by good advice, had his main company (*battle*) and wings arm, charging every man to keep himself close, and praying them all to be of good cheer. When they were ready, he asked what time of day it was and they said 'prime'. 'Then' said our king, 'Now is a good time for all England is praying for us. Therefore be of good cheer, let us go into battle.' Then he said in a high voice 'In the name of almighty God and St George, advance banners. St George, give us this day your help.'

Then the French came pricking down as if to override all our men, but God and our archers made them stumble. Our archers shot no arrows off target; all caused death and brought to the ground both men and horses. For they were shooting that day for a wager. Our stakes made them fall over, each on top of the other so that they lay in heaps two spear's length in height. Our king with his company and his men-at-arms always fought on, for he battled with his own hands. When the archers ran out of arrows, they laid on with stakes. In this way almighty God and St George brought the enemy to the ground and gave us the victory that day. There were slain of Frenchmen that day in the field of Agincourt more than 11,000, without counting the prisoners who were taken. The French had numbered that day in the field more than 120,000, and of Englishmen there were no more than 7,000 but God fought for us that day.

Afterwards, news came to the king that there was a new battle of Frenchmen drawn up ready to steal upon them and come towards them. Immediately the king had it proclaimed that every man should kill the prisoners that he had taken, and straightway drew up his battle line again ready to fight with the French. When they saw that our men were killing their prisoners, they withdraw, and broke up their battle line and their whole army. Thus our king, as a worthy conqueror, had that day the victory in the field of Agincourt in Picardy.

Then our king returned again to where the engagement had been to see who were dead on the English side and whether any were injured who might be given assistance. There were dead in the field on the French side the duke of Bar, the duke of Alençon, the duke of Brabant, the count of Nevers, the chief constable of France and 8 other counts, and the archbishop of Sens and over a hundred noble barons, and of worthy knights of good family and armorial bearings, 1500. Of the English, there died that day the duke of York and the earl of Suffolk, and of all others of the English nation there were no more than 26 dead, thanks be to God. And this battle was on a Friday, the feast of St Crispin and Crispinian, in the month of October. The king immediately ordered the dead to be buried and the duke of York and earl of Suffolk to be carried home with him. There were taken as prisoners the duke of Orléans, the duke of Bourbon, the count of Vendôme, the count of Eu, the count of Richemont and Sir Bouccicaut, marshal of France. Many other worthy lords were taken at this battle of Agincourt and brought to the town of Calais and then overseas with the king into England.

b. *Brut* 1377–1437, British Library, Harley MS 53, narrative written *c.* 1437, completed 1452–3, modernised from Brie, *The Brut*, pp. 554–8.

Kingsford suggested that this was a longer original of the English Chronicle published by Davies.[60] Its account of the campaign is slightly different from that of other versions of the *Brut*, especially in the fact that it gives lists of hostages at Harfleur and of French slain at Agincourt (where it is very close to the London Chronicle in British Library, Cotton Cleopatra C IV). It also has an interesting version of the origins of the stakes, making York responsible for giving the *whole army* stakes, and linking this to the king's initial mistrust of the duke. If Kingsford is right in his dating of the manuscript to 1452–3, this may be an example of pro-Yorkist sentiment at a time when Richard, duke of York was aiming to gain a greater say in the government of Henry VI. The inclusion of the story may suggest, however, that the text post-dates the Yorkist accession of 1461.

Then the king moved on from Harfleur with his army and went towards Calais by land, to the number of 8,000. As the French had broken all the bridges whereby he might have crossed, he sought a route by other routes and came to a place called Agincourt, at which all the power of the French were gathered, ready to stop his advance and to give him battle. When the King saw this he prayed to God for help, and with the people he had (scarcely 8,000) he made ready and drew up in battle formation. At the

[60] *EHL*, pp. 123–5. See below Text D 2a for the account of the king's entry to London as given in this version of the *Brut*.

time the king mistrusted Edward, duke of York. The duke was well aware of this and came to the king asking that he might have command of the vanguard that day. The King granted him this. Then the duke went forth and ordered and commanded every man to provide himself with a stake sharpened at both ends, and put in the ground in front of him at an angle so that the French men could not override him, for their intention was to override them as they numbered 120,000 or more. All the night before the battle the French made much revelry, crying and shouting all night, and played for Englishmen at dice, every archer for a *blanc*. On the morning at about prime the King ordered every man to make himself ready for battle saying these words, 'Sirs. Think this day to acquit yourselves as men, and fight for the right of England. In the name of Almighty God, advance banner. St George, give us this day your help!' Then our men knelt down all together and made the sign of the cross on the ground and kissed it, and put himself at the mercy of God.

The Frenchmen came on ferociously and with great pride and our archers shot freely. At last both the battles joined and met, and fought fiercely together. The Frenchmen pressed so thick and fast on our people that they fell on the stakes which were planted in the ground, horse and man, so thick, each on top of the other, that a great number of them were slain without making any stroke. The King fought right manfully on that day with his own hands, so that one piece of his crown was broken, which afterwards was found and brought to him. So at last Almighty God gave His grace that the King should have victory over his enemies, for all their pride, and slew 12,000. The names of the lords and other men of rank who were killed follow in this table below:

[list]

and many more as has been said before. These were the names of the French lords who were taken prisoners in the battle [list] and many others to the number of 800. And these were the names of the lords who were killed on our side; the good and noble duke of York in the vanguard, the earl of Suffolk and other yeomen to the number of 28. This battle was fought on 25 October, the day of St Crispin and Crispinian, in the year of our lord 1415, of which a versifier makes mention saying 'By Crispin the English race laid low many French'. Then came tidings to the King that a new battle of Frenchmen was ready to fight with him again. The King immediately charged and commanded that every man should slay his prisoner. When the French saw this, they withdrew and went on their way.

c. Version of the *Brut* written 1478–9, Lambeth MS 84, modernised from Brie, *Brut*, pp. 596–8.

As Kingsford notes, in this version 'for the battle of Agincourt there is a peculiar narrative'.[61]

> Then the sun rose and the day began; the king, acting on good advice, arranged his main force (*battle*) and his wings, and charged every man to keep his position (*to keep them whole together*), and prayed them all to be of good cheer. When they were ready, he asked what time of day it was and they said 'prime'. Then said our King 'Now is a good time for all England prays for us. And in remembrance that God died on the cross for us, let every man make a cross in the earth and kiss it as a token that we would rather die on this soil than flee'. And when the king of France saw our king and his people fall down to the ground, he asked 'What are they doing?', and a French knight standing nearby said 'Forsooth, Sire, they intend to die on that ground today rather than to flee'. And then our king with all his people rose up and said in a high voice, 'In the name of almighty God and of St George, advance banners, and St George give your aid on this day'. Immediately trumpets sounded, and the Frenchmen came galloping down (*prykiyng*) with the intention of over-riding our men. But God and our archers caused them soon to stumble, for our archers did not shoot a single arrow which did not kill and bring to the ground man or horse, for they were shooting that day for a wager. Our stakes made the French fall headlong, one on top of another so that they lay in heaps. Our king with his retinue (*menie*) and with men-at-arms began to lay on with their weapons for it was necessary for him to fight on that day with his own hands. Our good archer who lacked arrows laid on with stakes. On that day the Frenchman saw St George in the air over the host of the English fighting against the Frenchmen, and as a result they worship and esteem St George in England more than in any other land. Thus almighty God and St George brought our enemy to the ground and gave us victory that day.
>
> There were slain of Frenchmen that day in the field of Agincourt 11,000, not counting the prisoners who were taken. The number of Frenchmen in the field that day was more than 120,000 and of English only 7,000. But God and St George fought for us on that day. The Frenchmen who were in Paris had spread the rumour that our king had been overthrown on the previous day, for the *prekers* of the French who kept the out-watch met with some of our king's carts and rifled through them, removing our king's coronet and taking it to Paris, and telling those in the city that our king had been defeated, bearing the coronet around the city

[61] *EHL*, pp. 125–6.

in processions for joy. Afterwards when they saw Frenchmen coming home much wounded they marveled greatly and asked them, 'What cheer' and they said 'nous sommes tous morts' ('no som to mors'), we be killed and overthrown'. Then a great crowd of women and other folks came together to the field where the battle was in order to see which side had been defeated, and they stood upon a hill next to the field where the battle had been. When the English army saw this, the rumour went round that those people were another army of Frenchmen. In time tidings came to our king that there was another army of French, all in battle array, drawn up ready to steal upon him. Immediately our king had it cried that every man should slay the prisoners that he had taken. That was a mighty loss to England and a cause of great sorrow to France. When that had been completed, our king ordered his army again ready to fight with the Frenchmen. When the latter saw that our men had killed their prisoners they withdrew and broke ranks. So our king, as a worthy conqueror, had on that day the victory in the field of Agincourt in Picardy, thanks be to God.

Then our king returned again to where the battle had been to see what dead there were both French and English, or if any were wounded that might be assisted. Of the French were slain in the field the duke of Berry, the duke of Alençon, the duke of Brabant, the count of Nevers, the high constable of France and 8 other counts, and the archbishop of Sens, and of barons over 100 and of worthy knights of good pedigree (*of great alliance of cote armours*) 1,500. Of the English were killed that day the good duke of York, Edmund [*recte* Edward], who died without issue. In succession to him, his brother's son Richard, who was son of Richard, earl of Cambridge who had been beheaded at Southampton, was made duke of York, as you will hear more fully later. There also died the earl of Suffolk and of all the English no more than 26 were dead, thanks be to God. This battle was on a Friday which was the Crispin and Crispinian' day, in the month of October. [Verses in Latin follow. 'In the year of our lord 1415, the third year of Henry the fifth, king by right of his father, Maurice made Harfleur and Crispin the victory called Agincourt, where Christ gave him the omen.']

A 10. The London Chronicles (later fifteenth century, Middle English)

London Chronicles developed from glosses added to the lists of sheriffs and mayors. They thus dated their entries from the election of the mayor which took place on 29 October.[62] The oldest date from the thirteenth century and were composed in Latin. There is one in French for the period 1259–1343, but by the

---

[62] For a general discussion, see *Chronicles of London*, ed. C.L. Kingsford (Oxford, 1905), *Six Town Chronicles of England*, ed. R. Flenley (Oxford, 1911), and *Manual of Writings in Middle English*, 8, pp. 2647–50.

early fifteenth century, the chronicles were written in English. They were anonymous and not compiled on any official basis in the City although they certainly drew on official pronouncements, newsletters etc. It has been suggested, for instance, that the list in British Library, Cotton Cleopatra C IV of the French lords killed at Agincourt came from an official bulletin.[63] They were undoubtedly written for a London audience, and may offer us a useful insight into 'popular' opinion, although that term still needs to be defined rather carefully; they were patrician rather than plebeian in focus. They are useful, for instance, in providing material on commercial matters, although this is not particularly relevant to the material on Agincourt. They also drew on contemporary poetry, in one case, Cleopatra C IV, citing an extensive part of a ballad on Agincourt (see text D 7a below).

The textual history of the London Chronicles is complicated. Kingsford suggested that there may have been a common original in English to about 1414, but that there were several versions thenceforward, although he also speculates that the divergence from 1415 was 'due only to the exceptional interest of the year'.[64] It also seems that many versions have been lost. Recent work has concluded that the relationship between the different versions is perhaps more complicated than Kingsford suggested, and that although there are cross fertilisations and borrowings, each chronicle is essentially unique.[65] In some cases the chronicles occur alongside poems and other materials in compilations of historical texts made for the consumption of individual Londoners, demonstrating the taste for history in the second half of the fifteenth century.[66]

Many of the London Chronicles were compiled in their final versions later than the events they describe and thus often project a Yorkist perspective. They also provided a source for the *Brut* and its continuations, but as noted earlier, the exact link between the two forms of chronicles is extremely complex. The London Chronicles are particularly difficult to date, and may have drawn on the *Brut* rather than being a source for it. The sixteenth century saw editions, abbreviations, versions and continuations of the London chronicles written in the previous century, such as the *Chronicle of Robert Fabyan* and the *Chronicle of the*

[63] Kingsford, *Chronicles of London*, p. xxv.

[64] Ibid., p. xix. In *Chronicles of London*, Kingsford printed several versions, including an example of the abbreviated form from British Library, Cotton Julius B II.

[65] Gransden, pp. 228–30 gives a detailed analysis of the links between the versions. For further recent work, see two articles by M-R. McLaren, 'The aims and interests of the London chroniclers of the fifteenth century', *Trade, Devotion and Governance. Papers in Later Medieval History*, ed. D.J. Clayton, R.G.Davies and P. McNiven (Stroud, 1994), pp. 158–76, and 'The textual transmission and authorship of the London chronicles', *English Manuscript Studies 1100–1700*, 3 (Oxford, 1992), pp. 38–72.

[66] An interesting example is to be found in *The Historical Collections of a Citizen of London in the Fifteenth Century*, ed. J. Gairdner (Camden Society, new series, 17, London, 1876), where a version of the London Chronicle possibly associated with William Gregory of the Skinners Company, mayor in 1451, is found alongside John Page's poem on the siege of Rouen and John Lydgate's verses on the kings of England.

Greyfriars of London.[67] Many others, including John Stow, followed the format of dating. There can be no doubt that such sixteenth-century historians drew information from the fifteenth-century London Chronicles.[68] It is likely too that, by the later fifteenth century at least, other towns kept similar chronicles based on the mayoral year. Richard Ricard, town clerk of Bristol from 1479 to 1503, certainly did so but gave no entry for 1415 beyond the name of the city officials.[69]

One example is given below. Extracts from a further example, British Library, Cotton Cleopatra C IV, are given in chapter 3 as it contains a poem on the battle which also begs interesting questions on how the London Chronicles were compiled. Taken together, these extracts show how the memory of Agincourt was preserved in London, although they do not contain anything surprising or particularly unusual on the battle itself. In fact, there seems to have been a marked reluctance to go into military detail in these works. Not surprisingly, however, the London Chronicles show an interest in the king's entry to London. The Great Chronicle and Cleopatra C IV also give lengthy accounts of the surrender of Harfleur which are not given here due to constraints of space. It may be that the city had a particular interest in the fate of the town. As we shall see in chapter 3, the king sent a newsletter to London about the siege and also efforts were made to encourage settlement of merchants and craftsmen after the capture.

*

Modernised from *The Great Chronicle of London*, ed. A.H. Thomas and I.D. Thornley (London, 1938), pp. 91–4.

This could be a very late compilation, with Robert Fabyan suggested as author. The manuscript certainly dates to the early sixteenth century but it is likely derived from earlier versions.

---

67 *Chronicle of the Greyfriars of London*, ed. J.G. Nichols (Camden Society, first series, 53, 1852). This chronicle, found in the register book of the London Franciscans, covers the years from 1189 to 1556, and was consulted by John Stow. It reveals how shaky the historical memory could sometimes be, with several errors concerning names of those English peers who died on the campaign. Its London interest is revealed by the fact that it is the only one to mention the death of a Londoner, Sir John Philpot, at the siege.

68 John Stow probably owned what is now 'A short English chronicle' in *Three Fifteenth-Century Chronicles*, ed. J. Gairdner (Camden Society, second series, 28, London, 1880), p. 55. This version of the London Chronicle was written early in the reign of Edward IV, terminating with the coronation of Elizabeth Woodville in 1465. It is really three chronicles, an abridgment of the *Brut* from the foundation of Albion to the beginning of the reign of Henry IV; a rather generic account in London Chronicle form of the reigns of Henry IV and Henry V; and a more independent version of subsequent reigns. The manuscript also contains Lydgate's verses on the Kings of England and historical memoranda compiled by Stow. The text is not significant enough to be included here.

69 *The Maire of Bristowe is Kalendar*, ed. L.T. Smith (Camden Society, new series, 5, London, 1872).

1414   Thomas Fawconer mercer (mayor), John Mychell and Thomas
Aleyn, sheriffs, year three

Soon afterwards the king with his army rode from Harfleur for 21 days
through the realm of France towards Calais. The French heard that he was
coming and broke all the bridges that he would have had to cross so that
any crossing he took he would have to meet with the French host. On
Friday, the feast of St Crispin and Crispinian, all the royal power of France
came before the king and his little blessed company. Then they saw that
the dauphin, the duke of Bourbon, the duke of Bar and all the lords of
France were positioned before our king, as he passed en route to Calais,
ranged in three battles to the number of 60,000 men-at-arms. That was the
fairest sight of armed men that ever anyone had seen in any place. The
King saw that he could not pass without battle. Then he said to his little
company 'Sirs, those fellows yonder will prevent us passing, and they will
not come to us. But now let every man prove himself a good man this
day'. The king rode forth with his bascinet on his head, and all the other
men went on foot in their whole array for an English mile before they
assembled. Through God's grace the King made his way through the
thickest of all the battle. There were slain the duke of Alençon, the duke
of Bar, the duke of Brabant and six counts, as well as the constable of
France, the seneschal of Hainault and the master of the crossbowmen, and
many more lords. There were taken prisoner the duke of Orléans, the duke
of Bourbon, the count of Richemont, the count of Eu, the marshal of
France, Bouccicaut. Five thousand Frenchmen, lords, knights and squires,
were slain. As for the English, in all ranks of the English there perished
only 28 men, and of men of high station, the duke of York, the earl of
Suffolk, two knights, Davy Gam, and of gentlemen no more. After this
had happened the king went to Calais with his lords and his prisoners and
his army.

B. Chronicles written in France

B 1. The Religieux (Monk) of Saint-Denis, *Histoire de Charles VI* (c. 1415–22, Latin)

Translated from Le Religieux de Saint-Denis, *Histoire de Charles VI*, ed. L.
Bellaguet (Collection de documents inédits sur l'histoire de France, 6 vols,
Paris, 1839–52), 5 (1844), pp. 542–81.[70]

[70] Reprinted as *Chronique du Religieux de Saint-Denys* (Paris, 1994).

This chronicle covers the whole of the reign of Charles VI (1380–1422). The author is anonymous, but there have been several attempts to identify him.[71] The most likely candidate is Michel Pintoin (d. 1421) who was monk and *chanteur* (precentor) at the abbey of Saint-Denis. The abbey of Saint-Denis, rather like that of St Albans in England, had a tradition of chronicle writing.[72] To some degree, its chronicle writers were the 'official' chroniclers of the French monarchy and certainly had access to documents emanating from the royal chancery, citing some verbatim, although none in the account of the battle. The royal family are always treated with respect, and his stance is decidedly royalist and patriotic. At this stage of the reign the author was pro-Burgundian in sympathy.[73] He thus explains the relative lack of Burgundian troops by the fact there was hostility to the duke amongst the other princes, and highlights the valour of Anthony of Brabant and the seneschal of Hainault. But this did not prevent an independence of approach or even a criticism of policy. The chronicler often uses the first person to express his views, and gives us a good impression of the disbelief and soul searching that followed the defeat.[74] He was critical of the pride of the nobility and the rashness of youth, with the duke of Alençon being particularly singled out for criticism. The author was not, of course, an eyewitness to the battle, although he seems to have been present with the armies, and in the entourage, of Charles VI on several occasions, such as at Le Mans in 1392. In 1393 he was asked by the duke of Berry to keep an exact note of what happened at the peace negotiations with the English at Leulinghen, material which found its way into his chronicle.

It is not entirely clear how close to the event he was writing. His portrayal of Henry V, however, is most definitely not one of a bloody aggressor: the king intends to avoid engagement both when he leaves Harfleur and on the eve of the battle, and he limits the killing of the prisoners. This may indicate a final compilation after the treaty of Troyes. But the main function of the way he pictures Henry is to create a juxtaposition with the folly of the French nobility (though not King Charles himself, who plays no part in the narrative, nor is there any mention here of the nature of his incapacity, although elsewhere the monk gives us more details on Charles' madness). The two armies are also portrayed in contrasting fashions. The steady, well-disciplined English (who commit fewer

---

71 N. Grevy-Pons and E. Ornato, 'Qui est l'auteur de la chronique latine de Charles VI, dite du Religieux de Saint-Denis?', *Bibliothèque de l'école des chartes*, 134 (1976), pp. 85–103. See also H. Moranvillé, 'La Chronique du Religieux de Saint-Denis', *Bibliothèque de l'école des chartes*, 51 (1890), pp. 5–40, C. Samaran, 'Les manuscrits de la chronique latine de Charles VI dite du Religieux de Saint-Denis', *Le Moyen Age*, 18 (1963), pp. 657–71, and P.S. Lewis, 'Some provisional remarks upon the chronicles of Saint-Denis and upon the [Grandes] Chroniqes de France in the fifteenth century', *Nottingham Medieval Studies*, 39 (1995), pp. 146–81, which cites recent work by Bernard Guenée in note 16.
72 G. Spiegel, *The Chronicle Tradition of Saint-Denis. A Survey* (Brooklyn, Mass. and Leyden, 1978).
73 Bacquet, *Azincourt*, p. 15, considers him to be an Orleanist supporter, however.
74 See below text E 2.

atrocities than the home side), draw on the strength of the lightly armed archers. In comparison, the heavily armed, bombastic French knights, are so presumptuous of their success that they reject the aid of the Parisians and send home the crossbowmen. The author is not well informed on the deployment of the troops of either side at the battle. He has Henry tell his men before the battle that he has 12,000 archers who 'will range themselves in a circle around us to sustain as best they can the shock of the enemy', which gives a different, if imprecise, idea of the positioning of the archers. There are no stakes, but the English archers do drive off an opening cavalry attack intended to outflank the English. Henry's battle speech, particularly with regard to the possibility of victory with small numbers, has similarities with elsewhere, but also is of a general, and classically influenced form. As noted in the introduction to this chapter, the author goes out of his way to provide us with a whole range of reasons for the French defeat. As we shall see in chapter 3, he also launches into more religious interpretations in subsequent chapters where he tries to outline the root cause of the French humiliation and to set it in a historical context. Never had the French been brought so low. Here there are similarities with the Bourgeois of Paris. The Parisian focus of the chronicler is also clear, with his knowledge of the processions for the king's success. But there is a sense all the way through of a good story teller, who chooses his words with care, and who makes it seem, perhaps, as though he knows more in detail that he really does.

The chronicle was certainly drawn upon by Jean Juvenal des Ursins for his own *Histoire de Charles VI*. It is also possible that the Berry herald drew on it. It became more widely known in later centuries by virtue of the fact that Le Labourer's *Histoire de Charles VI* was in part a translation of the chronicle from Latin into French.

*

[Chapter 7] The king of England entered Harfleur in victory, offered thanks to God, and arranged his conquest as he wished. He treated the knights and esquires whom he had captured with more softness and generosity than one might have expected. He gave most of them licence to go where they wished after they had given their oath that they would return to him by Martinmas. He ordered the lives of unarmed civilians to be spared, but he had taken to England the wealthiest among them to keep them prisoner until they paid ransom. He left the youngest and most robust men for the defence of the town, booting out the sick, the poor and the elderly. As for women, he allowed them, out of compassion for their sex, to go off in full freedom and without impediment, with their clothes and all that they could carry. He then decided to go back home after putting a garrison in the town. A mortal epidemic brought about by intolerable shortages had already carried off many of his troops including those of high rank, and as winter approached he was persuaded to break off military operations and to seek winter quarters. On the advice of his most important men, he did not wish to trust to the dubious fate of military engagement with troops so unequal in number. So he decided to go to Calais and to await there the spring which would be much more suitable for military action. He made for Calais with long days of marching but when he arrived at the bridge over the Somme which he hoped to cross, he found it destroyed and partly broken and he was forced to go back on his steps.

At this news, and hearing that contrary winds had driven off his ships, the lords who were in control of the government of the kingdom ordered on the king's authority that men-at-arms from all areas should assemble in full haste, without stopping in any village for more than one night, telling them that fortune would render to them their enemy trussed up and would give them a clear victory. This order was addressed to all the *baillis* and *prévôts* of the king with the command to communicate it to all on pain of death. But the soldiers who were in the service of princes and who were for the most part foreigners, illegitimate and of insignificant origins, exiles and outlaws, keener on pillage than accustomed to military discipline, paid no regard to the orders to the king and made the inhabitants of the kingdom suffer even more than was usual. With a rapacity hitherto unheard of, they forced them to sell their carts, their beasts of burden and their own homes. They took off anything they could carry and forcibly removed the animals, even the horses who were used for agricultural work. In short, they committed more crimes than the enemy himself save for murder and arson.

The king [Charles VI] arrived at Rouen towards the beginning of October at the head of a mighty army which should have been enough to wipe out several barbaric nations. He had with him more than 14,000 men commanded by the most illustrious leaders whose names deserve mention here, for they were mainly of the royal blood and exceeded all others in authority. There was the duke of Guienne, eldest son of the king, the dukes of Berry, Orléans, Bourbon, Alençon, Bar and Brabant, the counts of Nevers, Richemont, Vendôme, and 15 more besides, of whom many were brave knights, famous barons, all burning with the desire to have revenge on the English for the injuries which the king and themselves had suffered. Duke John of Burgundy had also raised his troops in Burgundy, Savoy and Lorraine but the king was not advised to summon his assistance, for the other princes did not have affection towards him and preferred to finish the campaign in full honour without him.

In addition to the warriors who came in response to the royal summons, the townsmen of Paris offered him 6,000 fully equipped men, demanding that they should be placed in the front rank if it came to battle. As the duke of Berry boasted of this offer in the presence of his knights, one of them, called Jean de Beaumont, said with disdain 'the king should not accept the help of these rude mechanics for we are already three times more numerous than the English'. He did not see that plebeians were worthy of bearing arms, even though many such men had great honour by their deeds. Moreover, since antiquity, the fact that merit had been respected in whatever rank it had been proved was something which had caused the kingdom to increase. It can be seen in the histories of France that knights had used this kind of presumptuous talk at the battle of Courtrai and soon they had been thrown headlong into deep ditches, cleverly covered by light planks, where they were killed by the Flemish. At Poitiers, the illustrious King John was taken prisoner, and in Hungary, the Christians were overcome and massacred by the Turks. I do not think that one should agree with such a way of speaking.

I now return to the enemy throng of the English. Some say that it was due to their bravery that they left the coastlands, but I think that they were forced to do so by lack of victuals. They preferred to chance the fortune of combat than to see themselves decimated by lack of nourishment and continual privations. Making a virtue out of a necessity, they advanced into the interior of the kingdom. Making their way through the dense woodlands of Gournay, situated in the region of Beauvais, 22 leagues inland from the sea, they met with no obstruction and carried out actions as one might expect of an enemy. After about four days, although this is by no means exact, they turned towards the city of Amiens. I know by accurate information that they were so pressed by lack of food that instead of ransoming the inhabitants of the towns and countryside for money they asked them for victuals, and that they often cursed the French traitors who had advised them to seek France that they should receive their eternal reward like Dathau and Abiron. They always had to their rear and in front, as well as on their flank, illustrious dukes and earls with large troops of men, who guarded the rivers, roads, public highways and crossings with care so that they might cut off their retreat. If the French had persisted in their wise action they would have gained a triumphant victory against the enemy without much blood being spilled. But the English advanced to the River Somme so that they could cross it by a wooden bridge, but finding it cut and broken they threw themselves with fury on the villages round about and put them to the torch. After that they gathered together all the workmen and carpenters and ordered them to build a new bridge with trees from the nearby woods so that they could get across the river.

The garrison of Calais made up of 300 crack troops (*strenui stipendiarii*) did not know the troubles the king was experiencing and rushed off to meet him to give the honour due to him. But on their march they found Picards and rather foolishly engaged in conflict with them and were soon forced to flee. A few of them were killed in their attempt to get away but many were put to ransom. The admiral Clignet de Brabant, the marshal Bouccicaut, the bastard of Bourbon and other captains made other similarly successful sorties with other troops. In some, they surprised the enemy who were scattered here and there for purposes of foraging, and killed them or else wounded many. Their prowess and memorable exploits would have won them eternal glory if they had been written down. But not bothered about their renown, they were content to have their achievements heard of by repute or by the approbation of the crown.

Chapter 8. *How the French were defeated by the English.*

The speed of my account has made me omit something which I should have mentioned earlier. The favour of heaven was beseeched for the king's expedition. After he had left Paris, there were many processions from church to church; public prayers were addressed to God and there were solemn masses sung. At Paris a great number of prelates, dressed in full pontificals and accompanied by the clergy and the venerable university, took full part in these devotions. In order to boost the zeal of the huge crowd of men and women who were following them, they all had in their hands lighted candles. They flattered themselves with the hope that Providence would raise up their fervent prayers, for the rumour was already spread around that the enemy, exhausted by hunger and cold, were almost unable to defend themselves, and that the French army pressed them so close that if they remained in that position they would bring them low with ease and without shedding of blood. But suddenly, at the order of some leaders whose names I do not know, the French were ordered to change their position and to move off to establish themselves elsewhere. They obeyed, but not without regret, for they foresaw that this manoeuvre was to the benefit of the enemy. Indeed, the English passed over the Somme without obstacle and directed themselves slowly, and for the most part on foot, towards Calais. But arriving three leagues this side of Hesdin and being no more than nine leagues from Calais, they met again the Picards who prevented them from going any further and forced them to stop.

The king of England, alarmed by such difficulties, held council with the principal leaders of his army about the action they should take. At first they were all of the opinion that it would be necessary to open a passage with their arms in their hands and to chance battle. They ordered at the same time the churchmen who were with them to address their prayers, as was the custom, to the Lord during the divine office, to ask him to give the English the victory. But when they saw that they would have to fight against troops four times more numerous than their own, and commanded by the principal dukes, counts and barons of France they sent representatives to these lords on 24 October to offer them reparation for all the damage which they had caused and the restitution of all that they had taken on condition that they would agree to let them return freely to their own country.

The annals of earlier reigns ought to have served as lesson for the lords of France that the rejection of such reasonable conditions had often been cause for repentance. They even had an example from recent times in the person of the illustrious king of France John, who for having attacked the English under similar circumstances had been defeated and taken prisoner. But having too much confidence in their forces and guided by the poor advice of some of their company they rebutted all proposals for peace and made reply to the king of England that they would give battle on the next day. The king communicated the reply to his whole army: 'Brave companions in arms, he said to them, and you all, my faithful subjects, here we are reduced to having to chance a combat full of risks. Let us hope for the assistance of God. He knows that the offers we made were reasonable and that the enemy rejected them out of pride because of over confidence in their numbers without realising that God loves peace and that he often gives the victory to a handful of men rather than to the most mighty armies.' After he had said these words, he had his army advance about a bow shot and seeing that hey were in a vast plain added, 'we must stop here, regather our courage and await the enemy on firm ground in close battalions without dividing our forces. Our 12,000 archers will range themselves in a circle around us to sustain as best they can the shock of the enemy. Be mindful of the valour which your ancestors showed when they put to flight Philip of Valois, and when they defeated and captured the King John, his successor, and when later they crossed France six times without being prevented. Now is the occasion to use all your intrepidity. The needs of the moment should boost your courage. Rather than being scared of doing business with so many princes and barons, be of firm hope that their large number will turn, as in the past, to their shame and their eternal confusion.'

Credible witnesses of whom I have enquired carefully about the condition and array of the enemy have assured me that up to that moment they had had little cheer and that they had had great difficulty in getting hold of food, and that they had considered it as an almost unpardonable crime to have in their camp women of evil life, and that they showed more regard than the French for the local inhabitants who had declared themselves in their favour, that they strictly observed the rules of military discipline and scrupulously obeyed the orders of their king. His words, too, were received with enthusiasm. Not only the leading commanders, but even the infantry and the other light troops who formed the vanguard as was customary, promised to fight unto death.

In the absence of the king of France and of the dukes of Guienne, Brittany and Burgundy, the other princes had taken charge of the conduct of the war. There is no doubt that they would have brought it to a happy conclusion if they had not shown so much disdain for the small number of the enemy and if they had not engaged in the battle so impetuously, despite the advice of knights who were worth listening to because of their age and experience. You know, O Jesus, our sovereign lord, you who can read the hearts of men, what was the first cause of this great sadness which I cannot think about without shedding tears, and which covers France and its people with shame and confusion. I will acquit myself, however, of my duty as a historian, however painful it is to me, and will transmit for posterity the account of that sad day so that such faults can be avoided in future. When it came to putting the army into battle formation (as is always the usage before coming to blows) each of the leaders claimed for himself the honour of leading the vanguard. This led to considerable debate and so that there could be some agreement, they came to the rather unfortunate conclusion that they should all place themselves in the front line. Almost everyone in the camp flattered themselves in a vain hope, especially the young men who headed nothing but their own excessive ardour. Thinking that they could control at their own will inconstant fortune, they persuaded themselves that the sight of so many princes would strike terror into the enemy and would cause them to lose their courage, and that, in order to win the day, they had nothing to do but charge quickly and boldly. The leading lords forgot on this occasion that, whatever confidence could inspire the boldness of youth, the experience and authority of old age should prevail in the making of decisions. Accepting the least wise advice, they formed two other bodies of men who were to follow their lead and decided that they would put themselves in the front and approach the enemy from about 2,000 paces, a movement in which they had to overcome difficulties of all kinds. Was it ignorance, or was the advice given by certain traitors? I'm not sure but they had to bivouac in a terrain of considerable extent, newly worked over, and that torrents of rain had flooded and converted into a quagmire. They had to pass the night without sleeping and to await the day, to their great displeasure, marching through the middle of the mud where they sank up to their knees. So they were already overcome with fatigue even before they advanced against the enemy and they took little time to realise to their cost that the outcome of combat depends not on human forces but on fortune, or, more precisely, the sovereign arbiter of fortune. Four thousand of their best crossbowmen who ought to have marched in the front and begun the attack were not found to be at their post and it seems that they had been given permission to depart by the lords of the army on the pretext that they had no need of their help.

Between nine and ten in the morning the admiral of France, Clignet de Brabant, Louis Bourdon and the lord of Gaule were charged to go with 1,000 crack men at arms who had the best mounts to disperse the English archers who had already engaged in combat. But at the first volley of arrows which the archers caused to rain down upon them they turned and fled, to their eternal shame, leaving their leaders stranded in the midst of danger with only a small number of brave hearts. They piled up in great haste towards the centre of the French army and, as if they had fled before a tempest, spread terror and confusion amongst their companions. The English, however, thanks to the disorder brought about by their archers whose shots, as dense as a hailstorm, obscured the sky and wounded a great number of their opponents, arrayed in a line of battle in front of the royal army and, without being afraid of the multitude of the French as our young hot heads had predicted they would be, marched in resolute fashion on the French, determined to hazard the chances of combat, and exhorting each other to fight valiantly to death according to the oath they had sworn earlier.

At almost the same moment the illustrious dukes and counts of France, having invoked the assistance of heaven and made the sign of the cross, said adieu to each other and kissed each other affectionately; then they advanced against the enemy at the head of their men at arms, with a bold countenance, crying loudly 'Mountjoye, Mountjoye!' O blindness and lack of foresight of moral men! They scarcely realised that this presumptuous joy would soon be succeeded by grief and sadness. I have learned from a reliable source that each side fought until mid day in the most bitter fashion using all kinds of weapons, but that the French were too restricted and weighed down in their movements. Their vanguard, composed of about 5,000 men, found itself at first so tightly packed that those who were in the third rank could scarcely use their swords. That taught them that if the large number of combatants was sometimes an advantage there were occasions when it became a hindrance. They were already exhausted by a long march and were suffering under the weight of their armour. They were also saddened by seeing the two illustrious knights who commanded the vanguard, the count of Vendôme, cousin of the king and leader of his house, and Guichard Dauphin, both equally renowned for their prudence as for their valour and their fidelity, forced to retreat in the face of the enemy archers after they had lost several of the bravest of their men.

In the opinion of the French, it was precisely what injured the most their enemies which assured the English of victory, especially the continuous way in which they had rained down on our men a terrifying hail of arrow shot. As they were lightly armed and their ranks were not too crowded, they had freedom of movement and could deal mortal blows with ease. In addition many of them had adopted a type of weapon until then unknown – great lead-covered mallets from which one single blow on the head could kill a man or knock him senseless to the ground. They kept themselves with advantage in the middle of this bloody mêlée, not without losing many of their own men but fighting with so much passion, for they knew that for them it was a matter of life or death. They finally broke, with a desperate effort, the French line of battle, and opened a way through at several points. Then the nobility of France were taken prisoner and put to ransom as a vile troop of slaves or else perished under the blows of a faceless soldiery. O eternal dishonour! O disaster forever to be deplored! If it is usually a consolation for men of heart and a softening of their sadness to think that they have been beaten by adversaries of noble origin and of a recognised valour, it is on the other hand a double shame,

a double ignominy to allow oneself to be beaten by unworthy and vile
men.

This unexpected defeat put terror into the two lines of the army which
remained. Instead of marching to the aid of their companions who were
yielding, they heard only their terror. No longer having anyone to lead
them, they abandoned in cowardice the field of battle. This ignominious
flight brought upon them eternal opprobrium. At this very moment a large
group of warriors finding themselves at the very edge of the vanguard
made a movement to the rear in order to withdraw from the blind fury of
the victors. The king of England believed that they were intending to
return to the charge and so ordered that all the prisoners should be killed.
This order was executed quickly and the carnage lasted until he had realised and seen with his own eyes that all the men were thinking of flight
rather than of continuing the conflict.

Chapter 9. *Reproaches addressed to the French because they did not
accept wisdom in their counsels.*

[See Text E 2 below]

Chapter 10. *Events after the battle was won.*

I shall return to my narrative. After this bloody battle, the king of England
and the nobles of his army bought from their men, and also from working
men and the lower folk, the most important of the lords of France so that
they could put them to ransom and gain great sums of money. The English
put to ransom all the others, even those who were lying on the ground
amongst the dead and who were still breathing and giving signs of life.
The king went off some distance from the battlefield and assembled his
victorious troops, and after making a sign that they should all be silent he
thanked them for having so bravely risked their lives in his service and
encouraged them to preserve a memory of that brilliant success as a clear
witness of the justice of his cause and of the efforts which he was making
to recover the lands of his ancestors which had been unjustly usurped. He
also urged them not to let themselves be blinded by pride and not to attribute their victory to their own strengths but to accord all the merit to the
special grace of God who had delivered into their small company such a
great multitude of the French and had brought low the latter's insolence
and pride. He added that they must thank God that almost none of their
own men had fallen on the field. He declared himself horrified that so
much blood had been spilled and that he felt great compassion for all the
deaths and especially those of his comrades in arms. He had them pay
their last respects, and ordered that they should be buried so that they

would not remain exposed to the weather and that they would not be devoured by wild animals or birds of prey. He also allowed the same respects to be paid to the French and agreed that the bishop of Thérouanne should bless the unhallowed place so that it might serve as cemetery. He allowed this favour at the beseechings of the princes of the blood of France whom he treated as his beloved cousins, trying to console them and encouraging them to resign themselves to this cruel blow of fortune which by virtue of its accustomed caprices had totally reversed their great hopes of success, and which they should attribute to their lamentable disorder.

Chapter 11. *Of the French taken prisoner and killed in the battle.*

When news of this sad outcome was known by the king and his subjects, there was general consternation. Each felt a bitter sadness in thinking that the kingdom had been so deprived of so many of its illustrious defenders and that the revenues already much diminished in order to pay the troops would be completely ruined by the ransoming of the prisoners. But what was most galling was to think that the reverse would make France feeble and the laughing stock of other countries. The king had demanded from those bringing the sad news how many dead there were. They replied that seven of his close cousins had fallen whilst behaving most honourably. They were the duke of Bar, one of his brothers, their nephew Robert de Marlay, the count of Nevers, Charles d'Albret, constable of France, the duke of Brabant who was Anthony, brother of the duke of Burgundy, a young prince who was well loved on whom one had placed great hopes for the well being of the kingdom, if he had lived, and who, abandoning the command of the troops placed under his orders in order to distinguish himself by some act of prowess, had gone off to join the leading barons who had flocked to the front in their rash and imprudent haste, and finally the duke of Alençon who stood out from all the other princes by virtue of his agreeable personality and by his immense wealth, and who until them had enjoyed a great reputation for wisdom. But carried away by a foolish passion and by an overwhelming desire to fight, he had left the main body of the army over which he had the command and had thrown himself boldly into the middle of the mêlée.

'In addition to these princes', added the messengers who brought the sad news, 'there had also fallen the master of the crossbowmen of France, the lord of Bacqueville, bearer of the oriflamme, Guichard Dauphin, several of your *baillis* and seneschals, old knights renowned by their birth and their long service, and whose wise counsels had aided the government of the kingdom. They were all to be lamented for they had been opposed to giving battle even though they would have all rather faced the hazards of the fight than to dishonour themselves by returning home.' They indicated the names of each of them (how these names deserve to be written in the book of the living!) and they noted that amongst the clergy only one, Montague, the archbishop of Sens, had dared to take part in that bloody battle and that as he was dealing blows on the enemy to right and left, like his comrades, he paid with his life for his bold enterprise, along with his nephew, the *vidame* of Laon. That was also the fate of a large number of knights, esquires and noble townsmen who had pawned the best part of their belonging to go in suitable array to put themselves under the banners of the lords and to find an opportunity to mark themselves out by some notable deed. The messengers cited as particularly regrettable the loss of so many noble strangers who had joined with the lords of France on this occasion, especially several famous knights of Hainault, amongst whom was the seneschal of that area who by his proven valour and his exploits in various places had been deemed worthy of being called the most shining example of bravery.

'Most serene prince,' they finished by saying, 'it is difficult to indicate with certainty the number of the dead. However, if one can believe the rumours more than 4,000 of the best troops of your kingdom perished in fighting with courage and there is nothing more to do than to raise to heaven fervent prayers so that they might share eternal blessing with the saints. Your beloved cousins the dukes of Orléans and Bourbon, the counts of Vendôme and Richemont and 1,400 knights and esquires have been taken prisoner and put to ransom. Others in larger number yielded to their fear and are covered with eternal infamy for fleeing without being chased.

B 2. *Geste des nobles françois* (?late 1420s, French)

Translated from text given in *Chronique de la Pucelle ou Chronique de Cousinot*, ed. A. Vallet de Viriville (Paris, 1859, reprinted Slatkine-Megarotis Reprints, Geneva, 1976), pp. 155–7.

Guillaume Cousinot was an advocate at the parlement of Paris in 1405 who subsequently became chancellor of the duke of Orléans who was captured at Agincourt. Vallet de Viriville considered him the author of the 'Geste des nobles françois descendus de la royalle lignée du noble Priam de Troye, jusqu'au noble Charles, filz du roy Charles le sixyesme, qui tant fut aimée des nobles et de tous autres',[75] but believed that another Cousinot was the author of the better known *Chronique de la Pucelle*. The early sections of the *Geste* are compiled from other chronicles, but the account from the accession of Charles VI in 1380 to the termination of the work in 1428 is essentially original. Two copies of the work

---

75 'Deeds of the noble French descended from the royal line of the noble Priam of Troy, down to the noble Charles, son of Charles VI, who was loved by the nobles and all others'.

are known. That from which Vallet de Viriville prepared his edition of the sections from 1403 to 1428 is taken from the copy believed to have been executed for John, count of Angoulême, younger brother of Charles, duke of Orléans, who was a hostage in England from 1412 to 1445. De Viriville suggests that it might have been sent to him in England. One might have hoped, therefore, given the link with the house of Orléans, for some original material on the battle, but the account is rather thin. Note, however, the later reference to those who fled from the battle. Although anti-Burgundian elsewhere in the work, the author is here critical of the count of Armagnac.

*

Chapter 140. *Battle of Agincourt.*

King Henry wished to return to Normandy after the taking of Harfleur, in the month of October 1415. So he took his way on dry land, aiming straight for Calais, and had his ships follow up the Picard coast. During this time, the king issued orders to his nobility, who pursued with a great force the king of England, and advanced close to Hesdin where the king had pitched camp for the night at Agincourt. There gathered, for the king of France, the dukes of Orléans, of Brabant, of Bourbon, of Alençon and Bar; the sire d'Albret, constable of France, the count of Nevers, the count of Eu, Jean, monseigneur of Bar, the Marshal Bouccicaut, the lord of Hangest, the lord of Torcy, the seneschal of Hainault, the lord of Crouy, the lord of Heilly, and a large number of other nobles of France.

The duke of Brittany came with a large company, arriving at Amiens to be present at the engagement. He sent on in advance his brother Arthur, count of Richemont. But the duke of Bourbon was so keen to fight with the English that he did not want to wait for the Bretons, so he drew up his battle lines. All the lords wanted to be in the vanguard, against the opinion of the constable and the experienced knights. On the day of St Crispin, 25 October 1415, they engaged in battle, and the French were defeated.

In this battle were captured the dukes of Orléans and of Bourbon, the counts of Eu and Vendôme, the Marshal Bouccicaut and other lords and barons. There were killed the duke of Brabant, the count of Nevers, the constable of France, John, monseigneur of Bar, the archbishop of Sens and other noble lords. By virtue of this extremely sad day, the noble chivalry of France was much weakened. When news came to the King and duke of Guienne at Rouen, they fell into great sorrow. The count of Armagnac was elected and hastily appointed at constable. The king and his son accompanied by the duke of Berry came to Paris, to where also came the count of Armagnac. He was given the sword of the constable, and went into Caux with a large force, fortifying the strongholds with men and victuals. These garrisons made frequent sorties right up to the gates of Harfleur.

[In chapter 142 it is noted, 'In this time (1416) the count of Armagnac, constable, was in Normandy. He had the town of Honfleur strongly fortified and made attempts to raise an army. But as he held in little regard the nobles of France, Picardy and Normandy, he did not receive them into his army. He despised them for retreating from the battle of Agincourt. He found few nobles who would obey him save for Gascons and others from his own area.']

B 3. Pierre Cochon, *Chronique normande* (?early 1430s, French)

Translated from text given in *Chronique normande de Pierre Cochon*, ed. C. de Robillard de Beaurepaire (Société de l'Histoire de Normandie, 1870), pp. 273–6.

The author of this work is not to be confused with his more famous namesake, the bishop of Beauvais who was involved in the trial of Joan of Arc. Our Pierre Cochon (d. 1456) was a priest and *notaire apostolique* of Rouen, whose continuation of the *Chronique normande* to 1430 offers useful material on the impact of this period of war on his home city. Only one copy of the work is known. He shows himself to be opposed to the Armagnac group and generally espouses the cause of the dukes of Burgundy, although in his treatment of the battle of Agincourt one can see some criticism of Duke John by virtue of his supposed conspiracy with Henry. Cochon is anti-English. As a loyal Frenchman who sees the disastrous effects of civil and international war on his homeland. But he is not always well-informed, and confuses the events of 1416 and 1417. Historians are also generally agreed that there was no deal between Henry and the duke of Burgundy before the invasion of 1415, but the account is useful in revealing contemporary perceptions that there had been. The exact date of composition is not known. Cochon mentions himself in the text under the year 1425, and further references in the manuscript suggest he was in Rouen in 1406 and 1433. His view of the impact of battle is therefore based on a degree of personal experience.

*

When John, duke of Burgundy, saw that he had too much against him and that he could not fulfil his intention, he went to Calais and found there Henry, king of England. There they made an agreement and alliance with each other, and then each went home. The king of England saw to his needs and made all preparations necessary to embark from his own land in order to conquer lands in France. He knew that he would find there a large number of friends. So he put to sea.

Chapter 28. *Henry V disembarks at La Fosse-de-Leure. Battle of Agincourt.*

Henry V of Lancaster, king of England, landed at La Fosse-de-Leure and disembarked without anyone offering resistance. Once landed, he laid siege to Harfleur on Friday 16 August 1415. There were strong attacks but also strong defence, and the siege lasted until Thursday 19 September. Then he entered in procession and installed a garrison of his soldiers to guard the town. The king then left Harfleur to go to his town of Calais. At this point a large number of the lords of France, such as the duke of Alençon, were at Rouen. They set off, along with a large number of other lords from the whole realm, on the trail of the English, making for the area of Hesdin, and pursuing them to a village called Agincourt. There the French and English gathered on Friday, the day of St Crispin, 25 October 1415. As the night had seen much rain, the ground was so soft that the men-at-arms sank into it by at least a foot. The two armies drew up against each other. The French thought that they would carry the day given their great numbers, and in their arrogance had proclaimed that only those who were noble should go into battle. So all the men of lower ranks, who were enough to have beaten the English, were pushed to the rear. In addition there was a great division between the parties of the duke of Orléans and the duke of Burgundy. The two hosts engaged in a hard fight but at the end the English defeated the French.

These men died at the battle: the two brothers of Philip [recte, John] of Valois, then duke of Burgundy (and if the duke of Burgundy had himself been there, he would have met with the same fate); the duke of Alençon, the sire d'Albret, then constable of France; the brother of Montague, then archbishop of Sens in Burgundy; along with a very large number of nobles of France. Many prisoners were taken, to wit the duke of Orléans, nephew of Charles VI, the duke of Bourbon and many other great knights, bannerets and others. This was the ugliest and most wretched event that had happended in France over the last 1,000 years.

But that is how the battle went. The king of England's pride was greatly boosted by having such good fortune and God suffered as a result those who had died in the battle were each taken to their own lands for burial. Those who were still alive were taken by the king of England to his country, to his great honour but to the great confusion of the kingdom of France, as you will hear later. As soon as the duke of Burgundy heard what had happened, he no longer had an alliance with the king of England as they had had. But when the deed was done, the matter had been so. But let us leave off this topic.

[In chapter 30, Cochon is in error in claiming that Henry landed in France at Saint-Vaast-La-Hogue in 1416; it was not until 1 August 1417 that

Henry began his second campaign at Touques. But the passage is worth including here for its vivid description of Henry's soldiers.]

Chapter 30. *Henry V lands again at Saint-Vaast-La-Hogue. Description of the English soldiers. The Burgundians at Rouen.*

The English king was in his own country with his prisoners. He never slept but continually looked to his interests and made alliances and provision, as he saw fit, of young men from various lands, some Irish, all with bare feet and no shoes, dressed in scruffy doublets made out of old bedding, a poor skullcap of iron on their heads, a bow and a quiver of arrows in their hand and a sword hanging at their side. That was all the armour they had. There was also a large quantity of scum (*menues merdailles*) from several lands. He gathered his troops on the lands and put to sea in 1416 and landed at Saint-Vaast-La-Hogue and disembarked, spending a great time in unloading their carts with their provisions on 1 August in the year abovementioned.

B 4. *Chronique anonyme du règne de Charles VI* (?early 1430s, French)

Translated from text printed in *La Chronique d'Enguerran de Monstrelet*, ed. L. Douet-D'Arcq (Société de l'Histoire de France, 6 vols, Paris, 1857–62), vol. 6 (1862), pp. 228–30.

This is an anonymous chronicle often called the 'chronique dit du cordelier' (i.e. Franciscan) as the sole manuscript came from a house of that order in Paris. It begins with the creation of the world and ends in 1431. It may have been written by a Picard. It has been suggested that it was drawn upon by Monstrelet. There are inaccuracies, however, in the list of English names. The duke of Bedford, for instance, did not go on the campaign at all.

*

In the month of August, the new King Henry, son of Henry, king of England, put to sea. With him were the dukes of Clarence and Bedford, his brothers, the duke of York, the earls of Arundel, Warwick, Kent and Huntingdon, Lord Roos, Lord Scales and his brother, and many others. He landed at Harfleur, to which he laid siege, being there for about nine weeks before it was surrendered to him by treaty by the lord of Gaucourt who was captain there and who was an adherent of the Orléans party.

At this point the princes and lords of France gathered in great strength to advance against the English. When the king of England knew that they had assembled, he departed from Harfleur, leaving there the duke of Bedford, and desiring to return with all his men to Calais via the area of

Artois. But the princes and lords of France pursued him right into Artois so that he could not escape without giving him battle, despite the fact that he had already crossed the rivers Oise, Authie and Somme. They were blocked and hemmed in close to Agincourt and Ruisseauville. The English were very upset about this, because against them was the flower of the chivalry of the kingdom of France, and they were outnumbered four to one by the French.

The French army was led and commanded at the battle by the duke of Orléans. With him were the dukes of Alençon, Bourbon and Bar, the counts of Nevers, of Richmond, Eu, Vendôme, Marlay, Roussy, Tonnoire, Vaudemont, Dammartin and Salebruce, Charles d'Albret, constable of France, John of Bar, Ferry of Lorraine, the vicomte of Narbonne and all the flower of the chivalry of France, Picardy and Hainault. But from the lands of Flanders and Burgundy there was only one lord, Louis de Ghistelle, son of the lord of Ghistelle.

On 25 October, the French and English assembled for battle around the hour of prime in a place near Agincourt and Ruisseauville. The English began to fire on the French. The English were in two groups (*basquès*) and the French main battle (*bataille*) was between them with the intention of meeting the main battle of the king of England which was in front of (*au dessus de*) his archers. The French were in newly worked land which made it very difficult for them to cross. They were heavily armed and the ground was soft, so they were exhausted and much troubled in their advance, for they were on foot. When they engaged with the main battle of the king of England, many of them were so worn out that they could scarcely move.

The English were fresh and unwearied as they had not moved from their advantageous position. They began to strike in a most violent fashion against the French and knocked to the ground many who could not get up again. Most had no one with them to help them up because they had not wanted to take with them any of their lower ranks (*varlets*), for the gentlemen had wanted to have the honour deriving from battle. But they had made a ghastly mistake. They were all dead or defeated for few escaped. The battle did not last long. Right at the point of defeat, the duke of Brabant arrived with only a few men, those of his household alone. He threw himself keenly into the battle, in which he was almost immediately killed, along with two knights, the sons of the sire of Lens in Hainault, and brothers of the then bishop of Cambrai.

In this battle were killed the duke of Brabant, the duke of Alençon, the duke of Bar, the counts of Nevers, Marlay, Roussy, Vaudemont, Dammartin, Vendôme, Eu, and Salebruce [Salm?], the constable of France, Jean of Bar, Ferry de Lorraine, Louis de Ghistelle, and all those of gentle birth who had fought at the battle of whom few escaped save for those who were taken alive. These included the dukes of Orléans and Bourbon, the counts of Vendôme and Richemont and some others, who would never return from captivity. On the side of the English no men died save the duke of York his uncle and a handful of other gentlemen.

After this battle the king of England went to Calais very swiftly because he feared that those who had fled or survived the battle might reassemble to fight him again. For this reason he departed and made to return to England, taking with him all his prisoners.

B 5. *Mémoires de Pierre de Fenin* (?1430s, French)

Translated from *Mémoires de Pierre de Fenin*, ed. E. Dupont (Société de l'Histoire de France, Paris, 1837), pp. 58–67.

Pierre Fenin came from a noble family of Artois. His career is difficult to reconstruct because it is not clear whether all of the references are to the same man. A Pierre Fenin was admitted to the royal chivalric order of the Cosse de Geneste in 1411, served as *garde du scel* (keeper of the seal) of the *prévôté* of Beauquesne in Picardy and in the Vimeu, as *prévôt* of Arras, and as *pannetier du roi* (probably of Charles VI). It is also difficult to tell from his text precisely of what political persuasion he was, although he came from an area under Burgundian influence and is thought to have gleaned information from the same sources as Monstrelet. He speaks kindly of Charles VI, sees Henry V as worthy of praise because of his desire for justice, and is slightly disparaging elsewhere of the dauphin, later Charles VII. He includes one or two remarks which suggest Burgundian leanings. It may be significant, for instance, that he omits the name of the duke of Alençon from the list of the dead. His chronicle covers the period from the murder of Louis, duke of Orléans in 1407 to 1427. Fenin may have died at Arras in 1433, but even here there are difficulties, for there is an implication in some passages in the work that the author knew of events after this last date. It has even been speculated, although without much conviction, that Pierre Fenin was in fact a continuator who died in 1506, and that the original work was by someone else whose identity is not known. It gives a reasonable account of Henry's march, and some bare details on deployment at the battle. It includes an account of the attack on the baggage by Isambard d'Azincourt, adding that the resultant loss of horses was much damaging to the English.

*

In the year 1415, King Henry of England, who knew all too well the discord which existed between the lords in France and that they were constantly struggling to destroy each other, issued his orders in England and assembled a great force of English. Then he put to sea and landed near Harfleur, to which he laid siege by land and sea. The town of Harfleur was well provided with good men-at-arms, who guarded it well. But King Henry was there for so long that the French had to surrender the town to him, because they could wait no longer for help. And so began his con-

quest of Normandy. Whilst Henry was laying siege to Harfleur, the lords
of France assembled large numbers to resist him. Charles d'Albret, who
was constable, put himself into the field with a large force, as did the
Marshal Bouccicaut, the lord of Dampierre, admiral of France, and many
other great princes, that is, the dukes of Orléans, Bar, Bourbon, Nevers
and the count of Beaumont. These lords had assembled all their armed
might to fight King Henry of England.

After King Henry of England had conquered the town of Harfleur and
some other places in Normandy, he left with all his armed strength to go
to Calais, and made his route straight through Normandy. Before the town
of Eu there was a great skirmish of French and English at which died Lancelot Perre, a valiant and much renowned man of war, and also he killed
the Englishman whom he had mortally injured. From Eu, King Henry
continued his chevauchée towards Abbeville. Many hoped that he would
cross at Blanchetaque but this he did not do, but made for the Pont-de-
Rémy and assaulted the town in order to cross there. But it was well and
securely guarded by the lord of Wancourt, who was lord of the place, and
his two sons who were knights of great courage and renown, and who
were also well provided with brave soldiers and with military equipment.
As a result, the men of King Henry could not effect a crossing and lost
many of their number.

After King Henry realised that he could not cross at Pont-de-Rémy, he
made his way towards Arraines, and, from there, towards Amiens, and
passed before the town without incurring any losses, moving on to lodge
at Boves. The armed might of King Charles constantly pursued King
Henry, so that there were only five to six leagues between the two hosts,
and as every day dawned, the French wished to fight. But they did not
find a place to suit them, and also they were waiting for the duke of Brittany who was coming to their aid with a large force. So the French
pursued King Henry each day, and Henry crossed the River Somme at
Eclusiers and went to lodge around Miraumont. The French lords were
lodged at Péronne, and their men in the countryside around Miraumont.
King Henry took a direct route to go straight to Calais, and lodged at Forceville, and at Acheux and in the neighbourhood of these villages. The
French drew ahead towards Saint-Pôl. Then the King lodged at Bonnières
on the Wednesday before All Saints in 1415, and his advance guard
lodged at Frévent. And indeed, the English were that night in seven or
eight villages. On Thursday next King Henry decamped and went on past
Frévent, and from there, he chevauchéed up to Blangy-sur-Ternoise, and
passed beyond it to lodge at Maisoncelles. At that place all his army
lodged together. That same day the lords of France came to lodge at Ruisseauville and at Agincourt and in several villages thereabout, then put
themselves in the fields, and lodged so near to the host of King Henry that
there was only about four bowshots between the two armies. They spent
the night without doing anything to each other. When Friday morning

came, the lords of France drew themselves up into battle order. They established a vanguard where they put the majority of their nobles and the flower of their men, and made an extremely strong [centre] battle and a rear-guard. In very truth the French were incomparably greater in number than the English and had there an extremely fine company of men.

King Henry also drew up his battle order, and ordered a vanguard and a large [centre] battle and put all his archers each with a stake sharpened at both ends, fixed in the ground in front of them. On this day there was a great discussion between the two sides, and King Henry had grave doubts about the engagement. But they could not come to any agreement, with result that they had to draw up for battle. The lord of Heilly, who had been a prisoner in England for a long while, came to speak to King Henry. He desired that the French should have the day accorded to them. But it went completely the other way. For when it came to engaging, the English had such a large quantity of archers who began to shoot strongly against the French. The French were heavily armed, and as a result they were much worn down even before they reached the English lines. There a great battle arose on one side and the other, and the English were much knocked back at the start. But the advance guard of the French were in great disarray and began to gather into little groups and the English fell upon them and killed them without mercy. So the battle opened up and the English entered into it. Then the French were in great disarray and began to break up into little groups. And also the centre battle and rearguard did not assemble with all men and thus all took to flight, because all of the princes had placed themselves in the vanguard and had left their men leaderless. As a result there was no control or discipline amongst their men. There was a high mortality rate amongst the French on this occasion because they had been completely defeated; there died on the field between three to four thousand, not counting those who were taken prisoner, of whom there were a great number. Whilst the battle of the French and English was going on and the English were almost on top, Isambart d'Azincourt and Robert de Bournoville accompanied by some men of low rank launched an attack on the baggage of the English making great affray. As a result the English feared that the French would come upon them to do them harm. Thus the English killed many of the prisoners they had. Isambart and Robert were later much blamed for this and also they were punished by Duke John of Burgundy.

That engagement, which was on Friday before All Saints in the year 1415, between Maisoncelles and Agincourt in the county of Saint-Pôl, was called the battle of Agincourt, and at it died a great swathe of the nobility of France; including Charles d'Albret, who had been constable of France, Marshal Bouccicaut, and the lord of Dampierre, who was admiral of France. The duke of Bar died there, as did the count of Marlay, the count of Blancmont, and also there died Duke Anthony of Brabant and the duke [*recte*, count] of Nevers, his brother, who were brothers of Duke

John of Burgundy. Many other great lords met their death there. The duke of Orléans, the duke of Bourbon, the count of Richemont, the count of Eu were all prisoners and were taken to England, and many were the other great lords taken there with those whom I cannot name. Thus, and in this manner, was this day lost for the lords of France, which was a cause of great damage for the kingdom of France. For, of all the nations of the kingdom, the flower of gentility had been there, and many evils later arose as a result. And still the dissension between Duke John of Burgundy and the lords of royal blood consumed all. On the day of the battle the duke of Brittany was at Amiens coming to the aid of the French with all his great power of men, but it was too late.

After King Henry had won this engagement against the French he went back to lodge at Maisoncelles where he had been the night before. On the morning of the next day he broke camp and went to pass amongst the dead where the battle had been, and there he waited for a long time, and took prisoners of those amongst the dead, and led them away with him.

Of the men of King Henry there died about four to five hundred. The duke of York, who was the uncle of King Henry, had been killed here. The English were much upset at having their horses taken, because there were many wounded and sick who made their way there to Calais in great pain. But none the less, they did go to Calais and there they were greeted with much joy. After King Henry had refreshed himself and his men in the town of Calais, he went to England where he was fêted most highly and great reverence was paid to him throughout the whole kingdom of England.

The duke of Orléans and the duke of Bourbon spent the greater part of their life in England from that point onwards, and with them the count of Eu and the count of Angoulême, brother of the duke of Orléans. After this saddest of days, and when all the parties had retired home, Louis of Luxembourg who was bishop of Therouanne, had several grave pits made in the place where the battle had been, then gathered up all the dead from both sides and had them buried there. Then the bishop blessed the place and had it enclosed with strong hedges all around in order to protect it from animals.

At the time of the battle, Duke John of Burgundy was in Burgundy and was much distressed by the French loss when he was told of it, and particularly by the loss of his two brothers, Duke Anthony of Brabant and the duke of Nevers. Soon afterwards he went to his lands of Flanders and Artois and took up government on behalf of his two nephews in Brabant.

B 6. *Chronique de Perceval de Cagny* (late 1430s, French)

Translated from *Chronique de Perceval de Cagny*, ed. H. Moranville (Société de l'Histoire de France, Paris, 1902), pp. 94–101.

Perceval de Cagny tells us that he entered the household of the counts (later dukes) of Alençon in 1390. He hailed from the Beauvaisis, held land in Picardy near Mondidier, and was esquire of the stable to Duke John who died at the battle. His work was composed in the second half of the 1430s and consists of two parts. The first is a set of genealogical notes on the Alençon line from the mid-thirteenth century to 1436. The second part is a chronicle from 1239 to 1438 but the principal emphasis is on the period from 1393 to 1438. It is not simply an account of the deeds of the counts and dukes of Alençon, being much broader in scope although setting them centre stage. This can be seen in the frequent mentions of the duke of Alençon in every discussion of French resistance to the English. There is also much stress on the fact that the duke of Brittany, ancient rival of the Alençon line, failed to attend the battle because he was too busy serving his own interests. A separate note is added on this, out of the chronological sequence. Somewhat intriguingly, however, de Cagny says nothing about the duke of Alençon's role and bravery in the battle, whereas English accounts give him a prominent place in a desperate final, personal attack on Henry.

   Although it was not fully written out until the 1430s it is possible that some sections existed earlier as notes. At his own admission, de Cagny wrote the chronicle not only to contribute to the glory of his masters but also so that his own descendants could see and learn about the lords he had lived with for most of his life. This emphasises the significance of service to men of de Cagny's station. In addition, he tells us that he wanted to put in writing 'a little of the misfortunes, wars and pestilences which had happened in France before his days and those of which he had personal experience'. His later sections on Joan of Arc are of particular importance to historians.

*

The siege of Harfleur.

In the year 1415 on the eve of the feast of our Lady in the middle of August, the king of England landed in Normandy in a place called *Quié de Caux* with an exceptionally large army, larger (or so say veteran knights and esquires) than any which had been led to France for the last hundred years. Its company numbered between 80 and 100,000 soldiers. . . . Once the king had garrisoned Harfleur with as many men and as much equipment as he deemed necessary, he began his march with his army hoping to reach his town of Calais.

The battle of Agincourt.

In the year 1415, in the first week of the month of October, the king of England leaving the said place of Harfleur, wished to cross the River Somme near a place called Blanchetaque. The duke of Alençon, being with the king at Rouen, knew what had to be done and by his diligence managed to reach the town of Abbeville before the king of England could effect his crossing, and cut off his route, so much so that the king of England had to go upstream in order to find another crossing. Whilst doing this, he and his men experienced a great lack of victuals because the duke of Alençon had the dukes of Bourbon and Bar, the constable d'Albret and other lords, knights and esquires, move up to Amiens, Corbie, Péronne and Saint-Quentin in the Vermandois and so give the English much trouble and anxiety as well as causing them much damage.

But nevertheless, despite the diligence of our lords, the English found one night a crossing over the river between Péronne and Saint-Quentin. The duke of Alençon had placed the latter place under the command of the *bailli* of Vermandois and other officers of the king of the area, but these officers were with him at Péronne, so that that crossing and others over the river might be broken and prevented, and he had thought it would be so. And when the duke of Alençon and our other lords saw that the English had got across they sent this information to Rouen to the king, the duke of Guienne and the duke of Berry, and to every other place where they hoped to raise men to fight against the English, and they positioned themselves between the English and the town of Calais, and so laboured that they put themselves near a place called Agincourt. At this place on 25 October the day of battle was given to the king of England and all his company, which was most wretched and a cause of great and unrecoverable damage for the king most of all, and for all the people of his kingdom, great, middling and small, because it was to the honour and profit of the king of England. And on that day quitted their mortal coil the dukes of Alençon, Brabant and Bar, and the counts of Nevers, of Marlay, of Dreux (who was the constable of France), of Vaudemont and of Braine, the lords of Preaulx, and John, brother of the duke of Bar, and many other barons, knights, esquires and other men of war, estimated to number five to six thousand. And at the battle were captured and kept as prisoners the dukes of Orléans, of Bourbon, the counts of Eu, Richemont, Vendôme and Beaufort (the marshal of France) and many other barons, knights and esquires.

The taking of Harfleur.

Everyone must know that when it came to the knowledge of the king that the king of England had landed, as was said, in the Pays de Caux and had laid siege before Harfleur, the king and his council tried with all their might to find a way of assembling men to resist and avoid the malice and intention of the king of England. They acted so that all the abovementioned lords might come to royal service in person accompanied by as many men as they could be. The lords did this willingly as they were bound to do and as events show. The duke of Brittany was ordered just like the other lords, and prepared to do so, coming to the town of Falaise. Whilst there, the king, the duke of Guienne and the duke of Berry, then at Rouen, informed him that the king of England had taken Harfleur and had started to make his way to return to Calais, and that the duke of Brittany should advance in order to place himself in the company of the other lords. Despite the haste which the king needed of the duke of Brittany, the latter remained at Falaise for eight days. After that time he came to the king at Rouen, and although he saw and realised clearly the needs of the king, he did not want to go on further until the king had had passed in his great council letters granting to the duke the town of Saint Mâlo and all its appurtenances which none of his ducal predecessors had held in their possession or lordship.

B 7. *Chronique de Ruisseauville* (?1420s–1430s, French)

Translated from Bacquet, *Azincourt*, pp. 91–6.[76]

This account, written in a Norman dialect, derives from the abbey of Ruisseauville close to Agincourt. The text has never been fully studied and its editors merely state that 'we have been assured that it comes from the chronicle of the abbey which was once situated in the village of Ruisseauville, near Agincourt'. Interestingly, Monstrelet has the abbot of Ruisseauville involved in the burial of French dead, yet this account calls him the abbot of Blangy. Bacquet considers that the chronicle was written by someone with first hand information on the battle, but it does contain some unusual and unique material as well as obvious errors (such as the notion that Henry's brothers died in the battle). It is also written with someone who felt they had an axe to grind against d'Albret, de Gaucourt and Clignet de Brabant. It is highly unlikely, for instance, that d'Albret wined and dined with the English during the siege of Harfleur. It also criticises the behaviour of the French army as it assembled. This may reveal local fears, and is echoed in another monastic chronicle emanating from Bec.[77] The most

76 The full text is printed in 'Chronique de Ruisseauville', *Archives historiques et littéraires du nord de la France et du midi de la Belgique*, series 1, 4 (Valenciennes, 1834), pp. 136–44.
77 *Chronique du Bec et Chronique de François Carré*, ed. Abbé Porée (Société de l'Histoire de France, Paris, 1883), pp. 81–2. 'Around the same time the monastery of Bec was much damaged as was the whole region by the French army which had gathered there against the king of England. They stayed there continually devastating and destroying the whole region

striking impression here is that the writer had heard many rumours and stories associated with the battle. A good example of this relates to the attack by local men on the English royal baggage. It is not the only account to mention this, and several note the taking of a crown, but this is the only one to add in that King Arthur's sword was also taken. Another good example, and perhaps the sort of rumour which consternated monks, was the English propensity to raping and pillaging. There is therefore the obvious hypocrisy in Henry's after dinner speech! This was the wily old fox. Even his supposed standard of the tail of a fox on a lance proved it. But both this and the reference to the men at the back of the English host with pilgrim hats read like information picked up from someone who saw something but was not too sure what!

The date of the text is not known. It certainly was compiled after the death of Henry V for it mentions the return of de Gaucourt from captivity. But until it is possible to find out more about this intriguing account, its value must be doubted.

*

In the year 1415 after Easter the king of England, called Henry, son of King Henry of Lancaster, made a great and noble assembly both of great princes and lords and of fine men-at-arms and archers to come to France. He took with him two of his brothers and the Bastard of Portugal accompanied by the Portuguese and several princes of England and of several other countries, and also a large part of the navy from Holland and Zeeland, and arrived at the port of Harfleur in Normandy and laid siege to the place by land and sea. Charles d'Albret, constable of France, with a large quantity of princes of France and men-at-arms in his company approached close to the host of the English but Charles d'Albret, constable of France, went very frequently to eat and drink with the king in the English host, which did not please many lords of France. The English king was so long before the town of Harfleur that it surrendered saving the lives of those therein. It was commonly said that Clignet de Brabant and the sire de Gaucourt with the constable of France had sold it. The king of England entered Harfleur on 21 September and emptied it of all women, children and priests of the town, and had each of them given 10 *sous parisis*, and had it cried by sound of the trumpet that at the king's command no one should do anything to women or to the others under pain of death. But as soon as the women were some way from the town the French pillaged and violated them to a great degree. The king of England

from the month of August right through to the battle. So it was necessary to have munitions in the fortress of the monastery at the expense of the church, against the English invasion.' The editor notes an order issued by the dauphin from Vernon-sur-Seine on 22 September 1415 (citing folio 89v of the *Mémoires* of Dom Jouvlin, Bibliothèque Nationale, MS Latin, 13,905), that none of his officers should molest the monks or take foodstuffs from their estates. This would indeed seem to be at the very point when the army was being assembled.

then took a large number of men to England and kept as prisoner de Gaucourt and all the others, but they were soon delivered from captivity and returned to France.

It happened that after the feast of Saint Rémy in the same year the king of England left Harfleur and left the town well provided with good men-at-arms and archers and took his way to move towards Abbeville in order to cross there the River Somme. He intended to go from there with his men to Calais because otherwise he could not return to England for the navy of Holland and Zeeland had returned to their own country and also the navy of England had completely or in part been scuttled at sea by exceptionally heavy rain which had arisen in tempest. Thus they wished to return by the frontier but their passage had been blocked and they had to return through the vicinities of Amiens and Beauvais, always following the river Somme. But the French followed them and kept close to them all the time, and did nothing save robbing and pillaging towns, monasteries and abbeys and violating women. The English took their path so that they came towards Péronne to a town called Doing and thereabouts, and they crossed the river there quite peacefully for those who wanted to fight there at the passage escaped on foot. But the constable stayed in the towns and gave an order on behalf of the king forbidding anyone to fight. Then the count of Nevers came with a very fine company in order to fight them but the English made off. But it is true that they had a great lack of food and drink and were much exhausted with riding and going on foot because it was filthy, wet and windy weather. The English moved on until they came in Ternois to a village called Blangy and at which the constable of France and several princes of France advanced on them and came to a village named Agincourt, blocking their path.

Here are the names of the princes who were present on the day of the battle. First, Charles d'Albret, constable of France, the duke of Bourbon, the duke of Alençon, the duke of Bar and John his brother, the duke of Orléans, the count of Richemont brother of the duke of Brittany, the count of Nevers brother of the duke of Burgundy and to the duke of Brabant, the count of Eu, Ferry de Lorraine, count of Vaudemont, brother of the duke of Lorraine, the count of Vendôme, brother of the count of La Marche, the count of Marlay, the counts of Roussy and Braine, the count of Savigny, the count of Blammont and many other princes and great and noble knights and gentlemen who were all ready and intent upon fighting the English on Thursday 24 October after dinner but the courtiers did not want to suffer and said it was too late and that it would be better to wait until the next day, and thus was their cause ruined. It happened that during the night of the Thursday the heralds of England came to the French host and sought respite so that the English might on the next day (which was Friday and the feast of Saints Crispin and Crispinian, 25 October) have parley with the lords of France. This was allowed to them and all night it never stopped raining.

On the next day the French and English parleyed and the latter offered to surrender Harfleur and all the fortresses below Calais and 100,000 crowns so that they could go in safety to Calais. But the constable did not wish to agree to this and so the English retired to their host and straight-way put themselves into battle order. The English were lodged on the unploughed land and on firm ground, and the French were in the grain fields between a wood and a hedge of stakes (*haie de pieux*). The French vanguard were in much discomfort and their feet often sank deep into the ground. It was Friday at 10 o'clock. The English began to bray and to cry out and to shout three times whilst coming up against our men, the French. They came very quickly, the archers in front running without armour and with their breeches hanging down, always firing on the French, and our men of France advanced in fine fashion and without rushing. But they foundered on the grain fields where much damage occurred. Then Anthony of Burgundy, duke of Brabant, brother to the duke of Burgundy, came whilst they were fighting with very few men, but it had been ordered that Clignet de Brabant and the lord of Gaucourt and several others come with a very large quantity of good men-at-arms in front of the archers and their fire so that they might break their fire, but without any doubt, only few came and when they had made their course against the archers they turned back, because of the arrowfire which their horses could no longer endure, right amongst the vanguard and so the vanguard was all scattered in various places, and the English entered and passed through the vanguard, the main battle and the rearguard. The battle only lasted half-an-hour until all were completely discomforted, killed or captured, excepting a great number of knights and gentlemen and lower ranks (*gros varlets*) and pages who fled, because the French archers were not used and never fired, and also all the lords and gentlemen did not wish to have any of their lower rank soldiers (*gros varlets*). The king of England was mounted with a crown of gold on his helm, and had carried as a kind of standard the tail of a fox on a lance.

There was captured the count of Nevers and several others, but Clignet de Brabant gathered together a large number of men-at-arms to launch another assault on the English. When the English king saw that they were being launched, he had it proclaimed by sound of the trumpet that anyone who had prisoners should kill them. Then one could hear great and amazing cries both from the English and the French because of the good prisoners they had. In this discomfiture was killed the duke of Brabant who had come with few men and was not well armed and all were either killed or taken, except for those who fled. But when they were still fighting the men of Hesdin came with great strength to within the lodging of the king of England and pillaged all they found and took off the sword of King Arthur which was worth so much money that no one knew what to do with it, and two crowns of gold and of precious stones, one of which the English king would wear when he appeared himself before the people of France and the other crown to have himself crowned at Reims when he was consecrated and crowned. It is said that the men of Hesdin and the countryside thereabouts were strong enough to defeat all the English after the battle. It was the greatest pity that one had ever seen; given that the noble knights and gentlemen who were there, compared with the English, outnumbered the English ten to one. It is said that the *gros varlets* might have fought well against the English and all their power.

It was true that when the English realised that they were fighting they had behind them two men like monks who wore big hats with large shells on them, and who read their books and kept making the sign of the cross over the English for as long as the battle lasted. The battle was on the 25 October in the year 1415 in a place which is called Agincourt in Ternois, and there were killed many princes and great lords as much of France, Normandy, Picardy, Vermandois, Artois, Boulogne, Flanders, Brabant, Hainault, Cambrésis and many other lands. Here are the names of the princes and great lords. First those who were killed and died. Charles d'Albret constable of France. Some say that some lords of Picardy killed him at the beginning of the battle because they considered that he and others had committed treason, and also there died Anthony of Burgundy, duke of Brabant, and Philip of Burgundy, count of Nevers, brothers, and Ferry de Lorraine, count of Vaudemont and the count of Savines, the count of Roussy, the count of Braine and the son of the count of Blammont and many other great lords entitled to carry banners, and gentlemen and all the flower of lords of the county of Hainault such as the seneschal of Hainault and the lord of Hamede and the lord of Kievraing, seven bannerets with many others who were dead or captured.

When after dinner the king of England asked several lords of France who were prisoners how the day seemed to them, they replied that he had the victory and that the day was his. The English king then replied that he had done nothing, nor had the English; it was all the work of God and of our Lady and St George and due to your sins, for they say that you went to battle in pride and bombastic fashion, violating maidens, married women and others, and also robbing the countryside and all the churches; acting like that God will never aid you. Look at my men and all who came from England with me never mounted on women, or robbed men, or the church.

And soon afterwards they came before the king of France [sic] and begged and asked the king that they might to their duty, that is that they might go amongst the dead to see which lords were dead and which were not, and the king said that because of the hour they could not go then but on the next day they could. It happened that the king of England had 500 men well armed and sent them amongst the dead, to take off their coats of arms and a great quantity of armour. They had small axes in their hands and other weapons and they cut both the dead and the living in the face so that they might not be recognised, even the English who were dead as well as the others. There died the brothers of the king of England and two or three great princes of England and a good 600 English. It was found by the tally of the heralds between 1,600 and 1,800 coats of arms without counting the other gentlemen who did not have a coat, and in the defeat were killed 6,000 men in addition to the prisoners and those who had fled, being not even noble enough to engage with the English compared with those who had been defeated, for without doubt it seemed to be that the lords and gentlemen who came to fight the English came with great pride.

And the English, insofar as one can estimate their number, were about 8,000–9,000 including (*parmi*) the archers. It happened that on the next day which was Saturday 26 October the king of England with his whole company left the place and made their way to go to Calais with all the booty that they had taken and also all their prisoners, who were by estimation 2,200. There they stayed for five or six days and then went to England with the prisoners, who were as follows, first, the duke of Orléans, the duke of Bourbon, the count of Richemont brother of the duke of Brittany, the count of Eu, the count of Marlay, the count of Vendôme and several other great lords. The lord of Hainault, the lord of Lingue and his vassals and several others of many lands but during the time they were at Calais many lords put themselves to ransom and several were bought and also the men of Calais and those round about bought several from the English who would soon return to their country with God's grace. Since the battle, several princes and great lords had been found dead and disfigured whom they took back to their country. Then Louis de Luxembourg, bishop of Thérouanne, blessed the ground and the place where the battles [sic] had been, accompanied by the abbot of Blangy and made five graves, and in each grave were buried 1,200 men or more at his costs and expenses, and on each grave was placed a great cross of wood. It was forbidden that anyone should bring more dead on account of the fears and lamentations of the people, and so no one knows the exact number of dead, save the bishop of Thérouanne who had them buried and the man who actually buried them, but they took an oath and forbade that they should not reveal it save to those burying them. This is without those who were killed or felled by those of the Ternois and Boulognais when they found them between hedges and bushes, and after discovery, killed them and stripped them of horses, coats of mail and money, the *gros varlets*, pages and servants as well as others unless they were well escorted by men-at-arms.

B 8. Jean Juvenal des Ursins, *Histoire de Charles VI, roy de France* (1430–1440s, French)

Translated from *Nouvelle collection des mémoires pour servir à l'histoire de France*, ed. Michaud & Poujoulet, series 1, vol. 2 (Paris, 1836), pp. 518–20.

The father of Jean Juvenal des Ursins (d. 1431) was an advocate in the Paris parlement in 1400 and later chancellor to the Dauphin Louis (d. 1415), and Jean Juvenal himself (1388–1473) was an advocate in Paris at the time of the battle of Agincourt.[78] Father and son fled south when the Burgundians entered Paris in May 1418, and entered the service at Poitiers of the Dauphin Charles, later Charles VII. Jean senior became president of the parlement of Poitiers. His son was an advocate in that parlement, and was subsequently elevated to the bishopric of Beauvais in 1432, of Laon in 1444, and finally to the archbishopric of Reims in 1449. He thus had first-hand experience of the period of Anglo-French wars, and was totally committed to Charles VII's cause.[79] He was a prolific researcher and political writer, with a great interest in documentary sources. The exact date of compilation is not clear.[80] Although there seems to be some dependence on *Chronique du Religieux de Saint-Denis* at least to 1411 (he might have consulted the manuscript in the abbey after the Charles VII recovered Paris and Saint-Denis in 1436 perhaps), there are differences, and des Ursins gives effectively two versions of events, reflecting perhaps his research into the matter, for each is slightly different, including, for instance, varying estimates of numbers of troops. It is also likely that he drew upon the memories of his father. In many ways the first account he provides is an 'improved' version of the *Religieux*, giving more detail especially on discussions at the French war council. For the second version, he adds in information he has heard. He tells us at one point that some information came from a *valet de chambre* of Charles VI who had been captured at the battle. Des Ursins has also been accused of inventing material too, such as the idea of the archers being intended to ambush the French. In a subsequent additional section on Henry's battle speech, he also includes the notion of Henry ennobling all those involved in the battle.[81]

The *Histoire* was first published by T. Godefroy in 1614, with a second edition issued in 1653 with additional documentary material. It is a problematic chronicle to assess, not least because we do not know when it was compiled. There are obvious similarities with Monstrelet, but which drew on which? Most certainly, too, des Ursins adopts completely the opposite stance, being rabidly anti-Burgundian, not least because he is well aware that the defeat at Agincourt opened the way to Burgundian domination. There are also similarities with

---

[78] For a full biography and commentary on his works, see *Écrits politiques de Jean Juvénal des Ursins*, vol. 3, ed. P. Lewis (Société de l'Histoire de France, Paris, 1992).
[79] See p. 334.
[80] Bacquet, *Azincourt*, pp. 15–16 claims that it was written 15 years after the battle.
[81] See below, pp. 435, 460.

sections of the *Chronique de Ruisseauville*, but again the exact link is not clear. Moreover, it is not entirely certain that it is actually the work of Jean Juvenal des Ursins at all.[82] There is a need for much more critical work to be done on manuscripts of these texts.

*

After the king of England had taken Harfleur and was installed within he decided to return to England and to make his way towards Calais. He left the earl of Dorset in the place accompanied by a large number of men but he did not leave any baggage for he ordered that it should be put in the ships and sent to England, and that is what happened. The said king of England departed from Harfleur accompanied by 4,000 men at arms and also 16,000–18,000 archers, on foot, and other combatants, and he took his way towards Gournay and Amiens, committing countless evil deeds, burning, killing people, capturing and abducting children. When the French learned of his departure they began to assemble men of war as well as others. They even gathered together a large quantity of the communes, both from Paris and elsewhere, armed with axes, hammers of lead, who were very keen to get involved. But the soldiers (*gers de guerre*) despised and looked down on them as they had done at the battles of Courtrai, at the taking of King John at Poitiers and in Turkey, whereby, as was said, the French and the Christians had met with disaster. Marshal Bouccicaut, Clignet de Brabant and a bastard of Bourbon were ordered to ride out against them. This they did diligently and inflicted great damage on the English and killed many of them, and they did not dare to escape. Passing through woods and forests the French foot men also killed many and those whom they captured were not put to ransom or finance. From Calais about 300 English soldiers were despatched. Coming in advance of their men they were met by the valiant men of Picardy. And on this occasion several were taken or killed and the others who survived were forced to retreat to Calais.

When the English saw they were being so pressed they held themselves night and day in closed formation in the field and made several major offers that they might be allowed to pass in peace. They even offered, or so it is said, to quit Harfleur and return it to the possession of the French king, and to restore the prisoners without demanding ransom, or to come to a final peace and to deliver hostages to guarantee all that they now promised. The lords and captains were assembled to decide what to do. They had already diligently sent to seek the duke of Orléans, the duke of Brabant, the count of Nevers and others. There were diverse opinions and thoughts. Some said that they should let them pass without offering battle because to do so was certainly a dangerous thing to do. But many said that the company of [French] lords was large and powerful and the men well

---

[82] Lewis, 'Some provisional remarks on the chronicles of Saint-Denis', pp. 159–62.

armed and accoutred, and gentlemen who would not deign to make fault.
And that the English were very foolish, their armour in bad condition and
the *jacques* of the archers old and tattered. Moreover, seeing that they
were away from their own country and in danger, they would sooner sell
themselves than be defeated, or at least they would not do their duty. But
even supposing that God gave the victory to the French this might not be
without great damage. For the matter was very doubtful and often the
events of a battle were risky and perilous. For once the English archers
had engaged the French men-at-arms who were very heavily armed, and
once the latter had got out of breath, disaster might fall upon them. All
they had to do was besiege Harfleur and they would get it back easily.
And that if they decided to fight they should employ the communes and
that they should prove useful. It was said that the Constable d'Albret,
Marshal Bouccicaut and several other knights and esquires who had much
experience in arms, were of this opinion. The dukes of Bourbon, Alençon
and others were of the opposite opinion saying that in the light of offers
made by the English they had already in effect been defeated and that they
would not stay. And that they had enough strength without the communes
and that there was no need to summon them. They added that those who
were of the opposing opinion were scared. The others replied that experience had demonstrated that they were by no means afraid. Finally it was
decided that they would fight. It was ordered that there would be cavalry
to charge the English archers in order to disrupt their arrow fire (*pour leur
rompire leur traict*). This cavalry would comprise Gaulvet, sire de la
Ferté-Hubert in Soulogne, Clignet de Brabant and Louys du Boisbourdon,
all renowned for their valiance and who had long experience in arms.
Nobles arrived from all regions.

When the king of England saw that it would be necessary to fight and
that it seemed to him that they should all be reminded of their duty, he
spoke in fine fashion to his princes, knights, esquires and archers and
inspired them to defend themselves well and gave them great courage/
boosted their courage tremendously. He decided to wait for the French if
they were wished to fight him. The ground was much ridden over from
one side and the other. And they came to a field where the ground was
very soft for it had been raining for a long time and they sank into the
ground. The French were heavily armed and sank into the ground right to
the thick of their legs, which caused them much travail for they could
scarcely move their legs and pull them out of the ground. They began to
march until arrowfire occurred from both sides. Then the lords on horseback, bravely and most valiantly wanted to attack the archers who began
to aim against the cavalry and their horses with great fervour. When the
horses felt themselves pierced by arrows, they could no longer be controlled by their riders in the advance. The horses turned and it seems that
those who were mounted on them fled, or so is the opinion and belief of
some, and they were blamed much for this. The French were scarcely

harmed by the arrow fire of the English because they were well armed. So the French in the approach did not harm the English. But when they engaged, the French were out of breath because of the difficult going. There were great and valiant deeds of arms, they say that the duke of Alençon did wonders with his body. Finally the lightly armed English archers struck and knocked down the French completely and it seems that they were like anvils on what they struck. There were some who retreated or fled. The noble French fell one on top of the other, many were suffocated and others killed or taken.

After the defeat there came a rumour that the duke of Brittany was coming with a large company. As a result, the French rallied, which was a bad thing, for most of the English killed their prisoners. There died the dukes of Alençon, Bar, and his brother the duke of Brabant, the counts of Nevers and Marlay, the sire d'Albret, constable of France, the archbishop of Sens, and knights and esquires to the number of 4,000. There were a good 14,000 prisoners, amongst whom were the dukes of Orléans and Bourbon, the counts of Vendôme and of Richemont, and the marshal Bouccicaut. Of all those who conducted themselves well and valiantly and fought strongly, both the English and French gave the palm to the duke of Alençon, and it was clear on both sides, that he had conducted himself so valiantly that one could not have performed better. On the English side there were also deaths, but there was no real comparison. Amongst others, the duke of York died. Several French prisoners returned some on their oath, the others pledged by those to be taken to England. There was a gentleman who was *bailli* of Boulogne who did great deeds for some of the English recognised him as a worthy man, who at his *caution* delivered great resistance.

After the battle, the servants of those who died went to view the bodies to try to find their masters. Some were recognisable, but relatively few. There were several churches and cemeteries in the area where some of the dead were interred and others were buried in the fields. It was a great source of pity to see men mourning the French defeat and pointing out those who had retreated and fled from the battle. In many places of this kingdom there were ladies and young ladies who had been widowed, and poor orphans. Several were shocked by the fact that the duke of Burgundy, who had been quite close to the area where the battle was fought, had not been present or had sent assistance. It was commonly reported that he was not bothered in the slightest. Many different rumours circulated and everyone said what he thought without really knowing much about it. In Paris there were even some who seemed pleased and expressed sighs of joy, saying that the Armagnacs had been defeated and the duke of Burgundy would this time increase his position. Some who said this were brought to punishment. Men of worth said that it was divine punishment and that God wanted to bring down the pride of many.

On this matter some others have written in the manner which follows.

After the king of England had departed from Harfleur he took his route towards Fécamp, and went straight to Arques, finding nothing to prevent him. From there he went to the river Somme and found he was blocked by the bridges in several places having been broken. Finally he crossed without any disturbance or opposition, and went straight towards Saint-Pôl in Artois. Our men and all the lords of France were in the field. They had left at Rouen the king, the dauphin (monsieur de Guienne), the duke of Berry, the king of Sicily [the duke of Anjou], and a few men with them. An order had been made at Rouen to give battle to the English in the manner which follows. First, in the vanguard was ordered the duke of Bourbon, the Marshal Bouccicaut and Guichard Dauphin. In the main battle, the duke of Orléans was leader, with the duke of Alençon, the constable and the duke of Brittany. Several times the latter excused himself saying 'that he would not make one step if his cousin the duke of Burgundy was not there.' The other lords did not want this but they had it countermanded by the king, and had it forbidden that he should come, as far as they were able. The duke of Brittany said that there was great need for the duke of Burgundy to be there. Because when all the subjects of the king and his allies and well-wishers were there, there would be enough to do to defeat the enemy, who were very strong. It was true that the king of England landed in France with 4,000 men at arms, 4,000 *gros valets* [infantry?] armed with hauberks, great jacques and axes, and 30,000 archers with axes, swords and daggers. In the rearguard of the French were the duke of Bar, the count of Nevers, the count of Charolais, and Ferry, brother of the duke of Lorraine. And on the wings the count of Richemont, and Tanneguy (de Chastel), *prévôt* of Paris. And the cavalry, intended to break the battle order (*bataille*) of the English were the admiral and the seneschal of Hainault. And nothing came of all this order, for the duke of Burgundy remained at Amiens and the other lords went further towards Saint-Pôl and beyond.

On Sunday 25 October they informed the English that they would give them battle on the Saturday next. The king of England was very joyful at this news and gave the herald who brought the news 200 *écus* and a robe. Our men and the English were very close to each other. On the Thursday next, 24 October, our men discussed fighting on the morrow at the request of the English, who had had a shortage of victuals for three days and requested that they should be given battle, or victuals, or be allowed to pass. The French made only two battles out of all their men. All the lords wanted to be in the first battle, so that each would have as much honour as another, as they could not agree to do anything else. There was in number in this first battle 5,000 knights and esquires, who never wielded a blow. In the second there were 3,000, not counting the *gros valets*, the archers and crossbowmen. When the English knew this, they chose a fine position between two areas of woodland. In front of them but a little way off there was another wood where they put a large ambush of archers, and in one of the woodland areas which was on their flank they put a large ambush of their mounted men-at-arms.

The next day dawned, the 25 October 1415, feast of the blessed bodies of the saints Crispin and Crispinian, honoured at Soissons. Our men advanced towards the English, and in their path found the worked ground very soft because of the rain which had fallen that week, whereby they could not easily move forward. And when they wanted to find 400 horsemen whom they had ordered the day before to break the battle line of the English, they could find only 40. But when they came to attack, the archers and crossbowmen of our men never fired arrow or bolt. It was after eight o'clock in the morning. Our men had the sun in their eyes, so in order to better withstand and to reply to the English fire, they lowered their heads and inclined them towards the ground. When the English saw them in this position, they advanced on them so that our men knew nothing until they hit them with their axes. And the archers who were behind in the ambush party assaulted them with arrow fire from behind. Furthermore, the mounted men whom the English had put in the wood (as noted earlier) sallied out en masse and came from the rear onto the second battle of our men, who were close to the first battle – only two lance lengths away. The English horsemen made so great and amazing a cry that they scared all of our men, so much so that our second battle took to flight. And all those in the first battle, lords and others, were defeated, and were all taken and killed. The king of England had the victory that day. That event was the most shameful which had ever happened to the kingdom of France.

From there the king of England went to Calais taking with him all his prisoners, amongst whom were the duke of Orléans, the duke of Bourbon, the count of Eu, the count of Vendôme, the count of Richemont, and the marshal Bouccicaut. He entertained them to dinner on the Sunday following, and gave to each of them a damask robe. He said to them 'that they should not be amazed that he had been victorious against them. He attributed no glory to himself for this for it was the work of God. He was their adversary because of their sins. It was a great wonder that nothing worse had happened to them because it was evil and sin to which they had abandoned themselves. They had not kept faith or loyalty with any living soul in their marriages or in other matters. They had committed sacrilege in robbing and violating churches. They had taken by force all kinds of people, nuns and others. They had robbed the whole population and had destroyed them without cause. And for that reason they could not do well.'

These matters were reported by someone called Tromagon, the King's yeoman of the chamber, who had been taken prisoner and had come to seek his ransom, which amounted to 200 francs and the duke of Orléans had stood pledge for him, as is said. The *prévôt* of Paris was not at the battle as he had arrived too late. The constable, the duke of Bar and the count of Nevers died there, as did the archbishop of Sens, which was not much grieved over as it was not his function. Of the count [sic] of Alençon no one had any news, but he was later found dead. The count of Charolais had remained at Aire on the advice of the seigneur de Heilly, who had died in the place; they did not want him to be taken prisoner because he had previously reneged on his captivity in England. It is also said that when the duke of Brabant, brother of the duke of Burgundy, heard of the preparations that the king was making, he sent to him his worthy officer and *bailli* who, on behalf of the duke of Brabant, offered to the King, with the royal council present, 'to come to serve him with 1,400 knights and esquires and 600 archers, without counting his friends and allies'. To which reply was made that they had previously written to him asking him to send a certain number of troops, and the *bailli* replied that his lord had had no news of this. Then it was said to him that if the constable ordered it he should come. And the *bailli* replied that he doubted that he would come unless the king ordered it. The reply to this was that he would be given the order in good time. The *bailli* returned straightway. So it happened that the duke of Brabant was informed about the *journeé* late in the day, and as a result he had few men. But he came with a dozen or so, and went to the battle. He threw himself into the fray and died there with his brother, the count of Nevers.

As soon as the king of England had ascertained that the battle would be on the Saturday, he ordered all his captains and his men in companies (*par parties*). And he showed them, so it is said, that from time immemorial his predecessors had maintained their right to the kingdom of France, and that in good and just title it had fallen to him to do his utmost to conquer it. He had not come as mortal enemy, for he had not consented to burning, ravaging, violating nor raping girls and women, as they had done at Soissons. But he wished to conquer gently all that belonged to him, not to cause any destruction at all. For this reason he said to them that he had true hope in God of winning the battle because his enemies were all full of sin and did not fear their maker at all. And he commanded them that if any of them had quarrels against another that they should put themselves in peace and harmony and that all should confess themselves and be pardoned by the priests who were in his company, or otherwise good would not come to them. He exhorted them to be good men in the battle and to do their duty. And so that each of them would be a good man he granted that all the prisoners which any of them might take should be freely theirs, and that each of them should have all the profit from their prisoners without any reservation unless such prisoners were dukes and counts. Together with this he granted them that all of his company who were not noble he would ennoble, giving them letters, and that he willed that from thenceforward they would enjoy the same privileges as the nobles of England. And so that they might be recognised he gave them licence to carry a collar, made up of the letters of his order. Before the time that they came into battle order (*entrerent en bataille*) he had them kneel for a long while with their hands raised to heaven, and one of the bishops in his company gave them blessing.

It is commonly reported and is true that during the battle, at the time when the English were fighting with our men, some who had taken the initiative themselves went to pillage the baggage train of the king of England, and took some of it off to Hesdin, amongst which they found many jewels and other things of great value.

B 9. Enguerran Monstrelet, Jean Waurin and Jean Le Fèvre (1444–1460s)

There can be no doubting the importance of the accounts of all three writers. Monstrelet's chronicle was subsequently much used in both England and France, providing much material for sixteenth-century historians in particular, and it continues to be much cited. Waurin and Le Fèvre were both present at the battle, and although their chronicles were less used by early historians, they have been much exploited by recent writers on the battle and seen as particularly valuable because both writers were present at the battle, Waurin with the French army and Le Fèvre with the English. Waurin tells us that he was 15 years old at the time, and that Le Fèvre was aged 19. The latter seems to have been there in the service of the heralds. The exact function of Waurin is not known; it is not clear whether he was an actual combatant or not. Even if neither actually fought there, their presence on the campaign and at the battle ought to make their accounts of major significance to us.

However, the issue is not without its problems. It is generally agreed that neither Waurin nor Le Fèvre began to compile their chronicles until mid-century. Also there is clear evidence that their accounts were interlinked and interdependent. Indeed, both admit as much. A more problematic issue, however, is the relationship of their writings to the work of Enguerran Monstrelet. All three are part of the flowering of chronicle writing at the court of Philip the Good, duke of Burgundy.[83] All three pursue an obviously pro-Burgundian line, as is made apparent by their explanation of Philip's absence from the battle, which might have threatened to be an embarrassment in later years. All three recount the story of how he, as count of Charolais, was desperate to join the French army but was prevented from doing so by the machinations of his father, Duke John the Fearless (d. 1419). There are many other occasions where their devotion to the Burgundian cause is made manifest.

Monstrelet presented his chronicle to Philip the Good, duke of Burgundy, in 1447. There seems little doubt that both Waurin and Le Fèvre drew extensively

---

[83] See G. Small, *George Chastelain and the Shaping of Valois Burgundy. Political and Historical Culture at Court in the Fifteenth Century* (Woodbridge, 1997).

on Monstrelet.[84] The fact that they often say the same thing has been taken as proof of the veracity of their accounts of the battle. But if what we have before us is a case of copying, then there are difficulties in using them to confirm each other and we do need to look at all three chronicles together. Surprisingly, this has never been attempted before. Of course, there are variations between Monstrelet on the one hand and Waurin and Le Fèvre, taken together, on the other. Often the variations are common to both Waurin and Le Fèvre but sometimes we can see differences between their accounts. In the translation below, I have decided to use Monstrelet as the main text as it is the earliest, at least in terms of completion. I have then indicated where Le Fèvre and Waurin vary from Monstrelet by using bold type for what is essentially their shared account. Le Fèvre and Waurin are undoubtedly very close in content and wording. Only rarely does Waurin contain differences. I have indicated these by use of bold italics. This shows at a glance not only how close the dependence is on Monstrelet, and how similar Le Fèvre and Waurin are, but it also reveals passages unique to each writer. This is just about satisfactory for current purposes but there is a definite need for a full critical study of the three chronicles.[85]

It is not difficult to give reasons for the variations. Monstrelet provides more on the French court and army. It is perhaps surprising that Waurin adds little to his account of the latter given that he was present with the French army at this stage. That again makes me feel that Waurin is perhaps a less useful commentator than has sometimes been thought. Le Fèvre and Waurin are better informed about the march of the English from Harfleur to Agincourt, and about the English army on the eve of battle. As Le Fèvre was accompanying the English at least from the departure from Harfleur, I consider it likely that he was the source of information for Waurin. Indeed Waurin admits this when he comes to the section dealing with Henry's plans to cross at Blanchetaque.

It is helpful to know something about each writer and his work. Monstrelet was of Picard noble stock. He may have originated from the village of

---

84 Waurin mentions Monstrelet only once in his work, however, and it is not clear whether the latter was known personally to either Waurin or Le Fèvre. We are on surer ground that the last two met on several occasions. *Recueil des Croniques et Anchiennes istories de la Grant Bretagne a present nomme Engleterre par Jehan de Waurin*, ed. W.L. Hardy and E.L.C.P. Hardy, 5 vols (Rolls Series, London, 1864–91), vol. 1, pp. xiii–xiv.

85 Such a study would also need to bring in other works such as the *Chronique anonyme* (Text B 4), the *Chronique des ducs de Brabant par Edouard Dynter* (Text B 10), and the 'manuscrit de Tramecourt' which is essentially a reduced version of Monstrelet. (This in itself is significant in terms of the circulation of the latter's chronicle.) The manuscrit de Tramecourt is too derivative to merit inclusion here, and was not complied until the late 1450s, but is interesting for a note of authorship near the end of the account of Agincourt. 'Amongst the dead was someone called Hector de Magnicourt, lord of Werchin-en-Ternois, father of John, lord of Werchin, and he had been newly dubbed a knight at the battle, and 500 others. This Jean de Werchin, his son, later began to build in a new place the family seat of the Werchin in the year 1452 when he was 37, and it was completed, in its present state, in 1457. He wrote these present histories with his own hand and married Jeanne de Soutrecourt, by whom he had several children.' The section on the battle is printed in A. de Loisne, 'La Bataille d'Azincourt

Monstrelet which is a few miles from Doullens in the county of Ponthieu, and was probably born between 1390 and 1395. His work shows he had some familiarity with the language of Cicero and the works of Sallust and Vegetius, implying a good education. He may have served as captain of Frévent in the mid-1420s for the count of Saint-Pôl, who was the son of Duke Anthony of Brabant who of course met his end at Agincourt. By 1430 Monstrelet was *bailli* of Compiègne for John of Luxembourg, and in that capacity witnessed the capture of Joan of Arc. From 1436 he held various offices in Cambrai, becoming *prévôt* in 1444, and dying in the town in 1453. He tells us that he was resident in Cambrai at the time of the writing of his chronicle. He presented his work to Philip the Good in 1447, receiving 50 *écus* for his pains. The chronicle covers the years from 1400 to 1444 and was conceived as a deliberate continuation of the *Chroniques* of Jean Froissart, whose work ended in 1400 and whose memory is invoked in the Prologue of the work. As the opening of the work indicates, Monstrelet's principal focus was 'events and happenings of the kingdoms of France and England, and other matters between the two of them'. Like Froissart he intended to treat of 'great feats of arms and other matters worthy of record . . . and also the discords, wars and contests moved for a long time between the princes and great lords of the kingdom of France, neighbouring counties and other more distant areas'.[86] This was, as Boucquey has put it, essentially a 'histoire-bataille' – 'a battle history' – but one in which the deeds of the great and good would receive prominence. Monstrelet distinguished between two kinds of sources, what he himself had seen and heard, and what others had told him.[87] He tells us that he drew on the information provided to him 'by nobles and others, and also by kings of arms, heralds and pursuivants worthy of belief who were present at the events'.[88] Indeed, Boucquey suggests that his information was largely oral rather than written. It seems unlikely, for instance, that he used the chronicle of the Religieux of Saint-Denis, but there are some similarities between his work and the *Chronique anonyme dit du Cordelier*. His chronicle was itself continued by an anonymous continuator from 1444 to 1467. Kingsford suggests that it may have been used by the author of the Pseudo Elmham.[89] There can be no doubt that it was drawn on by the author of the *First English Life of Henry V* and other English writers of the sixteenth century.

Based on Waurin's comment that Le Fèvre was aged 19 at the time of the battle of Agincourt, the latter was born around 1395/6, probably in either

d'après le manuscrit inédit du château de Tramecourt', *Bulletin historique et philologique de comité des travaux historiques et scientifiques* (1887), pp. 77–82.

[86] *La Chronique d'Enguerran de Monstrelet*, ed. L. Douet-D'Arcq, 6 vols (Société de l'Histoire de France, 1857–62), vol. 1, pp. 2–3.

[87] D. Boucquey, 'Enguerran de Monstrelet, historien trop longtemps oublié', in *Les sources littéraires et leurs publics dans l'espace bourguignon XIVe–XVIe siècles*, ed. J. Cauchies (Publication du Centre Européen d'études Bourguignonnes, 31, 1991), pp. 113–25

[88] Monstrelet, 4, p. 128. That could have included Le Fèvre, of course, who was king of arms of the order of the Golden Fleece founded by Philip the Good.

[89] *The First English Life of King Henry the Fifth*, ed. C.L. Kingsford (Oxford, 1922), p. xv.

Avesnes, near Eu, or Abbeville. It is likely that by the time of the battle he was already an officer within the corps of heralds and poursuivants, possibly of the French crown or of the duke of Brabant. It is thought that he was present at the meeting of English and French ambassadors in Paris in March 1414. This contact may explain why he accompanied the English army from the time it left Harfleur up to the battle, although his exact status and function at this point remains unclear. At the end of the battle narrative he tells us that the heralds were together during the battle, but afterwards went off 'those of France to where it seemed best to them, and those of England stayed with their masters who had won the battle. But as for me I stayed with the English and later I heard many notable knights speak of it'. He singles out in particular Sir Hues and Sir Guillebert de.Lannoy who had been at the battle and who gave lengthy accounts of it, implying that this is where he derived his information on the French army and the battle itself. It could be, of course, that Monstrelet also gained information from the Lannoy brothers.[90]

There has been speculation that Le Fèvre was also in England in 1416 as he gives a detailed account of the visit of the Emperor Sigismund. In 1431 he was appointed king of arms of the order of the Golden Fleece, the order which Philip the Good, duke of Burgundy, had founded in 1429, and it is as 'Golden Fleece' that Waurin refers to him. He died in Bruges in 1468. He began writing his chronicle before the death of Duke Philip (d. 1467), in order, as he tells us, 'to escape laziness'. He intended to cover the period from 1408 to 1460 but only got as far as 1436. He also tells us that he intended to be brief, and his Agincourt sections are certainly more expansive than most of his work. The exact date of composition is not known, although the early 1460s have been speculated, which might put the composition of the Agincourt sections into the very same years as those of Waurin, and it seems that both men knew each other and their work. It has also been suggested that Le Fèvre's work first existed as 'a series of shorter narratives or reports which the herald would later fashion himself into a consecutive narrative. The writing of such reports was Toison d'Or's job. From the inception of the order, the chief herald had the task of providing material for the *greffier*, who was expected to record the business of the Golden Fleece and matters pertaining to its membership.'[91] Morand claims that 'there can be no doubt that Jean Waurin knew the original (of Le Fèvre) and that the transcriptions which he made for his own chronicle were made in his own hand.' She also provides us, at the end of her edition of Le Fèvre's chronicle, with a schematic representation of the relationship between his work and that of Monstrelet and Waurin.[92]

Waurin was the illegitimate son of Robert de Waurin, the hereditary seneschal of Flanders who had close connections with John the Fearless, duke of

---

90 *Chronique de Jean Le Fèvre, Seigneur de Saint Remy*, ed. F. Morand, 2 vols (Société de l'Histoire de France, 1876–81), vol. 1 (1876), pp. 267–8.
91 Small, *George Chastelain*, p. 140.
92 *Le Fèvre*, 2, appendix I and II.

Burgundy.[93] His birth has been placed in 1394 but he himself claimed he was 15 years old at the time of the battle of Agincourt. His father and half brother, who were killed at the battle, were amongst several Flemish fighting for the French although the area was under Burgundian rule.[94] Waurin was firmly in the Burgundian camp by 1420 and involved in several military engagements in the Anglo-French wars from 1415 onwards, being present with the English at the battles of Cravant, Verneuil and Patay. He then fought against the English, but retired from military service by 1445, if not earlier. By 1442 he had been rewarded by the grant of the lordships of Forestal and Fontaine. He also served at the ducal court and on various embassies in the 1460s, probably dying in the early 1470s. He was largely domiciled at Lille where he married the widow of a bourgeois. The precise date at which he began writing history is not known but it is unlikely to have been before 1446. A successful account of a naval expedition sent by Duke Philip to Constantinople in 1444 led to its commander, Waleran, lord of Waurin (and the chronicler's nephew) encouraging the composition of a longer work, the *Recueil des croniques*. This was in the tradition of the *Brut*, taking the history of Albion from the time of *Brutus* to the present day. The work was initially written down to 1413 and was probably completed by 1455. After the accession of Edward IV, Waurin continued his chronicle, initially to 1443 and later to 1471. Thus the section including Agincourt was probably written in the 1460s. It seems that he then presented the work to Edward IV but not to his Burgundian master. There can be no doubting Waurin's interest in military matters: as we have seen his writing career began with his account of a naval engagement, which he later incorporated into his main chronicle. He was also interested in English history, no doubt because of the Anglo-Burgundian link, and also provides valuable accounts of the Wars of the Roses. He drew on a variety of sources sometimes ascribing them.[95] He was, like Monstrelet, keen to write the chivalric chronicle and to applaud deeds of arms, and the prologue to his own chronicle echoes the sentiments expressed by Monstrelet whilst also adding in special mention of the desire to speak of the history of England.

These accounts undoubtedly provide the fullest versions of the battle. The list of dead and prisoners which Monstrelet gives is the longest and formed the basis of Belleval's study of the French there present. He also includes the full text of the royal order of summons issued on 20 September 1415. As noted earlier, he is thinner on details of the English march whereas Waurin and Le Fèvre are more expansive on this and provide the possibility of tracing the route of the march of the English in a way which fits well with the account in the *Gesta*. Both also give a very full account of the English camp on the morning of the battle, and include in Henry's pre-battle speech the idea that the French would cut off the

---

[93] *Biographie nationale de Belgique*, 27 (1938), col. 129–32. See also Gransden, pp. 288–93.
[94] *Receuil*, vol. 1, p. 3.
[95] Ibid., pp. li–cxx.

archers fingers if they were captured. This is thus a relatively late story, although other earlier writers make less specific allusions to how the French might treat their captives. All three writers give the same deployment of English troops, but this is rather unclear and potentially contradictory; the archers are put in front and 'then the men-at-arms', but this is soon followed by the making of 'two wings of men-at-arms and archers'. All three are full of detail on the commanders of the French army and make clear the French plan to launch a cavalry charge as well as why it failed. All three accounts mention the English sending a group of archers into a meadow, presumably to launch an unexpected volley from the flank, and the role of Sir Thomas Erpingham in drawing up the battles, though not specifically the archers. The role of the English archer in the mêlée receives particular emphasis especially in Waurin and Le Fèvre.

All are written in a much more matter of fact way than many English chronicles which tend to make much of stories and 'legends', and they are also less judgmental of the French, although this could also be due to the fact that they were written some while after the event, by which time French fortunes had revived and the shame of the defeat had been redeemed. These are the only real 'military' accounts which we have and are especially important because of that, even though they are written late in the day and have a complex inter-relationship. In addition, the early printing of Monstrelet's chronicle, with several printings shortly after 1500, made his account well known in both England and France, and much used by sixteenth-century English historians.

*

Translated from:

La Chronique d'Enguerran de Monstrelet, ed. L. Douet-D'Arcq 6 vols (Société de l'Histoire de France, 1857–62), vol. 3 (1859), pp. 89–124.[96]

Chronique de Jean Le Fèvre, Seigneur de Saint Remy, ed. F. Morand, 2 vols (Société de l'Histoire de France, 1876–81), vol. 1 (1876), pp. 230–69.

Recueil des Croniques et Anchiennes istories de la Grant Bretagne a present nomme Engleterre par Jehan de Waurin, ed. W.L. Hardy and E.L.C.P. Hardy, 5 vols (Rolls Series, London, 1864–91), vol. 2, pp. 185–222.[97]

In Chapter 143 Monstrelet deals with the Southampton plot and then moves on to the expedition. He gives the size of the English army at the siege as 6,000

---

[96] There is also a translation by T. Johnes (*The Chronicles of Enguerrand de Monstrelet*, 2 vols, London, 1840) but I have not found this to be totally reliable and have therefore provided a new translation based on the text in the Douet-D'Arcq edition.

[97] My translation is based upon that provided by the same editors in *A Collection of the Chronicles and Ancient Histories of Great Britain now called England*, 3 vols (Rolls Series, 1864–91), vol. 2 (1399–1422), pp. 187–226. The chronicles for the period from 1325 to 1471 are also printed in French in *Anchiennes Croniques d'Engleterre par Jean de Waurin*, ed. L.E.E. Dupont, 3 vols (Société de l'Histoire de France, 1858).

bascinets (i.e. men-at-arms) and 24,000 archers, not counting the *cannoniers* and other men connected with the ordnance, whom, he claims, were very numerous. It is noted that 400 French troops came to Harfleur to assist in its defence. Monstrelet also tells us that during the siege the king of France sent a force under the constable, the marshal Bouccicaut, the seneschal of Hainault, the lords of Ligny and de Hamede, Clignet de Brabant and others to Rouen to hold the frontier against the English. They prevent the English taking other towns and fortresses, which he claims that the English tried to do on several occasions. Also when the English rode out in search of victuals, the French prevented them from doing so and this contributed to a shortage of victuals on the English side, combined with the problems of disease, which killed 2,000 English at the siege. None the less, the garrison of Harfleur agreed to surrender if help was not forthcoming in three days, and the surrender took place on Saint Maurice's day. There is no mention of Henry's offer to fight in single combat with the Dauphin. The next chapter, 144, deals with the dispute between the town of Cambrai and the duke of Burgundy.

Le Fèvre begins his narrative of the expedition in his chapter 45 and Waurin in his chapter 5, with their accounts being very similar to each other and to Monstrelet. Both fail to give the size of the English army but say that the invasion was launched by 800 vessels laden with men and equipment. Le Fèvre and Waurin say that 300 French entered Harfleur to assist in its defence.

In chapter 145, Monstrelet tells us how the French king started to raise troops, and includes the text of an order sent out on 20 September. As this is of interest to how the French army was raised, and also makes some interesting observations on the response of the dukes of Burgundy and Orléans, Monstrelet's chapter is given in full below. Le Fèvre and Waurin mention that King Charles sent out such letters but they do not cite them verbatim. They also mention the duke of Burgundy's orders that the lords of Picardy should await his orders, with Waurin displaying his local interests by giving the names of some of the lords, but both claim that the lords obeyed the command of the king. They omit any mention of the response of the duke of Orléans.

(Monstrelet) Chapter 145. *How the king of France collects a great body of men-at-arms to oppose the English. The copy of the order which he makes on this matter.*

The king of France and his council, hearing of the surrender of Harfleur to the king of England, and, fearing that the latter would wish to make similar attacks on other towns in the kingdom, ordered from every part of the kingdom the greatest possible force of men-at-arms in order to offer resistance. To this end, he sent orders to all his *baillis* and seneschals stating amongst other things that he had sent ambassadors to England to offer his daughter in marriage to King Henry, with an immense portion in lands and money, to obtain peace, but that he had failed, and the king of

England had invaded his realm and besieged and taken his town of Harfleur very much to his displeasure. On this account, therefore, he required all his vassals and subjects to come to serve him without delay. He also despatched messengers into Picardy with sealed letters to the lords de Croy, de Waurin, de Fosseux, de Crequi, de Heuchin, de Brimeu, de Mammez, de la Viefville, de Beaufort, d'Inchy, de Noyelle, de Neufville and to other noblemen, that they should come to serve him with all their power, under pain of his indignation, and to join the duke of Aquitaine [the Dauphin] whom he had appointed captain general of his kingdom. The lords of Picardy delayed obeying, for the duke of Burgundy had sent them and all his subjects orders to hold themselves in readiness to march with him when he should summon them and not to attend the summons of any other lord, whatever might be his rank. This was the cause why the above-mentioned men-at-arms were in no haste to comply with the king's summons; fresh orders were therefore issued, the tenor of which was as follows.

'Charles by the grace of God, king of France, to the *bailli* of Amiens or to his lieutenant, greeting. Whereas by our letters we have commanded you to make proclamation throughout your bailliage for all nobles and others accustomed to bear arms and to all other men of war and archers living in your bailliage and on the borders of the same, to arms themselves and come quickly before us and our very dear and well-beloved son, the duke of Aquitaine, whom we have nominated our captain general of the kingdom. It is now some time since we have marched against our adversary of England who had, with a large army, invaded our province of Normandy and taken our town of Harfleur, which, owing to the neglect and delay of you and others, in not punctually obeying our orders, from want of succour our noble and loyal subjects within the town, after having made a most vigorous defence, were forced to surrender it to the enemy. And as the preservation and defence of our kingdom is the concern of all, we call on our good and faithful subjects for aid and are determined to regain those parts of which the enemy may be in possession and to drive them out of our kingdom in confusion, by the help of God, the holy virgin Mary and of our good and loyal subjects, relatives and friends, vassals and allies, of whom we are now requesting aid and succour.

We order and command you, expressly, relying by these presents on the faith and loyalty which you should have and on pain of forfeit to us, that, as soon as you have read these letters, you strictly issue orders to all others in your bailliage, to their persons and at their houses and residences, and to all men who are accustomed to arm themselves, by solemn proclamations in the *bonnes villes* and other places in your bailliage where it is customary to issue proclamations, so often that no one may plead ignorance of the same, under pain of being reputed disobedient and having their goods confiscated, that immediately after these proclamations, publications and command, they should come, armed and equipped adequately each according to his capacity, before us and our son, and that you should force them to do so by seizure of their good and bodies, placing foragers (*mengeurs*) within their houses at their expense, and by all other means employed on such occasions, to assist us in fighting against our enemy and his power and to expel him from our kingdom in great confusion.

You will also signify these things to the bourgeois and inhabitants of the *bonnes villes* of your bailliage ordering and commanding them on our behalf that they should send to assist us in this task all engines of war, cannon and weapons that can be spared, which we promise to restore at the end of the war. You will use every possible diligence in seeing to the execution of these our commands so that no inconvenience occurs to us nor our lordship or subjects, in full knowledge that if any things arise as a result of your default, we shall punish you in such wise that you shall serve for an example to all others. We command all our justices, officers and others our subjects punctually to obey all your directions and those of your commissioners or deputies in this matter. And you should send an acknowledgment of the receipt of these presents to our loyal subjects the officers of our *chambre des comptes* at Paris. Given at Melun 20 September in the year of grace 1415 and of our reign the 26th.'

When this proclamation had been published at Paris and Amiens and in other parts of the kingdom the king sent ambassadors to the dukes of Burgundy and Orléans to require that they would, without fail, instantly send him five hundred *bascinets* each, as he did not wish them to come in person as they had a major quarrel between them. The duke of Orléans was at first content to send his quota but afterwards followed with all his forces. The duke of Burgundy made answer that he would not send troops but would come in person with all those of his country to serve the king; however, because of distraction which arose, he did not attend himself, but the greater part of his subjects prepared and set off.

We thus take up Monstrelet's narrative in chapter 146 in the immediate aftermath of the surrender of Harfleur. For some of the narrative, setting aside minor semantic differences, Le Fèvre and Waurin give an identical account to Monstrelet. Where Le Fèvre and Waurin differ from Monstrelet, their versions are indicated in bold type. In general, Le Fèvre and Waurin give identical accounts to each other. The occasional differences in Waurin are indicated in bold italics.

Chapter 146. *How the king of England made his entry into Harfleur. The arrangements which he made concerning the march which he undertook to come to Calais. Concerning the disposition and government of the French.*

The fact is that once agreements had been made and concluded between the king of England and those of the town of Harfleur, the gates were opened and his commissioners went in. Then the king, entering by the gate, dismounted and took off his shoes, and walked barefoot to the parish church of Saint Martin and there prayed with great devotion, thanking his creator for his good fortune. After he had done this, he took as his prisoners all the noblemen and soldiers who were in the town and then let them leave the town, many dressed only in their doublets (*pourpoins*), on condition that they all had their names put down in writing and swore to surrender themselves as prisoners at Calais by the feast of St Martin next. On that condition they went off. A large number of the bourgeois of the town were also made prisoner and it was agreed that they should pay large ransoms. On that condition they too were put out of the town. Also driven out of the town were a large number of women with their children. They left with only five *sous* and some of their clothing. It was such a piteous thing to see and hear the sorrow and lamentations expressed by the inhabitants leaving the town with their belongings. All the priests and men of the church were also dismissed. As for the possessions found in the town, of which there was a large quantity, they all devolved to the king and he had them shared out according to his will. Two towers which were on the sea and were very strong held out for almost two days but then surrendered like the rest.

[Monstrelet] The king of England sent the greater part of his army to England by way of Calais, taking by ship the great booty, prisoners and engines of war. In this company were the principal captains the duke of Clarence, brother of the king, and the earl of Warwick.

[Le Fèvre and Waurin] 'The king of England sent some of his prisoners to England, that is to say, the lords of Estouteville and Gaucourt, on the ship whereon he had himself come, along with goods which he found in the town and also a large number of men who were sick, amongst whom were the duke of Clarence, the earl of Arundel and several other noblemen. They say that during the siege the king had lost 500 knights and esquires in addition to others who had all died of dysentery.' Le Fèvre (*but not Waurin*) also tells us that 'during the siege, several great lords of France had assembled, 500–600 mounted men who had been told to gather together as close as they could to the siege that the king of England was lying and to put in place great ambushes as close in as they could. Afterwards they sent out scouts to effect sorties against the English. These were noble men amongst whom was the sire de Lisle Adam and sire de Brimeu who were later members of the order of the Golden Fleece and who were captured on these sorties. For, as had been ordered, these scouts went to the siege and cried "to arms". The English immediately mounted and chased the French off. And refusing to retreat when ordered they captured the French out party. The English could have been in great danger that day if the matter had been well conducted, but the baron of Ivry showed himself too soon and the English left off chasing the French and returned to their siege with few losses. In this action were captured the lord of Lisle Adam and Jacques de Brimeu, taken by men of the lord of Robessart, native of Hainault, who had become English and was in the service of the king of England with his three brothers.'

The king repaired the walls and ditches of the town and then he placed in it a garrison of five hundred men-at-arms and one thousand archers under the captaincy of Sir John le Blond knight; he added a very large stock of provisions and of military equipment. [*Le Fèvre names the duke of Exeter as captain and give the number of archers as 1,500. Waurin also names Exeter but cites the same number of troops as Monstrelet and says that Sir John Blount was with the duke of Exeter.*]

After fifteen days the king of England departed from Harfleur intending to march to Calais, escorted by 2,000 men-at-arms and about 13,000 archers, and a number of other soldiers.

[*Waurin tells us more about the English army at this point. 'After the said king of England had sojourned fifteen days in the town of Harfleur he departed, endeavouring to go to Calais. At his departure he arranged his men in three battalions: the vanguard was led by the earls of Kent and [Sir John] Cornwall: in the centre division with the king were the duke of Gloucester, his brother, the earl of Huntingdon and his brother, the great lord Roos, with several others; the rearguard was commanded by the duke of York and the earl of Oxford. In this order the king of England journeyed in the midst of his troops through the lands of Normandy burning and destroying all before him; for he had in his army at least 2,000 men-at-arms and 14,000 archers.'*]

He lodged at Fauville and in the places thereabouts. Then, crossing the Pays de Caux, he made for the county of Eu. Some of the English scouts came before the town of Eu and several French men-at-arms sallied out to oppose them. In that number was a most valiant man-at-arms called Lancelot Pierre. Having attacked one of the English, he was struck by him with a lance which, piercing the plates of his armour, mortally wounded him in the belly. Whilst he was dying, he killed the Englishman. The count of Eu and many other French lords were much grieved and distressed at the death of Lancelot. From there the king of England marched through Vimeu with the intent of crossing the River Somme at Blanchetaque where his predecessor, King Edward, had passed when he won the battle of Crécy against Philip de Valois.

To this point the post-siege narratives of Le Fèvre and Waurin have essentially followed Monstrelet. The latter, however, now goes on to give a brief account of the march of the English up the Somme and of their eventual crossing of the river, whereas Le Fèvre and Waurin give a much longer account of this part of the campaign. They also go on to tell how the dukes of Orléans and of Bourbon sent heralds to the king of England to fix the time and place of battle. There is no mention of this incident in Monstrelet.

[Monstrelet] But learning from his scouts that the French had posted a considerable force to guard that ford, he altered his route and marched towards Arraines, burning and destroying the whole country, taking prisoners and acquiring great booty. On Sunday 13 October he lodged at Bailleul in Vimeu and moving across the countryside from there, he sent a sizable detachment to gain the crossing at Pont de Rémy, but the lord de Vaucourt, with his children and a great number of men at arms, gallantly defended it against the English. As a result the king of England could not cross and went on to quarter his army at Hangest sur Somme and in the neighbouring villages.

At that time, the lord d'Albret, constable of France, the marshal Bouccicaut, the count of Vendôme, grand master of the household, the lord of Dampierre, calling himself admiral of France, the duke of Alençon, the count of Richemont with a numerous and gallant body of men (*chevalerie*) were in Abbeville. On hearing of the route which the king of England was pursuing, they departed and went to Corbie and Péronne, with their army near at hand, in an attempt to guard all the fords of the River Somme against the English. The king of England marched from Hangest to Ponthieu, passing by Amiens, and fixed his quarters at Boves, then at Harbonnières, Vauvillers, Bayonvillers, with the French marching on the opposite bank of the Somme. At length the English crossed the Somme on the morrow of St Luke's day by means of the ford between Bethencourt and Voyennes, which had not been staked by those of St Quentin as they had been ordered to do by the king of France. The English army were quartered at Monchy-Lagache, near the river of Miramont, and the lords of France, with their forces, retired to Bapaume and the adjacent area.

[Le Fèvre and Waurin] [*Waurin tells us additionally that he was told what follows by 'a gentleman who was afterwards king of arms of the order of the Golden Fleece* [i.e. Le Fèvre], *in the household of Philip, duke of Burgundy, and who, as he said, was all the time with this company and was even one great cause of dissuading King Henry from crossing there.' Another manuscript of Waurin gives us further details of Waurin's informant 'who on account of his good sense and probity was chosen king of the said order, was at the time of the battle of Agincourt nineteen years old, and was in the company of the king of England in all the business of this time, and I the author of this present work, being then of the age of fifteen was in the French army. And we were acquainted and found ourselves together since that time, the said Golden Fleece and I, and agreed about these present matters by way of pastime, so that to drive away idleness, the mother of vices, I have taken pleasure in bringing together in writing the things which happened in our time and especially the great and mighty deeds of the kings of England.'*]

But when he came to two leagues off Blanchetaque, the men of his vanguard, spread out across the lands, captured a gentleman who was a native of Gascony, and a servant of Charles d'Albret, then constable of France. [*Waurin adds that he was handsomely mounted and armed.*] I do not know what to say about this wretch because of the crushing and terrible events which later came to pass. For if he had not been taken at this stage, the King of England would have crossed at Blanchetaque without being prevented, and then his men could have gone straight on to Calais and there would have been no sad and sorrowful day for the French at the battle of Agincourt. Speaking of this gentleman whom several Frenchmen call devil and not a man, it is the case that when captured by the English he was taken before the leader of the vanguard and interrogated about where he came from, of what country he was of and who was his master. He replied that he was a native of Gascony and that he had sallied out of the town of Abbeville, where he had left his master, the constable of France. After several interrogations he was asked if the crossing at Blanchetaque was guarded. He said that it was and that there were several great lords there [*Waurin names them as Sir Guichart Dauphin and the marshal Bouccicaut*] with about 6,000 warriors, and he swore that he was telling the truth. Because of this information the Gascon was brought before the king of England and questioned again, and all the English companies were halted.

After the king had heard him speak he called his princes and had the matter debated in council. This council lasted a good two hours, and ended by deciding that the king should choose another route because he believed that the Gascon was telling the truth. It is to be assumed that he said these things were true because he wanted a battle, for at this stage the French had not yet assembled and did not do so until eight days later. So having left behind the crossing at Blanchetaque the king chose a route to take him upstream trying to find a crossing over the river Somme. [*Waurin interposes here the following: 'And the same day the Gascon was taken the king and his army lodged quite near to Abbeville, at Mareuil, Pont-Rémy and other villages thereabouts, burning and destroying wherever they passed. And on the second day that the king of England had taken the road up the Somme, he thought to obtain a crossing at a narrow part; but the lords of Waucourt and Pont-Rémy accompanied by several Frenchmen prevented him; besides, the river there was very deep so the army past on and went to lodge at Crouy, Neige* [unidentified], *and other villages near Pic-quigny.*] He marched on until close to Amiens [*Waurin puts this as 'the third day the English arranged themselves in the order of battle on a fine plain before the town of Amiens'*] and then he made his way to Boves where he quartered.

In that village there were a large number of vineyards in which there was much wine in the presses. The English went there to look for wine, although the king was very annoyed about this. They asked why he had forbidden it and whether his troops could fill up their bottles. He replied that he was not troubled by the idea of bottles but that the problem was that many would have their stomachs as their bottles and that was what bothered him, for he was worried they would get too drunk. The village of Boves is on several watercourses. On a little rocky outcrop is a fine fortress belonging to the count of Waudemont. The king of England and his army were in great need of bread and the village was required to provide, by way of composition, 8 baskets of bread each to be carried by two men. These were given to the king by the captain of the fortress [*named by Waurin as Sir Jean de Matringuehem*]. The king had two gentlemen in his company who were very ill whom he delivered up to the captain, and each had to pay for their ransom two hackneys (horses). The captain conducted himself so well towards the king of England that it was later worth much to him. Leaving Boves, the king of England with his army took the road to Nesles in Vermandois [*Waurin adds here that he quartered at night in a large village called Cays* [unidentified], *near Nesle*].

When the king passed before the town of Nesle they had their walls covered with hangings which were mainly in scarlet. Whilst the king continued to follow the river trying to find a crossing (*Waurin adds here that although the bridge at Nesle was broken the archers were close to each other so the king of England and his army drew up here with the view of crossing over the river*), the constable, Charles d'Albret was at Abbeville with many other notable knights and other soldiers (*Waurin gives in addition the names of Bouccicaut, the count of Vendôme, grand master of the king's household, the lord of Dampierre, the duke of Alençon, and the count of Richemont*) and heard news every day about the route the king of England was taking. So he left the town and went to Corbeil and Péronne, keeping his troops close at hand, and trying to guard all the crossings of the river.

Speaking of the route of the king of England it is true that he and all his army dismounted and went down to the river, and they began to demolish houses and take away ladders shutters and window in order to make a bridge to get across [*Waurin explains that this was to make a bridge across the arches of the previous bridge*]. From 8am until nightfall the English did not cease in trying to make a crossing and so the men got across in dribs and drabs. First the archers went across without horses. [*Waurin says 200 archers on foot, then 500–600 gentlemen crossed with an ensign.*] When an adequate number had crossed, a standard crossed [*Waurin adds then 'afterwards there was given them an emblazoned pennon and then a banner*]. And when the whole vanguard had got across, all on foot, they passed the horses across. [*Waurin has the horses crossing after the vanguard.*] Then the main force and the rear guard crossed. As said earlier, it was night before they all crossed. [*Waurin places this on the day after St Luke's day.*] Even though it was dark the English continued to march on until the king quartered at Athies. The French were lodged in the area round there. [*Waurin, following Monstrelet here, has the English at Monchy-Lagache on the river Miramont and the French at Bapaume with their men in the neighbourhood.*] When the French were told that the English had crossed the river, they were very annoyed with those at St Quentin because they had been ordered by royal authority to break up the crossing by which the English had passed over the river.

The dukes of Orléans and Bourbon and the constable of France sent three heralds to the king of England and informed him that, to help him achieve his desire they had approached him for they knew well that, even from the moment he left his own kingdom, his desire was to give battle to the French. Moreover, they were three princes of the royal house of France who were ready to deliver and provide for his wish and what he was seeking. If he wished to appoint a day and place to fight against them, they would be pleased to have him do so. The details should be decided upon by the representatives of both sides and should not give unfair advantage to one side or the other, for such was the wish of the king, their sovereign lord. This was the content, or at least the substance of the letters which were sent to the king of England. He received them with great joy and also received the heralds with great honour, giving them large gifts from his belongings but sending them off without a reply. But he sent to the French lords two of his own heralds by whom he sent the following reply: he wished them to know that since he left the town of Harfleur he had sought and was still seeking to return to his kingdom of England, and had not stayed in any fortified town or fortress. Thus, if the three princes of France wanted to fight with him there was no need to appoint a time or place because they could find him any day they liked in open country and without any hindrance. This was his reply to them.

They again sent to their king to let him know that Henry had crossed the River Somme, because previously they had told the king the route that the English had taken. After the king of England was alerted to the fact that from all parts of the kingdom of France men were gathering to fight with him and to prevent his reaching Calais, being fully aware too of the desire of the three princes of France to give him battle, he put on his armour when he left his quarters and also had all his army put their armour on. In addition he ordered all the archers thenceforward to be provided with a stake sharpened at both ends and so he rode on each day up to the day of the battle.

[*At this point, Waurin chapter 8 begins, providing us with the same information as in Monstrelet chapter 147 about the deliberations at the French court. Le Fèvre alone goes on to tell us the following:* 'When the French saw that the English had chosen a route other than that over Blanchetaque and had gone up the river Somme, as was said, they sent to the king and the duke of Guienne to have leave to fight against the king of England. The matter was put to the council and it was decided that the king of England should be brought to battle. Immediately afterwards the king ordered his constable and the other princes with him to put themselves into the field with all the force they had and to fight the king of England. This decision was soon known in many places within the kingdom as beyond. Indeed at the battle which will be described shortly were several noblemen of the lands of Brabant, Hainault, Holland, Zeeland and elsewhere.']

Chapter 147. *How the king of France and several of his princes with him at Rouen decided in council to give battle to the king of England. And how Philip, count of Charolais did not go to the battle.*

[Monstrelet and Waurin] During this time the king of France and the duke of Guienne came to Rouen. There on 20 October a council was held to know what should to be done against the king of England. At this council were present King Louis (the duke of Anjou), the dukes of Berry and Brittany, the count of Ponthieu, youngest son of the king, the chancellors of France and of Guienne and many noble councillors numbering 35 in all. After several issues had been raised and discussed in the presence of the king about the matter, it was finally decided by 30 of the councillors that the king of England and his army should be brought to battle. The other five for various reasons counselled that it would be better, in their opinion, that they should not fight on the day which had been appointed. But at the end of the day the opinion of the majority held sway and the king immediately ordered his constable and other officers by letters signed with his own hand that they should assemble as soon as they could with all the force that they could get, and that they should give battle to the king of England and his army.

After this it was decreed throughout the whole of France that all nobles accustomed to bear arms and wishing to acquire honour should go by night and day in order to join the constable, wherever he might be found. Even the duke of Guienne had a great desire to go.

[Le Fèvre rejoins Monstrelet and Waurin with the mention of the duke of Guienne. Thus all three writers now give the following story of the count of Charolais (later Philip the Good, duke of Burgundy). Le Fèvre adds a few points: he notes a third governor of the count, the lord of Chanteville, and tells us at the end of the story that 'I have heard tell that the count of Charolais, even when he achieved the age of 67 was still annoyed that he had not had the good fortune to be at the battle, irrespective of whether he might have survived or been killed at it.']

All the lords and all soldiers went with great diligence towards the constable. The latter, moving towards the area of Artois, sent the lord of Montgaugier to the count of Charolais, only son of the duke of Burgundy to tell him of the decision that had been reached to fight the English and to request him, in all affection, on behalf of both the king and the constable that he might be present at the engagement. The lord of Montgaugier found the count at Arras and was most honourably received by him and his council. He told the count the purpose of his visit, in the presence of the latter's council. Reply was given by the sires de Roubais and de la Viefville, his principal governors, that he would respond diligently to the request as was right and proper, and on that they parted. However, although the count of Charolais desired with his whole heart to be at the battle to fight the English and although his governors had given him to believe that he would be there, nevertheless they had been forbidden to do so by Duke John of Burgundy, his father, who had ordered them to guard well that the count did not go to the battle. To that end, to keep him well out of the way, they took him to Aire, to where the constable again sent certain lords as well as Mountjoye, king of arms of France to make similar requests to the count of Charolais to those which had been made earlier. But to cut the story short, every time the matter was manipulated by the governors who found ways of keeping the count in the castle of Aire as securely and secretly as they could, so that he would not hear any news nor discover the intended day of the battle. However, many of the men of his household, sensing that the need to fight was approaching, left secretly without his knowing, and went off with the French in order to fight the English. The young lord of Anthoing and his governors stayed with the count. In order to appease him his governors told him that it had been his father who had forbidden them to let him go to the engagement. He was not very happy with this, and, according to what I have been told, because of his annoyance he took to his chamber in floods of tears.

But let us return to the king of England. From Moncy-Lagache where he had lodged, as we noted earlier, he went towards Ancre [now Albert] and lodged in a village called Forceville, with his men staying in Acheux and villages thereabouts. The duke of York, his uncle, leading the vanguard, lodged at Frévent on the river Canche. Indeed that night the English lodged in seven or eight villages.

[Waurin follows Monstrelet in the preceding paragraph, but Le Fèvre gives slightly different details of the first stops on the English march. 'After Henry had crossed the river Somme he lodged near Athies as was said before and then passed by Doing near to Péronne. Then he went to lodge at Miramont and thereabouts, and it was there that he heard definite news that he was going to be fought against. Then he made his way towards Ancre and lodged in a village called Forceville and his men lodged in the villages round about, always in such good order, as you have heard, and in their armour. (*Waurin adds this point too.*) And on the next day, which was a Wednesday, he rode close to Lucheux and went to lodge at Bonnières le Scallon, and his vanguard lodged at Frévent on the river Canche. (*Waurin follows Monstrelet in telling us that York was leading the vanguard.*) The accounts now diverge again.]

[Monstrelet] The English were not hindered at all for the French had gone on to get in front of the English towards Saint Pôl on the river Aunun. On Thursday the king left Bonnières and then rode in fine order to Blangy. There, when he had crossed the river [Ternoise?] and was on the higher ground, his scouts started to see the French coming from all directions in great companies of men at arms to lodge at Ruisseauville and Agincourt so that they could get in front of the English to fight them on the next day. On that same Thursday towards nightfall, after a few sorties, Philip, count of Nevers was knighted by Bouccicaut, marshal of France, along with several other great lords. Soon afterwards the constable arrived quite near to Agincourt in which place all the French assembled in a single army. They all bivouacked in the open fields close to their banners save for men of lower status who lodged in the villages close by. The king of England with all his Englishmen lodged in a little village called Maisoncelles three bow shots away from the French.

[Le Fèvre and Waurin] The French in order to be in front of them had drawn towards Saint-Pôl and the river Anvin. To tell the truth, the king of England had wanted to lodge in another village which had been taken by his herbergers, but he, who always observed proper and honourable practices, did what you will now hear. It is true that on this journey whenever he wanted to send scouts before towns or castles or on any matter, he had the lords or gentlemen take off their coats of arms when they went off and put back on again when they returned. It so happened that on the day that the king left Bonnières to go up close to Blangy, there was a village which had been commandeered by his harbingers, but he had not been told of it. Not knowing in which village he was supposed to lodge, he went on by a bow shot and rode past it. Then he was told that he had passed his lodging. Then he stopped and said 'As I have passed, God forbid that I should return as I have got my coat of arms on'. And he moved on and lodged where his vanguard were lodging, and moved the vanguard further forward.

On the next day, the king of England left in the same good order as he had on previous days and continued to make his way toward Calais. That day was Thursday 24 October, the eve of Saint Crispin. When the king of England had left his quarters and he and his battles had issued out from the villages, his scouts saw that the French were coming in large numbers from all parts intending to lodge at Ruisseauville and Agincourt so that they could get in front of him in order to fight him on the next day. But to return to the king of England, before he crossed the river at Blangy en Ternoise, because the crossing was narrow he had six bold men of his vanguard take off their coats of arms and cross over in order to find out whether the passage was guarded. They found that there was no one seeing to its defence, so the English crossed quickly. Then when they had passed the village of Blangy, the king was told by his scouts that the French had assembled in large number. Seeing all the French before him, the king of England had all his men dismount and put them all into battle formation. You could have seen the English, thinking that battle was to be given that Thursday, paying their devotions, all kneeling with their hands towards heaven, asking God to keep them in His protection. This is true: I was with them and saw what has been described. (*Waurin does not include this remark.*) The king stayed in this fine formation and in the same location until sunset.

The French, who could see the English, also thought they were going to fight on that Thursday and also stopped and put themselves into formation, putting on their armour, unfurling banners and dubbing many knights. There was knighted Philip, count of Nevers, by marshal Bouccicaut, along with other great lords and noblemen. Soon afterwards, the constable arrived near Agincourt (*Waurin does not mention the constable specifically*), at which place assembled all the French together in a single host. The English king, seeing that it was late, had all his battles move off to lodge at Maisoncelles which is near Agincourt. But before he arrived at his lodgings, he gave all the French, nobles and others, who were prisoners in his army, licence to leave and in return they promised that if the day of battle turned out in his favour and if God gave him the victory, that they would return to him and their captors, if they still lived. But if he lost the battle then they would be quit of their promise. After the prisoners had been released the king lodged in the village of Maisoncelles, as was said, very near to the place where his enemies were which was less than a quarter of a league away, so close that you could hear them very clearly and even hear them calling each other by name. As for the English never did anyone make such little noise. It was hard to hear them speak to each other for they spoke so low.

When the French saw that the king had lodged at Maisoncelles and that they would not be fighting on that day, they were ordered by the king and his constable to bivouac in the place he found himself. Then the banners and pennons were furled around the lances, armour taken off, and mules and trunks unpacked, and all the lords sent their men and harbingers to the nearby villages to find straw and litter to put under their feet and also to sleep on in the place where they were, which was much churned up by the trampling of horses. If that was not enough, almost all night it rained. There was also a great noise from pages and servants and all kinds of men, so much so that the English could hear in clearly.

But on the English side there was no noise, for that night all who could find one made confession to a priest. The men at arms got their aiguillets ready and did all they had to. Likewise the archers renewed their strings and also prepared what was necessary. Then when day dawned the king heard mass and heard three masses, one after the other, fully armed save for his head, dressed in his armour. After the masses he had brought to him his helmet which was a very fine bascinet with a visor on which was a very rich crown of gold encircling it like an imperial crown. When he was completely accoutred he got on his horse – a small grey horse – without his spurs, and without having the trumpets sound he had his troops move out of their lodgings and drew up his battles on a fine plain of young corn. He ordered a gentleman with 10 lances and 20 archers to keep the baggage of himself and his men, along with the pages of noble rank and others who were sick and thus could not be of help. He made only one battle. All his men-at-arms were in the middle of his battle and all the banners close to each other. On the two flanks of the men-at-arms were the archers. There were about 900–1,000 men-at-arms and 10,000 archers. Speaking of the banners there was for his own person five banners: the banners of the Trinity, the Virgin, Saint George, Saint Edward and the banner with his own coat of arms on it. There were several others, to wit, the banners of the duke of Gloucester, the duke of York, the earl of March, the earl of Huntingdon, the earl of Oxford, the earl of Kent, the lords Roos and Cornwall and of several others. When the king had drawn up his battle and made arrangements for the baggage he went along the battle line on his little grey horse (*Waurin omits mention of the horse*) and made very fine speeches, encouraging them to do well, saying that he had come to France to recover what was rightful inheritance, telling them that they could fight freely and securely in this quarrel and that they should remember that they had been born in England where their fathers and mothers, wives and children, were at this very moment. Because of that they ought to exert themselves so that they could return there in great honour and glory, and that the kings of England, his predecessors, had gained many splendid victories over the French and that on that day each should help in guarding him and the honour of the crown of England. In addition, he told them that the French had boasted that if any English archers were captured they would cut off the three fingers of their right hand so that neither man or horse would ever again be killed by their arrow fire.

Now we must speak of the French. On the Thursday night, as was said before, they lodged in the field between Agincourt and Tramecourt, where the battle on the next day. They stayed in that place until morning, hoping that they would not leave it until they had fought with the king of England. So they put themselves into formation.

[Le Fèvre and Waurin effectively rejoin Monstrelet here.] The French with all the other royal officials, that is to say the constable, the marshal Bouccicaut, the lord of Dampierre, the lord of Rambures, the master of the crossbowmen and several princes, barons and knights, planted their banners with great enthusiasm next to the royal banner of the constable in the field they had chosen situated in the county of Saint Pôl in the territory of Agincourt, through which the English would have to pass next day to reach Calais. That night they lit great bonfires close to the banners under which they intended to fight the next day.

Although the French numbered 50,000 men and had a great number of wagons, carts, canons, ribaudequins and other military equipment, they had very few musical instruments to cheer them up and hardly any of their horses neighed during the night, which some saw as amazing and a sign of things to come.

[The remainder of this section is not in Le Fèvre and Waurin. Instead, in relation to the 'evil omen' of the silent horses, Le Fèvre tells us 'this I know to be true by Jean, the bastard of Waurin, lord of Forestal. For in that assembling, he was with the French and I was with the English', and Waurin tells us at the same juncture 'I, the author of this work, know the truth about this for I was in the assembly on the French side, and for the English Golden Fleece (i.e. Le Fèvre) has certified the same thing.']

[Monstrelet] Throughout the whole night the English sounded their trumpets and all their many musical instruments so much so that the earth round about echoed to their sounds, despite the fact that the English were very tired and troubled by hunger, cold and other discomforts. They made peace with God by confessing their sins in tears, and many of them took mass, for, as was later revealed by some prisoners, they expected to die on the next day. That night the duke of Orléans ordered the count of Richemont who was leading the men of the duke of Guienne and the barons and had gathered 2,000 men at arms and archers, to go almost right up to where the English were encamped. The English feared that the French wanted to attack so put themselves outside the limits of the camp (*haies*) in battle formation and both sides began to fire on each other. The duke of Orléans and others were made knights on this night. After this sortie, the French returned to their billets and nothing else happened between the two sides for the rest of the night. At this time the duke of Brittany came from Rouen to Amiens with 6,000 combatants to bring aid to the French, if only they could have waited until the Saturday. Likewise the lord of Longny, marshal of France, came to the help of the French with 600 men-at-arms, sleeping that night only six leagues from the French army. In the morning he rose very early in the hope of joining them.

Chapter 148. *How the French and the English engaged in battle against each other at Agincourt, where the English won the day.*

[**Le Fèvre and Waurin rejoin Monstrelet here.** *Waurin adds that this was St Crispin's day.*] On the next day which was Friday 25 October 1415 the French, that is to say the constable and all the other officers of the king, the dukes of Orléans, Bourbon, Bar and Alençon, the counts of Nevers, Eu, Richemont, Vendôme, Marlay, Blammont, Vaudemont, Salines, Grandpré, Roussy, Dammartin and all the other nobles and men of war, armed themselves and moved outside their billets. [**Bourbon is not listed in Le Fèvre.** *Waurin omits the count of Nevers.*] Then the constable and other wise men of the council [*Waurin says the constable and marshals*] of the king of France ordered three battles to be made, that is, the vanguard, the main battle and the rearguard. In the vanguard were put 8,000 men-at-arms (*bascinets*), knights and esquires, 4,000 archers and 1,500 crossbowmen. [**Le Fèvre does not give the numbers of archers or crossbowmen but says simply 'and few archers'.**] The vanguard was commanded by the constable. With him were the dukes of Orléans and Bourbon, the counts of Eu and of Richemont, the marshal Bouccicaut, the master of the crossbowmen, the lord Dampierre, admiral of France, Sir Guichard Dauphin and some others.

The count of Vendôme and other officers of the king, numbering 1,600 men-at-arms [*Waurin gives the number as 600*], were ordered to make a wing to attack the English on the flank. The other wing was led by Sir Clignet de Brabant, admiral, and Sir Louis de Bourdon, with 800 mounted men-at-arms, all hand picked. [**Le Fèvre adds here 'as they say, and as I have heard say, for I was with the English'.**] These were to break the arrow shot of the English, and included Sir Guillaume de Saveuse, Hector and Philip, his brothers, Ferry de Mailly, Alain de Vendôme, Lanion de Launoy and others up to the number mentioned. In the main battle were ordered as many knights, esquires and archers as in the vanguard. [**Le Fèvre says merely, that 'in the main battle were ordered a number of knights, esquires and archers, whose leaders were the dukes of Bar etc.'**] Its leaders were the dukes of Bar and

Alençon, the counts of Nevers, Vaudemont, Blammont, Salines [Salm?], Grandpré and Roussy. In the rearguard was all the rest of the men at arms, led by the count of Marlay, Dammartin, Fauquembergue, the lord of Louvroy, captain of Ardres, who had led those from the marches of Boulogne.

After all these battles had been put into formation as described, it was indeed a most noble vision to behold. As far as one could estimate by just looking, the French outnumbered the English by six to one. **[Le Fèvre says 'three times to one'.]** When the formation had been made, the French were arranged in separate companies each close to their banner awaiting the coming of the English. They refreshed themselves and also made peace and unity between them out of the hatred, rumours and dissensions which had existed in the past. **[Both Waurin and Le Fèvre add here 'some of them kissed and put their arms around each others necks in making peace, and it was moving to see this. All troubles and discords which had been between them and which they had had in the past were changed into great feelings of love. There were some who ate and drank what they had.']** At that point, between nine and ten in the morning, the French were completely confident, given their great number, that the English could not escape from them. Even so, there were some wiser ones amongst them who were worried about fighting them in open battle.

[Le Fèvre and Waurin add here, 'These arrangements made, on the part of the French (as I have heard recollected by notable knights serving under the banner of the lord of Croy, eighteen gentlemen banded together and swore that when the two sides came together they would with all their might get as close as possible to the king of England that they should knock the crown right off his head, or else they would all die in the attempt. They did indeed do this. When they found themselves close to the king one of them with an axe in his hand struck on the king's bascinet such a heavy blow that it knocked off one of the fleurons of his crown, or so it is said. But soon afterwards all of the gentlemen were dead and cut to pieces; not a single one of them escaped. This was a great pity, for if everyone had behaved in this fashion on the side of the French it is credible that the English would have fared much worse. The leader of these eighteen men was Lauvelet de Masinguehem and Gaviot de Bournoville.']

[Le Fèvre and Waurin from this point diverge considerably from Monstrelet but remain almost identical to each other.]

[Monstrelet] Likewise on that Friday morning the English started to eat and drink seeing that the French were not advancing on them to fight. Calling on the aid of the Almighty against the French who despised them, they left the village of Maisoncelles and some of their scouts went to the rear of the village of Agincourt where they found no men-at-arms. There, in order to frighten the French, they burned a barn and house belonging to the priory of Saint-George of Hesdin. Elsewhere the king of England sent about 200 archers behind his army so that they would not be spotted by the French. They secretly entered a meadow near Tramecourt, quite close to the rearguard of the French, and held themselves there secretly until it was time to shoot. All the other English stayed with their king. He had his battle drawn up (*fist ordonner sa bataille*) by a knight grey with age called Thomas Erpingham, putting the archers in the front and then the men-at-arms (*mettant les archers au front devant et puis les hommes d'armes*) He made two wings of men-at-arms and archers (*et puis fist ains comme deux eles de gens d'armes et d'archers*), and the horses and baggage were placed behind the army. The archers each fixed in front of them a stake sharpened at both ends. Thomas exhorted them all on behalf of the king of England to fight bravely against the French in order to guarantee their own survival. Then riding with an escort in front of the army after he had set up its formation, he threw high into the air a baton which he had held in his hand, shouting 'nescieque'. Then he dismounted to join the king and the others on foot. At the throwing of the baton, all the English suddenly made a great cry which was a cause of great amazement to the French.

[Le Fèvre and Waurin also mention the archers sent behind French lines, and the role of Sir Thomas Erpingham but also include negotiations before the battle. What follows comes immediately after their mention of the activities of the eighteen French gentlemen, but the theme returns to the English camp. 'When the men of the king of England heard him speak thus, as you have heard before, and to make his remonstrances, their courage and hardiness was much increased. For they saw that it was time for everyone to defend themselves if they did not wish to perish. Some on the French side say that the King of England sent 200 archers towards the French and behind their army, secretly, so that they could not be seen, towards Tramecourt to a meadow close to where the vanguard of the French were positioned. The purpose of this was that when the French marched forward, the 200 archers could fire on them from the side. But I have heard said and certified as true by a man of honour who was there on that day in the company of the king of England that nothing like this happened. Then, as has been said, the English, hearing their king thus admonishing them, uttered a great cry, saying 'Sire, we pray to God that he will grant you a long life and a victory over your enemies.' Then after the king of England had thus admonished his men, again on his little horse, he put himself in front of his banner and then marched with his whole battle in very good order towards the enemy. Then he called a rest in the place where he stopped.

He sent men in whom he had great confidence to meet and talk with several notable Frenchmen. These French and English gathered between the two battles, it is not clear at whose request. But it is true that there were overtures and offers made on both sides to come to a peace between the two kings and kingdoms of France and England. On the French side was offered, or so I have heard, that if Henry would renounce the title which he claimed to have to the crown of France, and leave it completely aside, and surrender the town of Harfleur which he had recently captured, the king of France would be content to let him have what he held in Guienne and what he held by ancient conquest in Picardy. The king of England, or his men, replied that if the king of France would let him have the duchy of Guienne and five cities which he named and which belonged to the duchy of Guienne, the county of Ponthieu, a marriage to Catherine, daughter of the king of France, with jewels and garments to the value of 800,000 *écus (Waurin says 500,000 francs)*, he would be prepared to renounce the title to the crown of France and to surrender the town of Harfleur.

These offers and requests, made by each side, were not accepted, so each party returned to its own battle. There was no longer any hope of peace so each side prepared to fight. As was said before, each English archer had a stake sharpened at both ends which they put in front of themselves and by which they were protected. The truth was that the French had ordered their battles between two small woods, one close to Agincourt, the other to Tramecourt. The site was narrow and very advantageous for the English and the very opposite for the French. For the French had been all night on horse and it had rained. Pages, servants and several others in exercising the horses had completely churned up the ground making it so soft that the horses could scarcely lift their hooves out of it. In addition, the French were so weighed down by armour that they could hardly move forward. First, they were armed with long coats of armour, stretching beyond their knees and being very heavy. Below these they had 'harnois de jambes' (leg armour) and above 'blans harnois' (white i.e. polished armour). In addition they had 'bascinets de carvail'. So heavy were their arms that as the ground was so soft they could scarcely lift their weapons. There was a marvellous array of banners, and it was ordered that some should be taken up and unfurled. It was also ordered amongst the French that each should shorten his lance so that they would be stiffer when it came to fighting. They had plenty of archers and crossbowmen but nobody wanted to let them fire. The reason for this was that the site was so narrow that there was only enough room for the men-at-arms.

After the discussion had taken place between the two battles and the emissaries had returned to their own men, the king of England ordered a veteran knight, called Sir Thomas Erpingham, to draw up his archers and to put them in the front in two wings (*pour ordonner ses archiers et les mectre au froncq devant en deux elles*). Sir Thomas exhorted everyone on behalf of the king of England to fight with

vigour against the French. He rode with an escort in front of the
battle of archers after he had carried out the deployment, and threw
in the air a baton which he had been holding in his hand. (*Waurin
adds 'he cried "Nestroque" which was the signal for attack'.*) Then he
dismounted and put himself in the battle of the king of England who
was also on foot between his men and with his banner in front of him.
Then the English began suddenly to advance uttering a great cry
which much amazed the French.']

[Le Fèvre and Waurin rejoin Monstrelet at this point.] When the
English saw that the French were not advancing on them, they moved
forward in good order and again made another great cry before taking a
rest and catching their breath. Then the archers who were in the meadow
also raised a great shout and fired with great vigour on the French.
Straightway the English approached the French; first the archers, of
whom there were a good 13,000 [Le Fèvre says 10,000, *Waurin does not
give a number*] began with all their might to shoot volleys of arrows
against the French for as long as they could pull the bow. Most of these
archers were without armour, dressed in their doublets, their hose loose
round their knees, having axes or swords hanging from their belts [Le
Fèvre and Waurin add 'hatchets']. Many had bare heads and were
without headgear. [As well as noting that some were bare footed, Le
Fèvre and Waurin add 'and others had hunettes or cappelines of
boiled leather, and some of osier on which they had a binding of iron'
(*croisure de fer*).]
   The princes who were with the king of England were his brother the
duke of Gloucester, his uncle the duke of York, the earls of Dorset,
Oxford and Suffolk, the earl marshal and the earl of Kent, the lords of
Camoys [?], Beaumont, Willoughby and Cornwall, and many other
notable barons and knights of England. [This paragraph is not in Le
Fèvre or Waurin.]
   When the French saw the English come before them, they put themselves into battle order each under their own banner, placing their helmets
on their head. They were urged by the constable and other princes to
confess their sins in true contrition and to fight well and boldly, just as the
English had been. [Le Fèvre and Waurin put this sentence differently,
without reference to the confession of sins. 'The constable, the
marshal and the princes encouraged their men most strongly to fight
well and bravely against the English.'] Then the English sounded their
trumpets loudly and the French began to bow their heads so that the arrow
fire would not penetrate the visors of their helmets. [Le Fèvre and
Waurin put this sentence as follows: 'When they approached their
trumpets and clarions gave great noise. The French began to bow
their heads, especially those who had no shield (*pavaix*), because of
the English arrow fire. The English fired so vigorously that there were

none who dared approach them, and the French did not dare uncover themselves or look up.'] So they advanced a little against them, but then made a little retreat. But before they could engage together, many French were hampered and wounded. When they came together they were so closely packed one against the other that they could scarcely lift their arms to strike their enemy, save for those who were in the front who struck with their lances which they had cut in the middle so that they could be stronger and so that they could get closer in to the English.

Those who were supposed to break up the archers, that is Sir Clignet de Brabant and the others in his company were intended to number 800 men-at-arms, but there were only 120 of them to force a way through the English. In very truth, Sir Guillaume de Saveuses who had been ordered to be mounted with the others, broke ranks to be alone in front of his companions wanting them to follow him and went off to strike against the English. He was immediately shot from his horse and put to death. **[The wording of this passage in Le Fèvre and Waurin is slightly different. (*Waurin notes also, 'The said French had formed a plan which I will describe, that is to say'*) 'The constable and the marshal had set up a formation of 1,000–1,200 men at arms of whom half were to advance on the Agincourt side and the other half on the Tramecourt side in order to break the wings of the archers. But when it came to the time to attack they could only find 800 men. Clignet de Brabant was there with the special responsibility of carrying this out. (*But when it came to the time to attack there were but 120 left of the band of Sir Clignet de Brabant who had the charge of the undertaking on the Tramecourt side.*) Then Sir Guillaume de Saveuses, a very valiant knight, took the Agincourt side with about 300 lances; with only an escort of two he advanced before all the others who followed, and attacked the English archers who had their sharpened stakes placed in front of them. But the ground was so soft that the stakes made their horses fall. All of them returned, save for three men at arms of whom Sir Guillaume de Saveuses was one. (*Waurin puts this sentence differently, 'So the said Sir William and his two companions pressed on boldly'.*) It was their misfortune that their horses fell amongst the stakes and fell to the ground amongst the archers who killed them immediately'.]**

[Le Fèvre and Waurin rejoin Monstrelet here.] Because of the strength of the arrow fire and their fear of it, most of the others doubled back into the French vanguard, causing great disarray and breaking the line in many places, making them fall back onto the ground which had been newly sown. Their horses had been so troubled by the arrow shot of the English archers that they could not hold or control them. As a result the vanguard fell into disorder and countless numbers of men-at-arms began to fall. Those on horseback were so afraid of death that they put themselves into flight away from the enemy. Because of the example they set many of the French left the field in flight.

[Monstrelet] Soon afterwards the English fell upon them body on body. Dropping their bows and arrows to the ground, they took up their swords, axes, hammers, falchions and other weapons of war. With great blows they killed the French who fell dead to the ground. In doing this they came so far forward that they almost reached the main battle which was following in behind the vanguard. After the English archers the king of England followed up by marching in with all his men-at-arms in great strength.

[Le Fèvre and Waurin] And soon afterwards, the English archers, seeing the breaking up of the French vanguard, came out from behind their stakes) all together and threw down their bows and arrows, taking up their swords, axes and other arms and weapons (the weapon list in Waurin is *'swords, hatchets, mallets, axes, falcon beaks and other weapons'*). They struck wherever they saw breaks in the line. They knocked down and killed the French, and finally moved forward to the vanguard which had seen little or no fighting. The English advanced so far, striking from right and left, that they came to the second French battle which was behind the vanguard. They then attacked it and the king of England threw himself into the fight with his men at arms.

[Monstrelet] At that point Anthony, duke of Brabant who had been commanded by the king of France, rushed to enter the vanguard in the battle, accompanied by a small number of men. Because of the great haste with which he had come, he had left his troops behind. As a result, he was soon despatched to death by the English.

[Le Fèvre puts the story of the duke as follows, and Waurin's wording is almost identical to it. 'Then arrived Duke Anthony of Brabant, who had been summoned by the king of France, but who arrived so hastily with only a few men. His men could not follow him for he was so keen to get there. As he would not wait for them, because of the haste with which he had come he took one of the banners from his trumpeters, made a hole in the middle of it, and used it as his coat armour. No sooner had he dismounted that he was immediately killed by the English. Serious fighting began and many French were killed for they put up little defence. Because of the cavalry (*abovementioned*), the French battle line was broken.']

[Le Fèvre and Waurin rejoin Monstrelet here.] The latter pushed further and further into the French, acting together and with great energy, breaching the first two battles in several places, knocking men to the ground and killing them cruelly and without mercy. In this conflict several lords were recovered by their servants and led off the field. The English were so intent upon fighting, killing and taking prisoners that they did not bother to pursue anyone. The rearguard was still mounted but seeing the first two battles doing so badly, they took to flight save for some of the leaders. Whilst the battle had been raging the English, already with the upper hand, had taken several French prisoners. News then came to the King that the French were attacking from behind and that they had already taken the pack horses and other baggage. This was indeed the case, for Robinet de Bournville, Riflart de Clamace, Isembard d'Azincourt and other men-at-arms, accompanied by 600 peasants, had gone off to attack the baggage camp of the English king and had captured baggage and other things along with a large number of horses of the English whilst their keepers were involved in the battle.

[Monstrelet] As a result of this setback the English king was very concerned, for everywhere he looked in front of him the field was full of French who had taken flight but were regrouping in companies. Faring lest they might attempt to form a new battle he had proclaimed in a loud voice to the sound of the trumpet that each Englishman, on pain of penalty, should kill his prisoners so that they would not be able to assist their compatriots. There was immediately a great slaughter of French prisoners. Because of their activity Robinet de Bournouville and Isembard d'Azincourt were later arrested and imprisoned for a long duration at the order of Duke John of Burgundy even though they had given to Philip of Charolais, his son, a very fine sword adorned with valuable gems and other jewels, which sword had belonged to the king of England and had been found by them along with his other baggage. They had given him the sword so that if ever they fell into trouble or danger because of the matter the count might intervene on their behalf. The count of Marlay and the count of Fauquembergue, the lords of Louvroy and Chin, leaders of the rearguard along with the 600 men-at-arms which they had kept together with great difficulty, moved forward to attack the English with great valour. But this was to no avail, for they were soon killed or taken. Here and there in a few places the French tried to regroup in small units but they were all killed or taken by the English without putting up much of a fight.

[Le Fèvre and Waurin] In pursuing his victory and seeing his enemy defeated and that they could no longer resist him, they had started to take prisoners hoping all to become rich. That indeed was a valid belief for all the great lords were at the battle. (*The preceding sentence is omitted in Waurin.*) Once taken, they had their helmets removed by their captors. Then a great misfortune befell them. Many of the rearguard (*Waurin adds also 'the centre division'*), in which were several French, Bretons, Gascons, Poitevins and others who had previously been put to flight, regrouped. They had with them a large number of standards and ensigns and showed signs of wanting to fight, marching forward in battle order.

When the English saw them together in this fashion, it was ordered by the king of England that each man should kill his prisoner. But those who had taken them did not want to kill them for they were all hoping to collect a large ransom from their prisoners. When the King

was told that no-one was willing to kill his prisoner he appointed a gentleman with 200 archers to the task, commanding him that all the prisoners be killed. The esquire carried out the order of the king (*Waurin, 'without delay or objection'*) which was a most pitiable matter. For, in cold blood, all those noble Frenchmen were killed and their heads and faces cut, which was an amazing sight to see. When the wretched company of the French who had caused the death of these noble knights saw that the English were ready to take them on and fight with them, they all took to flight to save their own lives if they could. Most of those who were mounted did survive but those on foot suffered many deaths.

[Monstrelet] At the end of the day the king of England gained a victory against his enemy. About 600 English of all ranks were dead on the field, including the duke of York, the king's uncle. On that very day before they had come into battle array and during the night, the French had created a good 500 knights or more.

[Le Fèvre and Waurin] 'When the king of England saw and realised that he had gained a victory against his enemies he thanked Our Lord with his whole heart and he had good reason to do so, for only 1600 of all ranks had been killed of his own men. Amongst them were the duke of York, his great uncle, and the earl of Oxford. In very truth, on the day before they came into battle array, there had been made on the French side 500 knights or more.'

[Monstrelet] After the king of England had emerged victorious in the field, as has been said, and all the French, save for those dead or captured, had departed in flight to many different locations, he went over the field where the battle had taken place in the company of some of his princes. Whilst his men were busy in stripping and robbing those who had been killed, he summoned the herald of the king of France, the king at arms called Mountjoye, along with several other heralds both French and English, and said to them, 'It is not we who have caused this killing but God the Almighty, on account of the sins of the French, for so we believe.' Later when he asked them to whom victory should be accorded, to him or to the king of France, Mountjoye replied that to him was the victory and not the king of France. Then the king asked him the name of the castle which he could see close by. They answered that it was called Agincourt. 'As all battles', the king said, 'ought to take their name from the nearest fortress, village or town where they happened, this battle from hencefor-ward and for ever more will be called the battle of Agincourt.'

[Le Fèvre and Waurin] Afterwards, the king of England realised that he was victorious in the field, and that all the French had departed save those who had been taken prisoner or were dead on the field. (*Waurin, When the King of England saw that he was victorious in the field, and had got the better of his enemies, he humbly thanked God the giver of victory and he had good cause, for of his people there died on the spot only about sixteen hundred men of all ranks, among whom was the duke of York, his great uncle, about whom he was very sorry.*) He then called to him the other princes in the area where the battle had been. When the king saw the site, he asked what the castle was called that he could see nearby. They told him that it was called Agincourt. Then the king of England said, 'As all battles', the king said, 'ought to take their name from the nearest fortress, village or town where they happened, this battle from henceforward and for ever more will be called the battle of Agincourt'.

[Monstrelet] Since the English had been on the field for some time, having been delivered from their enemies, and that night was approaching, they returned all together to the village of Maisoncelles where they had lodged on the previous night, and there they lodged again taking with them several of their dead. After they had left the field some French came amongst their dead, dragging them throughout the night as best they might to a wood which was quite close to the field. There they buried several. Others went to various villages and to such other places as they could.

[Le Fèvre and Waurin] Then when the king and his princes had been there for a good space of time and no French had shown themselves to do him injury, seeing that he had been in the field for a good four hours, and also that it was raining and night was approaching, he went off to his quarters at Maisoncelles. In that place, since the victory the archers had been stripping the dead and taking their armour off. Turning over bodies, underneath them they found several prisoners who were still alive. One of these was the duke of Orléans, along with several others. The archers took the armour of the dead to their lodgings across horses, and also carried off the English who had been killed in the battle. Amongst the latter were carried the duke of York and the earl of Oxford who had been killed in the battle. In very truth the English had no greater loss save for those two. When night came, the king of England was informed about all the armour which had been taken to the billets. He had it proclaimed throughout his army that no one should take more than he was lacking for his own body, and that they were still not out of danger from the French. They had the bodies of the duke of York and earl of Oxford boiled so that they could take their bones back to England. Then the king of England commanded that all the armour which was surplus to requirements and in addition to what his men had carried off with the bodies of some of the English who had been killed in the battle should be put into a house or barn. There they were completely burned and so it was done.

[Monstrelet] On the next day the king of England and his English left the village of Maisoncelles very early in the morning along with all their prisoners and again went to the field. Those French whom they found still alive they took prisoner or killed. Then they departed from there, making their way to Calais. About three quarters of them were on foot, and were exhausted not just because of the battle but also because of hunger and other discomforts. Thus the king of England came to Calais after his victory without any hindrance, leaving the French in great distress because of the loss and destruction of their men.

[Le Fèvre and Waurin begin this section similarly but then deviate considerably from Monstrelet. 'On the next day, which was a Saturday, the English left Maisoncelles very early in the morning and with all their prisoners, again visited the field where the battle had taken place. There they found Frenchmen who were still alive and took them prisoner or killed them. The King of England stopped in the field, looking at the dead. It was a pitiable thing to see the great nobility who had been killed there by their sovereign lord, the king of France, for they were all naked just like those new born. (Waurin omits the reference to those new born but adds *'for during the night they had been stripped both by the English and by the local peasantry'*.) After this had been done, the king of England moved on and took his way towards Calais. It happened that, at a break for rest that he took on his route, he stopped his horse and had bread and wine sent to the duke of Orléans. But the latter would not eat or drink. News of this was brought to the king of England. Then the latter believing that the duke did not want to eat or drink out of displeasure, went towards him and said, 'Noble cousin, how are you?' And the duke replied. 'Well, sir'. Then the king asked him, 'Why do you not want to eat or drink?' The duke replied that indeed he was keeping a fast. So then the king said, 'Noble cousin, be of good heart. I realise that God has given me the grace of having a victory over the French, not because I am worthy of it, but I believe in full certainty that God wanted to punish the French. If what I have heard said is true, it is no wonder, for they say that there has never been seen such a great disarray or disorderly behaviour in excesses, sins and wicked vices as has reigned in France at present. It is pitiful to have it recounted, and horrible to those who hear of it. And if God is angry at it, it is no wonder, and no one can be surprised at it. Several discussions and conversations occurred between the King and the duke. They always rode in fine order just as they had always done, except that after the battle they no longer wore their armour (*cottes d'armes*) when riding, as before they had done. They moved on so that they arrived at Guînes where the king was received by the captain of the place in great honour and reverence. You should know that he always had his French prisoners placed between the vanguard and the main body of the army (*batailles*).

The king of England lodged in the castle of Guînes but the great mass of his men at arms moved on towards Calais, extremely tired and exhausted, encumbered by booty and the prisoners (save for the French dukes, counts and barons of rank whom the king of England kept with him). But when such men arrived at Calais where they hoped they could enter to gain refreshment and rest of which they had great need – for most of them had spent eight to ten days without eating bread and of other victuals, meat, butter, eggs, cheese always only the little they could find – they would have given anything to have it, more than you have ever heard of. For there was such a shortage of bread that they did not bother what it cost, but only that they should have some. It is bad enough to think of the poor French prisoners of whom many were wounded and injured being in great distress, for they all wanted to go into Calais. But those of the town refused to let them enter, save for some English lords. They did this so that victuals would not fail and so that the town, which lay on the frontier, would always stay well provided. (Waurin adds that the soldiers refused admission were '*very discontented*'.) Thus many of the men at arms and archers who were burdened with the baggage and the prisoners, sold their gear and enough of their prisoners to those of the town so that they could get money, and they did not care so long as they could get money and go to England. There were several who put their prisoners to a courteous ransom and who received them on their faith and on that day gave what was worth 10 nobles for four, and they did not worry so long as they could have bread to eat or that they could pass to England.

The king of England who was at Guînes heard what a shortage his men were experiencing and he made provision as soon as he could. With great care he commanded that shipping should be provided on which the men at arms, archers and their prisoners (*Waurin adds 'those who had any'*) crossed to England, some to Dover others to Sandwich. They were rejoiced to find themselves back in England, and also for the great victory which they had had against the French. So they went off each to his own home. Later the king, having stayed several days at Guînes, went to Calais. On the journey he spoke to the French princes who were his prisoners, comforting them in friendly fashion as one who knew well how to do this. And they rode on so that they came to Calais where the king was received by the captain and those of the town, who had come out to meet him almost to Guînes (*this point is omitted in Waurin*), and also the priests and clerks all in their vestments with crosses and banners of all the churches of the town, singing 'Te deum laudamus'. Men and women and little children rejoiced at his coming, saying, 'Welcome our sovereign lord'. (*Waurin adds that 'the little children cried "Noel"'*) And thus in great glory and triumph he entered into the town of Calais and stayed there several days. He celebrated there the feast of All Saints and soon afterwards had ships made ready to cross to England. When they

were ready, he left on 11 November' (*Waurin notes that this was St Martin's day*); **Le Fèvre and Waurin then deal with the return to England and entry to London.]**

[Monstrelet] Chapter 149. *Here follow the names of the lords and gentlemen who died in the battle of Agincourt on the French side.*

[list follows] In short, so many princes, barons, knights, esquires and other men were killed at the said battle, according to the declaration of several heralds and other notable people worthy of belief, that the total number was 10,000 or more. Many of these were removed by their friends for burial after the English had departed. Out of this number of 10,000 it is estimated that there were about 1,600 valets and the remainder of gentle birth. It was discovered that about 120 bannerets, including the princes, had died.

During the struggle the duke of Alençon with the aid of his troops had struck through with great valour almost the whole English battle, penetrating right to the king himself. He had fought so powerfully that he had knocked down and vanquished the duke of York, uncle of the king of England, and killed him. When the king saw what was happening he made to relieve the duke of York and bent forward a little, at which point the duke of Alençon hit the king on the bascinet with an axe which he was carrying. The blow was so fierce that it knocked off a part of his crown. The king's bodyguard in great strength surrounded the duke of Alençon. The latter, seeing that he could not escape death, lifted his hand to the king of England and said 'I am the duke of Alençon and surrender myself to you'. But just as the king was ready to take his oath, he was quickly killed by the bodyguard.

At about the same time the sire de Longny, marshal of France, who was mentioned above, arrived with 600 men of King Louis (of Anjou), to be at the battle. He was already about a league off when he met several French wounded, and others in flight, who told him that he should go home and that the chivalry of France had been completely annihilated by the English. When Longny heard this he was very upset and returned to Rouen to the king of France.

Here follow the names of the lords and gentlemen who were taken prisoner by the English at the said battle (*journée*), who numbered 1500 or more, all knights or esquires. [list follows]

[Neither Le Fèvre or Waurin tell us of the duke of Alençon or the sire de Longny. The names of the dead are given in chapter 73 of Le Fèvre, after a short introductory remark, 'So you have heard how the king of England came to his kingdom in great triumph. So we shall leave off speaking of him for a while, and shall speak of those who died in the

piteous battle of Agincourt and also of the prisoners. (He then gives the names of those who died in the battle.) To say by name and surname the barons, knights, esquires and nobles who died on this day would take us too far off the story. Indeed I have only given you the names of dukes, counts, knights and esquires for so many noble esquires died there and other valiant men that I saw with my own eyes that it was a pity to see and hear it told by the heralds (*officers d'armes*) who were at the battle, on both the French and the English sides. During the battle all the heralds, of both sides, stood together. After the battle those of France went to where it seemed best to them and those of England stayed with their masters who had won the battle. But as for me, I stayed with the English, and later I heard many notable knights of the French speak of it, and especially Sir Hues and Sir Guillebert de Lannoy who had been at the battle and who gave lengthy accounts of it. But as said, so many noble men died that they were reckoned to number 10,000, of whom 7,000–8,000 were noble and the remainder archers of others. It was found that, including the princes, 100–20 men entitled to banners. If the battle had been on the Saturday there would have been an even greater number so on all sides men were flooding in as if they were going to a festival of jousting, joust or to a tournament.

Waurin gives the names of the dead in his chapter 14. He ends the chapter by saying he has named only the most renowned and well known but otherwise follows the exact wording of Le Fèvre even to saying that he saw it with his own eyes and got information from the heralds and from the Lannoy brothers. Waurin omits the mention of their 'lengthy accounts' but tells us additionally that Sir Hues was taken prisoner and he escaped the same night. Waurin's comment on numbers dead is slightly different but he goes on to make the same remark about the Saturday. 'The number slain was ten thousand of whom it is thought about 1600 were varlets. All the rest were men of noble birth most of whose relatives carried the bodies from the field and buried them as they thought best. Among them were found six score banners. If the battle had been on the Saturday there would have been an even greater number so on all sides men were flooding in as if they were going to a festival of jousting, joust or to a tournament.

Le Fèvre gives the names of prisoners in chapter 74, following on directly from the end of the text in the previous note. Waurin puts this information at the end of his chapter 15 but the accounts are identical. 'Now as I have given you the names of those who died at the battle, I will tell you the names of those who were taken prisoner on the day. There were taken prisoner on that day 1600 men or thereabouts, all knights or esquires [list follows]. As you have heard, that is what happened on the piteous day of Agincourt. (Waurin puts this

last sentence, '*And now I shall leave of speaking off the day of Agincourt and proceed further in my proposed subject.*]

[Monstrelet] Chapter 150. *How after the departure of the king of England several French came to the field to find the friends of the count of Charolais whom they then buried, and other matters.*

After the king of England and his Englishmen departed on the Saturday to go to Calais, as was aid, several Frenchmen came back to the field. They again turned over bodies which had already been looked through once, some to find their masters and lords so that they might carry them off for burial in their own regions, and others to pillage what the English had left behind. For they had not taken off much gold or silver, clothing and hauberk, or other things of value. As a result a large amount of armour belonging to the French was found in the field. But relatively little was still there for they had all been stripped of their clothing and most of them had even had taken from them their underwear, sheets, shoes and other items of apparel by the peasants, both men and women, from the villages in the vicinity, and were lying completely naked in the field. On the same Saturday, and the Sunday, Monday, Tuesday and Wednesday following several princes and lords were taken up and washed, namely the dukes of Brabant, Bar and Alençon, the counts of Nevers, of Blammont, Vaudemont and Fauquembergue, and the lord of Dampierre, admiral of France. The latter was buried at Hesdin in the church of the Friars Minor. The others were carried away by their servants and friends some to their own lands and others to several churches. All those who could be recognised were taken up and carried away in order to be buried in the churches of their lords. Afterwards, Philip of Charolais came to learn of the harsh and piteous fate of the French and had a great sadness in his heart especially for his two uncles, the dukes of Brabant and the count of Nevers, who were naked on the field, so he sent men to seek them out. The abbot of Ruisseauville and the *bailli* of Aire were ordered to this task. They had a square measured out of 25 feet in which were made three ditches as wide as two men. In these they placed, according to an account kept, 5,800 men who had not been taken off by their friends. Also the others who had died from their wounds in the towns in hospitals or elsewhere in the villages and in the woods nearby, who were a large number as had been said elsewhere. The land and ditches were blessed and consecrated as a cemetery by the bishop of Guînes at the command of and acting as representative of Louis de Luxembourg, then bishop of Thérouanne. Afterwards thorny branches were placed above so that wolves, dogs and other beasts could not get in to defile and eat the bodies.

After this piteous and saddest of days, some clerks of the kingdom of France, in great wonderment, wrote the verses which follow: [see Text E 8 below]. Here follow the names of the principal men who were at the battle and who were neither killed nor taken. Firstly, the count of Dammartin, lord of La Rivière, Sir Clignet de Brabant, who called himself admiral of France, Sir Louis Bourdon, Sir Galiot de Gaules, and Sir Jean d'Argennes.

[Le Fèvre and Waurin do not include anything on the burial but go on to tell us (chapter 75 in Le Fèvre, 15 in Waurin) how news was taken to the king. 'Soon after the king of England had won the victory at Agincourt, news was taken to Rouen to the king of the sad outcome and loss of his men. There can be no doubt that the king, his men, princes and others had great sorrow in their hearts.' (*Waurin, 'As soon as the misfortune of the said field of Agincourt was known a number of horseman set out and made rapid way each striving to bring the first tidings of it to King Charles of France, the duke of Guienne his son and the other great lords of the blood royal then in the city of Rouen. With which piteous news all were greatly distressed and angry, not without cause, and so also were all the people of the realm, but for the present, nothing further could be done'.*)]

B 10. Edmond de Dynter, *Chronique des ducs de Brabant* (?early to mid-1440s, Latin)

Translated from *Chronique des ducs de Brabant par Edmond de Dynter*, ed. P.F.X. De Ram, 6 vols (Brussels, 1854–60), 3, pp. 298–304.

Dynter, who was born around 1382, was secretary of both Duke Anthony of Brabant, who was killed at Agincourt, and his successor, Duke John IV (d. 1427). The first five books of his chronicle trace the history of the duchy from the twelfth century to 1400. The sixth book covers the period from 1400 to 1442. The work was composed at the order of Duke Anthony's nephew, Duke Philip the Good of Burgundy, who became Dynter's new master and ruler of Brabant after Duke John IV's death. It was presented to Duke Philip in 1447 who then requested a translation into French, which was prepared by Jean Wauquelin.[98] Dynter was not himself present at the battle. He was due to follow Duke Anthony, who rushed ahead in order to participate, and was at Douai on 26 October where he heard news of the disaster. But he would have been in a good position to hear of what had happened from other members of Duke Anthony's household, not least the duke's confessor and valets of his chamber, who found the duke's body on the field on 27 October. Dynter's account is thus important to us. It has some similarities with the account of Monstrelet and the other Burgundian chroniclers so adding a further complexity to the issue of whose

[98] Small, *Georges Chastellain*, p. 103

account should be taken as the 'original'. In particular, Dynter may be the
source of the story of Duke Anthony's improvised armour, although he is the
only writer to suggest that the duke was not killed in the mêlée but as a prisoner
whose elevated rank was not obvious to his captors.

*

It is to be known that in the year 1415 on Monday 21 October, Duke
Anthony was in his castle at Louvain. In the evening, around 8 and 9
o'clock, there were presented to him letters written at Péronne in Vermandois on 19 October in the name of the duke of Bourbon, the duke of
Alençon, the count of Richemont, the count of Eu and the count of
Vendôme, of the leading *maîtres d'hôtel* of the king, of Charles d'Albret,
constable, and Bouccicaut, marshal of France, and also other letters
written in the same town on the same day by the seneschal of Hainault
and the lords of Waurin and Rons. By these letters the lords informed the
duke that he should set out in his own person, because in the following
week they intended to fight the English, telling him also that the king of
France and the dauphin of Vienne would be there in person. Once he had
received, had read out, and heard these letters, Duke Anthony immediately had his secretaries come before him and ordered them that that night
they should write letters close and patent to all his nobles, barons and
officers in his duchy of Brabant that without delay they should follow him
with as large a number of men-at-arms and archers as they could find,
making their way towards Cambrai, where they would receive news from
him so that they might go with him to join the French and the lords and
princes of France in fighting against the English, the ancient enemies of
France. And that very night he sent one of his esquires to the town of
Anvers [Antwerp] to make a similar request, and on the morning of
Tuesday 22 October, he went to the council chamber in the town of
Louvain and requested those of the town to give him men-at-arms, archers
and crossbowmen to use against the English, and he set out towards Mons
in Hainault, and then towards Cambrai, and there they had news of him.
That same day he went to Brussels where he made a similar request as at
Louvain and Anvers to the governors and council of the town. These three
major towns agreed to his request and made hurried preparations to have
their men arm and equip themselves, in large numbers and with much
apparel, and on the next day they all set out.

[Dynter then tells us more of the movements of the duke, mentioning
himself as his secretary.] On the morning of Friday 25 October, Duke
Anthony was at Lens in Artois hearing mass. Just as the host was being
elevated a man called Robin Daule brought him news that the English
were to be fought before mid-day. The duke and the other nobles who
were in his company put the sign of the cross on their clothing and coats
of arms, mounted their horses and set out quickly for the battle. They had
about 11 leagues to go to where the defeat took place, and alas, they died

piteously. [Dynter tells us here about how he subsequently heard news of the duke's death. He also reports how he later found out that the duke's brother, the count of Nevers, had sent letters on 22 October encouraging him to rush to fight in the battle. Other letters had been sent to the duke about the English movements. Dynter laments that the duke did not read all of these for if he had done so perhaps he would not have tried to move so quickly.]

Chapter 127.

Although this battle has little relevance to the *gesta* or chronicles of the land of Brabant, none the less, because of the case of the sad death of Duke Anthony, I must say something, but in as short a space as I can. It so happened that on 25 October the French on the one side and the English on the other both assembled in large number in the field. The king of England, seeing the multitude of the French was so much bigger and more powerful than his own, in great anxiety sent to the princes of France offering that if they would let him and his men leave in peace and freely from France, and to return to England, he would surrender to them Harfleur and all the other towns and castles which he might capture and that he would commit no further damage in the kingdom of France. The French princes refused his request. The king of England, having faith in Our Lord, for he could not expect victory from his numbers of men but only by virtue of a divine victory, ordered his battles as wisely as he could to meet the French, to wit the archers on one side and the men-at-arms on the other (*sagittarios ad partem unam, et homines armorum ad aliam*).[99] The French princes did the very opposite, for they put their archers, crossbowmen and infantry in the rear, not wanting their aid, and intending in their great pride to defeat and capture the English king and all his men by dint of their swords and hand-to-hand fighting, for there were ten French nobles against one English. To break the English archers, they ordered that Clignet de Brabant, with 1,200 horsemen who were well armed and mounted, should launch a charge against them in order to separate them from the English men-at-arms. Clignet tried to do this but could not because of the resistance of the archers, so he went on to the English camp to rob it. Meanwhile, the English archers caused maximum damage to the French with their arrows, so that they could not get close enough to the English to engage them in hand-to-hand combat. So it was to the English gain and the French loss that the latter had left their archers and crossbowmen behind.

---

[99] In Wauquelin's French translation this was rendered as 'fist ses archiers mettre devant très ordonnément sur les elles (wings) et ses hommes d'armes bien rengier et ordonner'.

When the two sides came to close combat, Duke Anthony arrived in the vicinity and stopped near a thicket. From there he went down with a few of his nobles. The other troops from the towns could not arrive as quickly, but he had ridden day and night fearing that he would arrive too late for the battle. They were still on their way and going as fast as they could. At the thicket, because his armour had not yet arrived and he had none of his own weapons or coat of arms, nor his standards and pennons, he put on the armour of one of his chamberlains, Gobelet Vosken, and for his coat of arms he took the blazon (*signum dictum blasoen*) of one of his trumpeters. With a hole cut in it he wore it as a tunic, and for a flag he took the blazon from another trumpeters and attached it to his lance. So he entered the battle with the handful of nobles then in his company, save for John de Grymberg, lord of Assche, who had the hereditary right to carry the Duke's banner. This he had refused to do. Indeed he had fled with his men and later had to excuse himself before the Three Estates of Brabant assembled at Fure for the obsequies of the duke. Then the duke with a flag, made as noted earlier, carried before him by Gobelet Vosken, threw himself into the battle along the route that Clignet de Brabant had gone in order to separate the archers from the men-at-arms. He first entered the fray with the cry 'Brabant, Brabant'. But alas, the battle did not last much longer for the French who, through their over-confidence, were captured or killed, and so the victory fell to the English.

Then Clignet returned not to fight but to pillage. The king of England, thinking that the French were wanting to fight again, ordered by the sound of the trumpet throughout his army that everyone should kill their prisoners. As a result, many princes and noblemen who were still alive as prisoners were killed. That Duke Anthony was one of these is well known, for after the battle he was found wounded only in the face and neck. This would not have been the case if he had been wearing his helmet. Also, he was found a long way from where the battle was fought, amongst other dead. Also many captives who survived said that they had seen him taken in the battle and still alive, but that they had not dared to speak to him in the hope that he might be put to a low ransom [i.e. by not being recognised as the duke].

This battle occurred on Friday, 25 October 1415, on the feats of Sts Crispin and Crispinian. On the English side were killed the duke of York, brother of the king, the earl of Arundel, and many other magnates and nobles. On the French side there died Anthony, duke of Brabant and Limburg, as noted above, the duke of Bar, the duke of Alençon, the count of Nevers, brother of Duke Anthony. But the duke of Orléans, the duke of Bourbon and several others of the great lords were taken prisoner and led to England. Of the company of Duke Anthony who had come with him, there died Henry de Liederkerke and Philip his brother. Englebert d'Ainghien, called Kettbetke, was found alive after three days amongst the dead, but died later from his wounds at Saint-Pôl, whence he had been taken. Jean de Fontaines of Hainault, then living at Brussels, Aleman d'Escaussines, knight, *maître d'hôtel* of the court of the duke, Thierry de Heetvelde, knight, Gobelet Voske, Jean de Huldenberghe, Henry de Woude and Jean de Halle, natives of Brussels, with several of their servants, also died. Jean de Rotslaire, Cornille de Liederkerke, brother of the Henry and Philip mentioned above, Nichoass de Saint-Géri, Jean de Glimes and Jean Cole of Brussels were taken prisoner along with several others from Brabant.

On the next day the English made for England with the best of the booty. They put bodies and much equipment in a big barn and burned them, although they took the bodies of the great nobles back to England. They left the bodies of the French naked in the field. After the English had gone off to Calais, several priests and servants of the French lords came to the field looking for their masters. Amongst them was Brother Hector, confessor of Duke Anthony, with several of the servants of the duke's chamber. On 27 October they found the duke's body a long way from the battle site and from where his men had been. It was naked and wounded only in the face and neck. They took it to Saint-Pôl where they put it in a lead coffin with spices and aromatic herbs. On the vigil of All Saints, the next Tuesday, the cortège went to Tournai where the bishop and chapter came out to meet it and accompanied it beyond the city with much lamenting. On Wednesday 1 November the cortège came to Hal and rested for the night in the church of St Mary, where vigils and exequies were performed. On the next day, 2 November, it was taken to Brussels and put in the church of Saint-Goule, where exequies were celebrated. Then the Three Estates assembled and accompanied the bier between Brussels and Hal. On 3 November it was taken to Fure where in the church of St John, after solemn requiem mass, the duke was buried alongside his first wife.

B 11. *Journal d'un bourgeois de Paris* **(?1449, French)**

Translated from *Journal d'un bourgeois de Paris de 1404 à 1449*, ed. C. Beaune (Paris, 1990), pp. 86–89.[100]

This is an anonymous chronicle written in Paris, whose author was more likely a cleric than a bourgeois, the latter being the title imposed by a seventeenth-century editor. Inevitably, there has been much debate over authorship. Longnon advanced the candidature of Jean Beaurigout, priest of Saint-Nicholas-des-Champs with Tuetey favouring Jean Chuffart, canon of Notre-Dame and rector

---

[100] There is also an English translation of the work in Janet Shirley, *A Parisian Journal 1405–1449* (Oxford, 1968), pp. 94–7. I have based my translation on that of Shirley but have made changes to bring it closer to the original French.

of the University of Paris, although Shirley speculates that the author may have been in minor orders and have had some connection with the household of Queen Isabeau. Whoever the author was, he provides much information on Paris, and makes particularly clear the impact of civil war in the city and in Northern France as a whole. Indeed, he tells us elsewhere that had it not been for the dissension in France between the Burgundians and Armagnacs, Henry V would never have dared to be so bold as to invade. The author's main loyalty was to the city. In time he came to accept the kingship of Charles VII, but he shows himself to be emphatically pro-Burgundian in the earlier stages of the war. Note particularly in this how the count of Charolais, later Duke Philip of Burgundy, is claimed to have been advancing upon the English, when in fact we have it from Monstrelet, Le Fèvre and Waurin that his father had had him locked up to prevent his entering into the fray. The Armagnac government is criticised not only for the heaviness of its tax but also for letting its soldiers pillage their own people in Normandy. Attention is also given to the disarray which followed the battle and in particular the response of the Armagnacs then in control of the city of Paris to the proposed arrival of the Burgundians. The comment that those who had been taken prisoner were considered by some to have been disloyal to those who died might also be a snub to the Armagnacs, for the first two deaths noted are of the duke of Burgundy's brothers. Perhaps too it was a counterblast to an Armagnac charge that those who fled from the battle as traitors were Burgundians. No detail on the battle itself is given. It merely serves as an opportunity for the author to express his anti-Armagnac feeling. He has an interest, however, in the dislocation caused by the death of so many officials (see text E 1 below) and mentions the local levies raised by the *baillis*, although there is no specific mention of any contingent from Paris.

The original manuscript does not survive, the earliest copy is incomplete and the precise date of composition is not clear. Moreover, it is more a memoir than a journal, for there is no firm evidence that it was written on a cumulative and regular basis. But it seems likely that it was written piecemeal because it is hard to believe that the prices of foodstuffs which are often cited could be remembered with accuracy at a distance of time. Some sections also use the present tense. The entries are often terse and in note form, with paragraphs introduced by the word 'item' ('also') much as one might expect for entries in an account book.

*

Item, at the beginning of the month of August, the king of England arrived with all his army in Normandy, disembarked near Harfleur and laid siege to Harfleur and the towns near by. Item, the duke of Guienne, eldest son of the king, left Paris on Sunday 1 September, in the evening, to the sound of trumpets, and he had only young men with him. He went off to fight against the English. The king of France, his father, left on the 9 September to follow his son, and went to lodge at Saint Denis. Immediately afterwards the heaviest tax that had ever been seen throughout the whole age of man was levied in Paris – it did no good to the kingdom of France; thus the confederates (*bandés*) controlled everything, for Harfleur was taken by the English during the month of September, on the fourteenth of the month, and all the countryside was devastated and pillaged. The French troops did as much damage to the poor people as did the English, and no other benefit came from them. The weather, some seven or eight weeks after the English landed, was as fine as anyone could remember its ever being in August and during the vintage (it was a good year for other crops too), but never the less, not one of the nobles of France came forward to fight the Englishmen there.

Item, on 10 October 1415 the confederates [i.e. the Armagnacs in the city of Paris] made a new *prévôt des marchands* and four *echevins* of their own choice, that is to say, as *prévôt*, Philippe de Breban, a tax-collector's son; as echevins Jean du Pré, grocer, Etienne de Bonpuits, furrier, Renaud Pis-d'Oue, money-changer, and Guillaume d'Auxerre, draper. The King and the duke of Guienne were now in Normandy, the former at Rouen and the latter at Vernon; but the people of Paris knew nothing about anything until after it had happened. The outgoing *prévôt* and *echevins* were very surprised to find themselves thus dismissed without any orders from the King or from the duke of Guienne and without the citizens' knowledge.

Item, on the twentieth of the month, the French lords heard tell that the English were moving through Picardy and that my lord of Charolais was pressing so hard and so close upon them that they could pass where they wished to go. Then all the princes of France, save for some six or seven, went off and found the English in a place called Agincourt near Ruisseauville. There they fought on the day of Saint Crispin and Saint Crispinian. The French were more than half as numerous again as the English, yet were defeated and killed, and many of France's greatest men were taken prisoner.

Item, first, the duke of Brabant and the count of Nevers, brothers of the duke of Burgundy, the duke of Alençon, the duke of Bar, Charles d'Albret, constable of France, the count of Marlay, the count of Roussy, the count of Salm, the count of Vaudemont, the count of Dammartin, the marquis of Pont. These all died in the battle and at least three thousand gilt spurs from the rest of the army. The following were captured and taken to England: the duke of Orléans, the duke of Bourbon, the count of Eu, the count of Richemont, the count of Vendôme, Marshal Bouccicaut, the king of Armenia's son, the lord of Torcy, the lord of Heilly, the lord of Mouy, my lord of Savoisy, and many others, knights and squires, whose names are not known. Never since God was born did anyone, Saracens or any others, do such destruction in France. Many *baillis* of France died too; they had brought the levies from their *bailliages* and all were killed – such as the *bailli* of Vermandois, with his men, the *baillis* of Mâcon, of Sens, of Senlis, of Caen, of Meaux, all with their men. It was widely said that those who were taken prisoner had not been loyal or true to those who died in the battle.

About three weeks later the duke of Burgundy came fairly near to Paris, very distressed by the death of his brothers and his men, wishing to talk to the King or the duke of Guienne. But a message was sent to him not to dare to come to Paris. The gates were hastily blocked up as they had been before and, because of the lack of lords, several captains established themselves in the Temple, in Saint Martin, and the places mentioned before. All the side streets around these places were taken over by the captains and their troops, and the poor people turned out of their houses. Only with great difficulty and much entreaty were they allowed the privilege of staying under their own roofs, and even then this riff-raff slept in their beds, as they did eleven or twelve leagues out of Paris. No one dared to talk about it or carry a knife for fear of being put in the Temple or Saint Martin or Saint Magloire, Tiron or some other prison.

B 12. Le Héraut Berry (the Berry Herald) (?1450s, French)

Translated from *Les Chroniques du roi Charles VII par Gilles le Bouvier dit le héraut Berry*, ed. H. Couteault and L.Celier, with M. Jullien de Pommerol (Société de l'Histoire de France, Paris, 1979), pp. 64–71.

Gilles Le Bouvier was born in 1386, probably at Bourges. He came to Paris in 1402 and was first attached to the household of the duke of Berry. At his death in 1416 he passed into the service of the dauphin, John, duke of Touraine, who died in the following year. At that point, Gilles moved into the service of the Dauphin Charles (later Charles VII). He fled south with the latter in June 1418. Charles subsequently set up his own group of heraldic officials for the lands loyal to him, naming Le Bouvier as Berry Herald and subsequently Berry King of Arms in 1420. His subsequent service as herald and diplomatic envoy can be traced until 1455. As his chronicle also ends abruptly at this date, it is likely that it marks his death.

He stands alongside Le Fèvre as a herald who also wrote a chronicle. It seems that the two occupations were much interconnected in this period, and heralds were in an enviable position in terms of access to military information and events and royal policy. Various other works of Le Bouvier are known, such as an *Armorial de France* (c. 1450), and he is also speculated to be the compiler of the *Chroniques de Normandie*.[101] He certainly composed a narrative of Charles VII's conquest of Normandy in 1449–50, which later formed part of the

---

101 Ed. Guillaume Le Tailleur, 1487, reprinted by A. Hellot as *Les chroniques de Normandie 1223–1453* (Rouen 1881).

chronicle now under discussion.[102] The chronicle is in annalistic form, giving an account of events year by year from 1402 to 1461, but the last six years are considered a continuation by others. The exact date of compilation is not known. The chronicle was printed very early, as part of the *Grandes Chroniques de France* published in 1476.

The whole of his chronicle is useful for its military detail, although its importance is greater for those campaigns of the 1440s of which he was an eyewitness. There is no suggestion that he was present at the battle of Agincourt. Indeed he does not give its name. But his account shows his connections with the court in later years through, for instance, his description of the troops in terms of their royal household links. There is useful material here on the French army, therefore, but little on the English side and no real account of what happened at the battle. He gives us some additional information on how Henry managed to cross the Somme, and emphasises French determination to bring the English to battle.

*

In the year 1415 the king of England landed at the mouth of the Seine and began to lay siege before Harfleur within which were installed the lord of Estouteville, the châtelain of Beauvais, the lord of Hacqueville and Lyonnet de Braquemont who had in their company a hundred knights and esquires. There arrived later the lord of Gaucourt, the lord of Guitry and others who also installed themselves in the town, which caused much joy to the lords and people therein. They defended and held the town for a long time in fine fashion. During the siege the constable of France, called Charles d'Albret with 1,500 men at arms, and the lord of Bouccicaut, marshal of France with the same number, were at Caudebec, holding themselves there and in other places around Harfleur in the hope of causing damage to the English who were laying siege. But the king of England was so well provided with weapons, bombards and all kinds of artillery, and with victuals. Provisions arrived every day from England by sea, and in such large quantities that the English never had to leave the siege to go off in search of victuals.

At the end it was necessary for those holding Harfleur to surrender it to the king of England, on condition that, if he was not brought to battle before he reached Calais, the knights who had held Harfleur against him would surrender to him as his prisoners. So the king of England left his uncle the earl of Dorset in Harfleur and left to make straight for Calais. When the constable of France got to know this, he informed the king and the whole kingdom how the king of England was heading for Calais. All the lords of the kingdom of France were informed that anyone who loved

[102] *Narratives of the Expulsion of the English from Normandy*, ed. J. Stevenson (Rolls Series, London, 1863).

honour should come to Picardy to fight the English. The constable and
marshal advanced before them to Abbeville in order to prevent the
English crossing the River Somme, and indeed they were successful in
doing this because they held them off for 15 days before they could cross
the river. But at the end they found a crossing between Corbie and
Péronne by which they traversed the river. This was the fault of certain
Frenchmen who were lodged at the crossing, expecting that the English
would cross higher up stream. These French fled during the night and
passing through villages said that the English had passed, so causing
those to flee who were lodged in the vicinity of the crossing. When it was
day, some English came to the river bank on the side where they were
lodging looking for something to eat because they had nothing to eat and
were finding it very difficult to get hold of any food. They entered a
windmill, from which they had a good view of the other part of the river
and that there were no French about. This made them bold enough to pass
the road beyond the windmill, where they found a village at the end of the
road. There they found a great quantity of cooked meat, boiled and
roasted, as well as bread and wine which the French had left behind in
their rush to depart. The English loaded themselves with these victuals –
even though they were on foot – and went back to their captains to tell
them what they had found. These captains left immediately to tell the
king of England. As soon as he knew the situation, he ordered his troops
(*fist ordonner ses batailles*) and sent men to find out what crossing was
possible and also if there were no French on the other side of the river.
They found that indeed there were none, and so straightway the king of
England and all his force crossed the river.

When the constable, the duke of Bourbon, the duke of Bar and the
count of Nevers who had just arrived at Corbie knew of this, they were
enraged by the news, and decided that they would demand that the king of
England gave battle on Thursday next at a place called Aubigny in Artois.
So they sent their heralds, to whom the king of England gave great gifts,
and accepted the challenge, promising to come to the field and to fight on
that day, without default. In effect, he did the very opposite, because he
passed by a place called Beauquesne so that he could reach Calais as soon
as possible. When the French lords knew this, they rode in advance of him
in order to cut him off in his route, and they sent to the king of France who
was at Rouen that he might wish to come to be present at the battle. But
the duke of Berry, his uncle, did not wish him to agree to this, and was
much annoyed that the lords had accepted to give battle. He did not want
the king to go there as he had many doubts about the battle, for it had been
at the battle of Poitiers that his father King John had been captured. He
said it would be better to lose just the battle rather than both king and
battle. For that reason, he would not agree that the king should go,
although the king would willingly have gone because he was a brave,
strong and powerful knight.

Then the constable and the lords (whose manpower was increasing daily) came before the English along a river to a village called Blangy and wanted to fight them that Thursday. But the English requested a truce until the next day, the which was allowed to them. On the morning of the next day, the king of England ordered his battles and at the same moment the dukes of Orléans and Brabant arrived, which caused much rejoicing in the French army, even though they came alone or at least with very few men. All morning, barons, knights and esquires arrived from all parts to assist the French. The French lords sent Guichart Dauphin, the lord of Torcy, the lord of Heilly and others to parley with the king of England. What offers the king of England made to them, no one knows, save the duke of Orléans, as all the others were killed in the battle, and he himself, as soon as he arrived at the battle, was taken prisoner. So at about 11 am in the morning on Friday 24 October the English marched in great array (*en grant ordonnance*) and shouting great shouts, and they came to assemble on the battlefield and against the wings of the lords of France. On the right wing of the French was the count of Richemont, and under him the viscount de la Bellière and the lord of Combourt, and he had on his wing 600 men at arms. The left wing was formed by the count of Vendôme, grand master of the royal household. With him was the baron of Ivry, the lord of Hacqueville, the lord of Aumont, the lord of La Roche-Guyon and all the chamberlains, esquires of the stables, *eschançons, panetiers*, and other officers of the King. On this wing was 600 men at arms. In the vanguard was the sire d'Albret, constable of France, and the Marshal Bouccicaut who had in their company 3,000 men at arms, the duke of Bourbon who had 1,200 men in his company and the duke of Orléans who had 600 men in his, commanded on his behalf by the lord of Gaules. In the [main?] battle was the Duke Edward of Bar who had 600 men in his company, and the count of Nevers who had 1,200 men, and the count of Eu, who had 300 men, and Robert de Bar, count of Marlay who had 400 men, and the count of Vaudemont, brother of the duke of Lorraine with 300 men, and the count of Roussy and of Braine, with 200 men, and the duke of Brabant, brother of the duke of Burgundy, who brought very few men, but all the barons of Hainault who were there put themselves under his banner.

In this company of French were 10,000 men at arms, most of whom were knights and esquires. The constable had ordered a certain number of horsemen to strike against the English, but they achieved little, and the chiefs amongst them were Geoffroi Bouccicaut, the lord of Graville, the lord of la Tremouille, Clignet de Brabant, Jean d'Engenes, Alleaume de Gripennes, Robert de Chalus, and Ponchan de la Tour. The last two died there, and the others – traitors – did not do their duty for they fled shamefully and never even attacked the English. The English king had in his company, along with those of his blood and lineage, 1,500 knights and esquires and 15,000–16,000 archers. He found the French in poor array and in small number, because some had gone off to get warm, others to walk and feed their horses, not believing that the English would be so bold as to attack them. As the English saw them in this disarray, they attacked and discomforted them. This was to the great pity and damage of the kingdom, because there died all the lords named above, save for the dukes of Orléans and Bourbon and the counts of Eu, Vendôme and Richemont, and the Marshal Bouccicaut, who were prisoners of the King and taken to England. On the side of the king of England there died the duke of York his uncle, and 300–400 English. On that field there died of the French 4,000 knights and esquires and 500–600 other men of war.

The King was at Rouen and heard the news, and also how the duke of Brittany had not been there when needed despite the fact that the King had given him 100,000 francs for the payment of his troops, as well as the town and city of Saint Mâlo so that he might be keener to come and serve.

B 13. *Chronique d'Arthur de Richemont* (1458–mid-1460s, French)

Translated from *Chronique d'Arthur de Richemont par Guillaume Gruel*, ed. A. Le Vavasseur (Société de l'Histoire de France, Paris, 1890), pp. 15–20.

Arthur, count of Richemont (1393–1458), was the younger brother of John V duke of Brittany, and was amongst those taken prisoner at Agincourt. The chronicle is essentially his life story, set against events of the Anglo-French war and of the French court under Charles VII, where Richemont became constable in 1425. The author of the work, Guillaume Gruel (c. 1410–1474/82), was a member of a Breton family from Quédillac near Montauban. He and his brother Raoul were raised in the household of the lord of Montauban. Raoul entered the service of Richemont around 1420 and Guillaume about five years later. Raoul's military service with Richemont can be traced, but the precise service and function of Guillaume remains unclear. It seems that he did not write the work until after the death of Richemont in 1458, completing it by the mid-1460s. It may have been based upon earlier written notes. Interestingly, it cites no written source and seems to have relied upon oral testimony. It is likely, therefore, that the account of the battle was learned by Gruel from Richemont himself. The writer tells us that towards the middle of 1436 his master passed through Agincourt again when returning from a journey to the lands of the duke of Burgundy, and that 'he explained to those who were with him how the battle had been' (p. 126). Perhaps Gruel was with him on this occasion. The account is mistaken, however, in thinking that the duke of Clarence was at the battle. It also gives little indication of the fighting, although the finding of Richemont under the bodies of others gives added weight to the notion of a pile up. No mention is made of any disfiguring wounds to Richemont's face, although he is believed to have suffered in this way at the battle.[103]

---

103 See E. Cosneau, *Le Connétable de Richemont* (Paris, 1886) for this and for a full discussion of his career.

Richemont went into captivity in England after the battle, where he was greeted by his mother, Joan of Navarre, duchess of Brittany, who had come to England as the second wife of Henry IV of England in 1403. He would only have been 10, of course, when she had last seen him, so perhaps it is not surprising that he did not recognise her. The story of the meeting, where she could hardly recognise him, may come from Richemont too or from the Breton servant, Catuit, who accompanied him in his captivity. Generally, however, Gruel has little information on what happened during the five years of Richemont's captivity, or else he chooses to skate over it. The work as a whole is valuable for its account of military events, which is not surprising given Richemont's later prominence in the army of Charles VII.

*

Chapter 13. *How Richemont left the siege of Parthenay and went towards the King.*

In the year 1415 Richemont laid siege to Parthenay because the lord of Parthenay supported the party of the duke of Burgundy. Before this, he had taken Vouvant, Mervent, Secondigny and Châtelaillon. Whilst he was before the town of Parthenay news came to him, and the king and duke of Guienne wrote to ask him to put everything else aside and to join them, telling him that King Henry of England had laid siege to Harfleur and that it could scarcely hold out. In order to help the king and the kingdom, Richemont raised his siege of Parthenay in order to go towards where the English were. He made his way to the duke of Guienne, who made him his lieutenant. Richemont gave the duke his standard and put the men of his household at his disposal. From Brittany there were a good 500 knights and esquires amongst whom were the lord of Combour, Bertrand de Montauban, John de Coetquen, Geoffrey de Malestroit, Guillaume Le Veer, and Oliver de la Fueillée, Edward de Rohan and the lord of Busson who carried his banner, and many other knights and esquires. My lord of Richemont went towards the River Somme in order to join with the lords who were gathering to fight the English. Amongst these lords were the dukes of Orléans and Bourbon, the count of Alençon, the constable d'Albret, the duke of Brabant, the counts of Nevers and Eu, Marshal Bouccicaut and many other lords and captains, and a great number of knights and esquires.

Chapter 14. *How Richemont was captured at Agincourt.*

In 1415, on 25 October [sic] they found themselves gathered together, and from the time of vespers lodged near the English in open country less than half a league from the host of the king of England. And on the Friday at daybreak, they began to put their men in battle order, and at about the time of tierce or later they assembled their battles in a place called Agincourt, which was too restricted to fight with so many men. There were a large number of horsemen on our side, Lombards as well as Gascons, who were supposed to make an attack against the English wings. When they experienced the arrowfire coming so thickly, they put to flight and broke the battle line of our men in such a way that they had great difficulty ever getting back into order, with the English always closing on them. As soon as the battle lines engaged, there was fierce and hard fighting. The duke of Clarence, brother of the king of England, was struck with a hammerstroke; the king his brother stood over him in fear that he might be killed, and received such a blow to his crown that he fell to his knees. Two others who were dressed just like the king were killed, and the uncle of the king, the duke of Exeter, was killed, as were many others. However, after less than an hour, according to the will of God who is master of battles, our men were discomforted, dead, captured or in flight. They had numbered 10,000 fighting men; the king of England had a good 11,000–12,000 men. There were captured the duke of Orléans, the duke of Bourbon, and the count of Richemont who was pulled from under the dead, a little wounded, being recognised by his coat of arms even though it was all bloody, for two or three had been killed over him. He was led to the king of England who rejoiced in his capture more than any other. There were also captured the count of Eu, the count of Vendôme and many other lords and captains. And there died in that engagement the following: the count [recte, duke] of Alençon, the duke of Brabant, the count of Nevers, the Constable d'Albret, John, lord of Bar. Under the banner of Richemont and from his company there died the lord of Combour, Sir Bertrand de Montauban, Sir Jean de Coetquen, Sir Geoffrey de Malestroit, the lord of Châteaugiron, Sir Guillaume de la Forest, Sir Guillaume le Veer and several others, and amongst those taken prisoner were Ydouart de Rohan, Sir Olivier de la Fueillée, Sir Jean Giffart and the lord of Busson.

Chapter 15. *How Richemont was left in the guard of the English.*

Then the king of England returned to lodge at Maisoncelles, the place he had left at midday. On the next day he departed and made for Calais, taking his prisoners with him, and from there he went to England. And with Richemont there remained only one servant called Jennin Catuit.

Chapter 16. *How the queen his mother had leave from the King to see him.*

Quite soon afterwards, when he was in London, the Queen, who was mother of the count of Richemont, asked leave of the king of England to see her son, who was a prisoner, and the king allowed her to do so. His guards led him towards the Queen, his mother. When she knew he was coming, she put one of her ladies in her place – a lady who would know how to speak to him and receive him – and placed herself in the midst of her other ladies, placing two ladies in front of herself. When Richemont arrived, he believed the lady who was pretending to be his mother to actually be her, and greeted her paying her his respects. The lady talked to him for a while then said to him that he should go and kiss the other ladies. When he came near the Queen, her heart melted, and she said to him 'My poor son, you did not recognise me', and both of them began to cry but afterwards were very happy. His mother the Queen gave him 1,000 *nobles* which he shared between his fellow prisoners and his guards. She also gave him shirts and other garments. He did not dare thenceforward to speak to her nor to visit her as he wished.

B 14. *Chronique de Normandie* (1460s, French)

Translated by the editor in *Henrici Quinti Angliae Regis Gesta, cum Chronica Neustriae*, ed. B. Williams (London 1850), pp. 216–21.

A manuscript of this chronicle in the Bibliothèque Municipale of Rouen is considered to be the hand of Georges Chastellain (1404–1474), herald of the order of the Golden Fleece and 'historiographe' and councillor of Philip the Good and Charles the Rash as dukes of Burgundy, although it may not be his own work.[104] It shows a pro-Burgundian line for instance in falsely accrediting Duke Philip with making the arrangements for burials. It also implies that the numbers of English dead were higher than others have said. Generally, the account of the battle is similar to that found elsewhere, with the notion of a company of French cavalry aimed at riding down the English archers. Interestingly, a copy of the chronicle was made by William Worcester, secretary to Sir John Fastolf.[105] Williams notes that it was drawn upon by Robert Fabyan and later by Thomas Goodwin.

*

Harfleur remained with the English from 24 September, on which account the Pays de Caux was ruined, and the smaller fortresses burnt and destroyed. The earl of Dorset remained in garrison at that town of Harfleur, with a strong company of English; the king of England, with all his army, set out on 10 October to go to Calais by land, but his brother, the duke of Clarence, went by sea on account of his sickness. The king of

---

[104] For a full study of the works of Chastelain, see G. Small, *George Chastelain and the Shaping of Valois Burgundy. Political and Historical Culture at Court in the Fifteenth Century* (Woodbridge, 1997).
[105] College of Arms, Arundel MS xlviii.

England then passed through the Pays de Caux, thinking to pass the Somme at Blanchetaque, but the people of the king of France, who pursued them, and were then at Abbeville, disputed the passage with them, and the English were obliged to proceed higher up the river as far as Abbeville, and thence to Amiens, to Corbie, and to Péronne, beyond which place they crossed the river at night.

In the town of Péronne were the dukes of Bourbon and of Alençon (who had been created a duke on the feast of Christmas preceding, when his county was changed into a duchy) the duke of Bar, the counts of Eu, of Vendôme, and of Richemont, the lord d'Albret, constable of France, and the Marshal Bouccicaut, accompanied by a great many horsemen, inasmuch that they were computed to be ten thousand men-at-arms, who pursued the king of England's army; but as soon as they knew that the English had crossed the River Somme, they took the field and pursued them, and so the English rode straight to Hesdin, because the two armies had promised, by their heralds, to give each other battle on Thursday 24 October, but the French who pursued them, immediately that they knew they had passed the Somme, took the field, and the English did not keep to their covenant that day, but held on their way more to the left than in their direct course; which when the French perceived, they rode forward straight across the country to get ahead of them, at the ford of a river which runs to Blangy in Ternois, so that on that same Thursday, at vespers, the two armies were in sight of each other, and encamped near each other that night.

On Friday the twenty-fifth day of the same month, being the feast of Saint Crispin, at break of day, both sides prepared for battle. At that hour the French were joined by the dukes of Orléans and of Brabant, and by the count of Nevers his brother, who had each brought his little band, resolved to stand or fall with them in the said battle. On that day they were drawn up in order of battle in a valley near Agincourt, and the French had then appointed 300 horsemen in armour to rout the English archers who were between the main bodies of the two armies, and when the horsemen had formed they thought to charge the archers, but the shower of arrows fell upon them so thickly, that they were compelled to retreat amongst their own people, by which they broke their vanguard, which was close by ready for action. At the same moment both the horsemen and the foot soldiers ran to fall upon and pillage the horses and baggage of the English which they had left in the rear during the battle. Such was the commencement of the battle on that day in the valley before mentioned, where the ground was so soft that the French foundered in it, for which cause and from their line being broken by their own horse, they could not again join battle, but were more and more defeated, and, as God would have it, lost the day. It was then a pitiful sight to behold the dead and the wounded who covered the field, and the number of men-at-arms who turned and fled.

When the duke of Alençon saw the French in such disorder, he mounted his horse and attempted to rally them, but in vain, for he could do nothing; and when he saw that there was no help for it, he returned to the fight, which still continued, where, as was said, he then performed such feats of arms, and fought so gallantly, that it was marvellous to behold, and so there he fell. Now, the duke of Brittany and his people, and the people of Louis the late king of Sicily, were not present on that day. On the Thursday they lay at Amiens, and as they were setting out on the Friday, they received the news of the defeat, on which account the duke returned, although they were numerous enough to have given the English battle again. In that battle died the dukes of Brabant, of Alençon, and of Bar, the count of Nevers, and the lord d'Albret, who was constable of France, with seven or eight thousand knights and esquires of France and of Hainault, besides several who were taken prisoner. On the side of the English died the duke of York and the earl of Suffolk, and of the other ranks a great number that could not exactly be known because the dead lay all together. The prisoners taken on that day were the dukes of Orléans and of Bourbon, the counts of Eu, Vendôme, and Richemont, the Marshal Bouccicaut, and many others. When the battle was over, the people of the king of Sicily came up, when the English feared that they should be again attacked, on which account proclamation was made that each man should put to death his prisoner, except the nobles, and for this cause many prisoners were put to death. The English encamped on the field that same Friday night, and stripped the dead of their arms.

On the morrow, Saturday, 26 October, the king of England, with all his lords who survived that battle, left the field, and rode towards Guines, and thence to Calais, where they refreshed themselves; and then the count of Charolais, eldest son of the Duke of Burgundy, who was at Arras, caused the field to be consecrated, and the dead to be interred, except the bodies of the nobility, whom he caused to be carried each to his own territory

B 15. Thomas Basin, *Histoire de Charles VII* (1471–72, Latin)

Translated from Thomas Basin, *Histoire de Charles VII*, ed. C. Samaran and H. De Saint-Rémy, 2 vols (Les Classiques de l'Histoire de France au Moyen Age, Paris, 1934–44), vol. 1 (1934), pp. 34–49.

Thomas Basin was born in 1412 at Caudebec in Normandy, so was a young child living close to Harfleur at the time of Henry's first invasion. When the conquest of Normandy began in earnest, the Basin family initially chose exile in Brittany but later returned. Thomas studied canon law at the University of Paris. He was involved as an envoy and in time acquired a canonry at Rouen as well as other benefices in English-held Normandy. After the English founded a University at Caen, he became professor of canon law there and was also a canon of Bayeux and vicar general of the dioceses of Rouen. In 1447 he was appointed to the bishopric of Lisieux, and also served as president of the Norman *chambre des comptes*. When Charles VII took the duchy in 1449–50, Basin soon changed his allegiance, and in time became a royal councillor. He supported the anti-royal side in the War of the Public Weal and so fell out of favour with Louis XI. He was obliged to renounce his bishopric, in exchange for which Pope Sixtus IV conferred upon him the honorary title of archbishop of Caesarea. He spent the rest of his life in exile first in Switzerland and later Germany. It was in Trier from 1470 to 1476 that he wrote all of his *Histoire de Charles VII*, part of his *Histoire de Louis XI* and an *Apologia*. He died at Utrecht in 1491.

The *Histoire de Charles VII* was probably written between 1471 and 1472. Basin was familiar with the historians of ancient Rome and keen to emulate them, seeing history as providing examples for future generations to follow. Many chapters include personal observations. Some passages suggest a familiarity with the works of Jean Juvenal des Ursins and Monstrelet. He later gives much space to the recovery of Normandy by Charles VII, and generally gives a very favourable picture of the monarch. But he also praises the English at least in the 1420s for their exercise of justice in Normandy, and for their bringing of some modicum of peace to a world devastated by civil war, though his growing disillusionment with English rule is also apparent – in this respect, his comment that the destroyers will in time themselves be destroyed. There is also an anti-Burgundian flavour to his account, claiming, for instance, that Henry invaded in 1415 with the support of the duke of Burgundy. The Burgundian attack on Soissons is also highlighted and Agincourt raised and then cleverly dismissed as a manifestation of God's punishment. Basin is also influenced by classical sources in Henry's battle speech and in the quote from Vergil.

*

Chapter 7. *How the king of England besieged and captured Harfleur.*

Having thus decided to invade the kingdom of France, Henry assembled a great fleet and an invasion force of hand-picked men, numbering no more than, or so it is said, 12,000–15,000 men, in addition to the pilots and the merchants who followed the army. Strengthened by the support and encouragement of the duke of Burgundy, he headed for the open sea [account of siege follows]. So began the English conquests in France and in Normandy: the citadel of Harfleur, which had been made famous by the exploits of its pirates, fell prey to its enemies. It is with good cause that our Lord, through the mouth of Isaiah, threatened in these terms similar destroyers, 'Woe be upon you. You who steal will you not be victims of theft yourselves. You who deceive, will you not yourselves be deceived. You who ravage, will you not also be ravaged yourselves?

Chapter 8. *How the king of England went into Picardy with his army crossing the Pays de Caux.*

After the surrender of Harfleur, as it was already the month of October, the king of England decided to take overland to Calais (which was on the frontier with Flanders) the expeditionary army which he had led to Harfleur by sea. Perhaps he could thus entice the French to fight with him. So armed, he took his path across the Pays de Caux, ravaging everything on his route. Then crossing the Somme he entered Picardy.

The princes and magnates of the kingdom of France thought that it would be a great dishonour to them if they let the English depart loaded with booty and leading a great crowd of prisoners after they had committed so much devastation throughout the whole of their long march. So they assembled, with all the nobility of the kingdom and the men-at-arms, a great army, four times as large and stronger than the English army. With justification could one apply to the English this verse of Vergil: 'Small in number yet most valiant in war'.

The French, on the other hand, although adequately vigorous, of warlike spirit and well instructed in the pursuit of war, lacked military order and discipline. Moreover, a long period of peace and tranquillity had made them lack experience in the exercise of arms. From all parts of the kingdom, great and less great princes, dukes, counts, barons, knights and nobles gathered in huge numbers and resolved to move to engage with the king of England and his army in order to prevent his advance. They did this in order to force him to fight. Some of them reported – we are not sure whether it really was like this – that the king of England realising that so large and strong and army was coming to meet him, had offered to surrender Calais and to pay a great sum in gold so that he might be allowed to return home without his men suffering any harm. But this offer was rejected and he prepared himself, as he was forced to do by necessity, to accept the challenge of battle.

The day approached when it would be decided. The troops (*acies*) of both sides were drawn up and ordered and the king of England spoke to his army in these words before battle was engaged:

'The moment has come, my fine and valorous comrades in arms, when we must fight not for glory and for the honour of your name, but for your very existence. We who are only too aware of the presumption of the French and their state of mind, we know for certain that if, by cowardice or fear you let them beat you, they will give no quarter to any of you. Whoever you are, whether noble or plebeian, they will slaughter you like beasts. Neither I nor the princes of my royal blood can expect such a fate for if they beat us they will hope to gain great sums and will thus take care to keep us alive rather than killing us. As for you, if you wish to avoid such a threat, cast all fear from your spirit and do not hope that the enemy will keep you in order to allow you to ransom your lives by money because they hate you with a hate as long-established as it is bitter. So, if it is sweeter to live than to die, remember, in the manner of strength, your nobility and the fame and glory won by the English on the field of battle and fight like men, with valour and courage, for the sake of your souls.'

As a result of the king's speech, the bravery of the English increased amazingly. They realised that they could not rely on their safety unless, by fighting more strongly, they overcame their enemy.

Chapter 9. *Battle of Agincourt between the French and English.*

Raising horrible cries, they began to bend their bows with all their might and to let fly arrows into the enemy in such quantities that their density obscured the sky just like a cloud. The arrows were so numerous that it seemed as though a thick harvest had suddenly sprung up in the field. They advanced whilst firing at the enemy wounding so many horses on which the French were mounted and men also, killing a good number, so that even before they came to hand to hand fighting, the French turned round and were suffocated in the crush. It was with little labour and without any damage that the victory fell to the English. It was a pitiful sight to see how, once their ranks had been broken, confusion spread amongst the French army, and how many of them tried to save their skins by fleeing. Ten Englishmen pursued a hundred Frenchmen, and one Englishman ten Frenchmen. When they were caught by the English they put up no resistance and put their sole hope in flight. They thus let themselves be killed or be led off as captives like a flock of sheep.

In this battle fell the duke of Alençon, the count [sic] of Albret and a great multitude of other counts, barons, knights and nobles. Anthony, duke of Brabant was killed with his company whose arrival as the battle had almost come to a close gave occasion to the English to kill many of those they had taken prisoner. Prisoners included the duke of Orléans, son of the duke whose violent death at Paris we have recorded earlier, the duke of Bourbon, Charles, count of Eu, and numerous counts, barons and nobles who were all taken by the victorious king to Calais and thence to England. It was an inauspicious day for the nobility and the kingdom of France for it destroyed a great part of those who could defend the kingdom against the enemy. This was a cause of great ruin and destruction to the kingdom, as we shall show throughout the pages which follow.

This unlucky battle was fought near to the town of Hesdin in the fields of two villages, the one Agincourt, the other Ruisseauville, in the year of our lord 1415, on the day of Sts Crispin and Crispinian. A year had passed since the French had wretchedly sacked the city of Soissons, as we recounted above, and amongst other sacrilegious acts, had despoiled the venerable monastery which was dedicated to those blessed martyrs. So it was commonly believed that this disaster was divinely inflicted on the

French because of their acts of impiety and their cruelty which they had committed in great numbers and to such a great degree by their sacking of that city and their plundering of the saints' shrines. Everyone can think what they will. We, however, will be content to tell the facts in true narrative fashion leaving the discussion of the arcane workings of the divine will to those who presume to do so.

In this battle John, duke of Brittany, although summoned, did not appear. He came to Amiens with a great number of his Bretons, estimated to be together 10,000 men, but preferred to await the outcome of the battle rather than to come closer to the danger. Once the battle was over, without even getting a sight of the enemy he returned home but not without committing damage to the places which he passed through.

B 16. *Chronique d'Antonio Morosini* (?1430s, Italian)

Translated from *Chronique d'Antonio Morosini*, ed. G. Le Fèvre-Pontalis and L. Dorez, 4 vols (Société de l'Histoire de France, Paris, 1898–1902), vol. 2 (1899), pp. 43–69.

Morosini was a member of a leading Venetian family, nephew of Michele Morosini who had been doge in 1382.[106] He came of age in 1377, was a member of the council of state of Venice in 1388, and was still alive in 1433. He was certainly already involved in historical writing in 1418 when he was ordered by the council to deliver two of his chronicles which were considered to contain materials of danger to the security of the state. These were examined and ordered to be destroyed but it is not clear how they related to his surviving work. The latter is essentially a history of Venice but the section from 1403 to 1433 takes the form of a diary and is written in a Venetian dialect. Morosini was particularly interested in the activities of Venetians overseas and in maritime matters, as the extract shows. The volumes were printed by the Société de l'Histoire de France because they contained so much material on events in France. Later sections contain interesting material on Joan of Arc, and also on the death of Henry V where there is a mention of rumours that he had died of leprosy.

The value of this account is that it shows something of the way in which news was carried overseas. Note too the rumoured size of the English army, as well as later rumours that the French thought they would soon have victory. But as Morosini was later informed, 'matters had gone from bad to worse'. The scale and impact of the French defeat were well appreciated in Venice, and it is a pity that there is not more time or space to explore this in writings from other countries.

---

[106] Le Fèvre-Pontalis provides a useful introduction in volume 4.

(p. 43) Then we learned that it was clear that the ambassadors of the king of France had returned to the king of England for discussions towards peace, and afterwards that they had achieved nothing in the matter of the marriage which was under discussion between the kings, and that the ambassadors had returned to France on 1 August 1415. In addition, by a letter coming from England and sent from there by Jacomo Sabbadini, written on 18 July 1415, the latter wrote in this manner to his brother Nicholas who was here in Venice, on [ ] August. He said that the Genoese were in open war with the English and that the latter had armed a great fleet (*armada*) to move against the Genoese, and he wrote that there was war to the death, more serious than ever before. The reason for this had been the capture by a Genoese carrack, of an English carrack loaded with much merchandise. Later we learned that the king of Portugal had taken into his pay all the ships he could get, to the number of 200, and that in addition the king had armed a fleet so that there was at sea 1,400 sail or more to fight with France. He said that it was rumoured that there would be 100,000 men or more coming out of the island of England, and that the duke of Burgundy was discussing matters with the king of France and had entered into his allegiance. [He repeats the failure of the French embassy to England, with the concluding line *Dio faza el meiody Christiany*! (God help Christianity!).]

By a messenger coming from Flanders, leaving there on 18 August, by numerous letters coming from our men in those parts, we heard news confirmed in substance by a letter of our Nicolas Michele to Castellano Michele de San Cassiano. The contents of his letter was thus. 'First he said that the fleet of the English King had begun to move in whole convoy and that many said that it had already started to cross but no one was sure about this, and that he himself did not believe it. Then that there had been a plot [an account of the Southampton plot follows].

Despite this turn of events, it seemed that the king was still disposed to follow his fleet, which could end in disaster, not just because other similar plots might arise but also because he was attacking a great power – all the lords of France were in agreement and were well provided. God put them in firm peace, for if peace did arise it would be to the great profit of commerce, but if war occurred, the opposite would be the case. I pray to God that he will dispose things for the best.' Following this, other letters received from several of our men mentioned that many ships of the English king's fleet had arrived in Normandy, on the coast of France. Likewise we learned from England, by letters written on 10 August that the king's fleet or at least part of it, had arrived in France in a place called La Fosse [de Leure], then at Harfleur on 14 August, and we learned that the French were handling the English roughly and that the English found the French very powerful so that they could not cause them damage.

These letters were received at Venice on 18 September 1415, and we learned that the duke of Burgundy had allied with the French and that there were hopes of peace. . . .

(p. 59) We had news by a ship coming from Flanders, by letters written on 12 September by our men there that our galleys in Flanders, captained by Pietro Loredano, son of Alvise, procurator, had left there (that is four loaded galleys) on 1 September with their loading scarcely completed and that they had left their merchandise on shore. We learned that if they had stayed longer, they would have been seized by the fleet of the king of England, as had happened to several other vessels and ships of all Christian peoples and races, in order to accomplish his designs against the power of the king of France.

And then we learned how a part of the royal fleet had arrived at the town of Harfleur and about 30,000 soldiers had disembarked, and that the king himself appeared a day and a half later. Then we learned about the same time that the English arrived there and gave battle three times a day to the French, finding their resistance very powerful, and that as there were about 500 barons of the kingdom of France with very great forces, they could no nothing against them. As a result it was thought, according to what had been written to us, that there could not fail to be a big battle where a great shedding of blood would occur on both sides with an immeasurable loss of life, and that there could be no question of an agreement. What new information we learn subsequently, we shall make full mention.

On Wednesday 16 October we learned that the fleet of the English king had arrived at Harfleur and that the captain of the place called [blank], there for the king of England, had surrendered to the English by means of a plot the place wherein were 10,000 Frenchmen, and we learned that the captain had defected to the English. In addition, it was said, by letters coming to Venice for the Florentine company of Giovanni de Cajano, that, at this news the king of France, fearing he would lose Paris, had negotiated with the duke of Burgundy and that the latter had returned to Paris to hold the peace in surety and guard against treason . . .

(p. 69) At this time news came to Venice from the region of Flanders, by one of our merchants, that the fleet (*armada*) of the king of England had left Harfleur, that men of the king of France intended to fight with the English, who had suffered 6,000 deaths [at Harfleur] and that as a result of such losses the English had withdrawn to go to Calais. We learned that the English had been trapped at the crossing of a bridge because the bridge had been broken, and that they thus could not escape from the French and were therefore compelled to give battle. We learned too that it was thought that the French would soon have victory with the aid of God, and that the plague was on a large scale in those areas.

Copy of a letter written from Paris on 30 October received in Venice on 1 December 1415, coming from Nicholas de Carcanetti de Lucca.

First of all the letter said that matters had gone from bad to worse. The lords of France had been routed in a battle fought with the English on 25 October in a location called Artois between France and Picardy, and at the battle had died the duke of Orléans and many other gentlemen, and amongst the prisoners were firstly the duke of Bourbon, then the duke of Alençon, the count of Nevers, the constable, the marshal, then monsieur Bouccicaut and the *maître* of the royal household, the admiral, and many other barons and lords, to such a degree that never had such bad fortune or such a great defeat been heard of. This letter also said that the kingdom had fallen into the wrath of God, and that it would soon be destroyed by its divisions, and that if things did not change, the kingdom would be lost. May God restore and assist them as necessity required. What would happen next will soon be known. This news was also received by the seignory by means of Genoa, Lucca and Verona. What followed we shall tell in due course, but it was a notable loss to our state of Venice.

I will write below the lords killed in the battle between France and England, then the French prisoners taken by the English, as appears below. First of all the dead – the duke of Brabant, the duke of Bar, the duke of Alençon, the constable of France, the count of Nevers, the count of Marlay, the brother of the duke of Bar, the Bastard of Bourbon, the lord of Waurin and his son, the lord of la Haimaide, the sire of Liederkerke, monsieur Erioch, his brother, the lord of Fosseux with his five brothers, the marshal of Hainault, the lord of Harnes, the lord of Roncq, monsieur Anthony de Graon, the prévôt of Paris, the lord of Nonzelar, esquire, monsieur Roland d'Oignies, the lord of Rasse. Total 26.

These are the prisoners – the duke of Orléans, the duke of Bourbon, the count of Eu, the count of Richemont, Bouccicaut, marshal, monsieur Louis de Ghistelle, the lord of Ligne and his brother, the lord of Heilly, monsieur Charles de Savoisy, monsieur Hugh de Lannoy, monsieur Guillaume, his brother, monsieur Atis de Brimeu. Total 13.

This news was confirmed more fully by a messenger who arrived, and we know with certainty that it was a notable loss to the French to the extent that more than 10,000–12,000 had fallen in addition to the barons who had been killed or taken prisoner, as noted in the list given above.

2

Sixteenth-Century Historians in England

In many ways it is difficult to say when 'chronicling' ended and 'history' began. Some of the writings of the sixteenth century were much influenced by the genres of the previous century. This is most apparent in the continuing legacy of the London Chronicle and *Brut* traditions, for many of the sixteenth-century writers of history were themselves based in London and keen to draw on and emulate the existing practices. But already towards the end of the fifteenth century, several developments occurred which were to have a marked effect on the nature of historical writing.[1]

One was the introduction of printing. At first, however, this had the effect of strengthening rather than undermining existing traditions for Caxton printed two editions of the *Brut* (1480 and 1482). Thus that style of vernacular chronicle became even more firmly and widely known. As the years passed, the power of the printer increased, and it is no coincidence that some of the authors considered in this chapter were printers as well as authors in their own right. Not only did they publish their own histories but they also put into print the works of contemporaries, and as significantly perhaps, some of the manuscript chronicles of the previous century. Thus Grafton printed Hardyng's chronicle in 1543, and Stow assisted Matthew Parker, archbishop of Canterbury, in a project to print several medieval chronicles amongst which were Thomas Walsingham's *Historia Anglicana* and *Ypodigma Neustriae* (1574).[2] These brought to a wider audience and to historians of the period sources to which they might otherwise not have had access, and was one of the explanations, although not the only one, which led to some of them citing a long list of sources on which they had drawn in the writing of their history.

The second development was the coming of the Tudor dynasty. The early Tudors were keen to fortify their position by whatever means they could and employed various techniques of what we would call propaganda to denigrate

---

[1] For useful general studies of the works of the period, see P. Levy, *Tudor Historical Thought* (San Marino, California, 1967) and M. McKisack, *Medieval History in the Tudor Age* (Oxford, 1971). Gransden and *EHL* also provide instructive insights. A listing of publications is to be found in *A Short-Title Catalogue of Books printed in England, Scotland and Ireland and of English books printed abroad 1475–1640*, ed. W.A. Jackson, F.S. Ferguson and K.F. Pantzer, 2nd edition, 3 vols (London, 1976–91).

[2] McKisack, *Medieval History in the Tudor Age*, p. 41.

their predecessors. This included the commissioning or encouragement of histories which justified their accession against the background of civil turmoil in the fifteenth century. Three works are relevant here. The first, the *Historia Regum Angliae* (History of the Kings of England) of John Rous (1411–91) takes the form of a general history from Brutus to the accession of Henry VII and was probably completed in 1486.[3] Although Rous had been a Yorkist supporter for most of his life, the coming of the new dynasty inspired a concluding section which praises the new king, Henry VII, and states hopes for the future under his recently born son, Prince Arthur. Interestingly, Rous's section on the reign of Henry V does not mention Agincourt by name nor is there any account of the battle. Rous merely mentions that in his time Henry V was second to none in terms of military prowess, that it was commonly held that he deserved perpetual praise for his prowess and his wisdom, that he conquered Normandy with a strong hand, married Catherine and became heir and regent of France. The lack of detail is surprising given that it is known that Rous drew on the *Brut* as well as the chronicles of John Streeche (who also hailed from Warwickshire) and of John Hardyng elsewhere in the *Historia*.[4] It might be dangerous to suggest, however, that Rous was deliberately omitting mention of the battle because of his desire to please the Tudors (or even the Yorkists) by denigrating their Lancastrian predecessors. It seems more a reflection that Rous's interests lay elsewhere, as is revealed by the other aspects of the reign which he mentions. Reference to Henry's 'pleasaunce' at Kenilworth Castle reflects Rous's local and antiquarian interests. The mention that Henry studied at Queen's College, Oxford, as prince, when Henry Beaufort was chancellor of the university, may reflect his desire to link the current monarch with his Beaufort Lancastrian forebears, but this, and the reference to the foundation of the University of Caen (which is wrongly placed in Henry's reign rather than that of his son) and to the new Scottish universities reveals Rous's own scholarly concerns and background.

Two later works were composed with a much stronger intention of showing how the Tudors had redeemed England from the turmoils of the past. Polydore Vergil's *Anglica Historia* was commissioned by Henry VII for this purpose, and later Edward Hall composed an even more obvious eulogy in his *Union of the Two Noble and Illlustre Families of Lancaster and York*, which gave a shape and unity to the history of the fifteenth century by seeing the turmoils arising out of the deposition of Richard II being settled by the accession of Henry VII, and even more cogently perhaps by that of Henry VIII who in his person embodied the 'Union' of York and Lancaster. Although this view of the past gave a generally critical view of the Lancastrian kings, both writers found it difficult to denigrate Henry V because of his military achievements and his reputation as a

---

3   *Johannis Rossi Antiquarii Warwicensis Historia Regum Angliae*, ed. T. Hearne, 1st edition (Oxford, 1716). I have used the 2nd edition of 1745, where the section concerning the reign of Henry V is pp. 207–9. For Rous and his works see Gransden, pp. 309–27.
4   Gransden, p. 322.

firm and pious ruler. Thus accounts of Agincourt in their, and in other, Tudor writings remained eulogistic, triumphant and patriotic in tone, as will be seen in the extracts given in this chapter. Hall even catered for English national pride antithetically by putting into the mouth of the constable of France several anti-English remarks whose effect is all the more potent when one knows the outcome of the battle, as all of his audience would have done: 'keep an Englishman one month from his warm bed, fat beef and stale drink . . . you shall then see his courage abated, his body wax lean and bare, and ever desirous to return into his own country'.

Such sentiments were further encouraged by the fact that the French remained the enemy for most of the reign of Henry VII and VIII at least, and there is a strong suspicion that the composition of one of the works considered below, the *First English Life of Henry V*, was in part stimulated by Henry VIII's own expeditions to France. Moreover, the new century was not without chivalric tastes. It has been suggested that Henry VIII and his circle were instrumental in reviving some of the knightly and courtly traditions of the past.[5] Thus in 1532, Lord Berners completed a translation into English of the chronicles of Jean Froissart which dealt with the fourteenth-century phases of the Hundred Years War and which had as their stated aim the recording of great deeds in arms. The *First English Life* also fits into this revived interest in chivalric achievement. Later in the century, John Stow included 'exploits worthy of great renowne' and 'incouragement of nobilitie to noble feates' in his justificatory preface.[6]

Many of the other writers from whom extracts are taken in this chapter were keen to 'enhance the fame of the heroes of the past'.[7] In this respect they were perhaps little different from their fifteenth-century predecessors, although it might be suggested that a third development had prompted them to this cult of heroes. This was the influence of humanism, as an element of a renaissance which had begun in Italy, and which had led to a renewed interest in, and knowledge of, classical sources. The latter was not lacking in the previous century, as we saw in the works of Walsingham, Tito Livio and the Pseudo Elmham, but it was more widespread as time went on and began to give much more of a shape and distinctive character to historical composition as well as a strong didactic element.[8] Polydore Vergil's *Anglica Historia* was an example for others to follow, and the rhetoric of humanist Latin also found its way into sixteenth-century English prose styles with the invention of speeches and moral exemplars. Hall was a master of this, especially in the use of orations. See too his comment at the end of the battle: 'this battle may be a mirror and glass to all

[5] Gransden, p. 476. See also A. Ferguson, *The Indian Summer of English Chivalry* (Durham, North Carolina, 1960).
[6] *A Summarie of Englysche Chronicles*, as cited in Levy, *Tudor Historical Thought*, p. 168.
[7] Gransden, p. 476 citing Hall, *Union*, p. v, and McKisack, *Medieval History in the Tudor Age*, pp. 105–6.
[8] There is a useful general discussion of humanism in England in Levy, *Tudor Historical Thought*, chapter 2.

Christian princes to behold and follow'. Later writers copied his style as well as content and method. This approach also gave much more place to the investigation of causes of events and of the motives of those who shaped them. Man was still not in complete control of his destiny, but in place of rather helpless fatalism or resignation to the hazards of fortune, there was a stronger notion of God working though man to create history. There was also much interest in the will and demeanour of princes and in the operation of power. History was also given a shape and a purpose, as in Hall's *Union*, which Gransden sees as a renaissance history with 'its emphasis on secular power and its predominantly secular tone, and in its literary and thematic unity'.[9] It also encouraged what we would term research, the desire to seek out sources. Polydore tells us that he 'first began to spend the hours of my night and day in searching the pages of English and foreign histories . . . spent six whole years in reading those annals and histories during which, imitating the bees which laboriously gather their honey from every flower, I collected with discretion material proper for a true history.'[10] He certainly drew on a wide range of chronicles, including Monstrelet, as well as on statutes and oral traditions. Actual physical collections of materials were made, as, for instance, by Stow, who was particularly energetic in consulting manuscripts as well as printed books. The nobility and gentry were also sometimes keen collectors: the library of John, Baron Lumley (d. 1609) contained a volume with extracts from the Pseudo-Elmham, which eventually passed into royal and, in time, national hands.[11] A similar fate awaited the collection of Sir Robert Cotton (d. 1631), now in the British Library, and of considerable significance because it contained manuscripts and copies of administrative materials as well as chronicles.

Efforts were also made to compare different versions, and to authenticate what was said in order to give authority and status to a work. This is revealed by the tendency to place at the beginning of a history a list of the materials consulted. Hall used a wide range, more than Polydore. Stow's list in the preface to the 1601 edition of the *Annales* is perhaps the most impressive, with references to many of the fifteenth-century English chronicles as well as to Monstrelet and the *Chroniques de Normandie*, Canterbury records, Parliament records, the register of the order of the Garter, and an entry termed rather mysteriously, 'old records'. There is little evidence of extensive work in official records but clearly there was some. In the 1586–7 edition of Holinshed, catalogues of writers were listed at the end of each reign. We see also the use of marginal notes which accredit the source of information. An early example of the latter occurs in the *First English Life*, and it is also found in Stow and Holinshed, although the use is often inconsistent.[12] Writers also include phrases

9   Gransden, p. 471.
10 As cited in *EHL*, pp. 256–7.
11 McKisack, *Medieval History in the Tudor Age*, p. 55, now British Library, Royal MS 13 A.XVI.
12 A. Patterson, *Reading Holinshed's Chronicles* (Chicago and London, 1994), p. 35.

of reference, such as 'Hall showeth', 'Enguerran (de Monstrelet) saith'. In the context of Agincourt, the consultation of French chronicles is of particular significance for it allowed both sides of the story to be seen, at least where it suited an English writer to do so. Monstrelet was much used for it was first printed in Paris in 1500 and then on at least six other occasions over the course of the century.[13] Writers debated their sources, as for instance in Hall's comments on the numbers of English dead – only a handful 'if you will give credit to such as write miracles, but other writers whom I sooner believe' give larger numbers, and he suggests they are more likely correct on the evidence that the battle was 'earnestly and furiously fought for the space of three long hours'. The consultation of a wide range of sources encouraged a stronger concept of historical truth, although this was by no means as complete as in today's empiricism, and there was a lack of real discernment, although writers might criticise each other's standards of scholarship as in the dispute between Stow and Grafton over the merits of their respective histories.[14]

This was, however, by no means exclusively 'secular' history. The Reformation had not led to the removal of God's will as a central cause, and there was still a strong concept of a divine plan.[15] The particular circumstances of the English experience had led writers to seek in medieval sources justification for royal supremacy and for a concept of an English church independent of foreign control, as in Hall and Redmayne in particular.[16] Hall's *Union* was included in a

---

[13] Most other French chronicles were not printed until the seventeenth century. Des Ursins was printed in 1614 and Le Fèvre in 1663. Although Waurin's chronicle was transcribed for Godefroy towards publication, it did not appear in print until 1863.

[14] Stow also got into trouble for collecting old, 'popish' texts, which allowed Grafton to accuse him of encouraging rebellion (Patterson, *Reading Holinshed's Chronicles*, p. 23). Richard Grafton (d. 1572) is an extremely interesting figure. A prosperous London merchant, it was his zeal for Protestantism which led him to have an interest in printing, being responsible for Coverdale's translation of the Bible and the first prayer book of 1549. He printed Hardyng's chronicle in 1543 with a continuation of his own which drew on Thomas More's *Life of Richard III*. In 1548 he printed Hall's *Union* with a continuation to the death of Henry VIII. He subsequently published under his own authorship *The Abridgement of the Chronicles of England* (1562) and *The Chronicle at Large* (1568). With these publications began a bitter feud with John Stow, who himself produced a similar brace of works (see below Text C 5), and who claimed that Grafton's work was inaccurate and of poor quality (see McKisack, *Medieval History in the Tudor Age*, pp. 111–13). Certainly Grafton's account of the battle of Agincourt in *The Chronicle at Large* (reprinted in 2 vols, London, 1809), vol. 1, pp. 513–20, follows Hall almost word for word save for the omission of the latter's lengthy invented speeches. For that reason it has been omitted from this collection, although the importance of Grafton as a printer must not be underemphasised, and there is some suggestion that he was a source for Shakespeare rather than Hall himself (L.B. Campbell, *Shakespeare's Histories: Mirrors of Elizabethan Policy* (San Marino, California, 1947), p. 72).

[15] McKisack, *Medieval History in the Tudor Age*, pp. 121–2

[16] Redmayne wrote a *Vita Henrici Quinti* which C.A. Cole included in *Memorials of Henry the Fifth, King of England* (Rolls series, London, 1858). Cole dated the work to the late 1530s or early 1540s, but R. Reid ('The date and authorship of Redmayne's "Life of Henry V"', *EHR*, 30 (1915), pp. 691–8) has argued convincingly that it was written between 1574 and 1578 by a Richard Redman (d. 1625) who was a lawyer and chancellor of the diocese of

list of banned books under Mary. Generally, however, as Protestantism won the day, it was as important to have histories in English as scriptures.[17] Interestingly, although Redmayne (as also John Bale), gave John Oldcastle a good press, this did not prevent Henry V having one too, despite his persecution of Lollardy.[18] The didactic purpose of history of the humanist tradition was fused with the moral examples of religious instruction. Gransden provides important quotations on this aspect from three of the writers cited below. 'To Edward Hall history was "the key to induce virtue and repress vice"; to Stow it provided "persuasions to honesty, godliness and virtue of all sort"; and Raphael Holinshed thought that chronicles (which "unto the holy scripture . . . do carry credit") were full of profitable lessons.'[19] It was partly the breaking up of monastic libraries which facilitated the research and collecting of materials. John Leland began this work, and later John Bale provided a useful list of materials, even urging the setting up of a national library.[20]

The form of the London Chronicle, based on the mayoral year, was continued in Fabyan, whose work should be seen as the last of the medieval chronicles rather than the first of the new histories.[21] Stow also used the London Chronicle's usual arrangement of the names of the mayors followed by the great events of that year in his *Summarie of English Chronicles*, but adopted a reign-based approach in his *Chronicles* and *Annales*. The use of medieval sources perpetuated the versions of history which they contained, for the art of criticism was not yet fully developed. The continuation of chronicles also remained popular. Grafton continued both Hardyng and Hall, for instance. As in the past, too, there

---

Norwich from 1588. She argues that the work is dependent upon Hall's chronicle, and also on Walsingham whose *Historia Anglicana* first appeared in print in 1574. Redmayne claims that he drew on some French sources. Indeed he implies that this fact was inappropriate for a great (English) hero, and he stresses how under Henry the French were often defeated. In the prologue to the work he also expresses the view that the memory of Henry has passed into oblivion in recent years and is thus no longer written about. Redmayne expresses his desire to remedy this, given the 'incredible' achievements and strength of character of Henry 'which puts him into strong contention for similar treatment as the Roman leaders of old have received, whose fame is celebrated by posterity' (*Memorials*, p. 6). Redmayne's account of Agincourt is not included here partly because of Reid's redating of the work, and partly because, as Cole allowed, 'Redmayne's sketch of the battle of Agincourt is so slight in its nature and so destitute of any feature approaching to interest or novelty that hardly a word of further comment is needed in reference to it.' It might, however, repay further examination in its original Latin in order to assess the classical influences on it. There are certainly borrowings from Cicero, Virgil and several other writers, alongside obvious Protestant leanings.

17 Patterson, *Reading Holinshed's Chronicles*, pp. 237, viii.
18 On the treatment of Oldcastle elsewhere, see Patterson, *Reading Holinshed's Chronicles*, pp. 130–49.
19 Gransden, p. 476.
20 McKisack, *Medieval History in the Tudor Age*, chapter 1. See *Commentarii de Scriptoribus Britannici, auctore Joanne Lelando*, ed. A. Hall, 2 vols (Oxford, 1709), and for Bale, *Illustrium Maioris Britanniae Scriptorum Summarium* (Wesel, 1548).
21 For other examples of sixteenth-century works in the style of the London Chronicles see Levy, *Tudor Historical Thought*, pp. 25–6.

was no shunning of plagiarism as a reading of Grafton and Holinshed against Hall shows. But inevitably some elements of contemporary life crept in, such as Tudor military terms like 'billmen'.

There is much of interest in the writers of the sixteenth century relating both to how they used older works and also to how they created their own narrative. There can be no doubt too that their works, at least those in English, became popular and well known, as is witnessed by the frequency of re-issues. There was an active market for history books in London and other towns.[22] Caxton's edition of the *Polychronicon* was undoubtedly one of his best sellers with 40 copies and many fragments still extant today, more than for any other work produced by his press.[23] Shorter works such as Grafton's *Abridgement of Chronicles* and Stow's *Summarie of English Chronicles*, as the sixteenth-century equivalent of a modern text book, sold well and went into several editions.[24] We know too that the cost of volumes of Holinshed was often relatively low if purchasers were willing to buy them unbound.[25] As Levy notes, 'from about the middle of the 1580s, a typical Englishman must have found it more and more difficult to avoid having any knowledge of the past. Regardless of his purse, his background, or his tastes, sooner or later he was bound to be exposed to history.'[26] They were already drawn on as part of a 'military education'. A late sixteenth-century pocket book includes within it a summary of the battle taken from Grafton (or possibly Hall) as well as notes on skirmishing, on 'men of occupation necessary in an army', such as bakers, armourers, carpenters, wheelwrights etc., and on the making of a bridge of boats.[27] The histories were often admirably readable, being imbued with their own sense of drama. It is not surprising, therefore, that Hall and Holinshed would be attractive sources for dramatists. Hall, for instance, is not satisfied to tell us simply that the French prisoners were killed, but has them 'sticked with daggers . . . brained with pole-axes . . . slain with mails, others had their throats cut and some their bellies paunched'. Through Shakespeare (and, for Agincourt, through Drayton too), even those not acquainted with the histories directly gained some impression of what they contained.

---

[22] A good example of a history produced for a more popular audience is *The Pastime of People or the Chronicle of Divers Realms and most Especially of the Realm of England, Briefly Compiled and Imprinted in Cheapside by John Rastell AD 1529* (reprinted by T.F. Dibdin, London, 1811). This account of the battle (pp. 248–50) was drawn largely from Fabyan and is not worth inclusion here, but the work includes woodcuts produced by Rastell himself and column-based tables showing events in other parts of Europe, although only the history of England is considered at any length. For further discussion, see McKisack, *Medieval History in the Tudor Age*, p. 97.

[23] See list of works in N.F. Blake, 'William Caxton', in *Authors of the Middle Ages*, vol. 3 (Aldershot and Brookfield, 1996), p. 57–63, and in general H.S. Bennett, *English Books and Readers 1475–1557* (Cambridge, 1952).

[24] *Six Town Chronicles*, ed. R. Flenley (Oxford, 1911), p. 51.

[25] Patterson, *Reading Holinshed's Chronicles*, p. 15.

[26] *Tudor Historical Thought*, p. 234.

[27] PRO, State Papers 9/36/7.

But many of them, particularly Stow and Holinshed, were agglomerations without much sense of discrimination or criticism. Levy calls them chronicles rather than histories, adding that the sources from which they were composed were 'never fully integrated'. As he puts it, 'the criterion by which a historian was judged was the quantity of information he managed to cram between the covers of his book'.[28] This was both a benefit and a danger: 'continual advances in the techniques of historical research . . . would, in the end, increase the amount of available information past all hope of intelligibility'. We could argue that this was a particular problem for Agincourt where there were already so many slightly different versions of events to which sixteenth-century writers had added their own gloss and embellishment. Moreover, the fact that the sixteenth-century histories were printed and in English, thus offering a mediation for less accessible Latin and French works, meant that historians of later centuries tended to use them in preference to sources written closer to the events, and so picked up their bad points as well as their good. This is particularly the case with accounts of Agincourt. Material from other sixteenth-century works was also drawn on, for instance David Powell's *History of Cambria (or Wales)* (1584), which ascribed additional activities in the battle to Davy Gam which are not found in any chronicle but which enabled him to have more personality and a more purposeful, heroic death.[29] It also meant that those chronicles, such as the *Gesta*, which still only existed in manuscript form and which had not been drawn upon by sixteenth-century writers remained largely unknown until the nineteenth and twentieth centuries. Moreover, the styles of historical approach which developed over the course of the sixteenth century continued into the next few centuries. Applied to Agincourt, this meant the agglomeration of material in a narrative fashion, and the elaboration of tales and legends, as well as the invention of impassioned speeches which served as material for Shakespeare and the 'Famous Victories'. This dramatic style is particularly prevalent from Hall onwards. With him, it can be argued, a definitive account of the battle was established and propagated. There was a false impression of both comprehensiveness and realism, and a stress on heroism and national prowess. The style sometimes overwhelmed the facts. There was no bar on copying, so that accounts were often remarkably similar. Arguably too, this was because the writers of the century had drawn on the same chronicle sources as well as on each other.

As will be seen in chapter 4, the subsequent influence of the Enlightenment was complementary rather than opposing. It pointed historical writing in the same basic direction, with further use of classical examples in the pantheon of national and noble heroes. It preserved the desire to tell an edifying and entertaining story through what remained predominantly a narrative account of the battle. In all these respects, Agincourt continued to offer an ideal vehicle for this style of history, and many later writers eagerly looked to the more conducive

---

28 *Tudor Historical Thought*, pp. 167–8.
29 See below pp. 372, 374.

and readable sixteenth-century works in English rather than to anything written nearer the time of the battle itself.

C 1. *The First English Life of Henry the Fifth* (1513, English)

Modernised from *The First English Life of King Henry the Fifth*, ed. C.L. Kingsford (Oxford, 1922), pp. 3–5, 41–66.

This work is based upon Tito Livio's *Vita Henrici Quinti* and is often now described as a translation into English of that work. The current title is one given to it by Kingsford. There are several references in histories produced in the late sixteenth century to the 'Translator of Livius'. It was not until the twentieth century, however, that the work was identified as existing in two early seventeenth-century manuscript copies, and that it was edited by Kingsford. The work is undated but Kingsford suggests that it was completed between 30 June 1513, when Henry VIII landed at Calais to invade France in league with the pope and emperor, and the autumn of the following year. As the prologue given below shows, it was intended as an inspiration to Henry VIII. This was not simply relating to his own invasion of France. Although it has been suggested that Henry VIII was keen to follow the example of his namesake in his martial ambitions in France,[30] the prologue does not dwell on the point at all, giving much more place to the hope that Henry VIII, now four years into his reign, will emulate Henry V's government in general, and in particular, perhaps, the fact that he reformed his morals upon his accession. There is, of course, a rather delightful irony in the last section given Henry VIII's later actions both towards his wives and towards the church.

The work is not in fact a simple translation of Tito Livio's *Vita Henrici Quinti*. It is more a paraphrase, although direct speech given in Tito Livio is almost always retained albeit in translation. The account of the campaign is in roughly the same chronological order as in the *Vita*, but the author of the *First English Life* has a tendency to break the narrative by moralisations and to add in expansions or interpretations of what Livio said. For instance, after following Livio's notice of the English soldiers taking a little piece of earth in their mouth, he adds his own gloss on the purpose of this gesture: 'in remembrance of that they were mortal and earth, or else in remembrance of the holy communion'. Moreover, as the author himself admits, he also drew on (the recently printed)

---

[30] S. Gunn, 'The French wars of Henry VIII', in *The Origins of War in Early Modern Europe*, ed. J. Black (Edinburgh, 1987), pp. 28–51. C.S.L. Davies, 'Henry VIII and Henry V: the wars in France', in *The End of the Middle Ages*, ed. J.L. Watts (Stroud, 1998), p. 237, n.7, is more sceptical, noting that 'what Gunn called "Henry VIII's almost ritualistic imitation of his namesake" did not extend, however, to having the translation and embellishment of Tito Livio Frulovisi's life, made 1513–14, printed, or even widely copied, although Holinshed used a copy owned by Stow'.

Monstrelet 'in such things as me seemed apt for my matter'. His debt to
Monstrelet is immediately apparent in, for instance, sections on the debate at the
French court and on the reasons why the count of Charolais was not present at
the battle. He also notes that he has 'added divers sayings of the English Chronicles'. These are most likely derived from Caxton's edition of the *Brut* and the
latter's own *Brut*-derived continuation in the *Polychronicon*. In addition, the
author of the *First English Life* adds in 'divers other opinions that I have read of
the report of a certain and honourable ancient person . . . the earl of Ormond'.
James Butler, fourth earl of Ormond (1392–1452) served on several French
expeditions including that which led to Agincourt, and may be the 'Jacques de
Ormond' knighted by Henry at Pont-Saint-Maxence.[31] Exactly how this information came to the author is not clear but up to nine stories concerning Ormond
are found in the work, including what the Emperor Sigismund is supposed to
have said to the duke of Gloucester in 1416.[32] Kingsford accepted the fourth earl
as the direct source, although, as he noted, 'It is curious and unfortunate that we
have no story from Ormond of the campaign of Agincourt in which he was
present.'[33] W.T. Waugh concluded that the author's informant could not have
been the fourth earl in person, but rather the latter's youngest son, the seventh
earl, who was still alive in 1513.[34]

The author notes in his margins whether his account is based on Livio or
Monstrelet, making this one of the earliest works in English to give attributions
as quasi-footnotes. There are also several passages where he debates his sources,
such as on the question of numbers in the English army. The text was certainly
drawn on by writers of the later sixteenth century. Holinshed mentions the
Translator of Livius in his list of sources, and says a copy was in the possession
of John Stow. The latter in his *Summarie of English Chronicles* also notes a
'Translator of Livius'. Indeed, it is likely that these authors used the 'Translator'
rather than the original *Vita* itself, and that it was an important source for them.
This is apparent by a reading of the text against those of Hall, Grafton, Stow and
Holinshed, although just as the author of the *First English Life* expanded on Tito
Livio so also these later writers expanded on his work.

*

Prologue

When I thoroughly had perused, perceiving that it served well to my
purpose afore rehearsed, I pained myself to reduce it into our natural
English tongue. And because the matter should be more fruitful, open and

---

31 Kingsford, *First English Life*, p. xvii, citing Hall, *Union*, p. 64, Holinshed, *Chronicles*, 2,
p. 75. The knighting of Ormond is first mentioned in the Chronicle of Peter Basset, College of
Arms MS 9, Text A 8 above. His career is outlined in *The Complete Peerage*, 10, pp. 123–6,
although his presence at Agincourt is not mentioned there.
32 *First English Life*, p. 67.
33 Ibid., p. xxxiv.
34 In Wylie, 3, pp. 445–8.

pleasant to the readers and hearers hereof, I have annexed to the same divers authorities of Enguerrant de Monstrelet such things as seemed apt for my matter, who, among all other French histories and chronicles that I have seen, indited most at large of the wars between England and France for those days; which two books, the one of Titus Livius out of fecund Latin, and the other of the said Enguerrant out of the common language of France I have translated and reduced into rude and home English, from whom all effective and famous inditing is far exiled. And to these two aforesaid books I have also added divers sayings of the English chronicles, and to the same matter also divers other opinions that I have read of the report of a certain and honourable ancient person, to whom as me seemeth for the gravity and experience credit is to be given. And that is the honourable earl of Ormond. I have contexed and adjoined to the authorities afore rehearsed in places for the same most apt and convenient, as by the book following shall be evident to all them that shall please to read the same, wherein they shall find entitled in the margin of the same of what authority every sentence is taken. And for as much as I have not enterprised the compilation of this present volume upon no presumption of wit, sentence, or cunning of myself, whereof I know me utterly destitute and void, nor for no reproof of vice nor default of virtue in the person of our before remembered Sovereign Lord, whom I see evidently to be excellently replenished of all natural virtues, as much, as I believe, as he of whom I intend to write, or more; but to this end I have been moved to the enterprise hereof, that his Grace, hearing or seeing, or reading the virtuous manners, the victorious conquests, and the excellent sages and wisdoms of the most renowned prince in his days, King Henry the Fifth, his noble progenitor (of whose superiority in all nobleness, manhood, and virtue, to my pretence, it is not read nor heard amongst the princes of England since William of Normandy obtained the government of this realm by conquest) his Grace may in all things concerning his person and the ruling of his people, confirm himself to his life and manners, which he used after his coronation, and be counselled by the example of his great wisdom and discretion in all his common and particular acts. And secondarily the principal cause of this my pain (for as much as we then laboured in war) was that our Sovereign Lord by the knowledge and sight of this pamphlet should partly be provoked in his said war to ensue the noble and chivalrous acts of this so noble, so virtuous, and so excellent a prince, which so followed, he might the rather attain to like honour, fame, and victory. But, praised be God, it is now much better for us, for that mortal war and hateful dissension is now changed into an amiable, toward, and peace honourable and also profitable (as we believe both to the King's Highness and to this realm). Therefore considered that my first motion to this enterprise hath only sounded to the true and faithful allegiance that I (as his natural subject) owe to bear to our Sovereign Lord, whom above all things I desire to be virtuous and victorious: instantly and in the form of humility I beseech his Grace and all other, as well men of honour as of the commonalty, benignly to accept this rude and simple, not rude but excellent of itself, howbeit in the compilation it is but homely and not much pleasant: and where any default is, through my negligence and small discretion, with charity (so it be with authority) to reform the same. And as to your Grace, my most dread Sovereign Lord, those virtues that by this pamphlet ye shall perceive to be used in his time of that most puissant prince, King Henry the Fifth, your ancestor, and namely three which I note especially with colour most necessary to every prince to ensue; whereof the first is Justice, whereby he shall best entertain the unity and wealth of his people: the second Continence, which of all men is to be observed, and namely of them that be professors to the Sacrament of Matrimony, which virtue, as I have heard of credible report, this noble prince, King Henry the Fifth, observed so constantly that from the death of the king his father until the marriage of himself he never had knowledge carnally of women: And the third excellent virtue that I note is Humility, and to eschew vainglory, lest a man ascribe laud to himself of that thing which is given to him of God, whereby he might lightly provoke against himself the indignation of God, by means whereof his prosperity and honour may be changed into adversity and dishonour: he gives to your Grace to use and ensue, and constantly to occupy to the pleasure of him, to the health of your Soul, and to the honour and prosperity of your royal person, realm, and commons, of whom ye have received so many and so great super-eminent virtues and graces. Amen.

*

When the gates of the Harfleur were opened, and that the king approached unto them in purpose to enter the town, he descended from his horse without the gate, and from thence, without hose or shoes, in great devotion he went immediately to the church of Saint Martin's, metropolitan of that town, and there he made his prayers devoutly in thanking and praising his Creator of his good fortune. O marvellous constance! that by the providence of God had made them habitation without mutability in this most noble prince, who in his youth was most mutable and void of all spiritual virtues.

And whom none for no persuasions or enhancements of fortune they suffered in his victories in anything to decline from the sovereign virtues of faith and humility. But void of all pride and vainglory, causeth him in great devotion, as well in the beginning, as in the achieving of his enterprise, at all times to thank, honour, and praise his maker, by whose only aid and comfort he undoubtedly believeth to attain with honour to the end of that he hath begun; not like unto the conquered, in most pomp and pride, delighting in vain praises and lauds of the people, and labouring to make the victories to be ascribed unto themselves, as if God intermeddled not of such affairs . . . These things [surrender of Harfleur] thus done and finished, the king assembled all his estates and lords of his host to council, which was to be done after the victory of this defensible and strong town, which they had conquered within thirty and eight days: notwithstanding that for the strength it ought to have feared a straiter siege of an whole year. It was then thought convenient by such their whole council, in as much as winter approached nigh, to return into England. But then it was debated amongst them upon their passage, whether they should return the next and surest way by water, or else they should pass through their enemies land by Calais. The more part condescended to go by land. But the duke of Clarence, with divers other lords, considering the great loss of those men that they had sustained by the death of the flux, that then reigned among them, and many other sick of the same, by which infirmity died the earl of Stafford, the bishop of Norwich, the lord Beaumont, and divers other noble men, and of the commons to the number of 2,000 and above, considered also the men they had left for the defence of Harfleur to the diminishing of their host, and most especially considered the great and infinite multitude of their enemies, which then were assembled to impede and let the king's passage by land, whereof by their spies they had knowledge, advised and counseled the return into England by water, as for the more fair passage. To whose council the king answered in this manner, saying, 'he greatly desired to see those lands, whereof he ought to be Lord.' 'And though,' said he, 'they prepare against us a great host of people, our trust and confidence is in God, that they shall not prevail against us, nor none of ours, nor we shall not suffer that they, that be inflated with pride, shall injuriously possess and enjoy that of right belongeth unto us. And if we should thus depart, they would say in reproof of us and of our realm of England, that for fear we left our right, and were so suddenly fled. Therefore we have at this time the stomach encouraged, and would rather submit our body to all perils, than they should into our kingdom the least note of reproof. We shall go, to the pleasure of God, without prejudice or peril. And, if they labour to disturb us of our journey, we shall escape their malice with honourable victory and great triumph.' And forthwith this sentence published and known moved the stomachs and encouraged the hearts of every man; nor there was not one that contraried his pleasures, lest they should be reproved by the king of fear and cowardice. Then with all speedy diligence was prepared for this journey by land with companies and retinues of man of war. The king ordained to go with him three battles and two wings, as thus of Englishmen is [accustomed,] of those men that were left unto him; of whom was no plenteous number, for, as is aforesaid, he had lost many by the infirmity of the flux, and many others there were that were diseased of the same sickness, which were left behind him. And also were left at Harfleur 2,000 soldiers of his host for the defence of the same. When the king had thus ordered his battles, and sent his brother the duke of Clarence into England by water with a great part of his army for the defence of his navy, which also greatly diminished his own company. After he had tarried at Harfleur fifteen days after the deliverance of the town and of the towers, he departed from thence and entered his journey towards Calais.

Whereof when his enemies were avertised, and also by what way he intended to pass, all the people of the country and also of the cities and of the towns were marvellously oppressed with fear, and mainly for the taking of Harfleur, wherefore they hastened them to defensible places, which, in all haste to them possible, as well as they could, they victualled both for men and also for horses. And other that were apt to war took them to their horses, and assembled them together in great number, with no small company of footmen, and in all that they might they oppressed the Englishmen. The king's host kept an easy pace, without making any haste, and when they approached the town of Eu their enemies, being there in arms and advertised to their coming, applied them in the field with great force and noise, where on both parties it was fought sore and vigorously, but the Frenchmen might no long endure the strength of the Englishman, wherefore they must of force recoil within the town; where they were in good sureties, for the king abode not to besiege the town.

At this encounter was slain a right valiant man at arms on the Frenchmen's part, whose name was Launcelot Piers, for those death the Frenchmen made great dole and sorrow. From thence the king departed and came to a passage of the River of Somme, which the Frenchmen call Blanckehestake or Blaunchtache, where long before passed over his ancestor and progenitor King Edward the Third, when he obtained the battle of Crécy against Philip of Valois, king of France. This passage at the coming to it was fixed with sharp stakes by their enemies of that country, so that they could not pass over the river there. And that the Frenchmen had so done to the intent that the king and his host should seek their passage over that river higher into France, and more near to the head of the same river. Thus the Englishmen were constrained to seek further, seeking their passage until they came directly to have the city of Amiens and the castle of Corbie on their left side. Then they of the said city, after they had perceived the ensigns and banners of the Englishmen, began with them a new fight both on horseback and on foot. And the Frenchmen with great number, with great clamour and noise, as the usage is among them, enforced them against the English host, of whom they were shortly vanquished and constrained to return to their holds. In this time it was complained to the king a certain Englishman in the host had violently taken from a church a pyx of silver. Then immediately after the king commanded his host to abide without moving until the sacrilege was purged. And first was the said pyx restored again unto the church, and the trespasser was led bound as a thief through the host, and after hanged upon a tree, that every man might behold him. After whose death the army was commanded to reprise the former journey.

O Marvelous God! that of thine infinite goodness amongst such and so many excellent virtues hast rooted in that most virtuous king so high and perfect degree of justice, that he as that other Joshua, that for his covetousness stoned to death Achan, put to death this his soldier for the offence, notwithstanding that he knew perfectly that the time approached right nigh wherein he should have great need of the aid and number of men; but what marvel he, that had his confidence only in God and Justice, and not in the number of people, loved better the absence of sinners than their company. And undoubtedly he that shall attain to conquests and honour must first by the example of this invincible conqueror confirm himself to semblable virtues. Then to return to our former purpose.

As the king journeyed by certain days seeking his passage over the river of Somme, by some Frenchmen that were prisoners in the host was shewed unto him a certain passage over the same river not much used, and before that day not known but of few, by which passage the Englishmen passed the river sure enough. The next day after the feast of St Luke the Evangelist the king passed the river of Somme at the passage of Voyennes and Bethencourt, which passages were not kept by them of St Quentin's as they were enjoined of the French king. When the king of England had thus passed the river he went to lodge him at Monchy-Lagache, from whence he advanced him towards the river of Miraumont. In this mean time the French king and the duke of Guienne, his son then dauphin, purposing to provide for the resistance of the Englishmen, came to Rouen, where the one and twentieth day of October was holden the council, which was to be done against the king of England. At which council was present Louis, the king of Sicily, the dukes of Berry and of Brittany, the earl of Ponthieu, the eldest son of the said King Louis, the chancellor of France and of Guienne, and of many other noble councillors to the number of 35; amongst whom, after they had devised and reasoned many things in the presence of the king upon this matter, at the last it was concluded by 30 of them that the Englishmen should be encountered and fought with at the appointed day; but in the end the opinion of the greatest part was approved and holden; whereupon in all possible haste the king sent his letters to his constable, and to others his offers, secretly commanding them that, immediately upon the knowledge of his commandment, they should assemble them together with all the puissance that might be had, and that they should encounter the king of England and his people. Then immediately was published through all France, that all noble men accustomed to bear arms, and that desire to require honour, should haste them night and day to the constable of France, wheresoever [he was]. And amongst all others Louis, duke of Guienne, then dauphin, had great desire to go to that field; howbeit he was commanded to the contrary by the French king, his father, and also by Louis, his council, king of Sicily, and of the duke of Berry he was letted from that purpose. Then from all parts, all lords, knights, and gentlemen, that already were prepared and entered into their journey for the same, hastened them towards the constable of France. And when the constable, with the more part of the lords and estates of the realm of France, approached the country of Artois, they sent the lord Mongoguier unto the earl of Charolais, the only son of the duke of Burgundy, to certify him of their enterprise, and to desire him affectuously in the king's name and in the constable's, that he would vouchsafe to be at that journey. This foresaid lord of Mongoguier found the said earl at Arras, of whom he was right nobly received, and also of all his lords. And after he had showed unto him his message, it was answered unto him by those lords, that were chief councillors of the earl, that he should make such diligence upon the king's request as should be requisite; and with this answer [they were] contented and returned to the constable. And where this earl of Charolais desired with all his heart to be at this journey against the king of England, whereunto also all his great councillors had advised him, yet nevertheless he was expressly commanded by John, duke of Burgundy, his father, that in no wise he should be at that journey.

This commandment was not given to the said earl by the duke his father, for no favour nor love he had to the English party, but only to the displeasure and variance betwixt the dauphin and him, and the duke of Orléans. And for because the said earl of Charolais should be the further place from the battle, his council caused him to remove to Arras, where notwithstanding the greater part of the people of his house, which was advertised of the day of the battle appointed, departed secretly without the said earl's knowledge, and accompanied them with the Frenchmen against the English host.

The disease and infirmity that reigned amongst the Englishmen, nor the small number of the king's host was not unknown to the Frenchmen; they also considered journeys that Englishmen had sustained long by land without any great corporal refection to repose for the maintenance of their strength; it was also remembered amongst them the great, puissant, and as an infinite, multitude of themselves, against whom, as they thought, it was impossible for so little an host (as the Englishmen were) to resist, mainly because that all the great princes of the realm of France were there assembled to disturb the king's passage; of whom the most principal were these: the dukes of Orléans, of Brabant, of Bourbon, of Alençon, and of Bar, the lord Charolais laboured [sic, recte Charles d'Albret], at this time the constable of France, whose progenitors were liege to the kings of England as of their duchy of Guienne, the earl of Nevers, brother to the dukes of Burgundy and of Brabant, the archbishop of Sens, and many other great lords and men of honour. These men, having their confidence only in their multitude, sent three of their heralds to the king of England to give him knowledge that he should not escape without battle; which heralds, when they came to the king's host, were first brought to the duke of York, and by him they were presented to the king, before whom they fell on their knees and, after they had obtained licence to say their message, they spake in this manner: 'Right puissant prince, great and noble is thy kingly force, that is reported of thy majesty amongst other princes and lords, they hear that by thy strength and prowess, though labourest to conquer towns, cities, and castles of the realm of France; they hear also of the great destruction thou doest on Frenchmen; for which causes, and for the performance of their oath that they have made to the king, many of our lords be assembled to defend this realm, the king's right and their own. And upon this by us they give thee knowledge, that, before thou come to Calais, they will meet thee in intent to fight with thee.' This victorious king, after he had heard their message, and understood the effect thereof, with a courageous heart, with a constant countenance, which neither ire nor displeasure moved, no colour of his face changing, with a moderate and soft speech, gave unto them this answer saying: 'At all things be done at the pleasure of God.' And when he was demanded of the herald, which way he would keep, he answered: 'To Calais'; and there too adding he said: 'If our adversaries do attempt to disturb us in our journey, they shall not do it without their own great prejudice and dangerous peril, we think; we seek them not, neither for the fear of them we shall not move the softlier, nor make the greater haste. Nevertheless we advise them they let not our journey, nor they seek not the effusion of so much Christian blood.' The heralds contented with this answer, and rewarded with an hundred crowns of French money, and licensed to depart, returned to their prince to whom they reported their answer that they had heard.

The king of England who was left at Monchy-Lagache, removed from thence and went to lodge him in a village called Forceville, advancing his host towards the river of Miraumont; and the next day, which was Wednesday, they passed by on horse, and lodged them that night in divers places. The king lodged him at Bonnières L'Escaillon, and the duke of York, his uncle, captain of the vanguard, lodged him at Frévent upon the river of Canche. And the residue of the Englishmen and host were lodged in divers other places, so that that night they were divided into seven or eight several places or towns. That notwithstanding they had no manner of displeasure of their enemies that night; for the Frenchmen were gone to be before them in their way towards St Pôl, and upon the River Miraumont. And the Thursday next ensuing the king removed from Bonnières and rode in right fair ordinance unto Blangy.

And forasmuch as he was advertised before of a river in that journey over which they must pass by a bridge, and if peradventure that bridge were broken by their adversaries he could not have passage without his great prejudice and peril, he sent therefore before certain noble horsemen, with them he assigned certain footmen, to defend and keep the bridge; where, at their coming thither, they found many Frenchmen, that enforced them to break the bridge, unto whom the Englishmen gave battle, and after a long and cruel fight betwixt them, many of their adversaries were slain, many wounded, and many taken prisoner, and all the residue put to flight. They won the bridge, and kept it from hurt. This day was the three and twentieth of November, upon which day is solemnized in the church the commemoration of St Romanus the confessor.

At which bridge when the duke of York, chieftain of the first ward, had passed the water, and had ascended the mountains, his spies perceived from all parts the Frenchmen coming by great multitudes of men of arms, which went to lodge them in Ruisseauville, and other places thereabouts, in intent to be before the Englishmen, and the next day to fight them. When the English spies had perceived the Frenchmen in so great number, one of them with fearful countenance and sorrowful sighing, reported unto the duke of York, that there were approached unto them an innumerable multitude of their adversaries; whereof when the duke had true knowledge by their spies and couriers, that had also been them, he gave to the king knowledge thereof; who, without fear or ire, gave to the middle ward, whereof he was conductor, charge to abide, and giving spurs to his horse he hastened to see his enemies, whom he perceived to be an innumerable host. Then he returned to his field with a constant mind, not moved with fear, but as he that putteth his whole confidence in God and in justice. After this he ordered his battles, and distributeth to every captain his number, and his order, and place of fighting, and in what manner. He kept his host ready ordered in the field until night; and when the day was passed, and that no light at all was perceived, he disposed him to get some harbour for that night, both for him and for his people, where they might have corporal refection and repose of their bodies. And in that night, whom a terrible battle was to follow, in that region unknown they could find no place nigh unto them, wherein to be refreshed, except that divinely there was shown unto them a certain white way; by the which they were led to a certain little village called Agincourt, where they were a little better refreshed with meat and drink than they had been in their journey before; where also the king for that night took a little house for his lodging. From that place where the king had set his battles in array until they came unto the town, by the commandment of the king, was no cry nor noise heard of the Englishmen, as they used before, but every man went peaceably. And when they came to the village aforesaid, they kindled their fires, and ordered and made watches. In like manner also did the Frenchmen, which scarcely were distant from the English the space of two hundred and fifty paces.

And the same proper Thursday towards the evening for certain courses Philip, the earl of Nevers, was made knight by the hand of Bouccicaut, the marshal of France, and with him were made knights many other great lords and gentlemen of France. This night came unto the French host the constable of France, who lodged himself nigh Agincourt. Then all the Frenchmen assembled themselves together in one host, and lodged themselves upon the plain field, every man as nigh to his own banner as he could, except some people of small estate, that lodged them in villages nigh unto the field. And the king of England with his Englishmen was lodged in a little village called Maisoncelles, three shots of a bow or thereabout from the Frenchmen.

Howbeit all other authors that I have read recite that he was lodged that night at Agincourt, but whereso he was lodged it was not greatly material, in as much as all mine authors accord in this point that the field was fought in a plain adjoining to Agincourt, and for that reason the field beareth the name of the town. The Frenchmen with all their great lords and captains fixed their banners and standards with great joy and mirth with the banner royal, whereof the constable had the conduct and charge, in the field by them devised and chosen, which was in the county of St Pôl in the ground of Agincourt, by which the day following the Englishmen should pass to go to Calais. And that night the Frenchmen made great fires, every man under his banner; and that night the Frenchmen, fishing before the net, played the Englishmen at dice, as if they had been assured of the victory, whereby the purveyance of God they disappointed.

And although the French were in number 100,000, whereof the most part had their horses with them there, and besides that they had many other horses in their chariots, wagons, and carts, and other wagons and carriages, whereof they had great plenty amongst them, they had few or no instruments of music to rejoice the companies with; nor of all that night before the battle right few, or in a manner none of their horses brayed or made any noise, whereof many men had marvel suspecting it to prefigure some marvellous fortune to come. But the Englishmen ceased not of all the night to blow or sound their business, trumpets, or other music, whereof they had great plenty, in so much as all the ground about them resounded at their noise. The night before the field the duke of Orléans accompanied with the earl of Richemont, who had the conduct of the people of the dauphin and also of the Bretons assembled them to the number of two thousand bascinets of other Frenchmen with shot, and went secretly to the lodges of the Englishmen, which by the good ordinance of the king, were all ready put in array doubting the invasions of their enemies. Then began the shot on both parties, which endured not long, but that the Frenchmen were constrained to withdraw them to their whole host. After which enterprise the said duke of Orléans and many other noble men were made knights; and thus they passed that night without doing any other feat of war on either party. During this time the duke of Brittany, notwithstanding that he had sent a part of his people before, was come to Amiens with 6,000 fighting men, in the aid of the Frenchmen, and had joined with them if they had tarried his coming till the Saturday. And in like manner the Lord Longny, marshal of France, accompanied with 600 men of arms, was also coming into their help, and lodged the same day of the battle six leagues from the whole host; and the morning next after he removed passing early, in trust to come to the field.

The 25th day of October, after matins, masses, prayers and supplications of the king's priests said and done with all devotion, that most Christian king of England in the morning very early sent forth his host in array. He commanded that his horses, and all other carriages and impediments, should be left in that village, where he had lodged that night, under the guard and keeping of a few persons, and with him he took nothing but men's bodies, harness, and weapons. The order of his field was: his own battle was not distant far from another. The middle battle, whereof the king was conductor, and wherein he intended to fight, was set in the middle of the field directly against the middle battle of their adversaries. On the right hand or side was the first battle, and therewith the right wing. And on the left side the last battle, and the left wing. And these battles joined nigh together, and by the purveyance of God was proved unto the king, which had his special confidence in God and in justice, a defensible place for his host; for the village, wherein he was lodged the night before, defended his host from all hostile invasions on the back, and the field, wherein he was, was defended on both sides with two small rivers. This noble king was armed with sure and beauteous shining armour, and upon his head was a bright helmet, whereupon was set a crown of gold replete with pearls and precious stones, marvellous rich; and in his shield he bare the arms of England and of France. And thus armed, as he that feared not to be known of his adversaries, he was mounted upon a great and goodly horse, and after him were led certain noble horses with their bridles and trappers of goldsmiths' work, marvellously rich, as the manner of kings is. And upon them also in the same work were beaten the arms of England and of France.

Thus this most victorious king, prepared and disposed to battle, encouraged his people to the field that approached at hand. And to one great estate of his company, which desired to the pleasure of God that every man of war within England were there with them presently ready apparelled for battle, the king made this answer: 'Truly I would not that my company were increased of one person more than now it is. We be, as to the regards of our enemies, but a very small number. But if God, of his infinite goodness, favour our causes and right (as we surely trust) there is none of us that may attribute this so great a victory to our own power but only to the hand of God; and by that we shall the rather be provoked to give him due thanks therefore; and if peradventure for our sins we shall be given into the hands of our enemies and to the sword (which God forbid) then the less our company be, the less sorrow and dishonour shall be to the realm of England; or else if we were in great number and should then have victory of our enemies, then our minds should be prone and ready to pride. And then peradventure we should ascribe our victory rather to our own strength than to the hand of God, and thereby we should purchase to ourselves his indignation. But be ye of good courage, and fight with all your might, and God and our right shall defend us, and deliver into our hands all this great multitude of our proud enemies that ye see, or at the least the most part of them.' The night before this cruel battle, by the advise and council (as it is said) of the duke of York, the king had given commandment through his host, that every man should provide him a stake sharp at both ends, which the Englishmen fixed in the ground before them in the field to defend them from the oppression of the horsemen. The Frenchmen had so much their confidence in the great multitude of their people, in their shining armour and beauteous, and in their great and mighty horses, that many of their great princes and lords leaving behind them their servants and soldiers, and namely leaving behind them their standards and banners, and other ensigns, came towards the Englishmen in right great haste, as if they had been assured of victory. Amongst whom the duke of Brabant, which for haste had left behind him his banners, took from a trumpet his banner of arms, and commanded it to be borne before him upon a spear instead of his banner.

And when they approached the English host with that knightly diligence that they might, they briefly ordered their battle in this manner. Early in the morning before the battle, which was the Friday the 25th day of October in the year of our Lord God 1415, the constable of France and other wise men of the king's council of France ordered of their company three battles, whereof the vanguard contained 6,000 bascinets, 4,000 archers, and 1,500 arbalesters [crossbowmen], of whom was the conductor the aforesaid Constable, and with him the duke[s] of Orléans, and of Bourbon, the earls of Eu, and of Richemont, and the Marshal Bouccicaut, the master of arbalesters, the lord of Dampierre admiral of France, and divers other great captains and men of honour. In the second battle were appointed as many men of arms, archers and arbalesters as were in the first, of which were conductors the dukes of Berry and Alençon, the earls of Nevers, of Vaudemont, of Blammont, of Salines, of Grand-Pré, and of Roussy. And in their rearward were all the residue of men of arms, archers, and arbalesters, the earl of Marlay, of Dammartin, and of Fauquembergue, and divers other great estates and noble captains. They ordained also two wings of horsemen to sever and break the array of the English host, wherein were 2,400 horsemen with such captains as were thought most convenient for the same. And the rather to encourage the heart of the young lords and gentlemen the constable of France the day and night before this field had made above 600 knights of the field and of his host.

And when they approached, the Frenchmen exceeded so far the Englishmen in number that of them was 31 men's thickness in every part of the field; nor the field, where they fought, suffered not to receive so great multitude of people as they were; and the English host was scarcely four men's thickness. At his departure from Harfleur he had in his host 2,000 men of arms, 13,000 archers, and other men of war a great number.

But of this number Enguerunt [de Monstrelet] putteth no certainty.

How well the English chronicle reciteth that he had at this field but 10,000 men of war in his host; and that seemeth me marvellous that he having 23,000 [sic] men at his commandment besides all them that were dead of the flux, and besides the garrison he left at Harfleur, would take so small an host with him, considering that he had knowledge before his departure from Harfleur of the preparation that the French made against him. But let every man give credence to whether part he will, and I will return to my matter. Howbeit Enguerunt reciteth that greater part of the English archers were without harness. The Frenchmen had also in his host many guns and engines of divers quantities and fashions, wherewith they shot and cast stones among the English host. These two hosts were distant one from the other scarcely three shots of a bow.

The Frenchmen abode in their array without moving until nine or ten o'clock of the day, being as ascertained that the Englishmen should not escape their hands, seeing how they exceed the English host in number. And when they had stood long thus the one against the other, without doing anything, saving that the horsemen of the French host ran divers courses upon the Englishmen, by whose archers they were at all times driven to their host, and that a great part of the short day was thus passed, the king counselled with his wise men what was to be done thereupon: amongst whom it was considered that long abiding in the realm of his adversaries, where they had no comfort, was unto them perilous and should turn to their great danger, and namely because they had scarcity of victuals, and that the Frenchmen being in their own country, where they had no enemies, and also they should daily increase in number and in strength. Wherefore it was concluded by them to go to their enemies, in as much as they came not to them. But before the king removed his host, upon surety safely to return, came unto the king three noble men of France, among whom was the lord de Heilly, which before time had been taken of the English soldiers, and was brought as a prisoner into England, from whence by breaking of prison he secretly escaped and returned into France. This lord spake unto the king in this manner: 'Noble king, it hath often been shown unto me, and also to others of our realm, that I should fly from you shamefully and otherwise than a knight should do, which report I am here ready to prove untrue. And if there be any man of your host hardy to reproach me thereof, let him prepare him to a single battle. And I shall prove it upon him before the matter, that wrongfully that report hath been imagined and furnished of me.' To whom the king made this answer: 'No battle shall be here fought at this time for this cause, another time shall be thereto more convenient than this. Therefore return you and call forth your company to the field, before the night approach. And we trust in God, that like as you having no regard to the order of honour of knighthood, escaped from us, so that [day] ye shall either be taken and brought to us again, or else by the sword you shall finish your life.' 'Noble king,' said the lord, 'for you I shall not warn my company, nor they shall in nothing attempt your commandment. Both we and you with your host be within the hand of the most Christian king of France, Charles, to whose commandment we shall obey and not to yours. And we that be his lieges shall come to battle at our own pleasure and not at yours.' 'Depart you from hence,' said the king, 'to your host, and we believe you shall not return with so full speed, but we shall be there shortly after you.' Then these lords departed.

And the king forthwith advanced his banners and standards to the French host. And he in his person, with his battle in the same order wherein they stood following, exhorted and encouraged every man to battle, notwithstanding he went to invade his enemies; yet [he] kept his accustomed order: that is, that the first battle went before, the second battle followed, and the third came immediately after. He commanded his priests and chaplains to abide in prayers and divine supplications; and his heralds bearing their coat armours to attain to their offices. Then every Englishman fell prostrate to the ground, and committing themselves to God, every one of them took in his mouth a little piece of earth, in remembrance of that they were mortal and earth, or else in remembrance of the holy communion. Thus all the carriages and baggages left behind, only charged with their harness, weapons, and stakes they marched toward their enemies with great noise. Then they began to sound their trumpets and their tabors, which greatly encouraged the heart of every man. Their enemies seeing them approach advanced themselves also, and met with them in the field, betwixt whom was began a marvellous fierce and cruel battle. The battles of the Englishmen were as long as the field, wherein they fought, would suffer; which was greatly to their advantage, for by that their enemies were let to come upon them at the sides and back of the host. The Frenchmen had ordained their battles with two sharp fronts like unto two horns, which always backward was broader; and these sharp battles set upon the king's middleward, in intent to run through the king's field. The order and array of the English had been sore troubled of the horsemen of France, if they had not been slain, beaten, and wounded by the bows of England, and by the help of the stakes that the Englishmen had fixed before them in the ground, whereby the horsemen were constrained to return, or else they must run upon the stakes, where many of them were overthrown and wounded, and many both men and horses slain. The battle and fight increased marvellously; every man enforced him to be a victor by the space of three hours, by which time without delay or respite endured this mortal battle; no man approached the place of the battle, but wither he must slay or else he was slain. There no man intended to prowess, but to victory; no man was taken prisoner, but an innumerable were slain. And when it came to the middle of the field the Englishmen were more encouraged to slay their enemies than before, as to whom was no trust of life but only in victory. They slew them that came first unto them, upon whose dead bodies an innumerable company were thrown and slain, and that the victory surely remained to the Englishmen. Thus after a long and cruel battle by the demerits of their great pride there approached no Frenchman to battle, but only to death: of whom, after that an innumerable company were slain, and that the victory surely remained to the Englishmen, they spared to slay and took prisoners of the Frenchmen both princes, lords, and gentlemen in great number. In this mortal battle the noble king never spared his body from labour, from perils, nor from fighting; nor he never failed his men for no danger of death, nor for no pain; but he fought with his adversaries with an ardent heart as a famished lion for his prey; in his helmet and in the residue of his armour he received many strokes. In this field as the puissant Duke Humphrey, duke of Gloucester, the king's brother, fought with great courage and force, he was sore wounded in the groin with a sword, and overthrown, in so much as he lay as half dead in the field, his head towards the Englishmen, and his feet towards his enemies, upon whom the king having brotherly love and compassion bestride him: and with most strong battle and labour, and not without his own great peril, the brother defended and succoured the brother from their enemies, and made the duke to be borne out of the field amongst the hands of his own men. At the last the victory obtained, and the great host of the Frenchmen slain, taken, wounded and vanquished, forth with another host of the Frenchmen, no less than the first, supposing the Englishmen now to be wearied by their long travail and fight, disposed them to recommence and begin again the battle anew; when the Englishmen (which had more prisoners than themselves were in number) saw this new field assembled to give them battle again, fearing lest in this new field they should fight both with their prisoners, and their enemies, they put to death many of their said enemies prisoners both noblemen and rich men. Amongst whom the duke of Brabant, who at that field was taken prisoner, was slain.

Then this noble prudent king, considering and seeing the resemblance of his adversaries, sent his heralds unto them commanding either forthwith to come to battle, or else immediately to depart; and if they delayed to depart, or else if they came to battle, both those of theirs that then were prisoners, and also all they that should after be taken, without mercy or redemption should be put to death. All this he gave in message to his heralds, which message when the Frenchmen had heard fearing the strength of the Englishmen, and also the death both of themselves, and also of those prisoners that were taken before on their party, with heaviness and with shame they departed forthwith. Then the king, assured of this great victory, gave the greatest thanks and laud to God that might be. And because that day the church solemnized the commemoration of St Crispin and St Crispinian (by whose suffrages it seemed him that this great victory was given him of God) he ordained during his life the commemoration of them to be said daily in mass he heard. In this cruel battle were slain on the French part the noble dukes of Alençon and Bar, and of

Brabant, and the Lord Heilly, who, as is aforesaid, came before the battle to purge himself before the king of his escape out of England.

The lord d'Albret, chief constable of France, the archbishop of Sens, eight earls, and one hundred and more of barons, 1,500 knights, and above 10,000 of all estates, whereof were not scarcely 1,500 persons that were soldiers, servants, or varlets, besides this great number. And all the rest were gentlemen of coat armour. At this battle besides this great murder were taken prisoners of the Frenchmen the duke of Orléans, and of Brabant, Arthur, brother to the duke of Brittany, the earl of Vendôme, the earl of Eu, the earl of Richemont, and Sir Bouccicaut, marshal of France, who was brought prisoner into England and there died. And many other men were taken prisoners unto the number of 1,500 persons, all knights and gentlemen. And on the English part were slain the duke of York, the earl of Suffolk, and to the number of an hundred persons in the vanguard. And of all estates as well of gentlemen as of commons on the English part were not found dead above 600 in the field.

When the day began to decline and the night approach, by the advice of his council that victorious king returned with his host into that village, wherein they harboured the night before the field, where he found his horses and other baggage and carriage that he left there before the field, stolen and carried away by robbers of the Frenchmen. Where amongst many other jewels of great price was stolen away a sword of great value, adorned with gold and precious stones, which after was given to Philip, earl of Charolais, son and heir to Burgundy.

The same day of the field at night, when the king sat at his refection in the aforesaid village, he was served at his board of these great lords and princes that were taken in the field. That night the king appointed good and sure watches throughout his host for fear of sudden invasions. But the Frenchmen were utterly divided and gone, without making or intending any new business; whereby the Englishmen were suffered in peace to take their rest that night. And the day next ensuing the king with his people entered his journey towards Calais; and as they passed through the field where they had fought the day before, they found all the dead bodies of the men despoiled as well of their harness as of their array by the inhabitants of the country both men and women. Notwithstanding, the bodies that might be known for Englishmen that were of any reputation, the king caused to be assembled and interred according to their estate. And so continuing his journey the king came to his castle of Guînes, and from thence he went to his town of Calais, with all his host and his prisoners, where he was received of his liegemen with great joy and with all due honour. And after that his host was something refreshed with meat, drink and sleep, the king counselled with his councillors if he should now return into France and pursue his enterprise begun, or else return with his host into England and refresh his people. Amongst whom it was considered that the number of his people was right small, and of them that were left many were troubled with the disease of the flux, and many so grieved of those wounds that they had received at the field. They considered also that long abiding at Calais should cause penury of victuals amongst his host. And on the other part in their own country the people should at their ease have refreshed them, and cure them of their diseases and wounds. They also considered that the time hitherto had not been unfortunate to them: but that with their honour they might return with their gain that they had conquered and gotten. They trusted also that the aid of God was not withdrawn from them, but that to his pleasure the king should right well obtain his desire in time to come. For which consideration the minds of all his councillors were condescended and agreed upon their return into England, thereby to rejoice the hearts of the people, where also they might refresh their bodies, and recover themselves of their diseases and wounds.

C 2. Robert Fabyan, *The New Chronicles of England and France* (1516, English)

Modernised from *The New Chronicles of England and France in Two Parts by Robert Fabyan, Named by Himself the Concordance of Histories*, ed. H. Ellis (London, 1811), pp. 573–81.

Robert Fabyan (d. 1513) was from Essex but followed his father as a clothier in London, becoming sheriff in 1493. He was in the tradition of the London chroniclers, as can be seen from the format of his work. He also drew on previous city chronicles and materials. But it has also been claimed that he was 'the first of the citizen chroniclers of London who conceived the design of expanding his diary into a general history'.[35] Thus his plan also has links with the general chronicles of previous centuries too. Six books of what he called the *Concordance of Histories* dealt with the period from Brutus to the Norman Conquest. The seventh took the account to his own day, and was dated as in the form of a London Chronicle from the reign of Richard I onwards. In his prologue he indicates his intention to deal with 'the fatall warre that hath dured so longe twene Fraunce and England, to both their damage'.[36] The text was printed after his death by Robert Pynson as *The New Chronicles of England and France*. A second edition was printed by Rastell in 1533 with a continuation to the death of Henry VII which may be the work of Fabyan himself.

Generally he does not give the source of his information, although he cites the French writer 'Gaguynus', that is, Robert Gaugin (d. 1501), who published the *Grandes Chroniques* and other historical and literary works. Flenley considers that Fabyan's work 'is poor in comparison with the chronicles written later in the century, yet it showed a great advance on the preceding and contem-

[35] *DNB*, 18, p. 13.
[36] Fabyan, p. 4

porary city chronicles'.[37] He drew on one of the London chronicles which is now lost, as well as a variety of other works and the Letter Books of London.[38] Thus, for instance, he tells us that the prisoners at Agincourt amounted 'to the number of 2,400 and above, as witnesseth the Book of Mayor'.[39] He also tells us of how the news of the victory came to the city: this detail is taken from an account in the Great Chronicle of London. He does not follow the number of troops given in the *Brut* or London Chronicles, suggesting 1,500 spearmen and 18,000 yeomen and archers, numbers which are suspiciously like ratios of these military components appropriate to the time he was writing rather than to 1415. He also gives, at 40,000, a lower total for the French than any fifteenth-century text. The chronicle proved popular and was printed three times within 50 years of the first edition. There is evidence of its use in other chronicles of the sixteenth century.

*

AD 1414		AD 1415
	John Mychell	
Thomas Fawconer, mercer		Year 3
	Thomas Aleyn	

Then the dauphin with other lords of France, which at the time had the realm of France in governance, for so much as the French king was visited with such malady as before I have shown, broke the bridge to let the king of his passage over the water of Somme. Wherefore he was constrained to draw towards Picardy, and so pass by the river of Péronne, whereof the Frenchmen being wary, assembled and lodged them at certain towns named Agincourt, Rolandcourt and Blangy, with all the power of France. And when King Henry saw that he was so beset with his enemies, he in the name of God and St George pitched his field in a plain, between the said towns of Agincourt and Blangy, having in his company of whole men that might fight, not passing the number of 7,000. But at those days the yeomen had their limbs at liberty, for their hose were then fastened with one point, and their jackets were long and easy to shoot in, so that they might draw bows of great strength, and shoot arrows of a yard long, beside the head.

Then the king considering the great number of his enemies, and that the act of Frenchmen standing much in overriding of their adversaries by force of spearmen, he therefore charged every bowman to ordain him a sharp stake, and to put it at a slope before him, and when the spears came,

---

[37] Flenley, *Six Town Chronicles*, pp. 38–9.
[38] As McKisack explains (*Medieval History in the Tudor Age*, p. 95), 'Fabyan cites the standard medieval authors, from Bede to Caxton, and seems to have had some idea of trying to reconcile them, but the task was beyond his powers.'
[39] Kingsford, *Chronicles of London*, p. xxxi.

to draw back behind it, and so to shoot at the horsemen. And the proper request of the duke of York he ordained him to have the vanguard of that field. And when King Henry had thus providently ordered for his battle overnight, upon the morrow being the 25th day of October, and the day of the holy martyrs Crispin and Crispinian, the king caused divers masses to be sung. And where the night before the English host was occupied in prayer and confession, he then caused the bishops and other spiritual men to give unto them general absolution.

And that done, with a comfortable cheer ordered his people as they should fight, having unto them good and comfortable words, and so abode the coming of their enemies, which of divers writers were and are remembered to be above 40,000 fighting men. The which about 9 of the clock in the morning, with great pride set upon the English host, thinking to have overridden them shortly; but the archers like as before they were taught, put their sharp stakes before them, and when they saw the French gallants approach, they a little rode back and received them, as hereafter ensueth.

That is to mean they shot at them so fervently, that what with the shot and goring of their horses with the sharp stakes, they stumbled one upon another, so that he or they which ran foremost, were the confusion of him or them that followed, so that in a short while a great multitude of horse and men were laid upon the ground. And after their shot spent, they laid about them with their glaives and axes, that by the great grace of God and comfortable aid of the king, the victory fell that day to the Englishmen, and with little loss of their company; for, after the opinion of sundry writers, were slain that day of Englishmen, the dukes of York and of Suffolk, and not over 26 persons more.

But of Frenchmen were slain that day, after English writers, over the number of 10,000 albeit that French Gaguynus saith, that of the English host were slain the duke of York and with him 400 men, and of French host 4,000 of men of name, besides others, which he numbered not. Also he affirmeth to be horsemen at that field, upon the French part 10,000, over and beside the footmen, and that the Englishmen were numbered at 1,500 spear men, and 18,000 of yeomen and archers. At this said battle was take prisoner, the duke of Orléans, the duke of Bourbon, the earls of Vendôme, of Eu, of Richemont, and Bouccicaut then marshal of France, with many other knights and esquires, which were tedious to name, to the number of 2,400 and above, as witnesseth the book of mayors. And in this battle were slain of the nobles of France, the dukes of Bar, of Alençon and of Brabant, eight earls, and barons above 80 with other gentlemen in coat armour, to the number of 3,000 and above; by reason of which pillage the Englishmen were greatly advanced, for the Frenchmen were so assured of victory by reason of their great number, that they brought the more plenty of riches with them, to the end to buy prisoners either of other. And also after the victory by them obtained, to show unto Englishmen their pride and pompous array; but God, which knew the presumption and pomp, turned all things contrary to their minds and intents. When the king by grace and power of God, more than by force of man, had thus gotten this triumphant victory, and returned his people from the chase of their enemies, tidings were brought unto him that a new host of Frenchmen were coming towards him. Wherefore he anon commanded his people to be embattled, and that done made proclamations through the host, that every man should slay his prisoner; by reason of which proclamation, the duke of Orléans and the other lords of France were in such fear that they anon, by the licence of the king, sent such word unto the said host that they withdrew them, and the king with his prisoners upon the morrow following took his way towards his town of Calais, where he rested him during this mayor's time.

C 3. Polydore Vergil, *Anglica Historia* (1513, published 1534, Latin)

Translated from *Polydori Vergilii, Anglicae Historiae Libri XXVI* (Basle, 1534), pp. 437–42

Polydore Vergil was born in Urbino, Italy in about 1470. He came to England in 1502 in the entourage of Adriano de Castello of Cornetto who had been appointed bishop of Hereford, and was appointed the bishop's deputy as collector of Peter's Pence, the tribute paid to the papacy by the English church. Four years after his patron was translated to the see of Bath and Wells in 1504, Vergil was appointed archdeacon of Wells. He was also used as an envoy to the papal court until he fell from Wolsey's favour in 1514. He remained in England until 1553, then returning to Urbino where he died in 1555. His *Anglica Historia* was begun under commission from Henry VII, although it is possible that he had already begun to collect information on his own initiative.[40] The first version to 1509 was completed in 1513 and dedicated to Henry VIII. It was published in Basle in 1534, the delay in publication probably being due to his fall from favour, although the place of publication may also reveal the author's intention that the work should be known on both sides of the Channel. Later editions were also delayed due to political developments in England. Second and third editions were published in Basle in 1546 and in 1555, the latter covering the period to 1537.

The work was within the humanist tradition, with much use been made of classical sources and classical-style rhetoric. Vergil's Latin style is also much purer and more precise than the fifteenth-century Latin writers noted in the pre-

---

[40] There is no modern edition or translation of the whole work but the section of the third edition covering the period from 1485 to 1537 is edited and translated in *The Anglica Historia of Polydore Vergil AD 1485–1537*, ed. D. Hay (Camden Society, new series, 74, 1950) with a useful introduction. See also D. Hay, *Polydore Vergil, Renaissance Historian and Man of Letters* (Oxford, 1952) and Gransden, pp. 430–43.

vious chapter. He also had a stated desire to seek the truth, and to establish causation based upon human rather than divine agency. As Ellis points out, 'it is the first of our histories in which the writer ventured to compare the facts and weigh the statement of his predecessors; and it was the first in which summaries of personal character are introduced in the terse and energetic form adopted in the Roman classics.'[41] Thus Vergil condemned the monastic chronicles as bald, uncouth, chaotic and deceitful.[42] Moreover, in the sections after 1066, he gave a reign-based structure to his work, probably influenced by Suetonius' *Twelve Caesars*, although there is less by way of summative judgments of each reign: the approach is overwhelmingly narrative. He also includes an index, which was a novel feature for the period, and he was much more discriminating in his use of sources than Fabyan had been.[43]

However, his work could not be totally objective given that it was commissioned by Henry VII. To 1400 there is no obvious bias but for the fifteenth century, and in particular the period of the Wars of the Roses, Vergil was keen to provide an account which would redound to the favour of the Tudors, rather as Hall attempted to do in the 1540s. This is not obvious, however, in the account of Agincourt, for here as elsewhere Henry V escapes the denigration given by the Tudors to their fifteenth-century predecessors. It is clear, too, that Vergil drew upon vernacular chronicles in England, especially the London Chronicles and the *Brut*, perhaps using the latter through Caxton's printing of it in his *Polychronicon*. The words he gives to Henry in response to the French heralds are very close to those given in Tito Livio and the *First English Life*. There are also references to the use of oral traditions, such as in mention of the popular fame of Agincourt.[44] Although the work was published abroad it was used by later writers, including Hall and Holinshed. It is notable for the level of explanation, on, for instance, the use of the stakes. It is a dispassionate and remarkably sensible account, although Henry is allowed a rhetorical flourish in his pre-battle oration. This is entirely in the classical tradition where the insertion of a speech before the action helps to heighten and maintain the tension. The excitement is also maintained by Polydore's frequent use in his Latin tense structure of the historic present. The influence of Livy as well as Suetonius is apparent.

*

Emboldened with joy and pleasure on account of that success [at Harfleur] the king thought that he should advance further but he was prevented by the onset of winter, which was now beginning to afflict them earlier than usual, and after calling a council of war consulted his officers about where now to march. Various opinions were offered, but one

---

41 *Three Books of Polydore Vergil's English History* (Camden Society, 29, 1844), p. xxviii. This is an English translation of pre-1066 sections of the work.
42 As noted in Gransden, p. 434.
43 McKisack, *Medieval History in the Tudor Age*, p. 100.
44 Hay, *Polydore Vergil*, p. 92.

seemed best of all, that they make for Calais and, so that their departure should not seem like running away, it was decided that they should go by an inland route through the middle of the enemy, which was judged to be that much more dangerous because the number of healthy soldiers had been greatly reduced, as many on all sides were dying from disease which at that time had spread through that region; that was also a reason why they had so quickly discussed a withdrawal. So the king, after leaving Thomas, earl of Dorset, with a garrison in the captured town, began to march with his column drawn up and hurried to Pontoise [sic] with the intention of leading his forces across the Somme before the bridges were broken down.

The French meanwhile got to know their enemies' plan and took in advance all the bridges and fords and also, wherever they guessed the English would try to cross, they despoiled the land of pasture, corn and any other foodstuff, in order to shut the enemy off from all routes equally and put pressure on him through lack of everything. The English, although affected at one point by inconveniences of that kind, were in no way dismayed, but, pressing vigorously to complete the journey they had undertaken, arrived at the Somme. There being informed that the bridges had been broken down by the enemy, without delay they sent light-armed horsemen to reconnoitre and find out what enemy troops, what ambushes, and what danger there might be to the right and to the left and also where there was a shallow part of the river that was safe to cross. The horsemen performed this duty and reported that everywhere was full of enemy troops. When the king learned this, he went forward slowly, just as he had started to do, and, managing his affairs well, he led his battle array against the enemy who were standing around on the right and the left in such a way that he seemed to carry in front of him an appearance which brought terror on those who were watching. By that means it was brought about that without the necessity of fighting being put upon him he advanced as far as Corbie. There he was delayed by the arrival during the night of the country-dwellers and in the morning of the soldiers who had been left as a garrison in the town, but that affair turned out well for him, for, when the garrison had been routed and driven back in flight within the walls together with the crowd of country-dwellers, on the following day he found a ford between Corbie and Péronne, which, so the story goes, had never been known before that time, crossed the river and accelerating his journey straightway made for Calais, and that though he had decided that he should not fight a battle on account of the small number of his men, unless the situation demanded otherwise, for he had with him up to 2,000 English cavalry and up to 13,000 archers.

The English were afflicted during their journey by innumerable inconveniences, since they had not prepared the food supplies necessary for so many days nor could they easily find any on the journey, as the corn had been removed beforehand by their enemies. Henry, however, restrained the hands of his soldiery in a situation of such shortage from acts of sacrilege, in that he had long since promulgated an edict in the following terms to his army: 'Let no soldier ever despoil sacred edifices or violate them; if you do this, you will expiate the crime with due punishment.' As a result of that, when he heard that a certain soldier had snatched from a church a small vessel in which the sacrament was reserved, it is said that he ordered his marching column to stop and did not allow it to leave the spot until the vessel had been restored and the soldier had paid the penalty with his life. Hence it came about that, when the report of that action had spread through the countryside, the inhabitants of neighbouring places, contrary to their orders, supplied food to the column.

The French were highly indignant that the enemy was slipping away without a fight and they sent an invitation to battle to Henry by means of messengers. To that the Englishman replied: 'It is my concern that nothing should be done other than as God wills and as is necessary: for I shall not take the initiative in attacking the French with arms, but, if I am provoked by them, I shall not refuse battle: meanwhile I shall proceed to Calais. But, if anyone tries to stop me on my journey, he will not do so without harm to himself. Therefore lest anyone rashly dare to do that, I am particularly keen that this land should not unluckily be soaked with Christian blood.' That said, he dismissed the messengers from his presence without a gift.

On receiving this response, the French leaders pitched camp near the town of Blangy and prevented the enemy from advancing further, prepared in any circumstances to join battle, and so they arrayed their line of battle. In the front line they positioned 3,000 cavalry, the second line was strengthened by Charles, duke of Orléans, Louis, duke of Bourbon, Edward, duke of Bar, and the count of Nevers, attended by much the most numerous multitude of infantry and horsemen. After these, in a disordered array an unnumbered throng of soldiers held the third line in order to bring help where needed.

When Henry saw that the battle was nearer than he had believed, and thought that he would not safely leave the nearby camp where he had established himself the day before, he led out his army to take up battle order on the nearest plain, which lay open and extensive around the town of Blangy: and in order that the site of the battle should not restrict his soldiers' valour he chose a place near the hamlet which they call Agincourt, behind which a small hill rose which was covered on both sides with a forest of trees and very thick thorn-bushes, which provided defences like a wall, to prevent the enemy attacking him in the rear. Here he drew up his battle line. On his right flank, which was against the enemy, he placed his archers, in command of whom he put Edward, duke of York, and on the left and around the sides he disposed his cavalry. He himself joined with the main strength of his soldiers in the middle of the line.

But, since the enemy were superior in the number of both infantry and cavalry, he was afraid that the battle would not be fought with the same intensity on his men's front and flank, and so to ward off the force and the charge of the enemy's cavalry and to prevent them disturbing the order of his infantry on which the whole strength of his army rested, and breaking it, he had fences made on each flank from stakes six feet or a little less long, shod with iron on both sides and sharpened, so that, if the horses ran into them, they would be suddenly transfixed, and to certain soldiers of the common sort he gave the task of refixing the stakes as chance and the situation required and again fixing them in that point of the location to which the infantry moved in the fighting. The infantry therefore stationed itself within these fences of stakes or a rampart of earth, but all the cavalry stood on the flanks outside the stakes. Even now the English keep this method of fortifying their battle-array, although other machines have been invented for this purpose by means of which cavalry are kept at a distance from their infantry, for, if horses run rashly into the devices themselves, either they are pierced through at once or, their feet wounded, they are forced to fall to the ground.

I return to my theme. When he had drawn up his battle line in this way, the king ordered the baggage to be thrown together into one place and a place left in the camp even though it was defended by only a small garrison. After that he made a speech to the soldiers and urged them to foster a good hope in their hearts; for, he said, they should convince themselves of that truth that they had come to that particular place, which was as suitable for a small force of solders to fight in as it was useless to a large number, with God as their guide, who did not favour treaty-breakers, who did not help those who laid their hands on what belonged to others, those by whose faults surely and whose crimes rightly they knew that the French were among their most clearly marked out enemies. Therefore they should not be afraid because the enemy were far greater in number, since they ought also to know that in a great multitude of soldiers it necessarily follows that the greater proportion of them are much the most inexperienced in warfare and that, whenever they are involved in fighting, they are wont to obstruct those soldiers who are brave and energetic. Moreover, even if all men were equally knowledgeable of military skill, they should not for that reason be terrified, since they had to fight for their country, on whose behalf nothing had to be done without a heart prepared for it. Further, although there would be loss of life, yet it would be glorious: if they were victorious, they should be assured that the victory would be ascribed by all peoples to their noble qualities, but, if they were defeated by so great a multitude of enemies, they should reckon that they themselves would incur no ignominy at all, because being few they had been overcome by many. And finally they should know for sure that victory was in their grasp, if at the first clash they entered battle with a brave heart; because, what taught them that they ought to do so was the fact that they knew well that the issue was between them and the French, whom they had very often defeated before and whom they had for a long time known were as very ready to join battle as they were very weak at bearing the burden of a longer fight.

While the king was speaking up to this point, the soldiers' ardour began to peak at such a level that with a huge clamour they demanded the signal for battle. The dukes of Clarence, York and Gloucester felt that that should be done quickly, arguing that delay was merely an advantage to the enemy, since new troops were flowing into him from all sides. The king, however, decided to delay a little so that he should not do anything without proper thought. But the French meanwhile scorned the small numbers of the enemy and considered them of no account and so much confidence and high spirits took hold of them that they no longer thought about the logic of warfare, but thought they had already won the day; they widely rejoiced, considered themselves to be in paradise, boasted and bragged that they had the English surrounded and that he was defeated with no effort of their part and was already in their hands. The leaders of the contingents were already dividing the spoils, casting lots for the prisoners and preparing a chariot, in which the captive king would be led in triumph; at the same time they encouraged their soldiers and shouted to them: 'Hurry to booty and to glory, so that we may now think about your rewards and about rendering our thanks.'

Vain though it was, their passion for rejoicing went so far that they sent messengers to the cities in every direction to order them to rejoice and publicly congratulate them on the victory, as if it was not still uncertain, and to give thanks to God, in no way suspecting that it would soon come about that the winds would snatch their joy away. From this one may gather that to judge anything as certain about the outcome of future affairs is as much a mark of madness as not to do so is of prudence. What about the fact that they sent a messenger even to Henry to ask how much he wished to pay for his own ransom! They say that Henry replied that he hoped that within two or three hours it would so happen that the French rather than the English would have to give consideration to ransoming.

But while these things were happening, the forces being drawn up by both sides on the 25th of October, which was the day of the battle, at around midday they came at last to grips, for, when the signal had been given at the same point of time from both sides, they ran eagerly at one another and began to fight in their different ways. Certainly the English archers so harried with their first attack the French cavalry and infantry who were positioned together against them, that for some long time afflicted by many wounds they could not easily mount an attack, and by falling all over the place they caused no small consternation to their own men and gave heart to their enemies. On the other hand, when hand-to-hand fighting began, a good part of the English archers, having quickly thrown away their bows as is their custom and taken up the daggers and the swords which they always had ready to hand, rushed at a great pace into the advancing enemy. Against them at every point the French pressed, threatened and strove hard; while some of the cavalry fought it out with the English infantry, others on the right wing, with their shields held before them strove with the utmost endeavour to attack the enemy from the flank, but not without slaughter and they were repelled first by the rest of the archers, then by the horsemen who were standing near the stockades. So, the contest was everywhere keen and it was in the balance; everyone straining on his own behalf where he stood and pressing forward with shields and swords without time to draw breath fought some for victory, others for survival.

After both sides had fought bravely for nearly three hours, the king, after leading round wings of his cavalry a short distance, himself attached the line of infantry from behind; the new clamour that arose from there so terrified the minds of the French that at once they began to retreat. But, when the king saw the standards in confusion and the battle-array wavering, he then encouraged his soldiers with a few words attacked them with such force that the French were suddenly put to flight and fled in different directions and, after throwing away their arms, praying only for survival, surrendered. Meanwhile the French cavalry with Robert Bournoville at their head, who had been the first to turn their backs, heard that the equipment of the English was far away from their armed men without a guard and unfortified, and stirred by eagerness partly to take booty, partly to remedy by some fine deed the misfortune they had suffered, made an attack on the camp which was empty of defenders and seized all the equipment capturing or killing those who had been left to guard it. When an alarmed messenger brought this news to the king and the clamour was heard of the young men and others, who on the arrival of the enemy had taken to their heels, and were shouting that the soldiers' goods were being snatched away and carried off in all directions, the king was afraid that the enemy might be gathered together from their scattered flight and renew the battle, and out of necessity going against the mildness of his spirit he ordered the prisoners themselves of whom there was a large number to be killed at once and instructed his soldiers to disencumber themselves again for fighting.

Carrying out his orders, they killed a good part of the prisoners, and, forgetting all the unexpected labour that they had endured through almost a whole day and their wounds, stirred themselves with a single shake just as if they were unharmed and fresh. They returned to their battle formation and then attacked the enemy with the greatest force they could. But since the enemy, having now obtained his booty, was too far away for them to overtake him, of their own accord they stopped pursuing him. So this was the glorious battle at Agincourt and a victory of the English people, recalled among their foremost victories. Ten thousand Frenchmen were killed in the battle; the number of those taken prisoner, if they had not been killed in their camp by the enemy, was almost as large; many on both sides died later from their wounds. Of the English, if we believe those who recount miracles, scarcely 100 perished, along with Edward, duke of York. Of the writers some record that 500 English were lost in that battle, others 600. I am not sorry not to be of the opinion of the latter; for, when the battle was hard fought for more than three hours, it is far from doubt fair to believe that the English who were involved in armed conflict also received wounds of their own.

But for the king who had won so great a victory nothing was more urgent than that at that place on bended knee he should say many prayers and give undying thanks to God to whom that day, which is sacred to Sts Crispin and Crispinian, has remained for ever dedicated. After that shortly before nightfall he returned to his camp, which, as he refilled it to some small extent with his spoils, when he had that night restored his soldiers who were weary from their labours. The next day he returned to the battle-field and honoured with burial all those alike, whether of his own men or of the enemy, who had been lost in that encounter, but he had the body of the duke of York transported back to England, in order that it might be placed in the tomb of his ancestors. This done, with the dukes of Orléans and Bourbon and other prisoners from the nobility he returned first to Calais and then to England.

C 4. Edward Hall, *The Union of the Two Illustre Families of Lancaster and York* (1542, English)

Modernised from *Hall's Chronicle Containing the History of England*, ed. H. Ellis (London, 1809), pp. 63–73.

Edward Hall (d. 1547) hailed from Shropshire. After studying at Eton and Cambridge, he entered Gray's Inn and spent most of his life in legal and political activity in London. He was a committed supporter of the Henrician Reformation: 'his historical studies were boldly applied to the maintenance of an extreme theory of royal supremacy'.[45] In 1542 he published his *Union of the Two Illustre Families of Lancaster and York Beyng Long in Continual Dissension for the Crown of this Noble Realm*, which was reprinted after his death by Grafton in 1548 and again in 1550. Unlike Fabyan, he chose not to cast his work in the style of the London Chronicle with the year by year list of officials, preferring rather a reign-based approach. He also gave a shape and an unity of purpose to his work by deliberately beginning it with Henry IV ('the first author of this division') and ending with the accession of Henry VIII ('the undubitate flower and very heir of both the sayd lineages'). This was an overtly political statement

---

[45] *DNB*, 24, pp. 63–4.

which contrasted the anarchy of the fifteenth century, caused by the continuing aftermath of the change of dynasty in 1399, with the peace brought about by the coming of the Tudors, who united the two warring houses.

Hall claimed that this made sense in terms of historical writing, although he was exaggerating somewhat when he said in his prologue that 'sithe the ende of Froissart which endeth at the begynnyng of King Henry the Fourthe no man in the English tongue hath either set furth their honours according to their desertes, nor yet declared many noble actes worthy of memory dooen in the tyme of the seven kynges which after King Richard succeeded.'[46] Hall used a wide range of source materials, and although he did not use marginal notes, he prefixed his work with a list of the authorities used. He divides this into Latin, French and English writers, and those relevant to the current study include Monstrelet, the Chronicles of Normandy, Fabyan, Hardyng, the Chronicles of London, Caxton and John Basset. This last reference is particularly interesting as there are distinct indications in his text that he did indeed draw upon the Chronicle of (Peter) Basset and Hanson which is now in the College of Arms. He did not, it seems, consult Tito Livio's *Vita Henrici Quinti*.[47] He praised Fabyan as one of the few adequate histories in the English tongue but he also used the manuscript London chronicles too.[48] Polydore Vergil was also an important influence if not source. Indeed it is claimed that there was a strong humanist influence playing on Hall, and that he was the first of the native sixteenth-century writers to use English in the fashion of the Renaissance in a work which deliberately covered a long and coherent period of time.[49] His chronicle is long-winded and he was keen to give his characters fictitious speeches. Roger Ascham accused him 'of making excessive use of what he called "indenture English", this is of synonyms and equivalent phrases', but as McKisack adds 'he had a sensitive ear for language and he was a master of the vivid phrase'.[50]

Hall treated Henry V as a great hero, subtitling his reign 'the victorious acts of King Henry V'. This tone is exemplified in the account of the battle which is exceptionally full although sometimes inventive. In many ways, Hall produced the definitive version of the battle, expanding upon the stories he found elsewhere, and establishing the orthodoxy for others to follow. The account is poetic throughout. Hall waxes lyrical on the killing of the prisoners, and gives a remarkable speech to the French king of arms after the battle as well as to Henry and the French constable before it.

*

King Henry, not a little rejoicing of his good luck and fortunate success in the beginning of his pretensed conquest, determined with all diligence to

---

[46] *Hall's Chronicle*, p. vi.
[47] Kingsford, *First English Life*, p. xlvi.
[48] Kingsford, *Chronicles of London*, p. xxxiii.
[49] Campbell, *Shakespeare's Histories*, p. 69.
[50] McKisack, *Medieval History in the Tudor Age*, p. 109.

set forward in performing his intended purpose and warlike enterprise, but because winter approached faster and more furiously than before that time had been accustomed, he was sore troubled and vexed. For the which cause he called together all the chieftains and men of policy in his army to consult upon the proceeding forward and to be sure of way and ready passage. After long debating and much reasoning, it was as a thing both necessary and convenient and fully agreed and determined to set forward with all diligence before the dead time of winter approached, toward the town of Calais. And because their going forward should be called of slanderous tongues a running or flying away, it was decreed that the whole army should pass the next way by land through the midst of their enemies, and yet that journey was judged perilous by reason that the number was much diminished by the flux and other fevers, which sore vexed and brought to death above 1,500 persons, which was the very cause that the return was sooner concluded and appointed.

When the king had repaired the walls, fortified the bulwarks, refreshed the ramparts and furnished the town with victuals and artillery, he removed from Harfleur toward Pontoise [sic, for Ponthieu?], intending to pass the river of Somme with his army before the bridges were either withdrawn or broken. The French king hearing that the town of Harfleur was gotten and that the king of England was marching forward into the bowels of the realm, sent out proclamations and assembled people in every quarter, committing the whole charge of his army to his son, the dauphin and the duke of Aquitaine, which immediately caused the bridges to be broken and all the passages to be defended, beside that they caused all corn and other victual to be destroyed in all places where they conjectured that the Englishmen would repair or pass through, to the intent that they might either keep them in a place certain without any passage or departure, and so to destroy them at their pleasures, or else to keep them in a strait without victuals or comfort, and so by famine with cause them to die or yield.

The king of England afflicted with all these incommodities at one time was neither dismayed nor discouraged, but keeping forth his journey approached to the river of Somme, where he perceived that all the bridges were by his enemies broken and unframed: wherefore he came to the passage called Blanchetaque where King Edward, his great grandfather, passed the river of Somme before the battle of Crécy. But the passage was so kept that he could not pass without great danger, considering that his enemies were at his back and before his face. Wherefore he passed forward to Arraines, burning villages and taking great booty and every day he sent his light horsemen abroad to spy and seek what perils there were at hand, what ambushes there were laid on the one side or the other, and to find out where he might most safely pass the river. The spies returned and declared for a truth that the country swarmed with men of war, whereof he being advertised, set forth in good order, keeping still his way forward and so ordered his army and placed his carriage, that having his enemies on both sides of him, he passed so terribly that his enemies were afraid once to offer him battle, and yet the lord d'Albret, constable of France, the Marshal Bouccicaut, the earl of Vendôme, great master of France, and the Lord Dampier admiral of France, the duke of Alençon and the earl of Richemont with all the puissance of the dauphin lay at Abbeville and durst not once touch his battles, but ever kept the passages and coasted aloft like a hawk that liketh not her prey. The king of England still kept on his journey till he came to the bridge of St Maxence, where he found above 3,000 Frenchmen and there pitched his field, looking surely to be set on and fought withal. Wherefore to encourage his captains the more, he dubbed certain of his hardy and valiant gentlemen knights, as lord Ferrers of Groby, Reignold of Greystoke, Piers Tempest, Christopher Morisby, Thomas Pickering, William Huddleston, [?] Hosbalton, Henry Mortimer, Philip Hall and William his brother, and Jaques de Ormond and divers others.[51] But when he saw the Frenchmen made no semblance to fight, he departed in good order of battle by the town of Amiens to a town near to a castle called Boves, and there lay two days, every hour looking for battle. And from thence he came near to Corbie where he stayed that night by reason that the common people and peasants of the country assembled in great number, and the men of arms of the garrison of Corbie skirmished with his army in the morning, which tarrying was to him both joyous and profitable, for there he discomfited the crew of horsemen and drove the rustic people even to their gates, and also found there the same day a shallow ford between Corbie and Péronne, which never was espied before. At the which he, his army and carriages the night ensuing passed the great river of Somme without let or danger, the morrow after St Luke's day [19 Oct.], determined with all diligence to pass to Calais, and not to seek for battle except he were thereto constrained and compelled, because that his army by sickness was sore diminished and impaired, for he had only 2,000 horsemen and 8,000 archers, billmen and of all sorts. The Englishmen were afflicted in this journey with an hundred discommodities, for their victual was in manner all spent, and new they could get none, for their enemies had destroyed all the corn before their coming: rest they could take none, for their enemies were ever at hand, daily it rained and nightly it froze, of fuel was scarceness and of fluxes was plenty, money they had enough but comfort they had none. And yet in this great necessity the poor folks were not spoiled nor anything without payment was of them extorted, nor great offence was done except one, which was that a foolish soldier stole a pyx out of a church and unreverently did eat the holy hosts within the same contained. For which cause he was apprehended, and the king would not once remove till the vessel was restored

---

[51] The source for this must be the Chronicle of Basset and Hanson now in College of Arms MS 9, see Text A 8 above.

and the offender strangled. The people of the countries thereabout hearing of his straight justice and godly mind, ministered to him both victuals and other necessaries, although by open proclamation they were thereof prohibited.

The French king being at Rouen, hearing that the king of England was passed the water of Somme, was not a little discontent, and assembled his council to the number of thirty five to consult what should be done, the chief whereof were the dauphin, his son, whose name was Louis, calling himself king of Sicily, the dukes of Berry and Brittany, the earl of Ponthieu the king's youngest son and divers others, whereof thirty agreed that the Englishmen should not depart unfought withal, and five were of the contrary opinion, but the greater number ruled the matter. And so Mountjoye king at arms was sent to the king of England to defy him as the enemy of France, and to tell him that he should shortly have battle. King Henry soberly answered: 'Sir, mine intent and desire is none other, but to do as it pleaseth almighty God and as it becometh me, for surely I will not seek your master at this time, but if he or his seek me I will willingly fight with him. And if any of your nation attempt once to stop me in my journey toward Calais, at their jeopardy be it, and yet my desire is that none of you be so unadvised or harebrained as to be the occasion that I in my defence shall colour and make red your tawny ground with the deaths of yourselves and the effusion of Christian blood.' When he had answered the herald, he gave to him a great reward and licensed him to depart.

When the lords of France heard the king of England's answer, it was immediately proclaimed, that all men of war should resort to the constable of France to fight with the king of England and his puissance. Whereupon all men accustomed to bear armour and desirous to win honour through the realm of France drew toward the field. The dauphin sore desired to be at that battle, but he was prohibited by the king his father, likewise Philip, earl of Charolais, son to the duke of Burgundy, would gladly have been at that noble assembly if the duke his father would have suffered him, but many of his men stole away and went to the Frenchmen.

The king of England informed by his spies that the day of battle was nearer than he looked for, dislodged from Bomers [?Boves] and rode in good array through the fair plain beside the town of Blangy, where to the intent that his army should not be included in a straight or driven to a corner, he chose a place meet and convenient for two armies to array for battle between the towns of Blangy and Agincourt, where he pight [arranged] his field.

The constable of France, the marshal, the admiral, the Lord Rambures, master of the crossbows and divers lords and knights pitched their banners near to the banner royal of the constable in the county of St Paul within the territory of Agincourt, but the which way the Englishmen must needs pass toward Calais. The Frenchmen made great fires about their banners, and they were in number 60,000 horseman, as their own historians and writers affirm, beside footmen, pages and waggoners, and all that night made great cheer and were very merry. The Englishmen that night sounded their trumpets and divers musical instruments with great melody, and yet they were both hungry, weary, sore travailled and much vexed with cold diseases: howbeit they made peace with God, in confessing their sins, requiring him of help, and receiving the holy sacrament, every man encouraging and determining clearly rather to die than either to yield or fly.

Now approached the fortunate fair day to the Englishmen and the infest and unlucky day to the French nobility, which was the five and twentieth day of October in the year of our Lord Jesus Christ 1415, being then Friday and the day of Crispin and Crispinian. On the which day in the morning, the French men made three battles: in the vanguard were 8,000 healms of knights and esquires and 4,000 archers and 1,500 crossbows, which were guided by the lord d'Albret constable of France, having with him the dukes of Orléans and Bourbon, the earls of Eu and Richemont, the Marshal Bouccicaut and the master of the crossbows, the Lord Dampierre, admiral of France and other captains. And the earl of Vendôme and other the king's officers with 1,600 men of arms were ordered for a wing to that battle. And the other wing was guided by Sir Guy Dauphin and Sir Clignet of Brabant and Sir Louis of Bourbon with 800 men of arms, of chosen and elect persons. And to break the shot of the Englishmen were appointed Sir William of Saveuses with Hector and Philip his brethren, Ferry of Maylley and Alan of Gaspanes with other 800 men of arms. In the middle ward were assigned as many persons or more as were in the foremost battle, and thereof was the charge committed to the dukes of Bar and Alençon, the earls of Nevers, Vaudemont, Blammant, Salm, Grand Pré and of Roussy. And in the rearward were all the other men of arms, guided by the earls of Marlay, Dammartin, Fauquembergue and the lord of Lourrey, captain of Ardres, who had with him men of the frontiers of Boulogne.

When these battles were thus ordered, it was a glorious sight to behold them, and surely they were esteemed to be in number six times as many or more than was the whole company of the Englishmen with waggoners, pages and all. Thus the Frenchmen were every man under his banner only waiting for the bloody blast of the terrible trumpet, and in this order they continued resting themselves and reconciling everyone to other for all old rancours and hatreds which had been between them, till the hour between nine and ten of the day. During which season, the constable of France said openly to the captains in effect as followeth:

'Friends and companions in arms, I cannot but both rejoice and lament the chances and fortunes of these two armies which I openly see and behold with mine eyes here present. I rejoice for the victory which I see at hand for our part, and I lament and sorrow for the misery and calamity which I perceive to approach to the other side: for we cannot but be victors and triumphant conquerors, for who saw ever so flourishing an army within any Christian region, or such a multitude of valiant persons in one company? Is not here the flower of the French nation on barded horses with sharp spears and deadly weapons? Are not here the bold Bretons with fiery handguns and sharp swords? See you not present the practised pickards with strong and weighty crossbows? Beside these, we have the fierce Brabanters and strong Almaines with long pikes and cutting *slaughmesses*. And on the other side is a small handful of poor Englishmen which are entered into this region in hope of some gain or desire of profit, which by reason that their victual is consumed and spent, are by daily famine sore weakened, consumed and almost without spirits: for their force is clearly abated and their strength utterly decayed, so ere the battles shall join they shall be for very feebleness vanquished and overcome, and instead of men ye shall fight with shadows. For you must understand, ere keep an Englishman one month from his warm bed, fat beef and stale drink, and let him that season taste cold and suffer hunger, you then shall see his courage abated, his body wax lean and bare, and ever desirous to return into his own country. Experience now declareth this to be true, for if famine had not pinched them, or cold weather had not nipped them surely they would have made their progress further into France, and not by so many perilous passages retired toward Calais. Such courage is in Englishmen when fair weather and victuals follow them, and such weakness they have when famine and cold vex and trouble them. Therefore now it is no mastery to vanquish and overthrow them, being both weary and weak, for by reason of feebleness and faintness their weapons shall fall out of their hands when they profer to strike, so that ye may no more easily kill a poor sheep than destroy them being already sick and hungerstarven. But imagine that they were lusty, strong and courageous, and then ponder wisely the cause of their coming hither, and the meaning of their enterprise: first their king a young stripling (more meet for a tennis play than a warlike camp), claimeth the crown, sceptre and sovereignty of the very substance of the French nation by battle: then he and his intend to occupy this country, inhabit this land, destroy our wives and children, extinguish our blood and put our names in the black book of oblivion. Wherefore remember well, in what quarrel can you better fight than for the tuition of your natural country, the honour of your prince, the surety of your children and the safeguard of your land and lives. If these causes do not encourage you to fight, behold before your eyes the tents of your enemies, with treasure, plate and jewels well stuffed and richly furnished, which prey is surely yours if every man strike but one stroke, beside the great ransoms which shall be paid for rich captains and wealthy prisoners, which as surely shall be yours as you now had them in your possession. Yet this thing I charge you withal, that in no wise the king himself be killed, but by force or otherwise to be apprehended and taken to the intent that with glory and triumph we may convey him openly through the noble city of Paris to our king and dauphin as a testimony of our victory and witness of our noble act. And of this thing you be sure, that fly they cannot, and to yield to our fight of necessity they shall be compelled. Therefore good fellows take courage to you, the victory is yours, the gain is yours and the honour is yours without great labour or much loss.'

King Henry also like a leader and not like one led, like a sovereign and not like a soldier ordered his men for his most advantage like an expert captain and a courageous warrior. And first, he sent privily 200 archers into a low meadow which was near to the forward of his enemies, but separate with a great ditch, and were there commanded to keep themselves close till they had a token to them given to shoot at their adversaries. Beside this he appointed a vanguard, of the which he made captain Edward, duke of York which of a high courage had of the king required and obtained that office: and with him were the lords Beaumont, Willoughby and Fanhope, and this battle was all archers. The middle ward was governed by the king himself with his brother, the duke of Gloucester, and the earls Marshal, Oxford and Suffolk, in the which were all the strong billmen. The duke of Exeter, uncle to the king, led the rearward, which was mixed both with archers and billmen. The horsemen like wings went on every side of the battle. When the king had thus ordered his battle, like a puissant conqueror without fear of his enemies, yet considering the multitude of them far to exceed the small number of his people, doubting that the Frenchmen would compass and beset him about, and so fight with him of every side, to the intent to vanquish the power of the French horsemen which might break the order and array of his archers, in whom the whole force of the battle did consist and in manner remain he caused stakes bound with iron sharp at both ends of the length of five or six foot to be pitched before the archers and of every side the footmen like an edge, to the intent that if the barded horses ran rashly upon them, they might shortly be gored and destroyed, and appointed certain persons to remove the stakes when the archers moved, and as time required: so that the footmen were hedged about with the stakes, and the horsemen stood like a bulwark between them and their enemies without the stakes. This device of fortifying an army was at this time first invented, but since that time, they have imagined caltraps, harrows and other new tricks to defend the force of the horsemen so that if the enemies at adventure run against their engines, either suddenly their horses be wounded with the stakes, or their feet hurt with the other engines, so that of very necessity for pain, the silly poor beasts are compelled to fall and tumble to the ground. When he had ordered thus his battles, he left a small company to keep his camp and baggage, and then calling his captains and soldiers about him, he made to them an hearty oration in effect as followeth, saying:

'Well beloved friends and countrymen, I exhort you heartily to think and conceive in yourselves that this day shall be to us all a day of joy, a day of good luck and a day of victory: for truly if you well note and wisely consider all things, almighty God under whose protection we be come hither, hath appointed a place so meet and apt for our purpose as we ourselves could neither have devised nor wished which as it is apt and convenient for our small number and little army so is it unprofitable and unmeet for a great multitude to fight or give battle in: and in especial for such men in whom is neither constant faith nor security of promise, which persons be of God neither favoured nor regarded, nor he is not accustomed to aid and succour such people which by force and strength contrary to right and reason detain and keep from other their just patrimony and lawful inheritance, with which blot and spot the French nation is apparently defiled and distrained: so that God of his justice will scourge and afflict them for their manifest injuries and open wrongs to us and our realm daily committed and done. Therefore putting your only trust in him, let not their multitude fear your hearts, nor their great number abate your courage; for surely old warlike fathers have both said and written that the more people that an army is, the less knowledge the multitude hath of material feats or politic practices, which rude rustical and ignorant persons shall be in the field unto hardy captains and lusty men of war a great let and sore impediment. And though they all were of like policy, like audacity and of one uniform experience in martial affairs, yet we ought neither to fear them nor once to shrink from them considering that we come in the right, which ever of God is favoured, set forth and advanced: in which good and just quarrel all good persons shall rather set both their feet forward, than once to turn their one heel backward. For if you adventure your lives in so just a battle and so good a cause, which way soever fortune turn her wheel, you shall be sure of fame, glory and renown: if you be victors and overcome your enemies, your strength and virtue shall be spread and dispersed through the whole world: If you overpressed with so great a multitude shall happen to be slain or taken yet neither reproach can be to you ascribed, either yet infamy of you reported, considering that Hercules alone was not equivalent unto two men, nor a small handful is not equal to a great number, for victory is the gift of God and consisteth not in the puissance of men. Wherefore manfully set on your enemies at their first encounter strike with a hardy courage on the false-hearted Frenchmen, whom your noble ancestors have so often overcome and vanquished. For surely they be not so strong to give the onset upon you, but they be much weaker to abide your strength in a long fight and tired battle. As for me I assure you all, that England for my person shall never pay ransom, nor never Frenchmen shall triumph over me as his captain, for this day by famous death or glorious victory I will win honour and obtain fame. Therefore now joyously prepare yourselves to the battle and courageously fight with your enemies, for at this very time all the realm of England prayeth for our good luck and prosperous success.'

While the king was thus speaking, each army so maligned and grudged at the other being in open sight and evident appearance, that every man cried forth, forth, forward, forward. The dukes of Clarence, Gloucester and York were of the same opinion, thinking it most convenient to march toward their enemies with all speed and celerity, lest in prolonging of time and arguing of opinions, the French army might more and more increase and multiply. Howbeit the king tarried a while lest any jeopardy were not forseen, or any hazard not prevented.

The Frenchmen in the mean season little or nothing regarding the small number of the English nation, were of such high courage and proud stomachs that they took no thought for the battle, as who say they were victors and overcomers before any stroke was striken, and laughed at the Englishmen, and for very pride thought themselves lifted into heaven jesting and boasting that they had the Englishmen enclosed in a straight and had overcome and taken them without any resistance. The captains determined how to divide the spoil: the soldiers played the Englishmen at dice: the noble men devised a chariot how they might triumphantly convey King Henry being captive to the city of Paris, crying to their soldiers, haste yourselves to obtain spoil, glory and honour, to the intent that we may study how to give you thanks for the great gifts and rewards which we hope to receive of your great liberality. The foolish folly of this vain solace broke out so far, that messengers were sent to the cities and towns adjoining, willing them to make open plays and triumphs, (as though that the victory were to them certain and no resistance could appear) and also to give God thanks for their prosperous act and notable deed, not remembering that the whirlwind shortly with a puff blew away all their foolish joy and fantastical bragging.

Of this doing you may gather, that it is as much madness to make a determinate judgment of things to come, as it is wisdom to doubt what will follow of things begun. I may not forget how the Frenchmen being in this pleasant pastime, sent a herald to King Henry to inquire what ransom he would offer, and how he answered that within two or three hours he hoped that it should so happen that the Frenchmen should come rather with the Englishmen how to be redeemed, than the Englishmen should take thought how to pay any ransom or money for their deliverance: ascertaining them for himself that his dead carrion should rather be their prey, than his living body should pay any ransom. When the messenger was departed, the Frenchmen put on their helmets and set them in order under their banners, richly armed and gorgeously trapped and caused their trumpets to blow to the battle.

The Englishmen perceiving that, set a little forward, before whom there went an old knight called Sir Thomas of Erpingham, a man of great experience in war, with a warder in his hand, and when he cast up his warder, all the army shouted, at the which the Frenchmen much marvelled, but that was a sign to the archers in the meadow, which knowing the token, shot wholly altogether at the vanguard of the Frenchmen. When they perceived the archers in the meadow, whom they saw not before, and saw they could not come to them for a ditch, they with all haste set on King Henry's forward, but ere they joined, the archers in the forefront and the archers on the side which stood in the meadow, so wounded the footmen, so galled the horses and so cumbered the men of arms that the footmen durst not go forward, the horsemen ran in plumpes [groups?] without order, some overthrew his fellow, and horses overthrew their masters: so at the first joining, as the Frenchmen were clearly discouraged, so the Englishmen were much cheered. When the French vanguard was thus discomforted, the English archers cast away their bows and took into their hands axes, mails and swords, bills and other weapons, and therewith slew the Frenchmen till they came to the middleward. Then the king approached and encouraged his soldiers, that shortly the second battle was overthrown and dispersed not without great slaughter of men: howbeit divers being wounded were relieved by their varlets and conveyed out of the field, for the Englishmen so sore laboured with fighting and slaying, and were so busy in taking of prisoners that they followed no chase, nor would once break out of the battle. The Frenchmen strongly withstood the fierceness of the Englishmen when they came to handy strokes, so that the fight was very doubtful and perilous. And when one part of the French horsemen thought to have entered into the king's battle, they were with the stakes overturned, and either slain or taken.

Thus this battle continued three long hours, some strake, some defended, some made a thrust, some traversed, some caused injuries, some took prisoners, no man was idle, every man fought either in hope of victory or glad to save himself. The king that day showed himself like a valiant knight, which notwithstanding that he was almost felled with the duke of Alençon, yet with plain strength he slew two of the duke's company and felled the duke: but when the duke would have yielded him, the king's guard contrary to the king's mind outrageously slew him. And in conclusion, minding to make an end of that day's journey, caused his horsemen to fetch a compass about and to join with him against the rearward of France: in the which battle were the greatest number of people. When the Frenchmen perceived his intent, they were suddenly amazed and ran away like sheep without array or order.

When the king perceived the banners cast down and the array was clearly broken, he encouraged his soldiers and followed so quickly that the Frenchmen turning to flight, ran hither and thither not knowing which ways to take, casting away their armour and on their knees desired to have their lives saved. In the mean season while the battle thus continued and that the Englishmen had taken a great number of prisoners, certain Frenchmen on horseback whereof were captains Robinet of Bourneville, Rifflart of Clamas and Isambert of Agincourt and other men of arms to the number of 600 horsemen: which fled first from the field at their first coming and hearing that the English tents and pavilions were far from the army without any great number of keepers or persons meet and convenient for defence, partly moved and stirred with covetous desire of spoil and prey, and partly intending by some notable act to revenge the damage and displeasure done to them and theirs in battle the same day, entered into the king's camp being void of men and fortified with varlets and lackeys, and there spoiled halls, robbed tents, brake up chests and carried away caskets and slew such servants as they could find in the tents and pavilions. For the which act they were long imprisoned and sore punished and like to have lost their lives if the dauphin had longer lived.

When the king by a fearful messenger was of this evil act suddenly advertised, and when the outcry of the lackeys and boys which ran away for fear of the robbers was heard into the field, saying that the Frenchmen had robbed all the tents and lodgings of the Englishmen, he fearing lest his enemies being dispersed and scattered abroad should gather together again and begin a new field, and doubting farther that the prisoners would either be an aid to his enemies or very enemies to him if he should suffer them to live, contrary to his accustomed gentleness and pity he commanded by the sound of a trumpet that every man upon pain of death should incontinently slay his prisoner. When this dolorous decree and pitiful proclamation was pronounced, pity it was to see and loathsome it was to behold how some Frenchmen were suddenly sticked with daggers, some were brained with poleaxes, some were slain with mails, other had their throats cut and some their bellies paunched: so that in effect having respect to the great number, few prisoners or none were saved.

When this lamentable manslaughter was finished, the Englishmen forgetting their wounds and hurts and not remembering what pain they had sustained all day in fighting with their enemies, as men that were fresh and lusty, ranged themselves again in array both pressed and ready to abide a new field, and also to invade and newly to set on their enemies, and so courageously they set on the earls of Marlay and Fauquembergue and the lords of Louray and of Thyne, which with 600 men of arms had all day kept together and slew them out of hand.

When the king has passed through the field and saw neither resistance nor appearance of any Frenchmen saving the dead corpses, he caused the retreat to be blown and brought all his army together about four of the clock at afternoon. And first to give thanks to almighty God giver and tributor of this glorious victory, he caused his prelates and chaplains first to sing this psalm *In exitu Israel de Egypto* etc. commanding every man to kneel down on the ground at this verse. *Non nobis domine, non nobis, sed nomine tuo da gloriam*, which is to say in English, 'Not to us lord, not to us, but to thy name let the glory be given': which done he caused *Te deum* with certain anthems to be sung giving lauds and praisings to God, and not boasting nor bragging of himself nor his human power. That night he took refreshment of such as he found in the French camp, and in the morning Mountjoye king at arms and four heralds came to him to know the number of prisoners and to desire burial to them which were slain. Before he could make any answer to the heralds he, remembering that it is more honourable to be praised of his enemies than to be extolled of his friends, and he that praiseth himself lacketh loving neighbours: wherefore he demanded to them why they made to him that request, considering that he knew not certainly whether the praise and the victory were meet to be attributed to him or to their nation. 'Oh lord' quoth Mountjoye king at arms, 'think you as officers of arms to be rude and bestial persons? If we for the affection that we bear to our natural country, would either for favour or mead hide or deny your glorious victory: the fowls of the air, the worms of the ground feeding on the multitude of the dead carrions, by your only puissance destroyed and confounded, will bear witness against us, ye and much more the captives which be living and in your possession with their wives and little infants will say we be open liers and untrue tale-tellers: wherefore according to the duty of our office which is or should be always indifferently to write and truly to judge, we say, determine and affirm that the victory is yours, the honour is yours and yours is the glory, advising you, as you have manfully gotten it, so politically to use it.' 'Well', said the king, 'seeing this is your determination, I willingly accept the same, desiring you to know the name of the castle near adjoining'. When they had answered that it was called Agincourt he said that this conflict should be called the battle of Agincourt, 'which victory hath not been obtained by us nor our power, but only by the suffrance of God for injury and untruth that we have received at the hands of your prince and his nation.' That day he feasted the French officers of arms and granted to them their request, which busily sought through the field for such as were slain, but the Englishmen suffered them not to go alone for they searched with them and found many hurt but not in jeopardy of their life, whom they took prisoners and brought them into their tents.

When the king of England had well refreshed himself and his soldiers and had taken the spoil of such as were slain, he with his prisoners in good order returned to his town of Calais.

When the king of England was departed the Sunday toward Calais, divers Frenchmen repaired to the plain where the battle was and removed again the dead bodies, some to find their lords and masters and them to convey into their countries there to be buried, some to spoil and take the relics which the Englishmen had left behind. For they took nothing but gold, silver, jewels, rich apparel and costly armour. But the ploughmen and peasants spoiled the dead carcasses, leaving them neither shirt nor clout, and so they lay stark naked till Wednesday. On the which day divers of the noblemen were conveyed into their countries and the remnant were by Philip, earl Charolais (sore lamenting the chance and moved with pity) at his cost and charge buried in a square plot of 500 yards, in the which he caused to be made three pits, wherein were buried by account 5,800 persons beside them that were carried away by their friends and servants, and other which being wounded to death died in hospitals and other places, which grove after was made a churchyard, and for fear of wolves enclosed with a high wall.

After this dolorous journey and piteous slaughter, divers clerks of Paris made many lamentable verses, complaining that the king reigned by will, and that councillors were partial, affirming that the noblemen fled against nature, and that the commons were destroyed by their prodigality, declaring also that the clergy were dumb and durst not say the truth, and that the humble commons duly obeyed and yet ever suffered punishment. For which cause by persecution divine, the less number vanquished, and the great was overcome. Wherefore they concluded that all things were out of order, and yet there was no man that studied to bring the unruly to frame. And no marvel though this battle were dolorous and lamentable to the French nation, for in it were taken and slain the flower of all the nobility of France, for there were taken prisoners [list follows] and divers other to the number of fifteen hundred knights and esquires beside the common people. There were slain of nobles and gentlemen [list follows] with divers other which I leave out for tediousness. But surely by the relation of the heralds and declaracion of other notable persons worthy of credit as Enguerrant writeth, there were slain on the French part above 10,000 persons whereof were princes and nobles bearing banners 126 and all the remnant saving 1,600 were knights esquires and gentlemen: so of noblemen and gentlemen were slain 8,400 of the which 500 were dubbed knights the night before the battle. From the field escaped alive, the Earl Dammartin, the Lord Delarivier, Clignet of Brabant, Sir Louis of Bourbon, Sir Galiot of Gaul, Sir John Dengermes and few other men of name.

Of Englishmen at this battle were slain Edward, duke of York, the earl of Suffolk, Sir Richard Kyghley and Davy Gamme esquire, and of all other not above twenty five if you will give credit to such as write miracles: but other writers whom I sooner believe, affirm that there was slain above five or six hundred persons which is not unlike, considering the battle was earnestly and furiously fought by the space of three long hours, wherefore it is not incredible nor yet impossible but more Englishmen than five and twenty were slain and destroyed.

This battle may be a mirror and glass to all Christian princes to behold and follow, for king Henry neither trusted in the puissance of his people, nor in the fortitude of his champions, nor in the strength of his barded horses, nor yet in his own policy, but he put in God (which is the corner stone and immovable rock) his whole confidence, hope and trust. And he which never leaveth them destitute that put their confidence in him, sent to him this glorious victory, which victory is almost incredible if we had not read in the Book of Kings that God likewise had defended and aided them that only put their trust in Him and committed themselves wholly to His governance.

C 5. John Stow, *The Chronicles of England* **(1580, English) republished in expanded form as** *The Annales of England* **(1592, 1601, English)**

Modernised from *The Annales of England, faithfully collected out of the most authenticall authors, records and other monuments of antiquities, lately corrected, encreased and continued from the first habitation until this present yeere 1601 by John Stow citizen of London* (London, 1601), pp. 348–51.

John Stow (?1525–1605) was a London tailor who in mid-life devoted himself to 'the search of our famous antiquities'.[52] He spent much time searching out manuscripts and printed books, gaining a great familiarity with such materials. He also became a collector of the same in his own right, and some of his manuscripts are today to be found in the British Library. He also assisted Archbishop Matthew Parker in locating and establishing texts of medieval chronicles for printing, such as that of Thomas Walsingham in 1574. His first publication was the works of Chaucer (1561). Four years later he produced the *Summarie of English Chronicles*, which was a brief survey of English history. In 1580 he published the first edition of *The Chronicles of England*, dedicated to the earl of Leicester. This was revised and expanded after extra research as the *Annals of England* (1592), which was reprinted in 1601. He lent materials to Holinshed and was involved in the revision of the second edition of the latter's chronicle.

Stow's interest in the traditions and history of London was particularly strong. The *Summarie* was dedicated to the mayors, aldermen and the commonalty of London, and in 1598 he produced his magisterial *Survey of London*. Of interest is his long-running intellectual feud with Richard Grafton, where both men impugned the accuracy and scholarship of the other, often in heated and abusive terms. This rivalry is not surprising given that both men brought out similar historical works in close succession. There can be little doubt that Stow was the more diligent researcher of the two, drawing on a more extensive range of original sources. Like others in this period, his works contain marginal notes on the source of information. His *Chronicle of England* was still in the annalistic form of the London Chronicle, and he has been seen as the last of the great London chroniclers. The *Annals*, despite the name, saw him drop this annalistic form and to adopt a continuous narrative. In this respect, and in the extent of his research, he also stands as an indication of future trends in historical writing, and there can be no doubt that his work, especially the *Survey of London*, was well known and much used in later centuries. As noted earlier a list at the outset of his work shows that he drew on a wide array of sources, including the 'Translator of Livius', of which he possessed a copy, and some official records such as the register of the garter and the records of Parliament on which no others are known to have drawn. He also put marginal notes giving the sources, although

---

[52] As cited in *DNB*, 55, p. 3.

by no means systematically. His account is much more business-like and less rhetorical than that of Hall and much closer to the *First English Life*.

*

After King Henry had remained at Harfleur fifteen days, after the delivery of the town and of the towers, he departed from thence towards Calais, whereof, when his enemies were advised, and also by what way he intended to pass, all the people of the country, cities, and towns were marvellously oppressed with fear, wherefore they hastened them to defensible places, and others that were apt to war took them to their hosts, and assembled them together in great number, with no small company of footmen, and in all they might they oppressed the Englishmen.

The king's host kept an easy pace, without making any haste, and when they approached the town of Eu, their enemies assailed them in the fields with great force and noise, where on both parties it was fought fierce and vigorously: but the Frenchmen drew back to the town, where they were in good surety. From thence the king departed, and came to a passage of the River Somme, which the Frenchmen call Blanchetoke, or Blanchtache. This passage, at the coming into it, was fixed with sharp stakes by their enemies, so that they could not pass there, but were constrained to go further, seeking their passage, until they came directly to have the city of Amiens and the castle of Corbie on their left side, where they of the said city began with them a new fight: but they were soon forced by the English to return to their city again. The nineteenth of October the king passed the river of Somme, at the passage of Voyennes, and Bethencourt, and went then to lodge him at Monchy-Lagache, from whence he advanced him towards the river of Miramont. In the meantime, the French king and the duke of Guienne his son, then dauphin, proposing to resist the Englishmen, came to Rouen, from whence they sent three heralds to the king of England, to give understanding that he should not escape without battle: unto whom the said king answered, 'All things be done at the pleasure of GOD, I will keep the right way towards Calais: if our adversaries do attempt to disturb us in our journey, we think they shall not do it without their own great danger and peril.' From thence King Henry removed to a village called Forceville, advancing his host towards the river of Miramont, and the next day they passed by the Cheve, and the king lodged that night at Gonvers-l'Estaillon. The next day the king removed on to Blangy. The next day late in the night the king came to a village named Agincourt, Enguerant saith Maisoncelles, where they lodged distant from the French host not above 250 paces. The Frenchmen tied their banners and standards with the banner royal, whereof the constable had the conduct in the field by them devised and chosen, which was in the county of St Pôl, in the ground of Agincourt, by which the day following, the Englishmen should pass to go to Calais.

The 25th of October, after prayers and supplications of the king, his priests and people done with great devotion, the king of England in the morning very early set forth his host in array: he commanded that his hosts and other carriages should be left in the village where he had lodged. The order of his field was thus: the middle battle whereof the king was conductor, was set in the midst of the field, directly against the middle battle of his adversaries. On the right side was the first battle and therewith the right wing: and on the left side the last battle, and the left wing. And these battles joining nigh together, by the providence of God, proved unto this king a defensible place for his host, for the village wherein he was lodged before defended his host from all invasions on the back, and the field wherein he was, was defended on both sides with two small rivers. This noble king was armed with fair and right beautiful armour: on his head a bright helmet, whereupon was set a crown of gold replete with pearls and precious stones, marvellous rich: in his shield he bore the arms both of England and France. And thus armed, he was mounted upon a goodly great horse, and after him were led certain noble horses, with their bridles and trappings of goldsmiths' work, and upon them also were beaten the arms of England and of France. Thus this victorious king prepared to battle, encouraged his people to the field that approached at hand.

The night before this cruel battle, by the advice and counsel (as it is said) of the duke of York, the king had given commandment through his host, that every man should purvey him a stake sharp at both ends, which the Englishmen fixed in the ground before them in the field, to defend them from the oppression of horsemen. The Frenchmen had such confidence in the great multitude of their people, and in their great horses, that many of their great princes and lords leaving behind them their soldiers, standards and other ensigns, came towards the Englishmen in right great haste, as if they had been assured of victory.

The king of England forthwith advanced his banners and standards towards the French host, and he in person with his battle in the same order wherein he stood, followed, exhorting and encouraging every man to battle, notwithstanding he went to invade his enemies, yet kept his accustomed order, that is, that the first battle went before, the second battle followed, and the third came immediately after, he commanded his priests to abide in prayers, and divine supplications, and his heralds in their coats of arms to attend to their offices. Then every man fell prostrate to the ground, and committed themselves to God, every one of them took in his mouth a little piece of earth, in remembrance that they were mortal, and made of earth, as also in remembrance of the holy communion. Thus all their carriages and baggages left behind, only charged with their harness, weapons, and stakes, they marched towards their enemies, with great noise. They sounded their trumpets, and struck up their drums, which greatly encouraged the hearts of every man. Their enemies seeing them approach, advanced themselves also, and met them in the field, betwixt whom was begun a marvellous fierce and cruel battle. The battle of the Englishmen was as long as the field wherein they fought, which was greatly to their advantage, for by that their enemies were allowed to come upon them at the sides and back of the host. The Frenchmen had ordained their battles with two sharp fronts, like unto two horns, which always backward was broader and broader: these sharp battles set upon the English middleward, intending to have run through the whole field, but the Frenchmen were slain and wounded by the English archers, and by the help of the stakes, which the Englishmen had fixed before them in the ground, whereby the horsemen were constrained to return, or else to run upon the stakes, where many of them were overthrown and wounded, and many both horses and men slain. The battle and fight increased marvellously, by the space of three hours, in all which time no man was taken prisoner, but an innumerable number were slain, upon whose dead bodies they that followed were thrown and slain.

Thus after a long and cruel battle, by the demerits of their great pride, there approached no man of the French to battle, but to death, of whom after that an innumerable company were slain, and that the victory surely remained to the Englishmen, they spared to slay and took prisoners of the French, both princes and gentlemen in great number. In this mortal battle, the noble king of England never failed his men, for no danger of death, but fought with his enemies with an ardent heart, as a famished lion for his prey, receiving on his helmet and on the residue of his armour, many and great strokes.

In this field, as the puissant prince Humphrey, duke of Gloucester the king's brother, fought with great courage and force, he was sore wounded in the groin with a sword, and overthrown, insomuch, as he lay as half dead in the field, his head towards the Englishmen and his feet towards his enemies: upon whom the king having a brotherly compassion, bestrode him, and with most strong battle and labour, not without his own great peril, like a brother he defended and succoured his brother from the enemies, and made the duke to be borne out of the field amongst his own men.

At the last, the victory obtained, and the great host of the Frenchmen overcome, slain, wounded, taken and vanquished, forthwith another host of Frenchmen, no less than the first, supposing the Englishmen to be wearied by their long travail and fight, disposed them to begin again the battle anew. When the Englishmen (which had many more prisoners than they were of themselves in number) saw this new field assembled to give them battle again, fearing in this new field, lest they should fight both against their prisoners and their other enemies, they put to death many of their said prisoners, both noble and rich men, among whom the duke of Brabant, who at that field was taken prisoner, was one.

The prudent king of England seeing the reassemble of his adversaries sent his heralds unto them, commanding them either forthwith to come to battle, or else immediately to depart the field, and if they delayed to depart, or to come to battle, both those of their company already taken prisoners, and also all they that should thereafter be taken, without mercy or redemption should be put to death: which message when the Frenchmen heard, fearing the strength of the Englishmen, and also the death, both of themselves, and also of their friends before taken prisoners, with great heaviness, and with shame, they forthwith departed. Then the king of England being assured of the victory, gave the greatest laud and praise to God that might be.

In this battle were slain on the French part, the noble dukes of Alençon, of Berry, and Bavere [Bar], and the Lord Heilly, the lord d'Albret, chief constable of France, the archbishop of Sens, eight earls, 101 barons, 1,500 knights, and above 10,000 of all estates, whereof scarcely 1,500 were soldiers or labourers, the rest were of coats armour (saith Enguerant) but Thomas Elmham saith archbishops, one, dukes, three, earls, five, barons and such like, 92 knights, 1,500, of esquires and gentlemen, 7,000, whereof he nameth the archbishop of Sens, the dukes of Brabant, Alençon and of Bar, the earl of Nevers, Dammartin, Marlay, Grandpré, Salines, and of Dansemonteul, the lord of d'Albret, constable of France.

In this battle were taken prisoners of the Frenchmen, the dukes of Orléans and of Bourbon, Arthur, brother to the duke of Brittany, the earls of Vendôme, of Eu, and Richemont, and Sir Bouccicaut marshal of France, and many others to the number of 1,500 knights and esquires: and of the English part were slain Edward, duke of York, buried at Fotheringhay, Michael de la Pole, earl of Suffolk, buried at Ewelme and to the number of 100 persons in the vanguard, and of all estates in the English party were not found dead above 600 in the field. When night approached, the king of England returned with his host into the village wherein they had harboured the night before, where he found his horses, and other baggages and carriages that he left behind him there before the field, to be stolen and carried away by the Frenchmen: where amongst many other jewels of great price, was stolen away a sword of great value, adorned with gold and precious stones, which was after given to Philip, earl of Charolais, son and heir to John, duke of Brittany [sic].

King Henry having gathered his army together, gave thanks to Almighty God for his so happy a victory, calling his priests and chaplains to sing the psalm *In exitis Israel de aegypte* [sic], and commanding every man to kneel down on the ground at this verse, *Non nobis Domine, non nobis, sed nomine tuo da gloriam* which being done, he caused *Te Deum* with certain anthems to be sung, giving laud and praise to God, not boasting of his own force or any human power. This night when the king sat at his refection in the aforesaid village, he was served at his board by those great lords and princes that were taken in the field. That night the king appointed good and fair watches throughout his host, for fear of sudden invasions, but the Frenchmen were utterly divided and gone without making or intending any new business, whereby the Englishmen were suffered in peace to take their rest.

On the next day the king with his people entered his journey towards Calais: and as they passed through the fields where they had fought the day before, they found all the dead bodies dispoiled, as well of their harness as of their array, by the inhabitants of the country, notwithstanding the bodies that might be known for Englishmen of any reputation, the king caused to be interred according to their estates, and so continuing his journey the king came to the castle of Guînes, and from thence he went to his town of Calais, with all his host and his prisoners, where he was received of his liege men, with great joy and due honour. After the king's host was somewhat refreshed with meat, drink, and sleep, the king conferred with his wise counsellors, if it were good now to return into France, to pursue his enterprise begun, or else to return with his host into England, there to refresh his people, among who it was considered that the number of his people was right small, and many of them with the flux, many sore grieved of their wounds which they had received at the field. Moreover, that their long staying at Calais should cause scarcity of victuals there, where as otherwise in their own country the people should at more ease refresh themselves, and also be better cured of their wounds: finally, considering the time had not been hitherto unfortunate, but that with honour they might return with great gain, which they had conquered, they doubted not, but by the aid of God, the king should right well obtain his desire in time to come, for which causes they all condescended upon their return into England.

C 6. Raphael Holinshed, *Holinshed's Chronicles of England, Scotland and Ireland* (1586–87, English)

Modernised from *Holinshed's Chronicles of England, Scotland and Ireland*, ed. H. Ellis, 6 vols (London, 1808), 3, pp. 76–84.

Holinshed probably came from Cheshire but came to London early in the reign of Elizabeth to work with the printer Reginald Wolfe.[53] The latter, who held the notes of the early Tudor antiquarian, John Leland, had an idea for the production of a universal history and cosmography, on which Holinshed worked, but this work was not ready for publication when Wolfe died in 1573. Three publishers took on the task but decided to limit the work to England, Scotland and Ireland, taking on others to assist. *Holinshed's Chronicle* was produced in two volumes in 1578, with woodcuts and with the intention of reaching a large audience.

[53] *DNB*, 27, p. 132.

After Holinshed's death in 1580, the publishers joined with others to produce a new expanded edition under the direction of John Hooker.[54] This appeared in three volumes in 1586–7. It was this edition which Shakespeare drew upon and from which he took phrases for his history plays and for Macbeth, King Lear and Cymbeline.

Holinshed was therefore only one of several authors but the work has continued to bear his name.[55] He used marginal notes to indicate his sources and he also listed some key works at the end of each reign. We thus know that he drew on a wide range of materials, including Tito Livio,[56] Hardyng, Walsingham, Monstrelet, Hall and the London Chronicles. He also used the verse work, *De Angliae Praeliis*, from which he cites a short extract on the numbers of French dead. Holinshed's chronicle was an extremely wordy production. There was also a desire 'to have an especial eye unto the truth of things'.[57] One of the reasons also cited for the publication of the work was 'to put men in mind not to forget their native country's praise'.[58] It would be fair to say, however, that there is nothing particularly different or superior about Holinshed's chronicle compared, say, with Stow or Hall, and that its claim to fame is perhaps dependent on the Shakespearean link. (Some of the errors in Shakespeare, such as Exeter and perhaps Clarence being present at the battle, come from errors in Holinshed, which he himself had copied from Hall and others.) In many ways, Holinshed is of crucial importance because it combined the traditions established in the *First English Life* and distilled through Stow, with the tradition established by Hall transmitted through Grafton, and is thus the greatest of the composite histories of the period.

*

The Englishmen were brought into some distress in this journey, by reason of their victuals in manner spent, and no hope to get more: for the

---

54 There is a helpful discussion of differences between the two editions in Levy, *Tudor Historical Thought*, pp. 182–6.
55 For a full discussion see A. Patterson, *Reading Holinshed's Chronicles* (Chicago and London, 1994).
56 Particularly interesting is the note on p. 136 of his chronicle. 'Titus Livius lived also in these days, an Italian borne. But since he was both resident here and wrote the life of this king, I have thought it good to place him among other of our English writers. One there was that translated the said history into English adding (as it were by way of notes in many places of that book) sundry things for more large understanding of the history, a copy of which I have seen belonging to John Stow citizen of London. There was also about the same time another writer who as I remember hath followed the said Livius in the order of his book as it were chapter for chapter only changing a good familiar and easy style which he said Livius used into a certain poetical kind of writing, a copy whereof I have seen (and in the life of this king partly followed) belonging to Master John Twine of Kent.' This is clearly a reference to the Pseudo-Elmham and is probably the work which Stow refers to in his marginal notes as 'Thomas Elmham'.
57 *DNB*, 27, pp. 130–32.
58 Cited in Flenley, *Six Town Chronicles*, p. 55.

enemies had destroyed all the corn before they came. Rest could they none take, for their enemies with alarm did ever so infest them: daily it rained, and nightly it froze: of fuel there was great scarcity, of fluxes plenty: money enough, but wares for their relief to bestow it on had they none. Yet in this great necessity, the poor people of the country were not spoiled, nor anything taken of them without payment, nor any outrage or offence done by the Englishmen, except one, which was that a soldier took a pyx out of a church, for which he was apprehended, and the king not once removed [*would not move on*] till the box was restored, and the offender strangled. The people of the countries thereabout, hearing of such zeal in him, to the maintenance of justice, ministered to his army victuals, and other necessaries, although by open proclamation so to do they were prohibited.

The French king being at Rouen, and hearing that King Henry was passed the river Somme, was much displeased therewith, and assembling his council to the number of five and thirty, asked their advice what was to be done. There was amongst these five and thirty, his son the dauphin, calling himself king of Sicily; the dukes of Berry and Brittany, the count of Ponthieu, the king's youngest son, and other high estates. At length thirty of them agreed that the Englishmen should not depart unfought withall, and five were of a contrary opinion, but the greater number ruled the matter: and so Mountjoye king at arms was sent to the king of England to defy him as the enemy of France, and to tell him that he would shortly have battle. King Henry advisedly answered: 'Mine intent is to do as it pleaseth God. I will not seek your master at this time; but if he or his seek me, I will meet with them God willing. If any of your nation attempt once to stop me in my journey now towards Calais, at their jeopardy be it; and yet I wish not any of you so unadvised, as to be the occasion that I dye your tawny ground with your red blood.'

When he had thus answered the herald, he gave him a princely reward, and licence to depart. Upon whose return, with this answer, it was instantly on the French side proclaimed that all men of war should resort to the constable to fight with the king of England. Whereupon, all men apt for armour and desirous of honour, drew them toward the field. The dauphin sore desired to have been at the battle, but he was prohibited by his father: likewise Philip, earl of Charolais would gladly have been there, if his father the duke of Burgundy would have suffered him: many of his men stole away, and went to the Frenchmen. The king of England, hearing that the Frenchmen approached, and that there was another river for him to pass with his army by a bridge, and doubting lest, if the same bridge should be broken it would be greatly to his hindrance, appointed certain captains with their bands to go thither with all speed before him, and to take possession thereof, and so to keep it, till his coming thither.

Those that were sent, finding the Frenchmen busy to break down their bridge, assailed them so vigorously that they discomfited them, and took and slew them; and so the bridge was preserved till the king came, and passed the river by the same with his whole army. This was on the two and twentieth day of October. The duke of York that led the vanguard (after the army was passed the river) mounted up to the height of a hill with his people, and sent out scouts to discover the country, the which upon their return advised him that a great army of Frenchmen was at hand, approaching towards them. The duke declared to the king what he had heard, and the king thereupon, without all fear or trouble of mind, caused the battle which he led himself to stay, and instantly rode forth to view his adversaries, and that done, returned to his people, and with cheerful countenance caused them to be put in order of battle, assigning to every captain such room and place as he thought convenient, and so kept them still in that order till night was come, and then determined to seek a place to encamp and lodge his army in for that night.

There was not one amongst them that knew any certain place whither to go in that unknown country: but by chance they happened upon a beaten way, white in sight; by the which they were brought into a little village, where they were refreshed with meat and drink somewhat more plenteously than they had been divers days before. Order was taken by commandment from the king after the army was first set in battle array, that no noise or clamour should be made in the host; so that in marching forth to this village, every man kept himself quiet: but at their coming in to the village, fires were made to give light on every side, as there likewise were in the French host, which was encamped not past two hundred and fifty paces distant from the English. The chief leaders of the French host were these: the constable of France, the marshal, the admiral, the Lord Rambures master of the crossbows, and other of the French nobility, which came and pitched down their standards and banners in the county of St Pôl, within the territory of Agincourt, having in their army (as some write) to the number of threescore thousand horsemen, besides footmen, waggoners and others.

They were lodged even in the way by the which the Englishmen must needs pass towards Calais, and all that night after their coming thither, made great cheer, and were very merry, pleasant, and full of game. The Englishmen also for their part were of good comfort, and nothing abashed of the matter, and yet they were both hungry, weary, sore travelled, and vexed with many cold diseases. Howbeit reconciling themselves with God by confession and shrift, requiring assistance at his hands that is the only giver of victory, they determined rather to die than to yield or flee. The day following was the five and twentieth of October in the year 1415, being then Friday, and the feast of Crispin and Crispinian, a day fair and fortunate to the English, but most sorrowful and unlucky to the French.

In the morning, the French captains made three battles. In the vanguard were eighty thousand healmes of knights and esquires, four thousand archers, and fifteen hundred crossbows which were guided by the lord d'Albret, constable of France, having with him the dukes of Orléans and Bourbon, the earls of Eu and Richemont, the Marshal Bouccicaut, and the master of the crossbows, the Lord Dampier, admiral of France, and other captains. The earl of Vendôme with 16,000 men at arms were ordered for a wing to that battle. And the other wing was guided by Sir Richard Dolphine, Sir Clignet of Brabant, and Sir Louis Bourdon, with 800 men at arms, of elect chosen persons. And to break the shot of the Englishmen were appointed Sir William de Saveuses, with Hector and Philip his brothers, Ferrie de Maillie, and Alan de Gaspares, with other 800 of arms.

In the middle ward, were assigned as many persons, or more, as were in the foremost battle, and the charge thereof was committed to the dukes of Bar and Alençon, the earls of Nevers, Vaudemont, Blamant, Salm, Grand Pré, and of Roussy. And in the rearward were all the other men at arms guided by the earls of Marlay, Dammartin, Fauquembergue, and the lord of Lourrey, captain of Ardres, who had with him the men of the frontiers of Boulogne. Thus the Frenchmen being ordered under their standards and banners, made a great show: for surely they were esteemed in number six times as many or more, than was the whole company of the Englishmen, with wagoners, pages and all. They rested themselves, waiting for the bloody blast of the terrible trumpet, till the hour between nine and ten o'clock of the same day, during which season, the constable made unto the captains and other men of war a pithy oration, exhorting and encouraging them to do valiantly, with many comfortable words and sensible reasons. King Henry also like a leader, and not as one led; like a sovereign, and not an inferior, perceiving a plot of ground very strong and meet for his purpose, which on the back half was fenced with the village wherein he had lodged the night before, and on both sides defended with hedges and bushes, thought good there to embattle his host, and so ordered his men in the same place, as he saw occasion, and as stood for his most advantage.

First he sent privily two hundred archers into a low meadow, which was near to the vanguard of his enemies; but separated with a great ditch, commanding them there to keep themselves close till they had a token to them given, to let drive at their adversaries: beside this he appointed a vanguard, of the which he made captain Edward, duke of York, who of an high courage had desired that office, and with him were the lords Beaumont, Willoughby, and Fanhope, and this battle was all of archers. The middle ward was governed by the king himself, with his brother, the duke of Gloucester, and the earls Marshal, Oxford, and Suffolk, in the which were all the strong billmen. The duke of Exeter, uncle to the king, led the rearward, which was mixed both with billmen and archers. The horsemen like wings went on every side of the battle.

Thus the king, having ordered his battles, feared not the power of his enemies, but yet to provide that they should not with the multitude of horsemen break the order of his archers, in whom the force of his army consisted (for in those days the yeomen had their limbs at liberty, so their hose were then fastened with one point, and their jackets long and easy to shoot in; so that they might draw bows of great strength, and shoot arrows of a yard long; beside the head), he caused stakes bound with iron, sharp at both ends, of the length of five or six foot, to be pitched before the archers, and on each side [of] the footmen like an hedge, to the intent that if the barded horses ran rashly upon them, they might shortly be gored and destroyed. Certain persons also were appointed to remove the stakes, as by the moving of the archers occasion and time should require, so that the footmen were hedged about with stakes, and the horsemen stood like a bulwark between them and their enemies, without the stakes. This device of fortifying an army was at this time first invented: but since that time they have devised caltraps, harrows, and other new engines against the force of horsemen; so that if the enemies run hastily upon the same, either are their horses wounded with the stakes, or their feet hurt with the other engines, so as thereby the beasts are gored, or else made unable to maintain their course.

King Henry, by reason of his small number of people to fill up his battles, placed his vanguard so on the right hand of the main battle, which himself led, that the distance betwixt them might scarce be perceived, and so in like case was the rearward joined on the left hand, that the one might the more readily succour another in time of need. When he had thus ordered his battles, he left a small company to keep his camp and carriage, which remained still in the village, and then calling his captains and soldiers about him, he made to them a right grave oration, moving them to play the men, whereby to obtain a glorious victory, as there was hope certain they should, the rather if they would but remember the just cause for which they fought, and whom they should encounter, such faint-hearted people as their ancestors had so often overcome. To conclude, many words of courage he uttered, to stir them to do manfully, assuring them that England should never be charged with his ransom, nor any Frenchman triumph over him as a captive; for either by famous death or glorious victory would he (by God's grace) win honour and fame.

It is said that as he heard one of the host utter his wish to another thus: 'I would to God there were with us now so many good soldiers as are at this hour within England!' the king answered: 'I would not wish a man more here than I have. We are indeed in comparison to the enemy but a few, but, if God of his clemency do favour us, and our just cause (as I trust he will) we shall speed well enough. But let no man ascribe victory to our own strength and might, but only to God's assistance, to whom I have no doubt we shall worthily have cause to give thanks therefore. And if so be that for our offenses sakes we shall be delivered into the hands of our enemies, the less number we be, the less damage shall the realm of England sustain: but if we should fight in trust of multitude of men, and so get the victory (our minds being prone to pride) we should thereupon peradventure ascribe the victory not so much to the gift of God, as to our own power, and thereby provoke his high indignation and displeasure against us: and if the enemy get the upper hand, then should our realm and country suffer more damage and stand in further danger. But be you of good comfort; and show yourselves valiant, God and our just quarrel shall defend us, and deliver these our proud adversaries with all the multitude of them which you see (or at the least the most of them) into our hands.' Whilst the king was yet thus in speech, either army so maligned the other, being as then in open sight, that every man cried: 'Forward, forward'. The dukes of Clarence, Gloucester and York, were of the same opinion, yet the king stayed a while, lest any jeopardy were not foreseen, or any hazard not prevented. The Frenchmen in the meanwhile, as though they had been sure of victory, made great triumph, for the captains had determined before how to divide the spoils, and the soldiers the night before had played the Englishmen at dice. The noblemen had devised a chariot, wherein they might triumphantly convey the king captive to the city of Paris, crying to their soldiers, 'Haste you to the spoil, glory and honour'; little knowing (God wot) how soon their brags should be blown away.

Here we may not forget how the French thus in their jollity sent an herald to King Henry, to enquire what ransom he would offer. Whereunto he answered, that within two or three hours he hoped it would so happen, that the Frenchmen should be glad to common rather with the Englishmen for their ransoms, than the English to take thought for their deliverance, promising for his own part, that his dead carcass should rather be a prize to the Frenchmen, than that his living body should pay any ransom. When the messenger was come back to the French host, the men of war put on their helmets, and caused their trumpets to blow to the battle. They thought themselves so sure of victory that divers of the noblemen made such haste towards the battle, that they left many of their servants and men of war behind them, and some of them would not once stay for their standards: as amongst other the duke of Brabant, when his standard was not come, caused a banner to be taken from a trumpet and fastened to a spear, the which he commanded to be borne before him instead of his standard.

But when both these armies coming within danger either of other, set in full order of battle on both sides, they stood still at the first, beholding either others demeanour, being not distant in sunder past three bow shots. And when they had on both parts thus stayed a good while without doing anything (except that certain of the French horsemen advancing forwards, betwixt both the hosts, were by the English archers constrained to return back) advice was taken amongst the Englishmen, what was best for them to do. Thereupon all things considered, it was determined that if the Frenchmen would not come forward, the king with his army embattled (as ye have heard) should march towards them, and so leaving their truss and baggage in the village where they lodged the night before, only with their weapons, armour, and stakes prepared for the purpose, as ye have heard.

These made somewhat forward, before whom there went an old knight Sir Thomas Erpingham (a man of great experience in the war) with a warder in his hand; and when he cast up his warder, all the army shouted, but that was a sign to the archers in the meadow, which therewith shot wholly altogether at the vanguard of the Frenchmen, who when they perceived the archers in the meadow, and saw they could not come at them for a ditch that was betwixt them, with all haste set upon the forward of King Henry, but ere they could join, the archers in the forefront, and the archers on that side which stood in the meadow, so wounded the footmen, galled the horses, and cumbered the men at arms, that the footmen durst not go forward, the horsemen ran together upon *plumps* without order, some overthrew such as were next them, and the horses overthrew their masters, and so at the first joining, the Frenchmen were foully discomforted, and the Englishmen highly encouraged.

When the French vanguard was thus brought to confusion, the English archers cast away their bows, and took into their hands axes, mails, swords, bills, and other hand-weapons, and with the same slew the Frenchmen, until they came to the middle ward. Then approached the king, and so encouraged his people, that shortly the second battle of the Frenchmen was overthrown and dispersed, not without great slaughter of men: howbeit, divers were relieved by their varlets, and conveyed out of the field. The Englishmen were so busied in fighting, and taking of the prisoners at hand, that they followed not in chase of their enemies, nor would once break out of their array of battle. Yet sundry of the Frenchmen strongly withstood the fierceness of the English, when they came to handy strokes, so that the fight sometime was doubtful and perilous. Yet as part of the French horsemen set their course to have entered upon the kings battle, with the stakes overthrown, they were either taken or slain. Thus this battle continued three long hours.

The king that day showed himself a valiant knight, albeit almost felled by the duke of Alençon; yet with plain strength he slew two of the dukes company, and felled the duke himself; whom when he would have yielded, the king's guard (contrary to his mind) slew out of hand. In conclusion, the king minding to make an end of that days journey, caused his horsemen to fetch a compass about, and to join with him against the rearward of the Frenchmen, in the which was the greatest number of people. When the Frenchmen perceived his intent, they were suddenly amazed and ran away like sheep, without order or array. Which when the king perceived, he encouraged his men, and followed so quickly upon the enemy, that they ran hither and thither, casting away their armour: many on their knees desired to have their lives saved.

In the meantime, while the battle thus continued, and that the Englishmen had taken a great number of prisoners, certain Frenchmen on horseback, whereof were captains Robinet of Borneville, Rifflart of Clamas, Isambert of Agincourt, and other men at arms, to the number of 600 horsemen, which were the first that fled, hearing that the English tents and pavilions were a good way distant from the army, without any sufficient guard to defend the same, either upon a covetous meaning to gain by the spoil, or upon a desire to be revenged, entered upon the king's camp, and there spoiled the *hails*, robbed the tents, broke up chests, and carried away caskets, and slew such servants as they found to make any resistance. For which treason and baseness in thus leaving their camp at the very point of fight, for winning of spoil where none to defend it, very many were after committed to prison, and had lost their lives, if the dauphin had longer lived.

But then the outcry of the lackeys and boys, which ran away for fear of the Frenchmen thus spoiling the camp, came to the king's ears, he doubting lest his enemies should gather together again, and begin a new field; and mistrusting further that the prisoners would be an aid to his enemies, or the very enemies to their takers indeed if they were suffered to live, contrary to his accustomed gentleness, commanded by sound of trumpet, that every man (upon pain of death) should instantly slay his prisoner. When this dolorous decree, and pitiful proclamation was pronounced, pity it was to see how some Frenchmen were suddenly stuck with daggers, some were brained with poleaxes, some slain with mails, others had their throats cut, and some their bellies cut open, so that in effect, having respect to the great number, few prisoners were saved.

When this lamentable slaughter was ended, the Englishmen disposed themselves in order of battle, ready to abide a new field, and also to invade, and newly set on their enemies, with great force they assailed the earls of Marlay and Fauquembergue, and the lords of Lorraine, and of Thine, with 600 men at arms, who had all that day kept together, but now slain and beaten down out of hand. Some write, that the king perceiving his enemies in one part to assemble together, as though they meant to give a new battle for preservation of the prisoners, sent to them an herald, commanding them either to depart out of his sight, or else to come forward at once, and give battle: promising herewith, that if they did offer to fight again, not only those prisoners which his people already had taken, but also so many of them as in this new conflict, which they thus attempted should fall into his hands, should die the death without redemption.

The Frenchmen, fearing the sentence of so terrible a decree, without further delay departed out of the field. And so about four of the clock in the afternoon, the king when he saw no appearance of enemies, caused the retreat to be blown; and gathering his army together, gave thanks to almighty God for so happy a victory, causing his prelates and chaplains to sing this psalm: *In exitu Israel de Aegypto*, and commanded every man to kneel down on the ground at this verse: *Non nobis Domine, non nobis, sed nomine tuo da gloriam*. Which done, he caused *Te Deum* with certain anthems to be sung, giving laud and praise to God, without boasting of his own force or any human power. That night he and his people took rest, and refreshed themselves with such victuals as they found in the French camp, but lodged in the same village where he lay the night before.

In the morning, Mountjoye king at arms and four other French heralds came to the king to know the number of prisoners, and to desire burial for the dead. Before he made them answer (to understand what they would say) he demanded to them why they made to him that request, considering that he knew not whether the victory was his or theirs? When Mountjoye by true and just confession had cleared that doubt to the high praise of the king, he desired of Mountjoye to understand the name of the castle near adjoining: when they had told him that it was called Agincourt, he said, 'Then shall this conflict be called the battle of Agincourt.' He feasted the French officers of arms that day, and granted them their request, which busily sought through the field for such as were slain. But the Englishmen suffered them not to go alone, for they searched with them, and found many hurt, but not in jeopardy of their lives, whom they took prisoners, and brought them to their tents. When the king of England had well refreshed himself, and his soldiers, that had taken the spoil of such as were slain, he with his prisoners in good order returned to his town of Calais.

When tidings of this great victory were blown into England, solemn processions and other praisings to almighty God with bonfires and joyful triumphs, were ordained in every town, city, and borough, and the mayor and citizens of London went the morrow after the day of St Simon and Jude from the church of St Paul to the church of St Peter at Westminster in devout manner, rendering to God hearty thanks for such fortunate luck sent to the king and his army. The same Sunday that the king removed from the camp at Agincourt towards Calais, divers Frenchmen came to the field to view again the dead bodies; and the peasants of the country spoiled the carcasses of all such apparel and other things as the Englishmen had left: who took nothing but gold and silver, jewels, rich apparel and costly armour. But the plowmen and peasants left nothing behind, neither shirt nor clothing: so that the bodies lay stark naked until Wednesday. On the which day divers of the noblemen were conveyed into their countries, and the remnant were by Philip, earl Charolais (sore lamenting the chance, and moved with pity) at his costs and charges buried in a square plot of ground of fifteen hundred yards; in the which he caused to be made three pits, wherein were buried by account 5,800 persons, beside them that were carried away by their friends and servants, and others which being wounded died in hospitals and other places.

After this their dolorous journey and pitiful slaughter, divers clerks of Paris made many a lamentable verse, complaining that the king reigned by will, and that councillors were partial, affirming that the noblemen fled against nature, and that the commons were destroyed by their prodigality, declaring also that the clergy were dumb, and durst not say the truth, and that the humble commons duly obeyed, and yet ever suffered punishment, for which cause by divine persecution the less number vanquished the greater: wherefore they concluded that all things went out of order, and yet was there no man that studied to bring the unruly to frame. It was no marvel though this battle was lamentable to the French nation, for in it were taken and slain the flower of all the nobility of France.

There were taken prisoner, Charles, duke of Orléans, nephew to the French king, John, duke of Bourbon, the Lord Bouccicaut, one of the marshals of France (he after died in England) with a number of other lords, knights, and esquires, at the least 1,500, besides the common people. There were slain in all of the French part to the number of 10,000 men, whereof were princes and noblemen bearing banners 126; to these of knights, esquires, and gentlemen, so many as made up the number of 8,400 (of the which 500 were dubbed knights the night before the battle) so as of the meaner sort, not past 1,600. Amongst those of the nobility that were slain, these were the chiefest, Charles, lord d'Albret, high constable of France, Jacques of Chatilon, lord of Dampier, admiral of France, the Lord Rambures, master of the crossbows, Sir Guischard Dauphin, great master of France, John, duke of Alençon, Anthony, duke of Brabant, brother to the duke of Burgundy, Edward, duke of Bar, the earl of Nevers, another brother to the duke of Burgundy, with the earls of Marlay, Vaudemont, Beaumont, Grand Pré, Roussy, Fauquembergue, Fois and Lestrake, beside a great number of lords and barons of name.

Of Englishmen, there died at this battle, Edward, duke of York, the earl of Suffolk, Sir Richard Kyghley, and Davie Gamme esquire, and of all other not above five and twenty persons, as some do report; but other writers of greater credit affirm that there were slain about five or six hundred persons. Titus Livius said that there were slain of Englishmen, beside the duke of York and the earl of Suffolk, an hundred persons at the first encounter. The duke of Gloucester the king's brother was sore wounded about the hips, and borne down to the ground so that he fell backwards with his feet towards his enemies, whom the king bestrid, and like a brother valiantly rescued from his enemies, and so saving his life, caused him to be conveyed out of the fight, into a place of more safety. The whole order of this conflict which cost many a man's life, and procured great bloodshed before it was ended, is lively described *in Anglorum praeliis*; where also, besides the manner of disposing the armies, with the exploits on both sides, the number also of the slain not much differing (though somewhat) from the account here named, is there touched, which remembrance very fit for this place it were an error (I think) to omit.

3

The Contemporary Reception of the Battle and Development of the Literary Tradition

It is clear that the battle of Agincourt had an impact on contemporary imagination. The chronicles have already revealed something of this, but here we shall concentrate on immediate responses to it, and on how it served as a stimulus to literary composition. The emphasis will again be on England, but as there are several highly important French literary works associated with Agincourt, these could hardly be overlooked. The battle was 'celebrated' in both senses of the word. In terms of the popular outpouring of emotion in the wake of the victory, as well as of official commemoration, the most significant event was the king's entry to London on 23 November 1415. It is possible that some of the verses in celebration of the battle were composed for this occasion, although some certainly had an independent existence and a later composition. Taking the other meaning of 'celebrated', we can see that the battle was such a famous (if not infamous) event that it even found its way into manuals compiled in England to assist in the learning of French, although one might wonder how suitable a topic it would have been for conversation with a Frenchman in this period! It is revealing to compare the English poetic response to the battle with that of the French. The latter was, not surprisingly, expressed in a more maudlin and reflective mood; the loss of so many of the 'flower of chivalry' was to be lamented, but blame also needed to be apportioned. The English remained triumphalist in tone throughout.

Admittedly, Agincourt is not unique in any of these contexts. It was neither the first nor the last battle to generate a poetic response. In both countries there was a strong tradition of political poetry. For England, we have the example of Laurence Minot's verses on various engagements of the time of Edward III, including the battles of Halidon Hill and Crécy, and the siege of Calais.[1] Poems were also written in connection with the emperor's visit of 1416.[2] Robbins'

---

[1] *The Poems of Laurence Minot*, ed. T.B. James and J. Simons (Exeter Medieval English Texts and Studies, Exeter, 1989). In this volume there is also a translation of a poem by an anonymous writer on the battle of Nevilles Cross.

[2] See, for instance, J. Taylor, 'The Chronicle of John Streeche for the reign of Henry V (1414–1422)', *Bulletin of the John Rylands Library*, 16 (1932), p. 155; J. Capgrave, *Liber de Illustribus Henricis*, ed. F.C. Hingeston (Rolls Series, London, 1858), p. 138; and *John Capgrave's Abbreviacion of Chronicles*, ed. P. Lucas (Early English Text Society, original

edition of political poems reveals works associated with the battle of Otter-bourne (1388) and the siege of Calais of 1436 as well as the wars in France of Henry VII.[3] For France, we have examples of lamentation and criticism in re-lation to the disaster at Poitiers in 1356. It seems clear, too, that memory of that great disaster affected the way some French writers contemplated Agincourt.[4] Moreover, we know that Edward III staged a ceremonial entry into London after Poitiers, although not quite so soon after the event as did Henry V following Agincourt. Edward was able in his entry, however, to display two glittering prizes brought about by English victories, the Scottish king, David II, who had been captured at Nevilles Cross in 1346, and the French king, John II, taken at Poitiers.[5] Spectacle of this kind, especially in London, was a regular occurrence in the medieval and early modern periods.

What is perhaps most fascinating and unusual about Agincourt is its lasting literary legacy in England. This is due in no small part to Shakespeare's *Henry the Fifth*, but there are other lesser known works in the ballad tradition which must be taken into account. In many ways it is rather misleading to separate treatment of these later literary writings from the discussion of early and later historians for the stimuli and context were essentially the same, even if the genre was different. Dealing with the later literary material in this chapter, however, helps to provide a link with, as well as a contrast to, the poetry of the fifteenth century. It also helps to emphasise the Shakespearean influence on later percep-tions of the battle.

D. England

D1. News of the battle

To some degree, the response to the victory was stage-managed by the king himself. In line with earlier expeditions, at least one newsletter had been sent back to London during the siege of Harfleur. This is given in full in Text F 5 below. It is likely that further news was sent back to England by some official and formal means. Riley claims that a message had reached London from Calais

---

series, 285, 1983), p. 248. The *Gesta Henrici Quinti*, ed. F. Taylor and J.S. Roskell (Oxford, 1975), p. 157, suggests that at Sigismund's departure from England, his entourage let fall broadsides with verses in praise of England written upon them.

[3] R.H. Robbins, *Historical Poems of the XIVth and XVth Centuries* (New York, 1959), pp. 64, 78–89, 96. V.J. Scattergood, *Politics and Poetry in the Fifteenth Century* (London, 1971), p. 29, suggests that many other battle poems have been lost.

[4] F. Autrand, 'La déconfiture. La bataille de Poitiers (1356) à travers quelques textes français des XIVe et XVe siècles', in *Guerre et Société en France, en Angleterre et en Bour-gogne, XIVe–XVe siècle*, ed. P. Contamine, C. Giry-Deloison and M.H. Keen (Lille, 1991), pp. 93–121.

[5] R. Barber, *Edward, Prince of Wales and Aquitaine. A Biography of the Black Prince* (1978, repr. Woodbridge, 1996), p. 142.

on 25 October saying that there was no indication as yet of the army's expected arrival there.[6] Within a few days, however, the reason for rejoicing was known in the capital. The *Letter Book* of the city of London records a solemn procession to Westminster made on morrow of St Simon and St Jude by the mayor, aldermen and a large number of the citizens, 'on foot like pilgrims', to give thanks for the news of the king's victory, before the new mayor was admitted and sworn before the barons of the exchequer.[7] The editor took this to be the actual feast day of the saints (Monday 28 October) but it is more likely to be the following day which is intended. Indeed the *Great Chronicle of London* tells us that the news was given to the mayor by Henry Beaufort, bishop of Winchester, on the day after the feast.

1415 Nicholas Wotton draper (mayor), Alan Everard and William Cambridge (sheriffs), year four

And in the same year on the morning after the feast of St Simon and St Jude, when the mayor rode to Westminster to take his oath, tidings of the battle came to London through the Bishop of Winchester who was chancellor at the time. For he came to London early in the morning and alerted the mayor. Then throughout London they rang the bells in every church and sang the *Te Deum*. At St Paul's at 9 o'clock the tidings were openly proclaimed to all the commons of the city and to all other strangers. Then the queen and all the bishops as well as all the lords who were in London at the time went to Westminster on foot in procession to St Edward's shrine with all the priests, friars and other religious devoutly singing the litany, and after making an offering, the mayor came riding home with his aldermen and commoners as they were accustomed to do.[8]

News of the victory was also sent to Bordeaux, reaching there by at least 23 November, as is shown by an extract from the archives of the *jurade*, or town council.

Meeting of 23 November 1415. [On that day the *jurade* decided to send an embassy to the king.] In addition, it was ordered that on the next day the commune should be gathered by trumpet call so that they should be told of the decision to send envoys to England to the king. This assembly was to be summoned so that the envoys might take their leave of the people, and also so that the people might have declared to them the good news which the *jurade* had

---

6   H.T. Riley, *Memorials of London and London Life in the 13th, 14th and 15th Centuries* (London, 1868), p. 620.
7   *Calendar of Letter Books of the City of London, Letter Book I*, ed. R.R. Sharpe (London, 1909) p. 144, where the editor notes that the usual custom would have been to go on horseback to Westminster on 29 October for the mayor to be sworn in. See also Riley, *Memorials*, pp. 620–22.
8   *The Great Chronicle of London*, ed. A.H. Thomas and I.D. Thornley (London, 1938), p. 94. This is also found in Fabyan, *New Chronicles of England and France*, p. 580.

received from the king, our lord, concerning his victory in Picardy (*la victoria de Piquardia*).[9]

To date, however, no text of an actual newsletter reporting the victory to England has been discovered. In the Ledger Book of the city of Salisbury there is an entry which might be derived from such a newsletter, although the text given there is in Latin whereas a newsletter would surely have been sent in English or in French. The entry is a bald account of the campaign, with much space being given to the French dead and prisoners. It has been suggested that the lists of French casualties given in the *Brut* and London Chronicles were derived from official circulars of some kind. Similarities between their lists and that in the Salisbury ledger are thus highly suggestive in this context, and make it highly likely that there had been some official communiqué circulated by the king either before or after his return to England.[10]

D 1a. Possible newsletter circulating in England after the battle (Latin)

Translated from Wiltshire County Record Office, Trowbridge, Salisbury Ledger book A (G23/1/1), fol. 55.[11]

This folio volume, covering the period from September 1387 to July 1456, deals with all aspects of the urban government. It is not possible to date the extract with great accuracy as entries do not follow a strictly chronological order, but there is no particular reason to doubt that it was placed in the ledger reasonably close to the event. The extract follows an account of the mayor, John Levesham, for payments made whilst he was in office. These include rewards to the minstrels of the bishop of Winchester, who may indeed have brought news of the victory to the city. Payments to minstrels of the king or of other great lords are frequent occurrences in urban records of this period. The text found in the ledger may also derive from an account of Henry's entry into London, to which it gives some space. We also know from references elsewhere in the volume that the city had lent the king £100 for the campaign through the mediation of the

---

[9] Original in French, translated from *Archives Municipales de Bordeaux, vol. 4, Registres de la Jurade: Délibérations de 1414 à 1416 et de 1420 à 1422* (Bordeaux, 1883), pp. 287–8.

[10] There is also an entry in the accounts of Winchester College which refers to news being brought 'from overseas of the dukes, counts, barons, knights and other gentlemen of France captured by our lord king of England in a certain battle fought at Agincourt in Picardy on the feast of the Sts Crispin and Crispinian in year three of his reign, and later brought to England with the said lord king'. This may also imply that a list of names had been circulated. Winchester College Muniments 22097. I am grateful to Dr M.K. Jones for this reference.

[11] Summarised in *Report of the Historical Manuscripts Commission on Manuscripts in Various Collections IV* (London, 1907), pp. 195–7. An eighteenth-century copy of the text is to be found in British Library, Lansdowne 1054. A.R. Malden, 'An official account of the battle of Agincourt', *The Ancestor*, 11 (1904), pp. 26–31, contains the Latin text and a translation as well as a brief note.

bishop of Winchester and duke of York, and that there had been some difficulties arising from the presence of troops in the area en route to Southampton.[12]

*

Be it known that our lord the king of England, Henry the Fifth, passed with his great army overseas towards Harfleur, and arrived at the said port on the vigil of the assumption of the Blessed Virgin Mary in the third year of his reign [14 Aug.], and laid siege to the town with the duke of Clarence, the duke of Gloucester and divers others, earls, barons and lords. And afterwards on 22 September, that is Sunday, the morrow of St Matthew the apostle and evangelist, in the year abovementioned, the said town surrendered and so the king doughtily got it. The town thus captured, he made orders for its safekeeping, appointing the earl of Dorset captain of it. When the king had done this he withdrew with his said army towards Calais on account of the grievous pestilence that was prevalent at Harfleur. While he was on the march, a great French host, some 100,000 strong, offered him battle: he had with him no more than 10,000. These said two armies doughtily joined battle, and at the battle were slain on the French side on the field of Agincourt on Friday the feast of Sts Crispin and Crispinian, that is, on 25 October in the year of our lord 1415, and the third year of the said King Henry the Fifth, to wit, the lord d'Albret, constable of France, the duke of Alençon, the duke of Bar, the duke of Brabant [71 further names are given, some in rather garbled fashion], and 4,000 valiant knights and esquires without counting the rest. And in like manner were taken as prisoners of our lord the king the duke of Orléans, the duke of Bourbon, the marshal of France called Bouccicaut, the count of Richemont, the count of Vendôme, the count of Eu and the brother of the duke of Alençon, and other gentlemen. And on the side of the king were slain the duke of York, the young earl of Suffolk, and of lords no more, but of their men about 15. Thus on that day our lord the king overcame all his enemies, giving thanks to the most high God and his mother, the Virgin Mary, and St George, and all the saints of God. And coming with his army to Calais, he rested there and refreshed himself, and sent whom he would of his said army to England there to refresh themselves. After this rest, the lord king, being encumbered by divers affairs of his realm, returned to England, reaching Dover on Saturday the feast of St Clement the Pope, that is, 23 November in the third year of his reign, bringing with him the said French lords his prisoners and captives. As he approached London he was met by an immense multitude of people of that city clad in red garments with white hoods, who attended him on either hand into the city on the following Saturday, that is the last day of

---

12 See below p. 435. Note that just before the extract there is a copy of a writ from the king to the mayor for the array of troops for defensive purposes. The text of this writ is damaged and a date cannot be identified.

the said month, the feast of St Andrew. So great was the multitude of both men and women who stood in the streets from the corner by St George's church in Southwark as far as Westminster that, starting at ten o'clock, the king with the said lords, his captives, was scarcely able to reach Westminster by the third hour after noon, which delay was also in part occasioned by the presentation to him of divers ordinances and gifts by the said city on his arrival. A great victory. Glory to God in the highest.

D2. Henry V's return and the entry to London

English chronicles such as the *Brut* suggest that Henry was greeted in some style at his landing at Dover. Elmham and Otterbourne also speak of his sojourn in Canterbury where he visited the shrines of St Thomas and St Augustine.[13] In terms of commemoration, however, by far the most important event was Henry's entry to London on 23 November 1415. It is realistic to see this as a joint effort by king and city to celebrate the victory, very much in line with other triumphs. The event is mentioned in most English chronicles but with variations in the space devoted to it and in the level of detail. The *Gesta* gives the longest and fullest account. This is taken to be the work of an eyewitness but it may perhaps have been based on some kind of official programme.[14] Supplementary material of a minor nature is found in Adam of Usk, where, for instance, it is said that the conduits ran with wine rather than water.[15] Not surprisingly, the *Brut* and London Chronicles give much space to Henry's entry because of their own links with the city. The first extract is thus from one of the versions of the *Brut*. Its story concerning the duke of Orléans' comment as he arrived in England provides an opportunity for patriotic gesturing and is similar to phrases in the *manière de langage* cited later in this chapter (text D 8). The *Brut* is one of several chronicles which provide us with an account of Henry's reception in Kent and of his actions thenceforward. It also places additional stress on the English devotion to St George. It was probably from a version of the *Brut* that Tito Livio derived his account of the king's return, which is also interesting given the latter's comments on the wealth of London and the king's humility in his entry to the city. Some chronicles also give more detail on the king's visit to St Paul's at the end of the pageant, and tell us of the funeral services there for the English dead, events omitted in the *Gesta*.[16] An example of this is provided in an extract from Walsingham who otherwise says little about the civic entry.

A recent work by Gordon Kipling has suggested that the entry to London had

[13] *Liber Metricus*, chapter 42; Thomas Otterbourne, 'Chronica Regum Angliae', *Duo Rerum Anglicanum Scriptores Veteres*, ed. T. Hearne, 2 vols (Oxford, 1732), 1, p. 276.

[14] *Gesta*, p. xxxvii.

[15] *The Chronicle of Adam Usk, 1377–1421*, ed. C. Given-Wilson (Oxford, 1997), pp. 260–61.

[16] York was subsequently buried at Fotheringay, and Suffolk at Ewelme (Wylie, 2, pp. 269–74).

a strong religious tone rather than merely providing an opportunity for the citizens and king to celebrate a great victory.[17] Kipling argues that the design and the theme of the pageantry were based upon the liturgy of the funeral office, and were conceived as 'a dramatically staged prayer'. The king's progress from the gate on London bridge to St Paul's dealt with the soul's coming into the celestial Jerusalem. This was portrayed in three stages, each with appropriate tableaux. First there was the entry into the gates of paradise, then the welcome by the ordered hosts of heaven, and finally the arrival before the throne of the almighty. 'Each of these pageants has welcomed the king to heaven by virtue of his faithful service to the lord rather than by right of his own earthly glory. But in bringing the conqueror of Agincourt before the king of heaven, the last pageant boldly contrasts the relative glory of God and man, showing that God's is not only greater but of an entirely different order.' This fits well, of course, with the frequent references to the humility of Henry in the face of his victory and his desire to ascribe it to God rather than himself. That said, the accounts of the entry also imply enough merriment and celebration, as well as expressions of civic pride. The presence of the captured prisoners must also have provided a patriotic as well as poignant reminder of the scale of the English triumph.

D 2a. The *Brut* 1377–1437, British Library, Harley MS 53 (narrative written *c.* 1437, completed 1452–53, Middle English)

Modernised from *The Brut, or the Chronicle of England*, ed. F.W.D. Brie, 2 vols (Early English Text Society, original series, 131, 136, 1906, 1908), pp. 557–8.

Then the king came to Calais with his prisoners, and thanked God for his glorious victory, and St George who had helped him to fight and who had been seen above in the air on the day that they fought. When the king arrived at Calais he rested there a while before taking ship and coming to England, landing at Dover and passing on to Barham Down where the representatives of the Cinque Ports met him with 10,000 men fully armed and arrayed. Then said the duke of Orléans, 'What, shall we now go again to battle?' The king answered saying, 'Nay, these are the children of my country come to welcome me home'. At that place the Cinque Ports presented the king with a ship which contained gold. Then he rode on to Canterbury where a procession met him outside the town, bringing him to Christ Church. The king made an offering at St Thomas' shrine, and from there rode on to Eltham from where he made his way to London. On Blackheath the mayor and aldermen met with him, with all the crafts of the city clothed in red to the number of 20,000. There they welcomed him

---

17 G. Kipling, *Enter the King. Theatre, Liturgy and Ritual in the Medieval Civic Triumph* (Oxford, 1998), pp. 201–9.

home, and the king thanked them. So he rode to London on St Clement's day when he was royally received with a procession and a song 'Hail, flower of England, knight of Christ of the world'. And when he came to London bridge, where there were two turrets on the drawbridge and a great giant. On the turrets stood a lion and an antelope with many angels singing 'Blessed is he who comes in the name of the lord'. He rode into London where the streets were royally hung with rich cloths. In Cornhill there had been made a fine tower, full of patriarchs singing 'Sing unto the lord a new song, praise to him, in the church of the saints'. They threw down birds which flew thick and fast around the king. When he came into Cheapside, the conduits ran with wine. On the great conduit were 12 apostles singing 'Bless the Lord, o my soul', and 12 kings kneeling, casting down oblations, and welcomed him home. The cross in Cheapside was royally arrayed like a castle with towers stuck full with banners, and angels inside them singing 'Nowell, nowell', giving *besants* of gold to the king. So he rode on to St Paul's where 14 bishops met him, and all the bells rang out for him. He dismounted there and went to the high altar. And they sang *Te Deum Laudamus*. From there he rode on to his palace at Westminster. Afterwards he rode about the land on pilgrimage and ordered Holy Church that St George's day should be kept as a high and holy day, as it had not been before that time.

D 2b. Tito Livio Frulovisi, *Vita Henrici Quinti* (c. 1438, Latin)

Translated from *Titi Livii Foro-Juliensis Vita Henrici Quinti*, ed. T. Hearne (Oxford, 1716), pp. 21–2.

When the fleet had approached Dover, the first port in England, innumerable people, monks, and priests both high and low ran down the paths to their king. So great was the love of the king and their enthusiasm that many walked into the sea by which the royal ship had come and carried him to the dry land on their shoulders. He remained at Dover several days and from there proceeded to the town of London. The people of that city held celebrations, more easily being able to celebrate with great pomp because of their greater riches. The mayor of the city came towards the king with his senators who are called aldermen and with all the people. The gates and the streets of the city were all adorned with tapestries showing the deeds, victories and triumphs of the great kings of England who had gone before, and they were placed so that the king openly saw what memorial of his great triumph would be made afterwards. The aqueducts throughout the city flowed not with water but with the sweetest wine. Small turrets were made through the public streets, furnished with banners and with most precious materials. At the top of them sat charming boys in English dress singing songs and praises with sweet voices. But in truth, the king did not suffer this honour to be ascribed to him, but put all praise and glory to God. Nor did he wish his helmet, with his crown which had been broken in the battle, nor his armour, to be shown to the people, shunning all this popular praise. After several days in London, he visited several places in his kingdom of England and was received by all with great joy.

D 2c. Thomas Walsingham, *St Albans Chronicle* (*c.* 1420–22, Latin)

Translated from *The St Albans Chronicle 1406–1420*, ed. V.H. Galbraith (Oxford, 1937), p. 98.

The king approached the church of St Paul and was solemnly received in procession by twelve bishops, who advanced towards him and led him to the high altar. Once his devotion was complete, he returned to the churchyard where meanwhile horses had been prepared for him and his men. Having mounted a charger, he set out for Westminster, riding thence in mounted procession through the middle of London. When he reached there, it was amazing that there ran up to meet him the greatest multitude of people that was ever seen in London. All the French watched this with downcast eyes. The abbot and convent of Westminster met him with a great procession, leading him to the church. With prayers discharged to St Edward, he approached the royal palace where he remained for several days. On 1 December, by royal order, the bishops and abbots set out for London in great number to be present at the most solemn funeral services of the Lord Edward, duke of York and of Lord Michael, earl of Suffolk, and of others, both English and French who had died overseas, which the king had arranged ordered to be celebrated with full royal munificence. To these obsequies came the captain of the aforesaid town of Harfleur, the uncle of the king, the earl of Dorset, who had previously made a sortie in the neighbouring region and had driven before him 800 captives whom he ordered to be kept in strict custody in the town of Harfleur.

D3. Parliament

Parliament, due to meet on 21 October, finally did so on 4 November, by which time everyone knew of the victory and the king's imminent return. By this period it was customary for the chancellor or another leading churchman to give an opening sermon which explained the reason for the summoning of parliament, and why the king was in need of a vote of taxation. On this occasion, the chancellor, Henry Beaufort, bishop of Winchester, gave the sermon, full of praise for the king and his victory. The commons responded by agreeing that the second instalment of the lay subsidy (tenths and fifteenths), voted in the previous year and due for collection from February 1416, should be brought forward to mid December, and that there should be generous grants of subsidies on wool and hides and of tunnage and poundage from September 1416 to endure for the lifetime of the king. In addition, the Commons granted a further tenth and fifteenth to be collected in November 1416. This was incomparable generosity on their part, and clear testimony to the euphoric response to the victory. Henry's plans for further activities in France led to constant need for taxation grants and for the support of the realm at large for military activity to be sought through parliament on many occasions during the reign. The battle continued to be useful as a way of reminding the members of parliament why they should assist their king. The battle is thus referred to in the opening sermons of parliaments which met in March 1416, October 1416, November 1417 and October 1419.[18]

D 3a. The roll of the parliament held at Westminster on Monday after the Feast of All Saints, in the third year of King Henry the Fifth since the Conquest (4 November 1415, Latin)

Translated from French and Latin in *Rotuli Parliamentorum*, 4, p. 62.[19]

And then the same chancellor, at the command of the said keeper [of the realm], declared the parliament open; and he said in particular that this parliament had been summoned for two reasons, the first for the good and wise governance of the realm during the king's absence, and the other to provide due and appropriate assistance, provision and wherewithal for the

[18] *Rotuli Parliamentorum*, 6 vols (London, *c.* 1783), 4, pp. 70, 94, 106, 116. The last two mentions are merely to the victory. The sermon of October 1416 stresses the large number of French dead and captured. The comment in March 1416 is lengthier: 'When our same most sovereign lord, within a short time after his most noble arrival near the town of Harfleur, had laid siege to it, the same town was surrendered to him; and afterwards on leaving there by land for his town of Calais, as a result of his most outstanding courage, with a small number of his men who were severely weakened from lack of food, encountered a very large army and a great number of soldiers from France, accompanied by men from the adjoining regions, and fought with them, until God from his bountiful mercy gave the victory to him and the enemy had been killed and defeated – the aforesaid enterprise, by that noble beginning has been and is truly and justly clearly determined and approved by God the Almighty.' Note too that Capgrave, *De Illustribus Henricis*, p. 118, tells us that 'on 1 March next parliament began at Westminster at which the bishop of Winchester, then chancellor of the realm and now cardinal, told the people how King Edward III had claimed the kingdom of France by virtue of his right, likewise Prince Edward and now again Henry V. In his speech the chancellor ordered that the people render services of thanks to God that our kings had acquired major ports to wit, Edward the port of Calais and Henry that of Harfleur. And what most stood as glory to the kingdom was how our king in this last battle had struck amazement and disbelief into the hearts of the French'.

[19] I am grateful to Professor Chris Given-Wilson for allowing me to draw on translations produced as part of the Leverhulme funded project to produce a CD ROM edition of the rolls of the medieval English parliament.

king's expedition to the parts of France, recently begun, to recover the rights of his crown: and he took as his theme, 'As he did unto us, so let us do unto him'. Whereupon firstly, concerning good governance, he declared how our said most sovereign lord since his coronation had continually striven and laboured for the preservation and reform of his laws and justice, and for the peace of the land, and for the benefit, safety and tranquillity of all his lieges, as is well known and acknowledged, as the counsel of the wise man says, 'Without justice, the public good will not prevail. And he inclined his heart, that he your statutes might perform'. And so for the intention of the first part of the aforesaid theme, 'As he did unto us, so let us do unto him'.

And moreover he said that despite frequent requests made by our sovereign lord the king to his adversary of France, in order to have peace, to avoid the shedding of Christian blood, and to have the aforesaid rights restored in the said parts of France, but being unable to secure restitution, and perceiving that he could not recover anything except by force of war, and, forsaking therefore all kinds of personal pleasure, comfort and safety, he undertook the same expedition (*voiage*) and venture for that reason, having complete faith in his lawful quarrel and in Almighty God, in accordance with the words of the wise man who says, 'Strive thou for justice, and the lord shall fight with you'.

And then he recited the manner of the king's noble passage and his arrival near the town of Harfleur in France, and how the same town, which was the strongest town in that part of the world and the greatest enemy to the king's lieges, was surrendered to the king after a short siege, without the shedding of his people's blood, by God's great gift and with His grace; and afterwards, how the king – notwithstanding that he had left a large garrison of his men in the same town for its safe-keeping, and also that the greater part of his army had departed from him, many of whom had died there through the visitation of a certain illness from God, and many had returned to England with the king's permission, for their safe recovery – took himself through the heart of France towards his town of Calais, and as a result of his most noble and most excellent courage, with few men in comparison with the might of his enemies, he encountered and fought with a large number of dukes, counts, barons and lords of France and other lands and countries overseas, and with all the chivalry and might of France and the same lands and countries; and how finally, with the Almighty's help and grace, all the French were defeated, taken or killed, without great loss to the English; and how he, after such a glorious and marvellous victory, has now arrived safely at his said town of Calais with his men and prisoners, praise be to God, with the greatest honour and gain which the realm of England has ever had in so short a time. For that reason, seeing as this propitious, honourable and profitable expedition has thus begun, which without assistance and support will be unable to continue, consider how such provision can be made in this matter by the lords and commons assembled here at present as will be appropriate for the execution and continuation of the expedition, and expedient for the king's well-being and honour, and that of all his realm.

D4. Convocation

The assemblies of clergy, meeting in convocation for the southern province at St Paul's from 18 November to 2 December 1415, and for the northern province in York from 16 December to 16 January 1416, were also generous.[20] The 'minutes' of the southern convocation show how on Monday 2 December the archbishop with all the clergy there present celebrated requiem mass at the high altar of St Paul's 'for the souls of the lords, knights, gentles and others of lower rank who had been killed in the army of the lord king at the siege of Harfleur and also in the battle of Agincourt in France, and for the souls of all the faithful who had perished, with solemn exequies on the Sunday previous'.

Between the opening of parliament on 4 November 1415 and of the southern convocation on 18 November, a letter was written to the king. We might be able to be more precise in the dating if we take the reference to the faithful people offering their good as implying that a vote of subsidy had already been made at the parliament, as it was on 12 November. The author is not known, but Henry Beaufort, bishop of Winchester and chancellor, has been suggested on the grounds that the letter somewhat resembles his speech to parliament. The writer calls himself the king's 'devoted chaplain'. This does not rule out Beaufort, who did indeed call himself the king's 'humble chaplain' in a petition addressed to Henry VI in 1426.[21] But the use of the term 'chaplain' led Wylie to believe that the writer was Thomas Elmham, whom he also, of course, considered the author of the *Gesta*.[22] The letter notes Henry's successful siege of Harfleur, which, it says, lasted nine weeks, the disease which beset the English and the great victory at Agincourt. It is full of hyperbole and, as in the *Gesta*, emphasises God's support for the English as witnessed by the manifest victories He has accorded to them. But it likewise urges that the credit should be given to God, and to the king as his minister (the 'prince of priests'), and that the English should not fall into the sin of pride on account of their great success. Henry is compared with Old Testament figures, and with Alexander. Although we do not know the author nor the precise purpose of the letter, we can be fairly certain that we have here a useful indication of a contemporary response by a well educated member of society.

---

[20] Wylie, 2, pp. 236–9.
[21] British Library, Cotton Cleopatra E III, fol. 30b.
[22] Wylie, 2, p. 247.

D 4a. Anonymous letter possibly related to convocation of 1415 (Latin)

Translated by the editor in *Letters of Queen Margaret of Anjou and Bishop Beckington and Others Written in the Reigns of Henry V and Henry VI*, ed. C. Monro (Camden Society, 86, London, 1863), pp. 1–6.

The original of this letter is not known. It exists as a copy which was transcribed, along with several other letters of the period, into a book towards the end of the fifteenth century. At the beginning of the book are the words 'constat Johanni Edwards', and it has been suggested that the original transcriber and owner was John Edwards of Chirkland who was receiver of Chirkland in the reign of Henry VII. The book was discovered at Emral, the seat of the Puleston family in Flintshire in 1861, and its contents published by the Camden Society two years later. All of the letters were transcribed by the same hand. They include several letters of Margaret of Anjou in the first ten years of her marriage to Henry VI (1445–55), seventeen letters of Thomas Beckington, bishop of Bath and Wells, in connection with his embassy to the count of Armagnac in 1442, and other miscellaneous letters of the period from 1415 to 1445. The letter cited here is the earliest in the collection.

*

Most glorious prince and invincible Lord, the devoted chaplain, in as humble wise as he can or may, recommends himself to his supreme Lord on earth. To the omnipotent king of kings, whose judgments are ever just, I humbly address such daily thanksgivings as I can. Now, what I long hoped for and wished to see before I left this world, I behold before my eyes, whereby I feel my heart warmed with special delight, viz. the glory and honour of the famous realm of England, for a long time wholly lulled to sleep and forgotten, roused from its heavy slumber. For now winter is gone – the winter, that is, of sloth and idleness, that I say not timidity or madness.[23] Flowers have appeared – the flowers of vigorous and warlike youth; and flourishing vines – whereby I understand that noble progeny of kings and nobles of England, which, rooted in virtuous arts, formerly spread their branches throughout the world, have given forth the odours of fame and of worthiest probity and of victory unheard of in all time; which to all the well-wishers of the realm are a savour of rare sweetness, to its enemies a terror, and deprives those who would cripple the rights of England of all courage for further resistance. National justice has required, the wisdom of the combatants has struggled, the prayers of the population have worked for [this consummation]. He whose victory is

---

23 Allmand, *Henry V*, p. 63 notes that this line from the Song of Songs was also used by Thomas Walsingham and Adam of Usk to symbolise the notion that Henry V's accession marked a new beginning, made all the more appropriate by the fact that there was a late fall of snow on the day of his coronation.

neither to the many or the few – who, the supreme judge of all, resists the proud and gives grace to the humble – hath looked on the combatants. What wise man, I ask, beholding, in future time, the success of such an expedition, will not marvel, and ascribe it to the power of God himself? How great are the events that have happened! when it is considered that, within nine weeks, a fortress of great strength, generally esteemed impregnable, and the safest port of the glorious realm of France, were taken; a progress opened through so many spacious and hostile provinces; and, finally, a victory obtained, which may well be deemed glorious in royal annals. Nothing like it has been heard or read of in all time. Not in the time of the Maccabees, whose history is still read in the church; not in that of Saul, the anointed of the prophet; not in that of David, the chosen king of the Israelitish people; not in that of Solomon, the wisest of men; not in that of Alexander, the most fortunate, has anything similar been read. Thy royal majesty deems and firmly holds, as I presume, that not thy hand, but the outstretched hand of God, hath done all these things, for His own praise, the honour and glory of the English nation, and the eternal memory of the royal name. In which it is chiefly to be considered what God has done for us; that whilst it was His will, perchance, to punish us to some extent, on account of our sins, he did not deliver us into the hands of our enemies, who know not how to spare; but he sent among us a plague, the rod of His displeasure; and, lest the glory of such a victory should be claimed by the men who perchance did not deserve it, it was His will that they should be absent, that the glory of the victory should be to Him, and to you as His minister. Chiefly let us beware lest, after such victories, the accompaniments of victory vanquish the victors – such as pride, vainglory, boasting, swelling words, cruelty, rage, and the fury of revenge; all of which are enemies greatly to be dreaded by conquerors, and by which the most famous victors have been themselves conquered. Much more let humility, modesty, giving of thanks, piety, clemency, and a warm desire to pardon, prevail. There remains, therefore, invincible prince, that, with our inmost affections, praises be rendered to God for these great things; and, living righteously and serving Him, let us suppliantly pray that He may bring so glorious a work to an end pleasing to Him. And you, most dread prince, receive not the glory of God in vain, but for the prosecution of your right, casting away the lust of power, go forward manfully (the false dealings of the adversary being retarded and put to flight) and insist, with the utmost vigilance, that he shall not regain his strength. No man putting his hand to the plough, and looking back, is fit for the kingdom [of heaven]; but continued effort usually leads to success; and, according to Tully, it is the part of true virtue not to look on what has been done, but what remains to be done; not what a man has, but what he is wanting in. Moreover, it is fitting that your royal highness should not boast of the past, but be anxious for the future; neither let the power of our enemies drag us back; let not their astuteness disturb us; nor let any fair promises seduce any one. Until you may be able to bring about and establish, on a basis of justice, a permanent peace, which has so long been the fixed desire of your heart, fitting matter will not be wanting, nor ought a careful executor [of the divine will] to falter, who, as far as possible, should spare Christian blood, and, tempering all things with mercy, bring them happily to an end. Truly, most worthy prince, it behoveth you not to fear for the subsidies of your realm, both spiritual and temporal, to be raised in this matter; because your faithful people so delight in their present happy auspices, that they offer to you themselves and their goods, and pour out for you unceasingly their devout prayers; and therefore they are now met together in Parliament; and the devout clergy of your realm will meet in London, on the octave of St Martin next coming. At which time, I doubt not that they will so regard their prince – (I allude to the phrase lately used by certain persons, 'the prince of priests') that it will appear plainly, that they not only laud you with their voices, but rather gloriously magnify you with their deeds, and heartily desire that you may long reign over them. To the honour of your realm of England may the Great God safely preserve your glory and majesty!

D5. The cult of saints and commemoration of the battle

As we have already seen, the chronicles mention three particular saints in connection with the English and the battle: St George is invoked in the battle cries, and the date of the battle is noted as the feast of Sts Crispin and Crispinian. In early January 1416 the archbishop of Canterbury, Henry Chichele, noting the consent of the whole convocation, ordered that the feast of St George should henceforward be a 'major double' in the whole province of Canterbury.[24] On a double feast, work was to cease and services to be attended. Even though the order does not contain any specific reference to the battle, St George is referred to as 'the special patron and protector of the nation', and it has been argued that the victory was behind this major boost to the status of the saint.[25] His invocation as one of a number of saintly guarantors of 'safety and victory to all English princes and armies' is evidenced as early as the late

---

24 *The Register of Henry Chichele, Archbishop of Canterbury 1414–1443*, ed. E.F. Jacob, 4 vols (Canterbury and York Society, London, 1943–7), 3, pp. 6, 9–10. In the same order, special devotions were also ordered for St David, St Chad, and St Winifred. One commentator at least suggests that this was 'especially to commemorate the glorious part shown by the Welsh during the battle' (J.H. Parry, *The Register of Robert Mascall, Bishop of Hereford 1404–1416* (Cantilupe Society, Hereford, 1916, p. v), but other longer term reasons are more likely.
25 O. DeLaborderie, 'Richard the Lionheart and the birth of a national cult of St George in England: origins and development of a legend', *Nottingham Medieval Studies*, 39 (1995), p. 44. This article, along with C. Tyreman, *England and the Crusades 1095–1588* (Chicago and London, 1988), pp. 14, 149, 272, 275, 287, 368, is the source of much of what follows.

eleventh century. A red cross had become fairly standard for crusaders, and remained so into the fifteenth century, with St George even being revived as a protector of Protestant soldiers in the late sixteenth century. A red cross was perhaps first worn by English royal troops at the battle of Evesham in 1265 in deliberate contrast to the white cross adopted by Simon de Montfort. This may still have been intended to invoke crusading rather than national or royal allusions, but by the time of Edward I's invasion of Wales in 1277, we have specific reference to the purchase of pennons for the king's army bearing the arms of St George. The connection of the saint with English royal military world was enhanced by his links to the order of the Garter. The chronicles suggest that there were several banners at Agincourt, including that of St George, and there is enough evidence to suggest that in campaigns both before and after the battle his device symbolised the English. It is difficult to know, however, whether English soldiers invariably bore the device: many may have worn the arms of their captain. It would be interesting to know whether the occurrence of it as the principal 'uniform' of the English army increased after Agincourt.[26] It must be borne in mind, however, that the English did not have a sole right to the saint, for the French also invoked him in a military context.

At convocation in April 1416, it was agreed that there should be special commemoration of the feast of the deposition of St John of Beverley (7 May).[27] In the specific instructions issued by Archbishop Chichele to the bishop of London in December 1416, the observance was ordered not only of the deposition of the saint, but also of his translation, which was the same date as the battle (25 October). It is in these instructions that full reference is made to the 'gracious victory granted by the mercy of God to the English on the feast of the translation of the saint to the praise of the divine name and to the honour of the kingdom of England'. There is also mention of how convocation had been told that on the day of the battle, drops of oil had emanated like sweat from the tomb of St John in Beverley.[28] The Lancastrian dynasty already held St John of Beverley in high regard: his shrine had similarly expressed oil at the very point Henry IV landed at nearby Ravenscar in 1399. Henry V may have visited the shrine in Beverley as prince in 1408, and he certainly did so again in his progress of 1421.[29] As the later visit was partly aimed at encouraging support for the war effort, it is tempting to see the king's devotions at the shrine as a means of bringing the great victory at Agincourt once more to mind. Yet none of

---

[26] Certainly the troops sent by the city of Salisbury for the relief of Calais in 1436 were provided with tunics bearing the cross of St George in the middle of which was sewn a blue letter 'S', presumably to symbolise 'Salisbury' (Wiltshire County Record Office, Trowbridge, G23/1/1, Ledger A.I of the Corporation of the City of Salisbury, 1387–1456, fol. 107).

[27] *Register of Henry Chichele*, 3, p. 14. For the life of the saint (d. 721), bishop of York and founder of the monastery at Beverley, see D.H. Farmer, *The Oxford Dictionary of Saints* (Oxford, 1978), p. 216.

[28] *Register of Henry Chichele* 3, pp. 28–9.

[29] Allmand, *Henry V,* pp. 33, 158, and J.A. Doig, 'Propaganda and truth: Henry V's royal progress in 1421', *Nottingham Medieval Studies*, 40 (1996), p. 170. Doig notes that,

the chronicles associate the saint with the battle, giving prominence instead to Sts Crispin and Crispinian. The instructions issued by Chichele in December 1416 in fact ordered that prayers on 25 October should be shared: the first third of the commemorative collects should be for Crispin and Crispinian, the middle third for St John of Beverley, and the final third for other martyrs.[30] Does this suggest that there was already a popular ground-swell of support for Crispin and Crispinian to be linked with the victory, or was the pressure coming from the king himself? Tito Livio, followed by the Pseudo Elmham, tells us that Henry ordered the Sts Crispin and Crispinian to be included in the prayers said at one of his daily masses. Yet there is no other evidence that this happened, or that there was any marked development of their cult in England by virtue of their association with the battle. Indeed, a close reading of the text of Chichele's December order suggests that emphasis was being still being placed on St John of Beverley rather than on Crispin and Crispinian.

There can be no doubt, however, that at least in the early years after the battle, 'jingles' were circulating linking the battle to the day of Crispin and Crispinian, and the surrender of Harfleur to the feast of St Maurice (22 September). The latter was particularly appropriate as Maurice was a third-century soldier martyr (d. *c.* 287). Tradition had it that on campaign against the Goths under the Emperor Maximian, he had refused to sacrifice to the gods for military success or to take part in the killing of innocent Christians. He was considered the patron saint of soldiers, and eight dedications of churches to him are known in medieval England. Interestingly too, he had been invoked alongside George as a protector of English armies in the late eleventh century.[31] Crispin and Crispinian were martyrs of the third century. The centre of their cult was at Soissons, to where their remains had been taken in the sixth century or earlier. In French tradition they were brothers of noble Roman stock who had preached in Gaul and practised as shoemakers. There was, however, a tradition that they had fled to Faversham in Kent; their supposed house there was visited by pilgrims down to the seventeenth century.[32] Given that the saintly brothers were themselves from France, there was extra piquancy in the fact that the English had defeated the French on their festal day. French chronicles regularly note that the battle occurred on their feast, and Basin tells us that some in France believed the defeat to have been divinely inflicted because of desecration of the shrine of the Crispins in Soissons as a result of conflict between the Armagnacs and Burgundians a year before the battle.[33] No churches are known to have been dedicated

according to the Pseudo Elmham, the Northern Chronicle and John Streeche, Henry prayed at the shrine of St John of Beverely and of Sts Crispin and Crispinian.

[30] *Register of Henry Chichele*, 3, pp. 28–9.

[31] Tyreman, *England and the Crusades*, p. 14. For his life see Farmer, *Oxford Dictionary of Saints*, pp. 272–3. As fellow soldiers under his command were believed to have been martyred with him, he is often cited as 'with companions'.

[32] Farmer, *Oxford Dictionary of Saints*, p. 93.

[33] See Text B 16.

to Crispin and Crispinian in England, but there was an altar in their honour in Faversham parish church, and they were commonly regarded as the patron saints of shoemakers and of leather workers in general. This last aspect may have helped to make them more likely saints to commemorate the victory than the less 'popular' St John of Beverley. Their fame was preserved by transmission through the vernacular chronicles, early histories and most of all Shakespeare, who has Henry mention them six times in his pre-battle speech.

The Latin couplets invoking Maurice and the Crispins were in the form of cryptograms and contrived constructions beloved of ecclesiastical circles. Significantly, the first known is in Elmham's *Liber Metricus*, but there are other examples, with minor variations, in the chronicle of John Streeche and in the annals of Bermondsey Abbey. A couplet is also given in Latin in one of the Middle English versions of the *Brut*, which may imply a circulation outside clerical circles.[34] So widespread was the couplet that Kingsford saw the verses as 'clearly common property'.[35] The couplet could be interpreted as form of intellectual jingle, which also served as an aide memoire, should anyone be likely to forget the year of the great victories. In the example given below, Usk gives the verse immediately after his account of the entry into London. He follows it with the explanation that the year, 1415, is revealed by adding together the Roman numerals which occur within it. Interestingly, a similar device is found in the chronicle of Mont-St-Michel, the abbey which lay on an island off the coast of Normandy, although the verse itself is different. These devices were not unique to Agincourt, but it is testimony to the fame of the battle that they are developed in connection with it. They are also the first example of several poetic responses to the battle.

No evidence has been discovered so far, however, of full-scale commemoration of the anniversary of the battle in subsequent years by the king or anyone else. Events moved on quite swiftly for Henry. The visit to England of the Emperor Sigismund (1 May – 25 August 1416) perhaps overshadowed or at least rivalled the euphoria occasioned by the victory, although in many ways that visit, and the negotiations which followed at Calais in September and October 1416 involving also the duke of Burgundy, were themselves brought about by Henry's success in the previous year. By then, too, the English had another victory to celebrate in that the duke of Bedford had defeated a French fleet off Harfleur on 15 August. The king celebrated this further manifestation of God's favour by going to the cathedral at Canterbury with the emperor and ordering a *Te Deum* to be sung as thanksgiving.[36] The king was certainly back in England by 25 October 1416 but no evidence has so far come to light that there was any

---

[34] 'Annals of the monastery of Bermondsey', in *Annales Monastici*, vol. 3, ed. H.R. Luard (Rolls Series, London, 1866), p. 484. The other examples are given in the relevant extracts in chapter 1.

[35] *EHL*, p. 50.

[36] Allmand, *Henry V*, p. 108, citing the *Gesta*, p. 151 and *St Albans Chronicle*, pp. 100–01.

formal commemoration of the battle at that point or in any future years. Indeed, anniversaries of this kind were not, it seems, part of the medieval way of doing things, but a development of much later centuries. Whilst Henry maintained an Agincourt herald for a couple of years after the battle, the title seems to have been dropped as the conquest of Normandy advanced and Henry became keen to be accepted as its legitimate ruler.[37] There is no proof that Henry ever revisited the scene of his triumph. One of his successors as king of England did, however, visit Agincourt, namely Edward IV during his French expedition of 1475. He may have intended this as a deliberate gesture to connect himself with his illustrious forebear, rather than its being simply the result of choice of route.[38] In a text of the late 1530s or early 1540s which urged Henry VIII to inaugurate annual triumphs against the pope, a yearly celebration at Calais of the battle of Agincourt is cited as an example of a comparable event already in existence, but so far no earlier reference to such a practice has been found.[39]

D 5a. Latin jingle in *The Chronicle of Adam of Usk* (c. 1416–30, Latin)

Translated by the editor in *The Chronicle of Adam Usk*, ed. C. Given-Wilson (Oxford, 1997), pp. 262–3.

As his name suggests, Adam was born in Usk towards the middle of the fourteenth century. He died early in 1430. An advocate in the Court of Arches, he initially enjoyed Lancastrian favour, but may have suffered during the Welsh wars because of his nationality. His attempts to gain papal provision to the see of Hereford in 1404 generated a serious rift with the English court. Two years later he defected to the Avignonese pope but returned to England under pardon in 1411. His chronicle, which exists only in one manuscript, was begun in 1401. Usk gives a perfunctory account of the 1415 campaign but is fuller on the entry

---

37 F. Devon, *Issues of the Exchequer* (London, 1837), p. 345 (February 1416). Exactly how long the title remained in use is not clear, but no references later than March 1419 have so far been found.

38 C.D. Ross, *Edward IV* (London, 1975), pp. 227–8. A letter in the Neville of Holt manuscripts from John Albon to Master Thomas Palmer relates to this visit to Agincourt but is undated and does not mention the king's name. Its editors wrongly dated it to 1417: *Appendix to the Second Report of the Royal Commission on Historical Manuscripts* (London, 1871), p. 94.

39 'For the victory that God gave to your most valiant predecessor, King Henry the Fifth, with so little a number of his countrymen against so great a multitude of the Frenchmen at the battle of Agincourt, your retinue at your noble town of Calais and others over there yearly make a solemn triumph, going in procession, lauding God, shooting guns, with the noise and melody of trumpets and other instruments, to the great rejoicing of your subjects who are aged, the comfort of those who are able, the encouraging of young children.' Modernised from S. Anglo, 'An Early Tudor programme for plays and other demonstrations against the pope', *Journal of the Warburg and Courtauld Institutes*, 20 (1957), p. 178. I am grateful to Dr David Grummitt for bringing this reference to my notice.

to London and gives not only the jingle below but also a longer poem connected
with the victory (D 6a). From 1415 to 1417 he treats Henry's French wars in
glowing terms, saying that the generosity shown by the parliament of November
1415 was 'no more than he deserved', as a recognition of his achievements. By
the end of the chronicle in 1421, however, Usk shows disillusionment, considering the war a waste of money.

*

Verse. The abovementioned capture of Harfleur and victory at the battle
of Agincourt are celebrated in this brief line: 'Harfleur Maurice hath
undone, Agincourt hath Crispin won.' ('Harflu fert Mauric', Agincowrt
prelia Crispin'). The date of our Lord 1415 also appears in this verse, by
adding together the following: M once, C three times, L twice, V twice
and I five times. It was the feast days of these saints that provided the victories.

D 5b. Latin jingle and gloss in *The Chronicle of Mont-St-Michel* (?1468, Latin)

Translated from *Chronique du Mont-St-Michel*, ed. S. Luce, 2 vols (Société des
anciens textes français, Paris 1879–83, reprinted by Johnson Reprint Corporation, 1966), 1 (1879), pp. 19–20.

This is a short chronicle covering 1343 to 1468. Up to 1448 it gives fairly bald
entries for each year, but then provides a longer account of the remaining years,
with disproportionate attention to the events of 1449–50. The island abbey of
Mont-St-Michel was the only place within Normandy which held out against
English rule throughout the whole of the period from 1417 to 1450. Not surprisingly, therefore, the tone is generally hostile to the English, and there is useful
information on military activity in the area close to the Mont. It is likely that the
work was penned by a succession of monks. The section from 1415 to 1434 is
notable for the fact that the writer includes from time to time in the middle of
the narrative a Latin verse which is intended as a mnemonic to commemorate
the date of certain great events. Agincourt is the first event to receive such an
aide-mémoire. Others include the battle of Baugé (1421), the death of Charles
VI (1422), the various activities of Joan of Arc, and military actions in Lower
Normandy in the vicinity of the abbey.

*

In 1415 the king of England, son of Henry, duke of Lancaster, came
before Harfleur and laid siege to it. It surrendered to him. Then he made
his way towards Calais pursued by the majority of the nobles of this
kingdom whom he defeated at Agincourt. This defeat was called the
wretched day (*la mauvaise journée*) because the dukes of Alençon,

Brabant and Bar, the count of Nevers and many others died there. The duke of Orléans, the duke of Bourbon, the count of Richemont and many others were captured. This *journée* of Agincourt and several other things which happened one can easily recall by certain verses mentioning each event individually. But is it is to be noted that certain letters, which add up to a number, teach us in which year such an event occurred:

HeV! nIMIs oCtobrI GaLLos Confregit AgInCoVrt. That is to know which year the said *journée* occurred, which was 1415.[40]

D6. Early literary responses in England

As we have already seen, some chronicles of the period were written in verse, such as Elmham's *Liber Metricus* (in Latin), and John Hardyng's *Chronicle* (in English). In addition to jingles noted in the previous section, other verses relating to the battle are also found in some of the prose chronicles. Finally, there are free standing poems which were written as a result of the battle, amongst them the Agincourt carol, and verses in ballad form ascribed to John Lydgate which some commentators have associated with Henry's entry into London. These various writings will be examined by genre, with examples of each being provided. Together they provide an important insight into contemporary reactions. As Kingsford noted, 'The student of historical sources can never afford to disregard contemporary poetry altogether. Least of all can he do so in such an age as the fifteenth century, when ballads are the most natural form for popular historical narrative, and verse is the commonest vehicle not only for political satire, but for political controversy as well.'[41]

D 6a. Latin poem in *The Chronicle of Adam of Usk* (c. 1416–30, Latin)

Translated by the editor in *The Chronicle of Adam Usk*, ed. C. Given-Wilson (Oxford, 1997), pp. 258–9.

It would be dangerous to say that all poetic representations reflect 'popular' responses to Agincourt. Many of the verses found in Latin chronicles are more indicative of their ecclesiastical origins and setting. Usk gives us a jingle and a longer verse in Latin although it is not certain that he was author of the latter. It is patriotic in tone, and stresses the misplaced pride of the French as well as the bravery and perseverance of Henry. Even so, praise for the victory is due by the English to Christ. It also mentions that the victory occurred on St Crispin's day.

---

[40] The numbers represented by the letters VIMICLLCICV need to be added together to give 1415.

[41] *EHL*, p. 228.

The rhyme structure in this verse is also a good example of contrivance, for in the Latin every line terminates in a word which ends in '-osa'. Equally contrived and so elliptical as to be almost untranslatable is an epigram of eight lines found in British Library, Harley 869. But its general message is much the same as we have seen elsewhere, that the victory at Agincourt was brought about by divine will.

*

[This poem is inserted following the account of the parliament which met in November 1415.]

This is what one poet wrote in praise of the king.

Verses. People of England, cease your work and pray,
For the glorious victory of Crispin's day;
Despite their scorn for Englishmen's renown,
The odious might of France came crashing down.
Invidious race of French, your scorn but taught
Our brave king's new heart, you it benumbed;
Praise be to Christ, from whom these gifts have come!
Thus artifice is vanquished, witchcraft gone,
Dull, downcast minds drink bitter, deep and long.

D 6b. Epigram on the battle of Agincourt (undated, Latin)

Translated from *Political Poems and Songs relating to English History*, vol. 2, ed. T. Wright (Rolls Series, London, 1861), p. 127, from British Library, Harley 869, fol. 282v.

Having overcome the beloved cross, the body of Christ, alone the victor,
brought death upon the French upon St Crispin's day.
Driving forward, Henry the fifth, was within the mutilated country.
With the right aid of Jesus, the king is victorious and suffers no harm.
His firm faith, good life, his prayers and his love [of the Church]
cause France to lose her flowers in the green woods.
As an hare he fled before; when as a lion he roars,
what now is an English town is surrendered by the French.

D 6c. The Agincourt carol and other carols

There are a number of poems in English, the most famous of which is perhaps the Agincourt carol. In fact the latter was only one of a number of 'carols' which were stimulated by the victory. 'The genre which the later Middle Ages designate by the term "carol" is distinguished from other Middle English lyrics by its form, which consists of a burden or chorus sung at the beginning of the piece and after each stanza and any desired number of stanzas of uniform verse-structure. It is a song designed for social singing.'[42] It is also a distinctively native form, and was the most popular musical form in fifteenth-century England. Many of the lyrics survive: there are fewer survivals of the music but still a useful number, the Agincourt carol being an example of where we have both words and music.[43] Although in earlier times the verse may have been intended to be sung by a soloist and the burden or refrain sung (or danced) by the group, many of fifteenth-century carols have polyphonic music for the verses too. Many use Latin phrases in the burden, as does the Agincourt carol where the refrain 'Deo gracias' follows naturally from the last line of the verses.

Most manuscripts containing carols come from religious houses, and the similarity between collections suggests that there was much interchange of carol texts and music in clerical circles. It is not likely, however, that carols were used in services in church, but more that both the overtly religious and the more secular carols formed entertainment at feasts or other gatherings in both monastic and secular contexts. The Latin phrases of the burdens were often taken from hymns of the Office or from other liturgical settings. Whilst the majority of carols are religious in tone, there are many other kinds ranging from the satirical to the amorous. Greene classifies the Agincourt carol as 'political', akin with, for example, those on the execution of Archbishop Scrope in 1405 and on the battle of Towton in 1461. Its text is certainly more secular in tone in comparison with the other examples cited but its refrain echoes the link with liturgical practice. It has been widely published and commented on elsewhere, and is the most famous carol of the period because of its subject matter.[44] The battle is also mentioned by name in the second verse of another Middle English carol, 'Enforce we us'. A third carol in English, 'The rose of Ryse', is not explicit in its mention of the battle but undoubtedly refers to Henry's victory in France. (Remember that the *Brut* has him called 'Flower of England' in one of the songs sung at the entry to London.) Finally, there are two carols in Latin, 'Exultavit cor', and 'Princeps serenissime', which allude to Henry's military success. Whilst it is always difficult to give a precise dating to these texts, especially as they usually exist in later manuscript copies, there is no reason to doubt that all of them were composed within Henry's own reign.

---

[42] R.L. Greene, 'Section XIV: Carols', in *A Manual of the Writings in Middle English 1050–1500*, vol. 6 (1980), p. 1743–52, at p. 1743. See also his *The Early English Carols* (London, 1935).

[43] M. F. Bukofzer, 'Popular and secular music in England', in *Ars Nova and the Renaissance 1300–1540*, ed. A. Hughes and G. Abraham (The New Oxford History of Music, vol. 3, Oxford 1960), pp. 119–26. There is also a useful discussion of the musical form in F. Harrison, *Music in Medieval Britain* (London, 1958), chapter 7.

[44] For a full bibliography on the piece see *Manual of Writings in Middle English*, 6, p. 2010.

1. The Agincourt carol (Middle English)

From Bodleian Library, MS 3340 (previously Arch. Selden B.26), fols 17v–18r.

This Middle English carol, also known by its first line, 'Our king went forth to Normandy' or by its burden in Latin, 'Deo gracias anglia', is found in two fifteenth-century manuscripts, both with music: Bodleian Library, MS 3340 (previously Arch. Selden B.26) fols 17v–18r, dated to *c.* 1450, and probably produced at Worcester Cathedral; and Trinity Cambridge 1230 (previously 0.3.58) no. 7, which is dated to the first half of the century.[45] It is difficult to know how close to the battle the carol was written. Robbins is amongst many who suggest that it was sung as part of the celebrations organised for Henry's triumphant entry into London. All accounts of that event suggest that the songs sung on that occasions were of an overtly religious nature, as a reflection of the king's desire for the glory to be ascribed to God rather than to himself. A tower in Cheapside, however, bore the legend 'Deo gracias', and a choir of maidens sang, presumably in English, 'a song of congratulation', following the text 'Welcome Henry the fifth, King of England and France'.[46] The mention of the entry in verse 5, however, reads as though that event had already passed. The references to Henry as 'our king' would suggest a composition date within his lifetime, but it is difficult to be more precise than that. The verse is for two voices. The burden begins with the voices in unison but then goes into two-part harmony in its second phase. The whole burden is then repeated with variations by a three-part chorus.

*

Burden: Deo gracias anglia
redde pro victoria
[To God give thanks, O England, for the victory]

Verses:
Owre kynge went forth to Normandy
With grace and myght of chyvalry;
Ther god for hym wrought mervelusly,
Wherfore Englonde may calle and cry.

---

[45] It is printed from the latter, with modernized musical notation, in *Musica Britannica. A National Collection of Music. IV, Mediaeval Carols*, ed. John Stevens (published for the Royal Musical Association (London, 1952), no. 8, p. 6, with a facsimile in J.A. Fuller Maitland, *English Carols of the Fifteenth Century* (London, 1891), frontispiece. The text is printed in its original Middle English from the Bodleian MS in R.H. Robbins, *Historical Poems*, pp. 91–2. A modernised version is in *English Historical Documents*, vol. 4, ed. A.R. Myers (London, 1969), pp. 214–15.

[46] *Gesta*, pp. 113, 111.

He sette a sege, the sooth for to say,
To Harfleu toune with ryal aray;
That toune he wan and made afray,
That Fraunce shal rywe tyl domesday.

Than went our kynge with alle his oste
Thorwe Fraunce, for alle the Frenshe boste;
He spared no drede of lest ne moste,
Tyl he come to Agincourt coste.

Than for soth that knyght comely
In Agincourt field he faught manly;
Thorw grace of God most myghty
He hath bothe the felde and the victory.

There dukys and erlys, lorde and barone
Were taken and slayne, and that wel sone:
And summe were ladde into Lundone
With ioye and merth and grete renown.

Now gracious God he save oure kynge
His peple and alle his wel-wyllynge;
Gef hym gode lyfe and gode endynge,
That we with merth mowe savely synge.

2. 'Enforce we us', 'exultavit cor' and 'princeps serenissime'

These carols are found in British Library, Egerton MS 3307, which dates to the middle of the fifteenth century. The manuscript is divided into two parts, the first containing mainly processional music for Holy Week, the second the music of 32 carols, a drinking song and a motet.[47] In the Middle English 'Enforce we us', the battle of Agincourt is referred to by name in the second verse. The music is set for two voices throughout. The Cistercian abbey of Meaux in Yorkshire has been suggested as the provenance of the manuscript. It is possible, however, that it comes rather from the Chapel Royal of St George at Windsor as it contains several invocations to the saint, including those in 'Enforce we us'. This provenance would also make sense for the Latin carols which were obviously written in honour of Henry. 'Exultavit cor' has music for two voices throughout, and 'Princeps serenissime' music for two voices in the verses and for three in the burden.

---

47 Its carols are printed in *Musica Britannica, IV.* For further discussion, see B. Schofield, *Studies in Medieval and Renaissance Music* (London, 1950), chapter 4, and his 'A newly discovered fifteenth-century manuscript of the English Chapel Royal', *Music Quarterly*, 32 (1946), p. 4.

*

'Enforce we us' (Middle English)

Modernised from *Musica Britannica*, no. 60, p. 49.

Burden:

Enforce we us with all our might
to love St George our lady [sic] knight.

Verses:

Worship of virtue is the mead
and is given to him of right.
To worship George then have we need
Which is our sovereign lady's knight.

He kept the maid from dragon's dread
And frightened all France and put to flight
At Agincourt, the chronicle you read
the French him see foremost in fight.

In his virtue he will us lead
against the fiend, the foul wight,
and with his banner us over spread,
if we him love with all our might.

'Exultavit cor' ('The heart rejoices') (Latin)

Translated from *Musica Britannica*, no. 61, p. 50.

Burden:

The heart rejoices in the Lord, now let this assembly sing together.

Verses:

1. For the help of the lord, a most mighty king has been given to us
2. Henry the fifth, by battle [the line is incomplete here]
3. Confusion being brought to the impious and protection to the pious,
   O Jesus our redeemer,
4. Now in harmonious music let us sing with a good heart in order to
   bear true witness
5. Let us bless the Lord who in the kingdom of heaven reigns eternally.

'Princeps serenissime' ('O most serene prince') (Latin)

Translated from *Musica Britannica*, no. 62, pp. 50–51

Burden:

O most serene prince, we praise you in song.

Verses:

1. O lord, because of your good governance you deserve the gift of the year.
2. That the Light from Light may bestow on you today He who is born of a virgin,
3. In the palm of victory, the crown of justice and the love of England.
4. And at the end of your earthly like to live for ever with the celestial host.

3. 'The Rose of Ryse', or 'The Rose it is the fairest flower' (Middle English)

Modernised from R.H. Robbins, *Historical Poems of the XIVth and XVth Centuries* (New York, 1959), pp. 92–3.

This carol is less explicit in its references to the battle but is clearly referring to Henry's victory and using similar themes to those found elsewhere. The 'rose on a branch' was a common theme and prompted by connections with the symbolism of the Virgin, as well as by analogy with England. It is assumed that this carol was used at Christmas time. Its music is not extant, but its Middle English lyrics are in British Library, Add. MS 31,042, fol. 110v, a manuscript containing romances and religious narratives along with many shorter items, compiled by Robert Thornton around 1440. Robbins suggests that the text of the carol may not be complete, for the two following pages of the MS are missing.[48]

*

Burden:

The Rose is the fairest flower of all
that ever was or evermore shall be

---

[48] Robbins, *Historical Poems*, p. 92. Further references are given in *Manual of the Writings in Middle English*, 6, p. 2011. Note that a poem for victory in France 1492, which is printed in Robbins, *Historical Poems*, p. 96 has considerable similarities with the 'Rose of Ryse'. The poem is dedicated to King Henry the seventh. The refrain (modernized) is as follows, 'The rose will into France spring, Almighty God him thither bring! first verse 'And save this flower which is our king, Which is called a noble thing, This rose, this rose, this royal rose, the flower of England and rose our king'. The rose here is red. The poem also invokes St George as England's protector, and seems to be written in advance rather than after the campaign.

The Rose on a branch
Of all these the rose bears the greatest price.

Verses:

1. The rose is the fairest flower
    The rose is sweetest in odour
    The rose in care it is comforter
    The rose in sickness is healer
    the rose so bright
    In medicines it is most of might.

2. Witness this clerks who are wise
    The rose is the flower most in price
    Therefore I think me that the fleur de lys
    Should worship the rose of *ryse* [on the branch]
    And be in its thrall
    And so should other flowers all.

3. Many a knight with spear and lance
    Followed that rose to his delight,
    When the rose took its chance,
    then faded all the flowers of France
    And changed hue
    In pleasance of the rose so true.

D7. Other poems in Middle English

There are three further poems of the fifteenth century which refer to the battle. One occurs within a version of the London Chronicle and is discussed below. The second can be glossed over for, as a eulogy of Henry V written by John Audeley around the time of his son's coronation in 1429, it mentions the battle only briefly.[49] The longest, the 'Battle of Agincourt', also given below, was traditionally viewed as the work of John Lydgate (*c.* 1370–1449). A monk of the Benedictine abbey of Bury St Edmunds, Lydgate has been credited with a very large amount of writing which cannot all be by him, and it is now doubted whether the 'Battle of Agincourt' is his at all. Erdmann has suggested, however, that in 'The siege of Thebes', which Lydgate completed just a few years after Agincourt, Lydgate modelled his hero, Tydeus, partly on Henry V. When ambushed by the Thebans, Tydeus retaliates 'like a lion rampant in his rage', standing firm like the boar. This, Erdmann suggests, may have been inspired by Henry's firm and courageous stance at Agincourt. Renoir is more sceptical of

---

[49] 'A recollection of Henry V', in Robbins, *Historical Poems*, pp. 108–9.

this direct link, suggesting that the story offered plenty of opportunity 'for pointedly relevant advice on the context of royalty in war, but could also be fashioned into an over-sized exemplum to be foisted on the dashing and reckless young king who had led the English at Agincourt'.[50] Just as Lydgate has now been dismissed as an 'Agincourt author', so too we must dismiss Thomas Hoccleve (*c.* 1386–*c.* 1437). Although his poem on John Oldcastle was written whilst Henry was at Southampton in August 1415 preparing to depart, the 'Balade to King Henry V', which has been dated to November 1415 on the grounds that it celebrated Henry's return to England, is definitely referring to the king as regent of France and thus must date to Henry's return to England in February 1421, after the treaty of Troyes had made him heir and regent of France.[51] In terms of literary achievement, neither of the poems given below rate particularly highly, but they both have something to say about near contemporary perceptions of the victory. It is difficult to give a precise dating for the works, since the manuscripts we possess may be later than the original composition.

D 7a. 'Poem on the battle of Agincourt' (*c.* 1443, Middle English)

Modernised from C.L. Kingsford, *Chronicles of London*, pp. 120–2, from British Library, Cotton Cleopatra C IV, fols 25v–26v.[52]

Within a version of the London Chronicle eight stanzas of a ballad on the battle are given, which Kingsford judged to be, despite being incomplete, 'the best and most spirited of the Agincourt poems'.[53] Robbins suggests that the verses were part of what was a much longer ballad already in existence at the time the chronicle was compiled. 'The writer describes the events preceding the battle of Agincourt, and uses a contemporary ballad to fill out the battle scenes, at first transposing it into prose, and then, as he wearied, gradually allowing a few rhythmical and then a few rhymed phrases to creep in . . . finally, the writer discards pretence since he was merely transferring lines into prose, and honestly copies what is left of the ballad as verse.'[54]

---

50 A. Renoir, *The Poetry of John Lydgate* (London, 1967), pp. 27, 112–13. See also *Manual of the Writings in Middle English*, 6, section XVI on Lydgate.
51 The 'Balade' is printed in *Hoccleve's Minor Poems*, ed. I. Gollancz (EETS, extra series 73, London, 1925), pp. 34–5. For the misdating see W. Matthews, 'Thomas Hoccleve', in *Manual of Writings in Middle English 1050–1500*, 3 (Newhaven, Connecticut, 1972), p. 754.
52 The text is also given in Nicolas, pp. 281–2, in *Political Poems and Songs relating to English History*, vol. 2, ed. T. Wright (Rolls Series, London, 1861), pp. 125–7, and Robbins, *Historical Poems*, pp. 74–7. For further bibliography, see *Manual of Writings in Middle English 1050–1500*, 5, p. 1664.
53 *EHL*, p. 240.
54 *Manual of Writings in Middle English 1050–1500*, 5, p. 1426; Robbins, *Historical Poems*, p. xxiii. On pp. xx–xxi Robbins notes other examples where poems, for instance a carol

The dialect of the poem is of London, and the story told is certainly very close to that in several of the English chronicles. This cross influence is intriguing, not least as it suggests that ballads of this kind were a source for the compilers of the vernacular chronicles. The celebration of the deeds of arms of individually named lords is symptomatic of a ballad form, and also reveals how chivalric heroes were also popular heroes. There is also the invocation of God's help, and as in the carols, a poetic unity (and perhaps also a popular appeal, especially if the poem was recited) is generated by the similarity of the last line of each stanza.

Before its account of the battle, it gives a long and detailed account of the surrender of Harfleur which may derive from an eyewitness, and which is slightly different from that in the Great Chronicle. It is also possible that the lists of prisoners and casualties are based on official bulletins. Kingsford noted similarities with those in the Salisbury Ledger Book entry.[55] It would be fair to say, however, that the author was 'geographically challenged' in his list of places that the king passed by between Harfleur and Calais! The closing attack on the Flemish suggests that the poem was written after the defection of Philip, duke of Burgundy, to the French in 1435. As Philip was ruler of Flanders, his subjects also passed into French allegiance at this point, and there are several propaganda works written in the late 1430s which pour venom upon them.[56]

*

In this manner did the king have surrender of the town [of Harfleur], appointing the earl of Dorset to be its captain. Our king stayed there until 1 October. On that day he moved off, making his way through Normandy and Picardy towards Calais. These are the towns which our king rode by whilst he moved through France. First Harfleur, the second in Honfleur [sic], the third Barfleur, the fourth Montivilliers, the fifth Fécamp with its abbey, the sixth Arques, the seventh Dieppe, the eighth Dieppe [sic], the ninth is the city of Eu, the tenth the city of *Tewe*, the eleventh Nesles, the twelfth Amiens, the thirteenth Arras, the fourteenth the water of Somme, the fifteenth the city of Peronne, the sixteenth the water of Ternoise, and then the battle of Thérouanne. And in Agincourt field our king fought with the French on Friday before the feast of St Simon and St Jude. All the royal power of the French came there against our king and his little company, save for the French king, the dauphin, and the duke of Burgundy and the duke of Bar. Otherwise all the lords of France lay before the king, blocking his way as he wished to pass towards Calais, deployed in three battles, to the number of 60,000, as the French say themselves –

concerning the execution of Archbishop Scrope in 1405, are very close to the chronicle accounts.

[55] *Chronicles of London*, p. xl.

[56] J.A. Doig, 'Propaganda, public opinion and the siege of Calais in 1436', in *Crown, Government and People in the Fifteenth Century*, ed. R.E. Archer (Stroud, 1995), pp. 79–106.

and the fairest men-at-arms that anyone had ever seen in one place. Our king with his little company realised that he would have to fight or else he could never get to Calais by road. Then he said to his lords [Note that the following section betrays influence of the ballad.]

'Sirs and fellows, the army yonder intends to block our path. As they will not come to us, let every man prove himself a good man today, and advance banners to make it the best time of the year. For as I am a true king and knight, England shall never pay ransom for me this day. Before any man leave his mortal coil, I shall to death be plighted. Therefore, lords, for the love of sweet Jesus, help maintain England's right this day. Also, archers, to you I pray. Do not flee away before we are all beaten in the field. Think on; Englishmen will not flee in battle, for even though we are outnumbered by ten to one, Christ will help us in our rightful cause. Yet I would prefer it if no blood were spilt. Christ help me now to this end. The French have been the cause of this fault. When thou sittest in judgment, hold me excused before thy face, as thou art God Omnipotent. But pass we all now in fear, be he duke, earl or bachelor. We are made sick by our sins. Gentle Jesus, born of Mary, who died for us on Good Friday, as Thy will was, so bring us to bliss on high, and grant us there a place. Do this and into action.' Our king bid them all good cheer, and so did they at his word, lord, knight and archer. There men might see a sad sight which brought many to harm and affliction, for many a lord was brought low who was of full noble blood, by eveningtime, truth to tell. Help us God omnipotent.

[From this point the ballad is cited verbatim.]

Steeds there stumbled in that place,
that stood there stuffed under steel.
With groaning great they fell to ground,
Their sides cut through when they fell.
Our lord the king he fought very well,
Sharply on them his spear he spent,
Many of them sick he made on that day,
Through might of God omnipotent.

The duke of Gloucester also that tide
Manfully with his menie [company]
Wonder he wrought there wonder wide;
The duke of York also, lost,
For his king no fight would he flee,
Till his bascinet to his brain was bent;
Now on his soul have pity,
Merciful God omnipotent.

Huntingdon and Oxford both,
Were wonder fierce all in that fight
That first was laid, they made full wroth;
Through them many onto death were sent.
The earls fought with main and might,
Rich hauberk they tore and rent;
Our king to help they were full light;
Now bless them, God omnipotent.

The earl of Suffolk began to them assail,
And Sir Richard Kighley [Kyghley] in that stead,
Their lives they lost in that battle,
With wounds sore there were they dead.
If any man bid any good prayer
Unto God with good intent,
To those two souls it must be meet,
Gracious God omnipotent.

Sir William Bowsere [Bourchier], as foul in fright,
Pressed he there was upon his prey,
Erpingham he came him with,
Their manhood helped us well that day.
Of French folk in that affray
Three dukes were dead with doleful dent,
And five earls, that is no nay;
Their help is God omnipotent.

Lords of name a hundred and more
Bitterly that bargain bought;
Two thousand cote-armours also,
After their sorrow thither they sought.
Ten thousand Frenchmen to death were brought,
Of whom never none away went:
All her names soothely know I nought;
Have mercy on them Christ omnipotent.

Two dukes were taken in that stoure [combat],
He of Orléans and of Bourbon,
The Eu, and Arthowre [Arthur de Richemont],
The earl of Vendôme, and many one.
The archbishop of Sens came with our enemy,
. . .
He failed the winning of his spurs,
Through might of God omnipotent.

The false flemings, God give them care,
They loved us never yet by the rood,
For all their false flattering fair,
Against our king that day they stood;
But many of them their heart-blood
Unblithely bled upon that bent,
yet shall they never wait [be of value to] England good,
I swear by God omnipotent.

These be the names of the French lords that were dead at the battle of
Agincourt in the year of our lord Jesus Christ 1415, on Friday 25 October;
the constable of France, the duke of Alençon, the duke of Bar, the duke of
Brabant, the count of Nevers. [85 further names are given, plus the son of
one named, and the five brothers of another; a total of 96 dead in all].

D 7b. 'The Battle of Agincourt' (?1440s, Middle English)

Modernised from Nicolas, *Battle of Agincourt*, pp. 301–25.

This is a poem which in its fullest version contains three sections or 'passus'.
The first deals with the preparations for the expedition and with the siege of
Harfleur, the second with the battle and the third with the entry into London.
Three manuscripts are known. The version in British Library, Cotton Vitellius D
XII, was printed by Thomas Hearne at the end of his edition of the *Vita et Gesta
Henrici Quinti* (Pseudo Elmham) but was then destroyed in the fire of the
Cotton Library in 1731.[57] It seems to have been the earliest in terms of manu-
script, although it does not divide the poem into stanzas. In addition, it omits the
third passus and the first six stanzas of the first, though it adds about 70 additional lines to the second passus which are mainly concerned with the names of
French prisoners. The text in Bodleian Library, 11951 (Rawlinson C.86), folios
178a–186a, dates to the last 20 years of the fifteenth century and contains some
small variations of the full version. The fullest text, and that used below, is
therefore to be found in British Library, Harley 565, folios 102a–114a, which
Kingsford dated to 1443–4 on the grounds that the manuscript includes a reference to the fact that Henry VI had been on the throne for 21 years. Here the
poem contains in total in total 69 stanzas of eight lines and is divided into the
three passus. Almost all stanzas have the refrain 'Wot ye right well that thus it
was, Gloria Tibi Trinitas'. Nicolas printed the whole of the Harley text,
providing the Cotton Vitellius text alongside.[58]

---

57 *Vita et Gesta Henrici Quinti*, p. 359 fols. *Manual of Writings in Middle English
1050–1500*, 5, p. 1426, gives an incorrect date of 1410 for the Cotton Vitellius manuscript.
58 For the whole poem see pp. 301–29. A further printed edition from Harley 565 is provided
in *Chronicle of London*, ed. H. Nicolas and J. Tyrell (London, 1827) p. 216 ff, where it is

The poem has often been ascribed to John Lydgate, but MacCracken rejected this notion in 1911. In his view, 'it seems to contain the fragments of earlier, half-popular ballads on the subject. It is written in the style of the street with the rhyme equipment of a poor minstrel'. Kingsford also doubted that the work was by Lydgate.[59] He noted similarities with the *Brut*, especially in the third passus concerning the entry to London. It has been suggested, of course, that descriptions of the entry may have been based on some kind of official account, but Kingsford's conclusion was that the *Brut* may be 'in part at least derived from ballad sources'. He doubted, however, whether the poem under discussion was the one which was the source of the chronicle, arguing that the latter was more likely influenced by another Agincourt ballad which is now lost. He also considered that the 'Battle of Agincourt' was a late poem 'made up of earlier half-popular ballads'. Oscar Emmerig claimed that it was the first manifestation of the story of the dauphin's gift of tennis balls to Henry.[60] Indeed, he suggests that the story was made up by the author of the poem, and that Elmham took it from the poem for his *Liber Metricus*. This is difficult to prove one way or the other. Elmham certainly wrote his *Liber* within the lifetime of the king, but it is possible, following Kingsford's line, that the poem, or at least parts of it, were of early composition too. Certainly some stanzas imply that Henry is still alive, although the wording of the last would imply that the poem was written some time after 1415. Emmerig's further observation may explain why the story ever came about at all. He suggests that it has its roots in traditions surrounding Alexander the Great. One tale was that Darius had sent Alexander, as a taunting insult, a whip and a ball to play with, along with a golden casket. Alexander was certainly a popular figure in medieval literature, as hero and military leader, and the gift has similarities with, even if it is not identical to, the gift of a chest of tennis balls.

The passus below concerning Agincourt is in ballad form, with use of direct speech and a peppering of names of the great and good with a stress on their heroism. Here there is a similarity at least in tone with the extract from the London Chronicle given above. Very little is provided in the way of military information, with the rank and file mentioned briefly in one verse.

Passus 1, first stanza

God that all this world did make
And died for us on a tree,
Save England for Mary's sake

presented as the work of Lydgate. See *Manual of Writings in Middle English 1050–1500*, 5, p. 1665, for further bibliography.

[59] H.N. MacCracken, *The Minor Poems of John Lydgate* (EETS, extra series, 107, 1911 for 1910), pp. xlvi–vii; *EHL*, pp. 232, 238–40.

[60] '*The Battle of Agyncourt*' *im Lichte geschichtlicher Quellenwerke* (Nürnberg, 1906), reviewed in *EHR*, 23 (1908), pp. 197–8.

Sothfast [the true] God in Trinity;
And keep our king that is so free
That is gracious and good with all,
And grant him evermore the grace
By courtesy of Christ our king royal.

Passus 2

When Harfleur was gotten, that royal town,
Through the grace of God Omnipotent,
Our king he made him ready bound,
And to Calais ward full fair he went;
'My brother Clarence truly
Ye shall ride all by my side,
My cousin York ye take intent,
For ye shall also this tide.'

'My cousin Huntingdon shall with me ride,
The earl of Suffolk that is so free,
The earl of Oxford shall not abide,
He shall come forth with his men,
Sir Thomas Erpingham that never did fail,
And yet another so mote [tell] I thee,
Sir John, the knight of Cornwall,
He dare abide and that know ye.'

'Sir Gilbert Umfraville will us avail,
The Lord Clifford so God me speed,
Sir William Bourchier that will not fail,
They will us help when we have need.'
Toward Calais full fair they go,
In the country of Picardy,
And out of Normandy they began to ride;
Now Christ save all the company.

Our king rode forth, blessed he be,
He spared neither dale nor down,
By towns great, and castle high,
Till he come to the water of Somme;
The bridge the Frenchmen had drawn down,
That over the water he might not ride;
Our king made him ready bound,
And to the water of Turwyn [Ternoise] he came that tide.

Our king rode forth then full good speed.
Into the country of Turville,
To Agincourt now as he is ridden,
There as our king did his battle;
By the water of Swerdys without fail,
The Frenchmen our king they did espy,
And there they thought him to assail,
All in that field certainly.

The Frenchmen had our king umbast [surrounded]
With battle strong on every side;
The duke of Orleans said in haste,
The king of England with us shall bide,
Who gave him leave this way to ride?
By God, methinks, he was not wise,
Therefore shall ye now be his guide,
Or that he come to strong Calais.

The duke of Brabant answered then,
And said, 'By God in Trinity,
There be so few of these Englishmen,
I have no doubt them to see;
Alas! he said, what needeth us all,
Today so many for to come here,
Twenty thousand of us it will befall,
Of them on prisoner.'

The duke of Bourbon swore by St Denis,
And other lords many on,
'We will go play them at dice,
The lords of England every one,'
Their gentlemen said, 'By sweet St John;
Their archers be sold full fair plenty,
And all the best bowmen each one,
All for a blank of our money.'

And then answered the duke of Bar,
With words that were full much of pride,
'By God,' he said, 'he will not spare ye,
Over the Englishmen ye think to ride;
And if that they dare us abide,
We shall overthrow them all in fear;
Go we and slay them in this tide,
And come home again to our dinner.'

Our gracious king, that is so good,
He battled him full royally;
Stakes he hewed down in a wood,
Before our archers put them on high;
Our ordnance the Frenchmen can espy,
They that were ordained for to ride,
They lighted down with sorrow and cry,
And on their feet they abide.

The duke of York then full soon
Before our king he fell on knee,
'My liege lord, grant me a boon,
For his love that on cross can die,
The vanguard this day that ye grant me,
To be before you in this field;
By my banner slain will ye be,
Or ye will turn my back or me yield.'

'Gramercy [many thanks] cousin,' said our king,
'Think on the right of merry England;'
And then be gave him his blessing,
And bade the duke he should stand up,
'Christ' he said 'that shapes both sun and sound,
And art lord and king of might,
This day hold over me thine holy hand,
And speed me well in all my right.

Help St George, our Lady knight,
St Edward that is so free,
Our Lady that art Goddess bright,
And St Thomas of Canterbury;'
He bade all men blithe to be,
And said, 'Fellows well shall we speed,
Every man in his degree,
I shall have you quit full well your mede.'

Our king said, 'Fellows what time of day?'
'Sire,' they said, 'it is near prime;'
'Go we anon to this journey,
By the grace of God it is good time,
For all the Saints that lie in shrine,
To God for us they be praying,
The religious of England all benign,
'Ora pro nobis' for us they sing.'

The king kneeled down in that earth,
And Englishmen on every side
And thrice there kissed the ground,
And on their feet they then arose;
'Christ,' said the king, 'as I am thy knight,
This day me save for England's sake,
And let never that good realm for me be fright
Nor me on live this day be take.

'Avaunt banner, without letting,
St George before, avow we him,
The banner of the Trinity forth ye bring,
And St Edward 's banner at this time;
Over,' he said, 'Lady Heaven Queen,
Mine own banner with hire [her] shall be;'
The Frenchman said all be done,
St George all over our king they see.

They triumphed up full merrily,
The great battle together came;
Our archers shot full heartily,
And made Frenchmen fast to bleed;
Their arrows went full good speed,
Our enemies therewith down they fell,
Through breastplate, hauberk, and bascinet they went,
Slain there were 15 thousand on a row all.

Our gracious king men might know,
That day he fought with his own hand,
He spared neither high nor low,
There was no man his power might stand;
There was never a king yet in this land,
That ever did better in a day,
Therefore all England may sing one song,
'Laus Deo' we may well say.

The duke of Gloucester, there is no doubt,
That day full worthily he wrought,
On every side he made good way,
The Frenchmen fast to ground he brought.
The earl of Huntingdon spared nought;
The earl of Oxford laid on all so;
The young earl of Devonshire he also so wrought;
The Frenchmen fast to ground went.

The duke of Orléans, then was woe,
That day was taken prisoner;
The earl of Eu he was also;
The duke of Brabant slain was there;
The duke of Bar fast him by;
The duke of Launson [Alençon] went never away;
Nor the earl Nevers certainly,
Nor many other lords that I cannot say.

The earl of Richmond certainly,
That day was taken in the field;
The earl of Vendue [Vendôme] was right sorry;
And Sir Bouccicaut he gan him yield;
And thus our king conquered the field,
Through the grace of God Omnipotent;
He took his prisoners young and old,
And fair to Calais ward then he went;
The year of his reign the third this was.
Gloria tibi Trinitas.

Passus 3 final stanza

Christ that is our heavenly king
His body and soul save and see
Now all England may say and sing
'Blessed must be the Trinity'.
This battle (*jornay*) have you heard, now all be done
The date of Christ I know well it was
A thousand four hundred and fifteen
Gloria tibi Trinitas (Glory to you, the Trinity)

D8. *Manière de langage* (?1415, French)

Translated from *Manières de langage (1396, 1399, 1415)*, ed. Andres M. Kristol (Anglo-Norman Text Society, 53, London, 1995), p. 70.

One of the most intriguing references to Agincourt, emphasising its place in the popular psyche, occurs in an equally intriguing source. Towards the end of the fourteenth century, a new kind of aid, the *manière de langage*, was produced to assist those English people who wished or had a need to learn French. This took the form of a collection of model dialogues, aimed at providing phrases and vocabulary suitable for various occasions. This type of work seems to have originated in Flanders in the earlier fourteenth century, although there is no evidence that the Low Country examples influenced the later texts produced in England. A study of surviving English manuscripts from the early fifteenth century suggests that there were three main *manières* in use in England which can be dated to 1396, 1399 and 1415. It is the last of these which interests us for it includes a conversational sequence which refers to the victory at Agincourt.[61] Kristol claims that the author was William of Kingsmill who had a school in Oxford; section 5 of the *manière* gives publicity for the author by having a boy of 12 say that he is at school 'at the house of William Kingsmill scrivener', where he has been taught how to 'escrire, enditer, accompter et fraunceys parler'. It is claimed that the text was written towards the end of 1415 or shortly afterwards, as Agincourt is referred to as a very recent event, although it could be argued that the verb structures, with the varying use of present, past and future, are merely a device to teach the use of tenses.

The nature of the text as a whole would imply a readership of the middle as much as the upper classes in English society. Moreover, it is possible that the purpose of learning French was mainly social – it was still a mark of polite society in England – rather than being aimed at facilitating contact with continental Frenchmen. The reopening of war and the conquest of French territory by Henry V would no doubt have increased the need for some men to know French. The model conversation concerning Agincourt might provide key phrases for the reporting of events, but it would perhaps have been less useful as an opening gambit for a friendly exchange with a Frenchman! Whilst the *manière* of 1396 includes material on a journey to Paris, neither it nor the example of 1399 includes a passage of topical interest comparable with that of the 1415 text.

The *manière* of 1415 opens with a series of phrases of greeting and politeness. The second scene is given in full below, translated from the French.

*

'Sir, from which region do you come. Sir, I come from the regions of France. Sir, what news have you from there? Sir, the king is in a good state, thanks be to God, with all his company in the region of Normandy, and he is in good health himself but several of his men are ill and many of them are dead.'

And furthermore the king arrived in those parts near the town of Harfleur, and laid a great siege to the town with the number of 60,000 people, and by the grace of God, he conquered the said town, and left the siege, and his purpose was to go to Calais, across the territory of France.

---

[61] It is found in four manuscripts: Cambridge, Trinity College B 14.39 (this was first printed by P. Meyer in 'Les manuscripts français de Cambridge. III Trinity College', *Romania*, 32 (1903), pp. 47–58, and is also the text printed by Kristol, Cambridge University Library MS Dd. 12.23 (printed in B. Merrilees and B. Sitarz-Fitpatrick, *The Liber Donati: A Fifteenth-Century Manual of French* (Anglo-Norman Text Society, Plain Text 9, London, 1993)); British Library, Add. MS 17716; and Oxford, Bodleian Library, Lat. misc. e. 93.

And I have heard tell that a little later the lords of France with the number of 50,000 or 60,000 armed persons had met him en route, and that the king with the number of 10,000 persons fought with them at a place called Agincourt, at which battle were captured and killed 11,000 French, and were killed only 16 English, of whom the duke of York was one and the earl of Suffolk another. And the king had the field and the victory, thanks be to God. And he put all the other French to flight. And then the king makes his way towards Calais and intends to return to England, by the grace of God.

II. Furthermore, Sir, I tell you for certain that the French who were captured at the said battle of Agincourt, that is to say, the duke of Orléans, the duke of Bourbon, and many other counts, knights and valiant esquires, as much of other foreign lands as of France, will be brought next Thursday after the feast of St Martin towards London, and they arrived [this is given as 'sount arrivez', which is odd given that all the other verbs in this section are in the future tense] at Dover, and all the people of Kent and of Essex will muster in their finest array on the high road between Canterbury and London. And the people of London, well armed and arrayed, will muster on Blackheath to meet the French so that they might see what people had been left behind by the king in England for the safeguard of the kingdom itself.

D9. Later literary responses in England – the ballad

Over the centuries which followed, Agincourt proved a relatively popular topic for poetic composition. 'The batayll of Egyngscourte' is a short metrical account of 380 lines in four-stress cross-rimed quatrains, printed by John Skot in 1530. It is effectively a summarised version of the 'Battle of Agincourt', sometimes using the same words, as in its opening lines.[62] The battle also features in several ballads of the sixteenth, seventeenth and eighteenth centuries. The ballad has been defined as 'a traditional narrative song', being distinguishable from folk songs which are lyrical and folk tales or narratives which do not have musical accompaniment.[63] Many were reworked over the centuries, often being issued as broadsides, and thus are not easy to date or classify.[64] Many also

---

62 Printed in Nicolas, Appendix, pp. 69–77, and also in A.W. Pollard, *Fifteenth-Century Prose and Verse* (Westminster, 1903), pp. 2–12, where it is ascribed to John Lydgate. See also J.H. Wylie, 'The Agincourt Chaplain', *Athenaeum*, 120 (1902).
63 D.C. Fowler, 'Ballads', *A Manual of the Writings in Middle English 1050–1500*, 6 (1980), p. 1753.
64 See R.F. Green, 'The ballad and the Middle Ages', *The Long Fifteenth Century. Essays for Douglas Gray*, ed. H. Cooper and S. Mapstone (Oxford, 1997), pp. 163–84, for the view that some ballads were of considerable antiquity, although he does not mention any of the Agincourt texts.

contain allusions to earlier works, to traditions established in Shakespeare or in sixteenth-century histories. The first major collection of ballads is found in the Percy Folio manuscript of *c.* 1650 which was printed again in the mid-eighteenth century when ballads were once more a popular form. The major establishment of the canon came with Francis Child's five volumes of *The English and Scottish Popular Ballads*, between 1882 and 1898.

As the nineteenth-century editors of the Percy Folio note, 'Agincourt must have been a tempting theme to the ballad writer and poet of its day. The splendid pluck with which the little English army, wasted by dysentery, ill-fed, and harassed by long marches and hostile skirmishers, nevertheless went at its enemies, facing the terrible odds of more than six to one, and put to ignominious rout the vaunting knights of France, must have appealed to the English heart and the English pride, and ought to have been worthily sung. The ballad-writer especially was bound to take it up, for the class he wrote for led the van and won the field. As at Crécy, as at Poictiers, so at Agincourt the English yeomen humbled the gentlemen of France. Like the *feu d'enfer* of our rifles at Inkerman, the hail of yeomen's arrows gained England honour in the older hard-fought field. But though at Agincourt the rout of the first division of the French army was due solely to our bowmen, against the second, squire and knight, noble and king did well their part too – none better than the Harry who said 'We will not lose'.[65] The story of Agincourt therefore had a double appeal for the ballad writers, for it revealed the heroism of both the king and of 'everyman'.

Percy printed the Agincourt carol, and also another work of 180 lines, broken into four line stanzas ('A councell brave our king did hold'). This may date back to 1569. Its account of the battle is fairly predictable, but it ends rather picturesquely with Katherine, on her knees before Henry, desiring him that his wars would cease, and that 'he her love would be'. No sooner said than done, and Henry is, in the next and final stanza, crowned king of France in Paris!

A more famous ballad perhaps is 'Agincourt or the English bowmen's glory', dating to around 1600, where the common (English) man is much extolled. This is given below in full. A further ballad, 'King Henry V, his conquest of France, in revenge for the affront offered by the French king sending him (instead of the tribute) a ton of tennis balls', begins 'As our king lay musing on his bed'. It is undated but clearly existed in several versions, one of which, in Chetham's Library, Manchester, has the king reacting to the tennis balls by ordering the recruitment of men from Cheshire and Lancashire 'and Derby Hills that are so free'.[66] Marching into France 'with drums and trumpets so merrily', the battle is

---

[65] *Bishop Percy's Folio Manuscript. Ballads and Romances*, ed. J.W. Hales and F. J. Furnivall, vol. 2 (London, 1868), pp. 159–73.

[66] Ibid., pp. 597–9. Two versions different from it, and from one another, are given in Nicolas, Appendix 78–82, with refrains. The first version cited by Nicolas was he says communicated to him by Bertram Mitford of Mitford Castle, Northumberland, 'who wrote it from the dictation of a very aged relative'. A version with variants is also given in *The English and Scottish Popular Ballads*, vol. 3, ed. F.J. Child, (New York, 1888), pp. 320–26, where a first printing of *c.* 1714 is given.

despatched in four lines and the English march to Paris, where the king offers 'And the finest flower that is in all France, To the Rose of England I will give free', an interesting allusion back to a fifteenth-century images.

D 9a. 'Agincourt, or the English Bowman's Glory'

From *Bishop Percy's Folio Manuscript. Ballads and Romances*, vol. 2, ed. J.W. Hales and F.J. Furnivall (London, 1868), pp. 595–7.

This ballad, first referred to in 1600 as 'The Three Man's Song', was printed in full as a broadside in 1665 with the title 'Agincourt, or the English Bowman's Glory', to a pleasant new tune. All eleven verses end with praise of the bowmen.

Agincourt, Agincourt!
Agincourt, Agincourt!
　Know ye not Agincourt?
　Where English slue and hurt
　　All their French foemen?
With our pikes and bills brown,
How the French were beat downe,
　　Shot by our bowmen.

Agincourt, Agincourt!
Know ye not Agincourt,
Never to be forgot
　Or known to no men?
Where English cloth-yard arrows
Kill'd the French like tame sparrows,
　　Slaine by our bowmen.

Agincourt, Agincourt!
Know ye not Agincourt,
Where we won field and fort?
　French fled like women
By land, and eke by water;
Never was seen such slaughter,
　　Made by our bowmen.

Agincourt, Agincourt!
Know ye not Agincourt?
English of every sort,
　High men and low men,
Fought that day wondrous well, as

All our old stories tell us,
  Thanks to our bowmen.

Agincourt, Agincourt!
Know ye not Agincourt?
Either tale, or report,
  Quickly will show men
What can be done by courage,
Men without food or forage,
  Still lusty bowmen.

Agincourt, Agincourt!
Know ye not Agincourt?
Where such a fight was fought,
  As, when they grow men,
Our boys shall imitate;
Nor need we long to waite;
  They'll be good bowmen.

Agincourt, Agincourt!
Know ye not Agincourt?
Where our fifth Harry taught
  Frenchmen to know men:
And when the day was done,
Thousands there fell to one
  Good English bowman.

Agincourt, Agincourt!
Huzza for Agincourt!
When that day is forgot
  There will be no men.
It was a day of glory,
And till our heads are hoary
  Praise we our bowmen.

Agincourt, Agincourt!
Know ye not Agincourt?
When our best hopes were nought,
  Tenfold our foemen.
Harry led his men to battle,
Slue the French like sheep and cattle:
  Huzza! our bowmen.

Agincourt, Agincourt!
Know ye not Agincourt?

O, it was noble sport!
  Then did we owe men;
Men, who a victory won us
'Gainst any odds among us:
  Such were our bowmen.

Agincourt, Agincourt!
Know ye not Agincourt?
Dear was the victory bought
  By fifty yeomen.
Ask any English wench,
They were worth all the French:
  Rare English bowmen![67]

D10. Shakespeare's *Henry V*, and the anonymous play *The Famous Victories*

August Wilhelm Schlegel has a remark on his Historical Plays, Henry Fifth and the others, which is worth remembering. He calls them a kind of National Epic. Marlborough, you recollect, said, he knew no English History but what he had learned from Shakespeare. There are really, if we look to it, few as memorable Histories. The great salient points are admirably seized: all rounds itself off, into a kind of rhythmic coherence: it is, as Schlegel says, epic: – as indeed all delineation by a great thinker will be. There are right beautiful things in those pieces, which indeed together form one beautiful thing. That battle of Agincourt strikes me as one of the most perfect things, in its sort, we anywhere have of Shakespeare's. The description of the two hosts: the worn-out, jaded English; the dread hour, big with destiny, when the battle shall begin; and then that deathless valour; 'Ye good yeomen, whose limbs were made in England!' There is a noble patriotism in it, – far other than the 'indifference' you sometimes hear ascribed to Shakespeare. A true English heart breathes, calm and strong, through the whole business: not boisterous, protrusive; all the better for that. There is a sound in it like the ring of steel. This man too had a right stroke in him, had it come to that! But I will say, of Shakespeare's works generally, that we have no full impress of him there: . . . his works are so many windows, through which we see a glimpse of the world that was within him. All his works seem, comparatively speaking, cursory, imperfect, written under cramping circumstances. . . . Alas, Shakespeare had to write for the Globe Playhouse; his great soul had to crush itself, as it could, into that and no other mould.

So wrote Thomas Carlyle in 1840.[68] It was never going to be easy to portray a

---

67 In the original printing the word 'women' is printed here in error for bowmen!
68 Thomas Carlyle, *On Heroes, Hero-Worship and the Heroic in History* (London, 1840)

battle on stage. Carlyle's view that Shakespeare was constrained by the limitations of performance and playhouse is immediately reminiscent of the playwright's own words in the Prologue to the play in the Folio edition (lines 11–14):

> Can this cockpit hold
> The vasty fields of France? Or may we cram
> Within this wooden O the very casques
> That did affright the air at Agincourt?

Henry V is an interesting play in so many ways.[69] It seems to have first been performed between March and September 1599, and was possibly the first play to be presented by the Lord Chamberlain's men at the newly built Globe Theatre, although that has not been proved for certain. But August of 1600 a text of the play (the First Quarto, or Q) was printed. It is generally assumed that Q was 'an inaccurately reconstructed version of the one that was being performed in the playhouse', written up by someone other than the playwright himself, although there have been many other interpretations of its origins and purpose.[70] In 1623, *the Life of Henry the fift*, a version of the play over twice as long as Q, was printed within the First Folio (F) edition of *William Shakespeare's Comedies, Histories and Tragedies*. It is the F version which is generally accepted as the author's definitive text and is the text used in modern editions. It includes the Prologue and other interludes spoken by Chorus which are not found in the Q version. Q also lacks division into scenes.

Both versions include in Act 4 Henry's famous pre-battle speech, and the issuing of a final challenge to the French through Mountjoye, the French herald. The duke of York then asks for the leading of the vanguard. The king replies 'Take it, brave York. Now soldiers, march away, And how Thou pleasest, God, dispose the day'. Battle is thus begun. As the extract below shows, in F, Act 4, scene 4 opens with the stage instructions 'Alarm' and 'Excursions'. There is then a comic scene featuring Pistol. The boy's words which conclude the scene are heavy with premonition. The next scene in F, Act 4, scene 5, is played between the duke of Orléans, the duke of Bourbon and the French constable. The battle is in full flight. The French lords enter speaking French but soon move into English with the classic lines beginning 'shame and eternal shame, nothing but shame'.

---

from a series of lectures, the third of which, entitled 'The hero as poet', considered Dante and Shakespeare, and was delivered on 12 May 1840.
[69] The most useful critical editions are *King Henry V*, ed. T.W. Craik (The Arden Shakespeare, London, 1995), and *King Henry V*, ed. A. Gurr (The New Cambridge Shakespeare, Cambridge, 1992). See also G. Bullough, *Narrative and Dramatic Sources of Shakespeare*, vol. 4, Later English History Plays (London and New York, 1962), and the clear but now slightly old-fashioned L.B. Campbell, 'Henry V' in *Shakespeare's Histories: Mirrors of Elizabethan Policy* (San Marino, California, 1947), chapter xv. D.K.C. Todd, *Shakespeare's Agincourt* (Durham, N.C., 1985), is not particularly relevant to the present discussion but contains some interesting literary points.
[70] Craike, *King Henry V*, p. xviii.

In Q these scenes are essentially the same but are placed in reverse order. In both versions, however, what comes next is a scene played out by Henry and the duke of Exeter which leads to the king's command to kill the prisoners (Act 4, scene 6 in F, given below). In both versions the play continues with the reactions of Llewellyn and Gower to the French raid on the camp, in which the boys are killed (Act 4, scene 7 in F, given below to line 82). Then follows another of Henry's famous speeches. At this point, the French herald Mountjoye enters telling Henry, 'The day is yours'. The battle is over, and Henry names it. All that remains is for Williams to retrieve the glove which he had given to the disguised king. An interchange between Llewellyn and Williams follows (scene 8 in F) which concludes with the presentation of the lists of French and English dead. The scene (and with it the fourth Act) concludes with Henry's command 'Let there be sung Non nobis and Te Deum, the dead with charity enclosed in clay, And then to Calais, and to England then, Where ne'er from France arrived more happy men.'

Taken together, these scenes raise certain interesting points. We should not be surprised, of course, to find a juxtaposition of comic and serious scenes for this was a deliberate and common Shakespearean dramatic ploy. It is tempting to suggest, however, that Shakespeare decided that the scenes worked best with the serious element coming second and leading directly into the king's appearance. By such means too, as Gurr has noted, the disarray in the French camp could be juxtaposed with a clear demonstration of English order and decisiveness.[71] The French lords dwell on their shame; the English king addresses his 'thrice-valiant countrymen' and hears details of the heroic deaths of York and Suffolk. In the F version, the king is noted as entering not only with his train but also with prisoners. The Q version does not note the presence of prisoners on stage. It must be admitted, too, that Shakespeare's justification for the killing of the prisoners is confused. In scene 6 the king is moved to his order by hearing the alarm and by taking it to mean that the French are regrouping. Yet at the end of scene 7 he restates the order after discovering the attack on the English camp.

On the printed page of the New Cambridge Edition of the F text, the battle occupies no more than 9 pages out of a total of 140 for the play as a whole, and the spoken text of both versions requires no actual fighting to take place on the stage at all. Here of course, we have to take note of stage instructions rather than dialogue. The F version gives 'Alarm' and 'Excursions' at the beginning of Act 4, scene 4. These are not given in the Q version, but 'Alarm' is given later in both versions as a prompting for Henry's orders to kill the prisoners. 'Alarms' were sounded either by drum or by trumpet. It has been conjectured that the 'alarm' which precedes the entry of Pistol and his fellow players was given on the drum, for that was appropriate for the entry of infantry. It is perhaps more likely that the 'alarm' which alerts Henry to the danger of a French regrouping was sounded on the trumpet, but we cannot be sure of this. As

---

[71] Gurr, *King Henry V,* p. 177, n. 37.

Gurr puts it, ' "Excursions" is the only indication in F that any battle action was depicted on stage'. He notes elsewhere that 'the few ragged foils which the Chorus derides at 4.0.50 were not called on for combat, except when Pistol wielded his old "fox" broadsword in 4.4', although armour (probably gorgets, breastplates and helmet) would be worn.[72] We cannot know exactly how the term 'excursions' would be interpreted or played out on stage. Presumably it could be anything the players or director wished, and it is possible that those performing the play could extend Shakespeare's battle in an improvised fashion.[73] It would also seem that the noise of battle scenes was generated by banging swords on metal targets or shields.[74]

It would be easy to dismiss the issue as one of practicalities, perhaps even to speculate that the Prologue, as cited above, was added to the F version in order to excuse the lack of action in the original production. Yet Jorgensen has suggested that there is more to it. He argues that Shakespeare deliberately avoided the excesses and distractions of special effects and energetic actions employed by others on the late Elizabethan stage in plays with military content.[75] Battle display was excluded from both Henry V and other plays because Shakespeare wished to play on the imagination of the audience, to have them think about war, and to conjure up its image by words rather than by actions. Others have speculated that the play has a strong anti-war feel, and even an anti-war message, to it. Be that as it may, it is certainly the case that the play in both its versions is lacking in real military detail. There is no mention of the stakes as a form of defence. Archers are remarkably thin on the ground, and anyone reading the play without knowledge of other accounts of the battle could be forgiven for thinking that archers and their arrows play any decisive part in the English victory. Yet Shakespeare had plenty to go on from Holinshed and his other materials. This has led some commentators to suggest that this was a deliberate ignoring of the sources. In their eyes, the play is a deliberate extolling of the virtues of the nobility as the principal warrior group – a so-called 'Garter play'. Emphasis is placed on the officer cadre of such as York and Suffolk, whose heroism in the face of death is dealt with at some length, and not on the common soldier, who is portrayed at best as simple-minded and accepting, and at worst as comic or wicked. The middling sort, the NCOs such as MacMorris and Llewellyn, fare little better. It is interesting to note, for instance, that in Act 4, scene 7 the king's use of the glove which Williams had given to him during his eve of battle peregrinations serves as an opportunity for an oblique reference back to Henry's own combat in the battle against the duke of Alençon: 'When

---

[72] Ibid., p. 171, n. 0, p. 41.
[73] 'Actors and stage managers may well have extended certain of Shakespeare's battles in this impromptu manner – certainly there was swordplay on the Elizabethan stage – but for these extensions Shakespeare was not accountable'. P.A. Jorgensen, *Shakespeare's Military World* (Berkeley and Los Angeles, 1956), p. 2.
[74] A. Gurr, *The Shakespearian Playing Companies* (Oxford, 1996), p. 439.
[75] Jorgensen, *Shakespeare's Military World*, pp. 2–17.

Alençon and myself were down together I plucked this glove from his helm. If
any man challenge this, he is a friend to Alençon and an enemy to our person. If
thou encounter any such, apprehend him, an thou dost me love' (lines 137–42).
Many chronicles note Henry's fight against Alençon, but as Shakespeare had
not included a character of that name, the allusion had to be indirect. This could
be mere dramatic licence, but it is certainly an opportunity for a contrast to be
drawn between noble and commoner – all the more so as the glove becomes a
comic prop in the hands of Captain Llewellyn.

The jury will no doubt be out on such matters for a long time to come, but
this last reference reminds us of the need to consider the influences on Shakespeare more fully. There can be no doubt that Shakespeare's main historical
source were the *Chronicles of England, Scotland and Ireland of Raphael Holinshed*, probably consulted by him in the edition of 1587. Bullough claims that
there are clear signs the playwright used Holinshed and Hall, even suggesting
that he had them open at his side as he wrote some parts of the play.[76] Although
Shakespeare reorders the action, on occasion the verbal links between play and
chronicle are very close, as is revealed in Craike's edition where the passages
from Holinshed are printed underneath the script.

Shakespeare was not the first to write a play on the subject of Henry V and it
is entirely possible that he drew on existing works. There are several references
to new plays about *Henry V* in the mid-1590s.[77] We have the text of a play called
*The Famous Victories of Henry the Fifth: containing the Honourable Battell of
Agincourt*.[78] This was registered in the Stationers' Register on 14 May 1594 and
printed in 1598, but it is believed to have been produced as early as 1588. The
first half of it deals with the riotous youth of the prince (which was to form part
of the plot of Shakespeare's *Henry IV*), the second with his invasion of France.
There are some similarities of words and action with Shakespeare but the
Famous Victories is much less impressive in language and content. It does
however, contain more military detail. This is well evidenced in the scene (see
text below) which parallels that which Shakespeare places before the battle. In
the *Famous Victories*, Henry's battle speech is much more concerned with
numbers of troops than with rhetoric. York is given command of the van without
having to ask for it, and this gives Henry the opportunity to tell us more about
the deployment and command of his troops. The earl of Oxford is made
commander of the archers perhaps because the contemporary earl of that name
was patron of the company which produced the play. In lines 1174–80, there is
explicit reference to the archers being ordered to prepare stakes, and after the
battle, the common soldiers John Cobler and Robin Pewterer, refer back to them
with 'didst thou see what a pollicie the King had, to see how the Frenchmen
were kild with the stakes of the trees' (scene 16, lines 1277–9). There is, as in

---

76 Bullough, *Narrative and Dramatic Sources of Shakespeare*, 4, p. 352.
77 E.K. Chambers, *The Elizabethan Stage*, 4 vols (Oxford 1923), 2, pp. 144–5.
78 Bullough provides the text of this in his *Narrative and Dramatic Sources of Shakespeare*,
4. See also the facsimile in the series *Tudor Facsimile Texts* (1970).

Shakespeare, no real indication of how the battle was to be acted out on stage, although the stage directions given at the end of scene 14 are slightly lengthier. There is a direct parallel to the comic scene concerning Pistol and his French prisoner in scene 17, but there is no killing of the prisoners.

Neither play, therefore, is 'historically accurate' in every detail, nor should we expect them to be. Not only was Agincourt much distant by the 1590s, and as we have seen the subject of much writing and rewriting in the intervening 175 years, but also these plays were meant as entertainment, and edification not as education.

In the *Famous Victories* the battle is immediately followed by negotiations between Henry and the king of France in person, in which Henry claims the throne of France. Shakespeare is equally at fault in conflating the events of the years from 1415 to 1420, but is more accurate in ending the play with Henry as heir and regent of France and not as its king. We know that Agincourt was not the decisive element in this, and it is hard to believe that Shakespeare and the author of the *Famous Victories* were not equally clear on the facts, as they are clearly stated in Holinshed and Hall. Indeed, the *Famous Victories* even has Henry saying he is prepared to leave his siege (line 1317), which is presumably a reference to the siege of Rouen, 1418–19. In the F version of *Henry V*, the battle is followed by an interlude by Chorus telling us of Henry's going to Calais and his triumphal entry into London, which also alludes to the visit of the emperor, and to Henry's later campaigns. But the structure and intent of these plays was to make Agincourt the pivotal point, or as Craike puts it with reference to the F version, 'the predetermined climax of the play'.[79] This was partly for dramatic effect, of course, but also to show, as in the histories of the sixteenth century, how the actions of man and the intervention of divine will could determine the outcome of events. The full title of the *Famous Victories of Henry the Fifth* continues with *containing the Honourable Battell of Agincourt*. The Q version of Shakespeare's play bears the inscription 'The Chronicle History of Henry the fifth, with his battell fought at Agin Court in France. Togither with Autient Pistoll'. In Shakespeare, the part of the play which comes before the battle is essentially a preparation for it in both comic and serious scenes, with taxation voted for the war, the diplomatic activity and the raising of troops leading the invasion itself. God is already clearly on the king's side as the plot against him on the eve of departure is uncovered. Act 3 deals with the siege of Harfleur, a prelude to Agincourt and an opportunity for the king to show his inspirational leadership, before moving on to contrast the French and English as they move towards battle. Act 4 begins on the eve of battle when Henry goes amongst his men in disguise, and moves to the culminating moment when he gives his pre-battle oration just before the conflict begins. In many ways, therefore, there is no need for a full, actual battle to be shown for the moral victory is already so clearly Henry's. In the *Famous Victories*, too, the king has already shown his

[79] Craike, *King Henry V*, p. 35.

worth by his transformation from miscreant youth to wise prince. These were not simply 'history plays', therefore, but dramatic representations of how 'history' came about. In this respect, too, they drew not only on histories such as Holinshed but also on popular tradition and on classical exemplars, some of which were also transmitted through chronicles and histories. They also chose to omit material from the histories that did not fit or that detracted from the dramatic unity. Shakespeare, too, 'develops in plot and dialogue the Elizabethan philosophy of war', including much on the justification of war, a theme found in other texts of the period.[80] It may also be that the play was influenced by contemporary events, such as the tide of patriotism sweeping England after the Armada, and the continuing fears of invasion in 1598–9 after Henry IV of France had made peace with Spain.[81] Thus the play and the portrayal (or non portrayal) of Agincourt is very much of its period rather than an attempt to re-create 1415. There can be no doubt, however, of its influence of popular perceptions of Henry V and of his famous victory.

*

Shakespeare, *Henry V* (Folio version)

Act 4, scene 4

> *Alarm. Excursions. Enter Pistol, French soldier, Boy.*

PISTOL: Yield, cur!

FRENCH: *Je pense que vous êtes le gentilhomme de bon qualité.*

PISTOL: Quality? 'Colin o custure me'. Art thou a gentleman? What is thy name? Discuss.

FRENCH: *O Seigneur Dieu!*

PISTOL: O Seigneur Due should be a gentleman. Perpend my words, O Seigneur Due, and mark: O Seigneur Due, thou diest on point of fox, except, O Seigneur, thou do give to me egregious ransom.

FRENCH: *Oh, prenez miséricorde! Ayez pitié de moi!*

PISTOL: Moy shall not serve. I will have forty moys, or I will fetch thy rim out at thy throat, in drops of crimson blood.

FRENCH: *Est-il impossible d'échapper la force de ton bras?*

PISTOL: Brass, cur? Thou damnèd and luxurious mountain goat, offer'st me brass?

FRENCH: *Oh, pardonnez-moi!*

PISTOL: Sayest thou me so? Is that a tun of moys? Come hither, boy. Ask me this slave in French what is his name.

BOY: *Écoutez. Comment êtes-vous appelé?*

---

80 Campbell, *Shakespeare's "Histories"*, p. 285.
81 Ibid., pp. 10, 257.

FRENCH: *Monsieur le Fer.*

BOY: He says his name is Mr Fer.

PISTOL: Mr Fer. I'll fer him, and firk him, and ferret him. Discuss the same in French unto him.

BOY: I do not know the French for fer and ferret and firk.

PISTOL: Bid him prepare, for I will cut his throat.

FRENCH: *Que dit-il, monsieur?*

BOY: *Il me commande à vous dire que vous faites-vous prêt, car ce soldat ici est disposé tout à cette heure de couper votre gorge.*

PISTOL: *Oui, coupe la gorge, par ma foi,* peasant, unless thou give me crowns, brave crowns, or mangled shalt thou be by this my sword.

FRENCH: [Kneels] *Oh! Je vous supplie, pour l'amour de Dieu, me pardonner! Je suis le gentilhomme de bonne maison. Gardez ma vie, et je vous donnerai deux cent écus.*

PISTOL: What are his words?

BOY: He prays you to save his life. He is a gentleman of a good house, and for his ransom he will give you two hundred crowns.

PISTOL: Tell him my fury shall abate, and I the crowns will take.

FRENCH: *Petit monsieur, que dit-il?*

BOY: *Encore qu'il est contre son jurement de pardonner aucun prisonnier. Néanmoins, pour les écus que vous l'ayez promis, il est content à vous donner la liberté, le franchisement.*

FRENCH: *Sur mes genoux je vous donne mille remerciements, et je m'estime heureux que je suis tombé entre les mains d'un chevalier – je pense le plus brave, vaillant, et très distingué seigneur d'Angleterre.*

PISTOL: Expound unto me, boy.

BOY: He gives you upon his knees a thousand thanks, and he esteems himself happy that he hath fallen into the hands of one (as he thinks) the most brave, valorous and thrice-worthy seigneur of England.

PISTOL: As I suck blood, I will some mercy show. Follow me.

BOY: *Suivez-vous le grand capitaine.*

[Exeunt Pistol and French soldier]

I did never know so full a voice issue from so empty a heart. But the saying is true, the empty vessel makes the greatest sound. Bardolph and Nym had ten times more valour than this roaring devil i'th'old play, that everyone may pare his nails with a wooden dagger, and they are both hanged, and so would this be if he durst steal anything adventurously. I must stay with the lackeys with the luggage of our camp. The French might have a good prey of us if he knew of it, for there is none to guard it but boys.

[Exit]

Scene 5   *Enter Constable, Orléans, Bourbon, and Rambures*

CONSTABLE: *O diable!*
ORLEANS: *O Seigneur! Le jour est perdu, tout est perdu!*
BOURBON: *Mort de ma vie*, all is confounded, all!
    Reproach and everlasting shame
    Sits mocking in our plumes.

A short alarm

O méchante fortune! Do not run away.
CONSTABLE: Why, all our ranks are broke.
BOURBON: O perdurable shame, let's stab ourselves.
    Be these the wretches that we played at dice for?
ORLEANS: Is this the king we sent to for his ransom?
BOURBON: Shame, and eternal shame, nothing but shame!
    Let us die! In once more, back again,
    And he that will not follow Bourbon now
    Let him go hence, and with his cap in hand
    Like a base pander hold the chamber door,
    Whilst by a slave, no gentler than my dog,
    His fairest daughter is contaminate.
CONSTABLE: Disorder, that hath spoiled us, friend us now.
    Let us on heaps go offer up our lives.
ORLEANS: We are enough yet living in the field
    To smother up the English in our throngs,
    If any order might be thought upon.
BOURBON: The devil take order now, I'll to the throng.
    Let life be short, else shame will be too long.

             [*Exeunt*]

Scene 6   *Alarm. Enter the king and his train with prisoners.*

KING: Well have we done, thrice-valiant countrymen.
    But all's not done, yet keep the French the field.

      [*Enter Exeter by another door*]

EXETER: The Duke of York commends him to your majesty.
KING: Lives he, good uncle? Thrice within this hour
    I saw him down, thrice up again and fighting.
    From helmet to the spur all blood he was.
EXETER: In which array, brave soldier, doth he lie
    Larding the plain; and by his bloody side,
    Yoke-fellow to his honour-owing wounds,

The noble Earl of Suffolk also lies.
Suffolk first died, and York, all haggled over,
Comes to him where in gore he lay insteeped,
And takes him by the beard, kisses the gashes
That bloodily did yawn upon his face.
He cries aloud 'Tarry, my cousin Suffolk.
My soul shall thine keep company to heaven.
Tarry, sweet soul, for mine, then fly abreast,
As in this glorious and well-foughten field
We kept together in our chivalry.'
Upon these words I came, and cheered him up.
He smiled me in the face, raught me his hand,
And with a feeble grip says 'Dear my lord,
Commend my service to my sovereign.'
So did he turn, and over Suffolk's neck
He threw his wounded arm, and kissed his lips,
And so, espoused to death, with blood he sealed
A testament of noble-ending love.
The pretty and sweet manner of it forced
Those waters from me which I would have stopped,
But I had not so much of man in me,
And all my mother came into mine eyes
And gave me up to tears.
KING: I blame you not,
For hearing this I must perforce compound
With wilful eyes, or they will issue too.

Alarm

But hark, what new alarm is this same?
The French have reinforced their scattered men.
Then every soldier kill his prisoners.
Give the word through.

Exeunt

Scene 7

Enter Llewellyn and Gower

LLEWELLYN: Kill the poys and the luggage! 'Tis expressly against
the law of arms. 'Tis as arrant a piece of knavery, mark you
now, as can be offert, in your conscience now, is it not?
GOWER: 'Tis certain. There's not a boy left alive, and the cowardly
rascals that ran from the battle ha' done this slaughter. Besides,
They have burned and carried away all that was in the king's

tent, wherefore the king most worthily hath caused every
soldier to cut his prisoner's throat. Oh, 'tis a gallant king!

LLEWELLYN: Ay, he was porn at Monmouth. Captain Gower, what
call you the town's name where Alexander the Pig was born?

GOWER: Alexander the Great.

LLEWELLYN: Why, I pray you, is not 'pig' great? The pig, or the
great, or the mighty, or the huge, or the magnanimous, are all
one reckonings, save the phrase is a little variations.

GOWER: I think Alexander the Great was born in Macedon. His
father was called Phillip of Macedon, as I take it.

LLEWELLYN: I think it is e'en Macedon where Alexander is porn. I
tell you, captain, if you look in the maps of the woreld I warrant
you sall find, in the comparisons between Macedon and
Monmouth, that the situations, look you, is both alike. There is
a river in Macedon, and there is also moreover a river at
Monmouth. It is called Wye at Monmouth, but it is out of my
prains what is the name of the other river. But 'tis all one, 'tis
alike as my fingers is to my fingers, and there is salmons in
both. If you mark Alexander's life well, Harry of Monmouth's
life is come after it indifferent well, for there is figures in all
things. Alexander, God knows, and you know, in his rages and
his furies and his wraths and his cholers and his moods and his
displeasures and his indignations, and also being a little
intoxicates in his prains, did in his ales and his angers, look
you, kill his best friend Cleitus.

GOWER: Our king is not like him in that. He never killed any of his
friends.

LLEWELLYN: It is not well done, mark you now, to take the tales out of
my mouth ere it is made and finished. I speak out in the figures
and comparisons of it. As Alexander killed his friend Cleitus,
being in his ales and his cups, so also Harry Monmouth,
being in his right wits and his good judgements, turned away
the fat knight with the great belly doublet. He was full of jests
and gypes and knaveries and mocks – I have forgot his name.

GOWER: Sir John Falstaff.

LLEWLLYN: That is he. I'll tell you, there is good men born at
Monmouth.

GOWER: Here comes his majesty.

*Alarm. Enter King Harry, [Exeter, Gloucester, Warwick,
and English Herald,] and Bourbon with prisoners. Flourish*

KING: I was not angry since I came to France
Until this instant. Take a trumpet, herald.
Ride thou unto the horsemen on yon hill.
If they will fight with us, bid them come down,

Or void the field. They do offend our sight.
If they'll do neither, we will come to them,
And make them skirr away as swift as stones
Enforcèd from the old Assyrian slings.
Besides, we'll cut the throats of those we have,
And not a man of them that we shall take
Shall taste our mercy. Go and tell them so.

[*Exit English Herald*]

Enter Montjoy

EXETER: Here comes the herald of the French, my liege.
GLOUCESTER: His eyes are humbler than they used to be.
KING: How now, what means this, herald? Know'st thou not
    That I have fined these bones of mine for ransom?
    Com'st thou again for ransom?
MONTJOY: No, great king.
    I come to thee for charitable licence,
    That we may wander o'er this bloody field
    To book our dead, and then to bury them,
    To sort our nobles from our common men,
    For many of our princes – woe the while –
    Lie drowned and soaked in mercenary blood,
    So do our vulgar drench their peasant limbs
    In blood of princes, while the wounded steeds
    Fret fetlock deep in gore, and with wild rage
    Yerk out their armèd heels at their dead masters,
    Killing them twice. Oh, give us leave, great king,
    To view the field in safety, and dispose
    Of their dead bodies.
KING: I tell thee truly, herald,
    I know not if the day be ours or no,
    For yet a-many of your horsemen peer
    And gallop o'er the field.
MONTJOY: The day is yours.
KING: Praisèd be God, and not our strength, for it.
    What is this castle called that stands hard by?
MONTJOY: They call it Agincourt.
KING: Then call we this the field of Agincourt,
    Fought on the day of Crispin Crispianus.

*

The Famous Victories

[Scene 14]

Enters the king of England and his Lords.

HEN. 5. Come my Lords and fellowes of armes,
What company is there of the French men?
    EARL OF OXFORD. And it please your Majestie,
Our Captaines have numbred them,
And so neare as they can judge,
They are about threescore thousand horsemen,
And fortie thousand footemen.
    HEN. 5. They threescore thousand,
And we but two thousand.
They threescore thousand footemen,
And we twelve thousand.
They are a hundred thousand,
And we fortie thousand, ten to one:
My Lords and loving Countrymen,
Though we be fewe and they many,
Feare not, your quarrel is good, and God will defend you:
Plucke up your hearts, for this day we shall either have
A valiant victorie, or a honourable death.
Now my Lords, I wil that my uncle the Duke of Yorke,
Have the avantgard in the battell.
The Earle of Darby, the Earle of Oxford,
The Earle of Kent, the Earle of Nottingham,
The Earle of Huntington, I wil have beside the army,
That they may come fresh upon them.
And I my selfe with the Duke of Bedford,
The Duke of Clarence and the Duke of Gloster,
Wil be in the midst of the battell.
Furthermore, I wil that my Lord of Willowby,
And the Earle of Northumberland,
With their troupes of horsmen, be continually running like
Wings on both sides of the army:
My Lord of Northumberland, on the left wing.
Then I wil, that every archer provide him a stake of
A tree, and sharpe it at both endes,
And at the first encounter of the horsemen,
To pitch their stakes downe into the ground before them,
That they may gore themselves upon them,
And then to recoyle backe, and shoote wholly altogither,
And so discomfit them.

OXF. And it please your Majestie,
I wil take that in charge, if your grace be therwith content.
HEN. With all my heart, my good Lord of Oxford:
And go and provide quickly.
OXF. I thanke your highnesse.
HEN. 5. Well my Lords, our battels are ordeined,
And the French making of bonfires, and at their bankets,
But let them looke, for I meane to set upon them.

The Trumpet soundes.

Soft, here comes some other French message.

Enters Herauld.

HERALD King of England, my Lord high Constable
And other of my Lords, considering the poore estate of thee
And thy poore Countrey men,
Sends me to know what thou wilt give for thy ransome?
Perhaps thou maist agree better cheape now,
Then when thou art conquered.
HEN. 5. Why then belike your high Constable
Sends to know what I wil give for my ransome?
Now trust me Herald, not so much as a tun of tennis balls
No, not so much as one poore tennis ball,
Rather shall my bodie lie dead in the field, to feed crowes,
Then ever England shall pay one penny ransome
For my bodie.
HERALD A kingly resolution.
HEN. 5. No Herald, tis a kingly resolution,
And the resolution of a king:
Here take this for thy paines.
But stay my Lords, what time is it?
ALL Prime my Lord.
HEN. 5. Then is it good time no doubt,
For all England praieth for us:
What my Lords, me thinks you looke cheerfully upon me?
Why then with one voice and like true English hearts,
With me throw up your caps, and for England,
Cry S. George, and God and S. George helpe us.

Strike Drummer. Exeunt omnes.
The French men crie within, S. Dennis, S. Dennis,
Mount Joy, S. Dennis.
The Battell.

[Scene 15]

Enters King of England, and his Lords.

HEN. 5. Come my Lords come, by this time our
Swords are almost drunke with French blood,
But my Lords, which of you can tell me how many of our
Army be slaine in the battell?

OXF. And it please your Majestie,
There are of the French armie slaine,
Above ten thousand, twentie sixe hundred
Whereof are Princes and Nobles bearing banners:
Besides, all the Nobilitie of France are taken prisoners.
Of your Majesties Armie, are slaine none but the good
Duke of Yorke, and not above five or six and twentie
Common souldiers.

HEN. 5. For the good Duke of Yorke my unckle,
I am heartily sorie, and greatly lament his misfortune,
Yet the honourable victorie which the Lord hath given us,
Doth make me much rejoyce. But staie,
Here comes another French message.   [*Sound Trumpet*]

Enters a Herald and kneeleth.

HERALD. God save the life of the most mightie Conqueror,
The honourable king of England.

HEN. 5. Now Herald, me thinks the world is changed
With you now, what I am sure it is a great disgrace for a
Herald to kneele to the king of England,
What is thy message?

HER. My Lord and maister, the conquered king of France,
Sends thee long health, with heartie greeting.

HEN. 5. Herald, his greetings are welcome,
But I thanke God for my health:
Well Herald, say on.

HERALD. He hath sent me to desire your Majestie,
To give him leave to go into the field to view his poore
Country men, that they may all be honourably buried.

HEN. 5. Why Herald, doth thy Lord and maister
Send to me to burie the dead?
Let him bury them, a Gods name.
But I pray thee Herald, where is my Lord hie Constable,
And those that would have had my ransome?

HERALD And it please your majestie,
He was slaine in the battell.

HEN. 5. Why you may see, you will make your selves

Sure before the victorie be wonne, but Herald,
What Castle is this so neere adjoyning to our Campe?
　HERALD And it please your Majestie,
Tis cald the Castle of Agincourt.
　HEN. 5. Well then my lords of England,
For the more honour of our English men,
I will that this be for ever cald the battell of Agincourt.
　HERALD And it please your Majestie,
I have a further message to deliver to your Majestie.
　HEN. 5. What is that Herald? say on.
　HER. And it please your Majestie, my Lord and maister,
Craves to parley with your Majestie.
　HEN. 5. With a good will, so some of my Nobles
View the place for feare of trecherie and treason.
　HERALD Your grace needs not to doubt that.

[Exit Herald]

　HEN. 5. Well, tell him then, I will come.
Now my lords, I will go into the field my selfe,
To view my Country men, and to have them honourably
Buried, for the French King shall never surpasse me in
Curtesie, whiles I am Harry King of England.
Come on my lords.

[Exeunt omnes]

[Scene 16]

Enters John Cobler, and Robbin Pewterer.

　ROBIN Now, John Cobler,
Didst thou see how the King did behave himselfe?
　JOHN But Robin, didst thou see what a pollicie
The King had, to see how the French men were kild
With the stakes of the trees.
　ROBIN I John, there was a brave pollicie.

Enters an English souldier, roming.

　SOUL. What are you my maisters?
　BOTH Why, we be English men.
　SOUL. Are you English men? then change your language
For the Kings Tents are set a fire,
And all they that speake English will be kild.

JOHN What shall we do Robin? faith, ile shift,
For I can speake broken French.
　ROBIN Faith so can I, lets heare how thou canst speak?
JOHN Commodevales[82] Monsieur.
　ROBIN Thats well, come lets be gone.

Drum and Trumpet sounds:

[Scene 17]

　　　　Enters Dericke roming, After him a Frenchman,
　　　　　　　and takes him prisoner.

DERICKE O good Mounser.
FRENCHMAN Come, come, you villeaco.[83]
DER. O I will sire, I will.
FRENCHMAN Come quickly you pesant.
DER. I will sire, what shall I give you?
FRENCH. Marry thou shalt give me,
One, to, tre, foure, hundred Crownes.
　DER. Nay sir, I will give you more,
I will give you as many crowns as wil lie on your sword.
　FRENCH. Wilt thou give me as many crowns
As will lie on my sword?
　DER. I marrie will I, I but you must lay downe your
Sword, or else they will not lie on your sword.

　　　　Here the Frenchman laies downe his sword, and
　　　　　the clowne takes it up, and hurles him downe.

DER. Thou villaine, darest thou looke up?
FRENCH. O good Mounsier comparteue.[84]
Monsieur pardon me.
　DER. O you villaine, now you lie at my mercie,
Doest thou remember since thou lambst me in thy short el?[85]
O villaine, now I will strike off thy head.

　　　　Here whiles he turnes his backe, the French
　　　　　　　man runnes his wayes.

DER. What is he gone, masse I am glad of it,
For if he had staid, I was afraid he wold have sturd again,

82 Comment tu vas?, i.e., how are you?
83 Rustic, or clown.
84 'Sir, have mercy'.
85 'Beat me with thy short sword'.

And then I should have beene spilt,
But I will away, to kill more Frenchmen.

D11. Michael Drayton, *The Battaile of Agincourt* (1627) and the *Ballad of Agincourt*

Michael Drayton (1563–1631) was born in Warwickshire but lived most of his life in London. His first work was *The Harmony of the Church* (1591), a versification of passages of scripture. In 1593 he published *Idea, the Shepherd's Garland*, in emulation of Spenser, and went on to write several other poetical collections. His *Poems Lyric and Pastoral* (c. 1606) contains many of his most well known poems, including the undated *Ballad of Agincourt*.[86]

As noted in the previous section, there was undoubtedly much expression of English patriotism and nationalism in Elizabeth's reign, increasing as it neared its end. This is revealed not only by the apparent introduction to the English language of the words 'patriot' and 'national' in the last decade of the century, but also by writings which range from the straight historical such as Holinshed to drama and poetry.[87] Drayton followed this trend (and, significantly, numbered the antiquarians Camden and Stow amongst his friends). In 1593 there appeared the first of several long poems on historical topics, *Piers Gaveston*. Most of his subsequent works of this genre dealt with medieval themes, such as *Matilda* (1594 – not the daughter of Henry I but a fictional creation who prefers death rather than dishonour as King John's paramour), *The Tragical Legend of Robert, Duke of Normandy* (1596), *The Barons Wars* (1603, originally published as *Mortimeriados* in 1596), *Sir John Oldcastle* (1599), and *England's Historicall Epistles* (1597–8), which dealt with the fall of significant English personages. The *Battaile of Agincourt* was published in 1627. 'In all of these works Drayton sought to bring further glory to England through his poetic muse.'[88]

This was England's past greatness projected into the present, aimed at appealing to, and encouraging similar acts of patriotic fervour from, Drayton's audience of country gentlemen and lesser aristocracy. All these historical works are also reminiscent of the medieval didactic tradition whereby good and evil deeds are seen to gain appropriate reward from God and history to be determined by such divine intervention. In the same volume as the *Battaile* is found *The Miseries of Queen Margaret*, concerning Margaret of Anjou, wife of Henry VI of England. This juxtaposition was deliberate, being intended to demonstrate the contrast between the success and good fortune of England when united in war against a foreign foe, and the horrors and bad fortune when disunited and fighting against each other in civil conflict. It is significant that relations with

---

[86] Printed in *The Works of Michael Drayton*, vol. 3, ed. J.W. Hebel (Oxford, 1932), pp. 9–72.
[87] R.F. Hardin, *Michael Drayton and the Passing of Elizabethan England* (Lawrence/Manhatten/Witchita, 1973), p. 25.
[88] J.A. Berthelot, *Michael Drayton* (New York, 1967), p. 72.

France were at a particularly low ebb in 1627 and that in that year the duke of Buckingham undertook a failed expedition to relieve the French Protestants in La Rochelle, although a direct link between this campaign and the poem is doubtful.

The Battaile is a poem of 2,520 lines arranged in 315 stanzas of eight lines (ottava rima), of which the battle proper occupies about the last half. Drayton also added marginal notes of explanation where he considered necessary. The *Battaile* is too long to be reproduced in its entirety here, but its content can be summarised and discussed, and an extract concerning the duke of Alençon is given in full to give some impression of the poetic tone.[89] Unlike Drayton's earlier historical poems, here he focuses on an event rather than a person. He draws quite heavily on Holinshed and Speed. There are also passages reminiscent of Shakespeare, but there is no comic element in Drayton's work.

*

The *Battaile* begins with a brief survey of English history since 1399, mentioning the Lancastrian usurpation, the battle of Shrewsbury and the threat of Wycliffe. In the fifth stanza the bill moved in parliament against the church, the same bill as cited in the opening scene of *Henry V,* is mentioned. Archbishop Chichele then encourages the king to invade France, again following the Shakespeare line with a historical account of the claim of Edward III and of English successes hitherto, as well as the truth of Salic law. The speech generates enthusiasm for the war in parliament: 'so much men's minds now upon France were set', but Westmoreland urges 'with Scotland let us first begin'. But other lords urge an attack on France 'and instantly an embassy is sent'. The king's demands and the tennis ball story follow before preparations for war are made, not only in terms of the making and gathering of equipment (we see here an interesting mixture of perceived medievalism and of weapons of Drayton's own day), but also through the old man sitting by the fire (line 313) telling his son 'with tears of joy' of fourteenth-century English successes. Much contrived detail is given of the assembling of the fleet to transport the army, complete with invented names of vessels, and their hopes and experiences. Here we have a reminder, perhaps, that by the period of the poem, English greatness as well as action against her enemies was much predicated on naval endeavour.

The troops then assemble ('there might a man have seene in every streete the father bidding farewell to his sonne, small children kneeling at their father's feete, the wife with her dear husband n'er had done, Brother, his brother with adieu to gret, one friend to take leave of another runne; the mayden with her best beloved to part, gave him her hand, who tooke away her heart', lines 473–80). At the muster the various bands were identified by their 'armings' or their 'colours'. This leads into a county by county, or town by town description in the

---

[89] Berthelot, *Michael Drayton*, pp. 84–7, and Hardin, *Michael Drayton and the Passing of Elizabethan England*, pp. 66–71, for a further discussion of the poem. See also Ben Johnson's praise of the poem in 'The vision of Ben Johnson', where Drayton is compared to Homer.

form of the Homeric catalogue. 'The men of Essex overmatched by none, Under Queen Hellens Image martching downe; Suffolk a Sunne half risen from the brack, Norfolk a Triton on a Dolphin's back', lines 541–4). The Welsh 'who no lesse honour ow'd To their owne king, nor yet lesse valiant were, In one strong re'ment had themselves bestoew'd' (lines 586–9). They too are then described county by county.

The ships put to sea in line 625, when we are already a quarter of the way into the poem. The French reaction is one of panic, with their own reminiscence of Crécy and Poitiers. Henry arrays his army before Harfleur, issues his disciplinary ordinances; in their turn the French make preparations for war. The siege of Harfleur is then described in 19 stanzas. The old man sitting by the fire in Harfleur is a reverse image of his English counterpart seen earlier: the Harfleurais can do no more than try to still the crying of his little grandchild before a bullet hits the chimney and both old and young meet their maker. Much is made of the assault through the breach, for this account of Harfleur stresses an English offensive rather than the slow, drawn out nature of siege warfare. The commanders of Harfleur agree to surrender if help does not arrive. As it does not, the English enter the town.

Henry summons the dauphin to single combat, and then sets out on his march to Calais, on which Drayton dwells extremely briefly. Barely have we left Harfleur than we are across the Somme, and the scene changes to the French war council at Rouen. Here the duke of Alençon is given a speech against the English urging an attack on 'a route of tatter'd rascals starved so, . . . And to our people but a handful are', because of the effects of dysentery at Harfleur. The duke of Berry urges caution, invoking the memory of Poitiers, but the other lords voice support for battle.

When King Henry was told of the likelihood of battle, Davy Gam is made to jest that the English would divide the French army into three – 'one part we'll kill, the second prisoners stay, And for the third, we'll leave to run away.' An obvious literary ploy, to give some sort of flesh to the bones of a man who is himself to die in the battle. A few stanzas later, the duke of York is also mentioned as in command of the vanguard and indulging in some reconnoitring to view the French. The French boast about their forthcoming success. The English in the meantime prepare for the engagement, 'some sharpening are the pyles, the Archers grinding his barb'd Arrow head; Their bills and blades some whetting are with files', lines 1187–9). The contrasting nature of the two camps on the eve of the battle follows the Shakespearean imagery as does King Henry's own soliloquy on the coming day.

The day dawns in line 1241, about half way through the poem, and the preparations begin with Henry sending 300 of his best bowmen into a meadow. The English were up with the lark, whilst the French tarried in their beds. But then the two armies are drawn up and we are introduced to their commanders. York commands the van, the king is in the centre, but it is to Exeter that the rear is given, an obvious error for he has been left as commander in Harfleur in line 926. The stakes are planted against the French charge, which then commences.

Henry makes his battle speech in manner partially reminiscent of Shakespeare (including the king's response to someone who wished for more men), the charge is sounded. The English fall to their knees, and on rising 'such a shrill shout from their throats they sent, As made the French to stagger as they went'. Erpingham gives the signal to charge. The French cavalry at first move only slowly but then like 'th'unweldy tide . . . assayle the English to dispierce their force'. The archers in the ambush wait till the French horse come alongside and then let fly their arrows. The French attack the English 'thinking them to route', but instead their horses run upon the stakes and riders and horses are thrown into disarray, 'tumbling on heapes, somme of their horses cast With their foure feet all up into the ayre'. The English arrows continue to fly, but all this time Henry in his main battle had had no involvement in the fight, but now his battle 'Upon the hoses as in chase they flye, Arrowes so thick, in such aboundance light, That their broad buttocks men like Butts might see, Whereat for pastime Bow-men shooting be.' Drayton's emphasis remains on the crucial role of the archers.

At this point the two French wings of light horse are mentioned, but the narrative then becomes very confused, with Henry ordering York to cease his advance until he can bring up his own battle. There is much killing, and the French leaders become despondent. Châtillon, again in a Shakespearean echo, tells the Constable, 'Shift noble Lord . . . the day is lost, If the whole world upon the matche were layde, I cannot thinke but that Black Edward's ghost Assists the English, and our horse hath frayde; If not, some Divels they have with them then, That fight against us in the shapes of men.' Drayton then features individual French and English barons in acts of bravery and destruction, with invented valorous speeches and actions accorded to them. In a simile of the appearance of the battle, as Drayton puts it in a marginal note, the French are compared to a field of standing corn hit by a wind; in the next stanza we find the French mutilated, 'another runnes to ground with half a head; Another stumbling falleth in his flight, Wanting a legge, and one his face doth light'. French lords agree to surrender and are sent to Suffolk's tent; further acts of bravery are given. But then the French main battle advances and York is slain. The king vows revenge. There follow, again matching Drayton's marginal note 'the bloody scuffle betwene the French and English, at the joyning of the two main battailes, in five stanzas', with again the device of naming individual lords and recounting their deeds of arms. There are more bloody sections ('there drops a cheeke and there falls off a nose, And in ones face his fellowes braines are dashed' – no medieval chronicler would have presumed to wax as lyrically violent as this!). Huntingdon and Suffolk then get into dispute which is resolved by their attempts to outdo each other's bravery. (This is Drayton's invention and may be intended as flattery towards the peers of his own day.)

Alençon comes upon the king, and engages in single combat with Gloucester before striking the king himself. Henry knocks him off his horse before killing two gentlemen who attempted to come to Alençon's rescue. The king is about to accept Alençon's surrender but the latter's voice cannot be heard above the mêlée and he is cut down. His death demoralises the French. (This section from line 1846 to 1928 is given in full below.)

Further acts of English bravery, including those of Davy Gam, follow. Exeter then brings up the rearguard, proving victorious against the count of Vendome. Bouccicaut brings up the remnant of the French wing, Erpingham advances with the archers who had lain in ambush earlier, and Drayton indulges in another excess of violence ('the solyle with slaughter everywhere they load . . . The sunne that rose in water set in blood', lines 2017, 2022). The French are in retreat despite the efforts of the duke of Brabant, who as a Burgundian is given a bitter exclamation against French cowardice before going to his own death. A group of French then hole up in an old ruined fort (this again is pure invention). Woodhouse and Gam assault the fort. The latter meets his death, the former, according to the marginal note is given an extra honour for his bravery, 'a hand holding a club, with the word Frappe fort, which is born by the family of the Woodhouse of Norfolke to this day'. Woodhouse's prominence here and earlier in the poem betrays Drayton's local interests.

Bourbon tries to reassemble and regalvanise the French, hearing that the dauphin is soon to arrive with reinforcements. ('From Agincourt discover'd from a Tower', as we are told in a gesture of verisimilitude.) Another violent battle scene ensues involving Bourbon ('Here a cleft shoulder, there a cloven scull, There hang his eyes out beaten with a malle . . . The French cry "tue", and the English kill') Bourbon is taken prisoner, but Richemont continues the fight ('an ounce of honour cost a pound of blood') before he too is taken. Many French take to their heels as the English 'as victors may doe what they will, for who to this Conqueror to account doth call, In gore the English seeme their soules to swill, And the dejected French must suffer all'). The world is turned upside down ('that brave French gallant, when the fight began, Whose lease of lackies ambled by his side, Himselfe a lacky now most basely ran, Whilst a rag'd souldier on his horse doth ride'). But some of the French who had fled as cowards earlier in the battle now attack the English baggage. The king is alarmed at the possibility of a fresh attack by the dauphin and the remnants of Bourbon's force and orders the prisoners to be killed. Drayton then gives a stanza-long expostulation blaming the French for bringing destruction upon themselves indulging in several further stanzas on the massacre before returning to the theme that the French had brought it upon themselves. 'How happy were those in the very hight, of this great Battaile, that had bravely dyde, When as their boyling bosomes in the fight, Felt not the sharpe stele thorough them to slide. But these now in miserable plight, Must in cold blood this massacre avide, Caus'd by those Villaines (curst alive and dead) That from the field the passed morning', lines 2449–56).

The remainder of the poem is vague in its content. Drayton is light on detail here but rich in imagination of how the English looted the field 'Who scarse as shirt but the day before, Nor a whole stocking to keepe out the cole, hath a whole wardrobe (at command in store) In the French fashion flaunting it in gold, And in the Taverne, in his cups doth rore, chocking his croiwnes, and growes thereby so bold, That proudly he a Captaines mane assumes, In his gilt gorget with his tossing plumes' (lines 2481–88) – we have here a true seventeenth-century knight, I think. The poem is then wrapped up rather perfunctorily in a concluding stanza, lines 2513–20:

> Thus when the king sawe that the Coast was clear'd
> And of the French who were not slaine were fled;
> Nor in the file not nay then appear'd,
> that had the power againe to make a head; this conqueror excedingly
>   is cheer'd,
> Thanking his god that he so well had sped,
> And so tow'rds Callice bravely marching on,
> leaveth sad France her losses to bemone.

Overall, the poem is bombastic as well as patriotic, but it has an epic style to it with its juxtaposition of violence and individual acts of honour and dishonour. It is riddled with early seventeenth-century medievalism, although he is correct enough to deny the protagonists' guns. It is also a very class-ridden poem. The nobility are as significant as the king at least in the battle. 'Henry V is a great man placed at the head of his nation . . . the greatness if the King is defined by that of his people'. These aspects cater for the audience for which Drayton wrote: 'country gentlemen and lesser aristocrats sharing his conservative political, religious and intellectual outlook'.[90]

From *The Works of Michael Drayton*, vol. 3, ed. J.W. Hebel (Oxford, 1932), pp. 55–7, lines 1846–1928.

> But ô what man his destinie can shunne,
>   That Noble Suffolke there is overthrowne,
>   When he much valour sundry wayes had showne.
>
> Which the proud English further doth provoke,
> Who to destruction bodily were bent,
> That the maine Battaile instantly they broke,
> Upon the French so furiously they went,
> And not an English but doth scorne a stroake,
> If to the ground it not a Frenchman sent,
>   Who weake with wounds, their weapons from them threw,
>   With which the English fearefully them slue.
>
> Alanzon backe upon the Rearweard borne,
> By those unarm'd that from the English fled,
> All further hopes then utterly forlorne,

90 Hardin, *Michael Drayton and the Passing of Elizabethan England*, pp. 67, vi.

His Noble heart in his full Bosome bled;
What Fate, quoth he, our overthrowe hath sworne,
Must France a Prisoner be to England led,
  Well, if she be so, yet Ile let her see,
  She beares my Carkasse with her, and not me.

  And puts his Horse upon his full Careere,
When with the courage of a valiant Knight
(As one that knew not, or forgot to feare)
He tow'rds King Henry maketh in the fight,
And all before him as he downe doth beare,
Upon the Duke of Glocester doth light:
  Which on the youthfull Chivalry doth bring,
  Scarse two Pykes length that came before the King.

  Their Staves both strongly rivetted with steele,
At the first stroke each other they astound,
That as they staggering from each other reele;
The Duke of Gloster falleth to the ground:
When as Alanzon round about doth wheele,
Thinking to lend him his last deadly wound:
  In comes the King his Brothers life to save,
  And to this brave Duke, a fresh on-set gave.

When as themselves like Thunderbolts they shot,
One at the other, and the Lightning brake
Out of their Helmets, and againe was not,
E'r of their strokes, the eare a sound could take
Betwixt them two, the Conflict grew so hot,
Which those about them so amaz'd doth make,
  That they stood still as wondring at the sight,
  And quite forgot that they themselves must fight.

  Upon the King Alanzon prest so sore,
That with a stroke (as he was wondrous strong)
He cleft the Crowne that on his Helme he wore,
And tore his Plume that to his heeles it hong:
Then with a second brus'd his Helme before,
That it his forehead pittifully wroong:
  As some that sawe it certainly had thought,
  The King therewith had to the ground beene brought.

  But Henry soone Alanzons Ire to quit,
(As now his valour lay upon the Rack)
Upon the face the Duke so strongly hit,

As in his Saddle layde him on his back,
And once perceiving that he had him split,
Follow'd his blowes, redoubling thwack on thwack:
   Till he had lost his Stirrups, and his head
   Hung where his Horse was like thereon to tread.

   When soone two other seconding their Lord,
His kinde Companions in this glorious prize,
Hoping againe the Duke to have restor'd,
If to his feet his Armes would let him rise:
On the Kings Helme their height of fury scor'd;
Who like a Dragon fiercely on them flies,
   And on his body slew them both, whilst he
   Recovering was their ayde againe to be.

   The King thus made the Master of the Fight:
The Duke calls to him as he there doth lye:
Henry I'le pay my Ransome, doe me right:
I am the Duke Alanzon; it is I.
The King to save him putting all his might,
Yet the rude Souldiers with their showt and crie,
   Quite drown'd his voyce, his Helmet being shut,
   And that brave Duke into small peeces cut.

   Report once spred, through the distracted Host,
Of their prime hope, the Duke Alanzon slayne:
That flower of France, on whom they trusted most:
They found their valour was but then in vayne:
Like men their hearts that utterly had lost,
Who slowly fled before, now ranne amayne.
   Nor could a man be found, but that dispaires
   Seeing the Fate both of themselves and theirs.

*

The *Battaile* was not the only poem which Drayton wrote on Agincourt. *The Cambro Britons and their Harp, his Ballad of Agincourt,* also known as *The Ballad of Agincourt,*[91] was published along with his odes, all being poems in praise of valour, but Drayton chose to apply the title 'ballad' in a gesture of deliberate archaism. It has been suggested that *The Ballad* was Drayton's favourite amongst his own works: '[I] would at this time also gladly let thee understand, what I think above the rest, of the last ode of this number, or if thou wilt, ballad in my book: for both the great master of Italian rhymes, Petrarch, and our

---

91 Printed in Nicolas, Appendix, pp. 83–6, and in Hardin, *Michael Drayton and the Passing of Elizabethan England,* pp. 142–5.

Chaucer, and other of the upper house of the Muses, have thought their canzons honoured in the title of a ballad: which, for that I labour to meet truly therein with the old English garb, I hope as able to justify, as the learned Colin Clout his roundelay.'[92] It is likely that he had come across genuine medieval ballads through his connections with Camden and Stow. The poem is only 120 lines long, but in it he 'triumphantly managed a tight compression of the patriotic and militant spirit which had dully motivated his long, historical poems', using a verse form which was 'eminently suitable for the martial beat of the poem'.[93] It was intended to be sung, which helps to explain the dedication. Drayton also seems to have had a special enthusiasm for the Welsh. He may have been less enthusiastic about the Scottish, and in particular about James I, whom we know he criticised in his other writings. King Henry is more the centre of attention here than in the *Battaile*. It has been suggested that 'the closing lines [of the Ballad] were intended to bring the seventeenth-century reader back into the present, with a thinly concealed contrast between Henry V and James I. From them we may infer that James's weaknesses were two – being a pacifist and being a Scot'.[94]

From Nicolas, *Battle of Agincourt*, Appendix, pp. 83–6.

Fair stood the wind for France
When we our sails advance,
Nor now to prove our chance,
Longer will tarry:
But putting to the main,
At Caux, the mouth of Seine,
With all his martial train,
Landed King Harry.

And taking many a fort,
Furnish'd in warlike sort,
Marcheth tow'rds Agincourt,
In happy hour:
Skirmishing day by day,
With those that stop'd his way,
Where the French gen'ral lay,
With all his power.

---

92 From the preface to his odes, cited in Hardin, *Michael Drayton and the Passing of Elizabethan England*, pp. 6–7.
93 Berthelot, *Michael Drayton*, preface and p. 129.
94 Hardin, *Michael Drayton and the Passing of Elizabethan England*, p. 8.

Which is his height of pride,
King Henry to deride,
His ransom to provide,
To the king sending:
While he neglects the while,
As from a nation vile,
Yet with an angry smile,
Their fall portending.

And turning to his men,
Quoth our brave Henry then,
Though they to one be ten,
Be not amazed:
Yet have we well begun,
Battles so bravely won,
Have ever to the sun,
By fame been raised.

And for my self (quoth he,)
This my full rest shall be,
England ne'er mourn for me,
Nor more esteem me:
Victor I remain,
Or on this earth lie slain,
Never shall she sustain,
Loss to redeem me.

Poictiers and Cressy tell,
When most their ride did swell,
Under our swords they fell,
No less our skill is:
Than when our Grandsire great,
Claiming the regal seat,
By many a warlike feat,
Lop'd the French lilies.

The Duke of York so dread,
The eager vanward led;
With the main Henry sped,
Among'st his hench-men:
Exeter had the rear,
A braver man not there,
O Lord, how hot they were,
On the false French-men.

They now to fight are gone,
Armour on armour shone,
Drum now to drum did groan,
To hear was wonder;
That with cries they make,
The very earth did shake,
Trumpet to trumpet spake,
Thunder to thunder.

Well it thine age became,
O noble Erpingham,
Which didst the signal aim,
To our hid forces:
When from a meadow by,
Like a storm suddenly,
The English archery
Stuck the French horses.

With Spanish yew so strong,
Arrows a cloth-yard long,
That like to serpents stung,
Piercing the weather;
None from his fellow starts,
But playing manly parts,
And like true English hearts,
Stuck close together.

When down their bows they threw,
And forth their bilbows drew,
And on the French they flew,
Not one was tardy;
Arms were from shoulders sent,
Scalps to the teeth were rent,
Down the French peasants went,
Our men were hardy.

This while our noble King,
His broad sword brandishing,
Down the French host did ding,
As to o'erwhelm it;
And many a deep wound lent.
His arms with blood besprent,
And many a cruel dent
Bruised his helmet.

Glou'ster, that Duke so good,
Next to the royal blood,
For famous England stood,
With his brave brother;
Clarence in steel so bright,
Though but a maiden knight,
Yet in that furious fight,
Scarce such another.

Warwick in blood did wade,
Oxford the foe invade,
And cruel slaughter made,
Still as they ran up;
Suffolk his axe did ply,
Beaumont and Willoughby
Bare them right doughtily,
Ferrers and Fanhope.

Upon St Crispin's day
Fought was this noble fray,
Which fame did not delay,
To England to carry;
O, when shall Englishmen
With such acts fill a pen,
Or England breed again,
Such a King Harry.

E. France

As Wylie noted, 'No record now remains to indicate the manner in which the news of the tribulation of Agincourt was received in Paris.'[95] There was, it seems, no official mourning, although the University of Paris held a service of their own in memory of their friends and relatives who had been slain. The king returned to Paris on 29 November 1415. There were major fears in the city, which was at this stage controlled by the Armagnac party, that John, duke of

---

95 Wylie, 2, p. 276. There is no mention in the battle in *Le journal de Nicholas de Baye, greffier du parlement de Paris, 1400–1417*, ed. A. Tuetey, 2 vols (Société de l'Histoire de France, 1885–8). A version of a French poem included in Monstrelet (Text E 8) is found in the *journal* in a hand which is not de Baye's, although the latter has inscribed a title in Latin giving the year as 1415 (pp. 219–20).

Burgundy would attempt to stage a coup.[96] The civil war threatened to escalate but was temporarily averted by the death of the dauphin on 18 December, which was almost as great a blow as the battle itself to a kingdom whose king was incapable of ruling due to insanity. Local government was thrown into some confusion by the loss of life at Agincourt, particularly of men from northern France. This is revealed by an order, recorded in the register of the Paris *parlement*, sent out in the king's name on 29 October 1415 concerning the issue of appointments. Fears of Henry's possible plans to advance on the city are witnessed by a further order in the *parlement* register dated to 3 October.

There were several who lamented and tried to explain the defeat. The fullest statement comes in the Religieux of St Denis, where there is a stress on bad leadership as well as on the sinful ways of the nation which provoked divine judgment. Other treatises and literary works which were stimulated by, or which refer to, the battle were largely the product of the Armagnac group, who supported the last surviving son of Charles VI, the Dauphin Charles (later Charles VII). He fled south when the Burgundians took Paris in May 1418, and found himself disinherited by the treaty of Troyes which Henry V had engineered with the aid of the Burgundians. It could thus be argued that they reflect a particular, anti-Burgundian stance.[97]

The Burgundians were not slow in coming forward with a counterblast. On 25 April 1417 Duke John of Burgundy issued a manifesto at Hesdin against his enemies charging them with, amongst other things, 'deliberately permitting Henry V to invade France and win the battle of Agincourt'.[98] Later Burgundian writers, such as the author of the *Pastoralet*, who were influenced by the assassination of Duke John, place the defeat at the door of the Armagnacs.[99] But there was some weakness in the Burgundian position given the absence of the duke and his heir from the battle. Remember how much space was given by

---

[96] For a detailed account of politics in this period, see R. Famiglietti, *Royal Intrigue. Crisis at the Court of Charles VI, 1392–1420* (New York, 1986), pp. 170 ff.

[97] See, however, the attempt by the duke of Brittany and Yolande of Aragon in February 1419 to create peace and cooperation between the dauphin and the Burgundians, where Henry's success at Agincourt ('where there was much human bloodshed and a great discomforting of many of the royal blood and lineage, and others of the French party dead in great number and others taken away as prisoners') was portrayed as a direct result of political divisions in France and hence a reason why both sides should now seek harmony (Paris, Bibliothèque Nationale, manuscrit français, 2699, fols 211–14).

[98] R. Vaughan, *John the Fearless* (London, 1966), p. 215. Monstrelet, 3, pp. 174–5, mentions the manifesto but not its specific contents.

[99] See also another pro-Burgundian text in chronicle form, *Le Livre des trahisons de France*, written after 1465. This gives a brief narrative account of the battle, emphasising the bravery of Anthony, duke of Brabant, and Philip, count of Nevers, who both died in the battle 'which was a great pity for they were not polluted or sullied by treason as were the other princes who had always supported the Armagnac party' (*Chroniques relatives à l'histoire de la Belgique sous la domination des ducs de Bourgogne*, ed. K. de Lettenhove, 3 vols (Brussels, 1870–6), vol. 2, textes françaises (1873), pp. 128–9).

Monstrelet, Waurin and Le Fèvre to explaining the absence of Duke Philip from the battle: his father Duke John had prevented his going when he himself was keen to show his loyalty and courage. Writers who supported the Armagnacs and thus subsequently the Dauphin Charles, such as Alain Chartier and Jean Juvenal des Ursins, came to blame the Burgundians for Agincourt, being influenced no doubt by the eventual Anglo-Burgundian alliance which followed the assassination of Duke John at the hands of the dauphin's party at Montereau on 10 September 1419. Even before this date, however, the loyalty of the Burgundians was suspected. Soon after Henry's second invasion of August 1417, the duke was accused by the pro-Armagnac royal council of assisting the English, charges which he emphatically denied.[100]

Whilst emphasising the political dimension, we must not lose sight of the generally felt shock which the defeat engendered, nor the sense of demoralisation which was hardly redeemed by events after 1415. The stress on the cruel agency of Fortune is found in many works. Another example for instance, occurs in an anti-English treatise written in 1418–19 ('débats et appointements' or 'après la destruction de Troye'). Here the dead of Agincourt are dealt with in a section dealing with examples of 'misfortune' which has affected the French over the centuries. France is portrayed as a woman who laments 'And how she affected me when she caused the death of several dukes, counts and barons, issue of my wives and husbands, with the flower of my chivalry at the battle of Blangy in Picardy?'[101] As the years past the desire (and opportunity) for revenge grew. The battle was thus invoked by Jean Juvenal des Ursins in a work of 1446 addressed to Charles VII, giving the latter reasons why he should make war against the English rather than coming to a peace.[102] This was written during the truce of Tours when the future of the Anglo-French war was the subject of much debate. 'The first reason is the just quarrel you have. The late King Henry, even though he was offered all kinds of friendly openings towards negotiations, landed in Normandy well aware of and in consideration of the divisions in the kingdom, and conquered the duchy of Normandy, which your predecessors had held for more than 250 years in true and just title. Have not you therefore got a right quarrel towards recovering what is yours and what has been unjustly usurped from you by war. Should not you legitimately avenge the death of your relatives, your good and loyal subjects killed by your enemies at the battle of Agincourt, Verneuil and other engagements and assaults, and which have caused much destruction to the majority of your kingdom not only to the people but also to churches and lands?'

---

100 Monstrelet, 3, pp. 193, 197–8, 199–200. No specific mention is made of Agincourt by either party at this stage.
101 *'L'Honneur de la couronne de France', Quatre libelles contre les Anglais*, ed. N. Pons (Société de l'Histoire de France, 1990), pp. 31, 74–5.
102 *Écrits politiques de Jean Juvénal des Ursins*, vol. 2, ed. P. Lewis (Société de l'Histoire de France, Paris, 1985), p. 161, from 'Traictié compendieux de la querelle de France contre les Anglois, beginning Tres crestien, res hault, tres puissant roy'.

The impact of Agincourt on France and the French would certainly be a topic well worth pursuing in greater depth, especially as it produces some distinctive and original literary works, such as those of Christine de Pizan and Alain Chartier.

E 1. The register of the parlement of Paris (3 and 29 October 1415, French)

Translated from Paris, Archives Nationales, Xia 8602, fol. 304v.

Charles, by the grace of God King of France, to our beloved and loyal councilors the presidents of our *parlement*, greetings and affection. As our adversary of England has recently entered into our kingdom to make war, there is a need, in our good town of Paris which is the capital of our kingdom, to provide for the fortification, defence, garrisoning and other necessary and appropriate matters. As we are currently occupied in military affairs and so that the matter can be carried out by good advice and counsel, we order that, summoning those members of our council, the *prévôt* of the merchants and the *echevins* of our town and others who seem useful in your opinion and men expert in such matters, you provide on the issue such a suitable remedy that no inconvenience or damage can arise both with respect to repairs to walls, gates, ditches and outer ditches, roadways, and military equipment, and to stores and provisions of foodstuffs to provide for the revictualling of our town, and otherwise, with related matters, compelling all those who can be compelled without sparing any, and summoning them fully without delay as the case requires. In this matter we wish that you and your deputies and assigns should be obeyed, and all without prejudice to the rights, privileges and liberties of us and of our good town and of the said prévôt of the merchants and echevins in providing for the same, on this occasion, and because of the urgent necessity and by royal command, for so it pleases us and we wish it to be carried out by these present letters, not withstanding proclamations, orders or countermands to the contrary. Given at Paris on 3 October in the year of grace 1415 and of our reign the thirty sixth. By the king at the relation of the council.

Translated from Archives Nationales, Xia 8603, fol. 2.

Charles by the grace of God to all those to whom these present letters come, greeting. As immediately after the battle held at Agincourt against our adversary of England and even before we had certain knowledge of the outcome of the battle, certain persons came into our presence to ask for, request and demand certain offices, both bailliages, captaincies and other offices which were held by several knights, esquires and other men, our servants and officers, who were present at the said battle, to which persons making the request we inadvertently granted that several of the offices be given to them by our council and mature deliberation and also regarding offices which fell to election of persons who were suitable, and in following certain ordinances on this and to avoid the impression and importunate request of those making petition. Considering that no letters of grant or donation have yet been sealed by us concerning the said offices, we have revoked and now do revoke all such grants made by us of these offices to whomsoever they were made, and we do not wish that any of these grants or donations should have any effect nor that any letters should be sealed or delivered unless they be passed by our council or by our beloved son the duke of Guienne, dauphin of Vienne, and by full deliberation, summoning the men of our council to the matter. To our son we have given and now give by these present letters full power to provide for these offices by the manner aforesaid. We wish that all that is done by our son should take effect without any contradiction and that no obstacle should be put in the way of those whom our king appoint to the offices by the manner aforesaid and that there should be no opposition to the same. Thus we give in order to our beloved and loyal chancellor, to our beloved and loyal councillors who hold our *parlement* and who will do so in future, to the officers of our accounts and the treasurers at Paris and to all our other officers and justices and their lieutenants that they should carry out the aforementioned matters without infringement and that they should not allow anything to be done to the contrary. In witness of which we put our seal to the present letters. Given at Rouen 29 October in the year of grace 1415, and of our reign the thirty-sixth. Signed 'By the King in his council where the king of Sicily, my lord the duke of Berry, the chancellor of Guienne and others were present'.

E 2. The Religieux (Monk) of Saint-Denis, *Histoire de Charles VI* (c. 1415–22, Latin)

Translated from Le Religieux de Saint-Denis, *Histoire de Charles VI*, ed. L. Bellaguet (Collection de documents inédits sur l'histoire de France, 6 vols, Paris, 1839–52), 5 (1844), pp. 565–7, 576–81.

As noted earlier, this account of the reign, written by a monk of Saint-Denis, is the nearest we come to an official French royal chronicle. But that does not mean that it avoids apportioning blame for the defeat. As will be seen from the following extracts, it provides a clear account of the response to the battle. The tone tends towards sermonising, for the main stress is put upon the sins of the French. Similarities have been noted with the *Tragicum argumentum de miser-*

abili statu regni Francie written by a fellow Benedictine, François de Montebelluna, as a response to the defeat at Poitiers in 1356.[103]

Just before the battle the *Religieux* writes 'You know, O Jesus, our sovereign lord, you who can read the hearts of men, what was the first cause of this great sadness which I cannot think about without shedding tears, and which covers France and its people with shame and confusion. I will acquit myself, however, of my duty as a historian, however painful it is to me, and will transmit for posterity the account of that sad day so that such faults can be avoided in future.' Later he comments, 'Then the nobility of France were taken prisoner and put to ransom as a vile troop of slaves or else perished under the blows of a faceless soldiery. O eternal dishonour! O disaster forever to be deplored! If it is usually a consolation for men of heart and a softening of their sadness to think that they have been beaten by adversaries of noble origin and of a recognised valour, it is on the other hand a double shame, a double ignominy to allow oneself to be beaten by unworthy and vile men.' He continues in this vein in chapter 9 following his account of the battle.

*

Chapter 9. *Reproaches addressed to the French because they did not accept wisdom in their counsels.*

You, therefore, famous barons and princes who claim your origin from Francus of ancient Troy, and who take glory in being descended from the most noble ancestors, I consider you to have the hardest of hearts and a completely unfeeling soul if you do not bitterly deplore the shame with which you are covered in deviating from the glorious footsteps of your ancestors. You know all too well how they, wisest observers of military discipline, followed on every significant occasion the counsel of prudence and so led to a good conclusion all their enterprises by virtue of their courage and their indefatigable perseverance, and that it was thus that they spread throughout the whole of the world their reputation for valour. The true annals of times past bear witness to this. It is by following this rule of conduct that in the past, before the time that they embraced the Christian faith, they burned Rome, terror of the whole world, and that they were the first after Hercules to breach the high summits of the Alps despite the eternal snows which made them impassable. They subdued Pannonia and subjugated Greece and Macedonia which they shared with the king of Bythnia who had called upon them to give him aid, making common conquests and giving them as their share the area called Gallo-Greece. You know also how after their conversion to the faith of Christ, they deprived

---

[103] F. Autrand, ' "La déconfiture". La bataille de Poitiers (1356) à travers quelques textes français des xive et xve siècles', in *Guerre et société en France, en Angleterre et en Bourgogne xive et xve siècle*, ed. P. Contamine, C. Giry-Deloison and M.H. Keen (Lille, 1991), pp. 96–8, 107.

of life and of his throne the powerful king of the Goths. Penetrating Spain, they treated the King Amalaric in the same fashion. Then having defeated the Saxons they put to death all the warriors of that country who fell by the sword of their king, Clotaire. Remember too that under Charles Martel they exterminated in one single battle 324,000 infidels who wanted to invade the kingdom. And later Charlemagne, that glorious prince, whose memory will not fade whilst sun gives light to the earth, did not rest until with the help of his Franks he had become the peaceful possessor of Italy, Rome and Germany, and he had spread Christianity in Spain. And finally the kings who were his successors united to the French crown the rich duchies of Normandy and Aquitaine. It is through these memorable triumphs and others that they made, as you know, the glory of France so brilliant, whilst you, o shame, you have tarnished this brilliance by your ill considered rushing forward, your disorder and your ignominious flight. Also, yielding to the justified feeling of confusion that you conduct inspires in me, I would have rather buried in eternal oblivion events whose telling is more suited to the tragic muse than to history if I did not have a duty to transmit to posterity the reversals as well as the commendable deeds of France.

[As given in full in text B 1 above, chapter 10 of this chronicle tells of events after the battle, such as the burial of the dead. It begins 'When news of this sad outcome was known by the king and his subjects, there was general consternation. Each felt a bitter sadness in thinking that the kingdom had been so deprived of so many of its illustrious defenders and that the revenues already much diminished in order to pay the troops would be completely ruined by the ransoming of the prisoners. But what was most galling was to think that the reverse would make France feeble and the laughing stock of other countries.' In Chapter 11 news is brought to the king, and details of those killed and taken prisoner are given.]

Chapter 12. *The king is much affected by the wretched outcome for his men, which many put down to the demerits of the inhabitants of the kingdom.*

On hearing this sad account, the king and the dukes of Guienne and Berry were struck with a great sadness and fell into deep lamentation. They could not help displaying their troubled souls nor their despair by groans and tears. The lords of the court and all the inhabitants of the kingdom, of both sexes, meditating on this cruel twist of fate, reckoned that their century would be considered the most infamous and shameful by all posterity. 'In what malign days have we been born, who are to see such confusion and shame?' Everywhere the lords and ladies of rank changed out of their garments of gold and silk into the clothes of mourning. It was a sight to bring tears to the eyes to see some of the women crying bitterly at the loss of their husbands, others inconsolable at the death of their children and their closest relatives, but especially those who had fallen without glory having taken with them to the tomb those famous names of ancestors which had featured so prominently in the annals of war. There were those who in the bitterness of their grief, cursed divine providence and asked why France, who had previously been so beloved by fortune, had experienced such misfortune. I heard several men of wisdom reply that the misfortune had been caused to the realm by the sins of its inhabitants and that if they had deserved God to be their helpmate, they would without doubt have easily destroyed the force of their enemies and humbled their excessive pride. They came to the indisputable argument 'The French of the past who had been true catholics living in the fear of God had been replaced by corrupt offspring, the sons of iniquity, who held the faith as nought and rushed, without any concern or holding back, into all kinds of vices following evil and avoiding good, like those who said to the Lord God: Get thee away from us, we do not wish to know they ways. And the Lord, rightly angered, withdrew his grace.'

I am inclined to share the opinion of wise men, for in seeing the bad habits of the French one could say that never had a people been more prone to seeking out the pleasures of the flesh. They should be considered as those for whom their stomach is God. Debauchery reigned amongst them, so that the bonds of marriage were no longer upheld even amongst friends and relations, and fraud, ruse and intrigue lurked everywhere. Avarice which, according to the apostle, is the servant of idol, exercised such dominion that there is no fraud which the people will not commit, whether relating to the payment of tithes or in their commercial transactions. They blaspheme the name of the Lord every time they speak. For they say 'Why does God, who in the past used to spare a whole wicked people even if he found but ten just men amongst them, not spare our kingdom in which there are clerics, bishops and monks who serve him assiduously?' I think that observation is without justification. For it is such men whom God established to set the example of obedience to his commands, to be the mirror of honour, the model of chastity and abstinence, the rule of humility and patience, the bringers of consolation to the poor and afflicted, putting aside their passions, rejecting ambition and devoting themselves to prayer and giving their time to pious reading. But they have observed none of this. They have rushed headlong into vice without shame or reserve. The bishops, forgetting their duties, have become like dumb dogs who do not know how to bark. They have received people and anointed them with the oil of penitence and then like mercenaries abandoned them to the wolves who ravage the sheep who are entrusted to them. They do not spurn simony, they live in corruption and are covered with sins and blemishes. They do not hate avarice or bribes, they do not attack the sinful when the preach the truth, and instead of giving righteous counsel to the princes of the land they flatter them with soft words. Considering so many vices and so much indifference in place of what is holy, just, reasonable and honest, we can say with the divine Psalmist 'We are all fallen; we have all become useless. There is no one who does good, no one at all.'

I shall leave to those who are more circumspect to decide if we should attribute the ruin of the kingdom to the disorders of the French nobility, who as everyone knows have all fallen into luxury, delivering themselves up to all passions and vanities of the world, to the point where there is not a man amongst them who follows the ways of his ancestors. The knights and esquires have not forgotten that the dukes and princes of the kingdom, prompted by the devil, enemy of peace, have cast off the sentiments of mutual affection occasioned by the much to be lamented death of the duke of Orléans, and have committed themselves to a mortal hatred and have broken many times the oaths which they had sworn. They have also encouraged those who fight under their orders to put everything to the torch and to shed blood. These wicked servants, worthy of rejection by God and man, have not spared the goods of churches nor monasteries nor have they respected any of the privileges granted by the piety of princes to places of sanctuary. They have abused sanctuaries, committed sacrilege, taken off holy objects and put their impious hands on the holy saints. It is common knowledge that it was the obstinate divisions between the princes which inspired in the enemy the boldness to dare to invade the kingdom. Everyone knows too that it was against the advice of the most experienced knights that battle should be given, and that during that time, soldiers who claimed to be enrolling under their banners were committing terrible acts of brigandage in almost every province of France under the pretext that they had not been adequately paid for their services.

All these crimes and others worse still, to cut a long story short, have rightly stirred up the wrath of God against the great men of the kingdom so that he has taken from them the power of defeating their enemies and even of resisting them. One should not attribute this bad fortune to the conjunction of certain stars or to the influence of certain planets as certain charlatans have claimed in their misleading and excessive assertions. It is the Almighty, I say, who, pushed to the limit by the sins of the inhabitants, has inspired in one people the audacity to invade the kingdom and in the others the thought of flight. I do not think that France has experienced such a great disaster since fifty years ago, and which will have, in my opinion, as grave consequences. For the king of England has returned to his lands with the firm intention of raising new troops in even larger numbers to attack France a second time, as soon as the spring comes, and he has repeated to the lords his prisoners more than once, 'It is you, my dear cousins, who will pay all the costs of the wages.'

E 3. Christine de Pizan, *Epistre de la prison de vie humaine* (1416–18, French)

Translated from *Christine de Pizan's Epistre de la prison de vie humaine*, ed. A.J. Kennedy (Department of French, University of Glasgow, 1984), chapter 1, lines 1–73; chapter 8, lines 889–929.[104]

Christine de Pizan (1365–?1430) was of Italian origin but spent most of her life in France, where her father was physician and astrologer to the royal court. She married Etienne de Castel, a royal secretary, but was widowed at the age of 25. It was in part the ensuing financial difficulties which prompted her to become a copyist and writer. Her literary output is extensive and increasingly well known, given that she is one of the few female writers of the middle ages and also wrote several works in defence of womankind. She had connections with the French royal court and nobility and was an Armagnac sympathiser, forced to take refuge in the convent at Poissy when the Burgundians took control of Paris in 1418.

Several of her works were occasioned by civil war and English invasion – *Epistre à la Reine* (1405, addressed to Queen Isabeau), *Lamentacion sur les maux de la France* (1410), *Heures de contemplacion de la passion nostre Seigneur* (c. 1420), and *Ditié de Jeanne d'Arc* (1429). Arguably here we have a specific female perspective on warfare, although there was a strong political undercurrent, and an increasingly religious dimension to her writings as the years passed. The *Epistre de la prison de vie humaine* is a good example of this last development, being written as a consolatory treatise, perhaps for meditational reading by its recipient.[105] The work, which is found in only one manuscript, is addressed to Marie de Berry, duchess of Bourbon and Auvergne, and seems to have been written for but not necessarily commissioned by her. From internal references we know that it was written in Paris after the death of Marie's father, John, duke of Berry (15 June 1416, lines 79–80), and that it was not completed until at least 20 January 1418 (it ends with Christine's apology to Marie that she has not received the letter sooner, lines 1478–89). Agincourt is not mentioned by name in the work – an interesting parallel with the situation in Alain Chartier's *Livre des Quatre dames*. But there can be no doubt from the wording used that the consolation to be offered to Marie, and indeed to all women, was in specific response to the losses they had suffered as a result of the battle, although it also considered the broader context of the damaging effects of civil war and the loss of loved ones from natural causes. The link with Agincourt

[104] There is also a translation of the whole work available: *Christine de Pizan: 'The Epistle of the Prison of Human Life', with 'An Epistle to the Queen of France', and 'Lament on the Evils of the Civil War'*, ed. and trans. J.A. Wiseman (London, 1984).

[105] On this work, see also, in addition to the editions by Kennedy and Wiseman, S. Solente, 'Un traité inédit de Christine de Pisan: "L'Epistre de la prison de vie humaine" ', *Bibliothèque de l'école des chartes* (1924), pp. 263–99.

is further revealed by references to those killed or captured in the battle. Many of the persons mentioned are linked with Marie. Philip of Burgundy, count of Nevers, whose death 'in the said unfortunate battle, is noted in lines 922–3, was her son-in-law; Jean de Bourbon and Charles d'Artois, count of Eu, referred to as captured in lines 895–902, were her husband and her son by her second marriage respectively.

The title of the work reveals the principal argument within it that whereas those left alive, such as Marie herself, were in the prison of human existence, fully exposed to the slings and arrows of Fortune, those who had died had been freed from this earthly prison and were in paradise. The argument is sustained and explained by reference to scripture and to classical references, and Marie is provided with several reasons why she should bear with patience and hope the loss of her loved ones. Amongst these is the reminder that those who die in battle are particularly honoured in the ancient texts (chapter 4, lines 411–12). Christine also tells her that God has provided her with three gifts – Grace, Nature and Fortune – which will provide consolation. As Christine explains in chapter 8 (the extract given below), Marie was indeed most 'fortunate' given her royal position and her family. Those who have died will be received into paradise where a victor's crown of twelve stars awaits them, each star corresponding to one of the joys which awaits them (chapter 12). In conclusion, Marie should not grieve 'the death of your friends who have died by the grace of God . . . who will profit more from alms, prayers and good deeds than from tears, seeing the great benefits which await them, if it pleases God' (chapter 13, lines 1470–73). Whilst the work is written for personal consumption and has a strong religious feel to it, it is a further example of the dislocation and soul searching in France which followed the defeat at Agincourt.

*

Chapter 1. *Here begins the letter of the 'Prison of Human Life', and on having comfort in the face of the death of friends and patience in adversity.*

To find any remedy and salve for the grievous malady and infirmity of bitterness of heart and sadness of thought by which the flood of tears (which can have no profit for the soul nor value to the body) can be controlled and stopped, which flood has flowed and still (such a pity) does not cease to flow, even amongst the queens, princes, baroness, ladies, maidens of noble royal blood of France and generally of all ladies of honour struck by this pestilence in this kingdom of France, because of so many and various deaths and captures of those nearest to them, husbands, children, brothers, uncles, cousins, relatives and friends – some dead in battle, others dying naturally in their beds – as by many losses and other divers misfortunes and misadventures arising for some time, to advise how anything proposed and brought to mind might serve and be of any value as a source of comfort to the many affected, amongst whom, renowned princess, my lady Marie de Berry, duchess of Bourbon and Auvergne, you have not been nor are exempted or excepted (which weighs heavily on me). And thus, as the deserts of your lavish charity, extended to me in this present time of affliction when friends have failed, has aided my poor widowed state by bringing singular aid (may God by his grace reward you), thankfully acknowledging this and other of your good deeds, desiring to be able to serve you in any manner as I am obliged to do so, to you first of the princesses of this kingdom, although charged by the prompting of another [perhaps a reference to an original commission by Marie's father, John, duke of Berry], this letter of mine is addressed, which similarly and subsequently might be useful for all others who have fallen into such sorrows.

So, highness, I your humble servant, moved by pity and by loyal and true affection, as I had begun this present work long ago (the excuse for not finishing it earlier will be given at the end), but better late than never, and which (this weighs heavy on me) like leaves after August, seeing the miserable disposition of the season which still continues (may God by his grace remedy this before too long) is taken up again by me with intention of bringing it to a suitable conclusion, by God's grace. And because the occasion of the death of friends, which comes often, is the principal sorrow which has grieved the hearts of loyal ladies who love too well, as it is a thing which cannot be redeemed and is difficult to forget, it will be the fundamental aim of this my letter written on this topic to bring comfort. And although in your person, which has played its part well, I shall speak to all, acquitting my task through writing, according to my little knowledge and understanding, to show you reasons taken and extracted both from accepted histories such as the Holy Scriptures, which can and ought to move you to restrain and staunch the flow of your tears, which by great sorrow often grow abundant on your face because of the loss of French chivalry (*la perte de la chevalerie française*) and the great quantity of very noble and worthy royal princes of France, so close and near to your blood, either dead or captured, husband, son, father, cousin, dukes, counts and others of high birth, all without reproach being most honourable, dying, some from natural causes as Catholics with a glorious end and in knowledge of their Creator, in most Christian fashion and in great humility, others fighting against the English enemy on the one hand and defending them on the other, elected with the martyrs of God in just defence by battle, obedient right to death for the sake of preserving justice and the right of the crown of France and their sovereign lord, of whom and for whom and for their kind the Evangelist says, Blessed are those who suffer for justice.

Chapter 8

After such things, are those benefits of Fortune, which you have in such quantity, to be forgotten? Of what are you lamenting? Haven't you parents of high rank, daughter of the son of a king of France, married prestigiously to the line, and good John, duke of Bourbon? But what in the world is a greater joy for those married, especially those of high birth, to have beautiful children. Have you failed in this? Although you may tell me that your sadness came from this whereby your heart is in sorrow and can have no joy, because of your husband and your eldest son, the count of Eu by harsh fortune, as is said before, in doing well by exposing their bodies in chivalrous manner for their sovereign lord and, not by their own fault, falling into the hands of our enemies. (May God by his grace return them soon to you in joy, and all the other noble French who are in that position), to this I reply to you, my renowned lady, by repeating what was said before that hoping that God will do the best for them, and being patient will enable you to give grace towards our Lord to see them again very soon (which God will soon do). And as for that tribulation, although it is great, it is meritorious and God sends you it so that the benefits, prosperity and joys which you have in abundance in this world will not be so pleasant that you forget the way to heaven, which is your rightful heritage, to which one cannot go, according to Scripture, by pleasures of this world, but which by the merit of patience in tribulation can be reached. Haven't you other fine children, noble lady? Good joy God sends you when he gives you such children. To wit, the good and beautiful lady Bonne, countess of Nevers, although you grieve much and have pity for her widowhood, that at such a young stage she has lost her fine husband, Philip, count of Nevers, son of Philip, count of Burgundy, son and brother of the king of France, killed in the aforementioned unfortunate battle (*mort en la susdicte infortunée bataille*). But her wise and good government, notwithstanding her young age, in her discreet provision, nourishing and bringing up of her noble children and of the lands and lordships which remain to her will make you, by her noble person and wise demeanour, consoled and joyful. [Christine then goes on to speak of Marie's other children, Catherine de Bourbon, Charles, aged 15, and Louis, aged 8, and the joys they bring her.]

E 4. Alain Chartier, *Livre des quatre dames* (1416–18, French)

Extracted and translated from J.C. Laidlaw, *The Poetical Works of Alain Chartier* (Cambridge, 1974), pp. 198–304.

Alain Chartier (*c*. 1385–before 1440) was of Norman origin and already a secretary and notary at the court of Charles VI when he fled south with the dauphin in 1418. He was rabidly anti-Burgundian as well as anti-English, and was the author of several works which criticised the treaty of Troyes. He remained loyal to the Armagnac and dauphinist cause throughout. This poem is one of his early works but also, at 3,531 lines, the longest and most ambitious of his poetic compositions.[106] The exact date of composition is not known, but it is likely to predate the Burgundian capture of Paris. Agincourt is not referred to by name in the poem. Here as elsewhere it is called simply 'la malheureuse journée', the wretched day.[107] Moreover, the opening sections of the poem suggest that this is going to be a straightforward poem about love, for it tells of how the poet has lost his love, his Belle ('Beauty'). But there can be no doubt, however, that the battle is the focus of the poem. Whilst trying to assuage his own sorrows by a walk through nature, the poet meets the four ladies of the title. Each claims to be the saddest because of how the battle has affected her. The poet is asked to decide which has indeed the greatest cause for grief. After hearing their cases one after the other, he decides that he is inadequate for the task of deciding between then, so he tells the ladies that he shall ask judgment of Belle, for it is only right that a worthy woman should decide on a matter concerning her own gender. But we never hear of Belle's decision. It is possible, of course, that Belle is not a person at all but a personification of France. Elsewhere in Chartier's writings France is portrayed as a women, as for instance in the *Quadrilogue invectif* of 1422 where she is portrayed as a distressed lady of noble birth whose once beautiful robe, embroidered in part with the fleur de lis, is all dirty and torn, a reference to the divisions and destruction of France in the face of civil war and English invasion.

The *Livre des quatre dames* is a poem that operates at many levels. The four women have suffered in different ways. The first has lost her husband (or lover, the meaning is never too clear) for he has been killed in the battle. The lover of the second has been taken prisoner and is in captivity in England. The lover of the third is missing. In the case of the last lady her love fled from the battle as a coward. Attempts have been made to identify the four women. The second, for instance, is often claimed to be Bonne of Armagnac, wife of Charles, duke of Orléans, and cases have been discovered of men who were missing in action. But the main thrust of the poem is really to criticise those who fled from the battle as cowards and traitors. Thus the widowed first lady (who is given the most lines) blames such men for the death of her husband, the fourth lady gives an account of her own shame and grief brought about by her husband's cowardly deeds, and there is a return to this theme towards the end of the poem when the

[106] I am extremely grateful to Rebecca Griffiths for permission to draw on her unpublished MA dissertation, 'An Examination of French reactions in the aftermath of Agincourt: Christine de Pisan's "Epistre de la prison de vie humaine" and Alain Chartier's "Livre des Quatre Dames" ' (Graduate Centre for Medieval Studies, Unversity of Reading, 1996). See also E. Hoffman, *Alain Chartier: His Works and Reputation* (New York, 1942).

[107] Writing in the early sixteenth century, for instance, Philippe de Vigneulles of Metz tells us that the battle was popularly called *la malheureuse journée*: *La Chronique de Philippe de Vigneulles*, ed. C. Bruneau, 2 vols (Metz, 1927–9), 2, p. 169.

first lady is allowed a reprise. Although it is not explicit, and perhaps gained more force by virtue of not being so, it is possible that Chartier was thinking particularly of those 'traitors' of the Burgundian persuasion. Stress is throughout on the fact that the French lost the battle because of the behaviour of those who fled. This is thus a significant political poem as well as an unusually pointed discussion of the effects of war on the womenfolk of France. It does not as yet exist in an English translation, which is a pity because it contains much of interest. It certainly would repay further critical study as a political poem, in comparison with some of Chartier's later, better known works. I have given below extracts from the arguments put forward by each lady.

*

The first lady

Then she said in fine and pitiful words, having tears in her laughing eyes which were closed up by crying; 'Ah, cruel destiny, and that accursed day, sorrowful, and ill starred, which turned all my joy into discomfort! Alas, he is taken by death, the man that I loved so much and so strongly. Never had hearts of lovers been of such accord nor had they ever loved so loyally and for so long. But now he is dead that is an honour for him, but a cause of sadness for me. Ah me. (lines 537–52)

It is against reason. He was a flower in season and born of such a noble house. You have taken him against all reason. (596–9)

Ah, why was he in the front? Why did he not go in the rear when attacking his enemies? When acting with valour, he did such great deeds by axe and lance that no one doubted his power, by which he gave great honour to France. And if fortune would have preferred rather to make him prisoner, I would be one of the most relieved women under the moon. (613–23)

Well had he acquitted to heaven his faith, as should be in many a chronicle and writing already composed, for he had constantly dared to expose his body and life without being cowardly or lazy, as a valiant man against those who aggressively attack France, giving them, by his unfailing courage, something to think about. And if each man had been willing to do the same without defecting, the English would have achieved little but would have carried the woes which we now have, and would have gone home and departed, never to bother us again. (831–41)

Ah, those who have no loyalty, who love only status and jewels. You abandon all the royalty and turn your back on them, in your retreat, for you stay such a little time, and then you abandon them, like miscreants guilty of treason, and recidivists. The number of the French royalty is decreasing whilst English hearts are boosted. Acting like a herd of sheep, despite the cries and the rallying of the good, you hid your true intentions under your helmets. May your skin be flayed and so burning that you will never recover. Such men should be swineherds or doing dirty jobs in cities and towns when they are so useless in arms . . . they are ready to spend money but are slow to come to defend. One curses God, the other becomes quarrelsome because of drunkenness, and sleeps until ten out of idleness. But he knows well how to get his arse out of a tight corner in battle and to throw away his helmet for the need of the kingdom. He knows more about dice and tennis, he prefers to sleep in his bed than under the hedgerows. (885–932)

. . . they have abused and brought low their lineages. Many were the honours they lost which their fathers had held dear, those who claimed to be nobles from whom came those who did not keep up their good deeds or proper behaviour and who returned to shameful lives. (944–52)

Their flight was the cause, to their great blame, of the loss, and also of their own infamy. (962–3)

The second lady

The deaths of friends, wars and imprisonment, sorrow and loss, blamings by open lies, treasons, wicked covetousness. (1193–9)

But he was taken whilst defending himself from his adversaries, who were acting against his prince. (1236–9)

I pray God that He will bring him back to me by means of His kind pity.
(1256–7)

For this request I ask the ladies of England that I might have their pity, that they might go and find out, enquire and ask after him, for any of them might do something to help. (1797–1804)

The third lady

Alas, I do not know whether my love and my betrothed is dead, captured or put to ransom. Between hope and desperation I hover full of doubts, as someone who has a sadness and does not know why. I do not know by what name to call myself, whether I am a widow for love or a prisoner. And so I can find no proof or witness to say whether he is alive or not. It is a new sorrow. I fear so much. My sorrows speak to me, when I dread the battle. (2166–80)

The fourth lady

The force of grief overwhelms me and makes me tell you of my shameful case. Which makes me collapse in tears and to pay less attention to displeasure than to shame. I hear one of you saying that her grief is the greater because of me through him whom I thought to be better and whom I loved more than any other. . . . I loved more than he did, and loved him more than any other. You cannot speak of the same. For he fled as a coward and ran away, so abandoning his honour. And they say, 'Why were he and those like him there, for their damaging cowardice and their dishonourable flight has brought about the death of so many notable men, indeed thousands, and has brought about for France the loss of her knights who were her pillars of strength, who were taken off like yoked oxen to violent prisons where there is only foul water and lentils. So their smouldering cowardice has made so many women sorrowful and full of tears.

(2552–79)

So you together curse those who fled for their crimes, of which they will never be redeemed, when the good whom they affected are angered, for which I have a very sorrowful heart. Who can reproach me for having loved a cowardly and disgraceful fugitive, guilty of such dishonourable action, who was so led on by his own selfishness to flee from that place and to harm others, who made his bascinet shine and put on armour only to flee. Ah, what a day. (2584–99)

So they say still that it was their flight, an ugly and notorious deed, which gave victory to the enemy, rather than the valour and glory of those who acted better than them. (2768–72)

Ah, fleur de lis, where God in the past placed his delights, as we read in the texts, your name is not buried, nor are you undone by dishonour or counterfeit, for those of your house did you honour by perfect valour. Some are now reduced to ashes. (2824–33)

E 5. Alain Chartier, *Le quadrilogue invectif* (1422, French; mid- to late fifteenth century, Middle English)

Modernised from *Fifteenth-Century English Translations of Alain Chartier's Le Traité de l'Esperance and Le Quadrilogue Invectif*, ed. M.S. Blayney (Early English Text Society, original series, 279, 1974), pp. 190–92.[108]

---

108 For the French text see E. Droz, *Le quadrilogue invectif* (Paris, 1950), p. 31.

As noted above, Chartier was a strong supporter of the dauphin, later Charles VII, and in that capacity was particularly hostile to English political control of northern France after 1420. The *Quadrilogue*, a political treatise rather than a literary work, is essentially a reflection upon the state of the nation, written also in the hope of awakening support for 'French France' under Charles VII. It begins with a prologue which discusses the rise and fall of nations and gives a brief commentary on the state of France. The author then falls asleep and in his dreaming sees the ill-kempt lady, France, surrounded by her three sons, Nobility (or Knighthood), Clergy and People, who are to engage in the four-way debate of the title. France reproaches her children for their evil ways; amongst these are the lack of bravery and loyalty on the part of the knights. The People criticise the Knights for their failure to provide defence, whilst the Knight bemoans the lack of support from the People. The Clergy then discuss what is necessary for the prince to make war – wisdom, resources and obedience. At the end of the poem, France asks Chartier to write down the debate in order to inform and edify the French people. Reference to the battle of Agincourt occurs in one of the speeches given by the Knight in his defence against the People. It urges careful consideration of the situation, suggesting that it was as a result of impulsiveness that the battle was lost. This is reminiscent of other writings such as the chronicle of the Religieux of Saint-Denis, that some older, wiser knight had advised against giving battle but that the young and foolhardy had urged otherwise, and had won (but then not won!) the day. The work was well known in dauphinist circles in France and was one of several French texts to be translated into English in the third quarter of the fifteenth century.

*

Yet this advantage have the common people, for their purse is as a cistern which hath gathered and still gathers the waters of all the riches of this realm, for the coffers of the nobles and of the clergy are greatly diminished through the continuing of the war, for the feebleness of their money makes the payments less than should arise out of the rents owed to them by the people. And by what outrageous scarcity and by their labours, daily they heap up riches and now have they in their possession our chattels and goods. And yet they cry against us and blame us that we do not fight at any time, they would not fear to put into hazard without reason and order all the nobility of the realm. For they would have noble blood given up cheaply, and when all is lost, then will they weep later.

God forbid that we should not annoy and harm our enemies or fight with them in a place or time where any advantage may be found. For there are many worshipful knights and esquires in this realm who would desire nothing else but that the king would give them licence to set them to their duty. But there is also wisdom in matters of fighting to wait and to delay things in order to have the advantage, just as there is in commercial transactions or in other lesser occupations, and it ought to be realised and accepted as a greater wisdom and honour at the end of a battle to withdraw and wisely to save the host and keep them together, which is required of necessity, rather than through misplaced bravery leave aside the wisdom of restraint and moderation, thinking to get a reputation for knightly prowess.

To demonstrate this, it is not necessary to search out ancient stories of time past, for we may use as our lesson something that happened recently in our own days. For we may record in our hearts the cruelty of the unhappy battle of Agincourt, which we bought dear. And yet we lament the sorrowful fortune and bear upon us all that evil mischance out of which we cannot come save by diligent labour and wise suffering in chastising our perilous hastiness by the guarantee of restraint.

E 6. *Le pastoralet* (*c.* 1422–25, French)

Translated from *Le pastoralet*, ed. J. Blanchard (Paris, 1983), pp. 198–207.[109]

This anonymous allegorical poem of 9,141 lines, which survives in only one manuscript in the Bibliothèque Royale at Brussels, was probably written within a few years of the death of Henry V. It is rabidly pro-Burgundian in tone, as is demonstrated by the great sadness expressed at the murder of Duke John at Montereau, and the praise of the latter in the prologue as 'most worthy and valiant . . . who loved the King Charles VI, the kingdom and the public good with complete and total loyalty'. The poem deals with the divisions within the French nation and the ensuing desolation of the kingdom. It is particularly hostile to Louis, duke of Orléans, whom it accuses of trying to poison Charles VI as well as of having an affair with Queen Isabeau. It is essentially a narrative of events from *c.* 1404 to 1419, possibly based upon the Religieux of Saint-Denis or on the now lost Latin chronicle of the abbey of Cercamp in the county of St Pôl: its dialectical features fit with the latter as a possible area of composition. Its fictional characters of shepherds and shepherdesses represent the main historical personages. A key is provided near the end of the work (lines 8,878 onwards). 'Florentin' is Charles VI, 'Belligère', Queen Isabeau, 'Panalus', Henry V and 'Florymaie', Princess Katherine. The political orientation of the anonymous writer is further revealed by the names he gives to the leaders of the Burgundian and Armagnac groups. John the Fearless is Léonet, 'with the strong heart of a lion', whereas Bernard, count of Armagnac is Lupal, 'with the heart of a fox or of a wolf by virtue of duplicity, greed and ill will'. The Burgundians and Armagnacs are thus respectively the 'Léonois' and the 'Lupalois', with the English the 'Panalois' and the French 'la gent Florentin'. The duke of Alençon is Elesis, 'who was full of youthful bravado without any concern for his own

---

109 The poem was first published in *Chroniques relatives à l'histoire de la Belgique sous la domination des ducs de Bourgogne*, ed. K. de Lettenhove, 3 vols (Brussels, 1870–6), 2, textes françaises (1873).

safety'. Antidus is Charles d'Albret, the constable. Normandy is symbolised by 'le clos', which the enemy capture. 'The park which sits next to the sea' which Panalus takes by force is Harfleur on the coast (lines 9,048–51).' The battle of Agincourt (here called the battle of Ruisseauville) is the subject of the four-teenth chapter (lines 6,355–736); extracts from this are given below. In addition, a further mention of the battle is given almost at the end of the poem (lines 9,090–95).

When dealing with the battle, the author tries to keep up the allegory of the rural setting by using the names of agricultural implements in place of weapons, and by continuing to speak of the protagonists as shepherds. The account becomes more gruesome as it proceeds. As in Chartier's *Livre des quatre dames*, women are portrayed as victims of the war because of the loss of their menfolk. For Chartier, however, the Burgundians were the villains. In the *Pastoralet*, it is the Armagnacs – the Lupalois – who are the cause of the defeat, not the Burgun-dians (Léonois). It was the Lupalois who fled from the battle whereas the Léonois stood their ground and died in the field. Duke John of Burgundy had feared treachery. That was why he had absented himself from the battle (*ceste honnourable journee*). It was not fear of the enemy, for no one was braver than he, nor did the English fear anyone more. The poem is undoubtedly intended as pro-Burgundian propaganda, but reminds us yet again of the powerfully strong memories which Agincourt evoked in France.

*

Here follows the fourteenth chapter which contains the battle of Ruisseauville of the French against the English.

I wish to tell you the tale of a great and bitter battle (the most excessively so, for no one can ever hear of a greater one), because the time has come to tell it. The Panalois rush to arms without any delay . . . Because they are in such great number the Florentinois have no fear of loss or defeat. They make no battle order, but go into combat in disarray, as if they were going to play boule. They think that they will defeat the Panalois, and bring them all to death, but they may well repent of this. By over-presumption one loses the victory. Panalus remembers Pan [i.e. God], but Antidus forgets everything. He does not fear the Panalois one jot. In his great host he has so much confidence. However much a shepherd has, one might say to him, fearing shame, 'the largest does not necessar-ily have the advantage'. . . . Now the battles are ranged where new shep-herd's crooks are forged. . . . They sound the horn for the attack. The vassals approach each other fiercely. To the onlooker it would have seemed as though they were going to a feudal host, Christian against pagan. So many of them fell, and in great and hideous affray, at the begin-ning of the fight. The shepherds in that flat place cried out with great, strong and high voices making the deep valleys and high trees resound with such raging that it seemed all would fall into the abyss itself at the sound of the very cry.

Right at that point the great battle began, but the outset was so fierce, cruel and horrible, and wonderously terrible. In order to kill or slay, arrows, hard irons with sharpened tips, were made to fly through the air more densely than hailstones fly in winter in the cold wind. Thus they took more light from the sun than a black cloud would have done. Then they engaged, throwing three-pointed darts. Many were felled by these darts so harshly and to such an extent that, wounded, they were unable to rise to their feet ever again. Then without seeking any end to this, hand to hand they struck with their hoes and with their sharpened crooks, effecting great scything blows by the strength of their arms. . . . They each struck the other to the teeth with great and hard blows, and with cruel cutting down of shepherds, lying dead in the meadow. So many heads cut off, so many feet, fists, so many arms without hands. I think there never was so much shedding of human blood nor a slaughter more cruel.

So much did the shepherds mortally injure each other, cutting off limbs and heads. Because of the bloody tempest and the great October rain, the place was completely muddy where the combatants stood, bogged down, sullied and shamed by the muck. There in the dung, without a bed, were the dead sleeping, one on top of the other, in piles, heaps, some lying upwards, some face down. The field is covered with them. There were many who died lying among the dead without receiving a single blow. Oh the harshness and wickedness of it all! Oh the cruellest of battles. . . . The streams run through the valleys, the rivers run red. But so emboldened are the Panalois and so feared that the Florentinois are driven back. . . . The Florentinois flee, they who were ten against one, for everyone did not do their proper duty. If the Léonois, who were at the front, did well, the Lupalois, at the rear where they could not be reached, did nothing at all. The failure of the Lupalois gives the victory to the Panalois. . . . Many lively and noble shepherdesses are left alone without their lovers. For so many have died . . . Shepherdesses, weep for them, lament with great sobbing because you have lost your lover. Weep with your eyes, weep often, for here perishes fine youth. . . .

The Léonois would rather give up their souls than flee. Each one continues to strike without sparing himself, even up to the point of death. Had they been supported just a little bit by the Lupalois and had the latter come forward as the Léonois had done, then the Panalois would have been dead. But the Lupalois flee over hills and vales, outdoing each other in their efforts to do so, without any fear of reproach. The grassy byways and green fields are covered with treacherous fugitives. But many died in their flight, having a villainous death which they entirely deserved. The valiant were killed in the battle, and the miscreants in flight. . . . The Florentinois were foolish to consent to give battle without Léonet for the Panalois feared him. Because of the sayings of Merlin, they took him as an Apollo.

If his name alone had been cried boldly in the hard and fierce battle, the Panalois would not have lasted very long, but would have fled as does the hare from the dogs. . . .

E 7. Charles, duke of Orléans, *Ballade* LXXXIV (1420s–1430s, French)

Translated from P. Champion, *Charles d'Orléans, Poésies*, 2 vols (Paris, 1923–7), 1, p. 135.

Charles (1394–1465) was taken prisoner at the battle of Agincourt and remained in captivity in England until November 1440. During his captivity, he wrote poems in French as well as in English, with some existing in both languages, and after 1440 continued to produce poems in French. They cover a wide range of themes although many lie within the courtly traditions of love poetry. Certain poems written whilst in England are of a patriotic nature or include references to war.[110] *Ballade* XXV may, for instance, concern the siege of Orléans where he urges Loyalty to unfurl her banner. In *Ballade* LI he celebrates the French recovery of Normandy: 'now I see the English humbled, now it is England's turn to be hated by God'. In *Complainte* IV he also tells us that France was once a great nation full of loyalty, honour, prowess, but that it had been corrupted by excessive pride, gluttony, laziness, covetousness, luxury, and lack of justice. God had therefore seen fit to punish France for her sins, and he urges repentance as well as revival with reminders of the sacred banner, the oriflamme, and the battle cry 'Montjoye'.

Agincourt is not mentioned by name in any of his poems but it is suggested that *Ballade* LXXXIV, addressed to the duke of Bourbon who was also taken prisoner at Agincourt, is also concerned with explaining the French defeat along similar lines to the *Complainte*. 'God wanted to punish Christianity'. Not surprisingly, perhaps, Charles did not chose to write versions of any of these 'patriotic' poems in English.

*

My gracious cousin, duke of Bourbon, I ask you, when you have the leisure to do so, to give me, by ballade or chanson, some idea of your state. As for me, you must know that, without any lie, I feel my heart to be renewed with joy, hoping that good times will come through the good peace which God sends us shortly.

---

[110] See chapter 7 of N.L. Goodrich, *Charles of Orléans. A Study of Themes in his French and in his English Poetry* (Paris, 1967).

Every Christian who is loyal and good must rejoice greatly about the benefit of peace, seeing the great evils and destruction which war has brought about throughout the whole country. God wanted to punish christianity which had abandoned living a good life. But later He wished to rescue it, by the good peace which God sends us shortly.

And for that reason, my dear companion, may you banish your displeasure by forgetting your long period in captivity which has made you suffer much grief. Thank God, think to serve Him, He will keep for you in all things great joy and will make it possible for you to have your desire, by the good peace which God sends us shortly.

Awake in joyful memory for I hope to see you again, and myself too, in comfort and pleasure, by the good peace which God sends us shortly.

E 8. Anonymous poem in *La Chronique d'Enguerran de Monstrelet* (c. 1444, French)

Translated from *La Chronique d'Enguerran de Monstrelet*, ed. L. Douet-D'Arcq (Société de l'Histoire de France, 6 vols, 1857–62), 3 (1859), p. 123.

Having listed the fatalities and told us something about how the French dead were buried elsewhere or in the field, Monstrelet gives a short poem which, from its inclusion in the register of the Paris Parlement and other locations, was apparently fairly widely circulating after the defeat, which it places firmly in the context of weaknesses and divisions in France.

*

After this piteous and saddest of days, some clerks of the kingdom of France, in great wonderment, wrote the verses which follow:

Leader [king] removed by pitiable fortune,
Young regent full of his own self-will,
Blood so divided that no one cared at all for the other,
Council suspected of bias.
People destroyed by prodigality,
Forcing so many men to turn to begging
that each is in need of help

Nobility acting against its nature,
Clergy fearful and hiding the truth,
The humble commonfolk obey, and suffer
weak protectors who bring them danger.
But necessity causes so much suffering

such as has never before been seen or desired
that each is in need of help

Feeble enemy in great defeat
victorious and scarcely harmed.
Reassuring words which mean little
and about which nothing is actually done;
You the ruler persecuted by your own
Your end will come, and our final state will be
that each is in need of help.

E 9. Poem by Robert Blondel (1420–22, Latin and French)

Translated from *Oeuvres de Robert Blondel*, vol. 1, ed. A. Héron (Société de l'Histoire de Normandie, 1891), pp. 33–4, 126–8.

Robert Blondel (*c.* 1390–*c.* 1460) was a member of a noble family of the Cotentin. He chose exile from the duchy during the English occupation, initially in Angers. In 1436 we find him as a member of the household of Yolande of Aragon, duchess of Anjou, but by 1449 he was attached to the court of the duke of Brittany, being responsible for the education of the count of Etampes (the future Duke Francis II). The family fief of Ravenoville was granted to an Englishman, Thomas Craffort, as part of the Lancastrian land settlement, but on Charles VII's recovery of the Cotentin in 1450, the fief was returned to Robert Blondel. In 1454 he became tutor to Charles of France, duke of Berry and second son of Charles VII.

Four works of Blondel are known. Three were written in Latin. The poem, *Liber de Complanctu Bonorum Gallicorum* (*The Book of the Complaint of true Frenchmen*) was written in the last years of the reign of Charles VI in the light of the treaty of Troyes and was intended to encourage all true Frenchmen to reject Anglo-Burgundian rule and to rally to support the Dauphin Charles. The work was soon translated into French verse (*La complainte des bons françois*) by a Norman clerk called Robinet who had also chosen exile during the English conquest. Five manuscripts of the *Liber de Complanctu* are known, three of which also contain the French translation.[111] It is within this poem that the reference to Agincourt occurs as one of many examples of how France has suffered at the hands of both the English and Burgundians.

Two of Blondel's remaining Latin works were connected with Charles VII's defeat of the English in 1449–50. The *Oratio Historialis* was written in 1449 to encourage Charles VII in his reopening of the war, and the *Reductio Normannie*

[111] For a full discussion of these manuscripts, all in the collections of the Bibliothèque Nationale, see *Oeuvres de Robert Blondel*, ed. Héron, pp. xxxi–xliv.

(*The Conquest of Normandy*) written soon after the event as an account of the king's successful campaign of 1449–50. Héron's edition contains the texts of the *Liber de Complanctu* and of its French translation, as well as of the *Oratio*. The *Reductio* was published in 1863 as part of a Rolls Series volume entitled *Narratives of the Expulsion of the English from Normandy*. The fourth and last work, *Les douze perils d'enfer* (*The Twelve perils of Hell*) is in French but was in fact a translation and expansion of a Latin treatise which was undertaken at the behest of the queen, Marie of Anjou.

*

O day full of tears which France in exile curses, when you were stripped of the whole flower of knighthood, and when you lost all recreation and enjoyment, all sweet songs and knowledge, and when you gave tears and groans to all. Know this, whoever reads it, be he lay or priest, and do not scorn it. For one could, which is impossible, count the ears of corn of Beauce, or distinguish all the droplets of the Loire and its pebbles which it makes swirl, or repair all the ruins without any materials, more easily than one could relate the misfortunes which have happened in France.

Question – Who is the one who does not find sadness where it is common to everyone?

Further question – And of what place can one say with certainty that no ill-feeling was ever there?

Reply – In France there is no path or lane, town or borough, however wretched, which does not feel the wound, and where there are not some fugitives who have been terrorised because there is no one left who is disposed to love the lilies whom the wild beasts did not devour. The field of France is rough and empty, which one was not accustomed to, for the good French are all either in flight or dead. When in the noble orchard of France lily flowers used to flourish and never cease to give great abundance of fruit to all, every living man in this world thought to give her aid. But when adversity strikes her down, I do not think that there is any one of them [who will give aid]. The gentle wind of prosperity showed her many sweet talking friends but now the wind of adversity [blows], few of them show her loyalty.

E 10. *Le Jouvencel* (1461–66, French)

Translated from *Le Jouvencel par Jean de Bueil, suivi du commentaire de Guillaume Tringant*, 2 vols (Société de l'Histoire de France, Paris, 1887, 1889), 2, pp. 62–3, 269.

Jean de Bueil (1405–1477) came from Touraine. He first served the vicomte of Narbonne as a page and was present at the battle of Verneuil, after which his master was hanged by the English for his involvement in the murder of John the Fearless, duke of Burgundy. De Bueil subsequently served with La Hire against the English in Maine and Anjou, and in 1444 he accompanied the Dauphin Louis in a campaign in Switzerland. He participated in Charles VII's reconquest of Normandy and was appointed admiral of France and captain of Cherbourg in 1450. He fell into disgrace in the reign of Louis XI because of his involvement in the War of the Public Weal. It was during this period (1461–6) that he wrote *Le Jouvencel*, essentially an autobiographical account of his own military career, although not written in the first person and with names of places and key figures changed to fictional forms. Tringant was a servant and collaborator in the work and wrote his own commentary on it between 1477 and 1483.

It is from Tringant rather than de Bueil himself that we hear that the latter's father, Jean de Bueil IV, grand master of the crossbowmen, was at Agincourt along with other members of the family. We know that Jean IV's younger son, Pierre, as well as his son-in-law, Jean de L'Isle, baron of L'Isle Bouchard, were both killed at the battle. It is unclear what happened to Jean IV himself. In 1416 his widow declared that she had heard no news of her husband, despite making enquiries, since the time he went off to accompany the king 'in his campaign to Picardy (*voyage de Picardy*) against the English enemies of the kingdom'. This led the editor of *Le Jouvencel* to suggest that he was, like one of the husbands of the ladies in Alain Chartier's *Livre des quatre dames*, 'missing presumed dead'.[112]

Le Jouvencel also includes several sections of a quasi-didactic nature where comments are made on the conduct of war and politics. The assessment of Agincourt comes from such a section in chapter 17 where several battles are commented upon. Vegetius was the fourth-century author of *De Rei Militari*, a text much copied and consulted by men of war of all western European nations in the later middle ages. The identity of the character named Monsieur de Chamblay and noted elsewhere as a marshal, Guy de Fromentières, is not known but it is suggested that he was of a family from Maine. The essence of *Le Jouvencel* is how a young man learned his military training and how his own cunning and loyal service contributed to his rise to prominence. This section of chapter 17 is therefore couched in terms of lessons to be learned from past military actions, and from the advice of the great commanders. Louis de Sancerre

---

112 *Le Jouvencel par Jean de Bueil, suivi du commentaire de Guillaume Tringant*, 2 vols (Société de l'Histoire de France, Paris, 1887, 1889), 2, p. 307, 1, p. vi.

(1342–1402) had been marshal of France from 1369 and constable from 1397; the Jean de Bueil referred to was the author's own grandfather who had been royal lieutenant in Anjou, Touraine and Maine in 1368; La Hire was leading captain under Charles VII.

The lesson to be learned from Agincourt was that armies on foot should stay put and let the enemy come at them. Interestingly, French accounts do not always include a mention of the English forward movement but offer the notion that it was the French who made the move. The author also emphasises that an army needs rest before a battle. Several French accounts emphasise the hullabaloo in the French camp on the eve before the battle, and the discomforts they suffered, in bivouacking as well as in their advance, because of the muddy ground. The chronicles of France referred to by Tringant are most likely to mean the work of the Religieux.

*

Vol. 2, pp. 62–3.

After reciting information from Vegetius, M. de Chamblay said to the Jouvencel, 'The king has given us a little memoir in which is contained in summary several battles lost and won, and the reasons why, in his opinion, they were so, along with three words which three noble captains declared one should always take note of. If it pleases you, would you like to hear them read?' The Jouvencel replied, 'Monsieur de Chamblay, I thank the king most humbly and ask you to let me hear everything so that I might learn.' At that, de Chamblay called a secretary of the king, called Master Guiet, and said to him, 'Read this memoir.' So he began.

[There follow three sets of advice, of Louis de Sancerre ('win well and lose well'), La Hire ('If you want to stop yourself being frightened make sure you always strike the first blow') and Jean de Bueil ('Don't move, I know where they are going to go'). There is then a note on the battle of Shrewsbury, before a note on Agincourt. After the section on Agincourt, which is given below, the following battles are discussed: Cravant (1423), Verneuil (1424), Baugé (1421); Patay (1429), Formigny (1450); Castillon (1453); Basle (1444); Auray (1364).]

There was another battle in France called Agincourt[113] which King Henry of England won because he kept up the spirit of his men and kept saying that the night would serve to refresh them, whilst the French did the opposite. For at night they slept in a field with mud right up to their knees, and in the morning they marched across a great fallow field to meet their enemy. This took such a long time, so much so that when it came to fighting they assembled with too few men and with some arriving after the others, and they were out of breath. As a result, they were

---

113 One text adds here 'in the county of Artois'.

defeated. On this matter, an army on foot ought not to march but should always wait for its enemy. For when they march they will not all remain in one force, they cannot keep close order. It only needs one drink to split them up. A power which marches in front of another power is defeated, unless God gives them grace. So, take up the most advantageous position you can, and as soon as you can.

Vol. 2, p. 269 (from the commentary by Guillaume Trignant).

[This short note follows a section on the battle of Verneuil.] I was not at the battle of Agincourt, where were taken and killed many princes and great lords of France, knights and esquires, and much great nobility, as everyone knows, and even the father of my master, his brothers and his cousins. But on that event, I agree with those who know more, and with the chronicles of France.

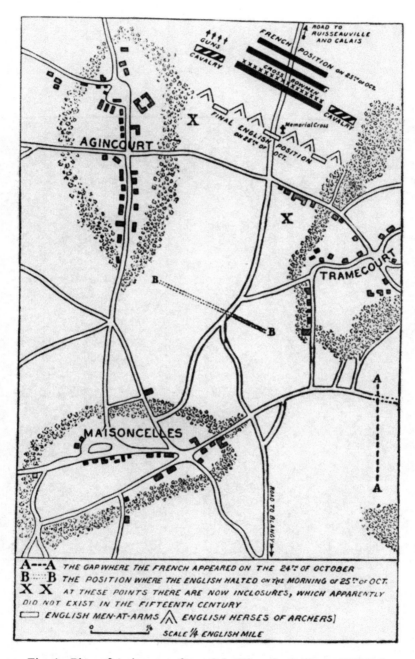

Fig. 1. Plan of Agincourt, from C.L. Kingsford, *Henry V* (1901)

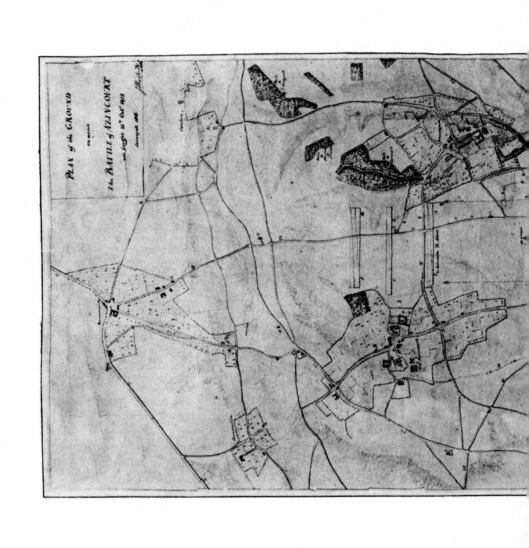

PLAN of the GROUND
on which
the BATTLE of AZINCOURT
was fought 25th Oct 1415

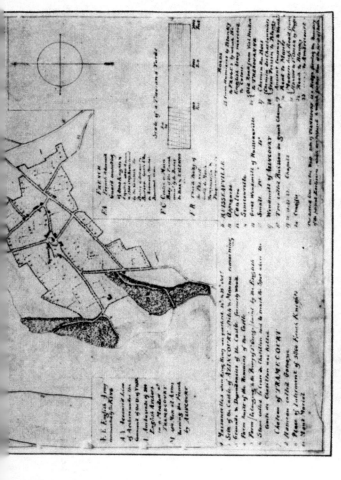

Fig. 2. Plan of the ground on which the battle of Agincourt was fought, drawn by Sir John Woodford, 1818 (from British Library Additional MS 16368, map C). By kind permission of the British Library

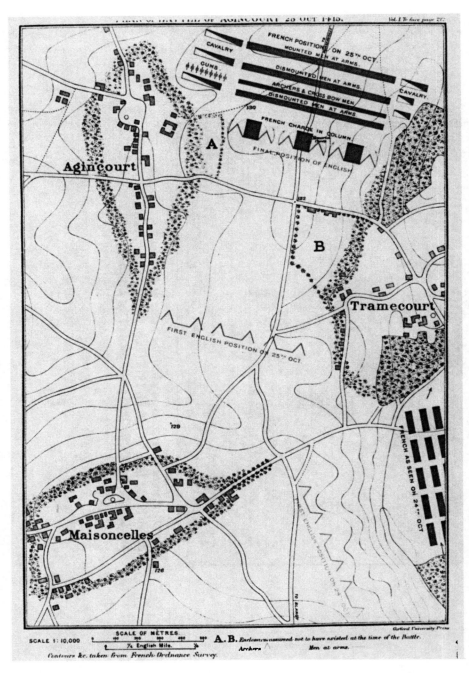

Fig. 3. Plan of the battle of Agincourt from J. Ramsey, *Lancaster and York* (1892)

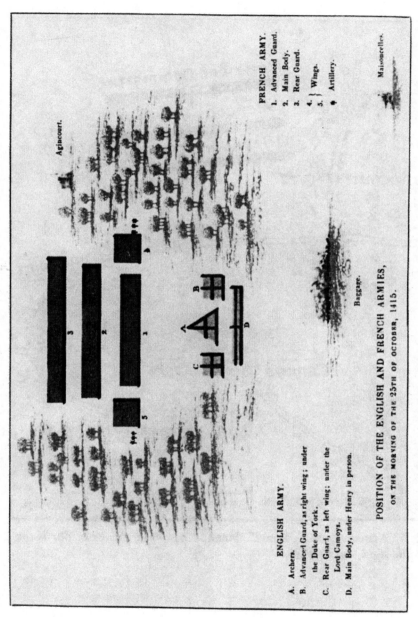

Fig. 4. Position of the French and English armies on the morning of 25 October 1415, from H. Nicolas, *History of the Battle of Agincourt* (2nd edition, 1832). Note that the village of Agincourt is placed in error on the right rather than the left

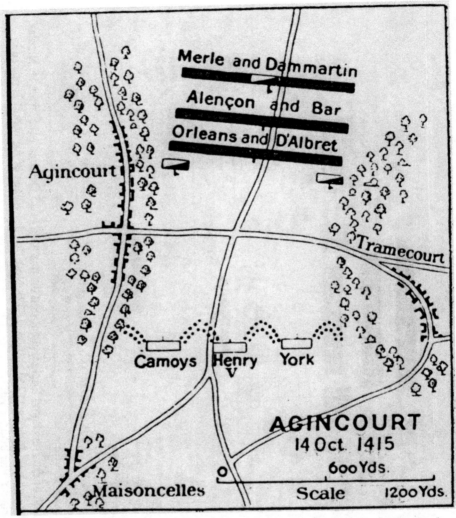

Fig. 5. Agincourt, 1415, from C. Oman, *A History of the Art of War in the Middle Ages*, vol. 2 (1898)

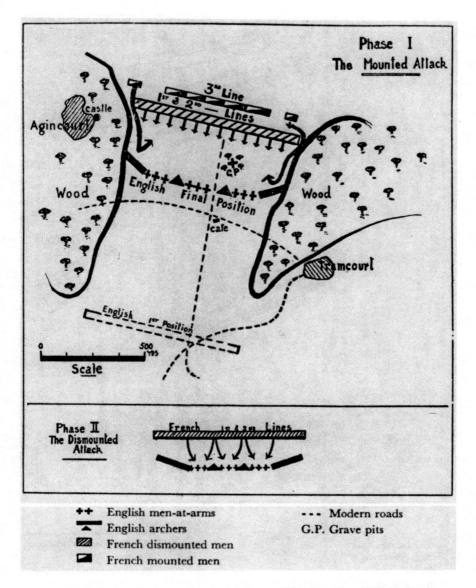

Fig. 6. Agincourt, 1415, from A.H. Burne, *The Agincourt War* (1956)

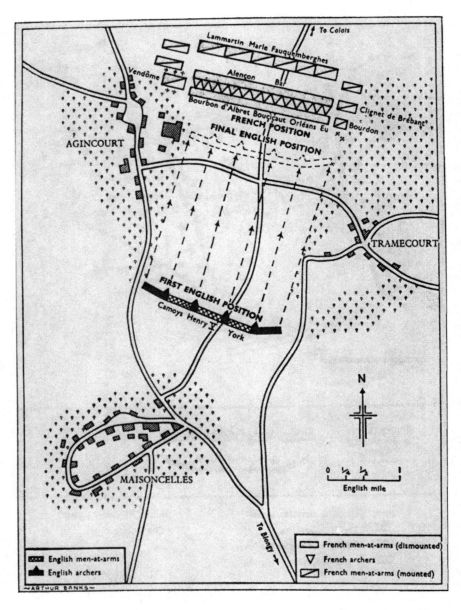

Fig. 7. Positions of the armies between Agincourt and Tramecourt, 25 October 1415, from C. Hibbert, *Agincourt* (1964). By kind permission of the author

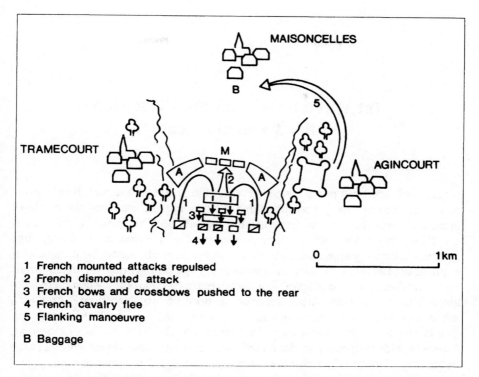

Fig. 8. The battle of Agincourt, from *Arms, Armies and Fortifications in the Hundred Years War*, ed. A. Curry and M. Hughes (Woodbridge: Boydell & Brewer, 1994). The three battles of men-at-arms are at M, with archers on the flanks marked A

4

Interpretations from the Eighteenth
to the Twentieth Century

It can be claimed that every century rewrites the history of the past. It is possible to detect contemporary considerations influencing the study of the battle of Agincourt over the last few centuries, but the debt both to specific chronicles of the fifteenth century and to certain historians of the sixteenth century also remains constantly apparent. Indeed, an examination of writings from the eighteenth to the twentieth century can reveal how frighteningly dependent historians were on what had gone before.[1] Why write one's own narrative when there were already some splendid earlier accounts in print on which to draw? And why, when they were so splendid, bother to draw on more than one? If the sense of drama flagged, there was always Shakespeare to fall back on. In this context, therefore, although many works do tell us of the battle, they do so without much in the way of personal comment or interpretation. Until the present century, and even within it, many studies of Agincourt have been almost entirely narrative in approach.

This is a sweeping statement. We must now be more discerning. It is necessary to distinguish between works not only from a chronological perspective, but also on the basis of genre. Most accounts of the battle occur within studies of the history of England as a whole. There are some, although perhaps surprisingly few, studies of the reign of Henry V alone. There are also discussions of the battle within military histories, and works which focus entirely on the battle itself. A seminal work of the latter type, Sir Harris Nicolas' *History of the Battle of Agincourt* (1827–33), must be mentioned right at the start, although it will be returned to for fuller discussion in due course. Nicolas provided the first serious

---

1   The exclusion of the seventeenth century needs a brief explanation. The period was not without history, nor of interest in the period. Around 1600, heralds were busy copying 'the Agincourt Roll', and in the 1660s examining the surviving indentures, as will be more fully explored in chapter 5. In the first quarter of the century, Sir Robert Cotton and others were collecting relevant texts, and towards the end of it, Thomas Rymer had been commissioned to collect and publish diplomatic and other documents. There were also some general histories, but the legacy of the works of the later Tudor period was considerable and I have not so far found any interpretations distinctive enough to merit inclusion in the current study. John Speed, *The History of Greate Britaine* (London, 1611), pp. 631–4, gives an account of Agincourt which is similar in content to those of Holinshed and Stow and which also provides marginal annotations of the source of information.

study of the battle and was all the more significant for bringing to public notice sources beyond the chronicle accounts. As we shall see, his near contemporary, Sir Joseph Hunter, also carried out important and in many ways more significant documentary work on the battle, but produced relatively little in print, and certainly nothing which has reached the readership of Nicolas.

My study of the interpretations of the last three centuries concentrates on works in English largely for the sake of space. Not surprisingly the French have not shown any inclination to write books on Henry V, so that their study of the battle has tended to arise within the context of general and military histories. But they have their own Nicolas in the shape of René de Belleval's *Azincourt* (1865). Both works show their antiquarian leanings in their desire to establish who was at Agincourt, but it is testimony to the contrasting outcomes and impacts of the battle for the English and French nations that Nicolas concentrates on those who participated in the campaign, and Belleval on those who died. This difference is also the result of the contrast between the surviving documentary sources for the English and French armies, and thus will lead us neatly into a more detailed examination of this subject in the next chapter.

Narrative histories from the early eighteenth to early twentieth centuries

The organisation of this chapter is not strictly chronological, for I have tried to bring out various themes and approaches rather than simply to consider each work in turn. But it is sensible to start with the first single volume study of the reign, Thomas Goodwin's *The History of the Reign of Henry the Fifth, King of England*, which was published in London in 1704. Christopher Allmand assessed this work as 'a promising beginning', whilst also emphasising its shortcomings.[2] We shall consider the latter in a moment, but it is important to place the book in its contemporary context. In 1704, England (or more correctly Great Britain) was at war with France in the War of the Spanish Succession. The dedicatory preface to John, Lord Cutts, who had himself taken up arms against the traditional enemy is unsurprisingly bombastic and patriotic in tone.[3] As Goodwin puts it 'our Black Prince's and Fifth Henry's wars are now no longer

---

[2]   C.T. Allmand, *Henry V* (Historical Association Pamphlet, general series, 68, London, 1968), p. 6. Goodwin (*c.* 1650– *c.* 1716), of nonconformist pedigree, was pastor of an independent congregation in Middlesex and published various collections of sermons (*DNB*, 22 (1890), p. 150).

[3]   For the career of Cutts, who had distinguished himself at the battle of the Boyne and was third in command at Blenheim, see *Complete Peerage*, 3, pp. 583–4. Jonathan Swift was less complimentary, describing Cutts 'as brave and brainless as the sword he wears' (cited in C.H. Knowles, 'Henry V and the historians', *Presenting Monmouthshire*, 21 (1966), p. 17).

acted only on our theaters [sic] but are revived in the field too'. The year his book appeared saw another great victory over the French at Blenheim (12 August). Henry's pre-battle speech is based on fifteenth-century versions but with certain new emphases which might have served to remind his military contemporaries of past English ambitions and glories. French disorder and cowardice is also stressed, as for instance in this extract towards the end of the engagement.[4]

> The French troops in the rear were yet in good order, and if they had not wanted courage might have renewed the fight, and made the victory yet doubt-ful; but when they saw the two first lines of their army entirely destroyed, they were disheartened; and their fears increasing, when they observed that the English horse by King Henry's order wheeled off to charge them in the rear, they fled without making any resistance. The English soldiers had now nothing to do but to kill and take prisoners, and the French were so dispirited as tamely to offer their throats to be cut or their hands to be chained.

The work is most emphatically a narrative history which derived its blow by blow account from chronicles and sixteenth-century histories. Indeed, it is perhaps the most obvious example of something noted earlier in this study – the piling up of all the various different accounts into one with no discrimination at all between sources written close to the event and those written later. Thus in the marginal notes, Stow and Polydore Virgil are cited alongside Le Fèvre, Monstrelet, Walsingham, the Religieux of Saint-Denis and other chronicles. Waurin does not seem to have been used. David Powell's *History of Cambria (or Wales)* (1584) is cited as the authority for the actions of Davy Gam before the battle.

> Captain David Gam, who attended King Henry with a party of valiant Welsh-men, having been sent to review the strength of the enemy, made this gallant report to his royal master: 'may it please you , my liege, there are enough to be killed, enough to be taken prisoner, and enough to run away. The king was extremely animated by this undaunted answer of a gentleman, whose actions afterward in the battle were no less surprising.[5]

Goodwin tells us in his preface that Thomas Rymer had communicated mate-rials to him. Rymer had been commissioned by the government in 1693 to search out and publish materials on diplomatic relations from the middle ages to the present.[6] The first volume of his *Foedera* was published, as was Goodwin's

---

4   P. 89. This is not to be confused with the killing of the prisoners which is ordered as a retaliation for the attack on the baggage. He cites as the source for his speech the Religieux of Saint-Denis (p. 87).

5   P. 81.

6   For the career of Rymer (1641–1713), see *DNB*, 50 (1897), pp. 65–8. Interestingly, Rymer also marked out Henry for praise in the preface to volume nine of the *Foedera*. See below p. 383. For the significance of the materials collected by Rymer, see below p. 410.

book, in 1704. Although the ninth volume of the *Foedera* dealing with the reign of Henry V did not appear in print until 1709, it is clear that Rymer had been collecting documents for it from the very start. From 1696 to 1707 he had employed as his assistant Robert Sanderson, who was thus partly responsible for the collection of materials on Henry V. Sanderson also prepared his own history of the reign. The latter was never published, however, and volumes survive in manuscript for the period from 1416 to 1422 only.[7] Many more documents were collected for the *Foedera* than were actually printed, as the surviving notes of both Rymer and Sanderson indicate. Even so, volume nine included important materials for the Agincourt campaign deriving from royal administrative records, and thus offered authors a useful complement to the chronicle sources.

Marginal notes in Goodwin reflect the information Rymer had supplied in advance of publication. For instance, Goodwin mentions the letter which William Bardolf, lieutenant of Calais sent to the duke of Bedford and which included a report that the duke of Lorraine was gathering troops to threaten the March. Goodwin gives as reference 'MS. in Bibl. Cott. Caligula D5': this text was later printed by Rymer in volume nine of his *Foedera*.[8] But such use of documentary materials is not extensive in Goodwin's account of the Agincourt campaign, and he cites no texts verbatim, whereas he does do so for later years of the reign. Allmand accused Goodwin of relying too heavily on sixteenth-century writers. In the Agincourt section this observation is not entirely justified, for there are many earlier works cited, although it is possible, for instance, that the references to Tito Livio are in fact not derived from the original *Vita* but from the *First English Life*, or even through Stow and Holinshed who themselves used the latter.[9] Goodwin appears to have consulted a wide range of narrative accounts, and most notably, referred to a number of French chronicles which had been printed by the Godefroys in the mid-seventeenth century, such as Jouvenal des Ursins, and de Cagny's chronicle of Arthur, count of Richemont (the story of Richemont's meeting with his mother, Queen Joan, being included, for instance).[10] Goodwin was also enough of a historian to include a short discussion on the different sizes of the armies put forward in various works.

Since his is a narrative history, it is not easy to characterise Goodwin's opinion on the battle, and his tendency to heap up material does not help. The king himself is spoken of highly. 'He acted not only the part of a general but of

---

[7] Sanderson (1660–1741) took over responsibility for the *Foedera* after Rymer's death (*DNB*, 50 (1897), pp. 65–8) and was also appointed master of the rolls and clerk (or keeper) of the records in the Rolls Chapel in 1726. The remainder of his 'History of Henry V' survives in the British Library, Additional MS 19979–84, along with a volume of his transcripts and notes in Additional MS 38525.

[8] *History of the Reign*, p. 76. See Text F 7.

[9] *First English Life*, p. xv. Hearne's printed edition of the *Vita* of Tito Livio did not appear until 1716. Goodwin's references are to folio numbers which may imply, therefore, that an original manuscript was consulted.

[10] Goodwin provides 'a catalogue of authors cited in this history' on pp. vii and viii of his *History of the Reign*.

a common soldier too, and excess of courage made him hazard a life on which alone depended the safety of his whole army.' Goodwin then uses the account in Le Fèvre of an attack on the king by eighteen French gentlemen, one of whom managed to come close enough to strike the crest of his helmet, although they were all cut down. But here again he uses Powell's *History of Wales* to give further personality to Davy Gam.

> Here it was that the valiant David Gam (whom we mentioned before) signal-
> ized himself in defending his prince, with loss of much blood and at last of his
> life, himself and two of his relations having received their mortal wounds in
> this encounter. The king was so sensible of their service that afterward, as they
> lay languishing in the field, he came to them and knighted them, this being the
> only acknowledgment he could make of their bravery, for they soon after died.

Oddly, however, Goodwin does not then give Gam amongst his list of the English dead a few pages later.[11] The lack of discernment in the use of sources and the following of the sometimes garbled sixteenth-century accounts also leads to oddities, so that the duke of Exeter and the duke of Clarence are both at the battle. The disposition of the army is particularly strange and reflects more about deployments at the beginning of the eighteenth century, with sixteenth-century overtones, than in the fifteenth. 'A strong body of horse being placed in the woods on the flanks and detailed to assault the enemy in the rear . . . a battalion of archers was placed in the van commanded by the duke of York . . . behind him was the main battle with King Henry at the head of it . . . the rear consisted of archers and such as were armed with spears, halberds and bills . . . led by the duke of Exeter.'[12] There was no thought here about whether the archers were intermingled with the men-at-arms in wedge-like formations, or whether they were on the wings.

History in the eighteenth century was taken seriously not least because of its didactic potential. The great deeds and statesmen-like acts of the past were seen as usefully instructive for gentlemen of the present. Take, for example the preface of Paul Rapin de Thoyras' *History of England*, published in French in 1723–5, and dedicated in its English translation (1726–31) to Frederick, prince of Wales.[13]

> For History, however useful to others, is infinitely more so to a Prince and par-
> ticularly the history of that crown he is born to wear. How instructive, as well
> as agreeable, must a fair and impartial narration of the lives and actions of a
> long series of predecessors be to him. And that such is the following history,

11 Ibid., pp. 88, 93.
12 Ibid., p. 84. See also the notion that they were drawn 'out of their intrenchments' to form the lines.
13 Rapin (1661–1725) was a French Huguenot who had fled to England and served in the army of William III, although his History was in fact written in the latter stages of his life at The Hague and Wesel (*DNB*, 47 (1896), pp. 297–300). The translation into English was by N. Tindal, vicar of Great Waltham in Essex.

originally penned by a foreigner, who had no party to serve or interest to promote, may be undoubtedly conducted from the universal approbation it every where meets with.

Rapin was the first historian to make extensive use of the printed volumes of Rymer's *Foedera*; this is revealed by the reference to 'Acta Publica' in his marginal notes. Indeed, Rapin had published French abridgments of each volume of the *Foedera* as it appeared. These were subsequently published in English by Stephen Whatley under the title *Acta Regia*. Rapin also consulted a wide range of chronicles, mostly the same as those consulted by Goodwin, and the latter work is also cited, with the Gam story being imported almost word for word. Not surprisingly the account of the campaign is close to Goodwin, but showing more of a tendency to judgment. This is well demonstrated in the following extract on the folly of the French commander's choice of battle site.

On 25th of October, the day appointed for the battle, the two armies were drawn up as soon as it was light. The constable d'Albret committed on this occasion an unpardonable fault in choosing for the field of battle a narrow ground, flanked on one side by a rivulet and on the other by a large wood. He thereby lost all the advantage which the superiority of number and especially in horse, could give him. It is most certain that this general ought to have posted himself in a large and green place, where he might have had it in his power to surround the English who were but a handful of men in comparison of his army. But by drawing up on so narrow a ground he was forced to make a front no larger than that of his enemies and thereby depriving himself of a very manifest advantage. Neither can it be said that the choice of field of battle was not entirely in his breast. As the English were marching to Calais, it was his business to expect them on a spacious plain, capable of containing his whole army, and where they might have all fought at once. His blindness therefore is astonishing, and can only be ascribed to his presumption. He seems to have intended to stop up that narrow passage that the English might not proceed without considering such a precaution can only be advantageous to the weakest. I have dwelt a little upon this error as it was, probably, the principal cause of the unfortunate success of the French in this action. The Constable, blinded by the number of his troops, drew them up, as I said, on this narrow ground, but so close that it was easy to foresee confusion would ensue during the battle.[14]

The generalship of Henry is contrasted with this lack of French leadership. Rapin claims that the English only had two battle lines because of the small number of their troops, the first commanded by York and the second by the king himself. The stakes are placed across the army as a whole, and are uprooted and planted again as the English army moved from its first position to its second. The archers, for whom there is no mention of being on the wings, or anywhere else for that matter, moved in front of the stakes to fire on the French cavalry

[14] *The History of England*, vol. 1 (London, 1732), p. 513.

and then 'nimbly retreated behind the stakes with a wonderful discipline in which the king had exercised them himself for some days'. Subsequently Rapin has the English first line engaging, and Henry then sending in his second line, as though his forces were grouped behind each other in eighteenth-century style, as implied in Goodwin, rather than being ranged across the field. Like Goodwin, Rapin also includes a discussion of the numbers of casualties which refers to the variance in different sources and historical interpretations. He notes that figures given by English writers for their own dead tend to be low, whereas 'Mezerai mounts the number to fifteen hundred and lowers the loss of the French to six thousand'.[15] He ends perceptively by observing 'it is very common, on these occasions, to see the like diversity in the historians of two opposite sides'.

Rapin's work remained the standard history of England, being reprinted several times in both its French and English versions, until the publication of David Hume's *History of England* between 1754 and 1762. Hume also displayed a critical eye.[16] He expressed scepticism of the excessively low numbers of English fatalities cited by many, and was also one of the few writers of the period to emphasise the significance of the French civil war as a key to understanding Henry's success.

> The success which the arms of England have, in different ages, obtained over those of France, have been much owing to the favourable situation of the former kingdom. The English, happily seated in an island, could make advantage of every misfortune which attended their neighbours, and were little exposed to the danger of reprisals. They never left their own country but when they were conducted by a king of extraordinary genius, or found their enemy divided by intestine factions, or were supported by a powerful alliance: as all these circumstances concurred at present to favour their enterprise, they had reason to expect from it proportionable success.[17]

Hume believed, like many modern historians, that Burgundy was a potential ally even if no formal alliance as yet existed. But it is the contrast in command which is later brought centre stage.

> The three great battles of Cressy, Poitiers and Agincourt bear a singular resemblance to each other in their most considerable circumstances. In all of them, there appears the same temerity in the English princes, who, without any object of moment, merely for the sake of plunder, had entered so far into the enemy's country as to leave themselves no retreat: and unless saved by the utmost imprudence in the French commanders, were, from their very situa-

---

15 Eudes de Mezeray wrote a three-volume history of France from the reign of King Pharamond to Henry IV which was translated into English in 1683.

16 Hume (1711–76) was a prolific and well-known Scottish philosopher and historian whose five-volume history ranged from the invasion of Julius Caesar to the Revolution of 1688. The edition used here is with a continuation to the reign of George IV by Hewson Clarke (vol. 1, London, 1823, pp. 438–40).

17 Hume, *History of England*, p. 438.

tion, exposed to inevitable destruction. But allowance being made for this temerity, which, according to the irregular plans of war followed in those ages, seems to have been, in some measure unavoidable, there appears in the day of action the same presence of mind, dexterity, courage firmness, and precaution, on the part of the English; the same precipitation, confusion, and vain confidence on the part of the French; and the events were such as might have been expected from such opposite conduct.[18]

But for Hume the battle was less significant than one might have thought. 'The immediate consequences too of these three great victories were similar; instead of pushing the French with vigour and taking advantage of their consternation, the English princes after their victory seem rather to have relaxed their efforts, and to have allowed the enemy leisure to recover from his losses.' As he notes, it was two years before Henry returned to France. 'The poverty of all the European princes, and the small resources of their kingdoms, were the causes of these continual interruptions in their hostilities; and though the maxims of war were in general destructive, their military operations were mere incursions, which, without any settled plan, they carried on against each other.' Hume was strikingly more perceptive than most, although his account of the battle proper was predictable and short, taking up less space than the general observation cited above. He was not, it seems, particularly interested in military matters.

The variations between accounts of the battle in the general histories of the eighteenth and nineteenth centuries are relatively few and far between for authors continued to draw on the same sources – and on each other. Many would fall foul of a modern university's rules on plagiarism. But it is perhaps in the minor variations and turns of phrase that we can see contemporary and personal perception most clearly. Thus in Carte's *A General History of England*, the killing of the prisoners was started without receiving orders from the king and in response to the attack on the camp, 'but they were stopped in taking this bloody, though necessary precaution by Henry's orders, who sending a herald to the rallied corps of the French with notice that if they ordered to advance he would put all the prisoners to the sword, that body retired immediately'.[19] Henry's own reputation was not to be diminished, and to this end most works gave considerable space to Henry's bravery in the face of the attack by the duke of Alençon and the eighteen French knights, in which Davy Gam might also feature. Some developed the theme of Henry's bravery by linking this incident with another, which also had its origins in several chronicle accounts but which could be embellished for the sake of the cult of the hero. Thus in F. P. Barnard's *A New Universal and Impartial History of England*,

Henry now darted into the thickest part of the battle, but his ardour and impetuosity again involved him in the most imminent danger. His brother, the duke of Gloucester, who had fought be his side, was struck to the ground and

---

[18] Ibid., p. 440.
[19] T. Carte, *A General History of England*, vol. 2 (London, 1750), p. 681.

the enemy pressed in crowds to avail themselves of the incident. Henry was again surrounded by a host of foes but being a stranger to fear, he covered the body of his brother with his shield and defended him with his sword. In this situation he received so violent a blow on his helmet with a battle-axe that he fell on his knees [this was not the same blow as that which was 'cleft the crown on Henry's helmet'; we have to wait for the next paragraph for Alençon to deal that one!] and would possibly have been seized by the enemy had not the duke of York advanced to his assistance at the head of a fresh body of troops. This intimidated the enemy; they fell back and Henry and his brother had time to recover from their alarming situation. Another reinforcement immediately followed that led by the duke of York, and Henry again attacked the French with such fury that they were unable to support the shock; they fell into disorder, and a dreadful slaughter ensued.[20]

York is then killed by Alençon but then Henry himself kills Alençon and the French flee. Barnard's account of the battle is mostly made up of a series of vignettes featuring the great and the good, as too is that given in Oliver Goldsmith's highly derivative *History of England*.[21] One might be forgiven for thinking from these accounts that the English army contained no rank and file. Although Barnard does allow Henry three divisions, the right and the rearguard are here considered as wings to his own centre division. He follows the notion that the rear was made up wholly of archers and 'such as were armed with spears, halberts and bills', under the command of the earl of Dorset (who was, of course, not present at the battle, but at least he is not anachronistically promoted to duke of Exeter in this account). Goldsmith displays no interest at all in the deployment of the king's army, but is one of the earliest to imply some conscience over the killing of the prisoners, the significance of which he is at pains to excuse. The killing is for him due to both the rallying of the French and the attack on the baggage.

Henry, now seeing the enemy on all sides of him, began to entertain apprehensions from his prisoners, the number of whom exceeded even that of his army. He thought it necessary, therefore, to issue general orders for putting them to death; but on the discovery of the certainty of his victory he stopped the slaughter, and was still able to save a great number. This severity tarnished the glory which his victory would otherwise have acquired: but all the heroism of that age is tinctured with barbarity.[22]

Sir James Mackintosh, who published his History of England in 1830, was more obviously critical.[23]

20 London, 1790, p. 224
21 *The History of England from Earliest Times to the Death of George the Second*, with continuation to the treaty of Amiens by Charles Coote, 4 vols (London 1812), vol. 2, pp. 21–6.
22 Goldsmith, *History of England*, p. 25. Save for the last sentence, the text is almost verbatim from Hume, *History of England*, p. 440.
23 *The History of England*, vol. 1 (London, 1830), p. 364.

A deplorable incident sullied the victory . . . a troop of peasants began to plunder the baggage: rumours of the advance of French reinforcements were spread, and Henry in an evil hour too hastily believed that the safety of his small army required the slaughter of his numerous prisoners . . . the greater part of the noble prisoners were slain, mutilated, disfigured, mortally or painfully wounded, before it was discovered that the whole was a false alarm, to which Henry had lent too credulous an ear. He stopped the massacre, but too late for the purity of his name.

By 1830, too, the national differences were again worth stressing.

Nothing was favourable to Henry but his own calmness, perhaps the coolness of his nation, and the inconsiderate impetuosity which has sometimes marred the brilliant valour of France. It is scarcely possible to doubt that the result of this famous battle must have been different if the two nations could have exchanged generals.[24]

As noted earlier, in many works, it is the bravery and courage of the king which is given pride of place. This was not surprising when a reign-based approach was used as the structure of the works. As the nineteenth century wore on, it also appealed to the increasingly large popular market for history. Thus the king's personal role features prominently in J.R. Green, *A Short History of the English People*, and is reinforced by a line drawing of the king's helmet, shield and saddle in Westminster Abbey.[25] It is a line which will be all too familiar to those brought up on the Ladybird and school history book tradition, and is one which has been fanned by the Shakespearean image of the king.

In 1901 C.L. Kingsford, who did much on a scholarly level to identify and explain the chronicle sources of the period, produced a 400–page biography of Henry in the 'Heroes of the Nations' series, which took as its motto, 'The hero's deeds and hard-won fame shall live'.[26] This, as he explains in the preface, was a development of his original article on Henry in the *Dictionary of National Biography*, but had involved a fresh look at the very abundant sources for the reign. Henry was 'the perfect pattern of the medieval hero', loved even by some of the French. But Kingsford was also a man of his time, one of many who saw the dawning of the twentieth century as offering a brave new world. The future did not lie with such as Henry. The modern order was not to spring from men like him 'who ruled a willing people as a trust from God, of a society based, *not on equality*, but on the mutual interchange of rights and obligations'. 'Europe, however unconscious, stood at the parting of the ways and must enter upon her inheritance of progress by a rough and novel road. Henry, for all his genius, was not fitted by temperament to be her leader.' Far too medieval!

Kingsford's book offers a fairly straightforward narrative of the battle, largely following the *Gesta* and Jean Le Fèvre. The strong discipline in Henry's

---

24 Ibid., p. 363.
25 Illustrated edition, vol. 1 (London, 1898), pp. 520–21.
26 *Henry V* (New York and London, 1901). His plan of the battle is printed on p. 139.

army is contrasted with the disarray of the French, which offers Kingsford one of many opportunities to emphasise the lack of supreme authority, and hence of unity, in the French army. The way the French were drawn up, in three dense masses one behind the other, also shows their division and poor counsel. He has the English line drawn up as four deep but with archers on the wings of *each* of the three battles. Thus he accepts the notion of six groups of archers, placed as inverted 'V's (or *herses*), suggesting that 'the wedges were formed with the apex in front, and the archers, being somewhat in advance of the men-at-arms, could use their weapon to the best effect' (see fig. 1). Kingsford does remark, however, that 'some authorities seem to imply that the whole of the archers were placed in two masses on the extreme right and left of the line'. Kingsford's plan of the battle was almost identical to that provided in Ramsey's *Lancaster and York* of 1892. Ramsey's two-volume study provided a well-referenced account of the fifteenth century which was much drawn upon by later writers. His plan has all the signs of nineteenth-century military organisation on it, especially with regard to the supposed positioning of the guns (fig. 3). Here the English are grouped into three battles. Each battle has wedges of archers on both flanks, portrayed by inverted v-shapes. Ramsey justified his interpretation thus:

> In view of his slender numbers [Henry V] drew up his force in one fighting line, without reserves. This line consisted of three little battalions of dis-mounted men-at-arms, each apparently with its complement of archers; slight breaks marking off the divisions. The archers seem to have been formed in wedges, with the points towards the enemy, the formation 'en herse' of Frois-sart, an excellent formation against cavalry. As the organisation of each div-ision seems to have been complete in itself, we must suppose that there were in all six wedges of archers, two to each battalion. But this cannot be asserted with confidence. It may be that there were only four bodies of archers; while Le Fèvre and Waurin seem to assert that they were massed in two bodies on the two flanks of the line. Yet Monstrelet again clearly understood that there were archers attached to each division; and to this view we must adhere.[27]

A good example of how history had developed towards 1900 is also provided by Charles Knight's *History of England*.[28] For Knight, Henry's men were 'formed in one line, the men-at-arms in the centre, with wings on the left and right, the archers being posted between the wings, with their stakes fixed before them', which seems to imply that there were only two groups of archers each positioned between the centre and one of the flanking battles. The killing of the prisoners is due to 'a momentary alarm' on the part of Henry, 'the hasty instinct of self-preservation dictated the order'. Henry's 'nature was not cruel' . . . he stopped the carnage when he found that the danger was imaginary', and, in case the point needed further reinforcing, 'the French chroniclers mention this horrible circumstance in terms of sorrow rather than of blame'. The account here is still

---

27 J.H. Ramsey, *Lancaster and York*, vol. 2 (1892), pp. 214–15. The plan is given after p. 212.
28 *History of England*, vol. 2 (London, 1862), pp. 57–64.

in the narrative form but in a less bombastic tone which more closely resembles the style we have become used to in our own century.

Battlefield and commemoration

Significantly, too, for the rise of empirical, investigative history, Knight had visited the battlefield.

> Between Agincourt and Tramecourt is a small enclosed piece of ground, which we saw planted with potatoes in the summer of 1856, where great numbers of the illustrious dead were buried. It is kept sacred to their memories; and here it is proposed, four hundred and fifty years after the eventful day, to erect a memorial chapel. There is nothing to tell of that time of bloodshed and terror. Now and then, indeed, the upturned soil gives forth evidence of the presence of the dead. In 1816 an English officer of the Army of Occupation found relics of the slain with many coins of Charles V and Charles VI. A peasant, now living in one of the farm cottages of Agincourt, shows a large thin gold coin of Charles VI, which he found in his field labours.

Writing in 1835, Charles Labitte tells us that before the French revolution, there was an expiatory chapel on the edge of the battle field, and that every twenty-five years a service was held on 25 October in memory of the French killed at Agincourt.[29] This 'chapelle de la Gacogne' had in fact been built in 1734 by the marquise de Tramecourt 'in accordance with a vow made for the return of her son from Italy'.[30] But this monument was destroyed in 1793 during the Revolution, and by 1835 its remains were being used as a stable by a farmer of Ruisseauville. Labitte confirms Knight's comments that, during the occupation which followed the fall of Bonaparte, the English undertook some excavations in the area where the French dead were buried, finding remains of armour and bones. He goes on to claim:

> Exalting in the memory of their recent victory [i.e. at Waterloo], the English had built a large grave casket in circular form where they deposited the bones found in their diggings. They wanted to take back to their homeland these sacred remains as a monument to their victory. But the authorities, who tended during that period to cave in when faced with the exigencies brought about by invasion, had on this occasion the strength to oppose with courage this arbi-

---

[29] 'Bataille d'Azincourt', *Revue Anglo-Française*, 3 (1835), pp. 13–47, at pp. 46–7.
[30] Wylie, 2, p. 225. La Gacogne is a hamlet within the commune of Azincourt. The chapel seems to have been built on the site of a major grave pit, which previously proved an object of some superstition for the local peasantry (R. Belleval, *Azincourt* (Paris, 1865), p. 121).

trary act and violation of tombs. . . .[31] The English were allowed to take back with them the remains of arms found in the ground, which they had gone over with a fine tooth comb. But the grave casket was buried in the cemetery of the church of Agincourt. No stone indicates where the French rest. Only the grave digger who buried them and who is still there could tell us the grass which covered them.

The excavations of the early nineteenth century were in fact undertaken by Sir John Woodford, a veteran of Waterloo, who was quartermaster-general in the Army of Observation in the Pas de Calais from 1815 to 1818.[32] Finds were taken back to England but are thought to have been destroyed by fire in 1874. A plan of 'the ground on which the battle of Agincourt was fought', which Woodford drew in 1818, does survive, however, in the British Library (fig. 2).[33] This is the earliest attempt at a graphic representation of the battle that I have discovered. It is interesting to speculate that it may have been consulted by later writers, although this can only be proved in the case of Wylie.[34] The plan marks roadways and landscape features presumably as they were in the early nineteenth century, although Woodford notes that enclosures to the west of Tramecourt are thought to extend further in his period than at the time of the battle. Woodford marked three lines of French. Nearest the English was an advance guard of 8,000 knights, 4,000 archers and 1,300 crossbowmen under the command of the constable, the dukes of Orléans and Bourbon, the counts of Eu and Richemont, and Marshal Bouccicaut. Behind this was the centre or main body of the French army under the dukes of Bar and Alençon, and at the rear a body under de Marlay, Dammartin and Fauquembergue. Woodford positioned the advance guard just south of the road between Agincourt and Tramecourt. The English he portrays in two main groups; at the rear, a thousand yards or so north of Maison-celles, is put the English army commanded by the king. In front of this Woodford placed the 'advanced line of archers under the command of the duke of York'. We must assume that he was here following the tradition found in Hall and others, based on the *Brut*, that York's van consisted exclusively of archers. For both parts of the English army Woodford indicates a forward movement towards the French advance guard by means of dotted lines. He also traces the routes of 200 English archers said to have been sent into a meadow near Tramecourt, and of '400 men-at-arms turning the French by Agincourt'.

Woodford also indicates the place of burial of 5,800 French knights north of the Agincourt-Tramecourt road. There were French efforts to set up a monument in the mid-nineteenth century, complete with wall mounted lists and armorial bearings of those who had died in the battle – 'véritable hécatombe de la

---

31 Other writers claim that it was the duke of Wellington himself who ordered an end to the digging after a remonstrance from the French government; Wylie, 2, p. 226.
32 There is a longer discussion of the excavations in Wylie, 2, pp. 225–9, and Belleval, *Azin-court*, pp. 121–2, with a note of a report in *Revue Anglo-française*, 1835, p. 148.
33 British Library, Additional MS 16368, map C.
34 Wylie, 2, p. 229.

noblesse française, et l'une des plus meutrières que l'histoire ait eu à enregis-trer'.[35] But it was the psychological impact of the Franco-Prussian war which led in 1870 to the erection, at the burial place indicated by Woodford, of a large calvary by the vicomte de Tramecourt and his wife in memory of the French soldiers who had fought so bravely in 1415.[36]

The issue of commemoration has certainly had some part to play in reflec-tions upon the battle. In his 'epistle dedicatory' to Queen Anne at the beginning of *Foedera*, volume nine, Rymer linked recent victories with Agincourt.[37]

May it please your most excellent majesty, with this volume you raise to life and set forth the acts and achievements of that most victorious prince, your royal progenitor, King Henry the Fifth. From whence the world may observe how well you trace, how justly you parallel, how far you surpass the most sur-prising actions of former ages. Armies and battles and victories and glory are become familiar, and an everyday entertainment, in the proceeding of your majesty's most auspicious reign, for some hundred years a long train of quar-rels, enterprizes and hostilities, yet no memorable battle ensued till the time of Edward the Third. His long (more than fifty years) reign was famous for Cressy and Poyctiers. And now in the time of King Henry the Fifth, for ever renown'd is the field of Agencourt; and to blazon on it the more, after the mode of the time, an herald is created by the name of Agencourt. Would your majesty, after so noble a president, go into that fashion and create a Blenheim herald, a Ramiles herald, an Audenard herald, a Blaregnies herald, where might you stop? But to go on to Paris and there erect a new college for your heralds in the Place of Victoire. Thus most redoubted sovereign, thus you set out, thus you begin your reign. These are the Dawn, the morning glympses, and first tokens of your rising sun. What must the world expect from your meridian splendour? Yet fortune has no share in your success: God Almighty is manifest in all you undertake, in all you do. And what may we not promise from the superior steddy conduct of your general, and the determin'd bravery of your troops, supported by your majesty's uplifted heart, your firm devotion and pious zeal for God's service? After various adventures, treaties of peace, and operations of war, this volume ends with a peace and a marriage. In the

---

35 Belleval, *Azincourt*, p. v.

36 H. Green, *Famous Engagements and their Battlefields Today* (London, 1969), pp. 29–3, who claims it is the place where Henry V's men inserted their stakes against the French cavalry. See M. Bennett, *Agincourt 1415*, Osprey Military Campaign Series (London, 1991), pp. 86–7 for illustrations and the added observation that it marks the site of extensive grave pits. Bennett suggests that this probably marks the centre of the French position. R. Hardy, *Longbow. A Social and Military History* (London, 1976, revised 1986) p. 119, notes 'a cross set up by the family who own and farm the battlefield today, as they did in 1415. They lost a father and two sons in the battle. A few hundred yards away is a memorial to another father and two sons of the family, killed by the Germans in the Second World War. In 1961 I visited the family to ask permission for cameras to film the battlefield. They were at first reluctant. I was told "It was a bad day, for you as well as for us, and many dreadful things were done by you to us here." I have a letter from them in which is written, "We defended our fields in 1415 and in 1915, in 1939 again, and often in between." '

37 As Kingsford notes, Rymer 'could find no nearer parallel for the victor of Blenheim and Ramilles than the victor of Agincourt' (*Henry V,* p. 389).

eighth year of King Henry the Fifth are brought to an agreement with him on his own terms. In this in the eighth year of his reign, the Great Peace, as they call'd it, and a royal marriage are concluded and solemnized. Whatsoever yet remains, which may add to the felicity and glory of your majesty, that God grant, is the prayer of your majesty's most devoted servant, T. Rymer.

Later in the century, however, Samuel Johnson was less effusive. When commenting on the famous line from *Henry V*, Act IV, scene 3 ('And Crispin Crispian shall ne'er go by/From this day to the ending of the world/But we in it shall be remembered'), he uttered a characteristically pithy remark:

It may be observed that we are apt to promise to ourselves a more lasting memory than the changing state of human things admits. The prediction is not verified: the feast of Crispin passes by without any mention of Agincourt. Late events obliterate the former: the civil wars have left in this nation scarcely any tradition of more ancient history.[38]

By sheer coincidence, the Charge of the Light Brigade at Balaclava (1854) also occurred on 25 October. As Kingsford observed in 1901, 'Now, almost into our own time, the charge at Balaclava has added fresh lustre to St Crispin's Day, and year by year the anniversary of the modern battle recalls to memory the hero of the ancient victory.'[39] Soon there was to be even more reason to call the battle to mind. In 1915, the five hundredth anniversary of the battle, Sir Herbert Maxwell wrote an article on the Agincourt campaign for the *Cornhill Magazine*.[40] This held extra piquancy by the fact of the war situation which then prevailed. Maxwell's account of the battle is unremarkable, but more significant is his observation at the end. 'It was a fruitless and costly enterprise, but one which contributed not a little to establish the prestige of British infantry, which is being so nobly sustained by King George's troops on the same old ground at the present time.' It was at this very time, of course, that stories were circulating about soldiers' visions of ghostly medieval archers.[41] Maxwell began his article with a contrast between the Kaiser and Henry V.

38 *The Yale Collection of the Works of Samuel Johnson, 8: Johnson on Shakespeare* (1968), p. 557. His *Preface on Shakespeare* and *Notes on Shakespeare's Plays* were published in 1765, twenty years after he began work on them. A similar condemnation of his own age is found in Johnson's early poem, 'London', written in 1738 as a sharp attack on the Walpole administration and other perceived vices of the time. 'Ah! what avails it, that, from slav'ry far/ I drew the breath of life in English air:/ Was early taught a Briton's right to prize/And lisp the tale of Henry's victories:/ If the gull'd conqueror receives the chain,/ And flattery subdues when arms are vain?' (lines 117–22).

39 Kingsford, *Henry V*, p. 389.

40 'The campaign of Agincourt', *Cornhill Magazine*, third series, vol. 39 (1915), pp. 524–41.

41 See above p. 8. As Brigadier-General Sir James Edmonds reminded the readers of the *Journal for the Society for Army Historical Research* in 1932, 'in the retreat from Mons in 1914, the 4th Division of the English Army crossed the Somme at Voyennes, at the same place as Henry V'. In his article, entitled, 'An early war diary – 1415', Edmonds described the *Gesta* as 'a first-class military record of the campaign, better kept than many diaries of 1914–18' (pp. 72–4).

Krieg ist Krieg is an axiom much in vogue in Potsdam circles at present. It is incontrovertible that war *is* war; but it has been reserved for the Kaiser and his generals to interpret the word as a synonym for rapine and sacrilege, slaughter of unarmed citizens and their children, violation of women, and senseless destruction of all that is beautiful but not portable. A year ago we were so simple as to believe that men had become more humane than their forefathers, and that means had been devised at the Hague and elsewhere to purge even war of the worst of its horrors. Certainly it is not to mediaeval chronicles that we should have turned for guidance in their merciful conduct of a campaign; yet the five-hundredth anniversary of the battle of Agincourt my remind us that Henry V of England, in setting forth upon the invasion of France (a campaign, be it admitted, of sheer aggression) issued the strictest orders against plunder of all sorts, burning of houses etc., sacrilege and violence to women under pain of death, and prescribed minor, but very severe, penalties upon soldiers who should wantonly injure orchards and vineyards.[42] All conception of war by those who have never been on active service and all experience by those who have so served, have been so utterly set at naught by the scale and fury of the conflict which has now raged for more than a year, that one might hesitate before reviving memories of less stupendous strife. It is somewhat remarkable, indeed, that among the myriad battle-fields of Europe, that of Agincourt should still be reckoned famous; for not only was the English army equivalent in numbers to no more that a couple of modern brigades, but the victory proved barren of all advantage to the conqueror and is memorable only as a soveran [sic] feat of arms.

In the school of decisive battles, Agincourt was indeed to have little place, but before we turn to how military historians dealt with it, we must retrace our steps to look at how work on both chronicle and administrative sources affected the historical study of the engagement.

The search for sources:
Sir Harris Nicolas, Sir Joseph Hunter and J.H. Wylie

Maxwell's account of the battle relied heavily on Ramsey's *Lancaster and York* (1892), and the plan he provided was identical to that provided by Ramsey. But he was able to add in references to the *First English Life*. Ramsey had not been able to use this text as it was only identified early in the twentieth century, and edited by Kingsford in 1911. Indeed, as the work of Ramsey and Kingsford shows, it was not the impulse of the desire to commemorate the battle or a study of the field itself which generated new insights. Such insights were only

---

[42] Maxwell conveniently overlooked here, of course, the killing of the prisoners; he does mention it towards the end of his account, with an attempt to see it as 'desperate remedy', albeit one 'which even self-preservation could hardly justify'.

achieved through fuller attention to the source materials. Already in the later Tudor period, the heralds had exploited a listing of men at the battle which certainly had its origins in the period itself. In the late seventeenth and early eighteenth centuries, Thomas Rymer and Robert Sanderson made transcripts and extracts from other royal records, some of which found their way into volume nine of the *Foedera* and thence, as we have seen, into secondary works. In the early 1700s too, Thomas Hearne produced editions of Tito Livio and the Pseudo Elmham. But it was the printing of the *Gesta*, or as it was then called, 'The Chaplain', by Harris Nicolas in his *Battle of Agincourt* (1827) and subsequently by Benjamin Williams in 1850, which contributed most to historians' accounts of the battle from the late nineteenth century to the present day. Williams produced a straightforward edition of the *Gesta* with some extracts from the *Chronicles of Normandy*. Nicolas had done much more by producing what is still the only extended study of the battle. But he was far from what we would now consider 'a historian' both in background and in approach. His career is so fascinating and his book so important that it is worth giving an outline of both.[43]

The end of the Napoleonic wars put Nicolas, like many other naval officers, on half pay; financial difficulties (a seemingly recurrent problem throughout his life) forced him to seek another career. He trained for the bar, being called at the Inner Temple in May 1825, and specialised in peerage claims lodged before the Lords, an activity which no doubt complemented his developing interests in the medieval and early modern periods. If the end of his navy career was one stimulus to his research, his marriage was another. His wife, whom he married in 1822, claimed descent from William Davison, secretary of state to Elizabeth I. This prompted Nicolas to research her illustrious ancestor. In 1824 he was elected as a Fellow of the Society of Antiquaries and joined its council in 1826, but after attending one meeting he never seems to have been present again. Whatever the precise circumstances there is every indication that he had fallen out with the Society. Alongside his impecuniousness was a propensity for arguing with members of the antiquarian establishment. He soon began to ask questions about the state of the Society of Antiquaries, demanding its reform. An unsurprisingly cool response from its officials led to his withdrawal from the Society in 1828. By 1830 he had switched his attention to the Record Commission (which the government had set up to investigate and publish records), inveighing against its constitution and cost. His views were communicated to Lord Melbourne in his 'Observations on the state of Historical Literature and on the Society of Antiquaries, with remarks on the Record Commission'. But his criticisms this time bore some fruit; a Select Committee was established to look into the Record Commission in 1836 and Nicolas was amongst those who gave

---

43 For his career see *DNB*, 41 (1895), pp. 41–4. There is also an extensive collection of his papers in the British Library which would repay detailed study. It is not surprising given his naval career that he should later be the author of an ambitious, if incomplete, history of the navy. His *History of the Royal Navy*, 2 vols (London, 1847) ends with the reign of Henry V.

evidence to it. Ten years later, he was engaged in another dispute with the director of the British Museum, Sir Anthony Panizzi. This stemmed from Nicolas' observations 'on the supply of printed books from the library to the reading room of the British Museum', a dispute which may ring many modern bells and which generated a good deal of pamphleteering and article writing in the *Spectator*. In October 1831 Nicolas was appointed knight of the Guelphs of Hanover, and later rose to chancellor and knight commander of the order of St Michael and St George (1832) and to the grand cross of the latter in 1840, honours which testify to his standing. It seems that his criticisms of the archival fraternity bore fruit for some reforms did ensue, and he was well regarded in retrospect, especially for his publication of records which brought materials to wider knowledge. But his parlous financial position was never successfully resolved, being exacerbated by his family of eight surviving children. In 1848 he was forced to leave London because of financial problems and took exile in a suburb of Boulogne where he died on 3 August of the same year.

The first edition (1827) of the *History of the Battle of Agincourt* was dedicated to King George IV 'under whose auspices the splendour even of that victory has been rivalled, if not eclipsed', as Nicolas put it rather obsequiously. As he explained, the stimulus for this book was his discovery in the British Museum (now Library) of an early seventeenth-century herald's copy of a list of the English army at Agincourt (Harleian 782). He initially intended to publish this with a few pages of background but subsequently resolved 'to collect all which had been said by contemporary writers of both countries on the subject; together with an account of the preparations for the expedition itself from the public records'. A central part of this project was a translation of the hitherto little known *Gesta*, against which he set translated extracts from other French and English chroniclers. He also drew on extracts from administrative records which had been prepared by Robert Sanderson for Rymer's *Foedera*, and which were by then in the British Museum, although unfortunately Nicolas gave an incorrect reference for these (Sloane 6400 instead of the correct 4600). To this he added much miscellaneous material from the *Foedera* proper, and from Cottonian manuscripts in the British Museum, a miscellaneous collection of copies and originals which enabled him to provide further details on the campaign and on the English army.[44] The *History of the Battle of Agincourt* takes the form of Nicolas' own narrative of the campaign, a translation of the *Gesta* from the point of embarkation to the morrow of the battle (which is glossed by comparisons with other chronicles), and numerous documentary extracts and listings, including the Agincourt roll. For a second edition in 1832, Nicolas reordered the book and added further materials to it.[45] The third edition of 1833 is essentially a reprint of that of the previous year.

What Nicolas did with some of this material was sometimes misconceived

---

[44] These had been collected or copied by Sir Robert Cotton (d. 1631) whose library formed one of the base collections of the British Museum.

[45] As he tells us in its preface, 'every statement has been collated with the authority upon

and led to some new myths and confusions, but there can be no doubt that he brought a vast amount of material into the public domain for the first time, including literary materials and administrative materials. Particularly significant was the fact that he based his account almost entirely on fifteenth-century chronicles rather than on sixteenth-century histories. This was a tremendous achievement, even if, to the modern eye, it is sometimes lacking in critical bite (especially on the chronicle sources which Nicolas tends to treat with some awe) and in a true understanding of the workings of medieval military administration. His account of the deployment of troops is not in itself odd.

> The main body of the English army consisting of men-at-arms was commanded by Henry in person : the vanguard, which at the particular request of the duke of York was committed to his charge, was posted as a wing to the right; and the rear-guard commanded by Lord Camois, as a wing on the left. The archers were placed between the wings, in the form of a wedge, with their poles fixed before them to defend them from an attack of cavalry; and the flanks were protected by hedges and coppices.

What is strange, however, is the diagrammatic representation which he gave of this where he had Henry's main battle at the rear across the width of the field (fig. 4). The van and rear guard are placed in front of it, with the archers positioned in one giant triangular shaped wedge between them.[46] There is no further discussion of this formation in the text of the book, but it is important to realise that Nicolas' plan of the field was probably the first to appear in print in Britain, as Woodford's plan of 1818 remained unpublished. Unfortunately, too, either Nicolas, or his printer, placed the village of Agincourt to the right rather than the left of the armies.

A shortcoming which is obvious to a modern eye is Nicolas' lack of use of original manuscripts from the public records proper.[47] With only one or two exceptions, every reference is to stray originals, copies and extracts in the British Museum collections. Nicolas lacked an overall context in which to place these. He also believed that he had established who was present at the battle. He based this assumption on his transcript of the list in British Library, Harleian 782, taken from a larger collection of materials assembled by Ralph Broke, York Herald in *c.* 1604. Nicolas collated this list of 'dukes, erles, barons, knights, esquires, serviteurs and others that wer withe the excellent prince King Henry

which it stands, and the extracts from contemporary writers are more copious than in the first edition . . . and as [the author] has left no available source of information unconsulted, or neglected any means by which the work could be rendered what it ought to be, he trusts that this account of the battle of Agincourt may be deemed worthy of the great event which it is intended to commemorate.'

46 The extract is cited from pp. 113–14 of the third edition, and the battle plan faces p. 113. This plan had been drawn for the second edition: the first edition contains only a map of the region.

47 Amusingly for the modern reader, perhaps, a review of the first edition of Nicolas in the *London Magazine* includes the remark, 'we do not recommend so arduous a task as a consultation of the original authorities' (cited in Wylie, 2, p. 77).

the Fifte at the battell of Agincourt' with a late sixteenth-century list in the College of Arms, believing the latter to have been transcribed from an original manuscript.[48] Both lists gave numbers of archers but not their names. Thus arose the myth that we did not know the names of the archers at Agincourt.[49]

Nicolas did not use original documents which were still kept in the ancient Exchequer repositories at the Tower of London and Westminster Abbey. This was partly because of the chaotic state in which the public records lay. As Nicolas himself lamented, such Exchequer records were 'now lying in bags in Westminster Hall, in their present condition perfectly useless, and as little heeded as if, instead of illustrating the history of this country, they were the papers of an insolvent tradesman'.[50] Indeed this gave him the opportunity to lambast the authorities once more and one cannot help feeling that one of the reasons for his lack of access to the public records may have been his truculent attitude towards the antiquarian and government establishment.

It fell to his contemporary, Sir Joseph Hunter (1783–1861), to begin the systematic search of the public records and to indicate their potential for the study of the battle.[51] As an establishment figure, his career provides an interesting contrast with that of Nicolas. Hunter was born the son of a cutler in Sheffield, but even as a child he developed an interest in antiquarian matters. After training for the Presbyterian ministry he moved to take charge of a congregation in Bath, but his first publication concerned the history of Hallamshire, his place of origin. Between 1800 and 1837 there were six Royal Commissions into the public records. The first (1800) recommended the publication of calendars as well as of whole texts in the case of significant manuscripts, and led to the setting up of the Record Commission. In 1833 Hunter was appointed one of the latter's sub-commissioners and moved to London. Here he edited several volumes of records, including the earliest known Pipe Roll of 1130–31. By the 1830s there was much criticism of the operation of the Record Commission, not least by Nicolas. Its operation was thus terminated in 1837 as a result of the last Royal Commission into the public records, which recommended instead the setting up of a proper Public Record Office. Hunter was immediately appointed an assistant keeper and given the task of compiling a calendar of the records of the Queens Remembrancer, part of the vast Exchequer collection, within which lay the materials concerning the Agincourt campaign. In 1850 he published *Agincourt. A Contribution towards an Authentic List of the Commanders of the*

---

48 College of Arms, MS M1, fols 17–34.
49 Wylie discovered a third, and probably earlier, list in the Bodleian Library compiled by Robert Glover, who was Somerset Herald from 1571 to 1588. J.H. Wylie, 'Notes on the Agincourt Roll', *Transactions of the Royal Historical Society*, third series, 5 (1911), pp. 105–40. For further discussion of these lists and of the *Foedera* transcripts see below pp. 407–8, 410.
50 Third edition, p. 166, note b.
51 On Hunter, see D. Evans, 'Joseph Hunter, Assistant Keeper of the Records, 1838–61', *Transactions of the Hunter Archaeological Society*, 7, part 5 (1963), pp. 263–71, and D. Crook, 'The Reverend Joseph Hunter and the Public Records', *Transactions of the Hunter Archaeological Society* (1983), pp. 1–15.

English Host in King Henry the Fifth's Expedition to France in the Third Year of his Reign.[52] In preparation of this small book, he examined many of the records which were at that stage still kept in rather random fashion in the ancient Exchequer repositories at Westminster Abbey and the Tower. (The search rooms in the Public Record Office did not open until 1866.) Some of the notebooks from his study of the Queens Remembrancer materials are still extant in the British Library.[53] Here he made abstracts of some of the accounts which captains presented to the Exchequer after the campaign. These are useful but are no substitute for reading the originals which are now helpfully catalogued in the Public Record Office, and which will be discussed in the next chapter. In fact, one does need to exercise some care in using Hunter's notebooks. Based on one of them, Allmand tells us that Sir Thomas Erpingham stayed at Harfleur after the siege, and thus by implication was not at the battle.[54] This may come as something of a shock to those who have read the accounts of Waurin, Monstrelet and Le Fèvre where Erpingham has a role in deploying the army and setting the battle in train, or of the many secondary works which put him as commander of the archers. In fact, the page in Hunter's notebook has been bound in the wrong way round, so that the reference is not in fact to Sir Thomas Erpingham. From the original materials in the Public Record Office relating to Erpingham's post-campaign account roll, on which Hunter drew and which he transcribed accurately, we can be certain that Erpingham was indeed at the battle, even if they cannot confirm the chroniclers' account of his specific military command.

Hunter's publication of 1850 shows that he was to some degree responding to a major obsession which exercised Nicolas and other antiquarian minds, namely who served on the campaign. He thus produced a catalogue of names organised under seven heads: princes of the blood royal; earls; barons; bannerets and knights; esquires and other persons who indented singly; persons indenting jointly; and persons not military, attached to the army. He also gave information about each person and his retinue based upon what he had found in the Exchequer material. A couple of examples will suffice:[55]

(Knights.) Sir Simon Felbrigge. He indented to serve with 11 men-at-arms and 36 archers. Robert Todenham and Bartholemew Appleyard, two of the men-at-arms died at Harfleur. Six returned home from Harfleur sick. The rest, and the 36 archers were at Agincourt.

(Esquires and others who indented singly.) Thomas Wilcotes. He indented to serve with one man-at-arms and 6 archers. The name of his man-at-arms was

52 John Russell Smith: London, 1850. The manuscript draft put before the Society of Antiquaries is to be found in British Library, Additional MS 24619, fol. 78 onwards.
53 British Library, Additional MS 24509–16, purchased in 1862. Those containing materials on Agincourt are 24512–13 and 24519. The fact that some of Hunter's volumes of papers bear the label 'Chaos' may bring a smile to the modern researcher. The British Library also holds volumes of his in-letters.
54 Allmand, *Henry V,* p. 212, n. 37, citing British Library, Additional MS 24513, fol. 23.
55 Pp. 35, 48.

William Wykham. On 28th September he and two of his archers had license to return from Harfleur, on account of sickness. The rest were at the battle. He appears to have died of the sickness, the Account being rendered by his mother, Elizabeth Wilcotes, who was his executrix, and John Wilcotes, junior, his brother and heir.

Hunter's 'authentic list' was accompanied by a short discussion of the organisation of the armies and the nature of the documentary evidence. He printed some useful specimen texts showing a full understanding of how the archives had come about, much fuller than that displayed by Nicolas who had not used the original materials. Hunter carried out pioneering work in the archive materials but he was well aware of the limitations of his 'small tract' and that it did not exploit the material to the full. At this stage, the Exchequer materials were difficult to use as they were largely uncatalogued. There are thus no document reference numbers in Hunter's published work, though some are supplied in his notebooks. He was also responsible for organisation of the Exchequer Accounts Various in which the Agincourt musters and other documents were placed.[56]

His book on Agincourt was not, it seems, widely known, but it stimulated at least one other commentator early on. In 1863, William Durrant Cooper produced a study of 'Sussex Men at Agincourt' based on surviving materials in the public records and giving complete transcripts of the names in some retinue rolls. There was a strong genealogical bent here. 'Many a familiar name, to be found alike in the following lists and in the recent muster roll of the Artillery and Rifles on Brighton Downs, will prove, however, that, after the lapse of four centuries and a half, the bearers of those names in our day are as ready to defend their own hearths and homes as were their predecessors to uphold the military renown of their sovereign before the walls of Harfleur and on the banks of the Ternoise.'[57] This statement makes more sense when we remember English fears of French invasion in the time of Napoleon III, and the elaborate and expensive fortifications along the south coasts which they prompted.

By the early twentieth century, the public records enjoyed a greater degree of organisation and accessibility. This is apparent from the work of James Hamilton Wylie (1844–1914), as manifested in his article on the Agincourt roll published in 1911.[58] In this, Wylie applauded Hunter's work as being 'of the first importance', and was fairly certain that he had been able to identify in the Public Record Office every document which Hunter had used in his book of

---

[56] For the catalogue of such records, see *PRO Lists and Indexes XXXV. List of Various Accounts Formerly Preserved in the Exchequer* (London, 1912). As its preface notes, the subject-based classification, which placed the Agincourt material within the category 'Army and Navy', was the idea of Hunter.

[57] *Sussex Archaeological Collections*, 15 (1863), pp. 123–37. Military continuity can also be noted for the neighbouring county of Kent where a favourite mustering site of the Hundred Years War period, Barham Downs, was much used by the militia in later centuries.

[58] 'Notes on the Agincourt Roll', *Transactions of the Royal Historical Society*, third series, 5 (1911), pp. 105–40. The paper was read to the Society on 27 April 1911.

1850. Wylie's article is of the utmost importance. Not only did it assess the heralds' Agincourt rolls and the list of retinues Nicolas had taken from materials associated with Rymer's *Foedera*, it also began to set in context the various documents from the Exchequer accounts.

Wylie's understanding of the procedures of the Exchequer and hence of documentary survivals was impressive, as is revealed by his *Reign of Henry V.* This was intended as an extremely thorough account of the reign, although such unmitigated comprehensiveness places the work still in an antiquarian tradition. Whilst many primary materials were used by Wylie, so too were many secondary. He tended to treat all the information he had collected as of equal veracity, and he was the master of the gratuitous and tangential footnote. As a result, there is no hierarchy of facts and often no critical discussion of events. Wylie was not an academic by profession but spent most of his life as HM Inspector of Schools, although the respect with which he was held in the scholarly world is testified by his being Ford Lecturer at Oxford in 1900.[59]

As noted in the introduction to this present book, Wylie died before completing his study of the reign of Henry V. The first two volumes, together numbering more than 1,000 pages, take the story to 1416. These were his own work, whilst the third volume, covering the remainder of the reign in less than 500 pages, was written by W.T. Waugh, although drawing wherever possible on Wylie's notes. There is much in the first volume on the preparations for the campaign. Henry prepares to set sail at the very end of it, and lands in France at the beginning of the second volume. The siege of Harfleur, battle and its aftermath occupy over half of the latter's 480 pages. The style is on the whole narrative, but Wylie shows a good grasp of the administrative records. On the latter, his footnotes are a mine of information although the organisation of the work can make it difficult to pull the various references together. In chapter 35 of volume 2, he shows his awareness of the hazards involved in using chronicle sources for a study of the battle.

> It remains therefore to look as narrowly as we can into such scattered evidence as has come down to us from eye-witnesses or at least contemporaries. The usual plan has been to call out everything that is picturesque in the accounts of the various writers who narrated the events anytime within the succeeding century and blend them together into a patchwork whole, provided that they do not carry contradiction on the face of them. My own effort has been to depend for essentials only on the statements of those who saw the battle with their own eyes or had good means of information at the time.[60]

Wylie's analysis of the reliability of the chronicles is broadly the same as my own. He subsequently tries to establish the 'just estimate of the causes of the

---

[59] *Who was Who, 1897–1916* (London, 1920), p. 784. He was also the author of a four-volume study of *The Reign of Henry IV.* This is also a very detailed study but the accumulation of material is less intensive and more processed than in the *Reign of Henry V.*
[60] Wylie, 2, p. 193.

gigantic failure of the French . . . out of the mass of contradictory evidence contained in these various writers'. Here, however, he succumbs to mixing early and later interpretations so that the resulting analysis is confusing. He observes that in the nineteenth century, criticisms of the French began to be supplanted in their own histories and even in some English works, by a stress on French 'bravery, devotion and folly'. He notes that Jules Michelet praised Nicolas' study for its impartiality, and even claimed Nicolas as French because his great-grandfather was a Huguenot.[61] Wylie also observes perceptively that 'it did not take long before swarms of circumstantial myths began to gather round the story, and so deeply have they struck their roots that we may despair of ever again being able to read it in its original simplicity'.[62] Here again, however, he mixes texts of the period with those of later centuries, although his conclusions may strike a familiar chord.

> In short there is not a single detail of the battle that does not get transformed or turned completely upside down somehow or somewhere except the fact that the French lost and the English won . . . In presence of all these intricate contradictions it becomes a matter of some importance to enter a word of caution likewise against a peculiarly subtle and fascinating form of self-deception that will beset the student as he looks into the evidence for the details of the battle. For in the general dearth of anything approaching first-hand knowledge the Victorian publisher discovered that the reader could best be allured to accept a theory if it was illustrated by a plan or a map. Hence arose a great outburst of graphic representation in which a succession of modern savants have tried their hands at illustrating what they consider to have been the tactics of the field, even recording the changes at different hours of the day. But as these sketches, where not directly copied, differ wholly from one another in setting out their pretty squares, oblongs and triangles, with neat batteries of guns packed on either flank, they can but serve as a pictorial warning, and when we examine a few of them side by side that only help to emphasise the fact that we have not yet arrived a certainty in regard to the first essential details of that eventful day and on the existing data I fear we never shall.[63]

There is some hypocrisy in Wylie's view here, however, for whilst not stooping to the drawing of a plan himself, he did come to a conclusion on the positioning of Henry's troops based on an agglomeration of material from different chronicles. Henry 'put himself at the head of the main battle which was formed up in one unbroken line, four deep, in front of the wood at Maisoncelles . . . the king himself took command of the central portion of the main body, throwing out two wings to right and left in echelon . . . spanning his whole front and circling it from flank to flank like a crown were placed the archers, clumped in triangular

---

[61] Ibid., p. 204. Jules Michelet's *Histoire de France* (first edn, 1833–65) was a highly patriotic and influential work in France. He describes Agincourt (1855 edn, vol. 2, pp. 659–78) as a 'terrible event', 'an immense sadness', 'where France herself was taken prisoner'.
[62] Wylie, 2, p. 205.
[63] Ibid., pp. 213, 215–16.

wedges, each block being ranged in masses of about 200 men each in the usual open order like a hearse or harrow, with the apex tending inwards, thus presenting broad volleying faces in every direction.' Wylie then has the English moving forward, although he is vague about how far they moved and how in terms of time and space this related to the intended French cavalry assault on the wings 'who were to charge down upon the archers, trample them and drive them in and then roll up the main body by mere weight of numbers'.[64]

Wylie's book is not easy to use because of the heaping up of detail. In addition he cites contemporary and later sources without discriminating clearly between them. But in his defence, he was all too aware of the 'mass of contradictory evidence' and of the different perspectives of English and French chroniclers. He also includes a useful discussion of the 'circumstantial myths' which developed from the sixteenth century onwards.[65] Until there is a full study based upon modern historical standards, Wylie's account of the battle will continue to stand as the most comprehensive. It also gives us a fascinating insight into the styles of research and the formation of historical judgments in late nineteenth- and early twentieth-century Britain.

Military histories, military men

Wylie's vitriolic outburst about the folly of attempting diagrammatic representations is immediately followed by his restrained apoplexy on the interpretation of the battle put forward by Delbrück. The latter was one of several authors of the late nineteenth and early twentieth centuries to write a history of warfare covering an extended period. Indeed, this style of approach, with its handmaiden, the 'decisive battles' school, gave rise to works which have remained highly influential well into our present century.[66] There are two distinctive elements in Delbrück's interpretation. The first is that he sees Agincourt as demonstrating the application of the defensive tactics of Crécy to an offensive situation. The English army at Agincourt was similarly comprised of men-at-arms and archers, but with a much greater preponderance of the latter compared with 1346. The higher ratio of archers explains why Henry deliberately chose to move his men towards the French so that they might come within shooting range

---

64 Ibid., pp. 147–57.
65 Ibid., pp. 205–15.
66 H. Delbrück, *Geschichte der Kriegskunst im Rahmen der politischen Geschichte*, 3 vols (Berlin, 1907). For his section on Agincourt, see the English translation by W.J. Renfroe, *History of the Art of War within the Framework of Political History* (Lincoln, Nebraska, 1990), 3, pp. 463–70. J. Keegan, *The Face of Battle. A Study of Agincourt, Waterloo and the Somme* (London, 1976), p. 53, sees Delbrück as 'the pioneer of the modern "scientific" and "universal" approach' to military history.

of their enemy. Once there, they replanted the stakes in front of the archers on the flanks. The French foolishly 'allowed the English enough time to shift this part of their defensive tactics into the defensive'. Then Henry had his centre advance 'so that their hail of arrows against the French foot troops would force the knights to attack, leading them then into the volley of arrows from the with-held and palisaded English flanks'. The subsequent French error, Delbrück suggests, was two-fold. First, they adopted far too defensive a position them-selves and made no effort to move against the English. 'It would probably have been even more appropriate to attack the English somewhere during the preceding days of marching, since the French army, by its composition, was simply unsuited for the defensive.' Delbrück suggests that Henry had foreseen this possibility, which was why he had ordered his archers to prepare stakes during the march on the assumption that, with a gross imbalance of archers to men-at-arms, they would need to form a strongly defensive position whenever attacked. The second French error was to divide up their army. 'The French mounted units that were supposed to attack the archers were only a part of the French army, and in their advance they encountered the total strength of the English, whereas the main part of their army waited inactively in the defensive position . . . the defensive is a very poor form of combat for an army with close-combat weapons. The proper action for them would have been to move over into the attack with both their mounted troops and their foot soldiers at the moment when the English marksmen were close enough.'

The second distinctive feature of Delbrück's interpretation, and that which perturbed Wylie most, was the argument that the English outnumbered the French. He suggests that the reason why the French did not attack Henry after the latter's crossing of the Somme was that they were still awaiting reinforce-ments. Although the French moved faster and were thus able to get ahead of Henry and block his passage, this was 'at the price of preventing their reinforce-ments from catching up under such march conditions'. Although the duke of Brabant himself managed to appear at the battle it was without his troops. Thus, based on figures initially advanced by Niethe, Delbrück puts the English at the battle at 9,000 men and the French at between 4,000 and 6,000.

This argument on numbers was maintained by Ferdinand Lot in his general history of medieval warfare.[67] He expands on the view that chroniclers' numbers cannot be trusted: 'the number for them was a matter intended to produce an effect of astonishment and marvel on the part of the reader: it falls within the art of literature.'[68] In his account of the battle,[69] he considers that the situation of the French was 'not as advantageous as one might have thought. Their number, despite what has been said, probably did not exceed the number of the English if even it came as high, as we shall see'. He later suggests, however, that the

[67] *L'art militaire et les armées au moyen age en Europe et dans la Proche Orient*, 2 vols (Paris, 1946).
[68] Ibid., vol. 1, p. 15.
[69] Ibid., vol. 2, pp. 5–15.

French army cannot have been as large as the 6,000 he assigns to the English. This he argues on the basis of the width of the battle field, which he places at 700 metres. He claims that if the French had outnumbered the English by four to one, the weight and strength of their army would have been great enough to push back the English; they would not simply have piled up in front of the English as the chroniclers tell us happened. Moreover, when the French were mounted and in three lines one behind the other, there would only have been room across the field for 1,800 knights. Thus according to Lot, 'If one accepts the hypothesis that there was twice the number of archers and crossbowmen, one arrives at the conclusion that the French army was not superior but probably inferior in number to the English army.'[70]

Lot also blames the French for being slow in assembling an army, noting that Charles VI only took the oriflamme from St Denis on 10 September. By not mounting an immediate attack to relieve Harfleur, the French king had effectively to resummon his army at Rouen in order to pursue the English. Lot also blames divisions within the French even on the day.

> The constable d'Albret only enjoyed a minimal prestige in the eyes of the princes of the blood. He and the marshal Bouccicaut, mindful of what had happened in the past, were in favour of a defensive plan. They had dissuaded the king and the dauphin from going to the aid of Harfleur. At the moment that the battle was about to begin, they wished to temporise, believing that exhaustion, hunger, and sickness would yield up the English army without the need to fight. The young men, on the other hand, were in favour of a full and immediate charge, and they disputed bitterly amongst themselves the honour of being in the van. Finally they decided to stay on the defensive. The weather played its part. It rained all night and on the morning of 25 October, it was clear that a full scale cavalry charge by the French was impractical on the sodden ground. And furthermore, the narrowness of the battle field, 700 metres at most, made deployment of one single line impossible. They had to range their army in four lines: behind a van which was mounted [on the next page he has the first line of French as dismounted and weighed down by their armour], two lines of dismounted cavalry, in imitation of the English, and a third of mounted cavalry. As for the archers, they had them moved straightaway back to very rear for fear that they might share in the honour of the day for the French knights had no doubt but that they would be victorious. They were in such little doubt that they refused, in the early hours of the day, Henry's request that he should be allowed to pass on to Calais.

Lot has the first line of French going in on foot and driving back the English, but suggests that the situation was re-established by the English archers attacking the French in the flank. Though he does not mention a French cavalry attack here, he then has the first line retreating on foot or on horse, and thus harassing the second line as it advanced. Only 600 men could be gathered to form a third line. The blame must therefore lie with the French. 'Whatever is claimed, the

---

[70] He also plays down the numbers of French at the battle of Crécy, vol. 1, pp. 347–8.

French knights had displayed the same bravery as in the past but also had proved the same level of tactical incapacity.' But praise is also given to Henry for his confidence in daring to advance against the enemy, and for his planning, as in the use of the archers, although earlier Lot shows his patriotism by describing Henry as 'a bigot, consumed by ambition and an all consuming deceitfulness'.

Even if it is accepted that most chronicle estimates of French numbers are too high, it would seem difficult to accept that the French did not have the numerical advantage. Lot does appreciate, however, the difficulty of knowing the English deployment for certain. Although Waurin has the archers on the wings, other writers have them divided between the three battles. The latter version had already been accepted by Sir Charles Oman, who also wrote a general history of medieval warfare in the late nineteenth century.[71] For him, the English army was arrayed as at Crécy, with archers on each wing of each battle: 'they were in each case thrown slightly forward so that where the archery of the centre met those of the vaward and rereward two projecting angles were formed' (see fig. 5). He also has three French lines, as well as small cavalry groups to launch an initial attack. The latter were driven back but he does not have them *clashing* into the advancing van on foot, suggesting rather that the latter were weakened by 'having to open the ranks to allow the flight of the beaten cavalry'. When Oman wrote of the battle thirty years or so later in the *Cambridge Medieval History*, he expressed himself more convinced that Henry wanted a fight in 1415. 'Agincourt saw a new modification of tactics: finding the enemy's main body slow in coming on – the recent heavy rain had made the fields into a slough, and the French could only shuffle forward at a snail pace in their heavy armour – Henry took the offensive. He advanced against the enemy, halted long enough to let his archers riddle the front line with arrows and then ordered a general charge, in which the lightly equipped bowmen joined in with their hand-weapons.' Thus in this later account, Oman omits any mention of French cavalry charges as the first stage of the battle.[72]

Lot inveighed against the use of battles as the main illustrations of military development. This line has become a mantra of all modern works, so much so that recent general studies of medieval warfare, such as Contamine's *War in the Middle Ages*, have solved the issue by saying relatively little about Agincourt.[73] J.C. Fuller did not include it in his *Decisive Battles of the World*. This is perhaps not surprising for it was also omitted from the mid-nineteenth-century best seller, E. Creasey's *Fifteen Decisive Battles of the World*, on which Fuller was

[71] C. Oman, *A History of the Art of War in the Middle Ages*, 2 vols (London, 1898). Agincourt is dealt with in vol. 2, pp. 380–86, with the figure on p. 378.
[72] 'The art of war in the fifteenth century', *The Cambridge Medieval History*, vol. 8 (Cambridge 1936), pp. 651–2. Interestingly *The New Cambridge Medieval History*, vol. 7 (1998) does not mention Agincourt in its chapter 8 on late medieval warfare, whilst stressing elsewhere in the volume (p. 462) that Henry's victory was partly due to French political divisions, and that it much boosted his position at home.
[73] See, for instance, P. Contamine, *La guerre au moyen age* (Paris, 1980), translated into English by M.C.E. Jones as *War in the Middle Ages* (Oxford, 1984).

exceptionally dependent.[74] Agincourt's place in general histories of warfare is thus not substantial, perhaps because it was seen as a similar victory to those of the fourteenth century: indeed, I have been struck by the relative paucity of modern writings on the battle. Perhaps it was felt that the works of Nicolas and Wylie said all that was necessary. There is one group of writings, however, which deserves some further comment – the observations of serving soldiers and veterans upon military actions of the past.

We have seen already how the First World War stimulated interest in Agincourt. Even before this, however, soldiers were fascinated by it and other actions of the past, from which they hoped to draw lessons for the present and for the future. A good example of this is an article on the battle published by Major-General Sir Frederick Maurice in 1908.[75] Here we have the eye of the seasoned commander (assisted by Colonel Hime of the Royal Artillery who provided 'the sketch and description of the defensive preparation made to protect the front of the archers at the battle'), claiming that Henry V would not be best pleased to find his march from Harfleur criticised as rash or dangerous (as Wylie had done). As Maurice wrote, 'Now it seems to me that the essence of Henry's skill as a commander consisted in that apparently rash march which tempted the armed chivalry of France to attack him at a time when he was firmly convinced that, if he could induce them to do so, he had in the coming battle, surprises in store for them which would ensure him the victory.' These surprises included Henry's guns – pretty surprising for modern historians too as there is no documentary reference to justify that the English had any ordnance at the battle. Maurice remarked, 'It is probable that he [Henry] counted very largely on the heavy and cumbrous artillery that he dragged with him to the field; but as the guns required ten minutes or a quarter of an hour to load, they could not have effected much, as the battle lasted only three hours.' He went on to claim that the appearance of artillery at the battle was important as an indication of the change which was coming over the nature of warfare' [as he later notes, 'from the very first the new arm, the artillery, became in both countries part of the royal forces'], but for the time being the main surprise was the use of the archers, behind defences and in herse formation, with Henry V being, according to Maurice, the *first* to realise the advantage of the long bow.

Worse is to come. 'The effect in England of the fact that the Norman king [here he means Henry V] and his chief barons had become by the battle popular heroes was of great social influence in this country in blending together the two races: and that the victory should have been won by the Saxon yeomen under the leadership and by the skill of the king, tended very greatly to make a nation out of elements that had only hitherto consisted of a dominant and a subject race.'

---

74 E.S. Creasy, *The Fifteen Decisive Battles of the World from Marathon to Waterloo* (London, 1853); J.C. Fuller, *Decisive Battles of the Western World* (London, 1955). Creasey and Fuller do include Crécy amongst their decisive battles, although arguably it was no more decisive than Agincourt.
75 'The battle of Agincourt', *Cornhill Magazine*, third series, 25 (1908), pp. 789–93.

This is as near as we get to a Whig interpretation of the battle and its effects. It is also applied by rather dubious means to France by reference to the end of the great feudatories such as Burgundy under Louis XI. Agincourt is thus ascribed an overwhelming importance in historical change.

> It is in the promise for the future that the battle of Agincourt throws a light upon this dark time – order coming out of disorder, national strength out of internecine squabbles that were making it impotent against any force from without. Properly speaking the battle, closed up the conditions of the Middle Ages, and opened the beginning of the new era. Thus the battle has a far greater historical importance than has usually been attributed to it. I venture to hope that our modern historians may look into the matter for themselves, and accept my suggestion as to the mode in which the presentation of the case to the generation that succeeds ours needs to be amended.

Another form of this quasi-empathetic stance is illustrated by *Famous Engagements and their Battlefields Today*, published by Lieutenant-Colonel Howard Green in 1969.[76] This was essentially intended as a guide to what can be seen from the battlefield today. Although Green was of the opinion that certain 'famous engagements' turned the course of history, he followed the line of Creasey and Fuller that Agincourt was not one of them. Instead he applies the eye and experience of the modern soldier to empathise with his military predecessors. So, for instance, he imagines the difficulties of transporting men across the channel with their horses and equipment. 'After their prolonged period on board the really very small ships in appalling discomfort, the men were very "soft" and not up to the hard work that was immediately required of them' and which 'taxed heavily their already lowered stamina', prompting them, in the hot weather, to eat fruit and to drink 'the unaccustomed wine', thus causing dysentery. And later, 'Prima facie the peasant population was naturally hostile to an invading army from a traditionally enemy country. Nevertheless the British soldier was, in 1415, as adept at making friends with foreign civilians, and especially the girls, as he was in 1914, and the local ale-houses were crammed in the evenings with thirsty archers and men-at-arms who had a little pay to spend.' There is a similar tone in W.B. Kerr's work: 'they had all the ups and downs of a soldier's life . . . they had felt the depth of gloom and the joy of deliverance . . . life for a short space had been full and varied'.[77] Note too Green's anachronistic use of 'British'. In article published in 1944, R.L. Mackie took to task a French writer for calling Agincourt a British victory, reminding his readers that 'since the few Scottish soldiers who did take part in the battle fought on the French

---

[76] The account of Agincourt occupies pp. 19–30, and was originally published in *The Army Quarterly and Defence Journal*, 91, part 2 (1966), pp. 230–36.

[77] 'The English soldier in the campaign of Agincourt: III. The battle of Agincourt', *Journal of the American Military Institute*, 4 (1940), pp. 209–24.

side, Scotland can claim no share in the glory or the guilt of Agincourt', and that it was Scottish soldiers who liberated the French peasantry in the 1420s.[78]

The most well known work by an ex-soldier must be Lieutenant-Colonel Alfred Burne's *The Agincourt War*.[79] Burne was much influenced, both in his account of Agincourt as of other engagements, by his own experiences as an artillery commander in the First World War, where he served with much distinction. He had much confidence in his ability to interpret the battle not only from the ground itself but also from 'inherent military probability', based on his own experiences and his reading of military history in general. He was thus dismissive of Wylie's account.

> Wylie was not a soldier, and if he visited the ground he did not attempt to draw a battle plan. One gets the feeling that he was so immersed in detail that he had not himself a clear idea of the actual course of events, still less of the lessons to be drawn from this famous battle.[80]

For Burne, there was a delightful order to the English army, 'a regular trained army of selected soldiers', whereas the French were 'a vast rabble-like horde of hastily raised troops, of a heterogeneous nature'.[81] The ground over which they fought was 'easily described for it is beautifully symmetrical. If the two contestants really desired a field that would give no advantage to either side as they declared, they certainly found it at Agincourt.' As Burne drew in a sketch map in his book,

> the arena formed a rectangle, the two sides being formed by the woods surrounding the villages of Agincourt and Tramecourt, the open space being 940 yards wide at the narrowest point and the two ends being formed by the two armies in line, just over 1,000 yards apart. There was a barely perceptible dip between the two armies, but the two flanks fell away appreciably, a surprising discovery to the visitor, for no account mentions the fact. Owing to the slight dip between them the two armies were in full view of one another, each army filled the open space, a newly-sown wheat field, and as the arena was slightly

---

78 'From Agincourt to Orleans. Scotland and the liberation of France', *Scots Magazine*, 42, no. 1 (1944), pp. 14–20.

79 *The Agincourt War* (London, 1956, reissued by Wordsworth Editions, 1999). Burne (1886–1959) became a well-known lecturer and writer on military history after his retirement from the regular army, being editor of *The Gunner* from 1938–57 and producing works as diverse as *Lee, Grant and Sherman* (1938), *The Campaign in Sicily and Italy* (1946) and *The Battlefields of England* (1949), as well as *The Crécy War* (1955) (*Who was Who*, 15 (1961), pp. 159–60).

80 He also criticised Wylie's following of the 'preposterous theory' that the two eyewitnesses, Le Fèvre and Waurin, copied from Monstrelet. 'Lessons from Agincourt', *Army Quarterly*, 62, no. 1 (1959), pp. 70, 75.

81 In an article published in the same year, he claimed that the victory could be 'summarized in a single sentence: a regular, trained and disciplined army defeated one that possessed none of these military virtues'. 'The battle of Agincourt', *History Today*, 6 (1956), pp. 598–605, at p. 605.

wider on the French side it follows that their line was slightly longer than the English, about 1,200 yards to 950.

Burne followed the same line as Kingsford in believing that each of the three divisions of the English army had archers on its wings, but he also spoke of the following:

> a strong force of what we should now call 'army archers' attached to no division but formed in two bodies one on each wing [see fig. 6]. The archers of the centre division would thus be in contact with the archers on the inner wings of the flank divisions: likewise the outside archers of the flank divisions would be in contact with the 'army archers'. Thus, looked at from the front at a distance as the French would see them (and this is important for my argument) the English army would appear to have men-at-arms in the centre, divided by two small clumps of archers, while the main archer force would be on the wings. I suggest that the army archers were about 3,100 strong and the divisional archers 1,850. Thus the biggest clumps, viewed from the front, would be on the wings, each nearly 1,900 strong. A simple calculation shows that such a formation should just fill the space of 940 yards between the woods.

Here as elsewhere Burne followed what he called 'Inherent Military Probability', based not just on common sense but also on his own experiences as a soldier. There is a major flaw in his interpretation to my mind. Whilst the chronicles do present problems over the positioning of the archers, there is no way by which one can calculate from them the relative numbers in each group, nor do they give adequate support for the notion of two different types of archers. But Burne was right in seeing the significance of the archers as more than a role as artillery to soften the French attack before it could reach the English lines. He sensibly stressed 'that glittering initiative', which led them to drop their bows and enter the mêlée, to kill with knives, daggers and even stakes. This was what for him carried the day for the English.[82]

It is easy to dismiss the judgments of soldiers of later centuries as anachronistic, and to criticise their selectivity when it comes to the use of sources (although Burne does include some assessment of chronicles). Burne was aware that 'the reconstruction of all history is largely conjectural, and this applies more to military than to any other branch of history'.[83] But he, like other military men, displays a desire to see military neatness and order, and to draw clear lessons from the past. In this context, therefore, such writings tell us as much about the period in which their authors were living and serving as about the era of Agincourt.

---

[82] *Agincourt War*, p. 93, 'Lessons from Agincourt', p. 77.
[83] *Agincourt War*, p. 12.

Recent studies

In the last thirty years or so, there have been several studies of the battle. Their authors have focused on the chronicle sources, whilst being all too well aware of the difficulties of using such sources. To quote Christopher Hibbert, for instance, writing in 1964, 'I have not, however, attempted to explain the wearisome processes which have resulted in my reconciling conflicting statements in the chronicles, since although the reconciliation has led me to an interpretation of some events different from that reached by previous writers of books on the subject, I can make no claims that I have proved anything. We are all merely guessing and the points at issue are, in any case, only relatively minor ones of time and place.' Hibbert accepts Burne's view that the archers were both in wedge-shaped groups positioned between the battles and also on the wings, curving into the centre 'so that the French, when provoked into attack, could be subjected to a hail of arrows not only from the front but from the sides as well' (see fig. 7).[84] John Keegan displays equal confidence in the chronicle sources, arguing that the events of the battle are 'gratifyingly straightforward to relate'. He provides us with the bare outlines of the battle,

> . . . as recorded by seven or eight chroniclers who do not materially disagree over the sequence, character or significance of events. Of course, even though three of them were present at the scene, none was an eyewitness of everything, or even of very much, that happened. An army on the morrow of a battle, particularly an army as small as that of Agincourt, must, nevertheless, be a fairly efficient clearing-house of information, and it seems probable that a broadly accurate view of what had happened – though not necessarily why and how it had happened – would quickly crystallize in the mind of any diligent interrogator, while a popularly agreed version, not dissimilar from it, would soon circulate within, and outside the ranks. It would seem reasonable therefore to believe that the narrative of Agincourt handed down to us is a good one; it would in any case be profitless to look for a better.[85]

Keegan gives the same version of the positioning of the archers as Hibbert, but adds wisely that we have no real idea of how the archers were commanded. He sees as crucial the fact that the French men-at-arms fell over, for otherwise their weight of numbers would surely have driven back the English, although he does not follow Lot's conclusion about French numerical inferiority. Once the French became stationary, the outcome of the battle was inevitable. As there were no French troops constituting a threat to them, the archers were able to come in for the kill, as Burne had also stressed.

---

84 *Agincourt* (London, 1964), pp. 5, 107.
85 *The Face of Battle. A Study of Agincourt, Waterloo and the Somme* (London, 1976), p. 85.

If the archers were now able to reproduce along the flanks of the French mass the same 'tumbling effect' which had encumbered its front, its destruction must have been imminent. For most death in battle takes place within well-defined and fairly narrow 'killing zones', of which the 'no-man's land' of trench warfare is the best known and most comprehensible example. The depth of the killing zone is determined by the effective range of the most prevalent weapon, which, in infantry battles, is always comparatively short, and, in hand-to-hand fighting, very short – only a few feet. That being so, the longer the winning side can make the killing zone, the more casualties can it inflict. If the English were now able to extend the killing zone from along the face to down the sides of the French mass (an 'enveloping attack), they threatened to kill very large numbers of Frenchmen indeed.[86]

Although this interpretation is inspired, as was Burne, by later analogies, it is altogether a more reasoned analysis. By the time Jim Bradbury considered the battle in his *Medieval Archer* in 1985, and Matthew Bennett published his study of the battle in 1991, a new document had come to light in the British Library, a French plan of battle.[87] This could be used as a check against the chronicle sources to explain French tactics. As Bradbury wisely notes, 'the plan shows that chronicle accounts of battles tend to prolong and separate movements that must often have been designed to coincide. There is clear intention to make one major effort, that would strike at vital points, at the same time engaging all the English forces so that there could be no reinforcement against a successful breakthrough.'[88] Also, because it seemed to have fallen into French hands before the engagement, the plan could be used to explain Henry's own actions, especially his ordering a defensive stake hedge for his archers. Bradbury is convinced that the archers were only on the flanks of the whole army, and provides a useful discussion of the issue, emphasising the potentially misleading phraseology of the *Gesta* where it claims that the king placed 'wedges' of archers between each wing (*intermisisset cuneos sagittorum suorum cuilibet aciei*). Bennett follows the same line (see fig. 8), and usefully provides a discussion of the debate.[89] Allmand is more equivocal in his biography of Henry: 'While it is possible that there were groups, or wedges, of archers between the three sections, it is clear that the majority of them were placed on the wings, looking slightly obliquely towards the centre of the French army which opposed them.'[90] Only Robert Hardy in recent years has followed the older view of

---

[86] Ibid., pp. 104–5.
[87] C. Phillpotts, 'The French plan of battle during the Agincourt campaign', *EHR*, 99 (1984), pp. 59–68. See below pp. 464–66 and 468–9 for this text and my own views thereupon.
[88] *The Medieval Archer* (Woodbridge, 1985), p. 125.
[89] *Agincourt 1415*, Osprey Military Campaign Series (London, 1991), pp. 66–8. See also his 'The development of battle tactics in the Hundred Years War', in *Arms, Armies and Fortifications in the Hundred Years War*, ed. A. Curry and M. Hughes (Woodbridge, 1994), pp. 1–20.
[90] *Henry V* (1992), p. 88.

archers being placed within the English line as well as on the flanks.[91] Bennett elucidates three phases of the battle: the English advance and French cavalry charges; the main French attack and mêlée; and the killing of the prisoners. In addition, he suggests that the French attack on the baggage was part of the original French battle plan, and not 'an extemporised attack by a greedy local lord'.[92] His book is particularly useful for photographs of the field and for coloured diagrams of the English and French positions, although these are by necessity stylised in form and we cannot be certain about the extent and nature of local vegetation in 1415.

Save for the issue of the archers' positioning, all modern writers have tended to rely in the main on the *Gesta*'s account. They have in general brought a number of other published chronicle and administrative sources to bear. Although there remains an occasional lack of discrimination in the use of chronicles, with faith continuing to be placed in late accounts and even sixteenth-century versions, recent writers have produced sensible narratives and discussions which are generally consistent with each other, and which benefit from our increased knowledge of medieval military matters as a whole. All modern writers emphasise Henry's generalship, and the folly of the French, although there remains some uncertainty over the exact tactics and deployment of the latter. But these two basic factors are seen to have combined to produce an overwhelming victory for the English, quickly and with relatively few casualties on the winning side. Such conclusions stand in a long and consistent tradition from the contemporary chronicles onwards, as mediated through histories from the sixteenth century to the twentieth.

One important change of emphasis can be detected, however. Authors of the eighteenth century, writing for an upper-class audience, tend to give most stress to the importance of leadership. It was in the nineteenth century that the English archers began to come to the fore, not so much in the work of Nicolas or Hunter, but more in works of a more popular nature, at least at first. Initially this was by virtue of patriotic leanings, and was a development of existing views of the French. The picture of the gallant but socially humble English archer pitted against the debauched and scornful French gentleman was one which appealed to the rising bourgeoisie of Victorian Britain.[93] One of the most extreme portrayals occurs in Charles Dickens, *A Child's History of England* with lines such as 'on the English side, among the little force, there was a good proportion of men who were not gentlemen by any means, but who were good stout archers for all that . . . the proud and wicked French nobility who dragged their country to destruction and who were every day and every year regarded with deeper hatred and detestation in the hearts of the French people, learned nothing, even from the defeat of Agincourt'. Dickens was, however, struck by 'the real desola-

91 'The longbow', in *Arms, Armies and Fortifications*, ed. Curry and Hughes, pp. 174–7. See also his *Longbow*, chapter 6.
92 Bennett, *Agincourt*, p. 84.
93 C. Dickens, *A Child's History of England* (1853), pp. 217–22.

tion and wickedness of war', a theme which has also coloured modern views, where there has been a much greater willingness to debate the killing of the prisoners, as for example in Keegan's *Face of Battle*, and to assess French mortality rates without patriotic hyperbole.[94] In recent times the English archers have been assessed on military rather than chauvinistic criteria. It is interesting to speculate that views were influenced by both the First and Second World Wars where massed and 'non-professional' troops were much deployed. In many ways, the Agincourt archer has been interpreted and portrayed as the 'Tommy' of the fifteenth century. As we observed earlier in this book, a direct link was drawn in the popular psyche in the First World War. Today we are more aware of the military significance of a massed firing of arrows in terms of its weakening the French before they were able to engage. In addition, it would appear to have been a tactic which prevented the French from pursuing their own intended plan of battle. Although there have been some variations in emphasis, in general all accounts over the centuries have suggested that the battle was as much lost by the French as won by the English.

---

[94] See, however, Charles Kightly, *Agincourt* (New Malden, 1974), p. 46: 'Though it is unfashionable to say so, it is also at least partly true that the English won the battle because most of them were brave men, and that the French lost it because many of them were cowards.' Kightly provides a useful campaign map (p. 9) which differs slightly in chronology from that provided in Bennett, *Agincourt*, p. 39.

5

Administrative Records

The English army

In the modern period, we might expect to find clear policy statements on the purpose and objectives of a particular campaign. For the middle ages, we are forced to rely more on actions themselves as indicators of intentions. Applying this to 1415, we have neither a specific statement by Henry on what his campaign plans were, nor do we have any kind of battle plan for how he intended to deploy his troops, although, as will be discussed at the end of this chapter, we do have a French text concerning their proposed 'order of battle'. We also have the demands Henry put to the French in the negotiations of 1414–15, which seem to show the seriousness of his intentions. This is also revealed by the size of the army he raised, which was intended to be in excess of 12,000. Not since 1359 had so large an army been formed; not since that date had a king campaigned on the continent in person. Not surprisingly, therefore, the surviving documentary materials on the administration of the army of 1415 are very extensive. They can give us an insight into Henry's possible plans both before and during the campaign even if they cannot answer all the questions we might pose about his war aims and battle deployment.

As we saw in the previous chapter, Joseph Hunter pointed the way towards how these records of the army could be used. After the foundation of a Public Record Office these archives gradually became more accessible, especially as their cataloguing advanced. It was this material, and more, which James Wylie tried to piece together in his own study of the reign. Ninety years on, we are able to set the documentation more easily in context thanks to the work of Allmand and others on Henry V, and on late medieval military organisation in general. The description of the sources provided in this chapter should by no means be considered the last word on the campaign, but as an indication of what does survive and what potential it can offer. We cannot give the subject the full treatment it deserves in the space available. The surviving documentation is so vast that it will take some time to process it fully. However, with the aid of computer-assisted analysis, it is hoped that, in due course, it will be possible to list and examine all the retinues and their members, to elucidate more systematically the financing of the campaign, and to set the expedition even more firmly in the context of military and political developments in the later middle ages.

Earlier writers were much concerned with who was on the campaign, and, more especially, present at the battle. It may seem a rather dry exercise to start with this topic but there are two reasons for doing so. The first is to make clear what sources Nicolas and others drew upon so that the value of their work can be more fully understood and exploited by those interested in the subject. The second is because a study of personnel can help us not only to identify Henry's strategies in general, but also to make some suggestions on the way he deployed his troops at the battle. The route to this final objective might seem long and tortuous, for we must first assess the listings of personnel in Nicolas, and then explain the administration of the army in general, before focusing on the campaign and battle itself.

The 'Agincourt roll'

As part of the Tudor interest in pedigree and the right to bear arms, heralds produced a list of those present at the battle. This list has commonly been called 'the Agincourt roll'. It was printed by Nicolas in his *History of the Battle of Agincourt,* and has been much relied upon by later commentators.[1] Three such lists are known with only minor differences between them. All occur within manuscripts which contain a wide range of heraldic and other materials, typical of the collections formed by the heralds of early modern England. The earliest is probably that in the Bodleian Library, Ashmolean MS 825 folios 15–35, compiled by Robert Glover who was Somerset herald from 1571 to 1588.[2] That in College of Arms, MS 1, folios 17–34, occurs within a collection made by Robert Cooke, Clarenceux herald (d. 1593), although there is a dispute over who penned the actual list. The third list is found in British Library, Harleian MS 782, a volume which has the name of Ralph Broke and the year 1604 inscribed on its first folio. Broke was York herald from 1593 to 1625.[3] It was this last version which Nicolas included in his *History of the Battle of Agincourt,* collating it with the version in the College of Arms. All three lists are organised

---

[1] Nicolas, pp. 331–64. Nicolas collated the Harleian and College of Arms lists in the second and third editions of his work.

[2] The dating and many other issues are discussed in J.H. Wylie, 'Notes on the Agincourt roll', *Transactions of the Royal Historical Society,* third series, 5 (1911), pp. 105–40. British Library, Additional MS 30323 contains a transcript taken from this Ashmolean MS by William Myton around 1733. Glover himself included a short and inconsequential account of the battle in his *Nobilitas Politica et Civilis* (1608), published in English as *The Catalogue of Honour* in 1610, and by the Folio Society as *The Kings of England* (1995).

[3] A *Catalogue of the Manuscripts of the College of Arms Collections,* ed. L. Campbell and F. Steer, vol. 1 (London, 1988), p. 92, claims that it is in the hand of Cooke but Wylie, 'Notes', p. 121 suggested that of Broke. British Library, Harleian MS 782, which later belonged to Thomas Cole, also includes a list of those present at the battle of Baugé and of towns taken in Normandy which Williams printed as appendices to his edition of the *Gesta Henrici Quinti,* pp. 274–9. Bradbury, *Medieval Archer,* p. 121 includes a facsimile of Harleian MS 782, folio 82b.

in the same way, with the names of each retinue leader being followed by the names of the 'lances' (i.e. men-at-arms) serving with his company. The number of lances is then totalled, as is the number of archers in each retinue, but no names of archers are given. Indeed, Glover explicitly tells us that the names of the archers have been omitted. The heralds of the late sixteenth and early seventeenth centuries presumably chose to ignore the archers as men of a lower social status, and hence of no interest in the search for the ancestors of the contemporary nobility and gentry.

It is impossible to tell whether the lists were taken from an original roll or from other earlier copies of an original, or whether they were copies of each other. Wylie concluded that Glover 'may have had before him not the original itself but some paraphrase of it which was circulating in his time'. But as Wylie went on to show, there can be little doubt that all three lists have as their ultimate source a roll submitted to the Exchequer in November 1416 by Sir Robert Babthorp, controller of the king's household. This is revealed by a paragraph in French given at the end of all three. I have rendered this here into modern English, with corrections to the translation given in Nicolas.

> Be it remembered that Robert Babthorp knight, controller of the king's household, did deliver to the barons of the king's exchequer, by the command of the king, on 19 November in the fourth year of our sovereign lord the king [1416], this roll containing 18 prests, the last prest indented with this bill, the which roll contains part [*parcell'*] of the names of the men who were with the king at the battle of Agincourt, that is to say, in the second quarter of the third year of his reign, for execution to be done to the profit of the lord King, and the which bill, thus taken from the said roll, was delivered by the said barons to the aforesaid Sir Robert.

Wylie could not find the original roll in the Public Record Office, and I have had no success in locating it either. But there can be no doubt that it once existed, nor that it was drawn up to assist in the final accounting in the Exchequer for the Agincourt campaign. As we shall see later, it is referred to in several documents of the period, where its description makes clear that the names of the archers were once included. Once we have established the context in which the original roll was compiled, we shall be able to assess its worth as a source for the battle.

The administration of the English army

The post-script to the Agincourt roll noted above emphasises a crucial point, that the army was administered through the Exchequer. Over the course of the fourteenth century, and most especially after 1369, a complex system of organisation had developed which continued for the rest of the Hundred Years War and beyond.[4] At its heart was an indenture, or contract, which a captain entered into

---

4   See J. Sherborne, 'Indentured retinues and English expeditions to France, 1369–80', *EHR*,

with the crown, to bring along, on a specified date and to a specified place of assembly, a particular number and type of soldiers for war service over a stated period. Captains then received pay from the Exchequer for distribution to their men. For campaigns intended to last less than six months, all the pay was awarded at the time of indenting. For a six-month campaign, half was given at the sealing of the indenture, and the rest at the muster. For longer campaigns, the first six months (or as it was more commonly expressed in Exchequer records, two 'quarters' of three months each) was paid in the customary fashion of half at the sealing and half at the muster, and special arrangements were laid down for the payment of the remainder. Exchequer officials checked that the right number and type of men had been brought along by undertaking an inspection (muster) just before embarkation. After the campaign, those who indented were obliged to make account to the Exchequer. This was partly because the crown was entitled to a share of the gains of war they and their men had taken. By this period, the crown took a third of the value of gains taken by those who had taken out indentures with it. In addition, leaders of retinues took a third of the value of the gains of their own men, with the crown creaming off a third of a third.[5] A further reason for the returning of accounts after the campaign was to allow for any deductions to be made in the case of indentees who had not been able to provide the number of men they had promised, and hence was an inevitable result of a system where wages for a campaign were paid in advance. As we shall see, these practices were followed in 1415, but there were some unusual arrangements concerning the issue of pay.

First of all we have the indentures. Most of these were drawn up on 29 April and follow a set format (see text F 1 below).[6] They tell us the conditions of service, the number and type of troops promised and the arrangements concerning pay. The indenture was so named because the same text was written onto the sheet of parchment twice. The two texts were separated across the middle of the document by alternate upward and downward cutting strokes, producing an edge which was 'indented', rather like a series of teeth (Latin, *dentes*). The upper copy of the text remained with the crown, the lower copy

---

79 (1964), pp. 718–46, and A. Curry, 'English armies in the fifteenth century', in *Arms, Armies and Fortifications in the Hundred Years War*, ed. A. Curry and M. Hughes (Woodbridge, 1994), pp. 39–68.

5   For the development of this system in the fourteenth century, see A. Ayton, *Knights and Warhorses. Military Service and the English Aristocracy under Edward III* (Woodbridge, 1994), chapter 4, and D. Hay, 'The division of the spoils of war in fourteenth-century England', *Transactions of the Royal Historical Society*, fifth series, 4 (1954), pp. 91–109.

6   As Allmand (*Henry V* (London, 1992), p. 72) has pointed out, preparations for the campaign had begun earlier in the year. Guns were being founded in December (*CPR 1413–16*, p. 292) and tents prepared in February (ibid., p. 294). An expedition was already been discussed in the privy council in February: *POPC*, 2, p. 145. On 10 March 1415, the mayor and aldermen of London were summoned to the Tower where the king informed them of his intention to cross the sea to reconquer the possessions of the crown, and of his need for money: *Calendar of Letter Books of the City of London, Letter Book I*, ed. R.R. Sharpe (London, 1909), p. 135.

with the indentee. In the case of any disputes, and in the drawing up of the final account, the two halves could be checked against each other. Fraud would be revealed if the two edges did not correspond or if there were any differences in one text from the other.

By the early eighteenth century, the indentures were housed along with other Exchequer records in the Chapter House at Westminster Abbey or in the Tower of London. In preparation of volume nine of the *Foedera* which covered the reign of Henry V, Rymer and Sanderson noted from these indentures the names of the indentees and the numbers with which they had engaged to serve. They then rearranged these names in alphabetical order to form a listing entitled 'the retinue of Henry 5 in his first voyage'. It may initially have been intended to put the whole list into the *Foedera*. This did not happen, although some specimen texts were included.[7] In time, the vast array of notes collected by Rymer and Sanderson passed into the custody of the British Museum, and the list was published by Harris Nicolas in all editions of his *History of the Battle of Agincourt*. Nicolas added to it further names drawn from the evidence of those who took out Chancery protections or letters of attorney for the campaign, a type of document which will be discussed more fully in due course. Nicolas' list of 'The Retinue of Henry the Fifth' has proved highly influential in all studies of the army of 1415.[8] It gives details of 290 retinues, containing 10,533 men, plus another 30 special companies, such as miners and gunners, contributing another 877 men, although many of these should probably be seen as non-combatants. In fact this list is not the only one to have been prepared from the indentures. A list of 184 of those who indented with the crown in 1415 exists in another British Library manuscript, Stow 440, folios 26 to 30, being drawn up by Sir William Le Neve, Clarenceux king of arms, and Sir Edward Walker, Garter King of Arms, around 1664.[9] In the early eighteenth century, the indentures for 1415 and for other campaigns were taken out of the Exchequer records for 'methodizing'.[10] Although they were subsequently returned, it is clear that over the years

---

[7] Rymer also collected materials from Chancery records and from the important collection made by Sir Robert Cotton, now in British Library, Cotton Caligula D V, from which similar selection was made for printing in the *Foedera*. There were plans sanctioned by the House of Commons in 1800 to publish the whole of Rymer's transcripts but this never happened: Wylie, 'Notes on the Agincourt roll', p. 108.

[8] Nicolas, pp. 371–400. Unfortunately, the reference he gave, Sloane 6400, was incorrect, although it has been followed by many later authors (see, for instance, Bradbury, *Medieval Archer*, p. 120, n. 14). The correct reference is in fact British Library Sloane 4600, which is also known as Additional MS 4600. He ascribed the protections and letters of attorney to the Norman rolls when in fact they are to be found in the French (or Treaty) rolls.

[9] This volume covered the wars from Edward III to Henry VIII and includes many fine illustrations of seals. The volume later belonged to John Anstis, Garter King of Arms, who prepared an index to it.

[10] As a note on the first folio of Stow 440 tells us. 'In the year 1719 they were placed with Mr Incledon, their housekeeper, by order of the House of Lords. They were afterwards delivered to John Anstis esq. by order of a committee of the Lords to be methodized and they remained at his house in Mortlake until 1756 when they were removed into the custody of Mr

some were lost. About 130 survive, now classified within the Public Record Class E101 (Accounts Various), and catalogued in List and Index Supplement IX.

Other sources can be used to compensate for the lack of surviving indentures. Once the indenture had been drawn up, the Chancery immediately sent to the Exchequer a 'warrant for issue', i.e. an order to release a sum of money to the leader of the retinue (see text F 2 below). This recites some, but not all, of the terms of the indenture. Most importantly for the purposes of calculating total effectives, it does cite the numbers and type of troops contracted. These warrants are to be found in the PRO class E404 (Warrants for Issue), also indexed in List and Index Supplement IX. Usefully, those warrants concerning military service have also been listed separately in the back of the volume with corresponding indentures noted where the latter survive. For the campaign of 1415, about 200 warrants survive, with slightly over half, 115, having matching indentures still extant.

Warrants for issue presented at the Exchequer led to a payment being made, and such expenditure by the crown was subsequently enrolled on the issue rolls (now classified as E403). Two issue rolls were drawn up each year, one for the Michaelmas term and one for the Easter term.[11] It seems, however, that most payments of wages for the campaign were put into special, separate issue rolls. Only one of these survives, now E101/45/5, which lists payments made to 210 indentees on 6 June (see Text F 3). The drawing up of special issue rolls suggests that the expedition of 1415 was perceived as such a large and distinctive undertaking that it was deemed best to keep separate records. The Exchequer officials no doubt hoped that this would make final accounting arrangements easier. Entries of payments to captains would all be listed in order rather than having to be found amongst a myriad of other entries within the standard issue rolls. In some cases a warrant for issue survives to tally with the entry in the issue roll, in some cases with an indenture, and in some cases both. All three texts exist for Sir Thomas Tunstall, as is revealed by the extracts given below. But there are some cases where we know of the retinue only through the entry in E101/45/5. In others we have indentures and warrants with no corresponding entry on the one surviving special issue roll. Considering all these sources together, the number of men bringing companies for the expedition totals at least 250, and nearer 300 if one remembers that some indented as groups rather than as individuals.

The first quarter's wages were paid in two instalments. The first instalment followed the sealing of the indenture, and is perhaps best seen as a kind of advance to assist in the recruitment of troops. The second was due at the time of

Carington, in whose possession they remained till 1770 when upon a representation of Messrs. Astle and Topham to a Committee of the House of Peers they were, by His Majesty's command, deposited in the State Paper office where they now remain.'
[11] The roll for the Easter term of 1415, however, is incomplete with no entries between 20 May and 2 September E403/621).

muster. The surviving special issue roll records the payment of the first instalment of wages on 6 June, but some, such as Sir Thomas Erpingham, had received payment earlier, in his case on 18 May. There is apparently no roll recording payment of the second instalment, but from accounts drawn up after the campaign, we can see that the Exchequer recorded this issue as mainly occurring on 7 July, although there is also evidence that some received the money earlier, in Sir Thomas's case on 1 July.[12] According to the indentures, no cash was to be distributed for the second quarter, but royal jewels and plate would be issued as guarantee of receipt of money in due course. The king was obliged to redeem the jewels within a year and seven months after the indentees had received them. The distribution of the jewels was envisaged in the indentures as happening on 1 June. For the third quarter, pay was to be given to the indentee within six weeks of the start of that quarter. No full arrangements were laid down for the payment of the fourth quarter. All that was said was that if the king could not give the indentee security by halfway through the third quarter, the latter would be able to discharge himself at the end of that same quarter.[13]

All this demonstrates an important point. Henry wanted to make a big show in France, yet did not have enough money to do so.[14] He did not have enough cash in hand to finance a six-month expedition, let alone a twelve-month expedition. But he was keen to keep his options open, allowing the possibility of twelve months in the field. This was not entirely without precedent, for a similar situation had existed in 1375 when 'the Crown promised payment for only six of the twelve months' service stipulated by indenture'.[15] Possibly Henry hoped that he might be able to gain some sort of pay-off within France from one of the warring factions in the civil war. In 1412 his brother, Thomas, duke of Clarence, had led an army to the assistance of the Armagnacs. On this occasion, pay for the first two months was issued by the English crown but it was anticipated that the following three months would be financed by the French allies. If this did

---

12 This is evidenced by an account drawn up after the campaign, E101/47/20, m. 3. Erpingham mustered on Southampton Heath on 13 July: E/101/44/30. The Exchequer accounted for payments to the contingents of Lancashire archers on 20 June and 21 July respectively. In the case of one of the leaders, James Harington, we have proof that he was paid the first instalment by an esquire of the sheriff of Lancashire at Winwick (Cheshire) on 27 June: E101/46/35.
13 There had been earlier discussion over the arrangements for payment. At a great council in March or April, it was noted that lords had already agreed to serve on the expedition with payment for the first quarter at its outset and for the second and third quarters at the end of the second quarter. But as funds could not be collected quickly enough, it was proposed that the payment for the third quarter would not be made till its end. The lords agreed so long as adequate security could be provided (*POPC*, 2, p. 151). We should perhaps see the final indenture terms as a compromise, for in effect payment for the second quarter was advanced to the outset of the campaign, albeit through the issue of jewels as security.
14 This is clear from council discussions from February onwards, especially as there were so many other costs to bear for Wales, Calais, the marches against Scotland and the keeping of the sea: *POPC*, 2, pp. 145–7.
15 Sherborne, 'Indentured retinues', p. 7.

not materialise, then the king was obliged to make a further payment to Clarence, although the indenture left the nature and duration of this payment vague.[16] But although we can see some similarities with other campaigns, what was unique about the situation in 1415 was the use of jewels as security for the second quarter, although they had been sometimes used previously as securities for loans to the crown in general. On 13 May, the king ordered Richard Courtenay, bishop of Norwich, keeper of the royal jewels, to issue jewels as required to the earl of Arundel as treasurer of England.[17] Jewels and plate were issued according to the level of pay due. This was done by calculating the weight of the precious metal in the object. Whereas a man who indented to bring along only a couple of archers in addition to himself would receive perhaps one piece of plate, those such as the duke of York or the king's brothers who had indented to provide hundreds of men were given extremely valuable and prestigious items extending even to royal crowns. All of this is revealed in warrants for the issue of jewels and receipts for the same, and in accounts drawn up after the campaign. Most of this material is to be found within E101, although, as we shall see in due course, there is also a special enrolled account, E358/6, relating to post-campaign accounting. It should be noted in passing that these records provide an extremely valuable source for the crown's holdings of jewels and plate.

What did the issue of jewels mean in terms of payment for service? We must assume that the retinue leaders would keep the jewels themselves and pay out money to their troops from their own pockets,[18] expecting recompense only after the campaign was over and the crown redeemed its securities. This is certainly what a petition put forward to Parliament in 1427 suggests (Text F 15). But could it be that some troops did not receive any pay for the second quarter? Having disbursed the money for the first quarter, the retinue leaders might have waited to see how long in practice the campaign would last. Whatever practices were adopted – and it is possible that a variety were used – it says much about attitudes to the campaign on the part of both retinue leaders and their men. Both were prepared to go to war without receiving the customary full cash in advance. We shall see that in fact the crown was extremely slow in redeeming the jewels, slower than the indentures laid down.

A further point about Henry's plans can also be made based on the pay clauses in the indentures. This relates to the proposed location of his campaign. Indentures for foreign service were often vague about the intended theatre of campaigning, using expressions such as 'France', etc. Most of the indentures of 1415 mention two possibilities, 'the duchy of Guienne (Gascony) or the

---

[16] *Foedera*, IV, ii, pp. 15–16. See also J. Milner, 'The English enterprise in France, 1412–13', in *Trade, Devotion and Governance. Papers in Later Medieval History*, ed. D.J. Clayton, R.G. Davies and P. McNiven (Stroud, 1994), p. 81.

[17] *Foedera*, IV, ii, p. 125.

[18] It is also possible that they could have placed the jewels with goldsmiths in return for ready cash.

kingdom of France'. If the campaign was to the latter, then the wage rates would be one shilling (i.e. 12d) per day for each man-at-arms and 6d per day for each archer. For Gascony, wage rates were cited in the indentures on a yearly rather than daily basis, namely forty marks *p.a.* for each man-at-arms and twenty marks *p.a.* for each archer. With the mark at 13s 4d, this was about equivalent to a daily rate of 18d for the men-at-arms and 9d for the archers, in other words 50% higher than for service elsewhere in France, presumably to reflect the higher costs of provisioning in the infertile south-west.[19] In both theatres, however, the same higher daily rates were payable to men of title: 2s for knights bachelors, 4s for knights banneret and barons 6s 8d for earls, and 13s 4d for dukes, although in military terms all such men mustered as men-at-arms.

When the first instalment of pay was issued, which for most indentees occurred on 6 June, it was at the Gascon rate. Hence in the extract from the special issue roll given below (text F 3), Sir Thomas Tunstall received £51 4s 8d: this covered 44.5 days service for himself at 2s per day, and for his men-at-arms at 18d per day and his archers at 9d per day.[20] Thus it would seem that Henry initially intended an expedition to Gascony. But was he simply trying to mislead the French into thinking that he would land in Bordeaux? Southampton was certainly a muster point suitable for expeditions either to the north or south of France, and had been Clarence's port of departure in 1412 too. The *Gesta* claims that Henry 'concealed from all save his closest councillors the destination of the ships'.[21] Allmand suggests too that 'at all costs, the enemy must be kept guessing'.[22] If there was any truth in the notion that those involved in the Southampton plot were in collusion with the French, then this subterfuge could have been doubly valuable. Remember too that there was a French embassy present in England from mid-June to early July.[23]

The question of the intended destination of the campaign is further complicated by references in the issue roll for the Easter term of the third year of the reign which begins in late March 1415.[24] Entries from 16 April to mid-May concerning the supplies of military equipment and shipping speak of the king's expedition (*viagium*) to Harfleur. The most interesting is perhaps the entry of 19 April where William Hoklyst was paid nearly £24 for the cost of a *jantaculum* (breakfast) at the palace of Westminster for the duke of Clarence and other lords so that the king might have their advice on 'his present expedition towards Harfleur and the region of Normandy'.[25] The issue roll for the preceding Michaelmas term shows preparations for the campaign from at least February 1415

---

19 This Gascon rate had been paid to Clarence's expedition in 1412: *Foedera*, IV, ii, pp. 15–16.
20 For other examples, and discussion of the destination of the campaign, see M.G.A. Vale, *English Gascony 1399–1415* (Oxford, 1970), pp. 72–4.
21 *Gesta*, p. 17.
22 Allmand, *Henry V*, p. 79.
23 Wylie, 1, pp. 485–92.
24 E403/621.
25 Ibid., m. 2. Allmand, *Henry V*, p. 78.

yet speaks only of a royal expedition overseas (*versus partes extraneas*).[26] This terminology starts in the Easter term issue roll from late May, but then there is a gap in this roll from 20 May to 2 September with no entries whatsoever. A marginal note simply says 'missing 249 entries'. But what are we to make of the fact that Harfleur was mentioned as the target in April and May, yet wages were issued in early June at the Gascon rate. Was it all a bluff on the part of Henry? Yet it might seem a rather expensive ruse to pay out the first instalment of wages at the higher Gascon rate if an expedition to Normandy had already been decided upon. Wylie suggests that the higher Gascon rate of pay may have been offered at the outset in order to attract men to serve.[27] But perhaps it was that Henry was already intending to campaign in Aquitaine, or at least making it the final destination of his expedition. This need not have ruled out a landing in Normandy for it was much cheaper to transport an army for a short distance by sea and then have them march by land to their destination. Nor does it make it impossible that Henry intended to take Harfleur as a bridgehead, although it is a slightly odd choice for the starting point of a chevauchée towards Bordeaux as it lay north rather than south of the Seine.

We can also draw here on evidence from the archives of Bordeaux (Text F 6). A letter of Benedict Espina, merchant of Bordeaux, written at London on 8 June to the mayor and *jurats* of Bordeaux, suggests that Henry was not going to go straight to the south, for why else would he be requesting the council in Bordeaux to send him siege engines?[28] This conclusion seems to be confirmed by the king's own letter to Bordeaux written sometime in June. Espina's letter does note, however, that the campaign was to continue into the autumn and winter, and the reply of the council at Bordeaux to him expresses a hope that the king might be persuaded to come to the south. At a meeting of 7 September, the council of Bordeaux still spoke of the possibility that the king might be coming to the city.[29] But was this by now wishful thinking? By 30 October the *jurats* were no longer convinced Henry would be coming to Bordeaux, although it is not clear whether at this stage they had already received news of his victory.[30]

Henry's plans for Gascony had changed much over the spring and summer of 1415. Intentions for Thomas Beaufort, earl of Dorset, to return there as lieutenant had been abandoned by 30 April, at which point Sir John Tiptoft was appointed seneschal. Henry subsequently made a series of changes to the size and nature of the company due to cross with Tiptoft. These moves suggest that the king was increasingly coming to the view that Tiptoft should cross with only a small force, thus freeing more men for the king's own expedition. Thus, for

---

[26] E101/403/619.

[27] Wylie, 1, p. 457.

[28] The siege engines never seem to have been sent: Vale, *English Gascony*, p. 75.

[29] *Archives Municipales de Bordeaux*, 4, p. 250, in the context of a discussion of levies on wine.

[30] Ibid., p. 279; Vale, *English Gascony*, p. 75. Vale claims that news of the victory did not reach Bordeaux until 23 November. That is the date on which it was announced publicly (see above pp. 262–3).

instance, John Fastolf and Henry Inglose were by 3 June ordered to be withdrawn from Tiptoft's company.[31] Both men subsequently crossed with the royal
army, as did the earl of Dorset. Tiptoft mustered at Plymouth with 80 men-at-
arms and 400 archers, and was in Bordeaux at least by 20 August.[32]

Henry's own army was intended to muster on 1 July. In fact most musters
were carried out almost a fortnight later. The second instalment of the wages for
the first quarter was due at the point of muster. The Exchequer accounted for
money paid out on 6 July, by the hands of John Everdon, clerk, assigned to pay
the wages of war, although there is no extant issue roll recording these
payments. But this time wages were issued which were appropriate for the
French not the Gascon theatre, with men-at-arms being paid at 12d instead of
18d per day, and archers 6d instead of 9d. In addition, a small sum was added in
for the men-at-arms to cover the regard which was payable in the French theatre
at 100 marks per quarter for every thirty men-at-arms. It would be convenient to
use Tunstall again as our example, but no account for his main retinue survives,
although we do have an account for the group of archers from Lancashire whom
he also led. But we can see the two different payment levels in the entry for
William Legh esquire of Cumberland in E358/6, a post-campaign account
whose significance will be explained in due course.[33] Here we see Legh
receiving £26 4s 6d on 6 June, which is the appropriate payment at the Gascon
rate for 3 men-at-arms, himself included, and 9 archers. On 6 July the payment
was £19 2s 3d, the appropriate total for the French theatre. Legh had not
received any jewels for the second quarter, but we must remember that many had
already done so, mainly in mid-June. The rate of payment of the second part of
the first quarter's wages suggests that Henry had decided at least by the beginning of July that the campaign was definitely going to northern France, and was
not going to move on to Gascony at all. Surely too, the issue of pay at rates
appropriate for the French theatre would make it likely that by the point of
muster, his troops *were* aware of the destination of the campaign, at least in
broad terms, despite what the *Gesta* says.

The *Gesta* also tells us that Henry crossed to Normandy 'in order *first*
(*primitus*) to recover his duchy of Normandy'.[34] Harfleur was known to be well
defended, and thus likely to be difficult and time consuming to take. It is
possible, therefore, that Henry had changed his mind about a Gascon objective,
perhaps because his expedition had been so delayed in leaving England. There
remains confusion, however, over whether Henry intended to move south after
the siege. A letter sent to Bordeaux by another Gascon, Jean Bordiu, from the
siege camp on 3 September, tells us of the king's plan to move on to further
places in northern France, and also mentions the king's intention 'to come there

31 E101/48/2, cited in Vale, *English Gascony*, p. 76.
32 *CPR 1413–16*, p. 347, order of 19 June 1415 to John Darundell and others to supervise the
muster of Tiptoft.
33 The entry occurs on m. 3.
34 *Gesta*, p. 17.

[i.e. to Bordeaux] before he returns to England'. The king's own letter to Bordeaux of the same date, however, says nothing of such plans (see texts in F 6).[35] What is not in doubt is that Henry had initially intended a long campaign. He had raised an army large enough to allow him to leave men in places he captured if he so wished. He had siege engines and siege specialists in his company, but he also had a fairly mobile army based on evidence of horses and proportions of mounted troops. Even so, Henry's objectives remain obscure and indeed may have changed over time anyway, for he was surely an opportunist.

The army began to sail from Southampton on 11 August, with the first landing at Chef de Caux at dawn on 13 August. It embarked without the crown having paid fully for its service, a case of mortgaging the future if ever there was one. This confirms the view of Henry as an opportunist. Perhaps Henry did anticipate being able to exploit divisions in France, as his father had done in 1412. We know that negotiations had been going on with John the Fearless, duke of Burgundy, before the invasion of 1415, and that Henry had already sent military support to Burgundy in 1411. Although we have no proof of any deal struck before embarkation, the impression gained from such negotiations may have been that Burgundy would ally himself with the English if the latter met with early success in their campaign.[36] Certainly there were rumours in France after Agincourt, fuelled by the duke's absence from the battle, that Burgundy had allowed Henry to invade. Even so, it is hard to escape the conclusion that the expedition of 1415 was a voyage into the unknown. This emphasises the bravado of Henry himself. The indentures could only guarantee him an army for nine months at best, perhaps less if he could not pay for a third quarter, and that surely would depend upon his success in France. The financial terms of the indentures and the size of his army also reveal the level of commitment he had been able to generate within England.

Personnel and organisation

As Hunter wisely observed, the Exchequer records can only show us which retinue leaders were *supposed* to be present at the muster.[37] They do not tell us which were they actually there, nor do they say anything about the men they intended to recruit beyond the number with which they had agreed to serve. It is interesting to speculate how these numbers were decided upon. Did indentees know already how many men they would be able to recruit, or were they taking a gamble in agreeing to a particular number in advance? There are sources we can

[35] Vale, *English Gascony*, p. 75, confuses the two letters and puts Bordiu's comments on royal intentions to march to Bordeaux into the mouth of Henry.
[36] English envoys had met with the duke in Ypres in August 1414 and discussed, amongst other matters, the military assistance which the duke might afford to Henry: Allmand, *Henry V*, p. 69.
[37] J. Hunter, *Agincourt. A Contribution towards an Authentic List of the Commanders of the English Host in King Henry the Fifth's Expedition to France in the Third Year of his Reign* (London, 1850), p. 4.

use to shed further light on this and other matters to do with recruitment, but as will be appreciated, this is a big topic deserving of fuller treatment elsewhere. The first source are the sub-indentures. Those who had indented with the crown themselves indented with others in order to raise troops. A number of sub-indentures survive in the Exchequer records for the earl of Salisbury and the earl of Dorset (see Text F 4 below). It is interesting to see how these compare with the terms of the indentures entered into by the crown.[38] We can speculate that these represent only a fraction of those which would have been entered into, for there was no real reason why they should find their way into the royal archives, being essentially private arrangements between the retinue leader and the sub-indentee.

The second source which can assist with the study of recruitment is the record of protections taken out by those intending to go on the campaign. This was a well-established practice aimed at protecting those in service overseas from damage to their property interests during their absence. Essentially it suspended any cases for a specified length of time, in this case for the antici-pated length of the campaign. Alongside this practice, men also might choose to take out letters of attorney to enable others to act on their behalf. Protections and letters of attorney were enrolled on the Treaty rolls, which are also more commonly known as the French rolls, and which form part of the Chancery archive, now classified as PRO C76.[39] As we saw, these were drawn upon by Nicolas to add to the names of retinue leaders he had derived from Rymer and Sanderson's listing of the indentures. Nicolas did not consult the French rolls themselves, drawing instead on the catalogue prepared by Thomas Carte in 1743.[40] In 1883, the French rolls for the reign were calendared in an appendix to the forty-fourth report of the Deputy Keeper of the Public Records, and are thus accessible in print today. About 500 protections and letters of attorney relevant to the campaign are enrolled between membranes 8 and 23 of the relevant French roll, C76/98. This reflects slightly fewer individuals since some took out both protections and letters of attorney. The name of the person is given as well as the name of the leader in whose retinue he was intending to cross to France. In the case of those who had indented directly with the crown, it was said that

---

38 For Salisbury, see E101/69/7, no. 508, and for Dorset, E101/69/7, nos. 488–505, and C47/2/49/7. Rymer, *Foedera*, IV, ii, p. 126, prints an indenture between Salisbury and William Bedyk which Nicolas translated in his Appendix, pp. 10–12, but it does not seem to be that still extant in E101/69/7, no. 508.

39 For earlier periods Chancery warrants for such protections survive, and are useful as they give further information, but such warrants are not extant for this period. The entries in the French rolls are terse and follow a set formula: an example follows from C76/98, m. 10. 'Protections. Thomas Rokeby knight who is to go with the king in the company of our beloved John, earl Marshal overseas there to stay in the obedience of the king has royal letters of protection with the clause *volumus* to last for one year. Witness the king etc. at Westmin-ster, 28 July.'

40 T. Carte, *Catalogue des rolles gascons, normans, et françois conservés dans les archives de la Tour de Londres* (London and Paris, 1743). Nicolas (p. 371) incorrectly described the information as coming from the Norman rather than the French rolls.

they were crossing in the retinue of the king. In a minority of cases, additional information is given such as a place of origin and occupation. The calendar gives the date on which the protection was taken out, which is a useful guide to how preparations for the campaign developed over time. The earliest occur around 22 April, implying that recruitment was occurring in advance of the indentures being sealed. Most were issued between May and August, but there are also a handful in September and even into October.

We must exercise some caution in using these records. They are not in themselves a totally reliable guide to those who participated in the campaign. They need to be viewed alongside the revocations of protections enrolled in the Patent rolls.[41] There is a further problem. The protections and letters of attorney do not distinguish between men-at-arms and archers, nor indeed do they distinguish between soldiers and civilians. Only one man is explicitly described as 'archer'.[42] In some cases, the occupation cited distinguishes them as craftsmen, such as bladesmiths, armourers, tailors etc., or victuallers, such as fishmongers, drovers, and were not therefore in military retinues and in receipt of royal pay. It stands to reason that soldiers took servants with them. We know too that the great lords travelled and lived in some style, even on campaign, and that captains were responsible for providing food and equipment for their troops. Royal records also show the significance of the provision of victuals, and of men such as tailors, tentmakers, carpenters and the like. We also know that the king summoned a number of clerks to his expedition for attendance upon himself and his council.[43] Thus we would be far too blinkered if we took all of those with protections as soldiers. Indeed, the fact that protections continued being issued after the departure of the army may suggest that the later ones were largely for non-combatants involved in the provision of victuals etc. But all non-military personnel did not take out protections. Although we do have one or two glimpses into this crucial group we cannot know exactly how large it was, nor whether such men might fulfil a military role if called upon, even if it was simply to assist in the defence of the baggage. This makes it impossible to know the total numbers on campaign.

We can be more certain of those crossing in a military capacity for they were to be in receipt of royal pay. The indentures, warrants and issues show us what the army was supposed to be like and what it was supposed to number. Most indentees were to provide mixed retinues comprising both men-at-arms and

---

[41] See, for instance, the revocation of protection for one year granted on 6 June last to Thomas Bernes going on the king's service beyond the seas on the king's service in the company of the king's brother, Humphrey, duke of Gloucester, because he delays in the city of London as appears by certificate of the sheriffs: *CPR 1413–16*, p. 360. Bernes' protection of 6 June is in the French rolls: *Annual Report of the Deputy Keeper of the Public Records 44*, (London, 1883), p. 571.

[42] John Riggele, alias Power, in the company of John Fastolf, protection dated 27 June 1415: *Annual Report of the Deputy Keeper of the Public Records 44* (London, 1883), p. 566.

[43] See, for instance, the summons to Richard Hals, treasurer of Exeter Cathedral, in PRO, E28/31/55.

archers usually in the ratio of one man-at-arms to three archers. This ratio seems to have become the norm during the Welsh wars of the reign of Henry IV and was to remain standard English practice to the mid-fifteenth century at least. Some of those entering into indentures in 1415 – men of noble or princely status – were contracted to bring large companies. The dukes of Clarence and Gloucester, the king's brothers, were indented to bring 960 and 800 men respectively. The duke of York, the earl of Arundel and the earl of Dorset were all due to bring 400 men. At the other end of the scale men might indent to serve with a handful of men, perhaps only themselves and an archer. There were even individual archers who engaged to serve directly with the crown. In between was a range of retinue sizes. What was unusual about the army of 1415 was the large number of men who had indented directly with the crown. No other army of the late medieval period was made up of so many retinues. As noted earlier, there were at least 250 men who indented with the crown to bring troops. Many of these (although the specific number remains to be calculated) brought less than 10 men. This reveals the energy with which Henry recruited for the campaign as well as the level of commitment in England to it. In terms of military activity the fact that the army was made up of a myriad of retinues raises important questions. Although it was administered and paid through the large number of individual indentees, it would stand to reason that the retinues were grouped together in some way right from the start. The need to group would have persisted during the siege, march and battle.

The indentures required troops to be brought to a certain place on a certain date. The area around Southampton was chosen as the point of muster early in the day, and ships were being impressed from late April onwards.[44] The indentures had envisaged a muster date of 1 July, but musters were not actually taken until mid-July. They gave rise to what remains an extremely important source for us today, muster rolls. It is only through such lists of men that we can be certain who actually set off on the campaign. In addition they can indicate whether retinue leaders had been able to bring along the numbers and types of troops for which they had indented. All surviving musters have been classified within E101 and catalogued under 'army, navy and ordnance' in List and Index XXXV, published in 1912 but based on a classification system devised by Joseph Hunter. Relatively few musters are extant but we can see that they come in several forms. Some are large parchment rolls on which many names are written. These were the master lists produced by the Exchequer clerks involved in the actual taking of musters. Examples include the musters of the retinue of Humphrey, duke of Gloucester, at Michelmersh, near Romsey, on 16 July, and of the duke of Clarence taken at St Catherine's Hill near the New Forest.[45] The

---

44 On 3 June the manors of Christchurch, Canford and Poole were granted to the earl of Salisbury for the billeting and support of his retinue: *CPR 1413–16*, p. 337. Orders for impressement of ships are also found in the *CPR* along with orders for the provision of equipment and food.
45 E101/45/13 and E101/45/4 respectively.

latter is undated. The first membrane of the muster of the duke of York's retinue is also damaged.[46] In addition there are some surviving lists of individual retinues, sometimes on paper, which may be drafts produced by individual retinue leaders.[47] Finally, there are some lists of individual retinues in indented form, so that the retinue leader could keep one part and the crown the other.[48] Unfortunately we do not have a full muster of the king's own company, although there are some miscellaneous survivals of musters of men known to be in his household, ranging from knights and esquires down to staff in the bakehouse and spicery.[49] Indentures and accounts drawn up after the campaign, along with the Agincourt roll suggest that there were many household officials and servants of all ranks on the campaign. As can be imagined, the surviving muster rolls offer tremendous potential for the detailed study of personnel.

The musters show how the army gathered at various points along the south coast in the vicinity of Southampton. The muster of Gloucester's retinue lists 190 men-at-arms and 610 archers, of the 200 and 600 he was under obligation to bring. The duke himself is not listed, so that it is possible that there was another roll for his personal retinue. The layout of the surviving roll indicates that there were 56 separate mixed retinues. This gives us a further insight into recruitment, suggesting that the duke attracted to his service 56 sub-indentees who themselves brought along their own retinues. Some of these, such as that of Sir William Beauchamp, were numerous, containing 9 men-at-arms and 30 archers. Twenty-four out of the 56, however, comprised one man-at-arms accompanied by two to four archers. Clarence's muster indicates at least 69 separate mixed retinues, of which 40 were of one man-at-arms and his archers. In some cases, men had brought more soldiers that they had been required to, and they were entered on the rolls as being 'above the number'.[50] It would seem that such men did not receive pay, but were no doubt deemed useful as possible reinforcements or substitutes. In other cases, men had not managed to find all the numbers for which they had indented. Some rolls show deletions and insertions of names.

In addition to the mixed retinues, there were specialist companies. Some might be classified as 'support services', men such as a company of miners from the Forest of Dean, or groups of cordwainers, tentmakers, and armourers, and even surgeons.[51] There was a company of crossbowmen from Gascony.[52] More

[46] E101/45/2.
[47] There are several such paper rolls to be found in E101/44/30. It is possible that these were submitted after the campaign for the sake of checking against the royal records.
[48] One such document survives recording the muster of Sir Thomas Erpingham's company taken by John Rothenale, controller of the royal household, and John Strange, clerk, on Southampton Heath on 13 July (E101/44/30).
[49] E101/45/18. One list in this set of musters is headed 'valets de diverses offices de l'ostell du roy'.
[50] Erpingham's muster shows 4 men-at-arms and 12 archers are 'in addition to his number' of 20 men-at-arms and 60 archers (E101/44/30).
[51] E404/31/386, 409, 416, 437, and 359 respectively.
[52] E404/31/315.

significant, at least in terms of numbers, were the companies of archers from Wales, Lancashire and Cheshire. These were areas which had a special relationship with the crown, and these companies were raised through the mechanisms of local government. Thus the chamberlain of South Wales, John Merbury, was responsible for bring a company of mainly foot archers. The documentation surrounding this company shows that the counties of Camarthen and Cardigan provided 10 men-at-arms, 13 mounted archers and 327 foot archers, with the lordship of Brecon providing another 10 men-at-arms, 13 mounted archers and 146 foot archers.[53] The Cheshire archers were raised from each of the hundreds of the county, and were paid out of local taxation at the Gascon rate. It is not exactly clear how many served. According to the reading of the indentures by Rymer and Sanderson, the chamberlain, William Troutbeck, engaged to bring 50 men-at-arms and 650 archers, but there seem to be pay records for only 247 Cheshire archers on the campaign.[54] From Lancashire 500 archers were raised, grouped into companies of 50 each under the command of a knight or esquire, who often led his own small company in addition.[55] This gives us 1,246 archers in addition to those raised in mixed companies through the indentures. The special issue roll indicates that there were also some archers who indented directly as individuals with the crown.

Commissions of array had been issued throughout England on 29 May.[56] Although these were theoretically aimed at raising men for defensive service within England (they had not been used for overseas service since the 1350s), it is possible that on this occasion they were used as a means of at least alerting archers in particular to the king's need for troops. Otherwise, no other general call ups or announcements are known, although we must suppose that recruitment had mainly taken place through those who took out indentures with the king, or by virtue of special relationships. Henry had certainly attempted to raise the service of those who held fees and annuities of the crown,[57] and as we have seen, large companies of archers were recruited from the crown's own principality of Wales, earldom of Chester and duchy of Lancaster. What we would much like to know is whether the resulting companies of archers were kept separate, or whether they were divided up and assigned to other existing retinues.[58]

---

53 E101/46/20. The lists reveal the numbers recruited in each commote.

54 Nicolas, p. 385. The account of the chamberlain of Chester for 1416–17 contains the names of 182 archers from the county who had served the king at Harfleur and Agincourt, but details 14 other companies from Cheshire serving on the expedition which contain a further 65 archers (SC6/776/4, m. 3d–4d). See also E403/624 m. 3, 629 m. 12.

55 There is much documentation on this group, but see especially the account of the sheriff, Sir Robert Urswyk, which gives details of all the companies: E101/46/35.

56 *CPR 1413–16*, p. 407.

57 See order of 22 March that such men should assemble for a meeting with the king on 22 April: Rymer, *Foedera*, IV, ii, p. 109. With further research it will be possible to see how many annuitants of the crown actually served on the campaign.

58 A question also asked by Allmand, *Henry V*, p. 208.

This is of particular importance when considering how the archers might have been drawn up at the battle.

A detailed study of all of this material, and of the accounts drawn up after the campaign, will permit us in the fullness of time to come to a firm conclusion on the total size and composition of the army, but it would seem to be at least 12,311 strong in terms of *indented* troops. The numbers actually serving are likely to be less, but we do not have enough musters to come to a definite figure. Over three-quarters of the troops were archers. The proportion may be as high as two-thirds because of the special companies from Cheshire, Wales and Lancashire. The issue of whether the archers were mounted and on foot is complex for the indentures and other documents are not always totally explicit. Rymer and Sanderson, followed by Nicolas, tended to assume that archers were foot unless otherwise stated. From the evidence of other fifteenth-century armies it is more likely to be the other way round, that archers were mounted unless they were referred to as foot. Moreover, there is evidence from post-campaign materials that foot archers did have horses with them. Nicolas has the earl of Oxford with foot archers, yet his return shipping account shows almost half of his archers with mounts.[59] Thousands of horses would have accompanied the army, not merely mounts but also pack animals and haulage beasts.[60] Much in the way of victuals and equipment was also despatched. There can be no doubt that this was a major effort, made all the more remarkable by the fact that an armed fleet was also sent out in the summer months, and that a company had been sent to Gascony under Sir John Tiptoft. Shipping had to be provided for all these purposes and to transport the main army. We know too that it did not prove possible to ship across to Normandy all of the men raised, and that some were thus left behind, although it is not possible to know how many.

Sources for the campaign

It seems highly likely that Henry issued disciplinary ordinances for the campaign. The *Gesta* implies this was the case, but to date it has not been possible to identify with any certainty a text belonging to this particular expedition.[61] We must rely on chronicles, most notably the *Gesta*, for the positioning of troops at the siege of Harfleur and for the ordering of the army on the march, but as we shall see in due course, the accounts produced after the campaign can be brought to bear on these matters as well as on the battle. But before we

[59] E101/46/36.
[60] Some of the indentures had specified the number of horses for each rank; see, for instance, that taken out by Henry, Lord Scrope, in *Foedera*, IV, ii, pp. 114–15, where he has 16 horses, his knights 6, the men-at-arms 4, and the archers one apiece.
[61] British Library, Additional MS 33191 is a possibility. C. Hibbert, *Agincourt* (London, 1964), pp. 160–67, published the ordinances issued by Henry at Mantes in July 1419.

discuss such records, we can pause to reflect upon a number of documents dating from the siege or shortly afterwards.

There were two letters sent to the mayor and council of Bordeaux from the siege camp on 3 September, one by the king and the other by Jean de Bordiu, chancellor of Guienne, who was present at the siege (and was once thought a possible author of the *Gesta*) (Texts in F 6).[62] The king gives nothing away as to his future plans. Bordiu is more effusive, with a mention of a plan to move on to other towns in upper Normandy and then to Paris itself, with the added promise of a visit to Bordeaux before the king returns to England. The latter cannot be taken of proof positive, however, that Henry proposed to undertake a chevauchée southwards to Bordeaux as his brother had done in 1412/13. It was equally important to keep those back in England informed as part of a more general policy to generate enthusiasm and to justify existing (and to encourage future) financial support. The campaign of 1415 had been costly to launch, with many loans having been raised from towns, merchants, clergy and nobility. The Londoners were particularly significant in terms of both political and financial support. It is not surprising, therefore, that a letter was sent to them by king from the siege of Harfleur on 22 September 1415 (Text F 5). It gave an account of the campaign to date although it did not provide a firm indication of future plans. Perhaps Henry was not too certain of his next move so shortly after the siege and when his army had been much afflicted by dysentery. A fourth letter is known, a personal summons issued by Henry to the dauphin, which was dated in the *Foedera* to 16 September but which Nicolas suggests may more likely belong to 26 September after the town had fallen.[63] The later dating would make sense of Henry's subsequent actions, for it allowed eight days for the Dauphin to reply. With no answer received, Henry prepared to leave Harfleur, with 6–8 October the most likely date for the commencement of his march towards Calais.

On 5 October, John, duke of Bedford, as guardian of England, issued a writ to the sheriffs to make proclamation for all knights, esquires and valets desirous of crossing to Normandy to go to the king's uncle Henry Beaufort, bishop of Winchester, chancellor and treasurer, and receive their wages. This also added that all merchants, victuallers and artificers who were willing to reside in the town of Harfleur should go there with all goods and harness: the captain of the town (Thomas Beaufort, earl of Dorset) would provide them with houses, and when settled there the king would grant them a charter of liberties.[64] An undated proclamation probably also belongs to this period; it likewise invites merchants

---

62 Vale, *English Gascony*, pp. 74–5. Bordiu himself received pay at the outset of the campaign: E101/69/8, no. 521.

63 Nicolas, Appendix, pp. 29–30, with discussion at pp. 71–2. The dispute over dating arises out of the fact that the fifteenth-century text, British Library, Cotton Caligula D V, was damaged in the fire of the Cotton Library. Hibbert, *Agincourt*, pp. 168–9 reproduces Nicolas' translation.

64 *Calendar of Letter Books of the City of London, Letter Book I*, ed. R.R. Sharpe (London, 1909), p. 159; Delpit, CCCXXX, p. 217, *Foedera*, 9, p. 314.

and others between now and a week hence to speed to the king, being at Harfleur, with all manner of victual, clothing, armour and artillery, and in the meanwhile to go to the mayor of London who would assign them shipping and passage.[65] These references, all from the records of the City of London, show what Henry's intentions were for his new conquest: it was to be a second Calais.[66]

A final letter, sent by the lieutenant of Calais to John, duke of Bedford, on 7 October, suggests that by then Henry's intentions to move towards Calais were known (one assumes messages had been sent thither from Harfleur, whether directly or via England), and that there was a need to act against threats to disrupt his passage in the north (Text F 7).[67] There are also some useful references to the post-siege period in the regular issue rolls. They show that victuals were indeed shipped to Harfleur from England, suggesting perhaps that the English army was better provided at the siege and as it began its march than might be thought.[68] Entries also reveal an order to recruit reinforcements to send to Henry in France at some point in October, although this was subsequently cancelled.[69]

We can know quite a lot about those who became ill at Harfleur. Particularly well known is the *congé* or licence to return home which Henry had issued on 5 October (Text F 8). It speaks of a list of those given such a licence, and indeed there are several known lists of the sick. One gives the names of the 'malades' in various retinues, including those of the royal household, the dukes of Clarence and Gloucester, and the earls of March, Oxford Huntingdon, and Suffolk. Interestingly, this does not restrict itself to soldiers, also giving the names of priests, minstrels, pages and servants who had become ill. It goes on to give the names of ships used to take the infirm back to England.[70] Allmand has calculated that at least 1,687 men were 'officially regarded as unfit for service'.[71] What is perhaps less well stressed is the fear of desertion at this point, which is of course the reason why formal licences to return to England were necessary. Such *congés* also imply that regular musters were taken, but only one muster actually drawn up during the campaign is known to survive. This is for the retinue of Edward, duke of York, and is marked 'for the second quarter'. It is doubly useful

---

[65] *Letter Book I*, p. 152. Vale, *English Gascony*, pp. 74–5 also notes supplies of war materials for Harfleur being sent from Bayonne and requested from Bordeaux.
[66] How many settlers crossed at this stage is difficult to tell. Certainly properties in the town were being granted to English settlers by the close of the year. See, for instance, *Annual Report of the Deputy Keeper of the Public Records 44*, p. 576, grant of inn at Harfleur on 22 Dec. 1415 to Richard Buckland of London who had assisted at siege with two ships, and p. 577, 29 Jan. 1416 life grant to Sir John Fastolf of manor and lordship of Frilense near Harfleur late of Guy Malet, seigneur de Gravylle. Fastolf had been placed in garrison after the town fell.
[67] Wylie, 2, p. 110.
[68] E403/621, m. 7.
[69] E403/622, m. 3 (entered under 23 October).
[70] See for instance E101/44/30 (roll 1).
[71] *Henry V*, p. 211.

as it indicates horses as well as men, and it notes those of the retinue who have died, become ill or been detailed to the garrison of Harfleur.[72]

We also have some shipping accounts concerning the return of troops from Calais to Dover after the battle. It may be too that in the Agincourt roll we do have a muster drawn up on the eve of or after the battle. We shall consider these sources more fully in the next section.

Accounts drawn up after the campaign

As noted earlier, those who indented were obliged to account to the Exchequer after the campaign. There was the added issue that the crown needed to redeem, by 1 January 1417, the jewels it had issued as security for the second quarter. The campaign had lasted for less than two quarters. There had been many changes to the number of men in each retinue as a result of the effects of the siege and of the need to garrison Harfleur. Gains of war had been made, most notably of prisoners. Given all of these factors, the post-campaign accounting was bound to be complicated.

In this context some crucial decisions were made by the king early in 1417. Until then, there was no full effort to deal with the financial aftermath of the campaign. The visit of the emperor, the cost of the defence of Harfleur and the need to fund another campaign to relieve Harfleur exacerbated Henry's lack of ready funds. Despite a generous tax grant in November 1415, prompted by euphoria of victory, and another in March 1416, there was still an anticipated deficit.[73] The parliament of October 1416 voted two tenths and two fifteenths, and the convocations of clergy at York and Canterbury were equally generous, making it now possible for Henry to consider paying off his Agincourt debts. He was under obligation to redeem the jewels used as sureties for the second quarter by 1 January 1417. He may have been prompted to account with those who had indented for the Agincourt campaign because he was already planning another expedition to France and may have hoped for their service again. Clearly the Exchequer officials were beginning to contemplate the problem before Christmas of 1416. As noted at the beginning of this chapter, the 'Agincourt roll' was handed over by Robert Babthorp to the Exchequer on 19 November 1416. The special issue roll for the campaign was handed to the clerk of Roger Leche, treasurer of England, on 24 November 1416.[74]

In early March of the following year, the king was asked to make a range of decisions concerning payments for the campaign. His replies were given in person on Saturday 6 March 1417 at a meeting held in the king's secret chamber in the Tower of London attended by the archbishop of Canterbury, the treasurer

---

[72] E101/45/19.
[73] R.A. Newhall, 'The war finances of Henry V and John, duke of Bedford', *EHR*, 36 (1921), pp. 172–98.
[74] PRO, E101/45/5 m.11d.

of England, the keeper of the privy seal and Sir Walter Hungerford. The questions and royal replies were jotted down, and survive today in British Library, Cotton Cleopatra F III, fol. 148, being printed also in Nicolas' compilation of the *Proceedings of the Privy Council*, and in his *History of the Battle of Agincourt* (Text F 9).[75] We shall look at these again to see how they and the resulting accounting materials can help us in a study of the campaign. But notice one point from near the end of the document which implies that a model account had already been drawn up concerning Sir Walter Hungerford, and presented to the king for his scrutiny and approval. It may be that the king had not found this account 'good and suitable', for this clause was not included when the full privy council ratified the decisions on 9 March.[76] Indeed a later set of enrolled accounts (E358/6) suggests that another model account may have been drawn up instead, that of Sir Robert Babthorp. On 9 March a writ was sent to the Exchequer officials ordering that all those who had indented for the campaign should appear before them and make account. Enclosed with this was a list of the persons who had so indented, along with copies of the indentures themselves.[77]

The accounting procedures duly began. They were bound to be complicated given that, for the first quarter, wages had been issued at two different rates, and for the second quarter jewels had been given in lieu of cash. The campaign had lasted an awkward length of time. It had been conducted entirely in the French theatre, so that the wage payments due would not tally easily with the advance of the first instalment. In addition, the retinues had suffered a variety of fates, with men dying, being invalided home or joining the Harfleur garrison part way through. For the accounting procedures, those who had indented needed to provide a copy of the indenture and details of any gains and prisoners they and their men had taken on the campaign. They also needed to inform the Exchequer of what had happened to their retinue, who had died at Harfleur, who had been invalided home, who had served at the battle. This would affect how much pay they were due. Thus retinue lists were drawn up by the retinue leaders indicating such matters against the names of their soldiers. These could be checked against the Southampton muster rolls as necessary, and presumably against lists made by the crown during the campaign, such as the Agincourt roll itself. In addition, the warrants for issue and the details of issue of jewels would need to be consulted to see how much each indentee had already received from the crown, and a final account drawn up whereby it could be revealed how much the retinue

---

[75] *POPC*, 2, pp. 225–7, with the points put forward for the king's decision at pp. 222–3. The text is in fact dated Sat. 6 March 3 Henry V but I would agree with Nicolas' re-dating to 1417. In 1417 the sixth of March fell on a Saturday whereas it did not in 1416. Moreover a date of 1417 fits with the officials mentioned and with other more firmly datable documents arising out of the decisions, such as the writ to the treasurers and barons of the Exchequer of 9 March, which was enrolled on the Memoranda rolls.

[76] Nicolas, appendix XI; *POPC*, ii, pp. 228–9 from British Library, Cotton Cleopatra F III, fol. 165v.

[77] *POPC*, 2, p. 224. See also p. 228.

leader owed or was owed, bearing in mind fluctuations in manpower, the need for the crown to take its share of gains, and to redeem the jewels as necessary.

As a manifestation of this process, we have several individual accounts as well as the supporting documentation which went with them, including the retinue lists on which it was noted what had happened to each man. Some sets have been divided up but others survive in their entirety, even occasionally within the small white leather bag marked with the name of the indentee and the date of the campaign. These bags would have been hung on hooks within the Exchequer awaiting and during the accounting procedure.[78] Others accounts are known only by virtue of enrolment. As with the issue roll before the campaign, the accounts for the campaign were enrolled on one, or perhaps more separate rolls, not on the Foreign Account Rolls (E364). One such enrolment survives in E358/6. This is made up of 11 *rotuli* (sheets) of parchment stitched together at the top. There is a referencing system by name of person at the foot of each *rotulus* enabling easy consultation. It is numbered roll six, implying that there may have been others now lost. It provides details of 59 indentees. The first entry is for Sir Robert Babthorp (who had replaced Walter, Lord Hungerford as steward of the household by 29 September 1421), and recites all the details of each stage of the procedure, being used as a point of reference for the remaining accounts in the roll. It recites the terms of his indenture, and of the various payments and decisions reached by Henry in March 1417. The account proper begins with his receipts in cash, the two payments relating to the first quarter, followed by his income from his share in war gains. His expenses are then calculated, being the wages due for the number of men he had had with him at various points in the expedition. There was an inevitable shortfall for the campaign had lasted longer than the one quarter for which wages had been received. The record of jewels given to him for the second quarter is then noted.

In 45 cases the entry in E358/6 can be matched by a set of surviving particulars. In a further 21 cases, we have only the enrolled entry or the particulars, not both. All these materials suggest that there was no urgency in dealing with the accounts of the campaign. Many were not dealt with until well into the reign of Henry VI. Certainly E358/6 dates from after 1422, although it reveals that some accounts were terminated within Henry V's lifetime. Some payments were made out of the issue rolls before 1422, and it would be relevant to search the later rolls to see if and when the debts were settled. All of this Exchequer material would repay further study in terms of what it tells us about royal finances, and indeed about attitudes to the campaign, for we need to explain why some of those who had served appear to have been in no particular hurry to be fully paid. The jewel accounts are particularly fascinating here. In some cases, including

---

78 Wylie, 1, p. 464. The list of sick noted earlier is found within such a bag (E101/44/30) on which is written in Latin 'musters of the time of King Henry the Fifth'. The bag also contains musters taken in the Southampton area at the outset of the campaign and other miscellaneous materials. The materials concerning the service of the Lancashire archers are to be found in another such bag, E101/46/35.

that of the earl marshal, the jewels seem to have been handed back without any money being paid by the crown.[79] In other cases indentees seem to have kept the jewels rather than having them redeemed for cash. Were they kept as a status symbol, proof perhaps of service on the campaign? Or was it that the crown could not afford to redeem them? Was it the crown that delayed payment deliberately? Petitions of the reign of Henry VI suggest that for some at least there was growing frustration in not having a settlement (Texts F 11, 14, 15). The fact that the settlement of accounts for service at Agincourt persisted well into the reign of Henry VI contributed to the increasing financial difficulties which the Lancastrian régime faced. This is another important topic on which further research is needed using the post-campaign materials.

But how can we use these accounts to tell us more about the campaign and battle? Let us look at the evidence they provide in the light of the king's decisions of 6 March 1417. He had helped the Exchequer by deciding on one date for the commencement of the campaign, Monday 8 July, even though some had not mustered until later and the whole expedition had not embarked until 11 August. This also made the quarterly payments easier to administer on the grounds that the first quarter could be taken as ending on Saturday 5 October, and the second as beginning on Sunday 6 October, the date which was duly adopted in the ensuing accounting procedures, and which was conveniently about the departure point from Harfleur. Henry had agreed that wages for the whole of the first quarter should be allowed even to those who had died or returned home during the siege, the latter including some who died subsequently from the illness contracted at Harfleur. Those who had been detailed to the garrison of Harfleur were to be paid until their entry to the garrison, the intention being that thenceforward they should be accounted as part of the cost of maintaining the new conquest. Any who had gone on to serve the king at the battle were to be paid for the whole of the period of the expedition. Henry further decided that the termination of the expedition should be taken as being eight days after his own arrival at Dover on 16 November, thus allowing for the fact that it took such a time for all of the survivors to be shipped home. Pay was thus due until 24 November. The campaign had thus lasted 140 days, or in other words, one whole quarter and 49 days, as was noted in the model account of Babthorp in E358/6.

As a result of the king's decisions, the accounts which the retinue leaders subsequently produced for the Exchequer reveal what happened to each retinue. First of all, we can see how many men died at the siege or were invalided home. Here, no doubt, the lists provided by the captains were checked against the lists of sick drawn up at the time. As we saw earlier, a list of those given *congés* to return home had been drawn up around 5 October, the end of the first quarter. Some conclusions can be tentatively drawn from the lists and account evidence. The first is that men-at-arms seem to have suffered the effects of dysentery more than archers. It is clear that the retinue of the duke of Clarence was much

---

[79] E101/47/37.

affected by disease. The duke himself was amongst those invalided home. This suggests that his troops were all stationed together, to the north-east of the town, where the land was marshy and conditions naturally unhealthy. It would also seem that those retinues which had mustered alongside his own before embarkation were also affected by dysentery, suggesting that they might have remained with him in the siege. In contrast, the duke of York's retinue does not seem to have lost many men at this stage. Of the 400 with whom he embarked, only 24 are noted as dying or being invalided home from Harfleur in his enrolled account in E358/6.

We can also see which men were detailed to the garrison of Harfleur. Here it is more difficult to see any pattern emerging. Only nine of York's retinue were placed in garrison, for instance. Those placed in Harfleur were paid by the Exchequer from 6 October to 6 January on the certification of their service by the earl of Dorset. In early 1416 a treasurer was appointed at Harfleur itself, and thenceforward the garrison was paid by him until January 1420, when the town was placed under the administration of the *chambre des comptes* which Henry had established at Caen on his second expedition.[80] The first surviving muster roll for Harfleur relates to the period from 31 December 1415 to 1 April 1416, but is not precisely dated.[81] It lists the earl of Dorset, four barons (Hastings, Grey, Bourchier and Clinton), 22 knights, including Sir John Fastolf, and 273 men at arms and 898 archers. Some of the names are certainly those of men known to have been detailed into garrison after the capture of the town, such as Fastolf, but it is possible, and indeed likely, that some of those originally detailed to garrison would have returned home and others would have taken their place by the spring of 1416. The garrison was reduced to 800 men in May 1416.

A more definite conclusion on how it was decided who should go into garrison might emerge from fuller study, but at this stage all one can say is that many retinues experienced a loss of men, whether by death, invaliding home, or detailing to garrison duty.[82] The organisation of the army had been dealt quite a blow. Some retinues were decimated, several had lost their leaders. It is likely, therefore, that there was some reorganisation at the point the army left Harfleur. Men from significantly reduced retinues were probably transferred to others. I think that this could be the explanation of why there is some difference in personnel between the muster rolls of the point of departure and the retinue lists which captains presented with their accounts. If one takes the example of the retinue of Sir Thomas Erpingham, for example, there is a good degree of consis-

---

[80] See A. Curry, 'L'administration financière de la Normandie anglaise: continuité ou changement?', *La France des principautés. Les chambres des comptes de xive et xve siècles*, ed. P. Contamine and O. Mattéoni (Paris, 1996). E36/79, E101/48/7, with particulars in E101/48/8 and enrolment in E364/63 m. 7.

[81] E101/47/39.

[82] Allmand, *Henry V*, pp. 212–13 has already shown the variety of experience using the examples of the retinues of Sir Roland Lenthale and Sir John Kyghley.

tency between the embarkation muster (E101/44/30) and the retinue list presented at the termination of the account (E101/47/20) in terms of the men-at-arms, but not of the archers.[83] There is also a strong suggestion that the royal household company had others detailed to it. Marginal notes made by auditors after the campaign in the special issue roll (E101/45/5) note several captains accounting 'in hospicio' (in the household), and there are further references to an account kept by Roger Leche, keeper of the wardrobe of the household during the campaign.

The evidence in the accounts and retinue lists also shows that some men died en route to Agincourt. These tend to be archers. That brings us to the battle itself. Here the king's decisions of March 1417 are not as helpful to us as they might have been, for he decreed that those who were killed at the battle should be treated in the same way as those who survived. They were all to be paid up to 24 November. There was therefore no need for deaths in the battle to be noted. Technically, therefore, what the documents show us is who was *present* at the battle. Indeed that is the wording used in the accounts and the retinue rolls. We can assume that the evidence presented by the retinue leaders on presence at the battle was to be checked against a master list drawn up by royal officials. We have no clear idea how such a list was drawn up, or indeed when. But the accounts refer to such a roll 'of dukes, earls, barons, knights, esquires and others who were with the lord king at the battle of Agincourt', which was delivered to the Exchequer along with other schedules (*cedula*) on 19 November 1416. We can be fairly certain that this 'master list' was what was copied by the heralds and printed by Nicolas – in other words, the 'Agincourt roll'.

It is not easy to count the names it gives because of variations in presentation (which suggests to my mind that it came from a copy and not directly from the original). Around 770 men-at-arms or lances are named, along with 2,496 archers, grouped into 68 or so companies. Yet it is certainly not a complete list of those present at the battle. This is revealed by the survival of particulars of accounts for captains who are not found on the 'Agincourt roll'. To cite but one example, that of Sir Simon Felbrigg.[84] The retinue list in the white leather bag containing his particulars indicates 6 men-at-arms at the battle including Felbrigg himself, in addition to one who died at Harfleur and 6 invalided home. All 36 of his archers were described as being at the battle, 'according to what Sir Simon says on his oath', implying perhaps that there was no muster to prove his statement. That could explain the omission of this company from the 'Agincourt roll'. A full study of all the surviving accounts is thus needed to come to a more accurate figure for presences at the battle, although it must be admitted that the survival of material is not so complete that it would ever provide a definitive figure.

---

[83] We have a further complication here, however, that Sir Thomas' account was not, in fact, presented until after his death in 1428, so it is perhaps possible that the inconsistency arises because after 13 years, no one was certain about the membership of his retinue.

[84] E101/45/3.

It is interesting to note that in Felbrigg's case, and indeed in the case of some of the companies listed in the Agincourt roll, the optimum ratio of three archers to every man-at-arms was no longer in place by the time of the battle. In some cases, there was a disproportionate number of men-at-arms, as in the case of the earl of Huntingdon who is given in the Agincourt roll as having 16 men-at-arms but only 35 archers. In others, the imbalance was in the number of archers, as with Felbrigg, and, in the Agincourt roll, Sir Roland Lenthale, who had 8 men-at-arms but 33 archers. This again confirms that each retinue suffered the effects of the campaign in different ways. The army was always likely to contain more than 75% archers, of course, because of the additional companies from Lancashire, Cheshire and Wales. According to the Agincourt roll, 209 Lancashire and 180 Cheshire archers were at the battle. This contrasts with the possible original numbers of 500 and 650 respectively. But the administrative records cannot clarify where they were positioned.

Henry's decision in March 1417 that those who died at the battle should none the less be paid for the rest of the quarter meant that there was no particular need to record English casualties in preparing the accounts. Thus, neither the Agincourt roll nor any of the surviving accounting materials can be relied upon as a guide to the numbers of the English army who died at the battle. We may therefore be gaining a false impression of the low level of English losses. Did Henry come to his decision to allow the continuation of pay to those who died because he wished to make it seem as though English losses were slight? Or was it simply a reward for those who had been present at his glorious victory? Or was it indeed true that English losses were slight, and therefore did not need to be a consideration in the accounting process? As it happens, some of the retinue lists and accounts do record fatalities at the battle. In the case of the duke of York's retinue, for instance, whilst only 24 were lost as a result of the siege, 93, including the duke himself, died at the battle; his casualties were thus a quarter of the retinue which had accompanied him from Harfleur. The retinue roll for John, earl of Huntingdon, on the other hand, names one man-at-arms and four archers as dying at the battle.[85] It is difficult to know, because of the king's decision, whether the accounts and retinue rolls do provide a comprehensive and accurate numbering of the dead. If they do, then English fatalities were indeed low, but by no means as low as chroniclers tell us.

The accounts also give details of the capture of prisoners, because of the need to pay to the king his share of the gains of war. Some are noted as being taken by two men together, such as a Frenchman called Le Sire de Corps who was captured by William Callow and William Kempton who were men-at-arms in the retinues of Sir Robert Babthorp and Sir William Phelip respectively.[86] Their captains were members of the royal household, so it is perhaps not surprising that the two men-at-arms should be fighting close together; indeed, there is at least one other example of a prisoner taken jointly by men-at-arms of household

[85] E101/45/7.
[86] E358/6.

retinues. Other prisoners are noted as being taken by individual men-at-arms: the duke of Bourbon, for instance, was captured by Ralph Fowne, a man-at-arms in the retinue of Sir Ralph Shirley.[87] Some – although at this stage in my research I would suggest relatively few – are noted as being taken by archers. The accounts also bear out the comment of chroniclers that some prisoners were sold at Calais rather than being taken back to England.

We can see from the accounts and Agincourt roll that the army remained for administrative purposes set into the retinues which it had contained from the outset. Yet these retinues had all suffered different fates, and it is highly likely that there had been regroupings. Those who had indented as individuals or with small companies must always surely have been attached to larger groupings. The chronicles speak of three battles on the march, and it is tempting to assume that these were already as they were to be in the case of battle, under the king, the duke of York and a third commander who is less easy to identify. If this is the case, then men who found themselves fighting side-by-side may well have known each other for some time. This would have contributed to the cohesiveness of the English forces. We are left, however, with a dilemma. The army was paid largely as mixed retinues, save for the extra companies of archers. Yet did it fight in this way, or were the archers of all retinues separated from the men-at-arms and put together? The accounting materials cannot tell us this, although perhaps the high numbers of casualties in York's retinue of both men-at-arms and archers do imply that his men were somehow together in his own battle. But how together is impossible to tell. Perhaps more detailed analysis of the surviving materials might reveal more on these matters, but we must admit that they were not compiled to answer the questions we would most like to ask.

The survivors marched on to Calais, with the king at least reaching it on 29 October. The king was obliged by the terms of the indentures to provide and pay for return shipping for the troops and their horses. Here surely we must accept that the numbers given are of survivors. Unfortunately there are few surviving detailed records of the shipping, but entries also occur in the enrolled account and in the particulars. The shipping account for the return voyage of the earl of Oxford's company, for instance, shows that 39 men-at-arms had 69 horses between them, and were each accompanied by one page. The earl had 12 horses for his own use, along with 6 horses for his cartage and 6 men to look after the horses and harness. Of 84 archers, 37 returned with horses, 47 without.[88] In some cases there is enough to help us estimate the number of horses lost on the campaign. Clarence's retinue returning from the battle (742 of his original 960) had with them 1,225 horses, 1.65 per head. The 283 survivors of York's retinue, on the other hand, had only 329 horses, 1.16 per head. These differences may simply be the result of an indiscriminate attack on the baggage camp, but it is also interesting to speculate that they do somehow link with the higher number of casualties in York's company. What accounts also show is that those invalided

[87] E358/6.
[88] E101/46/36.

home from Harfleur did not always take all their horses back with them. This is particularly noticeable in the account of the earl marshal where those who finally cross from Calais to Dover have with them their own horses and 'those of their sick comrades'. Although the earl himself was invalided home from Harfleur (along with 12 men-at-arms and 45 archers), his 24 horses had, it seems, accompanied the march northwards.[89] Thus those who undertook the march had with them a larger supply of horses than might have been expected. We know too that supplies were brought in from England after the town was captured, which might also have provided better conditions on the march than the chronicles suggest. Moreover, the survival of large numbers of horses right through the campaign would suggest that fodder was not a problem on the march.

All in all, therefore, there is a vast amount of documentation for the Agincourt campaign. There are some regrettable lacunae, however. As we saw, it seems that part of the financial administration was carried out through the royal household. There was once a book of particulars of account of Sir Roger Leche, keeper of the wardrobe of the household, covering the period from 1 October 1414 to 31 December 1415, which was used to verify some of the indentees accounts, but this book seems no longer to survive. There can be no doubt that the royal household was central to the expedition. This is obvious in all stages from indenting onwards, so that the loss of this book and other household materials for the period is a pity. The administrative and financial legacy of Agincourt continued to be felt for several years to come, in a fashion which may even have taken some of the gilt off the success of the battle itself. It was a costly victory, even if fatalities on the English side were low, and its financial burden was exacerbated and prolonged by Henry's later campaigns. But we should perhaps be thankful for the hard work of the fifteenth-century accountants which bequeathed to us today such a valuable legacy of documentation. There can be no doubt that fuller study of this rich archive will reap even greater rewards for the student of the period, and will provide a significant complement, and in some cases corrective, to the extensive chronicle accounts which have so far tended to predominate in discussions of the battle. That is not to say that administrative records could ever reveal the whole picture. Unlike the chronicles they cannot generate a feeling of what it was like to be there nor provide a full insight into what the battle meant to both English and French.

Other administrative records

As we have seen, many accounts took years to settle, and some may never have been settled at all. This led to a number of petitions to the council and to parliament. Examples of some of these are given below. They confirm the administrative nightmare that the peculiarities of the financing of the campaign had

[89] E101/47/37.

produced, and also tell us more in some cases about those present on the campaign. The case of Thomas Hostell is particularly instructive (Text F 10). Bradbury and others have claimed him to be an archer, but from a study of the original muster rolls, we can be certain that he was a man-at-arms under Sir John Lumley, whose retinue mustered with the duke of Clarence at St Catherine's Hill.[90] Hostell tells us that he served at Agincourt and that he was also in royal service in the naval battle at the mouth of the Seine (15 August 1416). His petition also shows the wounds which combatants might suffer, and the destitution which could arise, problems witnessed for soldiers in all ages. Disputes also arose over prisoners, and these, like disputes over pay, could drag on for several years. An example arising out of one such dispute is given below (Text F 12). As we have noted earlier, it is difficult to prove that there was continuing formal celebration of the battle but for those involved the memory and even kudos of being present must surely have meant much. In this context one of the most interesting, although at the same time perplexing documents, is the order of 1417 concerning the wearing of cote armours, which has been taken as indicating that all those who fought at Agincourt were as a consequence entitled to coats of arms (Text F 13). It is now thought more likely that what the document means is that those eligible to bear coats of arms had had their entitlement and presumably their arms checked when embarking on the campaign of 1415, and that such men did not need to subject themselves to a similar scrutiny when the next major royal expedition was under preparation in 1417.

This study has restricted itself to a consideration of materials in royal archives. It would certainly be possible to learn something from documents produced in other contexts. We have seen already relevant material in the Letter Book of the city of London. Records from other towns in England would also be worth investigating. The ledger book of the city of Salisbury, for instance, contains what may well be a newsletter produced after the victory. It also helps us to know something about the behaviour and movement of troops, for on 4 August a group of men from Lancashire under the command of James Harington, said to be about to go overseas with the king, assaulted a number of men of Salisbury at Fisherton, killing four citizens.[91] This may reflect the impatience with which the troops awaited embarkation from Southampton, or else that this company from Lancashire was relatively late in arriving at the muster point. Salisbury, like many other towns in England, also contributed loans to the king for the expedition, and may also have been a source of troops, although this is a topic on which little has so far been discovered.[92]

---

[90] Bradbury, *Medieval Archer*, p. 138; E101/45/4, m. 1.
[91] Wiltshire County Record Office, Trowbridge, G23/1/1, fol. 54v. For the account of Harington see E101/46/35.
[92] Allmand, *Henry V*, p. 207, cites E403/621 m. 4 for messengers sent to sheriffs and town authorities asking them to raise men. The text of the issue roll makes this clear that this was a commission of array for defence of the realm and not explicitly for the campaign overseas, but it is possible that it was used as an indirect means of raising men for the latter.

Another intriguing source for the campaign comes from the archives of one of the peers involved in it. Thomas Mowbray, the earl marshal (also earl of Norfolk and Nottingham), was invalided home from Harfleur, but we can see from the account of his receiver-general covering the period from Michaelmas 1414 to Michaelmas 1415 the preparation which had been made for the campaign.[93] Here are recorded the many purchases made by the earl's officials, which included a new latrine and tent, as well as an expensive 'cote armour' and horse trapping embroidered with his arms. The provision of victuals both before and during the campaign is instructive, as is also the list of medications which the earl took with him, although arguably the 'electura' against the flux was not as efficacious as might have been hoped. Purchases of armaments are also revealing, especially as it is clear that the earl was providing arrows and bowstrings to his men. The method of recruitment of his retinue is also made apparent. Two knights, Thomas Rokeby and Nicholas Colfox, and 32 esquires undertook to serve the earl, bringing with them a further 12 men-at-arms and 133 archers. In addition, 38 archers offered their service individually. This produced a total of 48 men-at-arms and 171 archers. The earl had actually indented with the crown to serve in person with 4 knights, 45 other men-at-arms and 150 archers, but had been able to recruit more archers than necessary.[94] Several of those serving were members of the earl's own household. In the case of Rokeby, we can also see how messengers were sent to his home in Yorkshire with his wages, and to order him to join the earl at Bosham on 1 July. It is unlikely that a number of similar accounts survive, but further searches in other local and private archive collections would be worth undertaking.

F 1. Indenture (29 April 1415, French)

Translated from PRO, E101/69/484. The original text of this indenture is printed in Rymer, *Foedera*, IV, ii, p. 116. Another translation is given in Nicolas, Appendix, pp. 8–10.[95]

---

93 The original roll is housed at Berkeley Castle, but a copy (Microfilm 12) may be consulted at the Gloucestershire Record Office.

94 There is no surviving indenture for the earl but the warrant for issue survives at E404/31/170, with an entry in the special issue roll, E101/45/5 m. 4d. See also the particulars of account in E101/47/37. The earl and others of his retinue were invalided home, as listed in E101/44/30 m. 8, and in E101/47/38. The remainder of his retinue, headed by Rokeby, went on to Agincourt, and is listed in the Agincourt roll, Nicolas, pp. 337–8.

95 There is also a protection for Sir Thomas Tunstall dated 14 June 1415 (*Annual Report of the Deputy Keeper of the Public Records 44*, p. 560). Tunstall also served on the 1417 expedition in the retinue of Henry, earl of Northumberland (E101/51/2), and in the coronation expedition of Henry VI in 1431, then becoming captain of St Lô and *bailli* of the Cotentin. He was dead by December 1432 (Bibliothèque Nationale, MS français, 26295/876, 26056/1986, Archives Nationales K 63/13/33, 63/19/4).

This indenture, made between the king our sovereign lord on the one hand, and Sir Thomas Tunstall on the other, bears witness that the said Thomas is bound towards our lord the king to serve him for a whole year on the expedition (*voiage*) which the lord king will make, God willing, in his own person, into his duchy of Guienne, or into his kingdom of France. The year will begin on the day of the muster to be made of the men of his retinue at a place which will be informed to him within the month of May next by the lord king, if he is then ready to make the said muster. Thomas shall have with him in the expedition for the whole year six men-at-arms, himself included, and 18 mounted archers. He will take wages for himself of 2 shillings per day. If Thomas goes to the duchy of Guienne in the company of the king, then he shall take as wages for the whole year for each of the men-at-arms, 40 marks, and for each of the archers, 20 marks. In the event that Thomas goes in the company of the king into the kingdom of France, he shall take as wages for each of the men-at-arms, 12*d* per day, and for each of the archers 6*d* per day, during the year. If the expedition is to France, then Thomas shall take the customary regard for himself and his men-at-arms, that is, according to the rate of 100 marks for 30 men-at-arms each quarter. Of the wages for the territory of Guienne, Thomas will be paid for half of the first quarter at the making of this indenture, and the other half when he makes muster ready to go to Guienne, if the King goes there or sends him there. If it happens that, after the muster, the king does not go to his duchy of Guienne, but does go to the territory of France, then Thomas shall be paid as much as shall be owing to him for the said quarter above the sum received by him, as mentioned above, for the wages and regard, both for himself as for the men-at-arms and archers crossing to France.

For surety of payment for the second quarter, the lord king will have delivered to Thomas on 1 June next, as pledge, jewels which, by agreement with Thomas, are worth as much as the value of the wages or wages and regard for that quarter. These jewels Thomas shall be bound to return to the lord king at the time he wishes to redeem then within a year and a half and one month following the receipt of the said jewels. It shall be permissible for Thomas or anyone else to whom he delivers the jewels to dispose of them after the end of the said month at their pleasure without prevention by the king or his heirs, according to the contents of the letters patent under the great seal to be granted to Thomas in this matter.

For the third quarter, Thomas shall be paid for himself and his retinue within six weeks after the beginning of it, according to the rate of the wages or wages and regard for the territory into which they have gone, or happen to be in during the said quarter. With regard to the payment of wages or wages with regard, as the case requires, for the last quarter of the year, if the king, our lord, does not by halfway through the third quarter give such surety to Thomas for the payment as he might reasonably accept, then at the end of the third quarter, Thomas shall be acquitted and discharged towards the lord king of the agreements specified in this present indenture.

Thomas shall be obliged to be ready at the sea coast with his men well mounted, armed and arrayed as appropriate for their rank, to make muster on 1 July next, and later, after their arrival overseas, Thomas will be obliged to muster the men of his retinue before such a person or persons as it may please the lord king to appoint and assign, and as often as Thomas shall be reasonably required to do so. Thomas shall have shipping for himself and his retinue, their horses, harness and provisions, at the expense of the king, and also return shipping, like others of his rank in the expedition. If it happens that Thomas is given orders to the contrary before he crosses the sea, he shall be bound to serve the king wherever it pleases the latter, for the same sum of money, with the said men-at-arms and archers, according to the rate of wages accustomed in the territory to which they shall be ordered by the lord king, except for those who die, if any do, in the mean time.

If it happens that the adversary of France, or any of his sons, nephews, uncles or cousins, or any king of any kingdom or his lieutenant, shall be captured in the expedition by Thomas or by any of his retinue, the lord king shall have the Adversary or other person of the ranks mentioned above who are captured, and shall make reasonable composition with Thomas or with the person who has effected the capture. With reference to other profits of gains of war the lord king shall have the third part of the gains of Thomas as well as the third of a third part of the gains of the men of his retinue gained during the expedition, relating to gains of prisoners, booty, money, all gold, silver and jewels worth more than 10 marks.

In witness of these matters, Thomas has affixed his seal on the half of the indenture remaining with the king. Given at Westminster 29 April the third year of our lord king.

F 2. Warrant for issue (29 April 1415, French)

Translated from E404/31/181. Printed in Rymer, *Foedera*, IV, ii, p. 116. The name 'Thomas Tunstall chivaler' is written vertically on the dorse. There is a filing hole in the centre of the document and parallel cuts in the top corners for the seal tag.

Henry, by the grace of God, king of England and France and lord of Ireland, to the treasurer and chamberlains of our Exchequer, greeting. We order you that having seen the indenture of our dear and faithful knight, Thomas Tunstall, by which he is retained before us to render us war service with 6 men-at-arms and 18 archers in the expedition [*viage*] which we will make shortly, God willing, that you make payment to him of what he should have and take of us according to the effect and content of the indenture aforesaid. Given under our privy seal at Westminster, 29 April, in the third year of our reign.

F 3. Issue roll (6 June 1415, Latin)

Translated from PRO, E101/45/5, m. 4d, special issue roll for the Easter term, 3 Henry V.

Thursday 6 June, to Sir Thomas Tunstall, retained by the king by indenture made between the king and Thomas for one year to go with the king in person to the parts of France or elsewhere, in money delivered into his own hands for his wages and those of five men-at-arms and 18 archers retained along with the said Thomas to proceed with the king towards the aforementioned area, by brief of privy seal amongst the orders of this term, as appears by the other part of an indenture, made between Thomas, earl of Arundel, treasurer of England, and Thomas Tunstall for the sum noted above, which indenture is retained in the Exchequer of Receipt of the King. £51.4.8*d*, for which he will account.

F 4. Sub-indenture (1 May 1415, French)

Translated from PRO, C47/2/49/7.

This indenture made between Thomas, earl of Dorset, admiral of England and Guienne on the one hand, and John Le Boteler,[96] esquire, on the other, bears witness that John is retained and will remain with the earl to serve him on an expedition (*viage*) that our sovereign king will make shortly in his own person with the grace of God towards his duchy of Guienne or into his kingdom of France for a whole year, the said year to begin on the day of the musters to be made by the men of his retinue in the place which will be appointed by our king. If he is ready to make his muster he will be informed of the place within the month of May. And the said John will have for the whole year and for the expedition for himself and for two men-at-arms (*lances*), himself included, and 6 archers with

---

[96] Identification is difficult here because of a common surname which can exist in various spellings. A John Boteler took out letters of attorney for the campaign (*Annual Report of the Deputy Keeper of the Public Records 44*, p. 569). A John Butler is found in the Agincourt roll in the company of Robert Alderton (Nicolas, p. 349). A William Boteler, but not, it seems, a John, is serving in the garrison of Harfleur under the earl of Dorset in March 1416 (E101/47/39).

him, adequately mounted, armed and arrayed as is appropriate to the rank of each of them, taking for himself and for the other man-at-arms 12*d* per day and for each of his archers 6*d* per day in the case of going into the kingdom of France, and for his regard for the whole expedition what is due to him at the rate of 100 marks for 30 men-at-arms per quarter. And in the case that our lord the king or the said earl go into the duchy of Guienne, the said John should take for his own person and for his other said man-at-arms 40 marks per annum, and for each archer 20 marks during the said year. And for the first quarter of the year, John will be paid in hand the half of the wages ordered for the expedition in Guienne and the other half after they have made their muster ready to cross over there where our lord the king goes or will send the said earl, and in the event that they do not cross to the territory of Guienne and go into France he will have rebated from the last payment for the quarter what he had received in excess for the wages (assigned for the said expedition and in the second quarter he will have payment or agreement in wages or jewels as the said earl has from the king)[97] within the 15 June next following, and for the third quarter John will be paid or have agreement for his wages within 6 weeks after the beginning of the said quarter, according to the rate of the wages which he should have for the territory into which the said earl goes , and in the case that John has no surety for wages from the earl which he is able to agree by half way through the said third quarter, then for the rest of this quarter he will be held as quit and discharged to go wherever it seems best to him. And the said John will be obliged to make muster of himself and of his men-at-arms and archers every time the earl informs him reasonably, either this side of the sea or overseas, and before anyone whom it pleases the earl to appoint and in any place. In addition John is obliged to be ready at the sea to make his muster of himself and his men-at-arms and archers on 1 July next following before whomever it pleases our lord the king to appoint. And John will have for the expedition adequate shipping and return shipping for himself and for his men-at-arms and archers, their horses and all their other goods and harness, that is to say, for himself and for his other man-at-arms each 3 horses, and for each archer, one horse, and in the case that the earl is countermanded by the king before his passage overseas after the first payment, John shall be obliged to pay service to the earl for the sum of money he has received wherever it pleases the king to send the earl with all his number of men-at-arms and archers according to the accustomed rate of wages in the territories where they are sent. The earl will have the third of all manner of gains of war which John gains, and the third part of the third of all those of his company, whether man-at-arms or archer, whether in persons, money, jewels and all other kinds of goods whatever condition or state

---

97 The bracketed section is a later addition.

they are. And in the case that John or any of this company taken any prisoner such as a king, son of a king and others of the blood royal, chieftains or other great captains, they are always obliged to surrender them and deliver them to the earl, as they are required to do by him or his deputies, taking for them reasonable recompense. In witness of which the earl and John have put their seals interchangeably on the indentures, Given on 1 May in the third year of the redoubtable King Henry the fifth since the conquest.

F 5. Letter of Henry V to the mayor and aldermen of the city of London (22 September 1415, French)

Translated from the text in J. Delpit, *Collection générale des documents français qui se trouvent en Angleterre* (Paris, 1847), CCCXXIX, pp. 216–17 from the Letter Book I of the City of London, and calendared in *Calendar of Letter Books of the City of London, Letter Book I*, ed. R.R. Sharpe (London, 1909), p. 131. Note that Delpit gives the date incorrectly as 12 September.

From the king.

Most dear, faithful and well loved, we salute you notifying you for your consolation that we are in very good health as regards our person, thanks be to God who has accorded this to us. After our arrival over here, we came before our town of Harfleur on Saturday 17 August last and laid siege to it as we have already written to you earlier by other letters, by the good diligence of our faithful lieges, who are presently in our company, and by the force and employment of our canons and other ordnance. The men who were in the town made much effort to have divers agreements with us, but nonetheless we made the decision to make an assault on the town on Wednesday 18 September. Those in the town realised this and made even greater moves than before to have agreement with us, and in order to avoid the shedding of human blood on both sides, we were inclined to hear their offer. We gave them reply on this and sent them the final expression of our will to which they agreed, for which we give praise to God for we believed that they might not have agreed so easily to our demand. On the same Wednesday there came out of the town at our command the sire de Gaucourt, the sire d'Estouteville, the sire de Hacqueville and other lords and knights who had the government of the town and handed over hostages. All of them, the lords, knights and the hostages, of whom some were lords and knights and other important burgesses, swore on the body of Our Lord that they would make full delivery of our town, and submit their persons and goods to our mercy without condition unless by Sunday next by one o'clock in the afternoon they were rescued by battle given to us by our adversary of France or his eldest son, the dauphin. Regarding the latter, we gave our letters of safe conduct to the sire de Hacqueville and others to the number of 12 persons to go to our adversary and his son to tell them of the agreement. The sire de Hacqueville and the others in his company returned on the day at 8am to our town without any rescue being offered by our adversary, his son nor of any other on their side, and the keys of the said town were fully delivered and handed over into our hand; and all those within the town submitted to our mercy without any condition, as said above praise be to Our Creator. We have placed in our town our beloved uncle the earl of Dorset and have made him captain of the same with an adequate garrison of men, of all kinds. We wish that you make humble thanks to Our Almighty Lord for this news, and hope by the fine power and good labour and diligence of our faithful people overseas to do our duty to achieve as soon as possible our rights in this area. We also wish you to let us know from time to time how it goes with you. May the Lord have you in his keeping. Given under our signet before our town of Harfleur, 22 September.

F 6. Extracts from the records of the city of Bordeaux (French)

Translated from *Archives Municipales de Bordeaux, vol. 4. Registres de la Jurade: délibérations de 1414 à 1416 et de 1420 à 1422* (Bordeaux, 1883).

Meeting of 7 July (pp. 193–4)

Delivered to my most honourable lords, the lieutenant and *jurats* of the city of Bordeaux.

My very honourable lords, I commend myself to you as humbly as I can. May it please you to know that the king wants to write to you to send two *brides* [trebuchets operated by a bridle?] and other things, for which purpose I do not know at present. What I do know is that when I had acquitted my duty towards the king and desired to go to Plymouth to deliver my other necessities, I met my lord of Dorset who told me to stay because the king wished to charge me to go to Bordeaux with letters and that I should take this charge to wherever the king will be. And if you wish to hear the news, the canons and *brides* are being loaded every day, and all the other equipment is greater than man can say. Twenty-two thousand mariners are in wages in the rolls to effect the passage of the king and his company. See if the number rises. Take account that they will arrive overseas with the intention of staying for summer and winter, for which they are making a great provision of victuals. All the mills of England are busy grinding flour from Holland. There ought to arrive 700 ships, and later, the wages. It is also said that the son of the king of Portugal is coming with a large company of galleys and men. Another contract has been made which has been three years in the making. It is not merchants who have made it but noble courtiers, and I dare not write to you about it. By the grace of God, it will be good for us. The duke of Alençon and the other French lords, the ambassadors, are to arrive in England. But the king has decided that they will not come to *Ronchestre* [probably Winchester], so that they will not be the cause of the king's preparations being disclosed. The truce is extended by one month. Between now and the end of the truce, the king will be ready, God willing.

With the grace of God I shall come with Sir John Tiptoft and bring you good news. It is ordered that he shall be seneschal. For the honour of God, may you collect the hearth tax and apply it to everyone as is right and proper and as you know how. Similarly, please see to it that the *brides* are ready so that the ships in which we will come can take them as soon as possible, so that the king will see that you are not being half-hearted in doing what he has ordered you to do. By such means you will be able to store up credit with him.

Please, my honourable lords, receive my little company which I commend to you. The true son of God hold you in His holy guard, and give you good and long life. Written at London 8 June, by your humble servant Benedict Espina.

Meeting of 27 July (p. 217)

To our dear and good friend Benedict Espina

Dear and well loved friend, know that we have received from you on 8 July a letter on the passage of the king, our sovereign lord (God by His holy mercy and pity keep him and govern him as his most noble royal person has need, likewise us and his other faithful subjects), containing in addition several other matters, for which news we thank you. Dear and loved friend, know that one of the engines is completely ready, and we want to act in such a way that it may be ready as soon as possible. And then, when the king, our lord aforementioned, wants this or anything else done, we, with the grace of God, will be ready to obey his orders as all true lieges are bound to obey their natural and sovereign lord. And when with the grace of God you have arrived here on the ship of which you have written to us, the engines will be completely ready to load aboard at the pleasure of the lord king. We draw great pleasure from the order which my lord of Dorset has given you on behalf of the king, our lord, for you to stay here. It is said that the king, our lord, had crossed, and for that reason we had postponed sending to him what we wished to send as commanded on other occasions. So in order to have certain news, it is ordered that the balenier [a type of ship] should go there. We pray you that you will work so that as soon as possible we have him here, for on receipt of certain news, what has not been done will be accomplished with God's grace.

And for love of you we have your house in our charge, and anything else that we may do for you, we will gladly. And God etc. Written at Bordeaux, 27 July. The mayor and *jurats* of the city of Bordeaux.

Meeting of 20 August 1415 (p. 232)

To our very dear, faithful and well loved mayor and jurats of our city of Bordeaux. From the king.

Most dear, faithful and well loved, we greet you. Since we are presently set, by the aid of God, to transport ourselves overseas in order to recover our right and heritage there, we will and pray you that, immediately after receipt of these letters, you order our beloved Benedict Espina of our city of Bordeaux to be sent to us, when you may know the place where we land over there, with two of the best engines called *brides*, and a master carpenter who is suitable and acceptable for overseeing there engines. May our lord have you in his keeping. Given under our signet at our palace of Westminster on [gap] June.

(p. 256) The next day, 1 October, towards the hour of vespers, there arrived Janicot de la Sala, master of a ship of Bayonne, who presented at the castle of Ombrières to some of the lords of the *jurade* a letter sent by the king, our sovereign lord, the contents of which are as follows:

To our very dear, faithful and much loved mayor, *jurats* and commune of our city of Bordeaux

From the king. Very dear, faithful and much loved, we send you frequent greeting, informing you that we are presently before the town of Harfleur in our land of Normandy, around which we have laid siege, with ourselves and all those of our company being in good health and disposition. For this, in all humility, we give thanks to our lord God the Almighty, hoping that, by His grace, He will give us, in pursuit of our right, the fulfilment of our desire and undertaking, to His pleasure, and for the honour and comfort of us and you, and of all our other faithful lieges and subjects. To this end we shall do our duty, so that, with God's help, our enemies will be henceforward less powerful to cause you trouble and harm than they have been in the past. We wish and pray you that you will offer all assistance to our dear and loyal knight John Tiptoft, our seneschal of Guienne, in resisting the malice of the enemy on your coasts, which will redound to the benefit and salvation of our land overseas. We also ask you to send us as quickly as possible such a quantity of wine and other victuals as you can provide from your area, for the refreshment of us and our men, without failing in any way, for the sake of the complete confidence we have in you. We reassure those who bring it to us that they will receive full satisfaction in payment. Most dear and loyal, and beloved, please let us know, as soon as you conveniently can, the state of our land of Guienne and of yourselves. May God have you in his keeping. Given under our signet at the said siege on 3 September.[98]

(pp. 257–8) Later, on the next day, 2 October, Janicot de la Sala delivered to the clerk of the town a letter sent from Jean de Bordiu to the mayor and *jurats*, of which the contents follow.

To my honourable lords, the mayor and *jurats* of the town of Bordeaux, my good lords and friends.

My honourable lords, I commend myself to your good lordships, and inform you that the king our lord has written to you his letters telling you of his good fortune. Although at present the fields are providing an adequate supply of corn, this cannot, however, meet the future requirements of the great army which is with him, and which increases every day. And thus I am informed that he would be pleased to have, for his money, a quantity of wine of between 500 and 700 tuns, as you will see from his letters which he showed to me, and which I sent to you by Janicot de la Sala, bearer of these present letters. My lords, do make every effort to please him, for he will look kindly on you in his heart, and has great confidence in you, and in the city [of Bordeaux], and it is his intention to come thither before he returns to England.

Honourable lords, please know that the town of Harfleur, with the aid of the Holy Spirit, will be in the king's hands before 8 days at most. For now it is well and truly breached on the landward side and on two flanks, and everything destroyed inside. Our king cut off the water supply before Montivilliers, which they had retained so that it could not run into the sea. He has had made great engines and cunning instruments for the protection of his people, and in order to take the town. And when he has taken it, I have heard it is not his intention to enter the town but to stay in the field. In a short while after the capture of the town, he intends to go to Montivilliers, and thence to Dieppe, afterwards to Rouen, and then to Paris.

Pray to God for him, for His great goodwill, with the prayers of his good people, will help him conquer what is his by right. Please you to write to him, and especially to my lord of Dorset, constable of the host, who is second in command. And help him with whatever food he needs, for which he will pay. He and his men are loudly complaining that there is no way of paying; but the king has great confidence in him. And so in all matters please you to keep him in the friendship of the city.

My lords, I am your good servant so I am answerable for my actions on your behalf. As you have heard tell, I am one of his doctors ordered to go

---

[98] Calendared in *Signet Letters of Henry IV and Henry V*, ed. J.L. Kirby (London, 1978), p. 197.

with him wherever he goes with his household and retinue. Therefore send me orders as soon as you possibly can. And I pray that you have me confirmed in my benefices, and that you guard me against wrongs and use of force if perchance there be anyone who in my absence wants to use arms against me. For I have a lord and master who will preserve my rights according to justice.

I know of no other reason to write to you at present, but I pray to God that He will keep you in His grace. Written in the camp near to Harfleur, 3 September. Yours, John de Bordiu, doctor of laws and archdeacon of Médoc.

F 7. Letter from William Bardolf, lieutenant of Calais, to John, duke of Bedford, keeper of England during Henry V's absence on campaign (7 October 1415, French)

Translated from *Foedera*, IV, ii, p. 147 (fifteenth-century text in British Library, Cotton Caligula D V).

To the most high and mighty prince and my most honourable and gracious lord, as wholly, affectionately and obediently as in any way that I know best and am able I recommend myself to your highness, good and gracious lord, giving thanks most humbly and often, as much as I am able, both on my own behalf as well as on behalf of all my companions in the March [of Calais], that it has pleased you in your nobility to have so dearly and tenderly taken to heart the well being, ease and prosperity of all of us and of the said Marches, by writing recently your honourable and gracious letters, and also by sending here into these parts the most honourable and wise esquires the sheriff of Kent, the lieutenant of the castle of Dover and the victualler of that town, your commissioners in this respect, my beloved and most dear companions, to find out how things were and in what state, the truth of which I signified and reported to them orally and to your nobility in obedient and humble manner by giving them knowledge both in writing and otherwise. By the relation of which esquires your will is well understood that we must make the most hard war that we can against the French, enemies of our most feared noble lord, in order to prevent those on the frontier crossing or advancing near to where he now is in person, to which purpose I received on the same day your letters of privy seal, the content of which commanded me, as it pleases God, to have carried out and performed at this time with all our power, diligence and strength, without failure.

Also, most high and mighty prince and my most honourable and gracious lord, as for news of this area, may it please you lordship to know that several good friends, who have come to this town and the Marches both from the areas of France and from Flanders, have told and reported to me clearly that, without doubt, the king, our lord, will have battle with his adversaries within fifteen days next coming at the very latest. And that also, along with the others, the duke of Lorraine will assemble very soon, according to what they say, with a good 50,000 men, and that once they are all assembled they will be no less that 100,000 or indeed, even more. Also they say for certain that a noble knight accompanied by 500 lances had been ordered to wait on the frontier under the governance of the sire de la Biefville in defence of the marches on the part of the enemy, and that because of that, most high and mighty prince and my most honourable and gracious lord, it seems to me that I would not acquit myself well if I did not certify to your highness what information had come to me. That is why I am writing now on these matters so that your noble wisdom will have knowledge of them and will order what seems to be best to be done.

May our Lord God, most high and mighty prince and my most gracious lord, have you now and henceforth in His holy protection, and give you long and joyful life, perfect health in mind and body, and all your wishes and desires, for His good grace. Written at Calais the 7th of this month of October. Your humble and obedient servant, W. Bardolf, lieutenant at Calais.

F 8. Licence to return home from Harfleur (5 October 1415, French)

Translated from PRO, E101/45/14.[99]

This licence is written on paper about 4 inches square, and has the marks of a red seal in the bottom centre. The names of those it applied to are provided on a small piece of paper attached by a paper tag. The end of the tag is secured under the seal impression. Seven names are given, headed by Ralph Shirley 'with one page' and John Huse 'dead'.

*

The king wills and grants licence (*congé*) to all those persons whose names are detailed in a schedule attached to this bill to go to England without hindrance. In witness of this the king has had put to this bill his signet by the chamberlain and steward of his household, 5 October 1415.

---

[99] Cited in French in Allmand, *Henry V,* n. 61, p. 81, with a facsimile in the frontispiece to J. Otway-Ruthven, *The King's Secretary and the Signet Office in the XVth Century* (Cambridge, 1939).

F 9. Discussions and decisions concerning the settlement of accounts for the Agincourt campaign (6 March 1417, French)

British Library, Cotton Cleopatra F III, fol. 148, printed in H. Nicolas, *Proceedings and Ordinances of the Privy Council*, vol. 2 (London, 1834), pp. 225–7.

Minutes of Council Saturday 6 March 1417.

1.   First that it should be declared whether the wages for the first quarter should begin on the first day of July in the third year of the reign, or else on the day musters were made.

The king's reply – wages and regards for the first quarter should begin on 8 July.

2.   Item, whether for this first quarter the absences (*vacatz*) of those dying and also those who had licence to return to England because of illness or other reasons should be allowed or not.

The king wishes that they have allowance for the first quarter, by the oath of those making account.

3.   Item, whether those making account for the first quarter whether for those who are still living or for those who are dead, should have allowance by their oath or by any other means.

The king wishes that the first quarter be allowed to both the living and the dead by oath of those making account.

4.   Item, whether those left for the safekeeping of the town of Harfleur from the time of their entry therein should be given allowance for their wages and regards as expressed in the indentures or otherwise for wages only, and also whether such allowance be made by their oath or by testimony of the captain of the place or of his lieutenant.

They should have allowance from the day they departed from England until they entered the town of Harfleur by their oath and by testimony of the captain there or of his lieutenant of wages and regards as expressed in the indentures.

5.   Item whether those accounting for men killed at the battle of Agincourt should have allowed to them the whole of the second quarter or only to the day of their death.

They should be allowed as the others are who are still living.

6. Item whether those who came to Calais with the king should be allowed for the whole of the second quarter or else for eight days after return shipping (*reskippeson*) had been delivered to them according to the content of the indentures.

They should be allowed for eight days after the arrival of the king at Dover.

Item that it should be declared what allowance those should have who were ready to depart on the expedition (*viage*) and who because of lack of shipping had to remain in England.

The king does not wish this.

And whether it pleases the king that Sir Walter Hungerford's account for the expedition should be accepted and that he should have allowance by his oath, and whether the order of this account is found by the king to be good and suitable, and if so, whether it pleases him that a similar order should be observed in the case of others making account for the expedition.

And also to know what should be done about those who were on their passage but then countermanded by the king.

Allowance should be made for them and their retinues who crossed with the king.

F 10. Petition of Thomas Hostell (temp. Henry VI, Middle English)

From *Original Letters Illustrative of English History*, ed. H. Ellis, second series, vol. 1 (London, 1827), pp. 95–6, from British Library, Additional MS 4603, no. 100.

To the king our sovereign lord

Beseeches meekly your poor liegeman and humble petitioner Thomas Hostell that in consideration of the service which he performed to your noble progenitors of full blessed memory King Henry the fourth and King Henry the fifth, on whose soul God have mercy, being at the siege of Harfleur, there smitten with a springolt [crossbow bolt] through the head, losing one eye and having his cheek bone broken, and also at the battle of Agincourt, and later at the taking of the carracks on the sea, there with a *gadde* of iron having his coat of plates broken asunder, and being sorely hurt, maimed and wounded; as a result of which he is much enfeebled and weakened, and now being of great age has fallen into poverty, being much in debt and unable to help himself, having not the means whereby he can be sustained or relieved save only by the gracious almsgiving of other men; and being for his said service not yet recompensed nor rewarded, may it please your high and excellent grace, having considered the above situation, to relieve and refresh your said poor petitioner at your discretion, by granting alms for the reverence of God and as an act of charity; in return he will pray devoutly for the souls of your said noble progenitors and for your most high and noble estate.

F 11. Petition of Thomas Strickland (1424, French)

Translated from Rymer, *Foedera*, IV, ii, p. 106.

To the king our sovereign lord and to the most gracious lords of the council, petitions most humbly a poor esquire Thomas Strickland,[100] formerly bearer of the banner of St George of the most noble King Henry the fifth, whom God absolve. May it please your good grace to consider the long service which the said suppliant has done for the late king overseas, right from his arrival at Harfleur, at the battle of Agincourt, and subsequently until the time that the city of Rouen was taken, and that the said suppliant has received no reward for his labour on the day of the battle, no further payment of his wages save for a half year, and how at present the said suppliant is discovered to be arrears in his account at the Exchequer for the sum of £14 4s 10½d for a certain silver vessel which is broken and which had been put in pledge to him by the late king, the which vessel the suppliant had sold and the money thus gained he had spent in the service of the late king. May it please your most wise discretions, for the reverence of God, and for the merit of the soul of the king, to grant to the said suppliant the said £14 4s 10½d, as reward for his service and in part payment of the wages due to him by the said lord king, and on this to grant sufficient warrant directed to the Treasurer and Barons of the Exchequer to discharge the said suppliant and to make him quit in the Exchequer towards the king for the £14 4s 10½d, and this for God and by way of charity.

[On 14 February 1424, this petition was granted by the Council and a warrant sent to the Exchequer officials to exonerate him of the sum he owed on his account for the Agincourt campaign.]

---

100 Strickland had taken out a protection for the campaign (*Annual Report of the Deputy Keeper of the Public Records*, 44, p. 566), and is listed in the Agincourt roll (Nicolas, p. 349). He crossed again in 1417 in the company of Sir John Neville (E101/51/2).

F 12. Case in Chancery concerning prisoners taken at Agincourt (temp. Henry V or VI, French)

Select Cases in Chancery 1364–1471, ed. W.P. Baildon (Selden Society, 10, 1896), item 112, p. 110.

To the right reverend Father in God, the bishop of Winchester, chancellor of England.

Most humbly beseech your poor servants, if you please, John Craven and Simon Irby,[101] that whereas they took certain prisoners at the battle of Agincourt, so it is that one William Buckton, esquire,[102] has by force and wrongfully taken the said prisoners from the said supplicants, and against their will and assent has ransomed them and delivered them up without any satisfaction made thereof to the king of what belongs to him, to the great damage and prejudice of the right of the same our most sovereign lord the king and to the utter undoing of the poor estates of the said suppliants if they do not have your most helpful aid and lordship now. And whereas the said suppliants have heard that a certain quantity of money, amounting to nearly the sum of 200 marks, part of the ransom of the said prisoners, is yet in the hands of one Maude Salvayn, the wife of the treasurer of Calais. May it please your right reverend paternity in God to grant to the said suppliants a writ directed to the said treasurer of Calais firmly charging and enjoining him that the said sum, being in the hands of his said wife, may be kept, and delivered to no one until it be tried by right and law to whom it belongs, and that our lord the king may have what is due to him. And further, of your most abundant grace to cause to come before your most gracious presence the said William Buckton to declare to you the names of the said prisoners. For God and in way of charity.

F 13. Writ concerning cote armours (2 July 1417, Latin)

From Rymer, *Foedera*, IV, ii, p. 201, with summary in *Calendar of Close Rolls 1413–19*, p. 433.

The king to the sheriff of Hampshire, greeting.

Whereas as we are informed, divers men who on expeditions made before this date assumed for themselves arms and tunics of arms called cote

---

[101] I have been unable to find further evidence of their service on the campaign of 1415. Irby crossed again on the June 1421 expedition in the company of Sir Geoffrey Hilton (E101/50/1). Craven was a member of the garrison of Poissy in 1423 (Archives Nationales, K62/7/2).

[102] Buckton had a long career in France, holding several captaincies including Bayeux and Lisieux, and the lieutenancy of Rouen under John, Lord Talbot.

armours, where neither they nor their ancestors had used such arms in times gone by, and who propose to make use of them in our present expedition [1417], God willing, and although the Almighty disposes his grace in natural matters according to His will, equally to the rich and poor, we, however, wishing that each of our lieges aforesaid should be dealt with and held according to the demands of his rank, order you that in every place within your bailiwick where by our writ we have previously ordered musters to be announced, you cause it to be proclaimed publicly on our behalf that no one of whatever status, rank or condition he might be assumes for himself such arms or tunics of arms unless he possesses or should possess the same either by ancestral right or by the grant of someone who had adequate power to make such a grant. And that he should demonstrate to persons assigned or to be assigned by us on the day of the muster by whose grant he holds these arms or tunics or arms, excepting those who bore arms with us at the battle of Agincourt, under the penalty of not being admitted to proceed on the expedition aforesaid within the number of the man by whom he is retained, and of the loss of his wages received by him for the said expedition, and also of the stripping off and breaking up of the said arms and tunics of arms called cote armours at the time of his mustering, if they shall have been displayed or found on him. And this in no way are you to default upon. Witness the king at the city of Salisbury, 2 July.

By the king. Similar writs directed to the sheriffs of Wiltshire, Sussex, Dorset under the same date.

F 14. Statute concerning payment for the Agincourt campaign (1423, French)

Translated from 1 Henry VI, c.5, from *Statutes of the Realm*, vol. 2, p. 215.

Item at the supplication of the lords and captains who are still alive who indented with the gracious King Henry, father to the present king, in all his wars, and also of the executors of those who had been commended to God who had indented with the King's father, made by their petition delivered to this parliament, the king, with the assent of all the lords spiritual and temporal and also of all the commons present in this parliament, wills and grants that the thirds and thirds of thirds of all kinds of gains, gained by means of war, belonging to the said king, the father, on the day of his death, as well as of prisoners captured and of other gains of war, may be deducted and rebated by lawful account in the king's Exchequer from the sums owed to them in wages by the king the father, according to the terms of indentures made on this. Provided always that what is found due on the said account by the said accountants in addition to their wages, should be paid to them on the said account, so that the said accountants, their heirs, executors and land tenants after the said accounts and agreement made, should be quit and discharged forever. And moreover, the king wills and ordains that with the assent of the lords and commons abovesaid, those to whom the king, the father, had pledged jewels and other things should be before the council of the king before the feast of St John the Baptist next following with the same things and jewels. And in case they are not then satisfied of their duties in that behalf, or within half a year after the same feast, then they, after the said half year, shall have all the said jewels and things in peace and without prevention by the king, paying to the king the value by which the same jewels and things exceed what they had in pledge, unless they be ancient jewels of the crown. And that they, and their heirs, land tenants, executors and each of them shall be and be quit and discharged against the king of the same jewels (with the exception of ancient jewels of the crown) and things, after the half year, forever.

F 15. Petition to parliament of Humphrey, duke of Gloucester, and Thomas, earl of Salisbury, concerning payment for the Agincourt campaign (October 1427, French)

Translated from *Rotuli Parliamentorum*, IV, p. 320.

16. Item another petition was presented in the same parliament by the illustrious prince Lord Humphrey, duke of Gloucester, and Thomas, earl of Salisbury, the tenor of which follows and is thus:

To the king our sovereign lord, Humphrey, duke of Gloucester, and Thomas, earl of Salisbury humbly request; whereas recently they were individually retained with the most noble King Henry, your father, whom God absolve, on several occasions to cross with his most noble person to his realm of France with certain numbers of men-at-arms and archers, and in particular on 8 July in the third year of his reign, at which time they each had their wages for the first quarter of the said retaining, and as guarantee of the payment for the second quarter of their retaining they each had from the said late king, and by his command, on 1 June then next following various jewels as pledge for their individual wages for the same quarter, the said jewels to be returned to your said most noble father whenever he might wish to pay them, within one and a half years and one month after the receipt of the same jewels. And otherwise, that it would be permitted after the end of the said month to them and to others to whom the said jewels had been given by the said suppliants to dispose of the said jewels at their pleasure without being prevented by your said father or by his heirs: within which second quarter and after the battle of

Agincourt, your said most noble father with several persons from his retinue and from the retinue of the said suppliants returned to his realm of England, that is, 48 days before the end of the same quarter, as a result of which the officials in your exchequer claimed to deduct the wages of the said suppliants and each of their soldiers for the said 48 days, notwithstanding that the said suppliants have each paid their soldiers for the full wages of the second quarter and that they were then prepared to remain in the realm of France in accordance with the terms of their retaining. And although various notable sums are still in arrears for the said retinues and are owed to each of the said suppliants both for the second quarter and for other times beyond the value of the said jewels, and more than the payments and loans and thirds and thirds of thirds and other profits of war individually taken, received and gained by the said suppliants and by their soldiers during the wars in the regions of France, legal action is taken and sued separately out of your said Exchequer against the said suppliants for them each to make and tender account and answer both for the said jewels and for their retaining, and payments and loans, and for the aforesaid thirds and thirds of thirds gained by the said suppliants and their soldiers during the aforesaid wars; because of which the same suppliants and each of them are greatly troubled and charged in important issues put forwards and returned against each of them in your said Exchequer, to their very great individual loss and damage unless they receive your most gracious favour in this regard.

May it please your most gracious lordship to consider the foregoing, and that there are many notable sums of money owed to each of the said suppliants for their wages of war, beyond the value of the said jewels, and of all the aforesaid receipts and payments, loans and other profits. And thereupon, by the advice and assent of the lords spiritual and temporal and the commons of your realm assembled in this present parliament, to grant, ordain and establish by the authority of the same parliament that the said suppliants and each of them, their heirs, executors and land-tenants, shall be quit and completely discharged towards you, most sovereign lord, and your heirs, of all kinds of jewels having been taken, had and received by them, or by either of them, for any of the abovesaid reasons; and of all kinds of loans, receipts, rewards and payments, and of the thirds and thirds of thirds and of all other profits of war, having been taken, had and received by each of them, and of the value of the same; and of all things, matters and causes which may fall or happen to the said suppliants or to each of them for any aforesaid reason, matter or retaining. And that the said suppliants and each of them, their heirs, executors and land-tenants from this day forward should be discharged of this, of every kind of account, and of every action of account, detinue and other action whatsoever; and of all that which might be adjudged by you for any abovesaid matter or cause; notwithstanding the fact that express mention is not made in this petition of the quantity of the said jewels, or of the value of them, or of the aforesaid profits of war, or of the loans, receipts, rewards or payments, or thirds, or thirds of thirds, or any special or general profits of war, nor the fact that express mention is not made in the said petition at the time of the retaining of the said supplicants, or of either of them, or how much the said supplicants have, should have, or how much either of them has or should have from the gift or grant of you, most sovereign lord, or any of your progenitors kings of England, or any of your ancestors; or the fact that express mention is not made here in this petition of the number of the soldiers retained with the said supplicants, or either of them, for the aforesaid wars; or any statute or ordinance made to the contrary. And this for God and by way of charity.

Be it remembered that this petition was read in the present parliament in the presence of the lords spiritual and temporal assembled in the same and – having had mature deliberation thereupon, and having diligently considered the motives and reasons specified in the same, considering also the many extraordinary and fruitful services expended in many ways for Lord Henry late king of England, father of the present lord king, by the illustrious and mighty prince Lord Humphrey, duke of Gloucester, the aforesaid most beloved uncle of the present lord king, at his great cost and expense, overseas, particularly in the realm of France and the duchy of Normandy, both in the siege and capture of his town of Harfleur and in his auspicious battle of Agincourt; considering moreover how afterwards the town and castle of Cherbourg and 32 castles, fortified towns and fortresses in the aforesaid regions, having been victoriously captured through the laudable labours and services of the same duke, were brought to the obedience and allegiance of the aforesaid late king; and that the same late king, on his last crossing towards the aforesaid regions, retained and appointed the aforesaid duke to proceed towards the same regions with 100 lances and the archers pertaining to the same; and although the same duke crossed to those regions with his retinue of this sort, except for four or six lances at most, who, on account of lack of time, he was unable to provide, the aforesaid late king did not permit any guarantee or reward to be allocated to the aforesaid duke for himself or his aforesaid retinue from the time of the aforesaid retaining, save from the time when the same duke mustered the complete and total number of the said 100 lances with their archers at the town of Dreux, at the very great expense of the duke; having been similarly mindful of and considering the indefatigable labours, not to mention the notable and most excellent services, displayed and exerted by the noble and mighty Lord Thomas, earl of Salisbury, beloved kinsman of our same present lord king, not only for our aforesaid present king, but also for his late father King Henry, in the tumult of the wars of the same kings in the said overseas regions for many years, both by fullness of counsel and strenuousness of arms, not without extreme danger of his person, but also to his excessive costs and expenses, both in the towns of Cravant and of Verneuil and in many other various ways: and to the end that the same earl will be encouraged and prompted with great fervour to more fruitful services of this kind to be performed henceforth for the present lord king in those parts, by which favour he will feel himself to be cherished, – the lord king, with the assent of the lords spiritual and temporal, and the commons of the realm of England assembled in the present parliament, has granted, ordained and decreed by the authority of the aforesaid parliament that the aforesaid duke and earl, and each one of them, and their heirs, executors and land-tenants, shall be quit and completely exonerated towards the said present lord king and his heirs of all kinds of jewels taken, had and received by them themselves or either of them, for any reason specified in the aforesaid petition: and of all kinds of loans, receipts, rewards and payments, and thirds, and thirds of thirds, and of all other profits of war taken, had and received by each of them themselves, and of the value of the same, and of all other things, matters and causes which might fall or pertain to the aforesaid duke and earl or to either of them for any cause, matter or retaining specified in the aforesaid petition. And that the same duke and earl, and each of them, and their heirs, executors and land-tenants shall henceforth be quit of all accounts, and of whatever action of account, detinue, and of other actions whatsoever: and of all that which might be adjudged by the aforesaid lord king on any aforesaid matter or cause; notwithstanding the fact that express mention is not made in the aforesaid petition of the quantity of the said jewels, or of the value of them, or of the aforesaid wages of war, or of the loans, receipts, rewards or payments, or thirds, or thirds of thirds, or any special or general profits of war; nor at the time of the retaining of the aforesaid duke and earl, or either of them, or of the grants or gifts made to the aforesaid duke and earl, or to either of them, by the aforesaid lord king, or any of his progenitors kings of England, or any of his predecessors, nor of the number of soldiers retained with the aforesaid duke and earl, or either of them, for the aforesaid wars, or any statute or ordinance made to the contrary. Provided always that the aforesaid duke for himself, and the aforesaid earl for himself, will remit and relax to the aforesaid late king and his executors, and also to our present lord king, each and every debt which either of them are owed by the aforesaid late king or his executors by reason of such wars or retaining by the said late king in such wars for the time of the same late king. And moreover, if within the next three years after the end of this parliament our same lord king pays or causes to be paid to the aforesaid duke or his executors, or to the said earl or his executors, each and every sums of money for the aforesaid jewels which have been pledged to the same duke and earl, or to either of them, for the reasons specified in the aforesaid petition; and also makes satisfaction to them or to either of them of the sums, costs and expenses expended and paid by the duke and earl themselves for the redemption and return of the same jewels, as the same duke and earl, or either of them, by their oath, or their sufficient deputy may wish or be able to affirm in this regard; then both the aforesaid duke and earl will be bound to give back and deliver each and every one of the jewels pledged to themselves, as said above, and remaining and being in their custody at present, to our lord king. Provided always that, by pretext of the present act, no prejudice will be caused to any soldiers of the duke and earl themselves, or of either of them, and that this grant will not henceforth be taken as an precedent.

The French army

There are some administrative materials concerning the French army, but the survival of material is considerably less than that on the English side, and as far as I am aware, there has been no attempt to pull it all together into a comprehensive study.[103] The following comments are based on an examination of printed materials only and do not claim to provide an exhaustive investigation into French archive sources.

The most important published work in this context remains René de Belleval's *Azincourt* published in 1865.[104] This includes an account of the campaign based on a wide range of French and English chronicles. It gives extracts from Nicolas and Rymer as well as some leads to French sources, but its main focus is an attempt to list the French who participated in the battle. It thus belongs to the antiquarian style of enquiry popular in nineteenth-century France where genealogy and the search for noble origins often took centre stage. Belleval took as his prompt the lists in the various manuscripts of Monstrelet of those killed and taken prisoner. To these he added further names from other chronicles and sources of any mentioned in any way in connection with the battle. By such means he created three alphabetical listings of 'princes: lords and French knights': those who were killed at the battle (pp. 125–270); those taken prisoner (pp. 271–97); and finally those who were present at the battle (pp. 299–336). He gave brief biographical details of each person, with information on their family and lineage and on their coats of arms. In some cases he was able to find very little, or even nothing at all, on the person. He also discovered that it was much

[103] Philippe Contamine, *Guerre, etat et société à la fin du moyen âge* (Paris, 1972), includes some useful material but not a study of the battle. His *Azincourt* (Paris, 1964) is more wide ranging than its title would suggest, covering the Hundred Years War as a whole and giving extracts from chroniclers and Nicolas but no observations or texts on the French army. B. Zeller, *La France anglaise. Azincourt et le traité de Troyes 1413–22* (Paris, 1886) is a collection of extracts from chronicles but for the battle only the account in Monstrelet is given in full with a brief addition from Juvenal des Ursins on the causes of French defeat (pp. 43–60). A fairly recent biography of Marshal Bouccicaut includes no details at all on the battle, although it does give some space to his captivity in England, where he died in June 1421. D. Lalande, *Jean II Le Meingre, dit Bouccicaut (1366–1421). Étude d'une biographie héroïque* (Geneva, 1988), pp. 169–73.

[104] J.-B. Dumoulin, Librarie Editeur (Paris, 1865), 391 pp.

more difficult to draw up the third list – those present at the battle but who were neither killed nor taken prisoner. The chronicles tend not to mention many names save for those dead or captured; Belleval found only a dozen or so others in the narrative sources. He was well aware that over the centuries family traditions had developed which claimed that ancestors had fought at Agincourt but realised that there was a need to exercise some caution in this area. He thus attempted to use the administrative records of the French crown to establish a more authentic list.

As was the case for the English army, such records derive from the financial administration of the crown, in this case the *chambre des comptes* (literally, chamber of accounts) of the French crown. In many ways the bureaucracy surrounding the raising of an army in France was remarkably similar to England, most men being raised by nobles, knights or esquires with the retinues then being put together into an army. One might expect to find *lettres de retenue* (letters of retinue) which were the equivalent of the indentures, but it does not seem that any have so far come to light for the campaign. Troops would then be mustered and paid, giving rise to *montres* (musters) and also to *quittances* which were essentially receipts for the payment of wages. In an ideal world, one might also find account books equivalent to the Issue rolls and other financial records of the English crown. Unfortunately the records of the French crown have experienced more vicissitudes than those of its English counterpart. The French Revolution led to the destruction of materials of this nature especially where they were seen to indicate noble status. But the archive of the *chambre des comptes* had already suffered as a result of a fire in 1737, and in addition materials had earlier been taken from it by successive generations of antiquarians, largely for the sake of proving or exemplifying titles of nobility.

Ironically we are now in the debt both of those who removed materials and of those who copied them before the fire, for by such means we still have examples at our disposal. Thus several musters survive in the Collection Clairambault in the Bibliothèque Nationale (called the Bibliothèque Imperiale by Belleval as he was writing during the reign of Napoleon III), which comprises the materials extracted and collected by Pierre Clairambault, 'royal genealogist' to Louis XIV. These were drawn upon by de Belleval, and consist of musters and quittances. Further documents of this kind are to be found in other BN collections, most notably in the vast *pièces originales*. Together they give evidence on some of the companies which mustered in September and October at Rouen as the French army gathered. Their dating can also be used to confirm the chronology given in the chronicles. Several musters and *quittances* are dated at Rouen between 18 and 30 September, and there is enough to suggest that there were major musters carried out on 24 September and again on 15 October. The earliest document is dated 29 August, although there are also some musters of companies preparing for the English attack as far back as early August.[105] The muster rolls are

---

105 See, for instance, the muster of Jean de Bethencourt kt. and his 9 men at Vitefleur en Caux, 4 August 1415 (Bibliothèque Nationale, MS Clairambault 14/93).

particularly useful as they give the names of the retinue leaders and of the men they had brought. They show that the army was made up of a number of retinues. The examples cited by Belleval show companies headed by knights and esquires ranging in size from 6 to 13 men. *Quittances* do not give names of individual soldiers but they do indicate the name of the commander under whom the company might be serving (several are under the duke of Alençon), and also recite some of the conditions of service, such as the obligation 'to serve against the English anywhere where it pleases the king'.

Belleval cites other sources from the royal archives. For instance, there are materials concerning ransoms in Archives Nationales series PP. These can be reinforced by archives in English repositories about the ransoms of those captured. As we saw, the accounts of gains of war in the particulars of account and in E358/6 also include references to prisoners taken and sold. In all such records there is some evidence of lower ranks but generally documents concerning ransoms relate only to French men of higher status. Presence at Agincourt is also sometimes noted in land disputes recorded in the Paris *parlement* and the *chambre des comptes*. For instance, in a dispute between Guillaume Rose and an Englishman named Richard Handford over a title to lands, heard at the *parlement* in 1428, it was noted that Jaquin Rose, seigneur of Bois Garnier near Meaux, son of Simon Rose and Pierette Doignon, and a relative of Guillaume, had been killed at the battle of Agincourt.[106] In a *chambre* grant of 1462 compensating for losses incurred during the English occupation as a whole, Jean d'O notes that his grandfather was killed at Agincourt when his father was only four years old.[107] The many deaths at the battle caused numerous wrangles over wardship and inheritance, and there is also evidence of dislocation to economies and administration of lordships, especially in north-western France.[108] The ranks of office holders were also much reduced (see text E 1 above), and indeed a way of detecting deaths is by evidence of changes in personnel.

We saw in chapter 3 that the husband of the Third Lady in Alain Chartier's *Livre des quatre dames* is missing after the battle: she does not know whether he is alive, perhaps as a prisoner, or dead. This category of the 'missing' can be substantiated by reference to land disputes. In the records of the Paris *parlement*, for instance, there is a letter of 1 December 1415 which gave custody of the lands and possessions of Charles, seigneur de Noviant, to his sisters and not

---

[106] C.T. Allmand and C.A.J. Armstrong, *English Suits before the Parlement of Paris 1420–1436* (Camden Society, fourth series, 26, 1982), p. 79, citing Archives Nationales Xia 4795, fol. 244r. See also p. 144 for a suit which refers to the death of John, count of Alençon at the battle, and p. 128 concerning lands held by Bonne of Artois, wife of Philip, duke of Burgundy, whose first husband, Burgundy's uncle, Philip of Nevers, had also been killed at Agincourt.

[107] Archives Nationales, microfilm 104, Collection Dom Lenoir, 75/263. These are transcripts taken before the fire in the archives of the chambre des comptes.

[108] See for instance problems in the barony of Neuborg evidenced in the surviving accounts for Feb. 1415–1416 (Evreux, Archives Départmentales de l'Eure, E3938, p. 70).

to his wife, Ysabeau la Mareschalle, because it was not clear whether his brother, Jean, who would otherwise have been his heir (there can have been no child of the marriage), survived the battle or not.[109]

> Charles was mounted and armed adequately at the battle which was recently in the pays d'Artois, between many of our blood and lineage and others of our vassals and subjects on the one side and our adversary of England and others who were his allies and accomplices, our ancient enemies, on the other. And there the said Charles was found dead. Also at the said battle was Jean de Noviant, brother of the said Charles and of the said ladies, about whose death or survival they have heard or know no news at all. Many of our subjects were captured and taken as prisoners into several lands and countries, so one cannot know the certainty of the matter.

It has been some time already, and the sisters have heard no news about Jean; no ransom demand has been received. As they will be inheritors of the Noviant estate if Jean is dead as well as his brother, they are entrusted with them, and are free to profit from them as if they were their own, although the governing of them still belongs in law to Jean to whom they must render account and inventory if he reappears. A note attached states that Charles' wife, Ysabeau, must turn to the sisters to receive any dower settlement in the meantime. As one might imagine, Ysabeau, as one of the queen's ladies in waiting, was not pleased by this decision, and requested view of all the documents produced for the court. A document concerning a similar case is provided below (Text G 2).

In addition, service at Agincourt often features in later claims to nobility. Gareth Prosser has noted one dossier in the archive of the *cour des aides* at Rouen which cites evidence by witnesses that Colin des Buats had survived Agincourt, and which contains an explicit statement that all who fought at Agincourt were reputed noble.[110] This a potential parallel to the right to bear arms in England being connected with service at Agincourt, and is certainly a line of enquiry which would repay further study. Philippe Contamine has also shown how these disputes over noble status and land holding can be used to reconstruct military careers. Sir Guillaume de Vendel, one of the *maîtres d'hotel* of Richemont, gives details of the military service of his ancestors as well as of his own, which included presences at Agincourt, at the later sieges of Avranches and Pontorson, at the defence of La Gravelle and at various other actions.[111] He also cites the example of Philippot Poitevin who was accused in 1451 of supporting the English and being ennobled by them because of his supposed presence at

---

109 Archives Nationales, Xic 110B (accords of the *parlement civil*, 8 August to 31 December 1415), no. 234, with additional note at 233. I am grateful to Dr Rachel Gibbons for this reference.
110 Rouen, Archives Départmentales de la Seine Maritime, 3B 1121. I am most grateful to Dr Prosser for this specific reference and for his generosity in suggesting other leads in French archives of this kind. As he has made clear, there is enough material for a major research project into the impact of Agincourt on French gentry and nobility.
111 P. Contamine, *Guerre, etat et société*, p. 259 citing Archives Nationales Xia 4799 fols 61v–62r.

Agincourt. This was not true, he retorted, for he had always served the French loyally in later actions.[112] Others speak of the presence of ancestors at the battle, such as Robert de Chabannes, a petty lord from the Limousin, whose presence indicates the wide geographical area from which troops were drawn.[113] Claude Gauvard notes that some remissions for later crimes were allowed partly on the grounds of service at Agincourt.[114] We have heard already the participation and fatalities of the families of Jean de Waurin and Jean de Bueil. In no records is it possible, I think, to distinguish between those who were killed as prisoners and those who fell in actual combat, but fatalities are also revealed by records of burials and tombs. Bacquet includes a good number in his study of the battle.[115] Some wills are also potentially useful: Belleval cites the example of that of Jean Boutin who died at Arras a few days after the battle.

Urban records are also valuable, principally for what they reveal about the lower ranks of troops, the archers, crossbowmen and infantry sent by towns in response to royal or ducal summons.[116] We can know, for instance, that Senlis was asked to provide men, and that archers and crossbowmen were definitely sent from St Omer. The records of Amiens are an exceptionally rich source not only concerning troops but also telling us something about local responses to the English invasion.[117] A register of deliberations shows us that on 13 October the inhabitants were summoned by the tolling of the bell to be informed of the request of the constable who was then at Abbeville. He had ordered the town to send him reinforcements to help defend the crossing of the Somme. The townsmen had expressed concern that this could weaken their own defences, but the constable persisted in his request. They thus agreed to send him 30 cross-bowmen and 20 *pavesiers*. But the latter probably did not depart immediately for new garments were ordered for the troops and a ship was drawn up on the quayside to transport the *matériel de guerre* downstream to Abbeville. By 16 and 17 October, large numbers of French troops were within Amiens itself. It seems likely that reinforcements were sent by the town to Corbie, against which Henry attempted a reconnaissance on 17 October. Earlier in the month the records of Amiens indicate that the townsmen had been trying out their artillery and had destroyed some bridges in the vicinity, thinking that this would help defend the town. This, combined with the initial reluctance to send out troops, reveals a fear that the English might make an attempt against a larger French

---

[112] Ibid., p. 475, citing Archives Nationales Zia 3119, fol. 46r.

[113] Ibid., pp. 414, 447, citing materials in H. de Chabannes, *Preuves pour servir à l'histoire de la maison de Chabannes*, 4 vols (Dijon 1892–7), with the reference to Agincourt at 2, pp. 452–3 and Robert's will in supplement 1, pp. 68–73.

[114] C. Gauvard, *'De grace especial'. Crime, état et société en France à la fin du moyen age*, 2 vols (Paris, 1991), 2, pp. 857, 919.

[115] G. Bacquet, *Azincourt* (Bellegrade, 1977), pp. 83–5.

[116] For the examples which follow, see Contamine, *Guerre, état et société*, p. 216.

[117] See J. Godard, 'Quelques précisions sur la campagne d'Azincourt tirées des archives municpales d'Amiens', *Bulletin trimestre de la société des antiquaires de Picardie* (1971), pp. 129–35.

city, although the chronicles, admittedly written with hindsight, make it clear that Henry had no intention of doing so. There was clearly a degree of panic occasioned by the presence of an English invasion force whose intentions were perhaps not entirely clear. This persisted after the battle. There were rumours at Amiens that Henry was going on to besiege Boulogne so reinforcements were to be sent there.[118] We know too that the town sent an emissary to recover from the battlefield *matériel* which belonged to it; three big canons and two smaller ones were brought back as well as damaged pavises and parts of tents. The town thus knew all too well the scale of the defeat. In addition, several leading French captains were buried at Amiens.

The records of Abbeville confirm the chronicler's story that there was initially a rumour that the English had been defeated, and that a feast was even held to celebrate the fact. A marginal note adds that this news was not true.[119] At Mantes, from which troops were requested for the company of the dauphin in 1415, the defeat was blamed on those who had fled the field. There was an order to guard the gates against the approach of such troops with the additional proviso that 'the men fleeing and returning from the host of the king should not pass through the town save in groups of 20 to 30 at a time'.[120]

The records of towns within Brabant, such as Louvain, Brussels and Anvers, are particularly valuable in showing how Duke Anthony of Brabant recruited at least part of his force, with requests being deliberated by some towns as early as 28 August, and orders being received subsequently for troops to assemble at Cambrai. Combining these with materials from the *recette générale* of the duchy and other ducal records, Boffa has been able to reach important conclusions on the duke's contingent, and his itinerary, which is all the more significant given the references in several chronicles to Anthony's rushing ahead of his main force with impulsive bravery.[121] Boffa estimates that the Brabanters, largely men of his household, fared very badly at the battle, with a half dying and a third being taken prisoner. Unfortunately the exact size of the company remains elusive, although financial records indicate that 219 horses were used in the expedition, and Anvers is known to have sent 57 men. But the records do show how information was being circulated in the weeks leading up to the battle. On 21 October Anthony was in the castle of Louvain when he was informed by a messenger of the route of the English army and that a French counterattack was imminent. He also seems to have received messages from his brother, the count of Nevers, whilst en route to Agincourt. He also received a letter sent from

---

118 See Bacquet, *Azincourt*, pp. 109–12 for extracts from the accounts of Boulogne 1415–16, now in Archives Nationales KK 280.
119 Ibid., p. 134, citing accounts which were, alas, destroyed by military action in 1940.
120 V.E. Grave, *Archives muncipales de Mantes. Analyse des registres des comptes de 1381 à 1450* (Paris, 1896), p. 14.
121 S. Boffa, 'Anthoine de Bourgogne et le contingent brabançon à la bataille d'Azincourt (1415)', *Revue belge de philologie et d'histoire*, 72 (1994), pp. 255–84. He makes much use of Dynter's chronicle (see above, Text B 10).

Péronne on 19 October by the leaders of the French army, and another from the seneschal of Hainault with further information. The latter also wrote to the town of Mons around 23 October saying that battle was imminent, having noted a few days earlier large numbers of English and French soldiers in the area.[122]

Duke Anthony's body was brought back to Brussels for burial. In early November the Estates of Brabant were convened there to install a council of regency for his young heir, John. Early in 1416 Duke John of Burgundy wrote to the Estates 'both to comfort and console them over the recent woeful death of our late very dear and beloved brother the duke of Brabant . . . at the lamentable discomfiture of the French at Agincourt, and to expound to the three Estates our rights to the guardianship and government of the persons of our nephews being minors, and of their lands and lordships.'[123] The duke of Burgundy had not, of course, been present at the battle. Vaughan suggests, based on his researches in the ducal archives that John the Fearless had intended to join the French army at least initially. A letter survives written by his son, Philip, count of Charolais (later Duke Philip the Good) to the *chambre des comptes* at Lille on 10 October 1415 which reads as follows:

> Dearest and well beloved, my father has recently informed me of his departure with all his power to advance against the English in the service of the king . . . and he wishes to have with him everyone in his lands who is accustomed to bear arms, including we ourselves in person and [the knights and esquires] of Flanders and Artois.[124]

There is also enough evidence that the duke had written to the king saying he would come in person at the head of his troops and not just send a contingent. His letters had been read and approved at the royal council around 11–12 October. Soon after 13 October the count of Charolais set out from Oudenarde with intention of joining army at Rouen. But at the end of the day Duke John never did set out and, as the chroniclers report, he prevented his son from going, detaining him at Aire in Artois. Yet it is not clear how many Burgundian troops did find their way to the battle under the count of Nevers and other leaders.

This can only be a brief glimpse at the subject. By piecing together a wide range of materials from the archives of the crown, of the dukes and of other noble families, and of the towns, it would surely be possible to come to firmer conclusions on the French army at Agincourt, although we would never be able to know as much as we do about the English army. This contrast is indicative of structural differences between the two armies. Whereas the English army was a discrete whole recruited under royal authority, the French army was made up of many diverse elements. Although at its core it was like the English army, namely

[122] *Cartulaire des contes de Hainault*, ed. L. Devillers (Brussells, 1889), pp. 46–7, cited in Allmand, *Henry V,* p. 86.

[123] R. Vaughan, *John the Fearless* (London, 1966), p. 238. Vaughan's book is useful for negotiations between Henry and Duke John before the invasion.

[124] Vaughan, *John the Fearless*, p. 208, from Archives Départmentales du Nord B17618. Vaughan is the source for what follows.

in that it consisted of the retinues of nobles, knights and esquires all grouped together, there were additional groups such as the urban militias and the ducal retinues which fell outside this. Moreover the English army had been together for some time before the battle. So had some French companies, but the whole army only came together shortly before the battle. An army which assembles on such an incremental basis raises considerable difficulties in command and in deployment. Thus the contrasting nature of the English and French sources does help us to understand, perhaps, why the French lost. But we must not assume that the French did not have an awareness of the problems they faced or that they had not made preparations to overcome them. This leads me to discussion of perhaps the most important source concerning the French army to survive, the French plan of battle.

Undoubtedly the most significant discovery of recent years was that by Christopher Phillpotts of a French plan of battle in the British Library. Although damaged in the fire of Robert Cotton's manuscripts, enough survives to establish a good text. Phillpotts argues that the plan was drawn up by Bouccicaut between 13 and 21 October, probably to deploy against Henry in anticipation of the latter being able to cross the Somme. The reason for thinking this is that the commanders listed in the plan were all those forming the advance guard under Bouccicaut and d'Albret which was already north of the Somme. It does not include the dukes of Orléans and Bourbon. They were with the main French army which mustered at Rouen on 17 October, crossed the Somme at Amiens and joined with Bouccicaut's advance guard at Bapaume on the 21st. It is not clear, therefore, whether the plan is linked in any way to the summons to battle presented to Henry on 20 October by heralds said by the chroniclers to have been sent by Orléans, Bourbon and d'Albret. According to Jean Juvenal des Ursins, the council of war at Rouen had itself drawn up a plan of battle, but it seems unlikely to be represented by this document for according to the chronicler it included the duke of Brittany, the count of Charolais and Tanneguy du Chastel, none of whom were in the field and who did not participate in the eventual battle. Both plans, then, were perhaps overtaken by events, or by changes in French strategy. Following the summons from the French heralds, Henry seems to have expected to fight near Péronne on 21 October. That certainly is the impression given in several chronicles. Phillpotts suggests that 'at this point there was an unexpected change in French strategy. The advance guard left Péronne and marched ahead of the English to join the main army at Bapaume. From there the united French army kept in front of the English and on their right flank, until it moved across Henry's path at Agincourt.'[125] This change was presumably because it was thought wisest to assemble as large an army as possible against Henry. Perhaps too it was felt that Henry's tail was up following the crossing of the Somme (as the heralds would have been able to report), and that it would be better to postpone an attack until the English had

---

[125] C.J. Phillpotts, 'The French plan of battle during the Agincourt campaign', *EHR*, 99 (1984), pp. 61–2.

been weakened by a further march. It is interesting to speculate, too, the effect on English morale to be led to believe that there would be battle on 21 October, but then to be left waiting, presumably in battle array, as some chronicles suggest. Henry might have portrayed this to his men as an example of French lack of resolve, but this would surely cut little ice when it was all too obvious how large an army the French now had at their disposal. The French were making it blatantly clear that they would be the ones who chose when and where to fight.

This raises questions of how and when the plan came into Henry's hands, none of which can be satisfactorily answered. Indeed there is no proof that it did do so until after Agincourt. It is possible, of course, that knowledge of it had informed Henry's decision that his archers should provide themselves with stakes to counteract specific cavalry attacks aimed against them. The *Gesta* places the order to prepare stakes between 17 and 18 October, although indicating the chronology by a rather vague 'meanwhile'. It also claims that the king's decision was occasioned by information divulged by prisoners. Could this signify the actual capture of the plan of battle itself? Stakes had been used at the battle of Nicopolis (1396), at which Englishmen had probably served, so it is equally possible that Henry had decided on the move without other impulse, or merely by anticipating what an obviously well-mounted French host might attempt.

Both Phillpotts and Bennett suggest that aspects of the plan do seem to have been put into effect at Agincourt by the French, including the attempt to override the archers, although this was carried out with many fewer men, it seems, than was planned.[126] The attack on Henry's baggage camp may also have been as envisaged in the plan. But the ordering of the French battles is not as in the plan, perhaps because of the arrival of Orléans and Bourbon, or perhaps, as Phillpotts suggests, because 'once arrived on the field of battle, the French found it too narrow to apply Bouccicaut's blueprint successfully to their swollen ranks'. Moreover, if there were to be 'two great wings of foot', does this imply that in the plan the first two main battles were intended to be mounted? The text is not clear on this, but we can be fairly certain that the main attack by the French at Agincourt was on foot. No such wings of foot seem to have been formed, and there was no use of the *gens de trait* [archers] as the plan had envisaged. The chroniclers, assuming that they can be believed, seem to suggest that at Agincourt the French simply advanced against the English on foot in three battles many men thick.

It is all to easy, perhaps, to say that the French lost because they did not stick to the plan, that once the whole army had assembled, the French command was racked by division of opinion on tactics, much as some chroniclers imply. Hence the French lords all wished to be in the front line, and were dismissive of the use of their own archers. Yet military commanders have to adapt according to

[126] Bradbury, *The Medieval Archer*, pp. 124–5, considers that 'the plan compares closely with what actually happened at Agincourt', but Phillpotts and Bennett are more circumspect.

circumstances, as the plan itself envisages at one point. The plan was appropriate against an enemy whose deployment was strung out widely, perhaps because of a piecemeal and diffuse river crossing. It was not appropriate, however, to a narrow site. There a tightly packed, narrowly focused and hard attack might have seemed the right course of action to break the English line. But the French reckoned without the effects of withering arrow fire on the English flanks. There is a further possibility which also gives the French a degree of greater credibility. Did they change their plan because they knew that it had fallen into the hands of the English? Is this why there was no battle on 21 October as they had threatened? Is this why they waited for the English in a position that would force the latter to have to compress their own battlelines? Whilst the plan is a fascinating and significant text (though not the only plan of battle to survive for the later medieval period),[127] it thus raises as many questions as it appears to answer. Text G 1 below, however, also indicates that the French had made some arrangements for their battle formation in advance of 25 October.

G 1. Succession dispute (1460, French)

Translated from Archives Départementales du Pas-de-Calais, Série B, registre 852, fol. 33 (original destroyed in 1915; text printed in *Bulletin de la commission des monuments historiques du P-as-de-Calais*, 1 (1890), p. 96).

... and that in the year 1415, the brothers Jean and Alain de Longueval went to the battle of Agincourt, in the service of the late king of noble memory, Charles, for the expediting of a matter of public interest against the English, the ancient enemies and adversaries of the kingdom. On the day (*journée*), the late Monsieur Jean, lord of Longueval, was in the main force (*la bataille*) in the company of the late count of Marlay, and Monsieur Alain in the vanguard, in the company of the late lord of Waurin. It is true that before the day of the battle, the method of fighting against the English had been pre-arranged by several lords and warriors of this kingdom, including Ghiscart d'Offin, the baron of Ivry and others who had on two occasions gone to the present duke of Burgundy, then count of Charolais, in order that he might be willing to be at the engagement. Afterwards it was ordered which lords should be in the vanguard, which in the main force and which in the rearguard, in which place and how the English should be fought against, just as it had been ordered, so it was done. For, although it was God's will that the battle and the victory should be the enemy's, on the part of the lords of France there was always a very

---

127 M. Bennett, 'The development of battle tactics in the Hundred Years War', in *Arms, Armies and Fortifications in the Hundred Years War*, ed. A. Curry and M. Hughes (Woodbridge, 1994), pp. 17–18.

fine arrangement of vanguard, main force and rearguard. The vanguard was a bowshot or thereabouts in front of the main force, as was and is well known to the kings of arms, heralds and pursuivants, as well as by others who can speak knowledgeably about the battle. The claimant says that the vanguard, in which was the late Monsieur Alain, had been broken up and those who were in it were not seen alive for some time before the main force engaged, and as a result there was absolutely no doubt that Monsieur Alain died there because afterwards he was not seen or noticed, and the said lord of Longueval was seen alive a long while after the said vanguard had been smashed and those in it dead and fallen. . . .

G 2. Petition of Jeanne de Gaillouvel (1416, French)

Translated from Bibliothèque Nationale de France, pièce originale 1504 (de Hellenvillier en Normandie) 56 (French, 9 May 1416, vidimus of July 1416).[128]

We have received the humble petition of our well beloved Jeanne de Gaillouvel, wife of our beloved and faithful knight Pierre de Hellenvillier, our bailli of Evreux, burdened with 7 children, containing how for some time the lands, lordships and revenues of Feugerolles in the vicomté of Beaumont-le-Roger and the mills of Les Andeleys held of the crown in the vicomté of Gisors, and the land of Guillemesnil in the same vicomté belonging to her husband have been taken into our hands because of the absence of her husband who is a prisoner in England as she says, she has obtained from us and our court certain letters of title which have been verified . . . by which we have granted that she can hold and exploit these lands, lordships and revenues until Easter next. And since she received our letters she has made diligent efforts to find out news of her husband. She heard some say that her husband was a prisoner of a knight of England called Cornwall [Sir John Cornwall], by which she hopes at the blessing of the Lord to have good and certain news soon, hopefully that her husband is living rather than dead. It would be a very hard, costly and damaging thing if it happened that the lands, rents and lordships should be governed by commissioners or other royal officers under the excuse that some presume that her husband is dead, about which she still knows nothing for certain . . . [Jeanne was given the right to hold the lands temporarily but without this causing any prejudice to the king's rights should her husband be dead.]

---

[128] I am grateful to Dr Prosser for this reference.

G 3. The French plan of battle (1415, French)

Translated from C.J. Phillpotts, 'The French plan of battle during the Agincourt campaign', *EHR*, 99 (1984), pp. 64–6, from British Library, Cotton Caligula D V, fols 43v–44r.[129]

This is how it seems to the lord marshal and to the lords who are with him, by the command of the duke of Alençon and of Richemont and the lord Constable, subject to the correction of these lords, for the matter (*fait*) of the battle.

First, in the name of God, Our Lady and Saint George, it is advised that there should be a large battle (*bataille*) which will be the vanguard. In this will be the constable and marshal with all their men.

Also, in this battle the banners of the constable and the marshal shall be placed together. That of the constable shall be on the right and that of the marshal on the left. And on the right the troops should be all men of the constable, together. And on the left all men of the marshal.

Also, there should be another battle near (*aupres*) that one, in which should be the duke of Alençon, the count of Eu and other lords who are not named elsewhere. And in the event that the English only form one battle, these two battles [gap in text, shall fight?] together; then they can join all together.

Also it seems that two great wings of foot ought to be made. Richemont should form one of them, which will be the one on the right, and he will have in his company, in addition to all his men, the lord of Combourg, and lord Bertrand de Montauban. And the other, which shall be on the left, will be formed by the count of Vendôme, grand master of the household [gap, Guichard Dauphin de?] Jaligny

[gap] the axes of the company and others who can be found elsewhere [gap] the two wings.

Item all the archers (*gens de trait*) of the whole company will be put in front of the two wings of foot, under the command of knights and esquires whom the leaders of the wings appoint, each on his own wing.

Also, a battle of heavy horse shall be formed of good men up to the number of 1,000 men-at-arms at least. This battle will be led by the master of crossbowmen, and he will be provided with this number from all the companies. This battle will hold itself off from all the other battles, on the left side, a little behind the last battle. This battle will be to attack the archers and will do the utmost to break them. And when it moves off in order to override the archers, the foot battles and the wings will march

---

[129] My translation, which is intentionally literal, is slightly different from that of Matthew Bennett, *Agincourt*, pp. 64–6, and of Christopher Allmand in *Society at War. The Experience of England and France during the Hundred Years War* (revised edition, Woodbridge, 1998), pp. 194–5.

to gather together (*aler asembler*). And this battle will have half of all the servants (*varles*) of the company mounted on the best horses of their masters.

Also there will be another battle of 200 mounted men-at-arms, along with the other half of all the servants mounted on the best horses of their masters, and this battle will be led by Monsieur de Bosredon. It will be to attack behind the battle of the English against their servants and baggage, and at the rear of the battle of the English. And this battle will move off when the master of the crossbowmen departs to attack the archers.

Conclusion

What this study shows is that history, like literature, is written for a purpose, or, to use a more modern allusion, with a specific agenda in mind. No account of Agincourt aims simply to tell us what happened on that fateful day of 25 October 1415. All, for one reason or another, place the battle within a broader intention. The study of chronicle sources reveals both national variations as well as differences arising out of date and style of composition. Later historians were moved by their own reading of the past, which was in turn influenced by their own present. Even today we are not immune from the effects of such baggage, or from the overwhelming desire to make sense of the inexplicable. After detailing the surviving sources, this may seem an admission of failure as well as a rather pessimistic viewpoint, but I would suggest that, despite the vast quantity of writing on Agincourt, or perhaps because of it, it is impossible to know what really happened. That is because of the nature of the event itself. No one could have a full knowledge or understanding of a battle even if they were there at the time. Mass actions are notoriously difficult to elucidate: witness more recent enquiries into disasters involving large crowds and high fatalities. Although early accounts exult or lament the outcome of the battle from a partisan perspective, all also contain, implicitly or explicitly, a sense of amazement. It is this, I think, which is the key to understanding the battle and subsequent responses to it.

The French had a numerically superior force, commanded by experienced generals and comprising many whose social status equipped them, both mentally and physically, for hand-to-hand combat of the most skilled type. The French leaders had chosen the site of battle, maximising the level of exhaustion and despair of their opponents by delaying the fight for as long as possible. Had the English lost, it is tempting to believe that the French might have gone on to assault Calais, as well as to pick off Harfleur at their leisure. Moreover, a victory won so near to Crécy would have counterbalanced the defeat of the previous century.

This is counter-history, of course; the French did not win. But they had been confident of victory, of that there can be no doubt. They faced a weak and less numerous army which had undertaken a forced march at speed and had already suffered attrition by siege and disease. At Henry's leaving of Harfleur the French were still cautious. There was certainly fear and uncertainty aroused in the Pays de Caux by Henry's march. We know with hindsight that he did not conduct a chevauchée of the customary kind where looting and burning were deliberate strategy. But initially the French could not have known that he would not do so. Spying must have subsequently revealed, however, that Henry was aiming to move towards Calais as quickly as he could. His attempt to cross the

Somme at Blanchetaque was a clear indication that he did not intend a move against important targets inland. Although he later managed to outwit the French by crossing the Somme unexpectedly, the French had already been given time to raise their army and to shadow him closely, eventually overtaking him and summoning him to fight. Even if Henry had by this time learned of intended French tactics as outlined in their battle plan and had begun to respond to them with his own plans for possible deployment, the strength of the army he was being called upon to engage would be all too obvious to him and his men.

Henry's response on 25 October can be interpreted as genius but it also falls into the category of subterfuge and desperation. The stakes would have made it difficult for the French to assess and locate their target. Archers on the flanks may have been hidden amongst the trees. Some may have been deliberately deployed out of sight, almost behind enemy lines. The narrative accounts of Agincourt do not give us, however, a clear picture of the deployment Henry used, or of which side moved first, and no amount of skilful reading of the texts can overcome these problems. An initial study of the administrative records for the English army suggests that the imbalance between men-at-arms and archers on the march and at the battle may not have been as great as the *Gesta*, with its figures of 900 and 5,000 respectively, suggests. Further research in the Exchequer records could produce more reliable figures. But whatever the numbers, the archers must still have outnumbered the men-at-arms by at least three to one, based on what we know of the ratio and composition of the army at the point of indenting. If the archers were entirely on the wings (which I person-ally find the most convincing argument), then they would perhaps have been positioned in two horn-like formations, curving round in such a way that they fired on the advancing French from the side. This would also allow them later to enter the mêlée, to come in for the kill at close quarters, in an encircling move. But all of this can be no more than speculation – even of inherent military prob-ability.

What we can be sure of, I suggest, is the murderous nature of the battle. The many were killed by the few. With further work on the English and French armies we might again be able to reach some firmer figures. The records of the English Exchequer are yet to be investigated fully. For the French there is much unexploited evidence arising out of the knock-on effects of mortalities on local society within France as well as the lists of dead which deserve further analysis. Even if English mortalities were higher than Henry wished or chose to admit, there can be no doubt that there was a tremendous imbalance between the losses of one side and of the other. Chroniclers might disagree on precise numbers, but there is enough consistency, backed up by hard evidence, that French losses were exceptionally high and English surprisingly low. This was a major theme in their writings, almost an obsession, one might suggest.

Herein lies the key to interpreting the battle. A small army can only defeat a larger one and cause so many fatalities under very specific circumstances. Several possibilities present themselves, and no doubt the battle should be seen as multi-faceted. It is easier for us today than it was for contemporaries to identify all the different aspects, although it remains difficult to weigh them one against the other, for in battle it is the cumulative effect which is crucial. Contemporary writers did not know enough individually. No one account could be comprehensive. Although, as pointed out in chapter 1, there is a danger in accepting everything any chronicler said as true and merely heaping up all of their observations in order to create a narrative, such an approach does at least enable us to appreciate the wide range of possibilities of explanation. Henry adopted a defensive position, yet one which was not lacking in offensive capability. The French failed to knock out the archers (and seem only have tried to do so on one flank rather than two). By virtue of flanking arrow fire, by difficulties in moving across the terrain, by packing caused by sheer weight of numbers (which was exacerbated by the effects of the English arrows and by the slow movement which was no doubt both demoralising and demobilising), the French assault lost its impact. Men slowed down and piled up, and were then easy targets even at the hands of archers who themselves had little defensive equipment but a myriad of weapons for close combat of a rather basic kind.[1]

But were the French targets for slaughter or for capture at this stage? Is this scenario of a pile up enough in itself to explain the high rate of death? Henry's order to kill the prisoners is perhaps more significant than it might appear. It must be assumed that a large enough number of prisoners had already been taken for Henry to be afraid of them as a drain on his own resources and as a potential military threat. Yet how does one take and keep a prisoner in the mêlée? Is it reasonable to suggest that the English had been socially selective in those they killed and those they captured? If that is so, then they must have had time and scope to choose, and for the few to capture the many – further indicators that it was the piling up of the French which was their essential undoing. The prisoners would surely have been grouped together, and disarmed, with their helmets taken off. The disproportionately large numbers of French dead of noble and gentle status arose in part because of the killing of men in this condition. Even some chroniclers, most notably Basset and Dynter, imply this. Moreover, the numbers of French prisoners are notably low. The Religieux suggests 1,400. Waurin, Monstrelet and Le Fèvre say 1,600, against a total French army size which they put at 50,000. Even if the latter figure is too high, the proportion of prisoners is unlikely to be anywhere near as high as at Poitiers where the estimate is 3,000, more than a quarter of the army.[2] Interestingly too there are relatively few ransoms noted in the accounts which English captains presented to the Exchequer after the campaign.

Agincourt was notable for contemporaries because of the high fatalities on the French side. It is impossible to know exact numbers or proportions, but chroniclers' estimates often fall in the 5,000 to 10,000 band. At Crécy 1,542

---

1   J. Keegan, *The Face of Battle. A Study of Agincourt, Waterloo and the Somme* (London, 1976), p. 101, sees the piling up as 'the crucial factor in the development of the battle'.
2   J. Sumption, *The Hundred Years War. II. Trial by Fire* (London, 1999), p. 247.

men of rank are said to have died.[3] Even allowing for omissions of the rank and file, the Agincourt losses would seem considerably greater. Of course, it is likely that the French army was larger in 1415 than in 1346, but even so, the Agincourt fatalities were still proportionately larger, especially of those of name. Even more worthy of note was the stark imbalance between English and French losses. This had been a feature of Crécy too, but it is tempting to say that the difference at Agincourt was even more marked and was a feature much stressed by chroniclers. Whilst all victories were ascribed to God, the battle of Agincourt, where there was such an obvious manifestation of his intervention on behalf of one party, gave an extra piquancy to the notion. The French were not merely demoralised, they were decimated. As the extracts in chapter 3 show, the French response was one of sorrow and recrimination on a scale greater even than that which greeted the capture of King John in 1356. For their part, the English were triumphalist, but less bombastically so than one might have expected. Henry's own response was one of humility in the face of victory. Was even he moved by the scale and nature of the carnage? The chroniclers' treatment of his viewing of the field on the day after the battle surely emphasises the scale of the horror felt on all sides. The poetic response in France and the religious tone of the entry to London, if Kipling's interpretation is to be believed, would support this interpretation.

Few medieval men experienced battle in their lives. Even fewer would experience a battle of this kind. It was hard to comprehend or explain by conventional means, and thus encouraged selective embellishment. Whilst we cannot prove that Crispin and those who fought on his day were 'forever remembered', as Shakespeare would have it, there can be no doubt that Agincourt was seen as a defining moment in the fifteenth century, returned to in later decades. This was fanned by the rise of English as a literary medium and by increasing national fervour, especially as English fortunes in France began to wane. In the writings of Tito Livio and the Pseudo Elmham, and in the *Brut* and London Chronicles, it served as a vehicle for Lancastrian, Yorkist or patriotic fervour as necessary. Later centuries of Englishmen were also keen to seize upon this particular victory, as opposed to the others of the medieval period, because of its scale and uniqueness. In time, the focus on the 'great and the good', which permeates the medieval writings, began to shift towards the rank and file, the archers. In the early modern period, the Englishness of the archer began to emerge, stout heart and all, but still fighting alongside the king and nobility who 'for famous England stood', as Drayton put it in his *Ballad of Agincourt*. As warfare itself developed, and an appreciation was gained of the efficacy of good generalship and massed fire, the military effectiveness of the archer became the central issue.

For such an overwhelming victory, it is perhaps surprising that Agincourt does not feature in the annals of decisive battles. Here we must remember

---

[3] For Crécy, see J. Sumption, *The Hundred Years War. I. Trial by Battle* (London, 1990), p. 530.

Henry's weakness before the battle which had made the victory his against the odds. Henry did not have the capacity to follow up his victory any more than he had had the financial wherewithal to launch it in the first place. For their part, a humiliation on such a scale was not likely to prompt the French into early negotiations or compromises. But Henry's victory plays a part in explaining French weakness and continuing political divisions in the face of his renewed attack from 1417 onwards. A full study of the effects of the battle on the nobility and gentry of northern France would be most useful in revealing how and whether the defeat affected the defence of the area thenceforward. Moreover, there can be no doubt that the Burgundians were less damaged than the Armagnacs. The duke's absence from the battle turned out to be fortuitous for him, for it removed actual and potential rivals either by death or capture, and facilitated his seizing control of the capital and king in 1418–19. What role, if any, it played in the duke's murder at the hands of the Armagnac group in September 1419 is unclear. Whilst historians would now argue it was this last event which opened the way for Henry to become heir and regent of France, the victory at Agincourt put him into a position to continue the war.[4] It had revived English interests in France which had been flagging since the 1370s. It bolstered support at home for the war, despite the debts which Henry had accrued in the campaign and which, combined with the costs of maintaining war over the next three decades, were to hang like a millstone round his son's neck.

Agincourt was a costly victory for the English even though they suffered few fatalities. But the battle persisted as a symbol of English success. It is perhaps not surprising that it should have generated a degree of mythology given that it was such an extraordinary and unexpected victory. This sense of amazement at the scale of the English victory persists down to our own age even if we can now set the battle in a firmer context and move away from over-reliance on narrative sources. And, whilst we can debunk the myths by realising that they mainly come from less reliable histories or from Shakespeare, we cannot destroy the significance of, or the interest in, the battle as a real event. The desire to 'know Agincourt' is destined to continue.

---

4   The successful defence of Harfleur over the course of 1416 is also important here.

Addenda

H1. Reminiscence of Ghillebert de Lannoy (1415–62, French)

Oeuvres de Ghillebert de Lannoy. Voyageur, diplomate et moraliste. Recueillies et publiées par Charles Poitvin (Louvain, 1878), pp. 49–50

Lannoy (1386–1462), lord of Willerval, was chamberlain of Philip, count of Charolais in 1415, and appointed captain of Sluys in 1416. Both before and after 1415 he travelled widely, writing accounts of his voyages. This reminiscence provides a valuable insight into the killing of the prisoners.

In 1415 I was at the battle of Ruisseauville where I was wounded in the knee and the head, and I laid with the dead. But when the bodies were searched through, I was taken prisoner, being wounded and helpless (*impotens*), and kept under guard for while. I was then led to a house nearby with 10 or 12 other prisoners who were all wounded. And there, when the duke of Brabant was making a new attack, a shout went up that everyone should kill his prisoners. So that this might be effected all the quicker, they set fire to the house where we were. By the grace of God, I dragged myself a few feet away from the fire. There I was when the English returned, so I was taken prisoner again and sold to Sir John Cornwall, thinking that I was someone of high status since, thank God, I was well accoutred when I was taken the first time according to the standards of the time. So I was taken to Calais and thence to England until they discovered who I was, at which point I was put to ransom for 1,200 golden crowns (*écus*) along with a horse of 100 francs. When I left my master, Sir John Cornwall, he gave me 20 nobles to purchase a new suit of armour (*harnas*).

H2. Chronicle of Verneuil (late fifteenth century, French)

Translated from 'Chronique d'un bourgeois de Verneuil (1415–1422)', ed. A. Hellot, *Bulletin de la Société de l'histoire de Normandie,* 3 (1880–1881), p. 218. (I am grateful to Linda Hutjens for bringing this text to my attention.)

This text, found in a *Histoire Universelle,* includes a short account of the battle. References to Verneuil persuaded Hellot that its author came from the town. After a short narrative of the siege of Harfleur and march to Agincourt (with the English being numbered at 10,000 and the French at 120,000), the author includes the following observation which embellishes des Ursins' claim that Henry ennobled all those who had fought with him. French fatalities are numbered at 12,000 and prisoners at 6,000.

Henry sought deals with the lords of France that it would only be the nobles who fought, and this was agreed with him. So King Henry returned to his men and told them of the agreement saying that he would make them all nobles (*quil les anoblissoit tous*). So all of the English fought against the nobles of France, and the lesser people of France did not fight at all. So the French by such means lost the battle.'

Index

Warfare in History

Lightning Source UK Ltd.
Milton Keynes UK
UKOW041707080213

206030UK00001B/1/P